For Prof. [illegible]
with best [illegible]

JOURNEY OF A KONKANI FAMILY
(*EKA KONKANI KUTUMBA PRAVASU*)

Journey of a Konkani Family
(*Eka Konkani Kutumba Pravasu*)

Mulki R. Bhat

AJJALKANI BOOKS

Published by
Ajjalkani Books
PO Box 705
Miller Place NY 11764-0705
USA
http://www.JourneyOfAKonkaniFamily.com

Manufactured in the United States of America.

ISBN: 978-0-9835757-1-9

Cover illustrator:
Jasmine Wabbington of Wabbington Studio; http://www.wabbington.com
Cartographer:
William L. Nelson of Bill Nelson Cartography; http://billnelsonmaps.esva.net
Designer:
Stephen Tiano of Tiano Book Design; http://www.tianobookdesign.com
Editor:
Katharine O'Moore-Klopf, ELS, of KOK Edit; http://www.kokedit.com
Proofreader:
Venkatesh Krishnamoorthy of Virtual Paper; http://www.virtualpaper.co.in
Indexer:
Cynthia Col of Cynthia Col Indexing and Editing; http://www.cynthiacol.com
Production, publication, and marketing:
Dick Margulis of Dick Margulis Creative Services; http://www.dmargulis.com

For Giridhar

Table of Contents

Preface

Journey of a Konkani Family, or *Eka Konkani Kutumba Pravasu* in Konkani, is the story of my family and our community. It is about a Konkani-speaking Gauda Sarasvat Brahmana (GSB) family from the South Kanara District of the west coast of India. We are a community of migrants. According to our traditions, the name Sarasvat is derived from the Vedic Sarasvati River, on whose banks we lived. Famine and other adverse living conditions forced us to disperse to different parts of India, eventually ending up in Goa. There were more migrations from Goa in the sixteenth century and later. Now quite a few of us are new immigrants in the United States.

I have always been intrigued by many questions about these migrations. Where and how did community members live? How did they interact with their neighbors and surroundings? Apart from their worldview as Hindus, what were their beliefs, their education? What were the mundane details of the texture and quality of their everyday lives? Above all, I wanted to know how they survived as a group, through all the vicissitudes and hardships of migrations. Unfortunately, we know very little of past history. There are very few written records—almost none. Some of the oral traditions are a mixture of myth and legend, with a few nuggets of truth in them. It is difficult to sort out the facts from later additions, embellishments, and poetic license that are part of oral traditions. Besides, these stories die out with the older generation and are lost forever. If we want to save the traditions of our family and community, we have to write them down. This has been my motivation for this book. My son, Giridhar, born and brought up in the United States, has always been interested in knowing about our family, the GSB community, their past, and their stories. Whenever I felt discouraged by the enormity of the task, he persuaded me to make a start on the book, keep at it, and bring it to a completion. Thus,

I dedicate this book to Giridhar, who asked for it. There are many young Konkanis who were born and brought up in the United States. If they are interested in our past too, I hope this book can satisfy their curiosity.

I have used all available records, written, oral, and a few tape-recorded interviews, in assembling this story. I have checked dates and events against more than one source where possible. If some information included here strains credulity, I say so. Because the purpose of this book is to tell the story of my family and our community, I have tried hard to keep any of my own biases, views, comments, criticism, and judgment to a minimum. Where these intrude on the main narrative, I point them out. In telling this story, I had to talk about Hinduism and its beliefs, which formed such an important part of our lives. Hinduism is a vast subject, and my own knowledge of it is very limited, so I am truly diffident in writing about it. There is no one correct way to write about any aspect of such a multifaceted subject as Hinduism. Each person's perspective, determined by personal experience, knowledge, and bias, is different, and no two statements regarding Hinduism need agree. Hence, I beg readers' indulgence in judging viewpoints or matters of detail that may be different from their own. Hinduism and its traditions are like a large mansion; it has room enough for many different points of view and opinions. However, if there are errors, I would appreciate it if you would point them out so that I can correct them. Because my knowledge of Sanskrit is almost nil, whatever little I know about Hinduism I have learned from the translations of scholars, both Eastern and Western. My debt to them is immense. I have acknowledged what I owe to these scholars by detailed references to their works. If there are any sources not properly credited, it is an oversight on my part and not an attempt at any claim of originality.

I am sure each Sarasvat family has its own stories to tell and traditions to recall. I hope this book will encourage them to write these down and contribute to the sum total of the human experience and collective memory of our community. Writing one's family history is always a hazardous project, with many opinions on its advisability. Some family members wonder whether it should be done at all. A few feel that the whole story is best forgotten; others think a sanitized version with a few selective lapses of memory are in order. Anyway, this is my version of our family story, which is also a platform for me to hold forth on personal views of life, especially on the power dynamics of human relationships involving the abuse of unrestricted power.

The first five chapters are the story of the past few generations of our family, ending up with our life in the United States. They also deal with the adventures of the GSB cluster outside Goa and their struggle for survival. Attached to this narrative are ten appendices treating a variety of topics. Appendix 1, "The

Cast," is meant to help the reader with the identities of people in the main narrative, so that they can keep the story line straight. Appendix 2, "Family Genealogy," and Appendix 3, "*Atri Gotra*, or Clan *Atri*," give more details on the family and its clan. Next are Appendix 4, "Kinship Terms in Konkani"; Appendix 5, "Hindu Rites of Passage"; and Appendix 6, "Feasts and Festivals." Appendix 7, "The Oracle, or *Darśana Sevā*," discusses the oracle at the Mulki Śrī Veñkataramaṇa Temple. Appendix 8, "Goa: A Paradise Lost?" is the story of our community in Goa some 450 years ago, before our exile to other parts of India. This is a sensitive, controversial topic on which there are many opinions, and it can evoke intense emotions. I hope that this version, narrated in a spirit of forgiveness, sheds more light and generates less heat. Appendix 9, "Guide to Konkani and Sanskrit Pronunciation," should be helpful with non-English words and with diacritics.

Throughout this book, I have given a short explanation of each non-English word immediately preceding or following its use in a sentence, so that readers can maintain their flow of thought without having to turn to the glossary (Appendix 10). Dipping into the glossary is worthwhile, however, because it contains other interesting information on etymology, similar words in Sanskrit or other languages, and related data. I hope that these help to expand readers' Konkani vocabulary painlessly, especially for those of the younger generation born and brought up in the United States. Diacritics have been used selectively to show the correct pronunciation of unfamiliar words. They have not been used with place and personal names or with other words in common use or those that have become part of standard English. Making the text user-friendly with diacritics has been more important than consistent or uniform usage. Some readers may feel uneasy when they face diacritics, which can be dealt with in two ways. The first is to get familiar with diacritics and, with a little practice, learn to pronounce words correctly. The second is to ignore them completely and plow right through the text. I leave this choice to the reader.

I have provided an extensive bibliography for those readers who would like to pursue matters discussed in the text in greater detail.

Mulki Radhakrishna Bhat

Author's Note on Usage

Some quotations from historical records included in this book contain offensive racial or religious epithets. These have been reproduced unsanitized, to convey the spirit and intent of the remarks and a flavor of the past. The author regrets any offense or hurt caused by inclusion of such language.

Map 1: Hindu Dispersal from Goa (Sixteenth Century and Later)

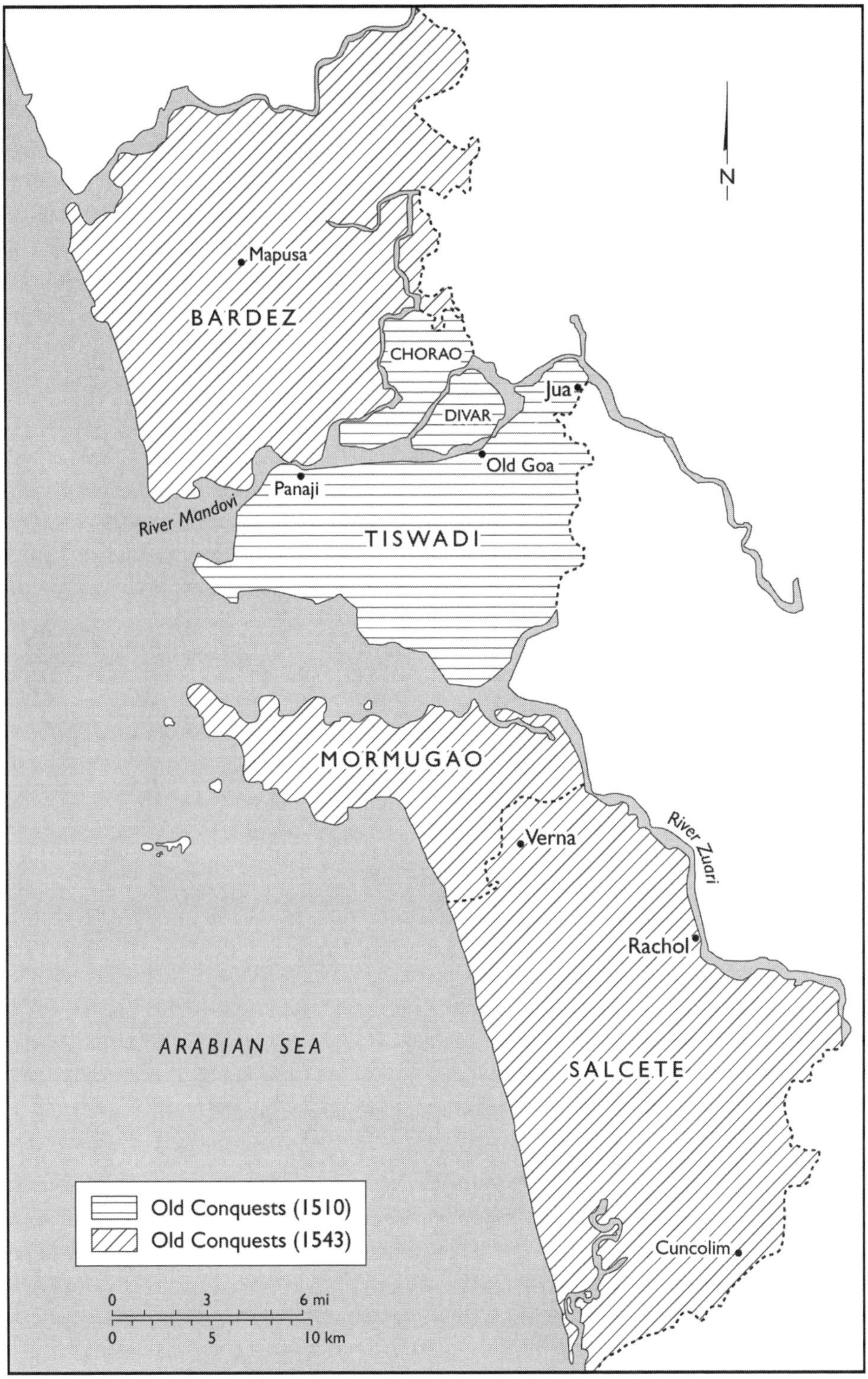

Map 2: Old Conquests in Goa by Portugal (1510–1543)

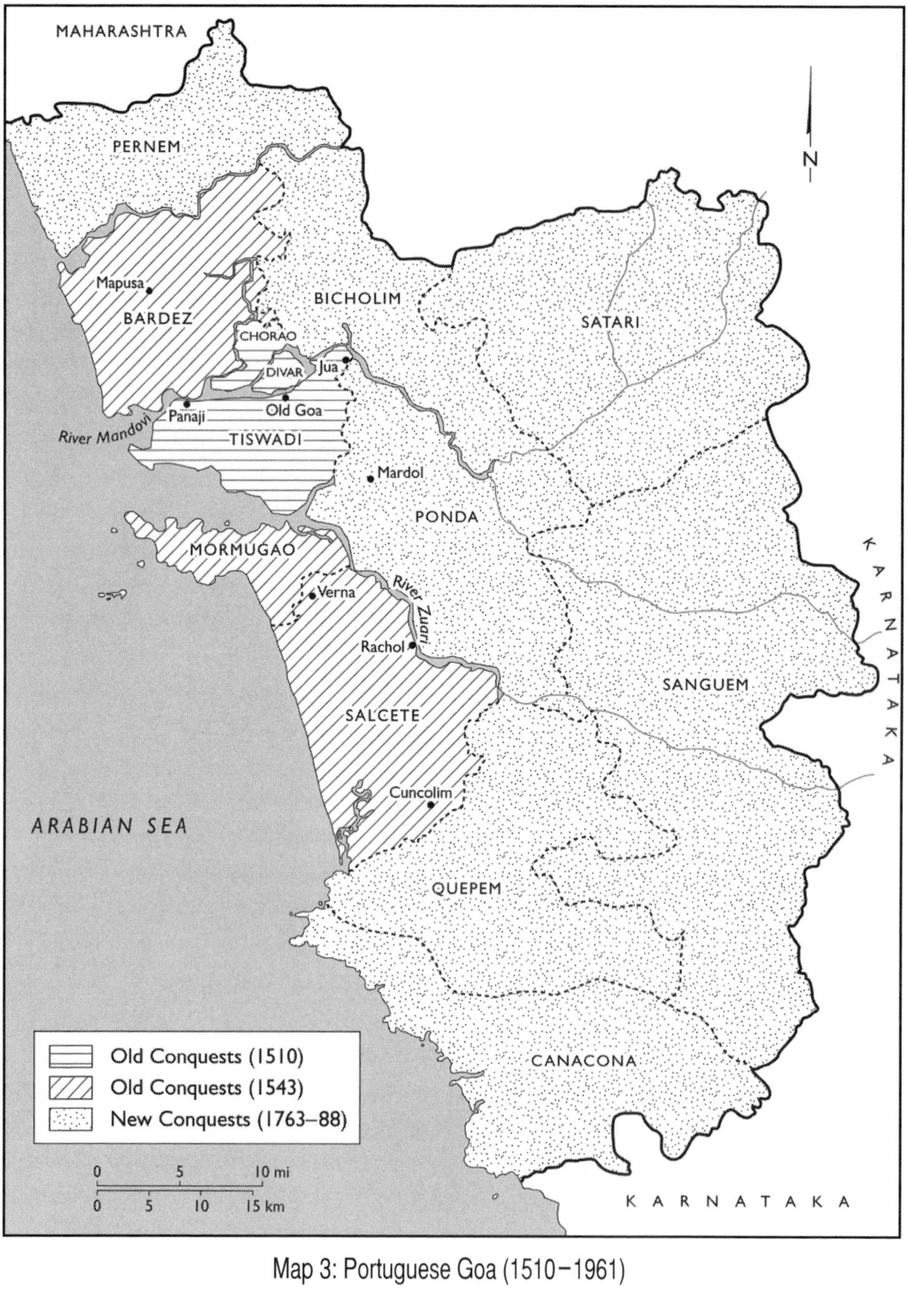

Map 3: Portuguese Goa (1510–1961)

CHAPTER ONE

Prabhus of Siddhapur

The man was lying facedown in the vestibule of the Kollur Mukhāmbikā Temple with his arms stretched out in supplication. Some said he had been there for a day; others said three days. Devotees looked at him with curiosity and went round his prostate body, in their *pradakṣiṇa* (circuits), and on round the sanctum. At the midday *mahāpūjā* (principal service), the vestibule and the surrounding areas were filled with worshippers gathered for the *darśana* (viewing) of the Goddess. Some were ringing the bronze bells in the temple and others were observing with rapt attention the *ārti* (waving of lights) in front of the image of Mukhāmbikā, their hands folded in prayer. At the conclusion of the *pūjā* (worship), the ringing of the bells stopped suddenly, and after a brief blessed silence, the chanting of the priests and the barely audible murmur of prayers of other devotees took over. Suddenly, the man got to his feet, and with tears streaming down his face and hands folded in prayer, he started singing the praises of Mukhāmbikā for favors granted. His song of praise was his own composition, created spontaneously. This was the rebirth of Siddhapur Venkataramana Prabhu—gambler, pot smoker, and wastrel—as a poet, an exponent of Hindu *purāṇas* (epics), and a singer of God's praise in *harikathās* (narratives of Hindu epics in song and story).

The Legend of Venkataramana Prabhu

Venkataramana Prabhu is my father's maternal great-grandfather. He was poor; my family does not know his date of birth. At the time he was born, most people did not bother to record their date of birth. He spent all his life in Siddhapur, a small village, in South Kanara District, cultivating a few fields for a living. He employed day laborers to help him with this hard work, but the income it produced barely supported him and his family. His education in a local school, *aigaḷa śāle*, was minimal—he could barely read and write. A compulsive gambler who indulged in smoking marijuana and drinking its decoction, *bhāṅgīpānaka*, he barely managed to survive. His younger brother, however, had been adopted by a rich family, the Nayaks of Gangolly. Whenever Venkataramana did not have enough to eat and hunger got the better of his self-respect, he would go to his brother to ask for a handout. The brother would load up a bullock cart with rice, dhal, oil, and other essentials and send them with his *aṇṇā* (elder brother) to help him out till the next crisis. But on one such occasion, the younger brother had had it. He was in a bad mood because he could see that helping out his elder brother was going to be a lifelong project. He started berating his brother about his bad habits, his wasted life, what a pain in the neck he was, and on and on, finally telling him not to expect any help from him starting right then. Poor Venkataramana, who was acutely aware of his own shortcomings, his wasteful habits, was devastated. The lecture hurt not only because it was delivered by his younger brother but also because what his brother said was all too true. Venkataramana thought of killing himself but decided against it for two reasons: First, suicide was forbidden for an orthodox Hindu; second, his wife would end up having to go to the same brother for help in performing his funeral rites. There was just no way that he could commit suicide. Finally, he decided to go to the Mukhāmbikā Temple at Kollur and take refuge in the Goddess. She had created him, so it was Her responsibility to show him a way out of his problems, to help him find some gainful employment. At the temple, he washed the small *muṇḍa* (oblong piece of cloth worn round the waist) that he was wearing, took a bath in the temple tank, and prostrated himself in the vestibule in his wet clothes, seeking refuge in the mercy of the Goddess. He begged for a miracle that would show him the way.

He soon found that his unshakable faith in Her had been rewarded with new talents: He could now create poetry as an exponent of *harikathās*—literally, "God's stories." He could spontaneously create songs in praise of the Gods; they seem to pour out of him without his conscious volition. For a barely literate man, this was indeed a miracle. He attributed his newfound talent entirely to the grace of the Goddess.

A few days after this event, the manager of the temple had a dream in which the Goddess commanded him to prepare a silver *mukha* (face) or representation of the Goddess, place it next to Her image in the main temple for *pūjā* for three days, and then give it to Her devotee, who would appear at the temple. Venkataramana also had a dream. In his, the Goddess commanded him to go to the temple to pick up the silver *mukha* that She was bestowing on him as a mark of Her favor. She commanded him to worship this image every day and keep it in his family for all time. This was Her gift to Venkataramana and his descendants. This *mukha* is still in the Prabhu family. It is a silver disk about six inches in diameter and about three-quarters of an inch thick, with the face of the Goddess in relief. It ends in a handle, which can be inserted in a support to install it for worship. In every Hindu family, there is a small niche, or cupboard-like enclosure, a *devā kūḍa* (family shrine), usually built into a wall, where the images of the deities are kept for daily worship. The lady of the house, after her morning bath, would formally open the enclosure and light a bronze oil lamp in front of the images. The lamp usually has five wicks fed by coconut oil. On ceremonial occasions, all of the five or seven wicks are lit; for everyday use, only one is lit, to save oil. Men of the family, who had gone through the *upanayana*, or the thread ceremony, could worship after their bath, when in a ritually pure state. In some families, a priest would visit every day to conduct worship and seek *prasāda* (grace) for the family. The *mukha* used to be kept in the house of Ananthayya, son of Venkataramana. Now it is with Srinivas, Ananthayya's great-grandson, who lives in Bangalore.

Harikathā has been a popular art form in South India for centuries. The event usually takes place in a temple in the evening and lasts for a few hours. Some performances dealing with complete epics could last for a few days, ending in a finale that sometimes involved a dinner for the whole community. The performer, or *Haridāsa* (God's servant), expounds an episode from one of the Hindu epics, interspersing the tale with songs, vivid imagery, mime, and humor. Before the advent of cinema and television, *Harikathā* was the only entertainment available to people. Outlines of these episodes, including the songs composed by famous *Haridāsas*, are available in books or as unpublished manuscripts. After his epiphany in the Mukhāmbikā Temple, Venkataramana became a famous *Haridāsa*. Each *Haridāsa* has his own ritual as part of his performance. Venkataramana had a wooden cradle made for his act. The *mukha* of the Goddess would be placed in it, draped with garlands of jasmine and other flowers hanging on the sides of the cradle. The ceremony would begin with Venkataramana doing the *ārti* (waving of lights) to the Goddess. With folded hands, Venkataramana would start singing Her praises, and then invoke Her blessings on his performance, while the rest of the devotees watched in rapt silence. After a while, the audience would see the cradle rocking gently, vouchsafing Her presence, and Venkataramana would begin his *harikathā*. Did the cradle really rock, or did it appear to rock because the strands of jasmine flowers with which it was draped moved gently? We do not know; Venkataramana and the devotees who formed his audience believed that they could see it rock. That was all that mattered to them. The songs he sang were mostly his own compositions, supplemented by those attributed to earlier poets and *Haridāsas*. My father remembers seeing notebooks of his original compositions. They were never published; I think they are lost now. These notebooks, along with his *tambūra* (three-stringed drone), used to lay in the attic over the kitchen in the house of his son, Ananthayya. It must have been discarded in one of the periodic cleanups carried out because the smoke from the kitchen coated everything in the attic with a fine layer of soot. Venkataramana also trained younger aspirants who wanted to become *Haridāsas*. One of these disciples was a Shivalli Brahman, Haridasa Lakshmi Naranappa of Pavanje, who composed the songs sung during the *pradakṣiṇa* (circumambulations) of the Venkataramana Temple at Karkal during the festivals (Kudva 1978, 203).

Venkataramana Prabhu Becomes a *Nāgapātri*

A short distance from Siddhapur, there is a village called Kammarsale, famous for its *nāgatīrtha* (pond sacred to cobras) in a cave. Cobras, *nāgas*, must have been worshipped as totemic deities in India even before the advent of Hinduism. Later, in a spirit of inclusiveness, they were merged into Hindu worship, especially that associated with Shiva. In a *nāgatīrtha*, there are usually many cobras, which are supposed to be harmless to devotees who approach them with proper reverence and in a state of ritual purity. However, people were afraid to take a dip in the pond, because one never knew what would happen. One day, Venkataramana decided to take a bath in the pond. We do not know whether he was egged on by his friends, did it out of bravado, or perhaps thought that if the cobras bit him, it might provide a brave end to all his financial woes. To his great surprise, he found that the cobras left him alone and were not aggressive. Word got around about his fearlessness in dealing with cobras, and people said that he must have a *garuḍa rekho* (*Garuḍa's* line) on his palms. In Hindu mythology, Garuḍa, part giant and part eagle, is the *vāhana* (transport) of Viṣṇu and is a sworn enemy of all cobras. Hindu folklore says that those with the *garuḍa rekho* on their palms are immune to the bite of a cobra and can handle them with impunity.

Shortly after this incident, Venkataramana had a dream in which a *nāga* told him to dig in a particular field and look for the buried image of a *nāga*, which he was to install in a temple. Sure enough, he found this image, which was installed in a small hut serving as a temple, or *gūḍi* (hut), and served as its priest. Soon after these events, Venkataramana developed eye problems that could not be cured by traditional, local medicine. This was an indication that the eye problems were due to the involvement of some supernatural forces and were most probably due to some sins of commission or omission. Tradition indicated that one sure way of finding the real cause of such problems was to consult an astrologer, who could divine the real reason by consulting the stars. The astrologer told Venkataramana that his eye problems were caused by his not cleaning properly the mud from the eyes of the *nāga* image. A thorough cleaning of the image, followed by other expiatory rites, was recommended. Venkataramana found that his eye problem cleared up by itself after he followed the instructions of the astrologer. Word of all these happenings got around, and his cure was declared a miracle, attesting to the sanctity of the *nāga* image and its power to cure human ills. Venkataramana welcomed all this attention to his small temple. Large number of devotees started coming to the temple with their problems and expectation of cures, and their offerings provided another source of income for him. This image is supposed to be a beautiful representation of a five-hooded *nāga*, carved out of black granite and about 3.5 feet high. My father remembers seeing it on a visit to Siddhapur.

This small *nāga* temple became quite famous in the immediate neighborhood of Siddhapur. If a cobra appeared in a person's house, it was considered to be a sign of displeasure by the cobra deity, and people would vow to convey specific offerings to the temple if only the cobra would leave them alone in future. Offerings to Nāga are also considered in the Hindu traditions to be particularly efficacious for childless couples who wish to have children. (Note the obvious phallic symbolism.) Word got around about successes in this regard, and the *nāga* came to be regarded as a *kārṇike devu* (powerful deity). These circumstances would have made any other person quite happy. However, Venkataramana, with his compulsive gambling and addiction to *bhāṅgi* (marijuana), never had enough money. He would pray to the *nāga* image to send him more devotees with offerings. To Venkataramana, the image was a living presence of the deity, who was his friend and patron, and he would have long soliloquies, one-to-one, detailing his financial woes and other problems. He would beg the *nāga* to be kind and gracious to his servant and send more devotees with rich offerings. If he thought that the deity was not responsive, he would resort to coercion. Sometimes he is supposed to have beaten the image with twigs to get the *nāga's* attention. He would coat the image with honey, which would then swarm with fierce fire ants. In his imagination, this was equivalent of a live cobra swarming with ants and being bitten by them. He believed that this would force the deity to induce more devotees to come to the temple with fresh offerings.

Venkataramana also used to earn some extra money as a *nāgapātri*, a medium who is possessed by the spirit of a *nāga* and who in such a state of possession serves as an oracle by answering questions of devotees regarding their everyday problems, such as the need for cures for illnesses that do not respond to traditional medicine, lost articles or animals, spells and incantations of enemies, begetting children, and whether to undertake new projects or business ventures. Such a ceremony, usually performed in a temple, is called *nāga darśaṇa* (Nāga's audience), and is performed regularly on certain auspicious days or on special occasions by request. A much more elaborate ceremony called *Nāgamaṇḍala* is performed to propitiate the serpent deity and is commissioned by a rich patron (Bhatt 1975, xxix; 1977). In this ceremony, the principal part is played by the *nāgapātri* (medium), who is accompanied by attendant *nāgakanyaks* (serpent maidens). The medium would normally carry cobras fashioned out of metal or wood, rampant and with their hoods spread, which when handled properly in his dance would appear to be alive. What was unique about Venkataramana's performance as a *nāgapātri* was that he would go to the nearest nest of cobras, *huththo*, and pick up a pair of live cobras, use them in the ceremony, dance with them, and let them go afterward. Such an act naturally inspired awe and gave great drama to his performances. He convinced the large number of devotees that this was a genuine thing and that he was really communing with the Nāga deity. In such worship it is customary to use the white flower pod, *bhiṅgāru*, of the local areca palm tree. At the conclusion of worship, Venkataramana would bow down with open palms, beseeching Nāga to bestow *prasāda* on the devotees. He and other devotees claimed that strands of these white flowers would miraculously fall into his palms, vouchsafing Nāga's grace. There are many other stories of the miracles he worked and the tests he passed to convince skeptics that he was really dealing with supernatural forces and was not a fake.

Because of his performances as a *Haridāsa* or as a *nāgapātri*, Venkataramana was usually away from home for many days at a time. His returns did not bode well for his wife. He was intensely jealous and would accuse his wife of infidelity, without any basis. She, poor woman, who was a virtuous, pious Hindu wife, had to put up with his temper tantrums, beatings, and physical abuse, in addition to his being an uncertain provider. As a general rule, a Hindu wife is a much-exploited person, abused by her mother-in-law and/or her husband. If she survives all of these trials and tribulations, she in turn will usually exploit *her* daughter-in-law, perpetuating the cycle of abuse and dominance.

Dominance and Hierarchy Among Chimpanzees and Humans

Dominance of one person by another and the power play involved in it have always puzzled and fascinated me. Ever since I learned to think for myself and assess the world around me, I realized that as the youngest member of the family, I was the beneficiary of much advice, criticism, and correction from the elders of the family. There was nobody whom *I* could advise, correct, or boss around. I thought this was unfair. Did age confer authority, knowledge, and wisdom automatically? In the traditional Hindu family in which I grew up, this was a tacit assumption. Most grown-ups felt that it was their duty to confer the precious boon of free, unasked-for advice on younger people, for the good of the objects of their attention. It appeared that the sole motivation for this act was their benevolence. But was it something else? Did they want to lord it over me just for the fun of it? Did they relish this exercise of authority? Was authority earned and achieved? These are some of the questions that used to bother me a lot. I learned the hard way that I had to put up with all this unequal distribution of power. In my rebellious teenage years, I talked back to air my feelings. I did it in no uncertain terms, till my elders learned to leave me alone. I also learned how to ignore all of this freely bestowed advice and do my own thing.

These ideas were floating in my mind for a long time without condensing into a coherent picture till I read a remarkable book: *Chimpanzee Politics*, by Frans de Waal, a primatologist (de Waal 1998). It was originally published in 1982, with a revised edition printed in 1998. I must have read the book soon after its publication, and I have reread it many times since and recommended it to my friends. The book describes the social life of about 25 free-ranging chimps at the Burgers' Zoo in Arnhem, Netherlands. Their behavior was studied and recorded meticulously for many years. Chimps' behavior is governed by their pursuit of food, sex, and dominance, in that order. Each chimp colony is always ruled over by an alpha male who controls access to food and sex by the rest of the troop. There is also an alpha female, with other female chimps occupying status niches in descending order. Thus, there is a hierarchy in each troop of chimps in which every adult chimp knows her or his place. Any challenge to this ranking is met with immediate physical punishment, unless the challenger is strong enough to fight back and make the challenge stick. This hierarchy is based on and maintained by physical strength. Baby chimps are allowed much freedom till they are old enough to know their place in the scheme of things. Babies of high-ranking females grow up to be confident and outgoing adults because they are treated better by other grown-ups under the watchful eye of the mother, who is always ready to fight for the interests of her offspring. The alpha male, once having achieved his rank, has to maintain it. There are always young interlopers looking for some signs of weakness in the aging boss and wanting to dethrone him. In most of the cases, the younger challenger is not able to defeat the alpha male by himself. Hence these young males have to look for support from other lower-ranking chimps, male or female, and form coalitions. This is where the politics of chimp behavior comes in, and the author notes that it is crafty, cunning, devious, and manipulative, worthy of a Machiavelli (de Waal 1998, 4). The challenger knows how to manipulate his coalition partners, use them to achieve his goals, and then discard them when they are no longer needed. Usually, the young adults ignore baby chimps as unworthy of their notice. However, when they want the help of the baby's mother, they show much kindness and attention to her baby, play with it, kiss it, and are nice to it. Chimps have been kissing babies to get mommy votes for ages, before human politicians learned the behavior! These themes are further developed and explicated by the same author in a later book: *Our Inner Ape* (de Waal 2005).

Primacy Drive and Primacy Pride/Conceit in Humans

This pursuit of food for survival, sex for the propagation of the species, and pursuit of power to feed the ego (or its chimp equivalent) is very much a part of chimp psyche and society. Power is the ultimate turn-on for males, who get addicted to its use (de Waal 2005, 49). As is noted later, female chimps too do not exactly shun power if they get it. Humans also strive for power after taking care of food and sex, and they appear to have essentially the same priorities as chimps. Humans have 98.5% of their genes in common with chimps. These circumstances suggest a plausible hypothesis: The pursuit of power by chimps and humans may be due to some of the same set of genes that are held in common. These set of genes must be our common genetic heritage, and we can explore where such a hypothesis leads us. Humans have much bigger brains than chimps, and their behavior is necessarily more complex than that of chimps. With our larger brains, this genetic heritage could lead us to much greater heights of sophistication, deceit, duplicity, and cunning, in pursuit of power. The idea I want to develop in this story is that the pursuit of power or dominance is the basic theme, and how humans use available opportunities, such as social, political, religious, economic, administrative, or any other institutions, to achieve this goal, are its variations. The motto is pursuit of power by any and every means; no opportunity is wasted. The available resources are used with much creativity, originality, and sophistication. This urge to be the first or the alpha of the group, I would like to call the *primacy drive.* It is defined as a basic need felt by each individual of a group to achieve the dominant or alpha status in it. Primacy drive is a plausible extrapolation from chimp behavior to that of humans. It motivates us to do strange things that determine the dynamics of our interaction with others of the group, bringing about changes in it. The primacy drive makes each individual try to dominate others in the group, to be the first or achieve alpha status. Dr. Samuel Johnson, a perceptive observer of the human scene, commenting on equality and subordination among men, said: "So far is it from being true that men are naturally equal, that no two people can be half an hour together, but one shall acquire an evident superiority over the other!" (Boswell 1960, 318, 15 Feb. 1766). As has been pointed out by de Waal, a desire to rank oneself against another is present in all of us (de Waal 2005, 49). If we are not happy with the outcome of such ranking, we will try to improve the situation by trying to dominate the other! One corollary of the primacy drive is the *primacy pride* or *conceit*, which impels the individual or the group to tell others that they have indeed achieved the goal of being number one. The pride is usually the result of measurable achievements, while the conceit is the product of one's illusions about them. The struggle for dominance can lead to social stratification within the tribe or group to form a power hierarchy with the successful individual at the very apex. This struggle may be the cause of violence among the primates (Goodall 1986; de Waal 1998; Wrangham and Peterson 1996). Under these circumstances, there is no such entity as a truly egalitarian group or society; it exists only in an idealistic utopia. History has many examples of groups that might have started as egalitarian, which after a period of group interaction and dynamics, end up stratified into a power hierarchy with an alpha at the apex and a supporting cast of subordinates. In ancient Egypt of the 5th Dynasty (~2494–2345 BCE), the pharaoh was at the apex with about two thousand grades of court officials, each with an official title, serving him in a well-ordered hierarchy (Wesson 1967, 110). Another good example is the early Christian community, a group of unprivileged, nondominant, like-minded persons, who considered themselves equal to one another in their membership of the proto-Church. The Christians were equal, meek, and humble and did not dominate or persecute anyone. Fast-forward to 440 CE, and what do we see? Pope Leo the Great (440–461 CE) is at the head of the Church, next stands the hierarchy, and the rest of the laity is somewhere down below, ranked by wealth. The meek and humble now dominate, and the persecuted are the persecutors (Küng 2001). The primacy drive has triumphed once again! This group dynamic is highly predictable. Once a person has been sensitized to look for the basic primacy drive, the why and how of our actions become more transparent, enabling a better understanding of our motives. I am not saying that this urge for dominance is the *sole* driving force in humans. Human brains are complex structures, and so are we. Our motivations for action are many, and they are not obvious even to us sometimes. All I would like to point out is that the urge for dominance over others of the group is one of the important or principal motivations. Whether the group dynamics involves two or more persons, whether it is a nuclear or a joint family, administrative structure of a business, community institution, religious hierarchy, or a nation, the underlying theme is the same; it is a pursuit of power and the urge to dominate, felt by each individual. Under ordinary circumstances, this pursuit of power and its exercise are constrained by social or religious moral codes, having to answer to a higher boss, human or supernatural, or being afraid to encroach on someone else's territory. These checks and balances usually keep humans and their actions within accepted bounds of sanity, moderation, and norms of behavior. However, once in a while a peculiar constellation of circumstances occurs where power is unlimited. Its use is motivated by an ideological zeal impervious to doubt or critical self-examination, with the result that there are no built-in self-correcting mechanisms. Under these conditions, humans and their institutions are corrupted by unlimited power; they are blind to common sense, fairness, and justice; and they commit the most monstrous crimes, even with the best of intentions. We can see an example of this in the persecution of the Buddhists, Hindus, and Muslims by the Portuguese state and the Roman Catholic Church in medieval Goa and the excesses of the Inquisition (see Appendix 8: "Goa: A Paradise Lost?"). My family's community, the Konkani-speaking Sarasvats, suffered much from these persecutions because in sixteenth-century Goa they faced a stark choice: convert to Christianity to be allowed to live in Portuguese Goa, or go into exile. My ancestors chose exile over conversion, and started on a journey filled with dangers and an uncertain future.

The human urge to dominate others has also led to wars of aggression, which result in other two major evils of human society: wholesale slaughter and slavery. Such pursuits are sometimes concealed under a nobler-sounding "pursuit of glory" to hide the resulting human misery. In this story, I give examples of such pursuit of glory, which depend on the killing of innocents, and also explain why people admire these serial murderers. As regards the story of my family, there are also the parallel interweaving themes of dominance and the pursuit of power. I invite the reader to keep an open mind about this added dimension to the story, waiting until the end to decide whether it is a plausible explanation and a conceivable scenario.

The single-minded ruthless pursuit of power in chimps is much softened in a related species, the bonobo, also wrongly called pygmy chimps (de Waal 1997; 2005). Bonobos show much greater empathy for other members of their group, temper competition with cooperation, and are more sensitive and less rough in their social relationships than chimps are, though they too pursue power. Female coalitions are more common among bonobos than among chimps. Such coalition partners have been known to gang up on the males of the group, deprive them of food, and make them beg for it (de Waal 2005, 64). Pursuit of power and the urge to dominate is gender neutral. Frans de Waal thinks that there is a bit of chimp and or bonobo in all of us. Dominance need not be asserted by physical force alone. Any form of intimidation, physical, psychological, or emotional, works equally well. This is where the originality of the individual fighting for the alpha status comes in. Mike was a low-level chimp of Gombe, in a hierarchy of fourteen males. He used two to three empty kerosene tins in his charging displays to scare and terrorize the more powerful, higher-ranking chimps. Using this novel method, he promoted himself to alpha status within four months (Goodall 1986, 426, 550). Mike's originality in his path to dominance paid handsome dividends. A parallel between Mike's charging displays of banging on tin cans to be an alpha and the rituals of promotion within academe should be noted. The scholarly drama (charging display) begins with the publication of significant new work, whose importance is attested to by its frequency of reference in a citation index. This is followed by invitations to the usual round of seminars at major universities and research laboratories. The proud author rehashes the same results, or bangs on the same tin drum, over and over again. This impresses (intimidates?) the power elite in the field to such an extent that they want the newcomer to be part of their high-status group. Fresh blood to rejuvenate the group of aging eminences is always a necessity. The upstart is rewarded by election to national academies, tenure and elevation to an endowed chair in a prestigious institution, a reserved parking spot with a nameplate, and other marks of distinction. This is the ultimate academic Valhalla for scholars, short of a Nobel Prize.

The insight provided by the chimps has been most helpful in understanding human behavior, including my own. Once the power structure of a new, strange group of humans is understood, their motivation and behavior become transparent. Each of us lust for dominance within our circumstances, shown by such markers as wealth, personal appearance, and education. Each of us is part of a hierarchy whether we are aware of it or not. Though a hierarchy gives a certain amount of stability and security to all the members of the group, the price they pay is dominance and exploitation by the higher-ranking members. Each group member in turn exploits the one below in the pecking order. Humans indulge in social behaviors that have striking parallels to what the chimps do. Chimps, both male and female, display: They work themselves into a frenzy, with their hackles raised, hooting loudly, rhythmically thumping their feet, throwing heavy objects around, and in general putting on a theatrical show of immense power. The other chimps get out of the way of the displaying chimp and let her or him calm down before they approach the displayer to participate in normal activities such as grooming. Such an intimidating display is very similar to the bursts of temper of the reigning matriarch or patriarch, whose unchecked rule is accepted by the lesser, dependent members of the family. Usually, he is the sole breadwinner, and all members of the family are beholden to him. When I lose my temper and have an irresistible desire to verbalize my frustrations and act up, I tell myself: "Don't be an ass and put on a chimp display." I see the humor of the situation and calm down immediately. Reading about the chimps has helped me to temper my own behavior.

Primacy Drive and Hierarchy

In this narrative, I draw more parallels between chimp and human behavior. My point is that hierarchies are just as much a part of human society as they are of chimp troops. I use here interchangeably the terms *hierarchy, power structure, social stratification, status,* and *dominance group* to denote essentially the same idea: the fact that pursuit of power or the primacy drive leads to dominance, which results in a hierarchy within a group. The term *dominance hierarchy* has Latin and Greek origins and may be replaced by the basic English phrase *ranked heap.* The word *heap* readily conveys the sense of a pile of sand with a broad base ending with a pointed peak, indicative of status ranking in the pile where available niches in the pecking order get fewer the higher you go. Both of these terms are used interchangeably in the following.

There is a ranking of status, and each individual in the group is aware of her or his position in it. Further, access to resources such as food and sex depend on the individual's position in the hierarchy. All it takes is two primates to interact before the process of eyeing each other begins, with the participants consciously or unconsciously assessing their relative standing and beginning to jockey for position to a more advantageous stance. Such behavior of course becomes more complex when extrapolated to a large group of humans. Humans have larger brains than chimpanzees do, and there are more reciprocal interactions between them than between chimps. However, some common features stand out as part of these rankings or hierarchies: dominance, exercise of power, and exploitation. Dictionaries define dominance as the relative position of an individual in a social hierarchy. Each individual is acutely conscious of her or his standing in the pecking order or dominance and is continuously working to improve it. The exercise of power goes along with dominance and very much depends on the individual. Power depends on the person who wields it and devolves on the individual who uses it. There are always individuals who take a relaxed view of the power they possess and who do not use it. A few push the limits of the power they have, to see how much they can get away with. Exploitation, the third factor, can vary over a wide spectrum. It can be the gentle persuasion of a good friend or a spouse to get what she or he wants, a religious hierarchy sanctioned by faith, or the aggressive misuse of a chattel slave by a master. Thus each niche in the dominance hierarchy has its obligatory exploitation hierarchy of debits or credits. Each member exploits those lower on the ladder and is exploited by those higher in the pecking order. This is life as it is, in its basic raw simplicity.

Alexander III of Macedon, Also Called the Great

Those of you who think that all this is some interesting bit of drivel, not applicable to people like us, let me give you another example. This has to do with our perpetual infatuation with individuals who exercised military power, were extremely successful at it, and have been immortalized in history and literature with the epithet "the Great." Examples are Alexander III of Macedon, also called Alexander the Great (Green 1991; Rogers 2005), and Charlemagne, also called Charles the Great (Bullough 1966). Each of these was a complex personality with many achievements to their credit—some constructive, others destructive. However, their military exploits form a significant part of their credentials for being called great. Historians and biographers have written hagiographies of these individuals full of admiration for their achievements, making their lives into romances of immense fascination, moving from one success to the next greater one. The stories or mythologies justifying these military actions are rehashed and the convenient excuses are retold for any incidental crimes they may have committed. The reader of these biographies savors the vicarious pleasure of the successes of their heroes, participates in their glory, tacitly identifies with them, and vaguely feels their power by proxy. Why do people admire these so-called greats? Because their struggle for and achievement of power resonate with the primacy drive in each of us. Somehow, we forget the immense oceans of human misery caused by this pursuit of personal glory that ultimately is built on the death and destruction of countless individuals, both soldiers and noncombatants such as women and children who unfortunately happened to be in the way of these heroes. Those who were not slain by these heroes were sold into slavery, to live out the rest of their lives as chattel, and dehumanized. It is only very recently that a few historians have dared to question the certainty of greatness traditionally assigned to these individuals (Green 1991; Rogers 2005). Green admits that Alexander's triumphal march of conquest was a trail of tears for the vanquished; they were pillaged, plundered, enslaved, or slaughtered (Green 1991, 477). To me it appears that the psyche of these individuals and their pursuit of glory built on the death of fellow humans is an indication of sick thinking. Alexander might have stood high and tall; however, he stood on an immense pile of human bodies and human misery. How come we admire these mass murderers and call them great? Why do we extol this form of psychopathology? I would like to suggest that it is because every one of us has the same genetic heritage that impels humans to dominate fellow tribe members, compete for the same resources, and exploit them if we can. Each of us, in our small way, is involved in these games of dominance, competition, and exploitation in our everyday lives. Hence the mighty deeds of these aberrant heroes strike a sympathetic chord in our individual psyches. The human misery involved is conveniently forgotten, especially if these killings happened in the distant past, to people whom we identify as "others," and we are deluded by the myths defending these "just wars." Thus Alexander's war against Persia and his burning of Persepolis in 330 BCE are justified as revenge for the destruction of the Acropolis of Athens and the burning of its temples by Xerxes 150 years earlier. Both acts were equally barbaric and reprehensible. The death or enslavement of innocent peoples in such battles as unavoidable "collateral damage" is totally unacceptable!

Genuine Human Greats

We do admire the person who proved Fermat's theorem or the painter of the *Mona Lisa* because these have reached such rare, unique peaks of human achievement. Their abilities are so completely and totally beyond the abilities of most of us that we cannot imagine ourselves in their shoes. However, dominating fellow humans and exploiting them are things we know only too well. The primacy drive is common to every one of us and to these immensely successful historical personages. That is why we admire these greats. The reader may dismiss this explanation as an interesting hypothesis, as difficult to prove or disprove—or as just a bit of hot air. If there is an alternate explanation for our general admiration of the military heroes, these rampant psychopaths and megalomaniacs, I would be interested in knowing it. I suggest that the truly great persons are those whose lives have contributed to a decrease of the sum total of human misery, such as Louis Pasteur, whose studies of microorganisms led to the cure or prevention of many diseases, or Norman Borlaug, whose discoveries in plant genetics resulted in the Green Revolution in agriculture that put food in many an empty belly. There are many others. Unfortunately, most of us do not even know or cannot recall the names of these truly great persons; instead we admire the serial psychopaths of military might. This reexamination of our admiration for the military greats of history and rethinking of their foul deeds, this appeal of reason to the human cognitive cortex—will it make us change our minds about warfare and dominance? Of course not! We will continue to fight wars—some just, others not so just—and to delude ourselves and others into believing that we should use industrial might to dominate others, indulge in games of hostile takeover in which we annihilate lesser opponents, play and enjoy aggressive competitive sports that stop short of murder, assert loyalty and support to our favorite teams with sports hooliganism and accidental murder . . . the list can go on and on. Dominance over others of the tribe originates in our genes and perhaps appeals to our brains at a level more basic than reason and compassion. We and our cousins the chimps bow to a similar genetic imperative, and it is their pant-hoots that echo in the caverns of our mind as we struggle to reach the top of the heap.

Primacy Pride and or Conceit

Does this cynical view of human society mean that it is past redemption? Are there no benign social interactions free of competition or the urge to dominate? Are there are no egalitarian societies? No, they exist, more or less, on paper. Egalitarian societies are part of the idealistic musings of social philosophers, of the ringing words of a constitution—on paper. But real life is entirely different. We humans are good at taking each and every label used in any classification, attaching a value to it, and claiming superiority whenever possible over someone else. These labels are used to anchor our overt or covert prejudices regarding skin color—black, brown, yellow, and white; ethnic origin—some deemed more desirable than others; religious beliefs—monotheism versus other belief systems; military might—superpower against lesser states . . . The list of human conceits that create an illusion of superiority over others is endless. It appears as though strict egalitarianism is a virtue that humans do not possess but would dearly like to claim. The yearning for this elusive, desirable label is so strong that some social scientists labor under the illusion that a few societies, including their own, are egalitarian, while others are not (Dumont 1980). I submit that just as is the case for our nearest cousins the chimps, competition and striving for dominance are built into our genes. We might as well accept it as a fact of human existence. Is this constant striving for dominance good for the individual and the species? This is an interesting question that must be answered by the ethologist, the anthropologist, or the social historian by looking at the data from functioning groups. We cannot, of course, ask the chimps; they seem to be quite happy with their lot. As for humans, we appear to be thriving under the competitive system. Individuals eventually reach the level of their competence in a hierarchy. If a person has the guts and gumption to reach higher, there are always openings for her or him to do it. In general this state of affairs leads to quite a bit of satisfaction with the status quo, making individuals feel quite good about what they have, what they are, or where they *think* they are. I am sure this has benefits to the individual, the group, and the species from an evolutionary viewpoint. It appears as if this sense of satisfaction extrapolates from individuals to groups, and then to nations and cultures, giving rise to some interesting cultural conceits. Each and every literate culture in history has left a record of claims for its exclusiveness and superiority over others with which it came in contact. They have been generous in bestowing on themselves accolades for these presumed virtues. Each culture has made exclusive claims to being civilized, cultured, noble, elect, select, chosen, central, extraordinary, and any other prideful conceit you can name, while the "others" are casually dismissed as barbarians, rude, crude, gentile, heathen, pagan, ordinary, and uncivilized. This claim to be the first, the best, and the exclusive possessor of eternal truths may be called a primacy pride or conceit and is found in all civilizations. What is the difference between these two states of mind? Pride is usually based on real achievements; the conceit is a product of illusions. *Primacy pride* is a cognitive state of an individual or a group that is convinced that it has indeed achieved the dominant or alpha status. This state of mind usually confers a sense of superiority and a desire to flaunt it. Self-delusion, which makes up for the difference between reality and one's self-image, causes primacy conceit. Both the pride and the conceit are obviously by-products of the primacy drive. It is a state of mind that results in much self-satisfaction. "I am the first" and "we are the best" are convictions created by the all-powerful primacy drive, in individuals or groups. All such claims result from the urge for dominance masquerading as presumed cultural superiority over others. Here is an example. Every American politician who opens her or his mouth has to state the obvious: We are the only superpower on Earth! We do not only flaunt it; we also rub it in. Does this mean that all societies are equally hierarchical? No, I do not think so; some are worse than others. Even the most egalitarian society's in-group is convinced of its primacy over other out-groups. For example, I think that U.S. society is more egalitarian than others I know of, rewarding hard work and enterprise and encouraging upward mobility. Is it as egalitarian as Alexis de Tocqueville thought (de Tocqueville 2004)? Perhaps not. I am sure that the U.S. society of his time was more egalitarian than the French or the European societies he was familiar with. However, social, political, and economic inequalities were very much a fact of life before and during his famous visit and his perceptive book, and they have been ever since then. If you have any doubts, compare the obscene, astronomical salaries of the CEO and upper management of any large corporation with the pay of its factory workers. Think of the prestige of an Ivy League university education versus that provided by a mere land-grant university; ponder the cachet of a Mayflower descendant versus that of a new immigrant; consider the privileges of old money versus the things that new money cannot buy. We humans are not egalitarian at heart; we like to compare and compete, to move up in the hierarchy.

Wife-Beating Among Chimps and Humans

Some male chimps in the Kibale Forest in Uganda have been observed to beat the females using large wooden clubs, a behavior researchers call wife-beating (de Waal 2005, 115–6). Parallels with episodes of domestic violence by Venkataramana Prabhu are obvious. It is sad to note that such wife-beating, accompanied by verbal abuse, was quite common among the traditional Hindu families of my ancestors and was made worse by the resigned acceptance of such behavior by the wife as a rightful male prerogative. Most of these characters must have put up many an intimidating display in between episodes of wife-beating. There were a few males who stand out for not abusing their women folk, and I will mention them as I go along. Hindu women are psychologically very vulnerable to being called a widow or, even worse, a widow and a whore (*rāṇḍa*). In traditional Hindu society, a widow's life is living hell. Hindu widows' property rights are almost nonexistent, and there is no second marriage for widows, at least among the orthodox (Derrett 1963; 1968; Lingat 1973; Parashar 1992; Kosambi 2000; Chakravarti 2006). I provide more details in Appendix 8: "Goa: A Paradise Lost?" Hence, it is the fervent wish of every Hindu wife to die before her husband and never become a widow. Their irascible husbands knew this fact well and would go out of their way to call their wives the *r*-word out of pure sadism and to assert their dominance. Uttering bad words is especially taboo at certain times of the day, such as morning, midday, or evening when the lamps are lit, because Hindus believe that words spoken at these times usually come true. The only way these bullies addressed their wives was with the *r*-word, though such behavior is expressly forbidden for Hindus.

Power Dynamics in a Joint Hindu Family

Young men with a Western-type education, known as an English education, were expected not to indulge in such a cruel treatment of wives and were at a premium as prospective sons-in-law. A young bride moving into her husband's family could and did expect autocratic rule by her husband, usually egged on by a coalition of the mother-in-law and sisters-in-law. The bride might learn to live with a tyrant of a husband, hoping that he would mellow with age and that eventually she would prevail, especially after she became the mother of a few children (read: boys). However, the mother-in-law clique is an ever-present nuisance, more like an arthritic joint pain that just will not go away. It is one of the evils of the Hindu joint family system. A Hindu joint family is intergenerational, with many generations living together under the same roof. Usually there are three generations; four is perhaps a maximum. The modern nuclear family has only two generations. Most often, the mother and sisters played a significant part in the choice of the bride in traditional arranged marriages. Besides, the bride is a stranger to the family, without record of feuds with its members, hence deserving all the courtesies accorded to an honored guest among the Hindus. It is a Hindu tradition to welcome the new bride as Bhāgyā Lakṣmī (Goddess of Prosperity) because she is an auspicious addition to the family and is the mother of future grandchildren. *"Bhāgyada Lakṣmī Bārammā"* ("Welcome to the Goddess of Prosperity") is the song that musicians play when a new bride enters her husband's home. However, the situation changes drastically after the initial welcome. It is downhill all the way in most cases. But what has the young bride done to merit a hostile reception from the clique of mothers-in-law and daughters? The answer is very simple: The young bride, just by being the wife of their beloved son or brother, has diminished whatever real or imagined dominance or power the mother and sisters had over him. This loss of power cannot and will not be forgiven. In the olden days, the young bride was uneducated, did not have an independent income, and was completely and totally dependent on her husband's family. Besides, the mother-in-law clique had the awe-inspiring weight of Hindu tradition to justify its dominance over the young bride. This situation was also partly due to the custom of child marriages prevalent in Hindu society. Was this phenomenon observed only among the simple uneducated village folk (*baḷḷentulẽ jenã*)? Could education and city-bred sophistication help the women of the groom's family to rise above such petty behavior? No. The best example of how more education does not help is the beastly treatment of Nehru's wife, Kamala, by his sisters and other senior women of his family. Nehru's sisters were perhaps one of the most highly educated women in India, sophisticated and cultured in the best sense of the word. However, in their meanness to their sister-in-law, they excelled and were in the same league as their village-bred sisters (Jayakar 1992). This is why Indira Gandhi never forgave her aunts and why, when she was the prime minister of India, she made sure that they felt her power and anger. Perhaps the deprivation of power among the primates elicits an immediate response from the basic reptilian, primitive part of the brain that cannot be overridden by the thin veneer of education of the newer cognitive cortex.

If there are enough brothers in a joint Hindu family and if the daughters-in-law have some backbone, they themselves will eventually form a power structure to counteract the in-laws. This could lead to a quasi-stable standoff between the two groups, with periodic squabbles, tears, and recriminations for all the past hurts, insults, etc. Are these confrontations necessary? Yes, of course, because they are very much part of the group dynamics and the drama of power plays in a joint Hindu family. There are at least three reasons for these episodes of confrontation, or displays: First, these are training sessions for each side to keep its battling skills up to snuff and to refresh the memory banks so that no single past hurt or insult is forgotten or forgiven. Second, it is payback time for each daughter-in-law for all her past sufferings as a new bride. She is now in a much better strategic position as the mother of a few children including boys, precious to any Hindu family. Her tactical skills would have also improved through past training sessions, and she has better knowledge of the lay of the land, including any enemy vulnerability, such as family skeletons the in-laws would be embarrassed about. Unexpected introduction of these side issues can always be expected to introduce an element of tactical surprise, catching the enemy off-balance, and is a useful battle maneuver. Third, and the main motivation for these encounters, is the perceived loss of power felt by each daughter-in-law by living in a joint family. Each woman would like to dethrone the mother-in-law and have her own home to preside over as the reigning queen. It is only natural that she ardently desire such dominance. These family quarrels usually build up till they assume a personality of their own, becoming a hungry demon of discord that can be satisfied only by the sacrifice of the joint family. The warring sides do a subconscious cost–benefit analysis and eventually realize that the energy expended in these squabbles is larger than what would be involved in a breakup of the family. They reach a stage where they don't give a damn about the social opprobrium attached to a breakup of their "happy" family. The joint family property is divided and the combatants move out with their spoils of war. The celebratory singing of the paean of the "Triumphant Wife" (O'Flaherty 1981, 290, 10.159), by each daughter-in-law would be appropriate here. This *Ṛgvedic* hymn celebrates the victory of a woman over her husband in gaining his undivided attention and in vanquishing her rivals (she calls herself "killer of rival wives"). Of course most of these problems were there in the olden days. At present, large joint families are not that common. Young men have jobs away from home and each have their own nuclear family. They may visit the ancestral home—once in a while when on vacation. The brides are also better educated, contribute substantially to the family earnings, and are not prepared to give up their hard-earned power and independence. The older generation can also sense a diminution of their power and have learned to temper their authority with common sense. They have learned the hard way to treat their daughters-in-law with kid gloves, as the very embodiment of the Goddess of Prosperity. All these changes are for the good. In the story of my family, I will point out these hierarchies and their interplay as I go along. Lust for power and hierarchies are very much part of all of us.

Some recent books have condemned the flagrant abuse of power by Hindu patriarchy in great detail (Kosambi 2000; Chakravarti 2006). If women had the same power as men, would the exercise of power by women be tempered by moderation and greater sensitivity? I do not know. The only Hindu matriarchy in existence is among the Nayars of Kerala, and I am not familiar with any detailed studies of power dynamics in an extended Nayar family. However, I propose that the ability of unchecked power to corrupt is gender neutral. If this proposition sounds farfetched, it is for anthropologists or sociologists to disprove it with hard facts from field studies. Until such verification, I will accept it as a given that absolute power corrupts and leads to abuses by both patriarchs and matriarchs. The mothers-in-law of joint Hindu families, immortalized in myth and legend, are an example. The raw, naked power of the triumphant wife in the Vedic hymn is another.

The Hindu Caste System

The Hindu caste system is an excellent example of a hierarchy. The founding charter of this social stratification is the *"Puruṣa Sūkta," Ṛgveda* 10.90. This hymn describes a fourfold ranking of society divided into priests, warriors, merchants, and laborers, on the basis of *varṇa*, a term meaning "color," "class," or "rank," and is translated as "class" in this book in subsequent discussion. To challenge this social division is to be branded a heretic by the orthodox Hindus. If the caste system is accepted as a Vedic tradition, are all such traditions unchanging? Of course not! Quite a few Vedic customs have fallen by the wayside and are no longer observed. One of these, the levirate, has been declared to be *kalivarjya* (forbidden in the Kali Yuga, the present Age of Kali; see the Glossary). Hence, there is room for reform and change in Hindu orthodoxy, and the fourfold class division of Hindu society can be declared no longer acceptable, or forbidden, in the present age. However, such a declaration on caste is possible only if Hindu society as a whole sees the basic unfairness and injustice of the caste ranking and wants to get rid of it. Unfortunately, two factors have prevented any reforms: first, the primacy pride or conceit of the higher or more dominant, and second, the tacit acceptance of the status quo by some of the less dominant groups so long as they can look down on other groups further down in the hierarchy. However, change is in the air and old customs are facing new challenges.

This fourfold class division has multiplied into the present system of a few hundred thousand *jāti* (birth groups), also called castes. Each birth group—Gauda Sarasvat Brahmana (GSB) is one example—is an endogamous unit in which interdining, marriage, and participation in social and religious functions as a means of cohesive bond formation is encouraged. Within each *jāti*, there could be subhierarchies based on wealth, education, lineage, and other measures of human conceit, leading to a complex group dynamics. This whole social system is almost fractal in its detail, complexity, ornamentation, and embellishments. How did such a complex system evolve? Perhaps for many reasons. It should be noted that barriers, impervious to the mingling of birth groups, are not possible. In the normal course of social interactions, a certain mixing of these groups is to be expected because of a form of diffusion at their boundaries, giving rise to new *jāti*. The three imperatives of all human existence—securing food, mates, and the primacy drive for power—influence such mixing significantly. Ideas of food pollution and ritual purity actually inhibit mixing of different castes. However, such restrictions are observed only by a small minority, usually priests, who can afford the luxury of these correct behaviors, in a stable, settled society subsidized by a wealthy dominant group. If the conditions for obtaining food are difficult because of war or famine, people get around such restrictions or modify them to survive. Survival is more important than correct practice, for most. A search for mates is quite opportunistic, and all available avenues are explored to satisfy the urge for the propagation of the species. The dominant groups of men could and did legally have wives from their own birth group and from castes below theirs. Thus a priest could have wives from all of the four *varṇa*, whereas a warrior could marry into three *varṇa*, excluding the priests, and so on (Kane 1974, 2:449). In addition, there were captures in raids and warfare, purchase for cash or kind, extramarital liaisons, and entanglements of all sorts. Bonded women and female slaves were readily exploited for sex by the owner or master. All these social transactions gave rise to a proliferation of new castes. The third imperative of pursuit of power resulted in many creative developments. An enterprising person from a low-status group could seize power by military might and expect recognition of his high status by his equals or subordinates. The priests could help by constructing a proper genealogy supported by a mythology, all written in Sanskrit, for a munificent fee. The upstart, now a newly anointed king, would be only too happy to record for posterity his generosity to the Gods, priests, and religion. Low-status groups can also move up in rank to satisfy their primacy drive, by copying rites, rituals, and social customs, such as restrictions on their women, from high-status groups. Means of production of goods and services, and methods of earning a livelihood influenced by better education and opportunities, have changed castes or communal groupings, over millennia. All these factors have lead to a multiplicity of castes. A large number of these birth groups can accommodate many egos: large, small, or in-between, which find full expression for their primacy drives. By multiplying these birth groups, *jāti,* persons belonging to them can feel superior to others *locally,* while conforming superficially to the fourfold varṇa, classification, *globally*. There could be another plausible reason for the birth of these new castes. The Indian mind revels in ornamentation and filigree for its own sake, just for the fun of it. Indians can take a simple idea and transform it into a complex system with large numbers, enormous distances, eons of time impossible to imagine, and subtle, complex philosophical ideas difficult to grasp. They have been at this game for centuries. Take for example, the simple idea of sensual gratification, or *kāma*, one of the four principal goals of human life, or *puruṣārtha*. Books on this subject, such as the *Kāmasūtra*, describe a variety of positions, gymnastic or otherwise, without much sweat (Daniélou 1994; Doniger and Kakar 2003). In their encounters with the locals, the missionaries with their one canonical position were totally outclassed and outgunned. They tried injecting sin and guilt into the discourse, hoping to curb such exuberance. The Indians were not fazed a bit, nor did the missionaries' teachings cramp their style. The Indians dismissed sin and guilt as not relevant to gratification, one of the goals recommended by the codes of law. The one idea that the Indians left untouched in its simplicity is that of the zero. This simple yet profound idea can be traced to the Buddha, who liked to present complicated concepts in simple terms. The Buddhist doctrine of *Anattā* (no soul or no self) was generalized into the concept of *Śūnyatā* (emptiness) of later Buddhist philosophy (Gethin 1998). People at large got used to the idea of emptiness as an entity in their centuries of contacts with Buddhist thought. This familiarity with "nothingness" enabled Indian mathematicians to make the conceptual leap of representing "nothing" by a symbol, and the zero and the place value system of numbers were born. The earliest recorded use of such a system occurs in a Jain cosmological text, *Lokavibhāga* (458 CE), and by the astronomer Āryabhaṭa around 510 CE (Ifrah 2000, 419). This contribution of India to world culture is simple, elegant, easy, and useful.

The caste system, including its corollary, the Dalits (the oppressed, formerly called the untouchables) and their treatment, is cruel, unfair, unjust, and iniquitous and will always remain a shameful blot on Hindu society. It is rigid, preventing upward mobility, because caste is determined by birth, or *jāti*. Learning and scholarship came to be confined only to priestly families for a variety of reasons, restricting them essentially to closed shops of trade guilds of priestcraft. In ancient India, knowledge was passed on from teacher to pupil by oral recitation because of the importance of correct pronunciation of the *mantras* (sacred words). Written manuscripts were rare, looked down on with suspicion, and rarely used. Extensive memorization was the only means of education. It had to begin at a very young age, and children of priestly families were inculcated with this behavior from watching their elders performing their everyday activities. As for others, education was possible only by living with the teacher as part of the household. Food habits, laws of ritual pollution, and other details of daily life assumed great importance in educating the young. Hence, priestcraft and its auxiliary branches of knowledge were taught only to the children of members of the guild—that is, to the Brahmans—and became esoteric—not available to everyone. This state of affairs is the reason learning and education came to be restricted to priestly families. There have been a few notable exceptions to this general rule down the centuries; however, these non-Brahman scholars were rare. Of course, all the blame for the masses not getting an education cannot be foisted on the hereditary teachers or Brahmans; there were many other reasons, such as poverty, reluctance to invest many years in education, and a lack of a state policy on education, that contributed to this problem. However, in situations where the Brahmans did not fulfill their role as teachers and denied education to non-Brahman children for any reason, they owe an apology to generations of lost pupils and, yes, lost teachers. Not fostering the growth of young minds is one of the gravest of social crimes a person can commit. Caste conceit and guild exclusiveness played an important role in perpetuating this restriction. This created the problem of mostly uneducated masses, usually exploited by the educated elite. The best antidote for this pervasive past problem is education for all concerned, the high and the low. Affirmative action by the government of India in providing better opportunities for education and employment should go a long way to redress past injustices to the lower castes and untouchables (Pasricha 2006; Guha 2007; Nilekani 2009).

It should be noted that the dominant Brahmana group is not a monolithic structure with all the members of the priestly caste marching in lockstep. The priestly caste is divided into two broad groups: the northern and southern, with five members in each. These are further divided into hundreds of birth groups, or *jāti* (Enthoven 1975, 1:213–54). Their first concern was to learn priestcraft and the codes of law (*dharma*) to earn a living. After having secured a means of livelihood, fighting among themselves, was their hobby, second only to acquisition of knowledge. Each of the birth groups was brimful with its own primacy conceit and fought for dominance, wanting to be declared superior to other groups by the local political power and accepted as such by other Brahmana. Each group questioned the origins and purity of other groups and sometimes claimed to be the only true Brahmana, with the others supposedly being not-so-good imposters. Apart from flattering their community ego, such declarations of superiority translated into donations of property and money for their community. Time and again, each group was fighting for the noble aim of maintaining Hindu codes of law, caste purity, and for the honor and dignity of their particular birth group (Wagle 1970; 1980). There were fights and legal challenges in the GSB cluster and GSB fights with the Chitpavans, the Deshasth, the Karhad, and other Brahmana (see Chapter 3: "My Maternal Grandparents"). The Chitpavan had political clout and state support under the Peshwa rule (1713–1817/18) of Maharashtra. Therefore, they were the most aggressive in these fights for dominance. A few of the other Brahmana groups went into exile outside the Peshwa rule to avoid this persecution. The priests were the most educated among the Hindus and supposed beneficiaries of the wisdom conferred by their scholarship. However, the reason and common sense of their cognitive cortex could not rein in the emotions of the more primitive limbic system of their brains. In the fights for dominance driven by the primacy drive, they were in the same league as all the rest of us or our cousins, the chimps.

Caste in a Changing World

Caste barriers are being broken because of changes in Indian society, especially those that have de-emphasized religious orthodoxy. Young men and women meet in schools and universities, fall in love, and marry without worrying about caste, religion, or region of their birth. The caste system is complex, with many facets that reveal themselves from different perspectives. The question of ritual purity versus impurity used to grade, assign, and justify caste distinctions highlights the religious viewpoint. Religious orthodoxy is being progressively diluted and eroded in India, and so is the problem of ritual purity. People are no longer isolated in caste-conscious villages; they live and work in big cities. Some of the problems discussed by Dumont, such as who will accept food or water from whom—that is, from which caste—are no longer relevant because people eat in restaurants without worrying about the caste of the cooks or the waiters there (Dumont 1980). Living in a big city where all people are busy with the immediate task of earning a living may be the best practical antidote to all forms of ritual pollution and associated caste conceits. The problem with life in small towns or villages is that people have too much spare time on their hands. This encourages them to be concerned with other people's business, engage in idle gossip, and worry about caste purity and similar antiquated trivia. The few ultra-orthodox, who may be still concerned about these particulars, will take their food with them while traveling or may eat only in the homes of families whose food habits and customs conform to those of their own home environment.

Does this mean that with the de-emphasis on religion, the caste system will eventually disappear? I do not think so. The reason is that in addition to the religious aspect, there is a strong status-conscious part to the system. Membership in a status group (a caste) and the power, prestige, and privileges associated with it are dear to every human heart and difficult to get rid of. The fact that some Christians and Muslims, converts from Hinduism, have maintained their caste-consciousness has been noted by anthropologists (Dumont 1980). Recent, post-Dumont thinking on the problem of caste, politics, and power is interesting (Searle-Chatterjee and Sharma 1994; Srinivas 2002). It shows that the religious justification for caste, based on Hindu ideas of purity versus impurity, is not really that important or relevant now. However, memory of the status of a group's caste, even many generations in the past, survives religious conversion and so must be important. It may be very difficult to get rid of caste, even though it is cruel, unfair, and unjust, for the simple reason that there is status associated with it, and every human loves status. Love of status transcends education, common sense, and sense of fair play. It is in our genes! It is a fact that caste respectability is partly built on the backs of its women.

Castes with severe restrictions on women, such as prohibitions against remarriage of widows or divorcées and denial of property rights and gender parity, usually claim a higher status. Women's education leading to economic independence and their challenge to age-old restrictions of their rights and liberties as individuals will be decisive in determining the future of caste. This is also a challenge to men of all castes, who demand equality as a human right. Are they prepared to concede the same rights to their women and accept gender parity? Answers to such questions will determine the future norms of Indian society, including castes. The resurgence of caste in the dynamics of power politics in a democratic India has been noted (Srinivas 2002, 251–76). These developments may even signal the beginning of a new era in which caste may have to be redefined as a more general grouping independent of religion. New rankings, permutations, combinations, and coalitions of different castes have been formed with the single aim of acquiring more economic and political power. It is the primacy drive using caste solidarity as a political tool. This creative use of old castes for the pursuit of power in new politics is a tribute to the native genius of humans. However, some have speculated about the end of the caste as a system and even hastened to write its obituary (Srinivas 2003). The classic caste system in its traditional form may be dying or in its last stages of life. However, caste as a type of power stratification will continue to live. It will morph into a new system of rank and status, which is cost-effective and efficient to suit changing social, economic, and political environments in pursuit of power. Future developments in India will tell us which will prevail—conceits of rank and status or a sense of fairness and justice. Stay tuned.

Some sociologists and historians like to point out the differences between the casteless, egalitarian West and the caste-ridden, iniquitous India (Dumont 1980; de Mendonça 2002). However, life is not as simple as that. Such naïveté is idealistic hogwash. While it is true that the West is casteless, it is not as egalitarian as sociologists would like to think. Each society, Western or Eastern, has its own stratification, where each rank in the social ladder is jealous of another rank's privileges, fawns on its betters (submissive greeting among chimps), and condescends to its inferiors (higher-ranking chimps ignore submissive greetings with lordly disdain). The butler is obsequious to the master of the house because he can dominate the lesser servants. The casteless hierarchies and their rankings can be as bad as the worst snobbery of caste. As an example, in Appendix 8: "Goa: A Paradise Lost?" I point out the many hierarchies in the "casteless" Portuguese society of sixteenth-century Goa and note that the Portuguese were not that different from the caste-ridden Hindus. Status matters! I hope the reader will excuse this digression into chimp behavior and power politics; I had to include it to illuminate the dynamics of the humans in this story. I hope it teaches us to see ourselves as we are and to be honest about it: We love status and are snobs at heart!

Ananthayya Prabhu

Ananthayya, the only son of Venkataramana, was born in 1872 or 1873. He did not have much schooling, perhaps a few years in the local *aigaḷa śāle* (school). These were usually one-room schools with a thatched roof where a single teacher, an *aigaḷu*, taught all the grades, and the pupils paid whatever they could, such as rice, vegetables, and oil, as school fees. The pupils could not afford the usual slate and pencil; instead, a pile of sand on the floor was smoothed in front of each student, and they traced the alphabet with their index finger and did their sums in the sand. I am not certain whether they had any books; perhaps they memorized their lessons, multiplication tables, and so forth, by repeating after their teacher. After his schooling, Ananthayya worked at several odd jobs such as a *kurbarānco* (cattle and/or sheep herder) and a field worker. Because he was an outstanding student, he is supposed to have substituted for the teacher on occasion. His handwriting was beautiful, and it helped him a lot, first as a lawyer's clerk and later on as a document writer. He wrote in the Kannada flowing, *mōḍi* (cursive) script, which was quite beautiful to look at; however, reading it requires some practice. My father, who was trained by Ananthayya, had a similar hand, and it is easy to recognize the thousands of documents written by these two in the script.

Ananthayya came to Udupi in 1890, when he was about 18. He stayed with his relatives in a thatched hut opposite our house in Tenkupet. Later, he bought that plot of land and the hut on it and built a new house there. He worked as a *gumāstu* (clerk), with Kumble Subraya Prabhu, a well-known lawyer at that time, in Udupi. He was hardworking, disciplined, and organized; had beautiful handwriting; and was absolutely honest and trustworthy. It was his apprenticeship with Kumble Subraya that taught him the basics of legal procedures and equipped him to be a document writer later on. In the legal hierarchy of Udupi, the local magistrate and the judge were at the top, followed by lawyers, and their clerks were near the bottom. Ananthayya could never hope to be a lawyer, because he lacked an education. However, his one fond hope was that his son would become one and rise up to be near the apex of the hierarchy. That was one grand unfulfilled ambition in his life, his reach for power and status!

Ananthayya was of medium height, with a long, aquiline nose and a serious face. His clothing was a bit old-fashioned. He wore the dhoti, topped by a black coat with a tight, closed collar, and a white turban on his head. On special occasions, he might put a black dot, *tīḷo*, on his forehead between his eyebrows. He carried a black umbrella and a stack of documents, the latter all securely tied with their individual pieces of string and the whole bundle wrapped in a piece of cloth. A pair of open leather *vhāṇa* (sandals) graced his feet. After an early breakfast, he would have his lunch at about 9 or 9:30 in the morning, and then would walk to his office near the courts. The courts usually opened at 10:00 in the morning. This custom of offices opening rather late in the morning, in a hot country such as India, was meant to give time for the lawyers, court officials, and so on time in the morning to take care of their morning devotions, or *pūjā*.

Kumble Subraya had two wives, the first one being Kitti Mai (Aunt Kitti) and the second one being Kanaka Mai. Narasingha, his son by his first wife, was a very bright and talented young man at the Canara High School in Mangalore. He was also a good public speaker and very popular with his classmates and teachers. Unfortunately he died of typhoid while at school. The state of medicine in Udupi at that time was not any help. Raaghu and Ramanath were Kumble Subraya's sons from his second wife. Raaghu was sent to Hyderabad to study medicine. There he got involved with Gandhi's freedom movement, was deported by the Nizams' government, and never completed his studies. Ananthayya worked with Kumble Subraya till the lawyer's death from a heart attack. In the meantime, Ananthayya had learned a lot about writing and executing legal documents and had become quite well known locally. At that time, Haradi Vasudeva Pai became a lawyer in Udupi. Ananthayya was very helpful in an orderly transfer of legal cases begun by his former boss, Kumble Subraya, and completed by Vasudeva Pai, and an equitable sharing of the legal fees between Subraya Prabhu's widow and Haradi Vasudeva Pai. Ananthayya worked with Haradi Vasudeva Pai till his death, caused by diabetes and carbuncles, a secondary complication of the disease. In those days, insulin was not available in Udupi, and changes in diet and traditional Āyurvedic medicine were not effective in controlling the disease. Haradi Keshava Pai, Vasudeva Pai's younger brother, was also a lawyer, and Ananthayya had worked in their joint practice. Keshava Pai wanted Ananthayya to continue to work for him, but Ananthayya decided to strike out on his own.

Ananthayya Becomes a Document Writer

Anantahayya was a lawyer's clerk till 1918; from 1918 to 1920, he worked at two jobs, trying out being a document writer also. A document writer does not have a law degree. However, he or she knows enough law and legal procedures to write and register at the local registrar's office legal documents such as property sales deeds, mortgages, wills, and promissory notes. He or she is an independent paralegal not attached to any lawyer. There was a conveniently empty niche in the legal hierarchy in Udupi, and Anathayya saw it as an opportunity and took it. Survival in an evolutionary regime involves finding an empty niche and grabbing it before others do. Ananthayya was quite good at his new job and decided to strike out on his own. On a day in 1920 determined by astrologers to be auspicious, Ananthayya opened his office near the law courts as a document writer. He could write and execute documents written only in the local language, Kannada. He rented a two-room office from Vakil Rama Nayak, and later from Vakil Rama's son Vakil Vittal Nayak on the road to the Christian high school, within walking distance of the law courts. Ananthayya and his clients would sit on *māndri* (woven grass mats) spread on the floor. In front of him was a wooden box about two feet long and about one foot high and wide containing all the stationery and other requisites of the trade. Initially there were no tables or chairs in the office, because such furniture was considered more appropriate for a lawyer who was the august member of the bar. Lawyers charged higher fees, and Ananthayya was perhaps afraid that all the office furniture might drive away clients by making them think that he would charge the fees of a lawyer. Ananthayya, by sitting on the floor, was tacitly acknowledging his lowly status in the local legal hierarchy. It was only much later that the office acquired standard office furniture, driven partly by his advancing age, arthritis, and stiff knees and painful legs from squatting on the floor and partly by greater professional confidence brought on by increased earnings. After he listened to the requirements of his clients, he would write a rough draft and read it back to them, because most of them were illiterate. The reading of the draft was quite a ceremony. The clients would brace themselves for the ordeal with a fresh mouthful of *phaḍpāna* (beetle leaf) or would light up a local country smoke (*beeḍi*) or a cigarette. They would listen with great solemnity and an occasional nod, to indicate understanding and appreciation of the fine points of law. Others would begin listening with great concentration, and then would slowly give up the struggle, their eyes glazing over, and gently nod off to sleep, especially if the document was long and complicated. After Ananthayya got their approval, he would write up a final copy on "stamp paper" purchased from the government for paying legal taxes due, depending on the amount of money involved and the type of transaction. The final copy would be read again, approved, duly signed or marked with a thumb print of the parties involved, and registered with the registrar of documents. And then the document writer would get paid for his services. If it was an important document that garnered a substantial fee, then on his way home Ananthayya would stop by at a restaurant or a sweets shop and buy sweets to take home to celebrate. This was how we children at home knew that an important legal transaction had been completed. If the clients were august personages, such as the heads of the local *maṭha* (monastery) or the head of our own *Kāśi maṭha* (monastic lineage) or were other persons who could not come to his office, Ananthayya would go to them to complete their legal requirements. This is how Ananthayya, and later on, my father, earned, supported their families and educated their children. Their professional reputations were excellent because they were honest, were truthful in all their dealings with their clients, and gave their clients their money's worth. In 1920 Ananthayya had the Nāga Temple in Siddhapur repaired. This was the temple first established by his father, and it had fallen into disrepair. The roof was leaking and was in danger of a collapse. I do not have any other details, such as whether daily worship still occurred there by that point or whether the temple could afford a regular priest at the time.

Ananthayya appears to have done quite well as a self-employed document writer, which, as you will remember, he became in 1920. On January 30, 1925, he dedicated a *bhāṇḍi* (small chariot) to the local Shri Venkataramana Temple, maintained by the GSBs. This chariot is a modest affair between fifteen and twenty feet high, with four wooden wheels and a representation of a many-hooded *nāga* carved in wood that serves as a seat for the image of the deity, *utsavā mūrti*, taken out in a procession round the perimeter of the temple on special festivals. A typical temple *ratha* (wooden cart) would be between fifty and seventy feet high, with an elaborate, intricately carved wooden base on four large solid wooden wheels, with a superstructure, and would need the muscle power of 50 to 100 devotees to push and pull it around. It is not an energy-efficient conveyance. On the base of the wooden chariot, carved in Kannada script is the date of dedication, the donor's name, and a note saying that it is an offering from his profits (*lābhādāyada seve*).

Sri Devi

Ananthayya was married to the daughter of Dasappa Kamath in 1880 or 1881 when he was about 8 years old, and the bride was 6 months younger. Child marriage was the norm among Hindus in those days. We do not know all the reasons behind child marriages and the period in which they became prevalent. Some blame the Hindu codes of law (*dharmaśāstra*), changed social conditions due to conquests, migrations, and similar events. It is possible that this custom evolved to become the norm, and then justification for this course of action was found in the codes of law. Anyway, it was a bad custom, which later social reformers tried hard to eliminate and passed laws, making it a criminal offense (see Appendix 5: "Hindu Rites of Passage"). During the wedding ceremonies and procession, the bride and the groom rode on the shoulders of their uncles so that they could be seen in all their finery and not lost in the crowd of guests. The bride's married name was Sri Devi; all of us used to call her *boḍemmā* or *boḍi āmmā* (literally "big mother" or "great-grandmother") and were terrified of her. Her coterie of friends used to call her Shirdevi, a colloquial form of Sri Devi. She was a tough, plainspoken, forthright lady, afraid of none, the living or the dead. She was the alpha of the dominance hierarchy in Ananthayya's home. Though he was the nominal head of the family, the real power resided with Sri Devi. As in all patriarchal families, the husband, who is perhaps the sole breadwinner, is the boss of the family, with the wife playing a strictly subordinate role. There are, however, a few cases where the husband abdicates his responsibility because of preoccupation with his job, intense religious devotion that does not leave him much time to attend to mundane affairs of the family, or just plain incompetence. In such cases, even the most retiring, self-effacing Hindu wife will take over the job of managing the family affairs and become the de facto head of the family. Power will not lie fallow; it always devolves on its user. She will say with some amusement and a touch of sarcasm, "With the Santa Tukārām,"[1] meaning that without her in charge, nothing will get done, and for the sheer survival of the family, she has to do it. Someone (meaning she) has to manage the household, find mates for her children, save money and collect jewelry for her daughters' dowries, and etc. Hindu women are instinctively keen students of applied human psychology. They know that the male ego is fragile and should be nurtured with tender loving care. Each woman will flatter her husband, make him appear strong and dominant in public, and may even walk three steps behind him as women of the last generation did, so long as she is the undisputed queen at home. Hindu women are quite good at creating the illusion of dominance and control in the mind of their husbands. Even if there is a mother-in-law in a joint family, the wife will have much influence over her husband, with a corresponding loss of power by the mother-in-law. It is this tension that leads to all the problems in an extended family. With Sri Devi, who had such a forceful personality, there was no question about who was the boss. I was too young to see the power play between her and Ananthayya. However, from the stories I have heard, there was no doubt as to her being the dominant partner.

Hoḍemmā was the de facto queen of Ananthayya's home. She was of medium height and build, with a long aquiline nose graced by a nose ornament (*nattu*) worn through a hole in the right nostril. The red dot of *kuṅkuma* on her forehead was not a small stylish dot but a big bold oval that proclaimed to the whole world her status as a *muttaide*, a woman whose husband is living.

---

[1] A poet-saint of Maharashtra (1607–1649) famous for his neglect of mundane affairs of daily life because of his preoccupation with the divine (Walker 1968, 2:524).

She was hardworking, frugal, outspoken, and forthright, and everyone was afraid of her. Behind her back, some people called her Khaḍga Rāvaṇa—that is, Rāvaṇa the demon king, brandishing a sword and likely to chop your head off! The money she saved from household expenses would be loaned to her friends, and her own set of clients, to earn some interest. By the late 1920s, she had accumulated enough money to give each of her grandchildren a necklace of interlocking gold discs (*cakrasoru*). When she died in 1936 or so, in addition to her jewelry, she had accumulated about 7,000 rupees, quite a sizeable sum for a lower-middle-class family like ours. Everyone in the family, including her son-in-law Madhava, was afraid of her sharp tongue. But because I was her favorite and only great-grandson, I could take liberties with her. Perhaps I was the substitute for many boys she had lost. Even when she was being strict with me, there was always a twinkle in her eyes that belied her sternness. After Madhava lost everything and was bankrupt, he moved with his wife, Bhavani, and family to Udupi. Madhava became the son-in-law in residence, *gharjāvãyī*, an unenviable position. Bhavani did all the cooking and household work, having in effect become the maid of all. Sri Devi developed arthritis and used to rest and sleep a lot. Perhaps the arthritis and lack of work and exercise fed on each other, and she spent more and more time resting, sleeping, and directing the rest of the household. In later years of her life, she became diabetic. She used to sleep on a *māñco* (bed) in the front veranda of the house, covered with a blanket for her arthritis, watching the passing scene, greeting her friends, and keeping a supervisory eye on things in general. As a special treat for me, she used to keep *drākṣa* (raisins), *khārooka* (dried dates), *jardala* (apricots), and *khaḍe sākkara* (rock sugar) in individual bottles under lock and key in her *kapāṭa* (cupboard) and dole out portions every afternoon. I felt that the portions she gave me were never adequate, and requests for more did not produce any results. Hence, I hit on the idea of holding her blanket hostage, releasing it only on payment of additional portions of the goodies. She, of course, would pretend to be angry and would shout, "Maddha, Maddha," for my grandfather, who was supposed to run after me to rescue the blanket and discipline me. If she was in a good mood, I would get a little bit more of the snacks with or without the release of the hostage blanket.

Infant Mortality and Local Beliefs

Ananthayya worked hard to better himself and suffered a lot in his personal life. After his first child, Bhavani (my father's mother), was born in 1891, he had five boys, four of whom died in infancy because of liver problems. Only one son, Seetharam, survived, but he lived only to age 16, dying in 1916. Some modern physicians have speculated that these liver problems were perhaps due to protein deficiency, resulting from a strict vegetarian diet. There was a high infant mortality rate due to the sorry state of medicine locally available in those days. Most of the medicine was of the traditional Āyurvedic type, supplemented by Western allopathic medicine, which was just then becoming available but was not much better and not much more effective. If medicine failed, people tried all sorts of magical or quasi-magical remedies. For some reason, these were called *muṭṭāsa* (quasi-magical "women's remedies"). Women usually whispered about them to one another, never discussing them in the open. Details about these desperate remedies were often too gruesome to be mentioned; many of the remedies supposedly would lose their potency if they were publicly revealed. The remedies are ancient, perhaps chthonic, and are usually known to the *Tuḷu*-speaking maids employed by middle-class families for sweeping and cleaning the house, washing clothes and dishes, and doing similar chores. Because many babies died of liver disease, one of the remedies was to cut open the dead baby and burn its liver, so that the next baby yet to be born would not have a liver problem! Another procedure was to cheat death by going through a symbolic burial by putting the baby in a ditch in the ground as if to bury it and then taking it into the house through the back door. Sometimes, on the twelfth or the naming day for babies, it was given to a woman of the untouchable caste, *mhāri*, as if a dead baby were being given to her for burial. The untouchable woman would then nurse the baby as if it were her own, whisper a name in its ear, and give the baby back to the parents. This symbolic ritual was supposed to cheat fate and save the baby's life. Ananthayya's second daughter, Sarasvathi—called Appi, or Bāppāmmā at home—lived to be 81, used to claim that her good health and longevity were due to the fact that she had been through such a ceremony and had been nursed by a *mhāri.*

Unfortunately for Ananthayya and his wife, Sri Devi, none of these remedies worked with their male children, and they lost all of them. In the backyard of the house, there was a piece of rock, *bhuttā phāttoru*, representing a spirit, Bhūtha, considered to be a powerful deity. When she was pregnant with the latest baby, Sri Devi had vowed to make certain offerings to the spirit if the baby turned out to be a boy who would survive any liver problems. The baby was a boy, and he died of liver problems in infancy. Sri Devi was angry; the spirit had not lived up to his end of the bargain! Sri Devi, after recovering from childbirth, is supposed to have taken a pick to personally remove the spirit stone, and to have thrown it into a ditch outside the compound wall to convey a strong message to the spirit. If the spirit did not listen to her supplications and would not or could not save her baby, she did not want to have anything to do with the spirit, so she got rid of it. She was one tough lady who was not afraid of anyone living or dead, human or spirit. Seetharam, the one son who lived to age 16 before succumbing to liver disease in 1916, was apparently well built and smart, doing well in school. Shiva Rao, MD, trained in London, was called to treat the boy. He apparently gave him an injection (the absolute latest innovation in medicine in Udupi in those days), to no avail.

Bhavani Marries Madhava

When Bhavani, Ananthayya's first child, was 12, Ananthayya decided to find a suitable groom for her. He had heard that there were many bachelor Bhats (priests) in Mulki, about 16 miles south of Udupi. He decided to go to Mulki to investigate the situation in person. In Mulki, in the neighborhood of the Sri Venkataramana Temple, he ran into Madhava Bhat, his future son-in-law and my grandfather. Madhava was whittling a stick to keep himself occupied because he did not have anything better to do. At that time, Madhava's father, Ganapathi, was dead; however, his mother was living. He was not much of a scholar, unlike his elder brother, Vasudeva. He had learned the essentials of different rituals, or priestcraft, *bhaṭṭvyāpti*, and that was about it. Because there was no paternal influence of any type to discipline him, Madhava grew up with his wild nature untamed, ready to explore life in all its aspects. Madhava's and Bhavani's horoscopes matched, the details of a wedding were negotiated to the satisfaction of both parties, and they were duly married in 1902. Kumble Subraya, the lawyer Ananthayya was working for, gave him 200 rupees to meet the expenses of the wedding. This was a princely sum in those days, and Ananthayya never forgot this act of kindness and generosity. The wedding was a five-day affair, which took place in Udupi, at the home of the bride. The groom's party would have traveled to Udupi from Mulki in bullock carts, which was the only mode of transportation other than walking. Though the wedding ceremony proper took only a few hours to complete, there were quite a few ancillary activities involving the newly married couple and the invited guests, which kept them occupied for five days. These activities involved various childish games that the bride and the groom were supposed to participate in, to the great amusement of the guests: the various acts of waving of lights (*ārti dākkocẽ*) and the sprinkling of rice in benediction (*śesa bhorcẽ*) on the couple. The ceremonial breakfast, lunch, afternoon tea, and the dinner had to be provided by the father of the bride for all of the visiting guests. In those days when people seldom traveled, weddings were a great excuse for the family to get together and catch up on all the latest family and community happenings and for the women to show off their latest acquisitions in saris and jewelry, gossip, and look over prospective matches for sons or daughters. Hence, Indian families made the most of these occasions, though it might send the father of the bride to the poorhouse. Extravagance from the father of the bride was expected, to keep up the good name of his family, and many people went into crushing, ruinous, lifelong debt to pay for a few days of living beyond their means. During all of the events of a wedding, it was customary for the groom's party to act hard to please and for the bride's relatives to go out of their way to keep them happy. Some of the details of these five- to seven-day weddings may be found in Kudva (Kudva 1978, Appendices I and II). Such weddings are of course, relics of the past, unless the father of the bride is filthy rich, in which case even now people waste money without feeling embarrassed about it.

Appi Marries Manjeshwar Narayana Bhat

Appi was born in 1899 and was the seventh and last child of Ananthayya and Sri Devi. Because the five boys born to them after Bhavani had all died in infancy, only one living into his teens, her parents were not sure whether Appi would make it into adulthood. It is possible that all the male babies had some sort of genetic defect, making them susceptible to liver problems. Of course, nobody knew about genetic diseases in those days. Yet Appi lived to the ripe old age of 81! When she was 11, she was married to Manjeshwar Narayana Bhat, who had been a bachelor. He was from the family of priests at the GSB temple in Manjeshwar, with a suitable background. He had finished high school and was employed by the postal department.

On marriage, Hindu women get a new name and assume the clan (*gotra*) name of their husband. Usually the new name for the bride is chosen to match the husband's name from Hindu mythology. Sometimes the name is that of a woman in the family who had died before her husband, and thus the name is considered to be auspicious. As I have already explained, the treatment of widows in Hindu society is cruel and atrocious. It is considered to be sign of great merit, *puṇya*, for a woman to die before her husband. It is fervently hoped that having the name of an *ayyapaṇāri gellili* (woman who died before her husband) will reflect that merit on the new bride, in the hope that she will die before her husband does, just as her predecessor did! Appi's married name was Sarasvathi.

At that time, the laws passed by the British Raj had designated 12 years as the minimum age for marriage; breaking this law was considered a criminal offense with the bride's father subject to a term in jail. Adding to his worries, Appi got pregnant with her first child when she was 11½. Fortunately for him, no one filed a complaint with the police, and a big weight was off his shoulders after an anxious year.

In those days, there were many ceremonies connected with the birth of the first baby, which somehow have fallen into abeyance these days. The details of the ceremony are interesting because they reflect traditions and customs no longer observed in the GSB community. My father remembers ceremonial feast conducted when he was about 5 years old, meant to honor a prima gravida, *phullaṭi gurbiṇi jevaṇa*, in the third trimester. The feast was in the home of Ananthayya's boss, Kumble Subraya, and organized by his wife, Kitti Mai. It was essentially a women's get-together, with the men of the family playing only a peripheral role. The hostess sent a formal invitation for the feast through one of her husband's employees. It was more or less a whole-day affair. Appi, Bhavani, and Sri Devi, with my father as the youngest of the family, went to the home of the hostess in the morning. A team of *vājpāncẽ* (musicians) had been hired to be in attendance for the ceremony for the whole day. They heralded the auspicious occasion by a brief performance in the morning to get the proceedings started. This was followed by a morning *pejje jevaṇa* (breakfast of rice gruel), accompanied by special dishes, such as mouth-watering hot pickles (*puḍye noṇcẽ* and *aḍgayī*). The women socialized while the guest of honor was ordered to lie down to conserve her strength. Lunch, the main meal of the day, was a ceremonial feast with special dishes, including five types of dessert, followed by a siesta for everyone. Later, at about 4 PM, there was *tiffin* (snacks) with tea or coffee, followed by the main ceremony. The mother-to-be was blessed by the *ārti dākkocẽ* (waving of lights), the *śesa bhorcẽ* (sprinkling of rice in benediction), and the giving of gifts. This was the portion of the festivities when the musicians had to perform the longest, to show off their virtuosity. The hostess would then bid a ceremonial good-bye to her guests. The guests who were younger than the hostess honored her by *pāyu dorcẽ* (touching her feet and craving her blessings), the senior women exchanged *kuṅkum* and flowers (*tīḷo lāvcẽ*) and thanked the hostess for her hospitality, and the guests were sent home accompanied by the musicians. I have described this day-long ceremony in detail to give a flavor of the times, when life moved at a more leisurely pace. Such elaborate ceremonies are a thing of the past except in families that are filthy rich and believe in ostentatiously displaying their wealth.

After a few months, Appi's first child, my uncle Narasimha Bappa, was born on July 12, 1912. He was followed by Shridhar Bappa, Ramanath Bappa, Rathna Akka, Yeshvantha, and Premananda—in all, five boys and a girl. In the meantime Appi's husband, Narayana, had found a job as a teacher in the education department and was posted to a town called Puttur in South Kanara District. After this event, he was called Grandfather from Puttur, or Puttur Ājjo. Narasimha did attend the local Christian high school for a few years, and then transferred to a high school in Puttur.

Ananthayya Builds a House

Ananthayya had bought the thatched-roof hut located at the corner of Tenkupet and Bhandari Voṇi. He decided to raze the hut and build a new house at the same location. In those days, most of the houses were built out of packed clay mixed with straw, *muḷye thaṇa*, for strength. Such houses, if properly built and topped by a roof that did not leak, could last for hundreds of years. The older parts of our current house has just such construction. Ananthayya's new house, however, was built with dressed laterite, a locally quarried stone. It had two floors and was topped by a roof with factory-made red tiles called Basel Mission tiles because they were initially manufactured and fired in a factory at Mangalore established by the Basel Mission, a German missionary society. The house had two entrances, the west entrance on the Tenkupet and the north entrance on Bhandari Voṇi. The north entrance opened on to a small yard surrounded by a wall. The yard had a *tulasī* plant (sacred basil), which one finds in all Hindu homes; at the northeast corner of the yard was a cowshed, with a hayloft for storing hay for the cows or buffaloes housed in the cowshed. Both entrances to the house led into an open *jagali* (veranda), which had a screen of wood laths on the north side. This screen, with its fixed laths, provided an ideal climbing device for small children, who just could not resist its invitation to observe the world from an adult's height. This we did in spite of all adult admonitions that we would fall and break our necks. At the far east wall of the veranda, there was a *māñco* (bed). You will recall that Sri Devi, Ananthayya's wife, used to sleep on this bed, so that she could observe the passing scene on the two streets as well as keep a supervisory eye on things in general.

Ananthayya, my father, and one or two clerks who worked with them, used the veranda as an office for their work as document writers. They sat on the floor, with a small wooden box containing paper, pens, pencils, and other articles of their trade. I suppose they could have afforded a table and chairs; however, as I mentioned earlier, they thought that sitting on the floor was more appropriate for document writers, who are subordinates to university-educated lawyers who were members of the bar. All the years of cross-legged sitting on the floor did eventually lead to arthritis of the knees, and my father in his old age suffered because of it. At the time of the Gaṇeśa festival, *Cavati* (Gaṇeśa *Caturtī*), the bed at the east wall of the veranda would be replaced by a table, on which the newly brought image of Gaṇeśa would be placed and worshipped. The veranda was also the place where more elaborate religious ceremonies involving ritual sacrifice would take place, to enable all of the smoke from the *homu* (sacrificial fire) to escape. The veranda opened into two rooms; one served as an office with one table and a couple of locked cabinets for storing important documents and law books. When I was little, my father, Ananthayya, and their clerks would come home at the end of a day's work and put away their records in this room before dispersing for the night. Before I started my school, my father had bought me a slate and some *kāḍḍi* (slate pencils), which were stored in the right-hand drawer of the table. I was so excited about the idea of the impending admission to the first grade and actually writing on the slate. I could not yet write on it, because I had to go through the religious ceremony of *akṣarābhyāsa* (beginning of studies) first. Every day, I would ask my father to open the table drawer, and then I would gaze on the slate and pencils with great fascination. I could not wait to be admitted to school. I was very curious about everything and asked a million questions, as children usually do. I was such a nuisance that my father used to call me *adhikaprasaṅgi* (excessive, impertinent questioner), and grown-ups would avoid me rather than face my questions that usually exposed their ignorance. I remember asking my father and others which was the richest country in the world. I also remember being crestfallen when told that the United States was the richest. Because I was born in India, I naturally assumed that India was the richest country—another example of primacy conceit. Little did I imagine that one day I would become an American citizen and spend more of my life in the United States than in India.

Ananthayya's office led to the stairs next to the south wall of the house and on to the second floor of the house. The whole of the second floor was divided into two rooms: one a big room extending over most of the second floor, and the second a storage area above the kitchen. The floor of this storage area was a wooden grating through which rose the smoke from the kitchen; however, there was no chimney to let the smoke out. This is a problem with most Indian homes: They do not have a proper chimney, smoke is not vented effectively, and soot accumulates in rooms immediately above the kitchen. This room was a spooky place because of the smoke-generated soot and cobwebs accumulated over the years. The bigger room upstairs was airy and well lit, and it had many metal trunks full of books and a central iron pillar to support the roof. A child could hold this pillar with one hand and go round and round the pillar, faster and faster, till dizzy. When finally the child would let go of the pillar and stand on wobbly feet, the room would continue to go round and round deliciously! I used to spend quite some in this upstairs room reading books accumulated by my uncle Shridhar Prabhu during his college years.

The first-floor veranda led into a small room, *vāsāro*, connected to a bedroom. At the east end of the house, there was one long room with a niche for the *devā kūḍa* (household shrine), the kitchen, and the dining area. The cooking area was a low platform about one foot high and six to eight feet long. There were three fireplaces: one *rānnaṇi* and two *vāila*, in which wood was burned and the everyday cooking of the house was done. An Indian homemaker has to be quite an expert in controlling the fire to suite the cooking and must watch over the different types of cooking, such as boiling, frying, and steam-baking. In most South Indian home cooking, ovens are not used, and one usually does not bake bread at home; it is always bought from a bakery. Western-style bread is a recent innovation, which orthodox Brahmans do not eat because of the use of yeast or toddy (fresh or fermented palm sap) in its preparation. When I was little, bakeries were a Christian monopoly, because their religion was not bothered by the use of yeast or toddy in baking bread and also because the technique of baking on the west coast had been introduced by the Portuguese. These days, anybody can be a baker. The kitchen led to a small room that had a big *ragaḍo* (grinding stone) at its northwest corner and a stone mortar sunk in the floor at its southeast corner. Both the grinding stone and the *vāna* (mortar) were made of the local granite. The grinding stone was a hemisphere about three feet in diameter, with a central depression about six inches in diameter and six to nine inches deep, surrounded by a less deep catchment area of two to three inches. The *ragaḍyā dāṇo* (ellipsoidal grinder), twelve to eighteen inches long and six inches in diameter, moved in the central depression to grind the spices, coconut, and chillies to prepare the *māsolu* (spice mixture) needed for the day's cooking. A person using the grinding stone would keep the central ellipsoid rotating with the left hand while feeding the mixture into the central depression with the right hand. Water would be added from time to time till the correct fineness and consistency of the spice mixture is attained. The fineness of grinding, consistency of the spice mixture, and its method of preparation are very much determined by the type of vegetable dish that is being prepared—that is, whether it is *ghaśi, āmbaṭa, koddela, sukhẽ*, or something else. In a few houses, there was a small depression under the grinding stone. The grinding stone would be pushed to one side, and women would deposit their jewelry in the hole as a temporary safe-deposit box for the night! In the good old days, each middle-class Hindu family in South Kanara used to have two or three *ceḍvã* (maids) for washing dishes and clothes, which would be done outside the house. They also swept the floor once or twice a day and wiped it with a piece of wet cloth, *āṅgti pussucẽ*, to remove the ever-present dust. The cooking was done by the women of the house, and the recipes for various dishes very much depended on and became more elaborate to fill the time slot available. Nowadays, with both the husband and the wife working, homemaking not being a full-time job, and modern electrical appliances such as blenders being readily available, use of the *ragaḍo* to obtain different degrees of fineness of the *māsolu* are things of the past. Most people are no longer knowledgeable about the the fine distinctions among spices for the various dishes. The *vāna-kāṇḍaṇa* (mortar and pestle), in which the pestle is about six feet long, were used rarely, for husking grains, by a person standing up and pounding using the two hands alternately.

This small room led into the *nhāṇi* (bathroom), which had two large (three to four feet in diameter) *bhāṇa* (copper caldrons) with wooden covers, *bhāṇā muccaḷa*, permanently embedded in a low earthen platform, about a foot high, rising from the floor, to the right of the passageway leading to the backyard. The caldron next to the wall was for cold water, *thanḍa utkā bhāṇa*, and the other caldron, *hoona utkā bhāṇa*, had a fire lit underneath it to provide hot water. Sri Devi, and later on my grandmother Bhavani, would light a fire in the bathroom, first thing in the morning, and then have a bath before beginning the day's cooking. It can be a bit chilly in the morning, even in India, and children usually sit in front of the fire while brushing their teeth, to get warm and to contemplate the dancing flames. Watching the flames of a fire has almost a hypnotic effect on humans and must be a favorite pastime all over the world, irrespective of culture. Next to these caldrons was a rectangular depression two to three feet deep, *nhāṇyẽ māddāḷẽ*, lined with granite. A person taking a bath would stand in it and dip a small copper vessel (*tāmbiyo*) into the hot water and then the cold water before pouring it on the body. Children cannot reach the water from the *māddāḷẽ*, so they stand on the ledge for their bath. The wastewater is discharged through a *tūmbu* (hole), at the bottom. When I was a kid, I never liked to stand in the *māddāḷẽ* to take a bath, because it was not brightly lit, and I was always afraid of stepping on a snake that might have crawled in through the discharge hole. After taking a bath, a person was supposed to alert the maid to fill up the caldrons, freshen up the fire, and so forth to get it ready for the next person. Use of soap was introduced in India in modern times. Before that, people used soap nut powder, *śikāyi*, a naturally occurring product. When I was little, soap nut powder was used almost exclusively by women for washing their long hair; nowadays, it is rarely used.

From the bathroom, a few steps led onto a brick pathway that led to a well in the backyard. This well supplied all the water needed for the house; it was quite large and lined with laterite. Next to the well on its right-hand side was a rectangular basin carved out of a single piece of granite, which used to be filled by the maid periodically. It was my favorite place for floating paper boats and in general playing in water. I used to blow bubbles with a metal *naḷi* (tube), about two feet long, used to get the fire in the bathroom going.

Once instead of blowing, I sucked in water, which went into my lungs and stomach; I was gasping for breath and thought I was going to die. I still remember being a scared little boy, trying to clear the water sucked in the wrong way, gasping for breath, and running for help. Perhaps the running cleared my lungs, because afterward, I could breath and was back in form. The backyard was full of trees: *nārlā rooku* (coconut palms), *poṇosu* (jack-fruit), *toranda* (pomelo), *papash phaḷa* (papaya), and many flowering shrubs. The pomelo trees had low-hanging branches and were ideal for climbing and hanging up a swing. Near the east end of the property was the outhouse, next to a second well that was used mainly to water the coconut trees in the garden in summer. The water was brought up from the well by a device called a *lāṭi*. This is an indigenous irrigation device much in use before the advent of electrical pumps. It was operated by two people. The device consisted of a long wooden beam supported on a fulcrum at its center. Attached to one end of the beam was a metal bucket suspended from a long piece of bamboo. A long rope was attached to the other end of the beam. One person guided the metal bucket to dip into the well, and when it was full, the other person would jump into a small pit while grasping the rope, thus bringing up the full bucket of water, which was then emptied into an irrigation channel. These shallow channels with the deliciously cool water were ideal places for splashing in, floating paper boats, or general messing around for little kids. These labor-intensive contraptions are rarely seen today, as they have been replaced by more efficient electric pumps. Much of the cheap labor available in South Kanara District in the old days goes now to the gulf states for better-paying jobs, and there is labor shortage. People have learned to do various and sundry jobs on their own instead of hiring someone else to do it. I personally think that this is good for their souls. When electricity became available in Udupi in 1940s, Ananthayya got his house wired for it. It was used only for lighting the house, as other appliances were not available in Udupi. Narrow strips of wood were nailed to the walls of the house for carrying the wires to the lamps that hung from the ceiling. The lamps were simple naked bulbs covered with a conical ceramic shade, white inside and a dark green outside and hanging from the ceiling with a length of wire. I still remember the first night when the electric lights were turned on. All of us went to Ananthayya's house just to sit around and bask in the bright light of electric lamps, which were much better than the kerosene or coconut-oil lamps, which continued to be used in our house for many more years. We would flick the light switches on and off just to enjoy the wonder of it all! At our home, and at most of other homes, no one would have even a radio until many years in the future.

In the Hindu calendar, there are many feasts and festivals (See Appendix 6: "Feasts and Festivals"). Hosting observances of these usually passes on to the eldest son of a family, down the generations. Because my grandfather Madhava was the younger brother, these festivals were observed and celebrated in the family of his elder brother, Vasudeva, in Mulki. Hence, we joined Ananthayya and his family for the observance of *Cavati*, the birthday of Lord Gaṇeśa, or *Aṣṭamī*, the birthday of Lord Kṛṣṇa. For the *Cavati*, a clay image of Lord Gaṇeśa is brought home, ceremoniously installed, and consecrated. There were people, usually of the potter caste, *kumbārānco*, who specialized in making these images, which had to be ordered months in advance. The wooden seat on which the clay image would be established was owned by each family and had to be given to the image maker along with the order. The traditional style called for a Gaṇeśa that was deep red (*sindūrā baṇṇu*), wearing a dhoti, and seated with a mouse, his transport (*vāhana*), close by. In the 1940s, at the height of Gandhi's independence movement, Gaṇeśa was used to make a political statement, in defiance of the British Raj. Thus the Gaṇeśa could be shown wearing a congress or Gandhi cap and seated at a spinning wheel as an ardent participant in the struggle for freedom. Gaṇeśa was also shown as part of a group containing his parents, Śiva and Pārvatī, and their entourage, against an elaborate backdrop of their abode on Mt. Kailāsa. There was an image maker in the lane next to the *Sodhe Maṭha*, who used to make Ananthayya's Gaṇeśa. Early in the morning of *Cavati*, always a holiday for which schools and most of businesses closed, Ananthayya and I used to go the home of the image maker to pick up our Gaṇeśa. At the home of the image maker, in the front yard, it was a glorious sight to see images of different colors, poses, and sizes. I would have loved to remain there for hours, inspecting all the latest styles and configurations of Gaṇeśa. Ananthayya, of course, had other things to do, and our Gaṇeśa would be bought from the maker, hoisted on the head of one of the coolies waiting nearby, and proudly brought home by us. The image would be placed on a table on the front veranda of the house, so that with the front door of the house open, passersby in the street could see our Gaṇeśa. Madhava would conduct all of the worship and the ceremonial offerings of food. The *Cavati* feast called for special dishes based on the fruit and vegetables in season; they were made of these items because by tradition, Gaṇeśa is supposed to be fond of them. We had an elaborate feast for lunch with many dishes and special desserts, held later than the usual lunchtime of noon. Madhava, who liked his lunch and the siesta that followed to be on time, was always impatient to finish all of the ceremonies and get on with the job.

The afternoon was devoted to visiting and seeing all of the Gaṇeśas in different private houses and temples, by children usually, with some men accompanying them. In some houses, people sometimes offer a little bit of *pañcakdāyi* (a mixture of beaten rice, brown sugar, grated coconut) as *prasāda*. Some of the Gaṇeśa displays were very elaborate, with waterfalls, background scenery, and figures of other Gods who are part of the Gaṇeśa mythology. The idea was to see more Gaṇeśas than your friends and to comment on the elaborate displays, as a connoisseur. After the evening *pūjā*, it was time to bid good-bye to our Gaṇeśa and his *visarjana* (ceremonial departure). The image would be carried to the well in the backyard and placed on the low wall surrounding it, *bāyncẽ āḍḍẽ*. There was a brief ceremony of *ārti dākkocẽ* there, and the image was dropped in the well, with all of us shouting "Govindā, Govindā," and then a final drawn-out "Govindā" in unison. The lighter wooden seat of the image would bob to the surface, and our Gaṇeśa would drop to the bottom of the well. As a child, I always used to feel so sad bidding farewell to Gaṇeśa, until the next year.

Krishna's birthday, *Kṛṣṇāṣṭmī*, or *Aṣṭamī* for short, meant a half-day holiday for school, because the bulk of the ceremony was at night, when Lord Kṛṣṇa is supposed to have been born. In preparation for the *pūjā* at night, we had to fast, or observe *upāsu*; that is, we would not eat rice, the everyday staple. We could have nonrice snacks using wheat or other cereals. In the evening, the participants in the *pūjā* would have a bath and then sit down to perform the worship special to *Aṣṭamī*. We had to get packets of leaves of holy basil, *tulasī*, and perform *Viṣṇu sahasranāma*. The thousand names of Lord Viṣṇu are invoked, and with every name, each participant offers leaves of the holy basil in worship. By the end of the ceremony, these form a sizeable pile in front of the household shrine, *devā kūḍa*, where the worship is conducted. At the end of this ceremony, a *pūjā* is performed, and special dishes prepared for Kṛṣṇa's birthday, including his favorites, are offered, followed by a grand feast.

Ananthayya and Sri Devi Adopt Their Grandson

One of the concerns of an orthodox Hindu is to provide for his or her afterlife, which highlights the importance of having at least one son for performing the obsequies and yearly offerings to the dead, *śrāddha*, for his parents after their death. If a couple has only daughters, then in theory, one of the sons-in-law can perform these ceremonies. However, it is considered better to have a son do these, even if it means having to adopt one. In Ananthayya's case, his elder son-in-law, Madhava, husband of Bhavani and an officiating priest, could have performed the *śrāddha*. However, Ananthayya did not trust Madhava, who was a ne'er-do-well and also something of a silent skeptic as to the efficacy of all ceremonies connected with the hereafter, to do these ceremonies faithfully every year. Hence, he and his wife decided to adopt a boy. His eldest daughter, Bhavani, had only one son, Narayana (my father) and three daughters. Narayana's first obligation was to *his* parents; therefore, he could not be adopted. Hence, Ananthayya and his wife decided to adopt Appi's second son, Shridhar, in February 1926. Ananthayya must have discussed this with his wife; otherwise, no one else knew about his plans for adoption. One fine morning, when he and his eldest daughter were alone, he brought up the topic with Bhavani to gauge her reaction. At that time, Bhavani and her family had moved in with Ananthayya for good, after Madhava had become bankrupt. Bhavani, in effect, had become a cook and maid-of-all-work for her mother and was living on the largesse of her parents; she was in no position to influence Ananthayya's decision one way or other. She told her father as much, and wished them, and her soon-to-be-adopted nephew, Shridhar, well. After adoption, Shridhar adopted Ananthayya's clan (Kaṁsa *gotra*) and family name and became his heir both legally and according to the Hindu codes of law. His new legal name thenceforth was Siddhapur Shridhar Prabhu.

Ananthayya Writes His Will

Ananthayya developed a growth of some kind in his nose in 1929, and the local physicians recommended surgery. In those days, any surgery, however minor, was a grave step and full of danger, only undertaken as a last resort. It was quite possible that he would not survive the experience. Ananthayya, being a methodical man, made preparations for the ordeal. On January 3, 1929, at age 57, he wrote his will and last testament. Three years earlier, he and his wife had adopted Shridhar; hence they had a son to do the obsequies, *śrāddha*, for them for their welfare in the hereafter. At least that problem was under control. It was a pity that their adopted son was not married yet and that Ananthayya and his wife had not seen their grandchildren. There was nothing they could do about it; it was their fate. It was decided that Ananthayya would go to the state (then called the presidency) capital at Madras (now called Chennai) for the surgery, because it was the only place in South India where the latest advances in medicine were available. He had never traveled outside the district and was worried about going to the big city of Madras. His son-in-law, Madhava, was an experienced traveler, having knocked around Bombay, Benares, and other places both in the north and the south, and would accompany him. This was an unexpected pleasure for Madhava, who was always ready for an excuse to get away from home to see the world. Narayana, my father, had been apprenticed to Ananthayya for the past four years and was quite experienced. Ananthayya was quite satisfied that Narayana could quite adequately take care of the legal business during his absence. Narayana's wedding in February 1929 had been set, and Ananthayya decided to buy diamonds for the diamond ear ornaments, *vajrā kuṭkā̃ jodu*, for the bride during his Madras trip. For a number of reasons, including ritual purity of food and drink, it was unthinkable for Ananthayya and Madhava to stay in a hotel. Arrangements were made to stay with relatives or friends in the big city. Madhava could also officiate as a priest during their stay, earning a few additional rupees as priestly gifts, *dakṣiṇā*. As Ananthayya said later, by the grace of God, his surgery was quite successful, their stay in Madras was enjoyable, the diamonds were bought, and he and Madhava came back home safe and sound.

Sri Devi's Death

Sri Devi was born into a nonpriestly family (*gṛasthā thancẽ*) and was used to eating onions, garlic, *ukdẽ śīta* (parboiled brown rice), and vegetables such as *vāḷi*, all of which are not normally eaten in priestly families (*bhaṭṭā thancẽ*). Because Madhava was an officiating priest in the Mulki temple, the priestly food taboos of Madhava's background were observed in Sri Devi's home. Once in a while, Madhava was obliged to go to Mulki for a week or two, to conduct worship because of ritual pollution, *vholẽ*, in the family of priests officiating at the Mulki temple. That was the only time when Sri Devi could indulge in some of these forbidden foods. Over the years, in addition to having arthritis, Sri Devi also developed diabetes. When she felt that her end was approaching, she decided to have a big meal of *ukḍẽ śīta, kuḷtā kaḍi* seasoned with garlic (*lośṇe phaṇṇa*), and her other favorite but usually forbidden dishes. The physician had recommended moderation in food and drink because of her diabetes. Sri Devi, being who she was, had her own view of things, including the competence of all physicians. A few days after this grand feast, she summoned me to her home. At that time we were living in our present house opposite Ananthayya's. She was in the kitchen wiping the floor, *āṅgtena nela pussucẽ*. I was six years old, and I remember the incident very well. She asked me to cup my hands, and then she poured 35 heavy silver rupees in it as her parting gift, though at that time I did not realize that that was what it was. She asked me to take the money home carefully and give it to my mother. I remember putting them in the pockets of my shorts, which almost slid to the floor because of the weight of the silver. I hung on to my shorts with two hands and ran home to show my mother and grandmother what I had gotten.

A few days after this, Sri Devi fell ill and took to her bed; she passed away sometime in July or August 1936. Early one morning, when she was near death, all of the family was summoned to her bedside, and each of us had to put a small *cippuṭa* (spoonful) of water from the River Ganges in her mouth. My grandfather Madhava had brought this water in a small bottle from one of his pilgrimages to Kāśi that he kept in a cupboard, to be used for just such an occasion. Water of the River Ganges, put in the mouth of a person on the point of death, by the children and grandchildren, is supposed to guarantee passage to heaven to the person's soul. Orthodox Hindu tradition, perhaps guided by hygiene, demands an expeditious cremation of the body. Hence, immediately after the death of a person, the family goes shopping for stout bamboo, for coconut coir for making the bier, and for the wood for the cremation, and so on. In Udupi, there are shops that specialize in providing all of these materials needed for a Hindu cremation as a package. I remember sitting on her erstwhile bedstead, *māñco*, in the front veranda, watching her body being prepared for the journey to the *smaśāna* (crematorium). I had been ordered to sit there, out of the way, so that I would not interfere by asking my usual multitude of questions. Funeral preparations, with problems of ritual impurity, were too solemn an occasion to satisfy childhood curiosity. The women of the family bathed the body, and it was dressed in one of her best saris. Sri Devi had realized the end desired and prayed for throughout life by every Hindu woman: to die before her husband. As such, she was garlanded with flowers, her forehead was decorated with a bold oval of *kuṅkuma*, and she was transferred to a bier made of bamboo. Four men carried the body to the crematorium. My uncle, Shridhar Bappa, as the adopted son, had had his head shaved except for the top knot, *śeṇḍī*, as a sign of mourning. He carried fire in a small clay pot, *ciḍki*, whose neck is set in a triangular frame of bamboo and is suspended from a piece of coir, to the cremation grounds and did all of the funeral rites for the next 13 days. The dead person's soul is supposed to be around the house till it is dispatched to heaven on the thirteenth and final day of the obsequies. Ananthayya commissioned a reading of the *Garuḍa Purāṇa* during this time. This took place in the room where Sri Devi had died. The priest would read the epic, *purāṇa*, in Sanskrit and translate it line by line to Ananthayya and me, who were usually the only two people who sat through the whole recitation. As the patron (*yajmāna*) who had commissioned it, Ananthayya had to sit through the recitation; I had to do so because of my curiosity about everything. The epic essentially describes scenes in various gruesome hells, involving different punishments for each type of sin, that the soul will encounter on its journey in the hereafter. Now that I think back on it, I am sure that such recitations, as well as all of the obsequies, are for the benefit of the bereaved family. As an orthodox Hindu, Ananthayya accepted the whole belief system and all of its implications. Constellations of beliefs, whether they be religious convictions, political convictions, or convictions about the merits of a favorite sports team, represent a way to say, "Do not bother me with facts or logical arguments. I believe, therefore it is." Hence, a skeptic's questions about how the departed soul can listen to and understand the epics without ears or sensory neurons for interpreting audio signals are not welcome and are at best considered as irrelevant impertinences. Of course, these questions occurred to me much later in life, definitely not to my 6-year-old self.

There is a grand feast on the thirteenth day called *Vaikuṇṭha Samarādhanā*, at which offerings are made to the dead person and he or she is supposed to go to heaven and officially join the souls of other ancestors, *pitrã*, already there. Three balls of rice, *piṇḍa*, are ceremoniously offered to the departed person, and before any one eats, some of that rice is taken out on a banana leaf and offered to the ubiquitous crows, *kāiḷe*. If the crows mob the offering and eat it up quickly, that is considered a propitious sign, indicating that the dear departed has indeed joined the ancestors in heaven, and the family can relax and enjoy the feast. If not, there is a problem (Kane 1973, 4:264). It is commonly believed that if the crows do not touch the rice, either the dear departed had some unfulfilled wish or something else was wrong. The story in our family was that at Sri Devi's funerary feast, though the crows gathered round the offered rice, they would not touch it. The ever-resourceful Madhava came to the rescue and made a gift, *dāna*, of one quarter of the merit, *puṇya*, earned by him from all his pilgrimages to holy places, *yātrās*, to the soul of Sri Devi. Then, and then only, the crows are supposed to have eaten all the rice offering, signaling Sri Devi's ultimate salvation and entry into heaven. The funeral rites and ceremonies in all cultures are for the benefit of the living, and it is these survivors who always have the last word, or the last laugh! So it was with Sri Devi's family, who had been afraid of her all her life. We do not know what she would have said about this unasked-for gift, especially from her never-do-well son-in-law, Madhava! The donor of a gift is always in a dominant position with respect to the recipient.

Ananthayya's Death

Ananthayya lived with his adopted son, Shridhar, and his growing family in the house he had built in Tenkupet. In our family, two parallel streams of the legal profession were represented: My uncle Shridhar Bappa was a lawyer, and Ananthayya was the nominal head of document writing, though most of that work was done by my father. Ananthayya had high hopes of seeing his adopted son flourish as a lawyer in Udupi. Unfortunately, for a variety of reasons, this did not happen. He lived long enough to see Shridhar give up his practice as a lawyer and move first to Poona and then to Bangalore to seek other jobs. These events were further complicated when Ananthayya suffered a stroke that affected the right side of his body, causing problems with his speech and making it difficult for him to move about freely.

One day in 1941, there was a *harikathā* performance at the home of Bailuru Vasudeva Rao, advocate, who lived on the same street as us. Shridhar Bappa attended the presentation, which had the added novelty of being performed by a girl. When my uncle returned home late at night and knocked on the door of the house, Ananthayya awoke and found that he could not talk or get out of bed. He had suffered a stroke in his sleep. Our family physician, Dr. Sunderram Pai, was summoned right away, and he gave Ananthayya an injection, the latest weapon in the armamentarium of physicians in Udupi. The consensus was that but for the prompt medical treatment, Ananthayya might have died. Later on, he received both allopathic and Āyurvedic treatment for his disability, but his condition did not improve. Because of the stroke, he was bedridden. He lived for only another six and a half years, and then passed away in 1948. Shridhar, by then the assistant registrar of the Indian Institute of Science in Bangalore, came to Udupi to perform Ananthayya's obsequies. I do not remember attending these and must have been in Mangalore at St. Aloysius College.

Ananthayya was a truly remarkable person. In spite of his minimal education, he worked himself out of the family profession of small-temple priest, or *Haridāsa,* like his father. He could have become a petty trader or opened a small shop selling miscellaneous items such as tobacco, soda, and bananas or opened a tea or coffee shop in his native Siddhapur. Instead, he made a clean break with his village and moved to the big city of Udupi in his teens. He made up for his lack of education by apprenticing himself to a lawyer and learning the legal profession from the bottom up. He led a life of discipline, honesty, and hard work to better himself and become a good, solid, middle-class citizen. His wife, Sri Devi, a person of strong character, was indeed a supportive wife. In his professional dealings, he was well known for his honest, truthful dealings and for not taking advantage of or cheating any of his clients, who were mostly illiterate. He was a good role model for my father and his other grandchildren. He was a good family man who assumed the added burden of supporting his elder daughter Bhavani and her family when they were destitute. He offered them food and shelter, gave his grandson Narayana, my father, a high school education, and taught him a profession. Ananthayya helped my father to transition from our family profession of temple priests to document writer. My father's hard work and his earnings enabled him to send me and my siblings to college and professional schools. This was the escape route to a better future for our family from the uncertainties of earning a living as a priest. We are all grateful to Ananthayya for his help, industry, and initiative.

Siddhapur Shridhar Prabhu

My uncle, born Manjeshwar Shridhar Bhat, changed his name to Siddhapur Shridhar Prabhu, after he was adopted by Ananthayya and Sri Devi in February 1926. His adoptive parents naturally lavished him with love, and he became the center of all their hopes and expectations for the future. After he completed high school in Udupi and then his undergraduate education in Mangalore, he went to Madras to earn a bachelor of arts at Presidency College. I always used to look forward to his trips back home during vacations, because in addition to being another person for me to play with, he used to bring all kinds of toys for me. I especially remember one toy, a man with a parachute that could be ejected by activating a spring. The toy man would pop up to the ceiling, and then gracefully float down with his open parachute. My uncle also had a Kodak Brownie camera with which he took some of the earliest pictures of me. He had also acquired a taste for Ovaltine, a thoroughly English, newfangled drink. I naturally had to have it. It tasted strange, foreign, and "European."

After he finished his baccalaureate, he went to law school to become a lawyer. I am not privy to all of the details, but my impression is that this choice of profession was entirely due to Ananthayya's single-minded insistence that Shridhar should become a lawyer. Ananthayya did not have much formal schooling—maybe just a couple of years in the local *aigaḷa śāle* (school) in Siddhapur. His work as a lowly clerk, *gumāstu*, for lawyers made him feel that being a lawyer was the ultimate goal in life, the pinnacle of one's career. Because he had not been lucky enough to be a lawyer, he wanted to do all he could to confer this unique boon on his beloved adopted son. This attitude was entirely in keeping with Indian tradition, in which the father decides a son's profession without consulting the son as to his preferences. A proper Hindu son is brought up to be obedient, respectful of his father's wishes and fulfill his obligations without any questions. Perhaps in some cultures, a son is supposed to compensate for the failed ambitions of a father as part of his filial obligations. Blindly obeying this tradition has caused much misery in many lives. If any one had bothered to ask Shridhar, perhaps he would have liked to become a teacher of English literature or to pursue an academic career. Later in life, Shridhar used to express frustration with his life as a lawyer, complaining about how he had been forced into it and how such a choice had ruined his life.

Shridhar was of medium height and build. As a college student in Madras, he used to wear Western clothes—a suit and tie—the first one in our immediate family to be so outfitted. After he was admitted to the bar in Udupi, he wore Western clothes whenever he was in the local courts. Later on, he switched over to the more comfortable dhoti worn by most lawyers, topped with a jacket and a white turban. He also hoped that the Indian dress would make him seem more approachable to potential clients, who might think that a lawyer in a Western suit charged higher fees and was out of their league. On the whole, unfortunately, Shridhar was not a successful lawyer. I do not know how well he knew his profession, but his heart wasn't in it. He used to consult often with my father on points of law, as did other lawyers in Udupi and the neighboring towns. Shridhar was a romantic at heart who loved literature and poetry, both English and Sanskrit, more than the dry, dusty tomes of law. In his backyard, on the left of the walkway from the house to the well, he had a low patio built, where he would sit in the cool of the evenings, declaiming and commenting on Sanskrit poetry to an appreciative audience of one consisting of Katapadi Maamu, husband of Manorama (Mannakka), my father's oldest sister. Shridhar would read aloud salacious passages full of erotic sentiments (*śṛaṅgāra rasa*) from Kālidāsa or Bhartṛahari in sonorous Sanskrit, and both of men would laugh appreciatively. This always used to intrigue me. When I asked the cause of all of the mirth, I was told that I was too young to understand.

Shridhar Bappa married Rathni, daughter of V.D. Kamath, sometime in 1935. V.D. Kamath was the chief engineer of the Madras harbor. Their wedding took place in Mangalore, the district capital and the seat of the local district collector, the administrative officer and member of the famed Indian Civil Service, today known as the Civil Services of India. The bride's party came by train from Madras and was stationed at a school building rented for the occasion. The groom's party went by bus from Udupi to Mangalore, a few hours' journey. Bus service in our district had been established in December 1914. It was the brainchild of entrepreneur Bolar Vittal Rao, who started a company called Canara Public Conveyance Ltd. that offered once-a-day service from Mangalore, the district capital, to Bantwal, a few miles to the east. The one-way bus fair was 6 annas (1 rupee = 16 annas), and the bus capacity was fourteen passengers. The body of the bus had been assembled locally on a Chevrolet chassis (personal communication from Pangal Rabindra Nayak, 2005). From these modest beginnings, the bus service had spread all over the South Kanara District and was a great improvement over the slow, creaky bullock carts that used to be the standard conveyance. In the 1930s, buses had open sides closed by flaps of tarpaulin in case of rain. Ananthayya had rented a whole bus for the wedding to accommodate all of the family. Shridhar Bappa and I were seated in the front seat, next to the driver, on our way to Mangalore. I distinctly remember the strong breeze in the front seat that nearly suffocated me, and how important and happy I felt riding on the front seat, next to the bridegroom. The unfamiliar surroundings of the wedding camp and the side trips to relatives and friends in Mangalore made the whole thing a big, enjoyable camping trip. At that time I used to walk barefoot, and I inadvertently stepped on a smoldering cigarette someone had thrown in the street. I still remember how painful this experience was. The details of the wedding ceremony are vague; all I remember now are a wedding *paṇḍal* (temporary structure of bamboo and woven coconut fronds) full of hundreds of people, loud music, and many dinners and *tiffin* (snacks). After the wedding ceremony, the bride and the groom were served separately in a room, and I remember sitting on the doorsill of the room, getting acquainted with my new aunt, *pācci*, whose married name was Srimathi.

Rathni, was born and brought up in Madras (now called Chennai), and to all of us, she was exotic for being a girl from a big city, knowledgeable about things we had only heard or read about. In turn, she did not know how countryfolk like us lived. There was intense mutual curiosity on both sides. She, poor thing, innocently asked whether "these" were the countryfolk (*baḷḷentulẽ jena*) she had heard about. Her choice of words was rather unfortunate, as it appeared to be condescending, and the poor girl was never allowed to forget them—or at least we carried on about the gaffe behind her back. A power block of the females in the family, headed by Sri Devi, the mother-in-law, was formed instinctively to put the new bride through her paces. I of course was too young to realize then that this was a dominance hierarchy; however, I do recall some incidents that prove its existence and how it functioned. However, this power block was fangless, because Sri Devi was more of a grandmother than a martinet of a mother-in-law, and the majority of the female hierarchy—my grandmother and mother—lived across from Ananthayya's house. Even a fangless Sri Devi was such a formidable character, however, that till the day of her death, her alpha status remained unchallenged. I will always be grateful to my *pācci*, though, for opening up a new world for me, that of English literature. At that time, I could not read and understand English, though I had begun English lessons in the second grade at age 6. Every afternoon, after her siesta, I used to bug her to read me stories. She would sit on the floor, I would lie down on my back next to her on the cool floor, and she would read a line in English and then translate it into my mother tongue, Konkani. I was curious about anything and everything under the sun, and Shridhar Bappa had many books in English I was interested in. She read me stories from the Hindu *purāṇas*, such as *Rāmāyaṇa, Mahābhārata,* and the *Pañcatantra*; the Greek classics *Iliad* and *Odyssey*; the *Arabian Nights*, and other books. I do not remember when exactly I made the transition from individual English letters and words to a connected sentence that I understood; that particular event is lost in the fog of my memory. However, my *pācci* certainly helped me to cross that eventful boundary, satisfying my insatiable curiosity and opening up the whole joyous world of a lifetime of reading. For this act of kindness, I will always be grateful to her.

I had a passion for reading; it was so elemental and visceral that I should really call it a hunger for books. I read any and every book I could get hold of: books around the house, those borrowed from my friends, or books from the school library. There was a grocery shop in the north end of our house, rented to a Mr. Kini. He used to receive bulk shipments of old U.S. newspapers, which he used for wrapping groceries. In those, I discovered American comics, including *Superman*, *Spiderman*, and my all-time favorite, *Li'l Abner*!

At that time, for some unknown reason, I was doing very badly at school. My grades were near the bottom of the class—in the range of 30 to 35, with 35 being a passing grade. This fact bothered me a lot; it bothered my father even more. Throughout his school, my father was a brilliant student who was always at the top of his class. He tried coaching me at home; however, it did not improve my performance at school, which remained as dismal as ever. After a while, he was at the end of his patience, and he essentially gave up on me, resigned to the fact that he had a dumb son who would never amount to much. However, I was blessed or cursed by some perverse self-confidence, which made me feel quite good about myself. Though I was doing poorly in my class, I knew I had more general knowledge than my classmates and, in some cases, my teachers—and I read a lot. Under these circumstances, when I told him I wanted to borrow books from the local municipal library, his answer was a definite no. He felt that my limited mental apparatus could not handle both schoolwork and extracurricular reading. Somehow, Shridhar Bappa talked him out of this stance, however, and got permission for me to accompany him on his visits to the local library, which at that time had a good collection of books. The first book I borrowed from the library was *Pātāḷadalli Pāpacci*—the Kannada translation of Lewis Carroll's *Alice in Wonderland*! The Kannada text was accompanied by the original John Tenniel illustrations, including the one showing the caterpillar smoking a *hookah* while sitting on a toadstool talking to Alice. I remember this illustration well because there and then, I decided that I was going to be a hookah smoker when I grew up. Though I never tried a hookah, I did smoke a pipe for a few years before giving it up for good many years later when my throat was sore and raw with a bad cold. I did not have any problems giving up tobacco; I am glad I gave it up. Shridhar Bappa could appreciate my love of books and reading just for the pleasure of it and not as part of obligatory schoolwork. I will always be grateful to him for encouraging my reading habit and thus introducing me to a whole new world outside my immediate surroundings in Udupi. One of my complaints about Udupi had always been that people wasted too much of their time in idle small-town gossip instead of reading good books or self-introspection.

As I mentioned earlier, Shridhar Bappa did not do well as a lawyer. It is possible that there was too much interference from Ananthayya, who was living his dream of being a lawyer vicariously through Shridhar. Perhaps there were too many lawyers in Udupi, more than the local litigious people could support. Ananthayya was incapacitated by the stroke he had in 1941 and essentially retired. Shridhar was forced to close his practice as a lawyer in 1941 because he did not earn enough. He moved to Poona to work in an ammunition factory during World War II. From Poona, he moved on to Bangalore in 1946, to work as an assistant registrar or an administrator at the Indian Institute of Science. He did quite well there, retiring as the registrar. My uncle's legal training and administrative skills enabled him to bring much sense and order to the administrative procedures of the institution. One day in 1950, he ran into Professor C.V. Raman, who was looking to hire young graduates as research assistants in the Raman Research Institute in Bangalore. I had just then graduated from Bombay University (now called Mumbai University), with a major in physics, and this led to my being hired to work as a research scholar under Raman. After retiring from the Indian Institute of Science, Shridhar lived in Bangalore, in a house he had built in the suburbs. My *pācci* passed away in Bangalore on January 11, 1986, and Shridhar passed away on October 28, 1989. I owe them a lot.

CHAPTER TWO

My Paternal Grandparents

Ananthayya Prabhu had been to Mangalore to be a *sākṣi* (witness) in a court case being tried there. He had taken the shorter coastal bus route to save time and money. This involved having to cross three rivers, at Udyavar, Mulki, and Panambur, between Udupi and Mangalore. The bus would drive up to the edge of the river, all the passengers and their luggage would be transferred to a long wooden *dōṇi* (boat), and the boatmen would punt them across. There were small stalls selling coffee, tea, snacks, cigarettes, and *beeḍis* (country smoke) on both sides at each river crossing. Passengers would wait in a bus station—an open shed with a roof—for the connecting bus. The wide-open fields at the back of the shed served as a communal comfort station for the men. When Ananthayya got off the bus at the river in Mulki, he was surprised to see his eldest daughter, Bhavani, her husband Madhava, and his granddaughters, Manorama and baby Mohini, waiting for the connecting bus to Udupi. Mohini, a 6-month-old, was sleeping on a quilt spread in the bus station.

"We are on our way to Udupi," said Bhavani, stating the obvious.

"Indeed, this is a pleasure," said Ananthayya, wondering all the while what his ne'er-do-well son-in-law, Madhava, was up to now and how much it would cost him to get him out of his latest scrape. What he did not know was that Madhava was bankrupt. He had sold his half of the ancestral home to his elder brother to pay off some urgent debts, did not know where his next meal was going to come from, and was leaving Mulki for good to escape his creditors.

On reaching Udupi, Ananthayya got the whole story out of Bhavani. Madhava was a pauper; he had lost everything in his irresponsible life by pursuing gambling, marijuana (a habit he had recently given up), and associated *durbuddhi* (vices). His small earnings as a priest were not sufficient to support all of his bad habits. He had opened a grocery store, which, because of his complete lack of business sense, went belly-up and lost him more money. He had nowhere to go and owned nothing, except for a few clothes. For the immediate future, Madhava and his family would be staying with Ananthayya for good. Madhava's eldest son, Narayana (my father), was already in Udupi, attending the local Christian high school in the fourth form (grade 9). The year was 1923, and Madhava and his family would be guests of his father-in-law for the next 10 years. Understanding the background of my grandfather Madhava's life in Mulki requires knowledge of the GSB (Gauda Sarasvat Brahmana) temple where generations of my paternal and maternal grandparents officiated as priests. This temple was the source of livelihood for my family, and their lives were centered round it.

The GSB Temple in Mulki

Shri Venkataramana Temple in Mulki is maintained by the local GSB community. There is no official history of the temple; however, three documents describe its origins: (1) *Pancayiti paisalu* (arbitration settlement), dated November 28, 1847; (2) court judgment of T. Jivaji, subordinate judge of South Kanara, dated March 17, 1919; and (3) a booklet published by the temple (Anon. 1847; Jivaji 1919; Anon. n.d.). The accounts in the first two documents are essentially the same and are grouped together here; the booklet has some additional information.

Pancayiti paisalu *of November 28, 1847 and the Court Judgment of March 17, 1919*

There are no dates or individual names in both these accounts of the history of the temple. Its origins are only incidental to the main narratives in these documents. The Konkanasth (Konkani-speaking) GSB community lived in Goa. After Goa came under foreign rule, some people of the community left Goa because of persecution, in three large vessels. One of these vessels sailed to Bhatkal (North Kanara District), and the remaining two went to Kochin. When the Savant chief of Mulki was in Bhatkal, he brought back with him five of the Konkanasth families. He built for them a thatched temple in the village of Manampadi and deeded some lands for its maintenance. This temple came to be called Manampadi Tirumala Temple at a later date. The guru of this community brought from Kochin and consecrated an image of Narasimha in this temple. When there were disturbances in Karkal, the local community brought an image of Venkataramana from their temple and immersed it in the well of the Manampadi temple for safekeeping. Later on when the Karkal people tried to retrieve their sacred image, they could not. Representatives of the Mulki community were told in a dream that Venkataramana wanted to stay in the Manampadi temple, hence the failure of the Karkal people to find the image. This image was retrieved and installed by the Mulki community. At a later date, the guru of the community installed an image of *Bindumādhava* that he had found while bathing in the Ganges at Kashi. This image was installed for use in processions and similar celebrations that commenced later.

A Booklet Published by the Temple

> The origins of the temple can be traced to a small structure called Vittala Gudi or Mulki Mata built by one Soira Vittala Bhat, an astrologer, who had come from Kumta in about 1260 CE [Anon. n.d.]. The image of Bindu Madhava was installed in 1774 CE for use in processions, which were celebrated after this date.

The one obvious discrepancy in these two accounts is about Soira Bhat's origin—was it Bhatkal or Kumta? The other problem concerns the date of the temple. I have not been able to locate a source for the 1260 CE date or verify its provenance. No one I have talked with in Mulki knows the source of this date. There are two points that call into question the correctness of this date. Did the local Sāmanta chief who helped Soira Bhat live that early? The earliest record available about these local chiefs refers to Duggaṇṇa Sāmanta and is dated 1378 CE (Bhatt 1975, 97). Hence, the fourteenth century is the earliest date one can assign to this dynasty or the temple, unless some other evidence is found for an earlier date. It is possible that a temple was built at an earlier date; however, there is no a written record to support such a claim. Soira Bhat is also described as fleeing Portuguese persecution. The Portuguese conquered Goa in 1510, and their persecution and forcible conversion of Hindus started at a later date and peaked in the 1560s (see Appendix 8: "Goa: A Paradise Lost?"). These dates are in conflict with the date of 1260 CE for the building of the original temple. It is quite possible that the narrative of the origins of the temple in the booklet telescope some events, resulting in a confusion of dates. Hence, this thirteenth-century date should be considered unproven until supported by records or other evidence.

The temple is supposed to have been a modest affair, a *gūḍi* (hut with a thatched roof). It was a shrine for the family deity, Vittala of Soira Bhat. We do not know the exact location of this structure; it is possible that it was at or near the location of the present temple. This Soir Vittala Bhat is the founder of the Vatsa *gotra* (clan) family of priests who officiate at the Mulki temple and is my ancestor on my mother's side of the family. The *pratiṣṭha* (installation) of the image, *pratimā,* of Shri Ugra Narasimha at the Mulki Venkataramana Temple by His Holiness Vijayendra Theertha, swami of the Kāśi Maṭha (Kāśi monastery) was on November 23, 1569 (Pai 1995, 715–7). At that time, His Holiness decreed that in addition to the Vatsa *gotra* priests already at the temple, only priests of Atri *gotra* could officiate. A priest belonging to this *gotra* and his family were brought from Kochin in Kerala. His name was Narasimha Bhat, and he was the progenitor of our family. It is estimated that he was born sometime around 1650 CE, nearly a century after the dispersal of the GSB from Goa in about 1560 when religious persecution there was at its most severe. (See Appendix 2: "Family Genealogy," and Appendix 8: "Goa: A Paradise Lost?" for details). What is known about the genealogy of his progeny is given in Appendix 2. If this progenitor of our family is assigned to the first generation of our family in Mulki, then Madhava and his brother Vasudeva belong to the thirteenth generation and my son Giridhar corresponds to the sixteenth generation after him. *Pūja* (worship) in Hindu temples is conducted according to the procedures laid out in specialized books called *Āgama*; in the Mulki temple, the *Tantrasārokta Āgama* is followed. The worship is modeled after the honors bestowed on a respected guest and may have evolved from the rituals of hospitality going back to the Vedic age (Kane 1974, 2:705–40; 1977, 5:35–7, 1120–31; Fuller 2004; Klostermaier 1994, 163).

The ownership of the Soir Bhat temple passed on to the local GSB community many years after his death. We do not know the exact date of this event; it is based on stories current in the family. The reason was the poverty of his descendants, who could not continue to maintain the temple and its daily services and ceremonies. They were too poor to afford even the oil for the lamps normally kept burning perpetually in a temple. A board of *moktessors* (overseers or trustees), made up of representatives of prominent local *grasthā thañcẽ* (householder) families, was appointed to manage the affairs of the temple for the community. Custom and tradition required that only a householder could ever become an overseer; a priest could not. In effect, the priests became the servants of the temple, with the community as a whole as their employers. This may be the reason for disqualifying priests from any involvement in temple management. This state of affairs put the temple priests in a subordinate position with respect to the trustees, and there were few checks and balances against their exercise of power. The GSB community as a whole was supposed to be the owner and supervisor of temple affairs.

The GSB Temple in Mulki and Its Surroundings

The bridge spanning the Mulki River was built in the 1960s. Before that, people crossed the river in boats along with their luggage. At the ferry in Mulki, the luggage was hoisted on to the head of a porter, and we would walk to the temple area through the coconut palm groves on the shores of the river. On the right-hand side of the road to the temple, first there was a Jain temple, a *basti*, along with a granite column, *mānastambha*, in front of it. The temple was on a steep rise of about 50 to 100 feet from the road, at the top of which one could see this granite column. Next, one passed a few homes on either side, along with the Umā-Maheśvara Temple of the Sarasvats on the right (Kramrisch 1988). The road then took a sharp, steep turn to the right, passing through a few low hills, with banyan trees on either side. On the left of the road was the *Pommatā guḍḍo*, a small hill to the southwest of the Mulki Temple and the back of the house of my maternal grandfather, Mulki Subraya "Subba" Bhat. We would go there for a walk or to fly a kite, after afternoon snacks. This brought one to an *aśvattha* (*Ficus religiosa*) on the right, growing out of the center of a platform. At the bottom of the tree on the platform, there were a few *Nāgā phāttora* (stones) that depicted a cobra with its hood spread. This area was called the *pāje kāṭṭẽ*, a term that refers to the road that led from there in a steep decline to the *rathāsuttu* (outer perimeter) of the temple. A few times a year, on special ceremonial occasions, the wooden temple cart, *ratha*, with the image of Bindumādhava, the *utsavā mūrti*, is taken round the temple in a procession. The *pradakṣiṇā* (circumambulation) of the temple is always done clockwise, so that the person's right side is toward the sanctum of the temple.

One turned left at the bottom of the decline, *pāje kāṭṭe*, to come to the Subba Bhat's house. When I was little, on the way to Subbajja's (Grandfather Subba's) house, there was the house of Venkataramana, a *ghāṇyānco* (oil presser), on the left. This house was at some elevation, reached by a number of steps, ending in a narrow pathway one had to squeeze through. Venkataramana belonged to the oil presser's caste, and was a retainer of sorts for Subbajja's family for an unknown number of years. He was always there doing odd jobs and running errands and had seen my mother and her sister and brothers grow up. When they were little, he used to carry them to school on his shoulders. In his house, there was an oil press whose motive power was provided by a bullock that slowly and patiently walked in a circle. Before the advent of electric oil mills, people would take to his house dried kernels of coconuts or other oil seeds, in a gunnysack, from which he would extract oil for them. Having a large number of dried coconuts is a by-product of being a professional priest. The residue, *pēṇḍi*, was used as a highly nutritious cattle feed. We children would ride on the long lever arm of the oil press pushed by the bullock. When I was a few years old, this ride was quite attractive and fun; at the same time, I used to be scared, because I was not used to heights and the dizzying circular motion. Modern oil mills soon put Venkataramana out of business. His children moved to Bombay and other cities, got good jobs, and sent money home. He eventually sold his old home, bought a plot of land on the way to the Mulki high school, and built a brand-new house there. I remember visiting his new house while in high school, looking for cashew apples, *kāju*, in his yard.

The outer perimeter of the temple has a moderate decline at this point and also turns right toward the east-facing main entrance to the temple. Both of these factors made the temple cart hit the compound wall of Subba Bhat's house, where there was a large mango tree that used to grow there next to a cowshed. The top parts of the cart would get entangled in the branches of the tree, and it would take quite some effort to get the cart moving again. Recently, this problem was solved by cutting down the tree, knocking down the cowshed, and shaving off quite a wide swath of the house to widen the outer-perimeter road. Farther down on this road is a *dharmaśālā* (pilgrim rest house) on the left and the temple tank, the *taḷẽ*, on the right. In the 1940s during my boyhood, there was a small GSB (read: ritually pure) coffee shop next to the tank. Early in the morning, my cousin Devaraya and I would stop by at this coffee shop on our way back from the temple. For 4 annas (one-quarter rupee), we could buy a packet of "mixture." This was a mixture of three snacks: *rulā̃vũ* (cream of wheat) and *caṇyā āni phovāupkari* (chickpeas and beaten rice) in a *poṭḷi* (package), tied up in banana leaves. There was enough of the tasty breakfast mixture for about six people. Of course, these days, 4 annas will buy you next to nothing. This coffee shop was next to the *Brahmarā* (a minor deity) *guḍi*, near the entrance to the temple. A big iron gate has been installed there recently, to block off the temple surroundings when needed.

There is a small lane that goes north past Subba Bhat's house, leading on to our present family home. When Narasimha Bhat first moved to Mulki, his house (hut?) was much closer to the temple, just outside where the present *agraśāḷā* (main dining hall) is. Later on, his descendants bought the present family home and moved there at date unknown, many years ago. The senior branch of our family, the great-grandsons of Vasudeva, live there. The lane is about 6 feet wide, with a wide, open sewer on the left and a *dharmaśālā* on the right. When I was little, there was a sizeable pond on the right, with *sāḷuka* (water lilies) growing in it. In the 1940s, the pond was built over into a large, deep well surrounded by the new wing of the *dharmaśālā*. Farther north was the older part of the *dharmaśālā* in which His Holiness the swami of the Kāśi Maṭha and other visiting heads of the *maṭha* (monastery) used to stay. The open sewer is filled with the fast-flowing waters of monsoon rains and is a good place to float paper boats. When the rains are over, some pools of water are left over in which one can see some small fish and tadpoles for a while, before they too dry up in spring and summer.

There are rice fields on the right next to the *dharmaśālā*. On the left is our family home, which faces east. We do not know when it was built and acquired by the family. It was initially partitioned between Vasudeva and his younger brother Madhava. Madhava mortgaged his half to Vasudeva, and then finally sold it to him to pay off his debts. There is a low door or gate at the entrance, leading to a quadrangle, at the center of which is a plant of holy basil, *tulasī*, found in all Hindu homes. On the right is a door leading to the back of the house; one can wash one's feet at the enclosure at the foot of a coconut tree, *māḍḍāyā kāṭṭẽ*, that is there, before entering the house. There is a wide veranda, a *jagali*, at the front of the house, where guests and visitors are usually received and entertained. The wall of the house is adorned with pictures of Hindu gods and goddesses, along with those of relatives, both living and dead. Only relatives and other GSB people go beyond the front entrance that leads to the household shrine, the *devā kūḍa*, and the kitchen and dining room on the right. The images in the family shrine are Vittala, Sita-Ramachandra, Vedavyasa, Kṛṣṇa, and Santana Gopala, a representation of Lord Kṛṣṇa that was given to our family by His Holiness the head of Kāśi Maṭha. The guru blessed the man who was then head of the family and his wife, *mātyāri bātu kāṇu*, vouchsafed them an abundant and healthy family, and gave them the image of Santana Gopala to be worshipped in perpetuity in the family shrine. The story behind this gift appears in Appendix 2: "Family Genealogy." I have never seen this image, because it is usually covered by a mass of flowers or *tulasī* leaves. I have been told it is about 1 to 2 inches high and shows Lord Kṛṣṇa holding a small baby in his arms.

The west wall of the kitchen is one long, low *rānye pedi* (fireplace), and people sit in two long rows, along the north and south walls of the kitchen, facing each other, for eating. They sit on low wooden platforms, *māṇayī*, and eat off metal plates or banana leaves on more formal or religious occasions. The food that is eaten is strictly vegetarian, with no meat, fish or eggs and plenty of milk, yogurt, and other dairy products. The one major change, introduced perhaps one or two centuries ago, was the use of coffee and tea as hot beverages. In the olden days, it was customary to drink *jīrā uddāka* (cumin water), a decoction of *jīrā* (cumin) flavored with jaggery (a traditional, unrefined sugar) or brown sugar and taken with or without milk as a medicine, digestive, or hot beverage. According to my grandfather Madhava, when he was young in the late nineteenth century, coffee was called *bunnā uddāka* (bunna water). I was skeptical about this story till I read that coffee beans are indeed called *'bunn'* in Arabic (Weinberg and Bealer 2001, 5–7). Legend ascribes the doughty act of introducing coffee to India to a seventeenth-century Sufi saint, Bābā Buḍān, who smuggled seven viable coffee beans out of Yemen in about 1670 in his waist-band while returning from a pilgrimage to Mecca (Chanda 2007, 88; Kamath 1982, 1:664). The ruler of Yemen used to export only boiled or roasted beans to make sure no one else could propagate them and challenge his monopoly over this precious commodity. The saint grew the first coffee bushes outside his cave on Bābā Buḍān Giri (Mountain) near Mysore, and he used the coffee to keep him awake during his meditations. The whole world is grateful to the saint for this bit of smuggling. At the east end of the kitchen are wooden stairs that lead on to the attic. Food is eaten usually with the fingers; a spoon may be given to visiting city folk at breakfast or *tiffin* (snacks) in the afternoon. At the end of a meal, one goes to the bathroom outside the kitchen for washing. The family cowshed is at the back of the house, along the north wall of the compound.

Priesthood as a Profession

Because we are a family of professional priests, religion is our family business in a way. If this sounds crass and commercial, it is not meant to be. However, if one looks at it dispassionately, the priesthood is indeed the family business. The religion professionals or priests are purveyors of comfort, hope, and reassurance in this world and promises of salvation in the next. This statement is not meant to be facetious or derogatory; it is an objective description of the transaction between the priests and their flock. Comfort, hope, reassurance, and salvation are commodities in demand by their followers, and the priests supply it. Market forces determine the interaction between these two groups. Comfort, hope, and reassurance are coping mechanisms; faith and belief are requisite for finding these in life. Salvation, as defined by *Webster's Dictionary* (*Ninth New Collegiate*), could be deliverance from the effects of sin or liberation from ignorance or delusions about the true nature of reality, thus covering a wide range of religious traditions or beliefs. Each person, with his or her own belief system, approaches the priests for relief from problems in this life as well as reassurances about the hereafter. The priests provide plenty of both, along with emotional support reenforcing the client's faith that he or she is doing the right thing in practicing the proper rites and traditions. These services could be provided gratis out of compassion or because the priests are supported by the community as a whole and are expected to serve it. For performing some rites and rituals, nominal fees are charged, because the priests have to make a living. Before the advent of psychiatry and psychiatrists, these spiritual advisors occupied a similar niche, providing moral and intellectual support to their community. As teachers and spiritual advisors, better educated than most in the community, priests did and still do form a dominance hierarchy. Today, psychiatrists, familiarly called shrinks, of course occupy a similar niche with respect to their patients. Whether practicing religion and going to a place of worship for solace is more cost effective than going to a shrink is a decision that each one of us has to make. Both of these groups promise much, and whether they deliver is, by its very nature, not subject to close scrutiny by truth-in-advertising laws. Client satisfaction is determined mostly by faith and belief.

Priests in GSB Society

Each family of priests caters to a set of client families, following a tradition extending over many past generations. The family priest, *purohit*, conducts all the rites and rituals for a client, *yajamāna*, for a gift or fee, *dakṣinā*. Hindu tradition ordains that a religious rite is never properly finished and the client accrues *puṇya* (merit) from it, unless the priest is paid his fees. Those priests must have had the same problems with deadbeat clients that modern professionals such as lawyers, physicians, and tax accountants face. The voluntary gift or fee depends on the finances of the client and his goodwill. Family priests conduct ceremonies for next to nothing and even provide materials for the rituals, if a family is facing hard times and cannot meet the costs. This symbiotic relationship is appreciated by both parties. People of our Konkani-speaking community owe allegiance to one of the four monastic traditions maintained at the four monasteries, *maṭha*, whose heads are the ultimate authorities in all matters pertaining to religion. They are, in alphabetical order, Chitrapur Maṭh, in the town of Shirali; Gokarn Partagali Jeevottam Mutt, in Partagal; Kashi Maṭh Samsthan, in Vārāṇāsi; and Kavale Maṭh, in Ponda. The first and last worship Śivā and the middle two worship Viṣṇu as the principal deity. These monastic institutions and their histories are given in detail by Kudva (Kudva 1978, 188–97). Hinduism does not have one central authority who governs all Hindus; the heads of these monasteries are as close as one can get to a central religious authority, at least as far as their followers in our community are concerned.

The symbiotic relationship, extending over generations of a priestly family, *purohita* with its clients, *yajamāna*, is determined by the clans, *gotra*, of the priest and the householder and is of ancient origin. Priestly families, in their turn, have other designated priestly families as their purohita. Thus, our family of Atri *gotra* are the *purohits* of the priests of my mother's family, who belong to the Vatsa *gotra*, and vice versa. The two broad groups—priests and householders—intermarry, interdine, etc., and are considered the same people or belong to the same birth group or caste. The priests have kept alive the ancient Hindu traditions of Sanskrit scholarship, customs, and strict rituals, whereas the householders are more relaxed about them. A householder can change his occupation and assume one of the priestly surnames, provided he knows enough Sanskrit and the rituals and observes other priestly customs, such as not eating fish, meat, onions, garlic, etc. Apparently, such changes did occur sometimes in the olden days. There is a tradition in our family that we were Nayaks or Pais before we became Bhats; we do not know the date of the change. Our family name, Bhaṭṭa (a learned Brahman), was originally a title conferred in recognition of scholarship of Hindu scriptures. This title can precede a name, as in Bhaṭṭa Nārāyaṇa, or follow it, as Nārāyaṇa Bhaṭṭa. It became a family name later on. At present, our family only has the title; there is no Sanskrit scholarship to deserve it. As regards priesthood as a profession, only one person, Srinivasa, a great-grandson of Vasudeva, has been trained to be a priest in our Atri *gotra* family. In my mother's Vatsa *gotra* family, there are no practicing priests. A priest could also change his profession and become a householder, as is quite common now. Both groups are gaining entry into the professions and moving away from their traditional occupations, rituals, and customs, which are fast disappearing into the sinkhole of memory.

Today, the hold of religion on everyday life is decreasing among everyone, including the GSBs. Hence, any power or prestige associated with traditional religious scholarship has diminished; it is almost nonexistent. Being a Sanskrit scholar does not earn you much money. It is as simple as that. The long apprenticeship of a budding Sanskrit scholar is not subsidized, and the young priest has to earn a living to survive. Further education in Sanskrit and Hindu traditions gets a second priority and is usually neglected. Even if a person becomes a Sanskrit scholar, there are no academic or equivalent jobs available for him to make a decent living. They have to depend on the seasonal, or occasional, precarious earnings as an officiating priest, and the generosity of their patrons. The patron–client relationship automatically puts the priest in a secondary, subdominant position. In a way I feel that the current state of affairs is a good thing because the priestly occupation is subject to the harsh realities of life in the Konkani society and hence will live or die, or be subject to Darwinian evolution, depending on the needs of society. This is exactly what has happened, and the profession is on a slope of certain decline. Young men of priestly families who can manage to get a college education are giving up their family vocation, getting out into the wide world, and competing with the rest. Those who cannot get an education are stuck with being a priest, carrying out the rites by rote without much understanding of their meaning and eking out a living. Traditional Sanskrit scholarship is hard to come by among the priests, and it would be difficult to respect many of them as scholars today. Here we have the situation of a community that does not respect traditional religious learning or subsidize it but having a set of priests who are not scholars and who are mere technicians of priestcraft. One group deserves the other!

It is also possible that one of the contributing factors to the decline of traditional scholarship among the GSB priests is the migrations of our society and its wholesale uprooting and the resulting instability (see Appendix 8: "Goa: A Paradise Lost?"). Fostering scholarship over a long period requires subsidies from the local power elite, such as monarchs, temples, or holders of a great deal of property. The migrations meant the end of existing subsidies and a search for new sources of support. They also ended any long-term teacher–student relationships through death or displacements. It was easier to find alternate means of earning a livelihood to suit the new conditions than to continue a tradition of learning and scholarship. The conditions of the sixteenth- to seventeenth-century migrations from Goa were particularly severe in this respect because they involved the wholesale destruction of temples or monastic establishments that supported scholarship and traditional learning in the GSB community.

Laukika–Vaidika Tension Among the GSB

Among the GSB, there is a division into two broad categories of *laukika* and *vaidika*. *Laukika* means "of the world" or "secular" and indicates that these people have some profession other than priest. *Vaidika* means "of the Vedas" and refers to the fact that these people are professional priests. The priests are specialists in the performance of Hindu rites of passage and other celebrations. This has given rise to the *yajamāna–purohit* relationship, where the former is the patron who pays the expenses and the latter is the craft specialist who performs the rites. The patron is naturally is in a dominant position with respect to the priest hired for the occasion, because he pays the expenses. There has always been tension between these two groups, influencing how they think about the other and deal with them. This is an example of these two groups positioning themselves for relative dominance, though both belong to the same dominant birth group of GSB. The result, unfortunately, has been tension in the community, and some rivalry detrimental to both. Such tension is much more muted now, like most other facets of community life. However, it does exist, especially in rural areas, where these small things assume great significance. Family names indicate where a person fits into one of these two broad groups. The householders, *g̣rasthāthañcẽ*, or *laukika*, have family names such as Baliga, Bhandarkar, Hegde, Kamath, Kini, Kudva, Mallya, Nayak, and Pai, and the priests, *bhaṭṭāthañcẽ*, or *vaidika*, have family names such as Acharya, Bhat, Joishy, Puranik, and Shastri. The first group is usually more relaxed about food taboos, rules of ritual purity, and customs and traditions of the community, whereas the priests observe them strictly.

The practicing priests undergo a period of training to learn the rituals and how to officiate at religious ceremonies such as weddings and funerals. Apprentice priests get their hands-on training helping their elders in the relevant ceremonies and rites. There are also centers of training where they go through a course of 3 to 5 years. Priests earn a living from the ritual gifts, *dakṣiṇā*, given at these functions, by reading and translating religious epics, *purāṇas*, or by conducting worship at a temple. They also get the coconuts, rice, and other grains that are part of offerings at these religious rites. This method of earning a livelihood is sanctified by centuries-old tradition. Unfortunately, it has not kept pace with the realities of inflation and the increase in cost of living in the modern age. The priestly families tend to be more conservative; hence, they were slow to take advantage of the new "English education" that was available starting in the 1860s. The householder families, however, used these new opportunities to become part of the government bureaucracy or go into private practice as lawyers or physicians. The Sanskrit-based education of the priests was not of much use in the new scheme of things and was irrelevant to the new survival skills needed in a changing world. All of these factors contributed to push the priests to the bottom of the economic scale compared with the householders, who, as merchants, property owners, or professionals, were men of wealth. Because money confers power and prestige, the householders look down on the usually poor priestly families with some condescension tinged with contempt, though there is an outward show of respect, especially at religious functions. This contempt is shown in various ways, some overt and a few covert, and has become part of Konkani vocabulary and usage. For example, piquant pickles, lively bursts of fire and spice on the tongue, spoil and develop a teeming swarm of small worms if not prepared properly. These are called *bhaṭṭu*, a curious word of unknown origin. This word is also used as a pejorative name for priests in many Konkani jokes about them. I have heard such demeaning jokes at least twice, and I protested strongly. These jokers who hope to stand tall on the backs of those whom they humiliate should take a good look at themselves sometime. The priests are usually poor, not very learned, and at the bottom of the social hierarchy; however, I very much doubt that they deserve such ridicule. Perhaps it is a sad reflection on the sense of values of the GSB community. With us, money talks to money, and lack of it calls for opprobrium and contempt. Money is power, and those without money are the losers. It is quite possible that I am particularly sensitive to the *laukika–vaidika* tension because I am from one of these *vaidika* families and have heard innumerable stories of these encounters.

The Cycle of Worship at the Mulki GSB Temple

The responsibility for daily worship and the celebration of special festivals and ceremonies at the temple is assigned to priests of the Atri and Vatsa *gotras* in a cycle of 12 years each. The 12-year period is divided into assignments for 1 to 2 years for the different families of priests of the same gotra or clan. This assignment is termed the family *paryāyu* (turn) and is important for remembering significant events in the family such as births, weddings, and deaths. The present sequence of these assignments follows an arbitration agreement (Anon. 1847) dated 28 November 1847. The decision to confine the worship at the temple to the Atri and Vatsa *gotra* priests was made by His Holiness Vijayendra Theertha, swami, in 1569, and became the custom thereafter. Priests of two different gotras are needed to take care of situations in which people of one gotra cannot conduct worship for a fixed number of days because of ritual pollution, *vholẽ*, resulting from births, deaths, etc. The 1- to 2-year assignments for each family enables the family to earn some material profit also. Such profit is supposed to supplement the uncertain earnings of the priestly profession so that the family can survive till its next assignment in another 24 years. The head of each family whose turn it is to conduct daily worship is responsible for the smooth working of all the ceremonies. The logistics of these procedures could involve as many as seven or eight people with responsibilities for individual areas.

The ceremony of transfer of responsibility of *paryāyu* at the temple is interesting. It takes place on *Mārgaśira Bahula Pratipāda*, or *pāḍvo*, or the first day of the dark half of *Mārgaśira*, the day after *Kārtipunnava*, according to the lunar calendar, or approximately in November–December. The incoming priest assumes responsibility for all the gold and silver vessels, the expensive jewelry used in the *alaṅkāra* (decorations), and worship of the sacred images, in addition to the orderly conduct of rites and rituals. He is expected to post a bond along with the surety of a person of means. A few days before the actual transfer of *paryāyu*, the incoming priest bows to God and offers a short *prārthana* (prayer) in the vestibule, *naḍo*, of the temple, and then tells the management his intention of assuming responsibility for worship according to tradition and to the hereditary right of his family. The temple management responds by fixing the date of the formal transfer and requesting that the incoming priest bring his bond and surety. On the day of transfer, the incoming priest's family, along with the image of his family deity, is brought to the temple in a formal procession accompanied by musicians, *vājjapānce*. The image of the family deity is installed in the temple along with the temple deities for worship. The incoming priest then has a ritual bath before entering the sanctum, and the keys to the sanctum are handed over to him. His term of worship is supposed to begin from the first *pūjā* he performs after entering the sanctum of the temple. The outgoing priest, along with his family deity and his family members, goes back to the family home in procession, accompanied by musicians.

Paternal Ancestors

The Atri *gotra* Bhats, our ancestors in Mulki, were not rich; however, they managed to survive on modest means. Their earnings from the *paryāyu* were supplemented by fees garnered from the performance of ceremonies associated with rites of passage, such as births and deaths, or *saṁskāra*. Madhava was the second son of Ganapathi (twelfth generation from Narasimha, our progenitor), whose first son was Vasudeva. Madhava was born in 1884 and had his *upanayana* (initiation ceremony) in 1893–1895 during the *paryāyu* of our family. During the *paryāyu* of 1917–1919, my father, Narayana, had his *upanayana*.

Vittala, Ganapathi, and Krishna were three brothers in the twelfth generation. We know very little about Vittala, the eldest, who did not have any sons. Ganapathi passed away when my grandfather Madhava was young, so we know very little about him either. Krishna did not have any sons—only three daughters, who will appear later in the story. He lived in the memory of his three daughters, who told us about a few events in his life. Krishna (Kuṭṭaṇi for short) passed away in 1917–1919 during this *paryāyu* when my mother was 3 to 5 years old. His wife had passed away earlier. After the partition of property between Vasudeva and Madhava, he had his meals with Vasudeva for a few years; however, because of some quarrel between them shortly before the beginning of the 1917–1919 *paryāyu*, he broke with Vasudeva and decided to dine with Madhava, his younger nephew. During the *paryāyu*, most of the activities of the household are transferred to the temple and its *bhojana śālā* (cooking and dining facilities). There is almost no cooking done at home, except for boiling milk or preparing baby food. Some men of the family also sleep on the inner veranda of the temple surrounding the sanctum. When my father was about 10, he used to sleep on the inner veranda of the temple surrounding the sanctum, along with his father Madhava, Krishna, and other males of the family. He can clearly recall the last few hours of Krishna's life. It was Krishna's habit to have some warm milk along with a light snack of cream of wheat with jaggery (*goḍḍā rulā̃vũ* or *nāñcaṇyā gūḷi*), made out of fried and ground millets (*nāñcaṇo*) mixed with coconut gratings and jaggery and kneaded into small balls. All of the grandchildren, including my father, used to wait patiently for him to have his snack so that they could help him finish it. After his snack that one night, Krishna lay down on his pallet and was soon writhing as if in pain. Madhava could see that there was a problem and that considering Krishna's age, it could be serious. Madhava and an assistant, Marthu, then carried Krishna out of the main building of the temple and propped him up with a few pillows on the veranda, *Vasantā jagali* or *Candra Śālā*, to the north of the temple. This was a precaution, to ensure that if he died, he did so outside the main building of the temple; otherwise, it would entail elaborate and costly purifying rituals. Madhava had guessed right; soon, Krishna breathed his last. He was cremated early in the morning.

Krishna, called Kuṭṭaṇi by everyone, had three daughters, Nethravathi (Nethru Mhava), Mathura, and Vedavathi (Vedu), and a son who died young. Krishna was the younger brother of Ganapathi, my grandfather Madhva's father. Hence, these three daughters and Madhava and his brother Vasudeva were first cousins. Nethru's life was very sad. She was born in 1880 and was married at a young age to Padubidri Srinivas Shenoy, a sickly man in his fifties. He had grown sons from his first wife who were married and had their own families. Such marriages were quite common in those days because the bride's father could more easily marry off a daughter to an older man without a large dowry or related wedding expenses. Daughters in a Hindu family are always considered a burden by the parents because of the problems involved in finding a suitable husband for them. Nethru did not have any married life as such. The only married "bliss" she experienced was short-lived and consisted of nursing and taking care of a sickly, diabetic husband. In a few years, her husband died, and Nethru, still a teenager, became a widow for life.

The misery of a widow's life in Hindu society is beyond description and can be truly considered life in hell (Kosambi 2000; Chakravarti 2006). The cruel, heartless treatment of widows is truly one of the low points of traditional Hindu society. On her husband's death, the young wife, wipes off the beauty spot, *tīḷo*, between her eyebrows, and can never wear it again. Flowers and perfumes are forbidden. All her jewelry, including the *maṅgala sūtra* (auspicious necklace) tied by her husband at the wedding ceremony, is removed, the glass bangles on her wrists are broken, and the gold bangles are removed. Her head is shaved, and she will wear for the rest of her life a particular type of sari, colored either red or white. Thus all the outward signs of a married woman, *savvāśiṇī* (with husband living), are obliterated forever, and in effect, she becomes a nonperson, as if she has ceased to exist. The symbolic significance of all these ceremonies, which are carried out as part of the funeral rites of the dead husband, and their psychological trauma must be truly devastating for a poor young woman. They overtly truly mark her passage to widowhood, stigmatized in Hindu society. She cannot marry again, and the death of her husband is usually ascribed to her bad luck or the unlucky constellation of planets at her birth, as if she were directly responsible for it. The father or brothers get no blame for giving a child bride to a sickly, much older man. If the husband's family allows her to live with them, she leads a life of deprivation, as if in expiation for her sins. Her future is an austere life of strict religious observances, prayers, ritual fasts, and hopes of a better life after the next birth. In some cases, the husband's family can pack her off to her parents or brothers, without any share of her husband's property.

Nethru had a small allowance from her husband, which provided savings for her pilgrimages and the bare necessities of life. She used to eat one meal a day, consisting of cream of wheat, *rulā̃vũ*, because she had given up eating rice as part of austerities. She fasted on many days in a month, repeated *Rāmnām* (Lord Rama's name) in her spare time, went on pilgrimages, and lived a life of great piety. I fondly recall Nethru Mhava, as we used to call her. She was a short, plump, kindly old lady who was very fond of us, her grandchildren. She was always an easy touch for pocket money, candy and sweets, toys, and other goodies that form such an important part of a child's life. Nethru Mhava passed away in 1946 when she was 66.

Mathura was married to Govind Bhat of Bantwal, a village on the Nethravathi River; he was a priest officiating in the Krishna temple at Panjalkatte, close to Bantwal. When I knew her, she was also a widow, but she had a few sons.

The third daughter, Vedu, was married to Mulki Subraya Bhat, my maternal grandfather. She appears again in Chapter 3, "My Maternal Grandparents."

Madhava and Vasudeva grew up to be quite different from one another. Vasudeva was a Sanskrit scholar well versed in the Hindu *śāstras* (codes of law), one who knew much more than was needed to officiate as a priest at ceremonies. He was nervous by temperament, constantly worried about unseen or unknown dangers lurking out there, and he needed reassurance and moral support before embarking on a course of action. Madhava was not a scholar; however, he had lots of common sense, was unflappable, and was rock solid in any crisis. He had intense curiosity and an urge to try out new things, especially those that were forbidden. Perhaps the "Imp of the Perverse" motivated him some of the time (Poe 1993; Baer 2002). This story by Edgar Allan Poe explores a primeval principle of action innate to humans, which Poe calls *perverseness.* What is perverseness? It is what makes us act, though reason tells us that it would *not* be prudent to do so (Poe 1993). Humans have a particular fascination with an act that logic tells us would end in certain disaster or death. When we look down from the top of a tall building, we contemplate the possibility of jumping off it, fully well knowing that it would result in certain death. In Poe's story the protagonist tells of a "perfect murder" he had committed, without the authorities suspecting it as such. The perpetrator has an irresistible urge to confess it, fully well knowing that he would hang for it. The story ends with a confession to the authorities and the impending punishment for the murderer. All of us may not follow the Imp; however, we are fascinated by *What if?*

I came to know of Madhava's urge to push boundaries from my father. In December 1986, my father consulted a famous astrologer from Kerala, Mr. Puduval, to find the reason we as a family were having many problems, great and small, with nothing seeming to go right for us. My father was an ardent believer in astrology and was convinced that the astrologer would provide a solution to all of our problems. This was many years after Madhava had passed away, and if he had been alive, he would have looked at this process of divination with some skepticism. Consulting an astrologer has the formal name of *aṣṭa maṅgala praśna*, and according to my father, it was up to his expectations and worthwhile. The astrologer recounted many past incidents pertaining to our family, some remembered and others forgotten, and prescribed expiations according to our *śāstras*. Among many other things, the astrologer said that Madhava had committed some ritual impropriety for which expiations had to be made. When I asked my father what exactly Madhava had done, my father told me: "I do not know the impropriety he committed. However, your grandfather, if he saw someone or something being held in great reverence or awe, he wanted to shake it a little bit to find out what gives or what would happen. That was his problem." This tendency, driven by intense curiosity, likely got him into all kinds of troubles and interesting situations in his life. I have a sneaking suspicion that I might have inherited this trait of basic skepticism and a desire to tweak the tails of sacred cows. He knew only enough Sanskrit to get by and earn a living as a priest. Pursuit of further knowledge and scholarship, he left it strictly to his brother. He was something of an epicurean who had an educated palate for good food, an aversion to hard work, a desire for fine things he could not afford, and a liking for irresponsible living. In short, he was a likeable character. In general, he had a decidedly positive outlook on life; something interesting or useful was right round the corner and was going to take place at any moment, and all was right with the world! His grandchildren were his pride and joy, and he loved all of them dearly.

Madhava's Asthma Is Cured by Marijuana

Both brothers were asthmatic. Vasudeva's asthma was treated by a local *Āyurvedic vaidya* (physician), but Madhava's asthma did not respond to the same treatment. One day, when Madhava was in his teens, he was wheezing past a group of wandering *saṁnyāsis* (ascetics) who had camped in the precincts of the Mulki temple. A kindly member of the group who was smoking marijuana (*bhāṅgi*) offered him his pipe for a few drags on it. This had two immediate effects: It relieved Madava's distressed breathing promptly, and it introduced him to pot. The added justification that he needed pot to cure his asthma was a creative thought on Madhava's part. He took to the pot with great gusto, smoking it on a regular basis even when he did not have asthma. According to the Hindu codes of law, drinking alcohol is one of the great sins, *mahāpātaka*, and is forbidden to Hindus and especially Brahmans. Hence, marijuana serves as a substitute mood-altering recreational drug. Madhava and his gambling buddies would also make a decoction, *bhāṅgi pānaka*, which they imbibed while playing cards. I do not know how good a gambler Madhava was—perhaps not very good, because he lost a lot of money. Being high on pot probably did not help either. He borrowed small amounts of money from his brother, his Uncle Krishna (also known by the diminutive Kuṭṭaṇi), and from friends to support his addictions. Between loans, he was usually broke. One day, when he needed some more pot and asked for additional credit from his usual pot merchant, he was told that his credit was no good and that he would not get any more pot. Madhava was desperate. He seized by force a sizeable cake of pot from the merchant and left for home from downtown Mulki's *peṇṭa* (shopping area). As he was passing by the *basti*, he was seized by remorse for what he had done. He, a priest born in a reputable family, had become a thief because of his addiction. He was overwhelmed by a great sense of shame for himself, his family, and his ancestors long dead. He could almost feel the presence of a long line of ancestors looking over his shoulder and tut-tut-ing in unison. Then and there, he decided to return the cake of pot to the merchant, apologize to him, and kick the habit. A local physician, Mr. Hedge, helped him through withdrawal from the pot with some medication. He never smoked either pot or tobacco after that. I heard this story from his own lips, and this memory was fresh in his mind when he related the incident. The one habit he did have was to chew on *phaḍpāna*, a mixture of *pāna* (betel) leaves, areca-nut pieces, quick-lime, and a small piece of tobacco as a breath and mouth freshener.

A Priest as *Purāṇik*

Some of the priests, who can translate Sanskrit into our mother tongue, Konkani, also serve as a *purāṇik*. A *purāṇik* reads aloud the Sanskrit epics, *purāṇas* such as the *Rāmāyaṇa* or the *Mahābhārata*, and translates them into Konkani, verse by verse. The family commissioning such a recital, along with friends and neighbors, form the audience, who listen with rapt attention and reverence. The recitals always begin on an auspicious day and time determined by the priest, who also serves as an astrologer. When I was a child, the priest would sit on the veranda, *jagali*, facing east, an auspicious direction, next to a bronze lamp, *kāśā divli*, which provided light and also defined a sacred zone for the recital. Each session lasted for quite a few hours and could occupy the better part of an evening and night. The books used in the recitation were usually palm-leaf manuscripts, *taḷti pustaka*, written on dried palmyra palm leaves, a few inches wide and about a foot long, with a metal stylus. Black ink is smeared on the pages and then wiped off, filling the indentations left by the stylus. Such manuscripts can last for centuries if they are kept with proper care. Unfortunately, termites, damp, or fire can ruin and destroy them. Each page of the manuscript had two holes in the middle, through which a red silk string was passed to hold the pages in sequence. All the pages were held together between two polished wooden boards, which might or might not have the title of the book carved into the wood. The whole manuscript was usually wrapped in a piece of red silk when in storage. The manuscript would be placed on an X-shaped wooden reading stand and unwrapped. These handwritten manuscripts have now been replaced by printed versions. However, their format as a collection of unbound printed pages is the same as the palm-leaf manuscripts. The *purāṇik* would invoke Sarasvati, the goddess of learning, bow to her, and start reading. Listening to the Sanskrit recital, which most people do not understand, and its translation is an act of piety, guaranteed to confer great merit on the audience. For Hindus, just listening to the sonorous Sanskrit recital itself is a great pleasure, inducing a pleasant, warm, cozy sense of the holy, full of virtue and merit. These recitals, which could extend over many days and are accompanied by appropriate worship, *pūjā*, at its conclusion, are an additional source of income to the priest. Shorter *purāṇa* recitals, lasting one or a few evenings, took place on joyous occasions such as the birth of a much-longed-for grandson or as part of the sad, solemn ceremonies accompanying the death of a person. Some of these *purāṇiks* were quite famous for their skills and were in great demand, especially in the olden days before the advent of movies and television.

One of our ancestors, a part-time *purāṇik*, managed to accumulate some wealth, by dint of hard work and prudent economies. He used it to purchase property at Kallmandkur, a village near Moodabidri in South Kanara, for 400 *varāha*, or about 1,600 rupees. A *varāha* was a gold coin in circulation in the Vijayanagara Empire (1336–ca. 1614 CE; Sastri 1966). We do not know the name of this worthy or the date of purchase of this property. This property must have been quite extensive by local standards, because its annual rent, *geṇi*, was 100 *mūḍo* (42 seers, or 40 kg per *mūḍo*) of rice, quite a substantial amount.

This property provided additional income and a much-needed cushion to compensate for the ups and downs of life, because priests depend solely on the income from the *paryāyu* at the temple once in 24 years and from officiating in the homes of the *yajamāna* of our family in between. However, this property did not last long. One of the curses of Hindu society, then as well as now, is the ruinous expense of a Hindu wedding incumbent on the father of the bride. For a number of reasons, including family pride and tradition, exorbitant demands by the groom's family, and a false sense of community expectations, it is usual for the father of the bride to borrow money and spend large amounts of it that he cannot really afford, burdening the family with debts it cannot hope to pay for generations to come.

One of our ancestors mortgaged the Kallmandkur property for 500 rupees to obtain a loan from the temple for a daughter's wedding. The family could barely pay the interest on the loan and could never hope to pay back the principal. My grandfather Madhava and his elder brother Vasudeva inherited this problem. The two brothers, instead of paying back the loan, trusted some bad legal advice that was based on some supposed arcane points of law and decided to fight it out in the courts. Both arbitration and compromise were out of question, being considered unmanly. Madhava and his brother were going to show the world how macho they were; they would not think of letting this opportunity go to waste. They could have sold part of the property to pay back the loan. One prominent lawyer of the community suggested arbitration. He told Vasudeva and Madhava that as a layperson, he did not presume to advise the two priests on the code of morality, *dharma*. However, he felt that they did not have a legal case and should pay up. He suggested arbitration, which would give the temple sole ownership of the Kallmandkur property in return for an annual payment of 50 *mūḍo* of rice in perpetuity to our family, and the loan would be considered paid. The two characters said no; they would fight it out in the courts! Over the course of years, the case made its way up to the High Court of the Madras Presidency in Madras. Their case would be argued by highly paid Madras lawyers wearing elaborate lawyer's robes (*cāri hāttā cogo*, a robe with four sleeves). This very fact was a matter of some local pride for these two characters. In the meantime, the legal fees had accumulated, and finally when the men lost the case in the High Court, they had to sell the property to pay back the original loan and the lawyers' fees. One of the local curses is "May you get involved in a civil suit!" This is guaranteed to bring about the ruination of the family involved. Apparently, Vasudeva and Madhava had forgotten this simple fact, and they paid for it dearly. Their actions showed a distinct lack of a moral compass.

The only memento of this property left is a huge wooden vessel, *koḷmbi*, about three or four feet in diameter and about two feet deep and made out of a single piece of wood from a huge jackfruit tree. The legend is that one could mix a *muḍo* of beaten rice, *phovu*, at a sitting in this wooden vessel. I do not know whether this is true. Looking back on these events, my father would say that the loss of property was a good thing for the family! Whatever happened was God's will, which in the long run, was good for us. This is an interesting bit of theology that ascribes occurrences due to chance, circumstances, and human folly to the will of Almighty God, who is directing the whole drama and is intimately interested in the welfare of everyone involved! Whether true or not, such thinking provides much comfort to the faithful in accepting the hard facts of life. It changed our mind-set of living from the earnings of landed property and the sweat of some poor peasants' labor. It forced us to seek education and earn a living in one of the professions. Education changed us, made us aware of the wide world outside Mulki, perhaps made us more humane, especially in the treatment of women and children, and got us away from the family business of the priesthood. We were poor and hungry; and hunger is one of the best motivators for innovative thinking. It got us away from Mulki to seek a livelihood elsewhere. There is a saying in our community that families that leave their native village always prosper; there is some truth in it.

Madhava Marries Bhavani

When Bhavani came of age (at about 12 years), Ananthayya began his search for a suitable husband for her. He had heard that in Mulki there were several marriageable boys in the Bhat families attached to the temple. When he went to Mulki to meet the prospective groom, he ran into Madhava, who was whittling a stick to keep himself amused and occupied. Madhava's father, Ganapathi, had passed away, and Ananthayya met Ganapathi's widow, Ammanni, and his eldest son, Vasudeva. The horoscopes of Madhava and Bhavani matched, the negotiations of dowry were amicably settled to the satisfaction of both parties, and their wedding date was fixed. Madhava and Bhavani were married in 1902; Bhavani was 12 years old and Madhava was 18. The wedding took place in Udupi, at the home of the bride's father. Ananthayya's boss, Kumble Subraya, gave Ananthayya a lump sum of 200 rupees to cover wedding expenses. Ananthayya was always grateful to Kumble Subraya for this act of generosity and kindness. Bhavani's married name was Padmavati. The wedding was true to form, with the father of the bride spending more than he could afford, and was supposed to have been a celebration spread over five days! The groom's wedding party was royally entertained with breakfast, lunch, afternoon tea, dinner, special oil baths, and other events indicative of GSB hospitality.

Madhava and His Travels

Marriage did not have much effect on Madhava in forcing him to settle down and take his family responsibilities seriously. The wanderlust in him was too powerful to be reined in by mere marriage. He left for Bombay in 1903 or 1904 for a stay of a few months. In those days, priests of our community were rare in Bombay. Hence, there was a great demand for priests from back home to officiate at rites of passage such as *upanayana* (initiation) and weddings. The visiting priest would stay with relatives or friends and earn some money, *dakṣiṇā*, in the course of a few months. Madhava had a great time in the big city, and he was in his element in exploring new things and places. Pilgrimages to sacred places, *yātrā*, on the way were guaranteed to confer merit, *puṇya*, and were an added bonus. However, there was an attack of bubonic plague in Bombay in 1904, and Madhava was infected. At the earliest sign of the sickness, Madhava decided to return home by one of the coastal ships to Malpe, near Udupi, serving as its port. All passengers from Bombay had to report to health authorities as part of quarantine. Madhava got worse after reaching Ananthayya's house in Udupi. There wasn't much hope for plague victims in those days, and his prognosis looked grim. Under the circumstances, Bhavani, made a vow, *āṅgvaṇa*, at the Mariamma temple of Kaup, a village near Udupi, to offer her nose ornament, *nattu*, as a thanks offering to the Goddess Mariamma if Madhava recovered from the plague. The nose ornament, along with other jewelry, is worn only by a woman whose husband is alive, *ayyapanā bāila maniṣi*, and is imbued with great significance to an orthodox Hindu woman. It was decided to transfer Madhava to Mulki, away from the close scrutiny of government health authorities in Udupi. The family was afraid that the authorities might forcibly remove him from home and admit him to a government hospital, which would be disastrous in view of all of the food restrictions he was expected to observe as a priest officiating in a temple. He was expected to report to the health authorities in Mulki every week to assure them of his continued good health. However, he was too sick to do that. Vasudeva, his older brother, came to the rescue. Every week, he would report to the health authorities in his brother's place and sign his brother's name. Madhava finally recovered, thanks to his own body defenses and not to the primitive medicine practiced in those days. As my father used to say, it was fated that he and Madhava's other children to be born—and therefore Madhava—survived the plague. Bhavani was greatly relieved. She made a pilgrimage to Kaup to offer her *nattu* to Mariamma as a thanks offering on the occasion of the *Darśana Sevā* (a particular religious ritual) at the temple. To her great surprise, the Goddess refused to accept the offering of her *nattu*; She ordered that Bhavani should wear it throughout her life and it should be offered only on her death. This was a pleasant surprise for Bhavani. This implied that she would die before her husband, because the *nattu* is worn only by a woman whose husband is living. Bhavani had been worried because an astrologer had predicted that there was a chance of her becoming a widow. Every Hindu woman wishes to die before her husband, *ayyapanāri morcẽ*, and thus not become a widow. Bhavani's devout wish was granted; on her deathbed, she reminded my mother about offering her *nattu* to Mariamma at Kaup, and it was so done. Bhavani passed away on December 25, 1958. Madhava, for some reason, did not expect to live much longer after her death. On her death, as the bamboo bier was being prepared, there was some bamboo left over. Madhava asked the people assembling the bier to save the remaining bamboo for his own funeral. Sure enough, within about six months, he too passed away—on June 13, 1959. I had left for the the United States in July 1956 and was not expected to return soon. When Madhava sensed that he was nearing the end of his life, he kept pestering my father as to the expected date of my return. When he realized that the date was not definite and that he would never see his favorite grandson again, he shed many tears. My father never wrote to me about my grandparents' deaths; he thought that I would be very upset. I came to know about their deaths in 1959 or 1960 from my cousin, Vivekaṇṇā, who was on a postdoctoral fellowship in St. Louis.

Madhava would get an attack of wanderlust, once every few years, and would decide to go on a journey combined with a pilgrimage to holy places he had never before visited. My father paid most of the traveling expenses, which were supplemented by Madhava's earnings in places such as Bombay, Calcutta, or Madras, officiating at religious ceremonies conducted in the homes of a settled GSB community of families from our district. He would stay with people of our own caste who would observe all of the food restrictions and taboos. The lady of the house had to avoid using onion, garlic, and certain vegetables such as cabbage and cauliower because these were forbidden to priests. If he was on his own, without any GSB homes to stay in, he would subsist on fruits and milk, *phaḷāru*. Giving up regular food and eating light was considered meritorious while on a pilgrimage. It also made good sense to eat light while traveling to lessen the chance of stomach upsets. If he felt like eating regular meals of rice and vegetables, once in a way, he did the cooking himself. After a bath and his daily twilight worship, *sandhi*, he would start from scratch and cook a simple meal of rice and vegetables. Meals at temples were acceptable because such food, *nivedyu*, offered to God was considered to be ritually pure. In the big cities, such as Bombay, he would do sightseeing and observe the curious ways of the city folk. These formed the substance of the stories of his adventures away from home, places foreign and strange that we folks at home never hoped to visit in our lives. At holy places such as Kāśi or Vāraṇāsi, Madhava could observe some obligatory rites performed, in addition to visiting the temples. On the third day after a Hindu is cremated, some of the bones remaining in the funeral pyre are collected, washed, and put in small earthenware pots to be buried on the south side of the holy basil plant, *tulasī*, which can be found in the front yard of every Hindu home. These are unearthed and taken to Kāśi for immersion in the Ganges after performing funeral offerings, *śrāddha*, on the banks of the river. These rites are done under the guidance of local priests, *paṇḍā*, who specialize in the performance of these ceremonies (Parry 1994). Pious Hindus believe that at the conclusion of these ceremonies, all the sins of the dead person are washed away in the holy Ganges and the dead soul is guaranteed an entry into heaven. One place that Madhava wanted to visit above all was the Badarikāśrama founded by the Śaṅkarācāryā in the foothills of the Himalayas, in the eighth century. The priests officiating at this temple are Namboodri Brahmans from Kerala, belonging to the same caste as Śaṅkarācāryā. The trip was arduous, hence more meritorious, and had to be done on foot for many days in the last stage of the journey. It is usually done in summer, though the weather could be rainy, and quite cold, especially for a person living in the hot climate of South India. The pilgrims walk, stick in hand and carrying their possessions, on a gradually climbing road in the hilly terrain, in large groups. They stay at rest houses, *dharmaśālā*, built by the wealthy to earn merit and provided with basic necessities. Madhava, unfortunately, never made it to the temple; he fell ill with dysentery, was quite weak and unable to go on, and must have been really worried about his chances of coming home alive. Anyway, the story he told us is that Lord Badrinārāyaṇa appeared to him in a dream and ordered him to return home, as he was not fated to complete the pilgrimage in this birth (*janma*). The dream might have been real, brought on by his concern for his life, his desire to go on, and his desire to find an honorable way out of the impasse. It might have provided a convenient justification for his decision to return home. One day, I think when I was in my second grade, I had to run home to get a pencil that I had forgotten. There was Madhava Bhat, large as life, back home from the latest pilgrimage. I was asked to bow to him and touch his feet, *pāyu dorcẽ*, to crave his blessings. This honor is shown to a person returning from a pilgrimage, because the person's feet have trodden the dust of many holy places; all those junior to the pilgrim do homage, *praṇāma*, to ask the pilgrim's blessings and transfer some of the merit that the pilgrim has earned. I was so happy and excited to see him, anticipating all the goodies and toys that I knew he would have brought back from his trip to exotic places. Sure enough, he did not disappoint me.

Madhava's Ghost Stories

At the evening meals, my father, Narayana, would eat first, along with some of the rambunctious children. He had not eaten since his morning meal at about 9 AM, except for a light snack in the afternoon. Eating with him was expected to keep the children less noisy and more manageable. It is an interesting observation to note that I and my immediate siblings were the more easily manageable, docile lot because we were more in awe of our father and elders. My younger siblings, however, were different; they carried on as usual at a high decibel level, with scant respect for their elders. When my father was having his dinner, it was usual to report to him all of the misdeeds, mischief, and troubles that I had caused during the day. My father would deliver judgment on the spot, threatening to send me to an *anāthaśālā* (orphanage) maintained by local Christians at the mission compound. There was no physical punishment, just the threat of being sent away to a strange place. Initially, I was worried; however, with resilience of youth and the short memory span of childhood, I soon forgot these threats till my next trial and court judgment. After the children and men had eaten, my mother and grandmother, *ānnammā*, would eat and then put away the leftovers, and then they could sit down for a while before going to bed. We would foregather in the front veranda of the house. My father would recline on the sole beach chair (called an easy chair) in the house, with my mother, grandmother, and grandfather sitting on the floor or a low bedstead (*māñco*). The brass container for the ingredients of *pāna* would be brought, and my grandfather would assemble a *pāna* for himself. Later on, my mother also took up this habit. There was always a general review of the happenings in the family, what the children were up to, visitors, local gossip, and the goings-on in our local GSB community.

My grandfather Madhava would then start on one of his stories. These would deal with his younger days, our ancestors and their adventures, the various *paryāya* cycles participated in by our family at the Mulki temple, and so on. For many years after the founding of the temple at Mulki, it was not prosperous and well known. The number of devotees attending the temple and its resulting prosperity really started to increase after the establishment of *Darśana Sevā* (for more details, see "Appendix 7: The Oracle, or *Darśanā Sevā*"). This religious function usually takes place on Wednesday, Saturday, and Sunday of every week, excluding some days determined by the Hindu calendar. The rite involves possession of a medium, *darśanā pātri*, by Kāla Bhairava, an incarnation of Lord Shiva. By tradition, the medium belongs to the Nayak family of Palimar. When in a state of possession, this person functions as an oracle, dealing with the problems of devotees, ordering expiations (*prāyaścitta*) for sins of omission or commission, driving out evil spirits possessing people, providing cures for illnesses that are not responding to traditional or allopathic medicine, and so on. Rangappa Nayak (1878–1924) was the most eminent person of the Nayak dynasty and is credited with the most famous cures and predictions under the auspices of the oracle (Anon. n.d.). The stories about the wonders he worked are legion, and my grandfather had the privilege of witnessing most of these in person. His first-person accounts of these happenings, embellished by his storytelling skills and vivid imagination, were truly fascinating, especially to a small, impressionable boy. I was enthralled with these stories, and I wish somebody had recorded them verbatim.

And then there were his ghost stories. In his younger days, there were no good roads and no adequate outdoor lighting at night. Travel was by a bullock cart or on foot. Priests going to religious functions in remote villages walked carrying the necessary articles in a wicker basket on their heads. There was no bus service back then, and later when there was such service, priests would not travel by bus, worried about ritual pollution from unknown people (read: people of unknown castes) traveling by the same conveyance. Religious ceremonies would be followed by sumptuous dinners, and the priests would walk back with the same baskets, now heavier with the added weight of some articles of clothing, rice, and other items offered to them as gifts (*dāna*). They had to walk on the low mud ridges, *gāddyā mēri*, separating fields of rice. There could be snakes, poisonous or not, on the footpath. More often than not, they walked barefoot, because ritual pollution brought about by wearing leather sandals was unacceptable. This was unfortunate because the open sandals worn by villagers are specially designed to creak a lot; their sound and vibrations warn snakes away from the beaten path. The priests would carry a bundle of dried fronds of the coconut palm, lit at one end, as a torch. This would momentarily flare up as it was swung back and forth as they were walking, providing a wholly inadequate source of light. Owls and other birds dive and screech at these people moving about in the dark and encroaching on their territory. Places reputed to be haunted, such as crematoria, *smaśāna*, or where people had committed suicide or had been executed, were of special concern, and people passed by them as quickly as possible, talking louder than usual to bolster each other's courage and hopefully discourage any ghosts or goblins from revealing themselves to the lonely, scared pedestrians. Perhaps the overactive imagination of these travelers played more havoc with them than any supernatural happenings did. Priests felt that their daily recitation of the sacred Gāyatri mantra endowed them with potent spiritual power that could overcome the baneful influence of any ghost, the walking dead (*mellelī*), spirits (*bhūtha*), or any supernatural being, however powerful. At the ruins of a town of a bygone era where there were the remains of an old fort or palace, there were reports of sightings of ghostly processions, with the full complement of palanquins and retinues of attendants, accompanied by music and paraphernalia of vanished glory, going about their unearthly business. These could be seen, provided that the phase of the moon, the alignment of the planets, and other conditions were propitious, and the people were particularly attuned to (read: scared or gullible enough to believe) these happenings. Some of these spirits could assume the form of a living person or acquaintance or of a beautiful woman of seductive speech filled with promise who would talk you into following them away from the beaten path, with fatal consequences. Apparently there is a spirit with a horrible grimace and long black hair that is covered with slippery moss (*pāmāji*) which runs past an unsuspecting traveler, screeching loudly in his face. If a bold person grasps the hair of this apparition and hangs on to it in spite of the slippery moss and fearsome appearance, the spirit is supposed to grant anything he wishes, including immeasurable wealth, as a condition for being set free. No one has ever been able to do this. Perhaps a night owl screeching past a traveler gave rise to this tall tale. Then there are those headless spirits that walk about, sweeping their arms to imprison and squeeze the life out of an unwary traveler. A person killed by a spirit in this manner is supposed to be doomed forever, becoming, in effect, a servant of the spirit.

I used to be fascinated by all of these ghost stories from my grandfather and enjoyed them immensely. However, payback time came after I had gone to bed. While I slept, there was a rerun of all of the evening's ghost stories, made lifelike by my vivid, overactive imagination. Any sound in the house, the street, or the garden of the house next door was enough to set my heart pounding and presaged the imminent arrival of some supernatural being bent on unknown or unpredictable mischief. The sound made by dead people, *mellelī*, going about their nefarious ghostly business at night was supposed to resemble the cry of an owl or some such bird of night. Whenever I heard such a sound and sensed it moving away or coming closer, I would vividly picture a dead person enveloped in a white funeral shroud, never at peace, walking about in the dark. There was some safety in burying my head under the bedclothes and keeping absolutely quiet, but I was never sure that this would work and so had difficulty sleeping. At that age, I used to sleep next to my grandmother, who was my only protection from any supernatural visitations. My grandmother used to get up at about 4 AM, have her bath, and then start preparing breakfast and the midday meal so that my father could have his lunch before leaving for work. I used to feel greatly relieved once she got up. With her moving about the house, I used to feel safe again and fall asleep, feeling that with at least one person awake, no ghost would dare to come into the house. It was only much later when I was older that I ceased to be afraid of or believe in ghosts and supernatural happenings. It was interesting to note that with better electrical lighting, the number of sightings of ghosts and other supernatural creatures decreased in number; they are almost unknown now. I am now convinced that one's own active imagination, abetted by the unknown fears of the dark, is the originator of all these supernatural happenings.

Madhava's Grocery Store

Madhava's earnings as a priest were not sufficient to meet his living expenses because he wasted money on gambling, pot, and other vices. He started a grocery store when my father was in school at Mulki. The shop, with a thatched roof, was on the right as one descended from the *pāje kāṭṭẽ* toward the outer perimeter of the temple. It was demolished later to build the present building, with a shop on the ground floor and a printing press above it. Madhava is supposed to have received about 900 rupees from his brother as his share of the 1917–1919 *paryāya* earnings. This was quite a substantial amount of money in those days. He might have invested part of it in the grocery shop and spent the rest on his various amusements. The shop did not prosper and was eventually closed, with a net loss of assets. My father's explanation of this debacle was a lack of any business sense on Madhava's part, lack of industriousness, and a casual attitude toward the whole project. Madhava had to have his leisurely siesta after a heavy lunch, the main meal of the day. He would ask his son to open the shop and wait on customers while he slept. Once, there was an attempted robbery on the premises, and he spent his money in securing the shop though he was not its owner, and it was rented from the temple. Madhava perhaps thought that all he had to do was to open a shop, and customers and money would start pouring in—that good times were ahead. Unfortunately, things did not work out that way, and he lost his investment. Madhava and Bhavani could manage for a while on his earnings in kind—the coconuts, rice and other grains, and a little cash as fees, *dakṣiṇā*, that he was given as an officiating priest. As time passed, things got progressively worse, with the result that when, as a small boy, my father asked Bhavani for 1 or 2 ruvvis (1 rupee = 16 annas; 1 anna = 12 ruvvis; 1 rupee = 192 ruvvis) for buying some puffed rice, *cārmburo*, she did not have the money. She felt so ashamed about it that she seriously contemplated suicide. Perhaps the thought of leaving behind a motherless child in the care of her thoroughly irresponsible husband must have deterred her. Finally, Madhava was left penniless; having mortgaged his half of the family home and borrowed as much as he could, he had to leave Mulki. I think that at one time, there was even a court decree against him for collection of the money he owed, and he could have been arrested and put in jail. Madhava's debts were finally paid by my father in the 1940s. When I was in middle school, his old cronies and creditors were invited to Udupi and fed a grand feast, and all of his debts, including any accrued interest, were discharged.

Madhava Moves to Udupi

Bhavani, my grandmother, was a model of the patient, self-effacing, long-suffering, hardworking, uncomplaining orthodox Hindu wife. It was the tempered steel in her character that held her family together and saw it through the hard times when they had to live off the charity of her parents. When Madhava and his family first moved to Udupi in 1923, my father was 16 and a student in the local Christian high school, old enough to understand the sad state of affairs of the family and sensitive to the problems of living on the charity of Ananthayya and his wife, Sri Devi. He used to tell me that it is better to live on whatever little one has, on *peja-mīṭa* (rice gruel and salt), in one's own house than to live off the goodwill of even the closest of relatives. Bhavani and my father, in later years, had a special rapport or understanding of two comrades-in-arms. They were the foot soldiers who had successfully fought to keep the family together and survived the 11 years of exile when they lived with Ananthayya. Once when I questioned her about the early days of their life when Madhava had lost everything in Mulki, she would tell me very little, except to say that her husband was thoroughly irresponsible as regards his family. As a devout Hindu wife, that was the worst she could say about her husband's conduct. The one good thing about Madhava was that he did *not* beat or otherwise physically abuse his wife. Wife beating and other physical abuse were considered the norm, well within the prerogatives of a husband in our community and social class in the India of those times. That Madhava did not engage in those practices was a definite plus in his favor.

When Bhavani moved to Udupi for good in 1923, Sri Devi, her mother, was about 50, which was considered to be early old age. Bhavani, in effect, became the maid, required to do all of the chores in Ananthayya's home. Sri Devi decided that it was a good time to hand over cooking and other household chores to her daughter and assume a strictly supervisory role. Bhavani did not have any choice in the matter and was happy to do her part; at least now she and her family had enough food to fill their bellies. She would get up at about 4 AM and have a cleansing bath before beginning the day's cooking. There was the morning breakfast, with coffee and some snacks. Later, Ananthayya and Narayana used to have an early lunch at about 9 or 9:30 AM before going to their office near the law courts. After lunch, there was time for a short siesta during the heat of the day, followed by preparations for the afternoon *tiffin*, which consisted of coffee and snacks. Next on the agenda was the evening meal, which had to be ready when the breadwinners, Ananthayya and Narayana, came home at about 7 PM. They had not eaten anything after their morning meal, except for a light snack in a restaurant on the premises of the court. After all of the men and children in the house had eaten, then the women of the house would sit down for dinner. In addition, some preparations for the next day's cooking had to be made, including applying a starter for the next day's yogurt or buttermilk, churning the buttermilk, and preparing dough for *iḍḷi* (a savory cake). It would be at least 10 PM before she could go to bed. Guests, festivals, birthdays, and other special events meant extra work. Bhavani was indeed a hardworking woman, taking on the responsibility for most of the cooking and other household work. For Bhavani, *puri*, also called *roṭṭi* (a particular kind of deep-fried flatbread), was her favorite dish, and her idea of the apex of good living was to be able to afford to have it every day for breakfast or the afternoon *tiffin*. A few years after her death, I requested that my father to be sure to serve *puri* at her yearly death anniversary rites (*śrāddha*). It did not matter whether she received any of these offerings; they were gestures of remembrance on our part. I have fond memories of both of my grandparents; they were a good and loving *ājjā* and *ānnammā*.

Religion

Religion as a Vocation

This is the end of my story of my paternal ancestors. Before I proceed further, I will discuss religion and its place in our society, because it plays such an important part in the story of my family. We were a family of professional temple priests, so religion was our vocation. Religion, and the beliefs and practices that go with it, is found all over the world, across many cultures and traditions. The one relevant question here is: Why do humans need religion? Are the religious beliefs and all the associated constructs common to all humanity because they are built into our genes? Recently, there have been suggestions that because of the structure and organizations of human brains, all of us are born with a supersense or a susceptibility to believe in the supernatural and the unseen (Hood 2009). Are religious commandments handed down from above by a supernatural power, as claimed by some traditions? The questions are endless. One possible answer is to look at religion as a cultural construct that humans have cobbled together as a coping strategy. It enables us to face the real or imagined stresses of human existence, nurture hope, and lead useful and constructive lives. What is this coping mechanism or construct? It is a set of actions that we take in trying to solve the latest problem or plan for a future course of action. These coping rituals can come in various shapes and sizes, covering a wide spectrum of activities. They can be simple and ordinary, such as taking a few deep breaths, counting to ten, or having a hot cup of tea or coffee while mulling over what to do next. Or they can be complicated and involve the whole apparatus of religious traditions of myth, theology, and rituals, which seek divine guidance by prayer or propitiation of unknown forces or beings. Performing the rites and rituals of one's favorite religion or belief system is guaranteed to reassure one that the Almighty is on one's side, lending a helping hand. These coping strategies relieve stress and emotional distress, give hope for the future, and perhaps help to solve the immediate problems of life.

Religion as a Coalition for Power and Control

Religion as a coping strategy is used within the context of the human primacy drive or the pursuit of power, which is the underlying theme in all human activities, as discussed in the previous chapter. Religion gives us an illusion of power, control, and certainty. Humans feel completely and totally helpless and powerless when confronted with natural phenomena, the unpredictability of life, and life's attendant problems. This total lack of control can cause immense anxiety and unhappiness. We often cannot make any sense out of all of these happenings around us. Humans, being story-telling or myth-making animals, put together stories, myths, or explanations of the origins of the Earth and the rest of the cosmos, humans, animals, and so on. These myths are woven against a realization of the utter powerlessness of humans individually and collectively. This lack of power can be compensated for only by positing an almighty, omniscient, omnipotent, omnipresent being who is benevolent, is forgiving, and—most important—is on our side and has our well-being or our interests at heart. Each human thus forms a coalition with the Almighty who occupies the apex of our favorite religion and who protects us. As far as alliances are concerned, this is the ultimate power coalition, because humans have endowed the supreme Alpha—the Almighty—superlative attributes. As part of the process of binding themselves to an anthropomorphic God, believers endow Her or Him with all of the desirable human qualities, in addition to the usual divine attributes. Of course, humans are good at forming coalitions in aspiring for power, just as our cousins the chimps do. This theme was introduced and elaborated on in the first chapter of this story. The power aspired to is the power obtained by fealty; by being under the protective aegis of the Almighty, humans feel some control over their lives, feel less anxiety about an uncertain future, believe in all the promises of the hereafter, and bask in the reflected power of the Protector. This transaction is especially appealing to the dispossessed, the powerless, and those who feel that the throws of dice in their lives are against them. It gives them hope through the expectation that fortune will ultimately favor the meek and weak. In return for any favors granted, the tribe has to placate the Almighty by obedience to Her or His rules and regulations, moral and tribal codes supposedly handed over by Her or Him, regular prayers and supplications, and appropriate sacrifices. In short, each individual who conforms to all these strictures gets some of the power of the Almighty by proxy and the certainty of protection of a very paternal God or a maternal Goddess. If we keep our noses clean and toe the line, the Almighty will take care of us, look after us, and ultimately bestow on each individual the joys of a paradise and an eternal life, or variations thereof. This acquisition of power by proxy is also accompanied by a feeling of greater control over life and a lessening of stress. Parallels between this act of submission and the kissing of the hand or the ring of authority of a feudal overlord as an act of fealty owed by a medieval peasant should be noted. Hence, belief in an almighty and conforming to a religious tradition are reducible to a pursuit of an illusion of power and control by fealty. It is perhaps the best bargain humans can get. I am not implying that this is the *only* motivation behind religious beliefs; that would be too simplistic. But this could be one of the important reasons humans are religious. I am sure that there are other reasons, equally significant, that explain human religiosity. Another comforting aspect of such a belief system is the utter certainties of its assertions, which provide a firm anchor in this life amidst its highly unpredictable happenings. Some people find it very diffficult to live with the uncertainties of life and very much need the firm certainties of religion. A devout person never presumes to ask, "How true are all these religious beliefs?" In the believing mode of thinking, such questions are forbidden. The explanations I have given make religion just a coping mechanism, similar to strategies for food gathering, courtship, mating, treatment of elders, bringing up of children, and other details of everyday life that are determined by the surroundings and circumstances in which a tribe finds itself. Hence, a proper arena for study of all religions is anthropology. Of course, human vanity and cultural conceit have given rise to claims as to the uniqueness of each tribal tradition, its superiority over others, and how each tribe is the sole custodian of the Truth. The priests, preachers, religious teachers, prophets, soothsayers, gurus, god-men and god-women, and others of similar persuasion support these assertions and also claim special privileges for themselves. They claim to be intermediaries between the Almighty and the members of the tribe, to have a direct line of communication with the Divine, and hence occupy positions of dominance. To this list I would like to add astrologers, soothsayers, psychics, and others who claim to read the future and who have become part of Hindu orthodoxy in the past several centuries. Instead of repeating this list time and again, I will call them religion professionals or priests. The dominance of each one of them depends on their personal charisma, claims to esoteric knowledge, scholarship in all the rules and regulations of their religion, knowledge of traditions of theology, and above all, their belief that they are something *special.* Hierarchy and dominance are built into the belief systems; they are *not* democratic. It is the tacit acceptance of this belief system by their followers, and the reassurance and comfort such a system provides in dealing with the tough problems of this life, that gives these religion professionals their place in the dominance hierarchy. Their power by proxy is most clearly shown when they point out to the faithful right from wrong, fulminate against deviations from acceptable behavior or other religious norms, or act as Her or His surrogates. Recently, books have been written pointing out problems with the concept of God in all religions: *The God Delusion* (Dawkins 2006) and the ringing condemnation of *God Is Not Great: How Religion Poisons Everything* (Hitchens 2007). It is unfortunate that the denunciations of God and religion by the atheists are as loud and thunderous as the fulminations of the "true believers" against the infidels. A reduction in volume of these condemnations could improve communication among all of the parties involved. It is true that both religion and politics, in their many variations and forms, have been part of human cultures all over the world. They have also been part of good and evil acts of us humans, or at least have been used to justify them. God or religion cannot be wished away or eliminated by fiat. Just as one cannot prohibit politics because it leads to war and slaughter, religions cannot be banned for the harm they have done. I would like to take a neutral position with respect to both religion and politics and accept the fact that they are part of human anthropology. The real problem lies with the practitioners of these religions or self-appointed spokespersons for God who claim to know His mind and intentions. These persons tacitly assume the mantle of God Almighty with its limitless power and omniscience, assign literal truth to their scared texts, and cause real problems with their pronouncements on all human problems, not tempered with doubt, critical self-examination, or common sense. The fault lies with the humans who abuse God and religion in pursuing their personal agenda for power, just as they do with state and politics.

Religious Tolerance

A person's beliefs are deeply held convictions, usually not supported by empirical data or verifiable by controlled experiments. If one accepts the proposition that all persons are equal and should be respected as individuals, the same should apply to their beliefs, religious, political, or any other, whether we agree with them or not. This attitude is essential to accepting religious pluralism, which respects all religions as equally legitimate whether we believe in them or not. This was best expressed in the rock edict 12 of Emperor Aśoka (ca. 274–232 BCE), who preached and practiced religious tolerance:

> King Priyadarśī (i.e., Aśoka) honors men of all faiths, members of religious orders and laymen alike, with gifts and various marks of esteem. Yet he does not value either gifts or honors as much as growth in the qualities essential to religion in men of all faiths.
>
> This growth may take many forms, but its root is in guarding one's speech to avoid extolling one's own faith and disparaging the faith of others improperly or, when the occasion is appropriate, immoderately.
>
> The faiths of others all deserve to be honored for one reason or another. By honoring them, one exalts one's own faith and at the same time performs a service to the faith of others. By acting otherwise, one injures one's own faith and also does disservice to that of others. For if a man extols his own faith and

> disparages another because of devotion to his own and because he wants to glorify it, he seriously injures his own faith.
>
> Therefore concord alone is commendable, for through concord men may learn and respect the conception of Dharma accepted by others. [Nikam and McKeon 1978, 51–2]

Dharma in general means law, usage, practice, or custom. Unfortunately, such an enlightened attitude is sadly lacking in current discourse. Instead, people want to run down other people's religions and question their legitimacy, as part of their fear and intolerance of the "other." They also assert the superiority of their own beliefs, as an expression of their primacy conceit. Some politicians and religious spokespersons mention only the three monotheistic religions as if other religions, followed by 47% of humanity (as estimated from the latest statistics from the World Almanac 2008, 711), do not exist or do not matter. The tacit assumption is that only the monotheistic religions matter and that the others are mere anthropological curiosities. This attitude is deplorable, as it forms the basis of hatred and intolerance of the "other," leading to discrimination, injustice, human conlict, and bloodshed. It should be noted that each of the monotheistic faiths, as spelled out in its sacred texts or "charter documents," declares itself to be the only "true faith," questioning the very *legitimacy* of other faiths (Kirsch 2005, 34). They declare that the God of their religion is the only "true" God, whereas all other Gods are "false." Hence, in each of these monotheistic faiths, there is a certain amount of built-in intolerance of other religions. This is another example of the primacy drive, which leads one to extol one's superiority and uniqueness. Whether this intolerance gets expressed or realized in practice depends on a number of circumstances, such as the number of true believers, their economic and political clout, and their motivation, especially if it is provided by a charismatic leader with her or his own agenda for power. If the conditions are not right, the same set of true believers can practice a limited tolerance of others for the nonce and bask in its virtues. These circumstances have resulted in overt or covert intolerance of other religions—monotheistic or polytheistic or any other persuasion—as attested to by history. Polytheism, however, has an easy time accepting other gods and belief systems and shows less conceit or has fewer delusions about its uniqueness or superiority over other faiths. All religions are dominance hierarchies, always jockeying for power in this world while extolling the glories of the hereafter. It is tacitly accepted by the believers that the promises of all faiths about eternity and related matters are not supported by empirical data or subject to the scrutiny of truth-in-advertising laws. In pursuit of power, all faiths, including the most tolerant, practice opportunistic intolerance that has less to do with theology and more to do with practical power grabbing. I consider all belief systems, monotheistic, polytheistic, or otherwise, to be the same. A hypothesis is a hypothesis, whether in the singular or the plural! The only reason to choose monotheism over polytheism is Occam's principle of parsimony, to keep beliefs simple. The following analogy may be helpful in grasping the concept of the basic equality of all religions. The many religions are like different geometries in mathematics. A variety of geometries, both Euclidean and non-Euclidean, are obtained, depending on the initial postulates. Similarly, different religions result from the mythology, rituals, and traditions one accepts and believes. Just as it makes no sense to argue that a specific geometry is true, better, or superior to another, it makes no sense to do so with religions either.

Christian Evangelization

In most cases, one's religion is an accident of birth and upbringing (or call it childhood indoctrination), and it is only natural that the person likes it or is most comfortable in its world. If a person expects others to respect her or his beliefs, simple reciprocity demands that she or he show the same respect to the beliefs of others. Respect for another person's beliefs tacitly assumes that the person loves her or his beliefs or religion as much as I do mine. This simple proposition has not been understood and appreciated in the centuries-old aggressive evangelization of the other, the nonbeliever, the "infidel" that continues today. Missionaries do not appreciate the fact that the person they are trying to convert loves her or his religion as much as they do theirs. Inducements of various types—money, free health care, better jobs, social privileges, and, if all these fail, naked force—have all been part of religious conversions (see Appendix 8: "Goa: A Paradise Lost?"). It is only recently that the World Council of Churches (WCC), a liberal Christian organization, has questioned the age-old mind-set on religious conversions and offered new alternatives. A correspondent for the newspaper *India Abroad*, catering largely to the community with origins in the subcontinent, interviewed Hans Ucko, a Swedish theologian, who heads the WCC's program for inter-religious dialog (Pais 2007). Mr. Ucko grew up in a nonreligious Jewish family, and he converted to Christianity in his twenties. As a convert, he was not particularly interested in converting others. He felt that Christians should live by their beliefs rather than convert others. As an individual, he did not want to be converted by anyone; he converted himself. He is not against conversions; however, the context of all aspects of conversion have to be considered. There are several possible motives for conversion: dissatisfaction with one's natal religion, a significant spiritual experience that leads to a change in belief, economic incentives, and coercion. The WCC has been looking critically at conversions for several reasons. Some Christian theologians feel that conversions should no longer be the main business of the church, in view of its past history of abuses. Conversions have been part of colonialism, subjugation, and exploitation of natives of many countries, with forced baptisms and belittling of their religions and cultures. WCC believes that conversions have become a threat to the plurality of religions as well as to their harmonious coexistence and cooperation. There are also the superior attitudes of the militant evangelizers. First, there is the arrogance of believing that they have a right to preach to and convert others. Second, there is their firm belief that any method of conversion, from persuasion to coercion, is acceptable, so long as it brings in new converts. What is disregarded in these encounters is that the right of the preacher to convert is opposed by an equally strong right of the preached-to be left alone to practice their religion in peace. Instead of running down other faiths or belittling them, members of all religions can work together for the betterment of the world. Aid-based evangelism, or trying to convert those one helps who are in distress because of poverty, ill health, or natural disasters, is unacceptable. Humanitarian aid, a primary commandment of many religions, should be given unconditionally, not used as an inducement to conversion. Any form of manipulation or enticement of others to convert to one's faith is immoral because it reduces others to objects of one's design rather than respecting them as autonomous human beings. True evangelism, or being a witness to the Christian faith, is the duty of every church and its members. This means that Christians must live by the faith that they preach, offering selfless service and even the knowledge of the message of Christ. Improper proselytism involves offering material or social advantages as an inducement to conversion by people in distress or involves denigrating other faiths (Pais 2007).

These sentiments and principles are admirable and should be commended. However, nearly half a century after the publication of this report, it is not clear how closely they are adhered to by missionaries in the field. The Right Reverend J. Jon Bruno, bishop of the Episcopal Diocese of Los Angeles, recently offered an unquaḷied apology from Christian community to Hindus worldwide for age-old religious discrimination and conversion attempts (Pais 2008). It should be pointed out that these enlightened views have not been articulated or adopted by other Christian denominations, including the largest, the Roman Catholic Church. There is still some hope for a more civilized dialog between different religions, for mutual respect and tolerance. In the meantime, each of these evangelizers will pursue their individual agenda for power while loudly proclaiming their good intentions.

Science Versus Opinion

Religious beliefs are a set of opinions, handed down by sacred texts, august personages, or the Almighty, who might have decided to get involved in these transactions, according to some traditions. By their very nature, these opinions, viewpoints, or perspectives cannot be subject to empirical verification. However, there are secular opinions that give rise to hypotheses about what happens around us, which can be empirically checked. Such an alternate course can lead to an understanding of natural phenomena instead of being afraid of them. Thus there is no mystery, mysticism, or supernatural origin to what occurs in nature. Natural phenomena are carefully observed, experimentally testable hypotheses are formed to explain them, and quantitative predictions are made and checked against experimental data. Initial hypotheses are modified on the basis of new data, and new experimental tests are proposed for further study. This is the way of science, which enables us to understand nature and use it for applications. Science may not be able to answer all of the questions humans pose; however, the limited knowledge it provides is insightful, illuminating, and useful. Human knowledge that is not science is opinion. Science does not answer questions about the purpose or meaning of life, for the simple reason that these concepts have a meaning only in the context of humans and are meaningless for nature. Trying to answer these questions is futile, as meaningless as using a mathematical function outside its range of definition or validity, which usually leads to nonsense. The oft-repeated claim that religions answer these questions of why is a false illusion perpetuated by its practitioners. Religion only claims to answer them. Weighty tomes of religious discourse, produced by much labor, sweat, and ink, usually declare answers to these questions mysteries beyond human understanding. Such a statement is no explanation at all! It is a form of intellectual humbug. Contemplating these mysteries may give some a warm, cozy, and comfortable feeling; however, most see them as intellectual deceptions. The limited explanations of science are better than the bottomless mysteries of religion.

Science provides limited control over nature in conformity with its laws and is an alternate answer to human belief. A study of fluid flow and aerodynamics enables us to design planes that can transport hundreds of people over huge distances. No amount of a priori reasoning or introspection will enable us to fly. There are some religious practices such as yoga that claim to endow its followers with the ability to levitate. There is no experimental evidence for levitation, which goes against the laws of nature. No one has used levitation as a means of transportation; all people, including the practitioners of these esoteric beliefs, buy tickets on commercial planes, just like ordinary folks. Another unique aspect of science is its democratic and truly egalitarian nature. Experimental data and their generally accepted interpretations are the ultimate authority in science. There are no *special* people belonging to an inner circle of acolytes with mystical, magical attributes who mediate between the masses and Mother Nature. Science by its very nature is democratic. Any person competent enough to do experiments can check on a theory and accept or reject it. By the same token, any person who claims special esoteric knowledge or authority in science does it at her or his peril. The history of science has few examples of some people who forgot this simple truth and cultivated pretensions to a privileged position. Eventually they fall flat on their faces and are reduced to the level of all practitioners of science, whose final arbiters are experimental data. The rules of the game in religion and science are entirely different; the first depends on belief that is not subject to scrutiny by logic or limited by empirical data, and the second is very much restricted by them. That is why it is best not to mix religion and science. Some religious traditions include miracles in which the laws of nature are broken under special circumstances by unique personages. It is a personal choice as to whether one believes in miracles. A significant number of people with their feet firmly planted on this Earth consider miracles to be examples of self-delusion and do not believe in them. For them, the laws of nature are miraculous enough! Miracles in the baggage of religions have become something of a problem. In the age of belief, they might have been useful to impress the gullible and recruit new converts; however, in the age of skepticism, they have become an embarrassment. The only problem is that the religious establishment does not know how to shed them gracefully.

Religious Experience and Brain Pathology

The association of epilepsy with religion is ancient; it is close enough for epilepsy to be called a sacred disease. Before the pathology of epilepsy was better understood, it was considered an altered state of consciousness in which the epileptic was in touch with the supernatural. Clinical observations have shown that in some people with temporal-lobe epilepsy, there is an unusual preoccupation with religion and with theological and philosophical questions. They also see profound cosmic significance in events that the rest of humanity sees as ordinary and trivial. Some of these patients claim to have seen God, that they are in frequent communication with Him, or that they themselves are the Almighty (Ramachandran and Blakeslee 1998). A temporal-lobe personality, known scientifically as Gastaut-Geshwind syndrome, with its own set of characteristics and occurring in some of patients with complex partial seizures, has been studied (Sadock and Sadock 2000, 267). It is not known how temporal-lobe epilepsy results in visions of the supernatural during seizures and a mystical religious affect between seizures. Perhaps an explanation of these observations lies in the future, when the brain and the mind it supports are better understood. However, temporal-lobe epilepsy, as a possible cause or originator of religion or religiosity in *some* cases, cannot be ruled out. Neuropsychological bases of God beliefs have been reviewed by Persinger (Persinger 1987). These include temporal-lobe transients, which could be induced by a number of physical causes such as low blood oxygen, low blood sugar, or certain forms of meditation or prayer. The same may be said of auditory hallucinations, either self-induced or organic (Smith 2007). There are many believers who may object to explaining religious experiences or events as brain pathologies and not miracles. However, the occurrence of brain pathologies, which follow natural laws, is more probable than miracles, which do not.

Some psychoactive mushrooms, plants, and isolated chemicals have also been found to induce profound religious experiences and have been used in many cults all over the world for thousands of years as part of many religious services (Furst 1990; Schultes and Hofmann 1979; Letcher 2008). However, religion and its experience can exist without brain pathology or ingestion of consciousness-altering substances. It should also be noted that affects of normal or abnormal brain chemistry, either organic or chemically induced, in the context of religious experience depend very much on and are modulated by a number of circumstances. These are the environment—sacred versus profane, ritualistic, or recreational; expectations—spiritual insight, liberation of one's self, or divine intervention to answer current problems; the beliefs, myths, and worldview and expectations of the person experiencing them, along with the support group of the rest of the community. Hence, explanations of religious experiences and their profound significance to humankind makes them complicated, and unraveling them only in terms of neurochemistry will be too simplistic. The Astonishing Hypothesis of Francis Crick, that the mental activities of a person are entirely due to anatomy, physiology, and normal functioning of the person's brain—nothing more, nothing less—can only be a starting point for solving the problem (Crick 1995, 271). Or, as LeDoux, a neuroscientist, would like to say: "You are your synapses" (LeDoux 2002, ix). Science has much to learn before it can clear up the exact mechanism of how nerve impulses in the brain are converted into subjective thoughts of consciousness; we may know the answer many years down the road (LeDoux 2002; Koch 2004). However, possible organic or chemical proximate causes of *some* religious experiences in no way debase or devalue them or make them less genuine either to the person who experiences them or to others who believe in these revelations. It has been pointed out by William James that the origins of religious revelations, whether ascribed to supernatural agents or to organic causes, are not very relevant in judging them. What matters is the pragmatic criterion of how effectively the religion works in practice, or how useful it is to those who believe in it and try to live by its precepts (James 1936, 21).

CHAPTER THREE

My Maternal Grandparents

The whole house had been astir since early in the morning. The *vājpāñce* (musicians) were there, playing festive music to herald an auspicious day. Vedavathi, or Vedu, was going to be married. She was a lucky girl because the prospective groom had an "English education," with a college degree and a good job in Bombay. He was from a well-known orthodox Acharya family of Mangalore. These modern boys were known to be kind and considerate; they did not beat their wives. She could expect a comfortable, cushy life in the big city away from all the problems of a small village. The bride's father, Krishna Bhat, whom everyone called Kuṭṭaṇi, was more worried that day than usual. His was a nervous temperament. He was always looking for the unexpected, which was out there waiting to pounce on him. This *adṛṣṭa* (unforeseen), capricious fate would not disappoint him that day. Before the day was out, it would do its worst to thwart his plans. However, because of the girl's good fortune, or the good karma of the ancestors, the rescue would be equally unexpected. Vedu's mother had died giving birth to her, so Kuṭṭaṇi, as a widower, could not participate in the ceremonies. He had asked his older brother, Ganapathi, to give away the bride. All Kuṭṭaṇi had to do was sit on the sidelines and observe the proceedings. This would allow Kuṭṭaṇi to give free rein to his fertile imagination, to think of all the things that could possibly go wrong, and to be worried stiff. He did not have to wait long.

The officiating *purohits* (family priests) for the wedding were Kuṭṭaṇi's cousin Panduranga, or Pandu, and his recently widowed son, Subraya (Subba), of the Vatsa *gotra* (clan). Kuṭṭaṇi's family of Atri *gotra* priests were the *purohits* to the Vatsa gotra family and vice versa. These two families had been exchanging brides for centuries and were closely related. Because both families officiated at the local temple, their young girls were quite familiar with all the rules of *anvāḷpaṇa* (ritual purity). It was such a bother to train a girl from a *grahastha* (householder) family who had not grown up with these rules. Pandu and Subba had started the ceremonies well ahead of the auspicious time fixed by the astrologers. The groom's party had arrived on time, and were received with all due ceremony. In Hindu weddings, there is a bit of playacting in which the groom pretends to go to Kāśī or Vāraṇāsī or Benares for further studies. The father of the bride stops the groom on the way and importunes him to change his mind, to accompany him to his home, and to marry his daughter. The groom had started on his journey to Kāśī, *Kāśīyātrā*, ready to be intercepted by Ganapathi. This is where fate struck. At that moment, the groom got cold feet, decided he did not want to marry after all, and walked out of the marriage *panḍal* (enclosure) and out of Vedu's life. Poor Kuṭṭaṇi was beside himself. What was he going to do? Where was he going to find another boy? After such a scandal, who would ever marry poor Vedu? Though it was not her fault, the wedding had fallen through, and the local people had much to gossip about. Someone in the assembly, however, came up with a creative solution to the crisis. Young Subba, officiating at the wedding, had lost his wife recently. Tradition dictates that a widower cannot conduct worship in a temple; hence, he was looking for a wife. Subba the *purohit* became Subba the designated groom. That is how Subba and Vedu, my maternal grandparents, got married. The marriage was happy by the standards of that time. Subba did beat Vedu once in a while; however, he did not make a regular habit of it. He was quite well to do and a good husband. Vedu did not expect much out of married life; she was not disappointed.

After about thirty or forty years, Nethru Mhava, Vedu's elder widowed sister, met the boy who had run away from the wedding, at Benares or Haradhwar, during one of her pilgrimages. He had wanted to renounce the world and become a *saṁnyāsi* (ascetic) all along, he said. His parents had forced him to consent to the wedding. However, he had found his backbone at the last moment and had decided to walk away from marriage. He asked about Vedu and how she was getting along. This man's cowardice in standing up for his rights had caused much misery in an innocent girl's life.

The Vatsa *Gotra* Priests of Mulki

Subba belonged to the Vatsa *gotra*, the other clan of priests with a hereditary right to conduct worship at the Mulki temple. The progenitor of his family was Soira Vittala Bhat, who migrated to the South Kanara District and was given land by the local Savanta chief, a Jain, to build a small temple for Vittala (see Chapter 2: "My Paternal Grandparents"). We know very little about this ancestor of ours; information on many generations after him is also missing from the genealogy chart. The original temple is supposed to have been a modest affair, a small hut with a thatched roof. In effect, it was an extension of the family shrine, *devākūḍa*, that is in almost every Hindu home. The priest's income was from the offerings of the devotees who visited the temple and from the *dakṣiṇā* (fees for a ritual), in cash and kind for officiating at *saṁskāra* (rites of passage) for the local families of his clients, *yajmāna*. At best, the life of the priests was precarious; they barely managed to eat and provide for the oil to light the temple lamps and to purchase some rice as a daily offering. These were the minimum expenses of maintaining a place of worship, and most of the time the priests had difficulty in meeting these. There is a local saying that compares the life of a priest to that of *dirbhāṅkuru* (a type of grass), which somehow survives even the worst drought. This type of grass never grows tall. It always grows low, hugs the Earth, and somehow manages to survive.

Panduranga

We know a little bit about Panduranga, Subba Bhat's father. When he was a little boy, his mother brought him to our home (that is, the home of the Atri *gotra* priests) one day to leave him as a surety, *aḍavu ghālcẽ*. Apparently there was a famine, and Panduranga's family was going through some rough times and did not have anything to eat. His mother wanted to borrow some rice and had decided to leave the boy with our family as surety. It would also mean one mouth less for her to feed. The two families were of course related by many exchanges of brides in marriage. Our family declined the surety and helped Panduranga's family through the hard times. Panduranga was educated in our family and became quite a Sanskrit scholar and a much-respected priest with his own set of client families. He became well known as an expositor of *purāṇa* such as the *Rāmāyaṇa* and the *Mahābhārata*, which earned him some extra money. He was a prudent man who saved money and lived within his means. This enabled him to buy some extensive areas of agricultural land, *guttu*, in the three villages of Manampadi, Kilpadi, and Yende. Panduranga had six sons: Narayana, Krishna, Srinivasa, Ramachandra, Padmanabha, and the youngest, Subraya. Panduranga is supposed to have died at the ripe old age of 105 years with all his faculties intact. Panduranga was in his eighties when Subba was born, which was about 1859. Subba died around 1948 at age 89. Because these dates depend on the memories of my relatives and were not officially recorded anywhere, they are approximate.

All of Subba's elder brothers died without having produced any children. Panduranga's property remained undivided within the family, and Subba inherited all of it at the death of his father. He was not a scholar; however, he was trained in the basics of priestcraft that enabled him to discharge his obligations in the temple as well as to the client families he inherited from his father. He had a big ego, a luxury he could afford in keeping with his status as an owner of three *guttu* with an annual income of about 150 to 200 *mūḍos* of rice. In those days, this was considered quite a substantial income, especially for a priest. He was easily manipulated by others with flattery and sweet talk, did not tolerate criticism or a realistic appraisal of the state of affairs, and was not blessed by sturdy common sense as a substitute for his lack of education. His closest advisors laughed at his naiveté behind his back, took advantage of him, and helped to ruin him with much glee and relish. They were envious of his wealth and helped to drag him down to their level of subsistence by encouraging him to commit a number of blunders whose significance he perhaps never understood. Of course, he alone was responsible for his missteps in his financial affairs. Before we proceed with his story, however, a detour through three problematic aspects of life for the Gauda Sarasvat Brahmana (GSB) in Mulki would be helpful because they had a direct bearing on the life and fortunes of my maternal grandfather, Subba Bhat: (1) the ever-present *laukika–vaidika* tension (the tension between the secular and religiously observant) amongst the GSB, (2) how the Sarasvats dealt with caste and politics in exile, and (3) the movement for unifying the different *jāti* (birth groups) of the community. The first problem deals with a struggle for dominance in the GSB community and is discussed in Chapter 2, "My Paternal Grandparents," in the context of Hindu priesthood as a profession. The second factor is about discrimination and challenges to the caste status of the GSB from other competing groups of Brahmans, and the third deals with a reform movement to unify the community that failed. All of these factors came together in the sleepy town of Mulki, resulting in the local *saṁyuktā galāṭo* (unification movement uproar).

The GSB Face Caste and Power Struggles in Exile Over the centuries, the GSB in Goa had become mostly merchants, earning a living by trade, except for a small group of professional priests, called *bhot* or *bhat*. The community as a whole had moved away from Vedic rites and religion, and priestcraft, as its primary focus. In Goa, the Sarasvats were in the majority and formed a dominant group that controlled seagoing trade, both foreign and coastal, domestic petty trade and commerce inside Goa, moneylending, trade in jewelry and precious metals, and other forms of lucrative business. The GSB community was at the top of the ritual and social hierarchy and did not feel threatened. There was really no upward mobility for the community as a whole; it was already at the top of the heap. Hence, the surplus energy of the people was expended in fights for relative dominance within the community—that is, amongst the various *jāti*. As has been noted by historians, in Goa there was a proliferation of these birth groups, some eleven to thirteen (Wagle 1970;

Enthoven 1975, 1:251). The GSB magnified any small differences between the different *jāti* and wasted their energy on mindless quarrels and claims of superiority over other *jāti*. From our modern perspective, it is difficult to justify dissension of this kind; however, considering the time and energy spent by the community on these quarrels, they must have been very important for them. The sectarian fighting between the Vaiṣṇavas and the Śaivas in the community is an example. Originally all members of the GSB were Śaivas (worshippers of Śiva). Sometime in the thirteenth century, a sizeable number became Vaiṣṇavas (worshippers of Viṣṇu). However, the two sects acted as one community, dining together and exchanging brides. All of this changed in the eighteenth century, and for reasons no one remembers, the two sects began quarreling. The fighting escalated until the sects requested that the Portuguese state and the Portuguese king, the former persecutors of the community, referee their quarrels (Priolkar 1961, 148). Yet the problems between the sects could not be resolved, and their fights did not come to an end. The Portuguese got sick and tired of their role as arbitrators, and finally, they gave the factions one month to reconcile or else split into two separate independent groups. Because these groups felt that their differences could not be reconciled, splitting is exactly what they proceeded to do. Each group decided to live in complete segregation from the other. Such a break was too much for many people in both groups. At least three women committed suicide because they could not bear the idea of never seeing their natal families again. The leadership of the community could not or did not want to heal these differences. The inter-*jāti* relationships were determined by tradition and the orthodoxy of the people involved. Some of these subcastes interdined and exchanged brides. A few others thought that such a social relationship implied ritual pollution that had to be cleansed with proper *prāyaścitta* (expiation). The heads of the *maṭhas* (monasteries) to which the subcastes owed allegiance enforced these rules of ritual purity. The followers of these monastic gurus clung to the rules tenaciously, like child clutching security blankets. In most cases, members of both groups either had forgotten why these barriers between them had been erected or were not interested in removing them.

Religious persecution in Goa, especially after the 1540s, forced a large number of the GSB into exile to the neighboring Hindu or Muslim kingdoms outside Portuguese control. Literacy, familiarity with many languages, and commercial experience were the strengths of the community. These skills could be used to earn a living in the new places where the GSB migrated. The Hindu kingdom of Shivaji, and later the states of the Maratha Confederacy, were attractive refuges for the new immigrants (Map 1). Each of these states was the preserve of a particular community of administrators and power brokers and provided different opportunities for the newcomers. The entrenched groups in these areas were the Deshastha, Chitpavan, Karhada, and other Brahmanas and the Chandraseniya Kayastha Prabhus (CKP). The CKP saw themselves as a warrior, or *kṣatriya*, caste, well educated and equally facile with a sword or a pen. They had functioned in Maratha history as military leaders as well as administrators or bureaucrats. Why did these communities monopolize the administrative jobs? Because these groups were the only educated people amongst the populace who could read and write in an age of general illiteracy. Each of these groups had found its own niche or theater of activity before the GSB appeared on the scene. The Deshastha were predominant under the Bhonsles of Nagpur, the Peshwa of Poona were Chitpavan who were in the majority there. The CKP were powerful in the state of Gaekwads of Baroda (now called Vadodara). The Shenvi subdivisions of the GSB spread to the states of Scindias of Gwalior, Holkars of Indore, and Dhara and later moved to other Maratha states of Madhya Pradesh and Gujarat, including Indore and Baroda (Vadodara). It was only natural that there would be struggles over territory between the old-timers and the newcomers. Because they were all intelligent people, they showed quite a bit of originality and creativity in the struggle for survival and fight for dominance. Their techniques included extolling the virtues of their *jāti* while running down others, employing and advancing the careers of their caste-fellows, discriminating against other groups, and reaping any financial or material benefits from their discrimination. A favorite pastime of this age was to challenge the caste status of another group and humiliate its members if possible, so as to eliminate them as competitors. This is precisely what the entrenched groups proceeded to do to the newly arrived GSB. The GSB made no secret about the fact that some of them ate fish; hence they were known as "fish-eating Brahmans." The other Brahmana groups would bring up this reason for declaring the GSB non-Brahmana who did not deserve all their privileges. Because caste and politics are both dominance hierarchies, people prominent in one could leverage the other to enhance status and benefits. This is exactly what the dominant groups already in power did to the new immigrants, the GSB. This intersection of caste and politics in Maharashtra has a long history that must be delineated for full appreciation of the problem.

Gaga Bhatta Declares Shivaji to Be a True *Kṣatriya* When Chatrapati Shivaji (1627–1680) wanted to be crowned according to the ancient Hindu rituals, there was the question of whether he was a *kṣatriya*. Only a *kṣatriya* could go through the coronation as a "twice-born." A learned Sanskrit scholar, Gaga Bhatta of Benares, was asked to deliver judgment on the matter. His verdict was that Shivaji was a true *kṣatriya* belonging to the Solar Sisodia clan of the Rajputs of Udaipur and thus entitled to a coronation ceremony according to the Vedic rituals (*Vedokta* mantras). Shivaji's coronation was celebrated on 6 June 1674 in conformity with the ancient Vedic rites. However, there were rumors that the sacred Gāyatri mantra had not been imparted to Shivaji at the coronation, and questions about the *kṣatriya* status of the royal family would surface time and again for the next three centuries (O'Hanlon 1985, 20, footnote 12). There were also questions about the status of other castes too. The CKP had played an important role in Shivaji's fight for freedom with the Mughal Empire. Baji Prabhu Deshpande sacrificed his life at the Battle of Ghod Khind to allow Shivaji to escape from the Mughals and was a CKP hero. Murar Baji Prabhu, a CKP, gave up his life at the battle for Fort Purandar in the service of Shivaji (Laine 2003, 67). The patriotic credentials of the CKP, and the part that CKP members played in the struggle for freedom by the great Shivaji, were impeccable. CKP members had achieved much with their native talent and were proud of it. They wanted to be recognized as a high-status group, or twice-born *kṣatriya*, and hence entitled to initiation, or the *upanayana* with *Vedokta* mantras. Competing Brahmana groups, however, declared that the CKP were *śūdra* (servants). Gaga Bhatta had visited Maharashtra on several occasions before the coronation and had declared the GSB to be Brahmana (1663) and the CKP to be twice-born *kṣatriya* (1669–1672) and hence entitled to the rite of *upanayana* (Laine 2003, 66). However, the caste status of the GSB as Brahmana would be challenged many times. The CKP had to prove that they were *kṣatriya* and not *śūdra*. These challenges and counterchallenges would go on for the next three centuries! The challengers declared that the GSB were only twice-born, or *trikarmi*, and not *ṣaṭkarmi*, as befits a full-fledged Brahmana.

The *Trikarmi–Ṣaṭkarmi* Controversy Who is a *trikarmi* and who qualifies as a *ṣaṭkarmi*? According to the Hindu codes of law, all three castes that undergo *upanayana*, the Brāhmaṇa, Kṣatriya, and the Vaiśya, are the twice-born, also called *trikarmi*. This means that their rights and obligations are three: self-study of the Vedas, offering sacrifices, and giving gifts. Only Brahmans have three additional rights: to teach the Vedas, officiating at sacrifices for others, and receiving gifts. They have thus a total of six obligations and are called *ṣaṭkarmi* (Doniger and Smith 1991, 244, 10.74–77). In spite of Gaga Bhatta's ruling in 1663 that the Sarasvats were full-fledged Brahmans with six rights and obligations, their credentials would be challenged again and again by other Brahmana, who said that they considered them to be only *trikarmi*. The reason was that some GSB ate fish, and that the whole community, who dined and married with them, were ritually polluted. The other Brahmana had two reasons for so designating the GSB. The first was their primacy drive, impelling them to declare themselves superior to the GSB by degrading their ritual status. The second reason was purely economic: By cutting out the GSB, they got a bigger share of the subsidies from the rich and powerful patrons. For the Sarasvats, such a move threatened their very existence. They claimed an ancient lineage going back all the way to the Vedic sage Sārasvat, which the *pañca drāvida*, or the southern Brahmana, such as the Chitpavan, could not. Hindu mythology declared that the sage Paraśurāma had only recently minted some shipwrecked sailors as Chitpavan Brahmana, who might not know the old traditions. However, there were Vedic scholars aplenty amongst the Chitpavan who knew that the codes of law allowed eating of fish and meat at special ceremonies (see Appendix 5: "Hindu Rites of Passage," the section under the heading "Transition from a Nonvegetarian to a Purely Vegetarian Diet"). However, they chose to ignore these exemptions in their zeal to be the holiest, and they declared that the GSB were not Brahmana. Each of these groups had its own primacy conceit that declared that its community was the best and the foremost amongst all Brahmana, and they wanted to humiliate the other.

The Peshwa and the Rise of the Chitpavan Brahmana The whole power structure in Maharashtra changed with the appointment of a Chitpavan as the chief minister of the king. Shuhji (died 15 December 1749), son of Shambhaji and grandson of Shivaji, appointed Balaji Vishwanath Bhat as his chief minister, or peshwa, effective 17 November 1713. Balaji Vishwanath (peshwa 1713–1720) was a Chitpavan from Shrivardhan on the Konkan Coast who had moved inland to escape persecution at the hands of the Sidis of Janjira. The rule of the Peshwa would last for 105 years till the end of Maratha independence on 17 November 1817, when the Union Jack flew over Shaniwar Wada, a palace of the Peshwas in Poona (Gokhale 1988). These were the golden days for the Chitpavans, who combined a high caste status with political and economic power and patronage. Because they represented the king, or the *chatrapati*, it was their responsibility to make sure that the subjects lived according to the dictates of the Hindu law, *varṇāśrama dharma*. The Peshwa became self-appointed guardians of Hindu orthodoxy, *jāti* boundaries, and caste status (Fukazawa 1968). The combination of political power and the obligations to police religious orthodoxy is always a dangerous mixture that can lead to abuses. It is difficult to judge where the religious zeal to enforce orthodoxy ended and persecution of other *jātis* began. Complaints about the high-handedness of the Peshwas and the Chitpavans, by the Deshastha, the Karhad, the GSB, and the CKP, have been documented (Wikipedia. "Deshastha Brahmin," http://en.wikipedia.org/wiki/Deshastha_Brahmin, accessed 19 July 2008; Desai 1980; Gokhale 1988; Deshpande 2004; 2007). A few of these communities, the Deshastha and the Pratihara (or Pathare) Prabhus, went into exile from the Peshwa dominions rather than submit to their harsh restrictions under Balaji Baji Rao, also known as Nanasahib (peshwa 1740–1761).

The Harassment of the Sarasvats The trials and tribulations of the GSB during the reign of the Peshwas were many (Wagle 1970; Desai 1980). In the state of Sawantawadi, there was a quarrel between the Sarasvats and the Karhads over some rituals, and the former felt that the state was being partial to the latter. The Sarasvats opted for exile from the Peshwa dominions rather than put up with state pressure and unfair treatment (Desai 1980, 52). During the reign of Madhava Rao (peshwa 1761–1772), the question of the ritual status of the GSB had come up for consideration. The peshwa's banker wanted to give an *agrahāra* (a village of tax-free land gifted to Brahmana) to the Brahmanas of Maharashtra, including the GSB. This raised the question of whether they were *ṣaṭkarmi* and hence fit to receive the *agrahāra*. This was decided in favor of the GSB by a panel of learned scholars, including the famous jurist Rāmaśāstri Prabhuṇe, chief justice (1759–1789) of the Peshwa. In 1788, the Deshastha, Chitpavan, Karhad, and Gujarati Brahmana challenged, in a court of law, the right of the GSB to manage the temples in Bombay at Walkeshwar and Bhuleshwar. Avid for the wealth of the temples, these communities appealed to the Bombay judicature to vacate the GSB ownership of the temples. The GSB had to obtain a certificate signed by eighteen pundits from a Benares tribunal in support of their status as Brahmana and their right to manage these temples. The Brahmana status of the GSB was tied to all the gifts they could receive from the state or other rich patrons. These included the very generous distribution of *dakṣiṇā* by the Peshwa once a year in July and August, exemption from taxes by the state, and any other gifts they were entitled to as priests. However, they had to face new problems regarding their caste status during the reign of Baji Rao II (peshwa 1796–1818). In his struggles to attain office, Baji Rao had come to see the GSB as his enemies. Once he became a peshwa, it was payback time, and he hanged many of them. However, he did not want to be accused of priest-killing, *brahmahatyā*, which is one of the great sins for a Hindu. He decided to declare that the GSB were not Brahmana but only *trikarmi*, thus minimizing his crime of hanging them. This he did with the help and approval of his caste-fellows, the Chitpavans. This peshwa also confiscated the previous gifts of land from the GSB, because they were not entitled to them anyway, and redistributed them to the Chitpavan, the Deshastha, and the Karhad Brahmana. The rule of the Peshwa and the dominance of the Chitpavan ended when Baji Rao II was deposed and sent into exile in 1818 by the East India Company. However, the harassment of the GSB by the Chitpavans, wherever they had local power, continued. They would withhold state subsidies in the form of *dakṣiṇā* or reimpose taxes excused by the state. The GSB objected and had to fight for their rights and privileges as Brahmana all over again. The Chitpavan would not recognize the

GSB as Brahmana or allow them into the inner sanctum of their temples. The GSB, of course reciprocated. The right of the GSB to maintain and manage temples was challenged again in 1850. This right was affirmed once more, by the judgment of a nineteen-member tribunal in Poona, mostly made up of Chitpavans. This tribunal further warned the Chitpavans not to bear false witness against the GSB (Wagle 1970). However, small skirmishes concerning the caste status of the GSB continued, and in each case, the people involved had to prove their caste status in a court of law, obtaining new rulings and certificates from an assembly of experts from Benares, or use earlier precedence and appeal to a higher administrative authority. There was the 1864 case concerning the right of a GSB to attend Brahmana meetings in Bombay, a case dealing with land taxes in Baroda, one dealing with the distribution of *dakṣiṇā* in Gwalior (1908), and maybe others. In the 1870s, these fights seemed to have escalated to blasts and counterblasts of outrage, in the press or in published books. In 1869, a GSB social reformer spoke in favor of widow remarriage as supported by the Hindu codes of law, "speaking as a Brahmana" (Conlon 1974, 354). His status as a Brahmana was immediately challenged by a Maharashtrian Brahmana. This was followed by a heated public exchange. A renowned GSB Vedic scholar, Narayana Bhatta Karnataki, visiting Bombay was dubbed a *trikarmi* and snubbed by the local Chitpavans and Karhades. This was an outrage for the GSB, who protested in public meetings, fiery speeches, and polemical books (Wagle 1970, 319). There were more books written glorifying the GSB and their Brahmana status, and then replies by the opposition, debunking them and questioning all these claims. This is one of those never-ending controversies that can go on and on, forever, so long as human egos and conceits are alive.

These questions of caste status for the GSB, whether major battles or minor skirmishes, had several permanent effects on the GSB community. At least for the time being, the different GSB *jāti* stopped fighting amongst themselves because they had to face many challenges from outside. It brought them together. The GSB moved to big cities such as Bombay, away from the Peshwa and the Chitpavans, to take advantage of new opportunities in education and commerce. These moves started soon after Bombay was transferred to English control in 1665. There was no religious persecution or forcible conversion under the English. There was a stable government with expectations of fairness and justice most of the time. The GSB found employment with the English, as interpreters, diplomats, or trade agents, because of their familiarity with English, Portuguese, and the local languages. Narayana Shenavi was an English agent at the court of Shivaji. Ramachandra Shenavi was employed as interpreter by the English in 1667 in settling property claims by the earlier

Portuguese settlers in Bombay (Wagle 1970, 314). The list of the GSB in English employment is quite extensive, and one finds favorable references to their honesty, integrity, business enterprise, and the importance they gave to educating their children. The English saw the Chitpavans, Deshastha, and Karhad Brahmana as seditious and favoring the Peshwa, who had lost the struggle for power. They knew about the GSB–Chitpavan hatred and came to consider the GSB as the good guys, a counterweight against the Chitpavan, and commented favorably on them. The GSB were pioneers in taking advantage of new educational opportunities. Thus amongst the first four graduates with bachelor of arts degrees from Bombay University in 1862 were two GSB: R.G. Bhandarkar and B.M. Wagle (Wagle 1970, 317). Ramakrishna Gopal Bhandarkar distinguished himself as a Sanskrit scholar, Indologist, and Hindu reformer and retired as the vice-chancellor of Bombay University (Dandekar 1976). The Bhandarkar Oriental Research Institute (BORI) in Pune (formerly called Poona), a center for research and studies in Sanskrit and Indology, is named after him. Narayanarao Ganesh Chandavarkar was another Sarasvat who graduated from the Bombay University with a bachelor of arts degree in 1876. He had a distinguished career as a lawyer, justice of the Bombay High Court, vice-chancellor of Bombay University, president of the Indian National Congress, and Hindu reformer; he held leadership positions in several civic institutions and was active in public service.

The GSB Stop In-Group Fights and Regroup The buffeting that the GSB received from other power elites on their caste status brought about much greater awareness of their subcaste, birthgroup, or *jātī*, and a few even thought of themselves as a single super birth group: the GSB cluster or family. They declared a temporary truce in their internal quarrels that had been so popular in Goa and decided to work together, at least for the time being. This feeling of caste solidarity gave rise to many caste associations in the big city of Bombay, beginning in 1870 and moving into the twentieth century. A partial list of nineteen of these associations established between 1902 and 1934 is given by Wagle (Wagle 1970, 328–9). These included social clubs, cooperative banks, housing societies, education, and loan and scholarship funds. Though some of these were initially confined to a particular subcaste, later on such restrictions were relaxed to include other groups amongst the GSB. Shripad Subrao Talmaki (1868–1948), a Chitrapur Sarasvat, was a pioneer in the organization and founding of these banking and housing cooperatives in Bombay, beginning in 1906. In addition to being an active member who took many initiatives in founding these societies, he was a visionary who could foresee inclusion of Sarasvats from all over India, outside the parochial boundaries of the Konkani speakers in Bombay and the south (Talmaki and Nadkarni 1998).

Away from the big city of Bombay, in Mangalore, Ammembal Subba Rao Pai (1852–1909), a lawyer, was active in local GSB affairs. He was instrumental in the founding of Canara High School (1891), Canara Girls' School (1894), and Canara Hostel (1904), which made it easier for young people of the community and others to get a good education locally (Wikipedia. "Ammembal Subba Rao Pai," http://en.wikipedia.org/wiki/Ammembal_Subba_Rao_Pai, accessed 31 July 2008). The conversion of three young GSB men by the Basel Evangelical Mission in the 1840s had convinced the GSB that the mission school was the center of Christian conversion activity. They stopped sending their sons there and decided to build their own schools (Conlon 1977, 79). Subba Rao Pai founded the Canara Hindu Permanent Fund, Ltd. in 1906, which later morphed into Canara Bank. He initiated the formation of Gauḍa Sārasvat Brāhmaṇa Pariṣad, which was the precursor to the United GSB Conference, discussed in the next section.

For the 1901 census conducted by the government, it was decided to rank castes in order of "generally accepted social precedence" while grouping them in the general scheme of the classic fourfold *varṇa* system (Conlon 1974, 1981; Bayly 2001; Dirks 2001, 212–24). This one simple act in which caste status was listed in black and white in a government publication gave it an official stamp of approval and thus politicized caste. Many people who were barely aware of their caste suddenly wanted to upgrade its status and bask in its added glory. There were many petitions to the government by hastily organized caste groups or associations to move their caste to a higher category or a more superior ranking. Each case was supported by hastily organized documentation, where there was none before. Caste histories were rewritten, new mythologies on caste origin were created, and fresh demands were made for revisions in the order of precedence. These attempts to move castes a little bit higher on the totem pole represent one of the best examples of the primacy drive and conceit working in harmony.

All of these factors were a prelude to the United GSB Conference described in the next section.

The United GSB Conference, or Saṁyukta Gauḍa Sārasvat Brāhmaṇa Pariṣad (1910–1917) The GSB community at the beginning of the twentieth century was a diverse group. A sizeable number of the group were urban dwellers of Bombay, Madras, Calcutta, and other big cities, including the capitals of princely states—part of the old Maratha Confederacy (Kudva 1978, 64). These people were usually better educated, having at least a high school equivalency or a university degree, "modernized" to different degrees, mildly skeptical about religion and older beliefs; some of them could at least feel the need for reforms and changes in the status quo. A few, such as R.G. Bhandarkar or N.G. Chandavarkar, had national and international reputations because they were significant achievers in their chosen fields and outspoken social and religious reformers. Many in the community lived in rural areas and were engaged in agriculture or petty trade, were conservative in outlook, and were guardians of tradition, its values and virtues. A few individuals, city or village dwellers, were quite wealthy, whereas most of the community was of the middle or lower middle class. There was a whole spectrum of people in between these two groups who had traveled outside their "native place" and had seen the big world outside, who could find change in tradition useful sometime but were afraid of being called modern or progressive. The conservative and orthodox living in small towns or villages outside the big cities such as Bombay far outnumbered the progressive and the reformers. They looked at their fellow caste members in big cities with suspicion because it was believed that they were so busy earning a living that they did not worry about ritual purity and ate food cooked by unknown people in Irani tea stalls (Conlon 1977, 152). The "unknowns" were, of course, people whose *jāti*, and hence their status as regards ritual purity, was not known. Big-city life was not compatible with the norms of orthodoxy. Presiding over this diverse group were the heads of the different monastic lineages, *maṭha*, who were the ultimate arbitrators on matters of religious correctness. They set the standards for orthodoxy, and anything they declared to be outside the bounds of religion was forbidden. The religious reformers, who were a small minority, always kept a watchful eye on their guru to make sure that they were not too progressive to be considered overstepping the bounds of orthodoxy and the approved norms. None of them wanted to be formally excommunicated from the community or saddled with expiations, *prāyaścitta*, some of which could be quite expensive, in addition to being a public embarrassment. No one wanted one of these punishments hanging over his head. Unless *prāyaścitta* were taken care of, a person would have difficulty finding mates for his children; performing rite-of-passage ceremonies such as upanayana, weddings, or funerals; and participating in community functions, being considered an outcast. That would really bring down the wrath of the women of the household, which was worse than any calamity this side of hell!

The Chitrapur Sarasvats, or Bhanaps, were the most progressive, among all the *jāti* of the GSB in the last decades of the nineteenth century. Many of them had good education and jobs, and they were progressive in their outlook on life. The Bhanaps were also the first community that had to deal with the problems of modernization and its conflicts with tradition. In 1885, N.G. Chandavarkar of Bombay was the first Bhanap to go to England. On his return, he was greeted with much pride and jubilation by his caste-fellows in

Bombay, whereas caste members from small towns in the south had some reservations about his trip and the ritual pollution from it. The question was whether he should undergo some *prāyaścitta* to atone for the ritual pollution resulting from foreign travel (Conlon 1977, 152–67). Chandavarkar did not see the need for any penance, because he had not committed any overt act making it necessary. This precipitated the community's crisis of social reforms, ritual pollution, atonement, and all the related problems. The fissure in the community over the issue of purification for foreign-returned members became so bad that it was noted in the 1911 census as the cause of forming two factions: the Londonwalas, those who had been excommunicated by the religious head of the community for dining with the London-contaminated Chandavarkar, and the non-Londonwalas, the orthodox (Enthoven 1975, 1:251). To understand ritual pollution and its transmission to others, one has to think of it as a type of infection by a virus or by bacteria. One foreign traveler, ritually polluted, can pass on such pollution to thousands of other caste members by the simple act of dining with them. The proper thing to do is to have him "cleansed" by required penances before he interacts with or dines with other members of the caste. The details of this crisis are discussed by Conlon and are representative of similar problems in other *jāti.* The progressive big-city folk were more relaxed about ritual pollution, whereas it was cause for grave concern for the rest of the caste, including the guru, or head of the Chitrapur *maṭha.* Religious orthodoxy was defined by their guru, and most of the reformers did not want to risk excommunication from their caste by going against his guidelines. Without the approval of their guru, no social reforms were possible.

It is against this background that we have to understand the progressive movements that took place in the big cities and the reaction of the residents of small towns in the hinterlands. The village folk in a small town such as Mangalore, in the South Kanara District, could appreciate and want the progress achieved by their kin in Bombay. The Bombay folks were better educated, had good jobs with the government, were rich, and had more conveniences. Their caste associations, banking and housing cooperatives, were well known and the envy of people in Mangalore. The Chitrapur Sarasvats, or Bhanaps, had taken the lead in these progressive movements in Bombay. The rural folk wanted the good things of these city people in their own towns. They wanted to send their boys to get an education, and later to look for good jobs, in the big cities of Bombay, Madras, and Calcutta. In 1906 all these ideas contributed to the planning of the GSB Parishad by Ammembal Subba Rao Pai of Mangalore and others. The parishad (assembly) held its first session in April 1907 in Mangalore. The objectives of the meeting were better stewardship of temple funds, provision of scholarships, implementation of improvements in the training of priests, and institution of changes that would result in better trade and commerce practices (Conlon 1974). The answer to the question of who could participate in the meeting was left vague. The second session of the parishad met in Mangalore in December 1908. Its stated objectives were the control of wedding expenses, the use of surplus temple funds for education, and the institution of measures for poverty relief. A constitution was adopted, limiting the membership of the parishad to the followers of the Vaiṣṇav Kāśī and Gokarṇa-Partagāli and to the Śaiva Kavaḷe *maṭhas*, thus effectively leaving out the Bhanaps. Most Bhanaps did not attend the first session, because they had felt unwelcome. However, some notable Shenvi were invited as honored guests from the Bombay presidency. The big-city folks felt that leaving out any *jāti* in the GSB cluster was parochial and small-minded and that the parishad should be open to all the GSB. This small urban minority was enthusiastic about unifying all the GSB *jāti* and bringing down the barriers of yesteryear, whose justification had been forgotten long ago. As a sign of this opening up of the meeting to all of the GSB with the avowed purpose of unifying the community, they were going to add the word *Saṁyukta* (United) to the name of the GSB Parishad. The hosts of the meeting in Mangalore, however, warned these unifiers that the majority of the GSB were orthodox and would be against such unification (Conlon 1974). The unifiers, however, hoped to drag the rest of the GSB into the modern age of a progressive, united, and a strong community to face the challenges of the twentieth century. The next session of the United GSB Parishad met in Belgaum in April 1910. The objectives were to facilitate educational and employment opportunities for the young men of the community, establish caste schools, and to establish scholarship funds. Most of the delegates were city dwellers who had at least high school competency—and some had had a university education—and were for unification. The rural orthodox, with a basic education and a limited worldview, were quite comfortable with the status quo, which left the caste barriers alone. Their opinion reflected the views of the heads of all the religious *maṭhas*, who were against removing caste barriers (Wagle 1970; Conlon 1974). These caste barriers could never come down so long as the GSB thought that interdining with other *jāti* or exchanging brides with them would result in ritual pollution. Unfortunately, there were no reassurances about these concerns from the gurus of the different lineages. This is the crux of the reason for the failure of the unification movement. The next session of the United Parishad was in Vasai in 1912. It stands out because of a speech made during its course by a female student volunteer who was applauded for her talk, "The Needs of the Times," which called for, amongst other things, more polite usage in society. In 1912, the Chitrapur Sarasvats, the most progressive *jāti* in the GSB cluster, went on record as being against unification, in a formal resolution put forth under the leadership of the head of their *maṭha* (Conlon 1977, 165). At the 1913 session in Karwar, the girl who gave the speech in Vasai was refused a seat as a delegate, the excuse being that the delegates should be householders. Ultimately, when an apology was offered, she scorned it, pointing out that the insult in not seating her was against all women. This issue would be resolved only in 1935, when women were accepted as full delegates. Education of women was then considered desirable and received support. The goal was to provide a pool of educated, sophisticated women as possible brides for the educated new young men of the community and thus prevent their marrying ("Heaven forbid"!) any of those foreign girls. The usual list of the great women of Hindu mythology was trotted out, the ancient women intended as role models for these young women who were never expected to go into a profession or be financially independent wage earners. They would be put on a pedestal with all due respect but would be exploited as usual! The parishad met in 1916 at Indore, in 1917 at Alibag in the Kolaba District, and for the last time in 1935. The reformers never came to grips with significant social reforms, such as widow remarriage and a minimum age for marriage of 18 for boys and 12 for girls, because they saw them as being too controversial and too far ahead of their times. In 1935 the parishad had run out of steam and was relegated to the archives of the past. The movers and shakers behind it had lost their enthusiasm or had moved on to other causes, such as national liberation. They could also feel the storm of anti-Brahmana feeling brewing in South India, Maharashtra, and other parts of India (O'Hanlon 1985). Those were not propitious times for talk of Brahmana caste–centered groups.

The Failure of Unification In retrospect, the question we can ask is: Why did the unification movement fail? The reasons are obvious. First, without the support of the heads of the *maṭhas*, unification did not stand a chance. Most GSB, urban or village dwellers, educated or not, could not live with excommunication from their *jāti* and the attendant problems of finding mates for their children, *upanayana*, marriages or funerals in the family, without the support of their caste members. Second, the worldview of the majority of the community was firmly rooted in earlier times, without any changes brought about by the uprooting of the community from Goa and its exile or by confrontation with evangelical Christianity or the new British Raj. Most of this majority were not educated enough to change their conservative views. Third, the women in each family, the keepers of orthodoxy, had changed the least. They would try their best to stamp out any changes proposed by reformers in the family, seeing these as errant nonsense. The heads of religious establishment, who could have spearheaded any reforms, did not lead. The conservative orthodox majority of the community and the gurus supported each other and were firmly against any reforms. The progressives were a minority who could be ignored with impunity. With these three big *no* votes, unification did not stand a chance; it was as good as dead. Did the unification movement achieve anything at all? The cooperative housing, banking, and educational societies, the schools and scholarship funds, survived the movement as its lasting memorials. These successes may have had a positive impact on the self-confidence of the community. The GSB realized that if they cooperated without indulging in petty bickering and quarrels, they could achieve much. Self-confidence was never a short commodity with the GSB. One of their conceits was that they were smart and had more new ideas as a group than the number of GSB in the group! As a community, they had survived the Adil Shahi dynasty of Bijapur; the Portuguese state; the evangelical zeal of the Roman Catholic Church and its Inquisition; the rule of the Peshwa; the challenges to its caste status from the Chitpavan, Deshasth, and Karhad Brahmana; and above all, their own internecine quarrels. Perhaps the GSB were only dimly aware of this history of tribulations; however, they were a community of survivors whose self-worth was never in doubt.

Would unification find any support today? Is it worth reviving today? Perhaps not. Religion has much less of a hold on the GSB community today. The educated and progressive are marrying people of other *jāti*, both inside and outside the GSB cluster, other religions and nationalities. The conservative and orthodox continue their old ways, their family traditions, ignoring the goings-on of all the city folk. People have migrated to other parts of India and to other countries and openly accept other cultures. There are no community watchdogs policing religious orthodoxy, and everyone is more relaxed now about rites and observances. Caste and unification have become irrelevant or nonproblems, perhaps for the better. Caste as a dominance hierarchy has been replaced by other modern, cost-effective hierarchies. Primacy drive and its attendant primacy pride and conceit are very much alive and well, but under new names.

Commotion from the Unification Movement How did the commotion of the *saṁyuktā galāṭo* play out in the villages of South India? When this newfangled idea reached the hinterlands, it was as good as dead because it was not supported by the heads of the *maṭhas*. Hence, a majority of the conservative rural GSB did not favor it. Unification meant interdining with other *jāti* in the GSB group and exchanging brides with them. Each of these *jāti* had been indoctrinated from childhood to think of such acts as strictly forbidden, ones that would result in ritual pollution and excommunication from one's caste, or *bahiṣkāra*. This was also true in the village of Mulki, South Kanara District.

Mulki, though a small village, is well known for its GSB Shri Venkataramana Temple, famous for the *Darśana Sevā* (see Appendix 7: "The Oracle, or *Darśana Sevā*"). After the inauguration of this rite sometime in the eighteenth century, the temple had become quite rich and famous. The management of the temple was a center of power in the Mulki GSB community. The people in Mulki could have let the *saṁyuktā galāṭo* pass into a quiet oblivion and forgotten about it. Instead, they used it to settle old scores and to continue their personal vendettas by other means. Much drama, amazing ingenuity, and many power plays were displayed in these encounters. It was the topic of conversation in Mulki for the next few years. It is quite possible that similar events took place in other GSB centers too. Hence, I will try to give the highlights of the upheaval, leaving out the legal details, which are boring. It was a power struggle, pure and simple, under the cover of religious orthodoxy. Information on this episode is from a court judgment delivered by T. Jivaji, subordinate judge of South Kanara, on 17 March 1919 in a related lawsuit (Jivaji 1919).

The Temple Management and the Community in Mulki There were four main groups involved in this drama in the village of Mulki: (1) the management of the temple; (2) a few local social reformers who were for unification; (3) the temple priests, or *arcakas*; and (4) the rest of the community. The standard mode of operation for these groups in dealing with each other was always confrontational and never cooperative. If they had any problems, they did not believe in talking them over, seeking a common ground, and resolving their differences by compromise for the good of the community. "Good of the community" was mentioned often; however, it was only a cover for advancing the power agenda by the principals in the quarrel. Compromise was seen as an insult to their "manliness" and was out of the question. Any differences could be settled only by legal suits and countersuits. The lawyers for these antagonists were the only people who benefited from these endless quarrels. The temple management, as the stewards of the temple, had responsibility for the proper execution of daily worship, the performance of special festivals, the preparations for *samarādhanā* (community feasts), the repair and maintenance of the buildings, and so on. This list is long, and looking after all these responsibilities was a full-time job. However, the trustees of the Mulki temple only got around to appointing a full-time manager with a salary at a much later date. Earlier, some of the trustees supervised the temple affairs on a voluntary basis, with no salary, in addition to their regular jobs. However, these trustees had immense power in the community and perhaps volunteered for the management of the temple because of it. One or more of these trustees, always from a householder family, would be the executive manager of the temple, taking care of the day-to-day functioning. So long as the executive had the nominal support of other trustees and the community at large, he could do what he wanted. These managers ended up becoming autocrats and petty tyrants, without any checks and balances on their power. Unlimited power corrupted them, and they succumbed to the temptations of abuse of power. It was easy for them to forget that they were indeed voluntary servants of the community and the temple. They made arbitrary decisions to show their power and emphasize the subordinate status of temple functionaries, including priests. With a false notion of authority, they accused the priests of disobedience if the priests were bold enough to fight for their traditional rights (Jivaji 1919, 30). If the executive trustees were not amenable to reason, compromise, or arbitration, the people who depended on the temple for their livelihood had no recourse. The management could always challenge the subordinates to take their problems to a court of law and fight it out. If the priests or other functionaries were too poor to afford a lawyer, they had to back down and live with such arbitrary behavior as best as they could. The rest of the community would watch this struggle for dominance, with the detached amusement they would give to a show, a *tamāso*, and did nothing to rectify the problem. In effect, the rest of the GSB community in Mulki abdicated their supervisory responsibilities. It is against this background that one has to see the unfolding of the *saṁyuktā galāṭo*.

Some four local unifiers or reformers had attended a meeting of the unification movement in Mapusa, Goa, in 1910 and were accused of having dined with members of other birth-groups or *jāti*, and hence, in a state of ritual pollution (Map 3). There was no hard evidence to support the charge of interdining—only allegations or hearsay accusations by people *who were not there*. After the unifiers returned to Mulki, they had attended an *upanayana* and the *Satyanārāyaṇā pūjā* following it. All of the people who attended these functions and shared food were therefore alleged to be ritually polluted. This was of grave concern to the temple management, who reported it to the head of the Kāśi Maṭha, with a request for guidance from their guru. This incidence was followed by meetings, criminal complaints to the police, injunctions to prevent some of these "polluted" people from attending temple functions, interdicts against them, suspension of temple functions such as *samarādhanā* and *Darśana Sevā,* defamation suits, and an exploration of the list of all available legal actions. The temple management claimed that their only motive behind all these legal actions was maintaining caste purity and other norms of behavior; however, they also hoped to settle scores with their enemies among the unifiers, the priests, and the rest of the community. They hoped to foist onto the unifiers any temple monetary losses from the stopping of its festivals (Jivaji 1919, 69). The Pandora's box of the legal system was opened, with no one realizing how long these processes would drag on. The temple management had the unlimited resources of the temple treasury to pay the lawyers, whereas their opponents had to use their own funds to fight them. As I have mentioned before, in Indian society, it is a customary curse to say to your worst enemy, "May you be involved in a civil suit." All of the parties in the dispute knew this bit of proverbial wisdom, but they jumped into the fray anyway.

The court ordered Subba Bhat, my maternal grandfather, to appear as a witness against the temple management in 1911. Subba did as ordered. The temple trustees thought this was a grave affront to their dignity, which demanded revenge. Thus, they put new restrictions on his traditional rights as a priest and encouraged others to bring lawsuits against him (Jivaji 1919, 69–70). His rights could be reinstated only by a court judgment, and he had to fight these and other frivolous lawsuits too. The rest of the community either did not see any unfairness in such high-handedness or did not do anything to correct what they saw. Finally, in 1915, a few GSB initiated legal action against the temple management, requesting the courts to order their removal for a number of causes, including mismanagement of temple affairs, and to appoint new trustees. This lawsuit dragged on four more years; a judgment was finally delivered in March 1919. The court judgment is 116 pages long, with details of the background of the case, past judgments, and other material that could be read and appreciated only by law mavens (Jivaji 1919). However, this document is interesting because it is an objective description of the state of affairs of the community and a unique snapshot of the GSBs in Mulki, circa 1915–1919. The court judgment also deals with a number of issues not generally recorded elsewhere, such as the stewardship of the temple, the mores of the community, attempts at social reform and the fate of the would-be reformers, and finally the battle for dominance in the community. The court found that there was no inventory of the jewels and cash belonging to the temple. Hence, it appointed a commissioner to prepare an inventory of temple property. The court noted the following from the commissioner's report:

> Before leaving the inventory a note must be made of an entry in it that 93 rubies, 13 emeralds, 7 sapphires, 125 pearls and 10 diamonds, etc., were found in the sweepings of the dust in the Chandrasala upstairs and the report further shows that a bundle of currency notes of the value of Rs. 4685 which was damp and mouldy on account of white ants about it was also found and that he replaced the same by cashing them into silver coin. [Jivaji 1919, 19]

It is obvious from this quote that the management was woefully lacking in its stewardship of temple properties. The trustees were ordered to pay back to the temple about 4,168 rupees (a huge sum in those days), which was the money they had spent in defending their actions in civil suits. The court declared that these expenses were unauthorized. Though the court found quite a few problems in the management of the temple by the trustees and declared that the executive trustee was "guilty of misfeasance and nonfeasance of his duties as a managing trustee," it did not remove them (Jivaji 1919, 69). The court ordered the litigants to come up with a new constitution for management of the temple and postponed any decision until that was in place. I have no information on the temple affairs after 1919. By this time, the unification movement and any social reforms suggested by it were long dead in Mulki. All that remained of this affair were the interminable lawsuits associated with it.

A Vedic Poet Praises Harmony This concludes the saga of the *saṁyuktā galāṭo*, or quarrels within the GSB community in Mulki, associated with unification. The obvious question is: Why are there so many quarrels within the GSB? Are they quarrelsome by nature, or did circumstances force them to act like that? Is the individualism in the community so strong that its members cannot get along with one another? Are their egos so big that they can never cooperate? Are the GSB so very competitive that they cannot work together? The community has achieved much of lasting value by cooperation among its members, but internal quarrels have left the GSB with hard feelings, inflexible opinions, and bitter memories and have kept in place the walls that have long divided them. Perhaps the GSB are no better or worse than other similar groups with intelligent, assertive members, full of initiative and enterprise.

Can they do better? In answer, I offer the following thought: The last hymn of the *Ṛgveda* is by Saṁvanana Āṅgirasa to Agni and Harmony (Bose 1966, 203; de Nicolás 1976, 233; Panikkar 1983, 863; Griffith 1963, 2:609, 10.191). This hymn (*Ṛgveda* 10.191) is a farewell message from the Vedic poets. It has only eight lines; the first two invoke Agni, and the remaining six praise Harmony. The poet exhorts his audience to be one in their hearts, minds, and acts, with a single goal and a united purpose (de Nicolás 1976, 233):

Hymn to Agni and Harmony

You take possession, Powerful Agni,
Of all that is precious for your friend.
As you are kindled at the Sacrifice,
Bring us all wealth.

Come together! Speak together!
Let your minds be in harmony.
As the gods of old together
Sat in harmony for their share of the Sacrifice.

Common is the counsel, common the assembly,
Common the mind; let your thoughts be common too.
I lay before you a common purpose,
With united minds we offer the Sacrifice.

Let your aim be one and single;
Let your hearts be joined in one;
Let your minds too be united,
Let all, about these, willingly agree.

It is quite possible that bitter conflicts were a problem even in Vedic times. That is why the poet was compelled to sing on the virtues of Harmony. In these days, people are only too ready to put the *Ṛgveda* on a pedestal and worship it. Few care to read, understand, and live by it. The GSB are proud of their ancient Vedic heritage. However, they seem to take perverse delight in going against every one of the noble sentiments of the Vedic poet and engage in thoughtless, mindless quarrels amongst themselves most of the time. The earnest plea for harmony by the poet is a message that transcends *jāti* (caste), *varṇa* (class), religion, nationality, and ethnicity and is applicable to the whole of humanity. If only all of us could work together, forgetting minor differences, we could stop killing each other and achieve much, and live in peace and harmony. Is anyone listening?

Subba Bhat After the Unification Movement

Here we pick up the narrative of Subba Bhat's life, at the end of our excursion into the doings of the GSB community at large. His problems with the temple management began in 1911 when he appeared as a witness against them in a lawsuit filed by one of the unifiers in the *saṁyuktā galāṭo*. As was noted by the court judgment, the management denied Subba many of his traditional rights as an *arcaka* (priest) and encouraged others to bring frivolous legal challenges without any justification, in a spirit of revenge tinged with malice (Jivaji 1919, 77–8). Instead of meekly acquiescing to the temple management, he chose to fight them, because he had the means to take the dispute to a court of law. However, he did not have much common sense or the legal acumen to manage his affairs properly. The temple management had at its disposal its own essentially limitless resources to finance the legal proceedings. Subba, however, had to spend his own money. The legal proceedings worked their way through the local, district, and finally the presidency (state) High Court, then in Madras, at an enormous expense in legal fees. He did win all of the frivolous cases brought again him by the management or their henchmen, and the courts validated his traditional rights. However, the price of justice was steep indeed. These court cases became a type of indoor sport for those who could not afford to take part in them, and whose significance and the larger picture of what was at stake was not clear. Both parties in these legal fights had big egos and little common sense. They were not embarrassed to wash their dirty linen in public and take their intracommunity fights for adjudication outside the small GSB community. Compromise by arbitration was unthinkable. The fact that their case was being argued in front of the presidency High Court itself was a source of pride and earned the parties involved some local notoriety. These legal goings-on, the huge fees, the qualifications that entitled the lawyers to argue in front of the august presidency court, and the official robes they wore (*cāri hāttā cōgo*, robes with four sleeves) were topics for gossip by the locals over innumerable rounds of *phaḍpāna*, coffee, or tea. The litigants did not even think about a cost–benefit analysis, and once they felt that their machismo was at stake, it was a fight to the death. Subba Bhat, after having exhausted his savings, had to borrow money from the temple to pay the lawyers' fees. In those days, there were no banks around, so people usually borrowed money from the temple. Though he won these cases and could assert his legal rights, it was at a great sacrifice and expense. Subba had been brought up in relatively comfortable circumstances, meaning that he had enough to eat and wear. With a steady income of about 150 to 200 *mūḍos* of rice from his properties and his earnings as a priest, he was quite well off. The property had been accumulated by the hard work of his father, and he could entertain a certain aristocratic lack of interest in or worry about the prudent management of his resources. This resulted in his having to feed and take care of some distant relatives, general hangers-on who sponged off him, resulting in much waste in the daily management of his household. His wife, my maternal grandmother, Vedu (short for *Vedavathi*), was a very mild, sweet person who just did not have the toughness to speak up and manage his affairs properly. Subba never listened to advice from his wife; after all, she was only a woman! Nothing would have been seen as out of the ordinary if his eldest son, Narayana, my maternal uncle, had taken charge of his father's affairs and managed them sensibly. However, he was as bad as or even worse than his father at managing money. All of these problems were exacerbated by the large loans Subba had to borrow from the temple to pay the lawyers for fighting his legal battles on several different fronts, leaving Subba with very little of his wealth. A few of his friends suggested that he sell off a part of his real estate to pay off his loans. Unfortunately, Subba did not see this as the most sensible solution to his monetary problems. For him, selling any of his property was an act of surrender to his adversaries, a tacit admission of his defeat. He did not have any other resources with which to pay off his debts. Instead of facing these hard facts of life, he chose fight his creditors in courts of law, egged on by the cabal of his cronies! He was too simpleminded to sense that he did not have a valid legal case. The final result was devastating: Subba Bhat incurred more legal expenses, and all of his belongings, including the house he lived in, were attached and sold at auction to pay off his debts. But perhaps the loss of all his property was a blessing in disguise. It forced his grandsons to give up any plans of using the priestly crafts as a means of earning a living, to get an education, and to leave the closed, gossipy society of Mulki to live elsewhere. Our family has certainly benefited from all of those changes. Instead of living off of the rental from real estate and the sweat of the poor tenants working the land, Subba's descendants got an education and learned to earn an honest living that was based on their own hard work. They were forced to get out of the closed, narrow-minded world of outmoded orthodoxy into the real world of change and challenge.

Subba Bhat's Domestic Problems Subba had one daughter from his first wife named Sundari. She was married to Baba Bhat, son of Majoor Bhat, who was a local *patel* (tax official). Her wedding was a grand affair that lasted seven days and provided a chance for the display of Subba's wealth and high social status—his primacy conceit. The guests were entertained royally, with lavish meals, and marks of hospitality such as oil baths and various auxiliary functions to keep them amused and occupied. A caparisoned elephant was brought from the Shri Krishna Temple in Udupi, at great expense, to lead the wedding procession for the bride and the groom. I do not know whether the groom had any education or means of earning a livelihood and thus deserved all this adulation. He seems to have spent his life sponging off his father-in-law as a son-in-law in residence, a *gharjāvāyı*. He had all the vices then in fashion amongst men of his class: gambling, *bhāṅgi* (pot), women of easy virtue. You name it, and he had it. There are some rumors that he also got infected with some venereal disease, which he may have passed on to his wife, but that was some years in the future.

In the meantime, he, his wife, and an ever-increasing brood of children lived with Subba. Sundari had eleven children by her early death at the age of twenty-nine! Childbirth was a major killer of women. Some women died in a difficult delivery; many others who survived it died after having a large number of babies in a short time. Their bodies could not support the demands of being a baby factory. It was a double whammy for women, and only a few tough, lucky ones survived.

As a son-in-law, Baba Bhat was entertained with great *sammānu* (ceremonious hospitality), befitting an honored guest. There were elaborate meals with many special dishes (*poḷi pīṭa*), breakfast, and snacks in between (*tiffin*), special *tellā nhāṇa* (oil baths), and general marks of respect and esteem. After these heavy meals, he would climb into a thick comfortable bed to sleep off the exertion of consuming them. This bed was kept always ready in the room assigned to him. Amongst orthodox Hindus, it is considered bad practice, *ācāru*, to keep a bed spread out during the day, because it is usually done only when a person is sick. To do otherwise when there are no sick people would be tempting fate and inviting sickness and disaster. However, Baba Bhat demanded it, and as a son-in-law, his smallest wish was a command. He borrowed money from his in-laws for his minor expenses such as *pāna* (betel) leaves, *beeḍis*, and cigarettes. During his residence at Mulki, my mother, Sharada (later to be called Laxmidevi once she was married), was a little girl. She remembers this character robbing her piggy bank, *ḍabbi*, by using a knife with a blob of wax, *meṇa*, stuck to its tip when he needed some ready cash in a hurry. A final adventure that landed him in real trouble was a botched robbery, which was really more of a comedy of errors. This rascal decided to rob a poor widow in his native town of Kapu. He had known her since childhood. He was also aware of the fact that she had a few pieces of jewelry that every Hindu woman has as a safety net for dire emergencies. He disguised himself as a Muslim, complete with a fez and a checkered cloth, *luṅgi*, or *muṇḍa*, of the style normally worn by Muslims. He was also accompanied by two of his Muslim friends. He broke into the widow's house at night to steal her jewelry. In keeping with his Muslim disguise, he spoke only in Urdu, a language normally used only by Muslims, in demanding the widow's jewels. However, this perceptive woman was not fooled by either his disguise or his Urdu. She recognized him, calling him *Babanna* (a familiar endearing form of his name), just as she had been used to calling him since his childhood. She started berating him in no uncertain terms, recalling his family and respectable ancestors and how his robbery was bringing shame and disgrace on all of them. This, of course, did not deter Baba; he went ahead with his nefarious plans anyway. The widow lodged a police complaint, the police found incriminating evidence against him, and Baba Bhat was in real trouble. Subba's daughter, Sundari, was in tears, begging her father for help to keep her husband from going to jail. This meant more lawyers' fees, adding to Subba's already heavy burden of loans from his legal fights with the temple management.

Subba lived for many years after he lost all his wealth and property in about 1929. He continued to earn a living as a priest, performing his *pariyāya* duties when it was his turn. However, by the time I came to know him as a grandfather, he was a mere shell of his former glory. All of his wealth was gone, and with it went his status. In the olden days, I am told, when he owned the three *guttus* (extensive cultivable property), his tenants would bring in the owner's share of the produce of their fields after the harvest. These tenants would stack the rice, cereals, and other produce in their landlord's house and were fed and entertained in return. When I was in grade school, I saw such a visit by Subba's few remaining tenants only once. I do not know to which village or property they belonged. They must have come from the last remnants of Subba's old holdings. They brought the produce of their fields in large open baskets or gunny bags. That was when I saw for the first and last time how to assemble a *muḍo* of rice. A *muḍo* contains forty kilograms of rice completely enclosed in a spherical shell, with a diameter of about two to three feet, of dried hay expertly assembled and tied with lengths of straw rope. A properly tied *muḍo* of rice can stand much rough handling, and was used in the olden days for the transport of rice in and around the South Kanara District by bullock carts. In those days, I am told that gunnysacks were expensive and hard to come by. To assemble a *muḍo*, one starts with a bundle of dried straw tied together in a tight bundle at one end. This bundle is then spread uniformly on the floor of the front yard, *āṅgaṇa*, with the tied end in the middle, positioned upright. The person tying the *muḍo* pushes down on the knot in the middle and starts pouring in the rice or cereal, and gradually begins building the outer shell of the container. He has one foot on the middle of the container he is assembling and the other foot on the outside to support and form the outer shell. He has also a wooden paddle in his hand with which he keeps pounding on the outside of the straw shell to firm it up, distribute the straw uniformly, and in general obtain a tightly wound assemblage. It is joy to watch an expert tie a *muḍo*, and it can keep the rice in good condition for years. I am told this is one of the skills that is dying fast, with very few of these experts still in business. The rice or grains in a finished *muḍo* are sampled by piercing the outer straw with a bayonet-shaped borer with a shallow depression running along its length for collecting the sample. The sample is put in the left palm, rubbed, and smelled to judge the quality. After all of this hard work, with the new harvest properly stowed away, these tenants had to be fed. The forecourt, *āṅgaṇa*, of the house was swept clean, and the tenants would sit down in front of a number of freshly cut banana leaves for their meal. Usually a professional cook, used to dealing with large quantities of food, was employed for the day. Most of the vegetables brought in by them, and huge amounts of rice, were cooked, and the tenants would have a grand meal till they could eat no more. The tenants would then walk back to their villages after having discharged their yearly obligations to their landlord, *guttināyā*.

In the last few years of his life, Subba became irrelevant to the running of the family, because his two sons, Narayana, the eldest, and Padmanabha, the third child, were grown up and earning a living. Somehow, his wife Vedu, my grandmother, kept the family going through all these years. His second child was Tulasi (Aunt Tucci, or Tucci Mhāva), and Sharada, my mother, was the last child. He passed away in 1948, when I was in my last year of undergraduate college. He was a kindly grandfather, always an easy touch for some spending money for festivals such as the Pratiṣṭha Pūrṇimā, a full-moon event celebrating the installation of Lord Narasimha at Mulki and usually occurring in November–December, and the Rāmanavami Rathothsava (the Cart Festival), usually occurring in March–April. He would give each of us 4 annas (1 rupee = 16 annas), which we would spend on toys or some other goodies from one of the small stalls erected in the front of the Mulki temple specially for the duration of the festival. Once in a while, he would visit us at Udupi for the Makara Saṁkramaṇa festival (a harvest festival celebrating a beginning of an auspicious phase of the year) at the Krishna temple. He would appear unannounced, followed by a porter carrying his small suitcase and a bedroll. All of his grandchildren knew immediately that this would be another happy visit, with their grandfather passing out some spending money for the festival. My grandfather Madhava would formally welcome his cousin and son's father-in-law, *sāḍḍu*, inquire about his health and general well-being, and talk about the grand old times of their youth. At Mulki, Subba used to sleep on large, deep wooden chest, *kaḷambi*, kept on the south veranda, called Grandpa's veranda, *ājjāli jagali*, as befitting the head of the family. The family used to keep heavy bronze and silver vessels and other valuables in the wooden chest. The chest's heavy lid was closed and locked, and he would then spread his pallet, *hāntuḷa*, on top of it. This wooden chest has been converted now into a large vertical cupboard. The key to the chest was looped onto his sacred thread, *jānnuvē*, as is the custom amongst Brahmans. The sacred thread would be looped over the right ear to get it out of the way when a person squatted down to answer calls of nature. Brahmans of his generation did not shave themselves. Once a fortnight or so, a local barber patronized by Subba would be summoned to shave his face and head except for the topknot, *śenḍi*, on his crown. Subba would then apply a paste of turmeric all over his face and head as a disinfectant. This interesting property of turmeric was recognized by traditional Hindu medicine in ancient times and has been verified by modern science. He would then have his bath. This was followed by the daily performance of morning worship, *sandhi* (short for *sandhyāvandanam*, or morning and twilight worship), and a visit to the temple. Next to Grandpa's veranda was a bedroom where I spent many happy hours reading in the afternoons during my summer vacations. Outside the house, near the south wall of the compound, there used to be a mango tree producing large, succulent Munḍappa mangoes. Further to the west was a cowshed for the family cows and buffaloes. All of these are now gone; they were demolished a few years ago to widen the street to provide a smoother passage for the temple cart, *ratha*. The cart used to get stuck at this corner, requiring much effort to free its superstructure from the branches of the mango tree and get it moving past the house.

Summer Vacations in Mulki Summer vacations, when I was in middle and high school, were always spent at Subba Bhat's house in Mulki. Most of Subba's grandchildren used to congregate there, and we could be as noisy and rambunctious as we wanted. At home in Udupi, we were always shushed and asked to be quiet so as not disturb Father, who used to work at home part time on weekdays and full time on weekends. Looking back on my childhood, I am amazed at the volume of noise we used to generate without trying. It is not that we wanted to be noisy on purpose; it is just that to children, most situations appear to demand a noisy response for emphasis. The only time we had to keep quiet in Mulki was after lunch, when the grown-ups hibernated and had a siesta in the hot afternoons after the main meal of the day. We children had too much energy to take a nap, and even after trying hard, things would get out of control and the volume of noise would go up. Sometimes things got so noisy that we would awaken Subba from his nap, and he would get up in a towering rage. He would be angry enough to chase us into the backyard, *hittaḷa*, waving a bamboo stick. We were, of course, too quick for him to catch, and he would finally give up only when he was too tired to follow us. It was always a time of great fun. In the attic, there were quite a few books to read. I also used to borrow books from anyone and everyone I could collar. I have always had a voracious appetite for books.

Amongst Subba's grandchildren in Mulki, the eldest and our nominal leaders of the gang were Vivekaṇṇā and Gopalakrishna Bhavaji, who were attending the high school in Mulki at the time. Vivekaṇṇā is the eldest son of Tucci Mhāva, my mother's elder sister, and Bhavaji is the eldest son of my maternal uncle, Narayana, my *hodu māmu* (elder uncle). Devaraya, Bhavaji's younger brother, also lived in Mulki. Then there were Gokulanna, Villa, Vasudevu, all children of my aunt, Tucci Mhāva. Together, my sisters Lalitha and Kasturi; my brothers Vasudev, Rathnakar, Shidhdha; and I formed our battalion from Udupi. There were also Vasanth, Pandu, and Saudhamini, children of my younger uncle (my *Panni māmu*), Padmanabha. When we ate, the kitchen and the dining area was filled to overflowing with a noisy group of kids. You sneaked into the bathroom for your bath whenever it was free. The maid, *ceḍū*, who washed clothes, did the dishes, and took care of other chores, also kept the two large copper cauldrons, *bhāṇa*, topped up continuously; one was for hot water, and the other one was for the cold water. The older boys would organize expeditions to collect mangoes. The semiripe fruit were harvested using a long, thin bamboo pole with a knife tied to one end, and the fruit were caught in a large piece of cloth stretched taut and held by two helpers under the tree. The fruit were allowed to ripen in layers of straw spread on the floor of the attic, *māḷi.* Every day, the mangoes were inspected to remove those that were ripe and ready to be eaten or cooked. When I was little, I was afraid of heights, and so the ladder to the attic was always a problem. The ladder did not end in a landing; instead it had one of those old-fashioned trap doors that was flush with the floor of the attic when closed. Standing on the last few steps, one pushed the two halves of the door open and up into the attic. The left half of the door rested against the attic wall, and you climbed onto the right half to enter the attic. For me, going up into the attic, because I was attracted by the smell of ripening mangoes, was easy. However, on my way down, transferring from the horizontal right half of the door to the vertical steps of the ladder by extending my left foot was always a problem that filled me with apprehension about missing my step and tumbling down the ladder. I am blessed with an active imagination; sometimes, however, it is too active for my own good. I could vividly imagine missing the step, falling down the steps, and breaking my neck. After many a false start and a tentative feel for the steps, I would finally manage to get down, to the great amusement and derision of the other kids.

We children engaged in other projects too, such as building a model of the water bucket, *lāṭi,* used to lift water from a well and pour into the network of channels used to irrigate coconut and other fruit trees in the backyard. The water bucket in our model was an empty cigarette tin, and the supporting cross-trees of the structure were formed by two stout branches stuck in the ground. In the backyard, there was a low mud wall, 3 to 4 feet high, just begging to be climbed. We would walk along it and jump off at various points, as dictated by fancy. The boys would also hold pissing contests while standing on top of it. The idea was to stretch out as far forward as possible without falling off the wall and see who could piss the farthest. We would drink large quantities of water, hold it in as long as possible to provide enough volume and pressure, and do our best as a sign of budding male prowess. One had to always watch out for a sudden gust of wind that sometimes caused the drenching of the puissant pisser, or one could lose balance and fall off backward from the wall while stretching out too far forward to gain distance. We could also pretend to be the characters from the epics *Rāmāyaṇa* or *Mahābhārata,* as portrayed in the latest local performance of field drama, *bayalāṭa* or *kheḷu.* Turbans tied with pieces of cloth, colored sections of *sāris* judiciously tied round the waist, and mustaches traced out in charcoal transformed us into the heroic characters of the epics. Banging on an upturned water pail, *bāldi*, in imitation of a drum, *cenḍo*, accompanied by our own vocal imitation of the master of ceremonies, *bhāgavatu*, and other actors, would enable us to work up quite bit of enthusiasm for the performance.

After the *tiffin* at 5 o'clock or so, all of us would go for a long walk in the direction of the Mulki high school. Venkataramana, the oil presser, *ghāṇyānco*, had built a new house in the neighborhood and had moved there from his old house on the outskirts of the temple. His grown-up children were living in Bombay, gainfully employed, and sending him money every month. This had enabled him to buy a plot of land and build a new house with a tiled roof, as opposed to a thatched hut like the one in which he used to live. The new house was solid proof of his doing quite well and of having moved up in life. In the olden days, during the childhood of my mother, aunt, and uncles, and when Subba was rich, Venkataramana used to be a sort of retainer at Subba's house. He used to do odd jobs round the house; take the children to and from school; and carry them on his shoulders to get a good view while attending festivals, wedding processions, and public outings. He had grown up with them. He had many cashew trees in the compound of the house, and we could always help ourselves to as many cashew apples as we wanted. These fruit are not worth much as a cash crop; they do not taste good and are tart, sharp, and pucker your lips and constrict your throat. Enjoying them as a grown-up is only possible as a means of reliving the happy days of one's childhood. The cashew nuts, growing in a hard shell and appended to the bottom of the fruit, are collected and sold to factories for roasting and further processing. We would return home after nightfall, having had a few cashew apples or talked about the good old days with Venkataramana. Sometimes we would go flying kites on the small hill, *Pommatā guḍḍo*, behind Subba's house. The steep side of the hill was toward the house, and the updrafts from this side were always helpful in getting the kite airborne before it could be coaxed to higher levels to catch stronger and steadier air currents.

We would freshen up and then go the temple as part of the daily ritual visit. We would normally have our dinner at about 8 or 9 o'clock, followed by a general gathering of the whole brood in the front veranda. The grown-ups would assemble the evening after-dinner *pāna*, recount the important happenings of the day, chew on the latest gossip, and reminisce about the stories, events, and happenings of the main characters of the family, past and present. This was the cauldron of our family memories that we were stirring, and we muttered the incantations of collective recall to give new birth and form to our family myths. The older family members would correct one another on minor points of detail and add their own amplifications and embellishments to suit the image of the family cherished by *them*. Because none of these stories were written down when they happened, we really do not know how true they are. Even if they had been written down, truth can be elusive, and there is no guarantee that a written record represents facts. In all cultures, the oral traditions are earlier than recorded history and must have evolved with each retelling before they were written down. This book, after all, is my version of our family stories, and I invite and challenge my relatives to retell these to suit their fancy. There were also stories about ghosts, strange and mysterious happenings in and around the temple, and supernatural beings. The golden age of the oracle, *darśana*, during the tenure of Rangappa Nayak was recalled by people who had lived through it, with an account of many of his predictions that came true, his exorcisms, and the number of devotees who used to attend these weekly sessions (see Appendix 7: "The Oracle, or *Darśana Sevā*"). The Mulki temple became rich, self-supporting, and famous because of the oracle and the extra offerings in cash and kind brought in by the devotees consulting it.

All of us used to sleep on the front veranda, *jagali*, of the house, next to each other, with our feet toward the street entrance to the house. It was much cooler on the veranda than indoors, and the early mornings could be quite chilly requiring a thin coverlet. Amongst Hindus, the direction in which your feet extend while you are lying down is important. For example, one does not usually sleep with the feet toward the south, because south is the direction of the abode of Yama, the God of death. A corpse is normally laid out with its feet pointing south while it is being washed and prepared for the final journey to the crematorium. One also does not point one's feet toward sacred objects held in great reverence, such as the household shrine, *devākūḍa*. Each of us had his or her own pallet (*hāntuḷa*), a pillow (*uśśē*), and a thin coverlet (*pāngurcē voli*), to keep the ever-present mosquitoes out. There would be the rehashing of a few funny stories or jokes, much shushing and many admonitions to go to sleep, tossing and turning, fake snoring, and finally, that would be the end of a tumultuous day of a summer vacation in Mulki.

Subba's second wife, Vedu, short for *Vedavati*, was my grandmother. Everyone called her Āmmi; short for *āmmā* (mother). She was a sweet, trusting, kindly lady, easily manipulated and used by others, and without even a scintilla of guile or deception in her. She had to have been born sometime around 1883, because she died in 1972 age 89. She was a great worrier; she worried about past mishaps, present problems, and all that could go wrong in the future. If by some chance there was nothing to worry about, this state of affairs was cause for great concern. It was only the calm before the impending storm, and one better batten down the hatches before all hell broke loose. I do not know whether there are any worry genes; if there are, I am sure all of her grandchildren must have inherited them from her. Once in a while, when I worry about things I cannot control, I think about these worry genes that I must have inherited. I ask myself to snap out of it, and mentally work hard to defeat them! That is one ancestral legacy I could do without. Vedu's mother died giving birth to her, and she grew up motherless. She might have inherited worry genes from her father, and that, compounded by her experiences in early adolescence, must have shaped her outlook on life.

Subba and Vedu had four children in all: two boys and two girls. In birth order, they are Narayana (my *bodu māmu*), my aunt Tucci Mhāva, my uncle Padmanabha (my *Panni māmu*), and Sharada (my mother). Tucci Mhāva was born sometime around 1905 and passed away in 1983. She was married to my uncle (*mhāntu*) Taranath Krishna Bhatt (1902–1987), a physician from Bombay with an MBBS degree, one of the new "English-educated" sons-in-law much in demand because they did not beat their wives. He practiced medicine at Shringeri, famous for its monastery founded by the great Ādi Śankara. My mother was born on 25 December 1914 and passed away on 22 January 1989. Vedu's deliveries were difficult, and the last one, which was the birth of my mother, was particularly so (see Chapter 4: "My Parents and My Childhood"). There were rumors afloat to the effect that after the birth of her fourth child, Vedu decided to have no more children. In those days, when the average number of children in a family was in the double digits, a family with four children was considered to be small. Infant mortality was high, and having a large number of children was insurance against the early death of a few. Any form of birth control or family planning was also considered to be a grave sin because it implied rejection of the precious gift of a child from almighty God. It must have taken quite a bit of guts and gumption on the part of an obedient, self-effacing Hindu wife to say no to her husband.

Āmmi was a great believer in education for both boys and girls amongst her grandchildren. She knew well that there was no future in traditional learning, following the priestly crafts and being dependent on the generosity of the priest's clients and the various survival strategies associated with a priest's life. She knew that the old Sanskrit education had limited value in the marketplace of life. She was only too familiar with the hard life of a priest's wife, the vagaries of a husband's temper tantrums, the beating and physical abuse of wife and children a husband could mete out, and husbandly vices such as gambling, smoking pot, and fornicating. She strongly encouraged her granddaughters to get an education leading to a profession, so that they could be financially independent of any husband. She was preaching women's liberation years before it became fashionable! Young men with an English education were known to be kinder and gentler with their wives and children than their traditional counterparts were. Hence, they were in great demand by prospective in-laws. Her first son-in-law, Tucci Mhāva's husband, was a physician, educated in Bombay. Her second son-in-law, my father, was a high school graduate. Neither man beat his wife. She wanted her grandchildren to make a clean break from the life of a priest's family, get educated to get a good job, preferably a well-paying government position, and get away from Mulki. She exhorted all her grandchildren, including girls, to study and work hard to get good grades in school. Getting a good Western education and a decent, well-paying job was the only way out of our situation. She had the zeal of a missionary in how much she stressed the importance of education and getting ahead in life. Āmmi was ecstatic when her granddaughter Villa qualified as a physician specializing in obstetrics and gynecology. "You are my blood. I am proud of you," is how she congratulated Villa. She lived to see most of her grandchildren, both boys and girls, get a university education and training in the professions. When ill, she insisted on being treated by her granddaughter, the doctor. In 1972, Āmmi died peacefully in Villa's arms, at age 89. In Indian society, Brahmans have a reputation for being smarter and cleverer than average citizens. I do not believe in this folktale of primacy conceit. I am a fervent believer in the equality of all people in an egalitarian society. I believe that Brahmans have, after all, the same number of neurons in their brains as anyone else. The only extra thing that they have going for them is a tradition of education and learning in the family, with all family members urging the children to get a good education and cheering them on. A Brahman family would skimp on the necessities of life, miss a meal or two, and live in poverty if that was the only way to save up enough money to educate a child. Hunger and poverty are great motivators for the single-minded pursuit of education. There is a Sanskrit proverb that says that education and knowledge are the only possessions none can steal from a person. Brahmans have always understood this to be true. My father always used to say that no free lunches for the GSB in our temples did wonders for the well-known entrepreneurial spirit of the members of the community! Years of exile, away from Goa, have forced the GSB community to adapt to changing circumstances and to be innovative in its strategies for survival.

CHAPTER FOUR

My Parents and My Childhood

The small *bāḷāntiryācẽ kūḍa* (birthing room) was dark. Its one window was shut, and the only dim light was from a *divli* (bronze lamp) in one corner. It was quite hot, humid, and stuffy in the room, though it was winter. There were four large iron rings attached to the center of the main beam on the ceiling, two on either side of it. Later, on the twelfth day after birth, the baby would be put in the *pāḷḷẽ* (cradle) suspended from these rings. They were bare now. The woman in labor, Vedu, was lying on the floor on a thin *hāntuḷa* (pallet), moaning softly. There were beads of perspiration on her brow, which the midwife was wiping away with a damp piece of cloth. The midwife was murmuring words of comfort and encouragement in, *Tuḷu*, her mother tongue, silently praying for a quick delivery. With each spasm of pain, the woman's body strained taut like a bow stretched to its limit. The woman would then audibly relax with a groan of relief. When the pain became unbearable, she would call out to the gods and her dead mother, imploring them to relieve her pain and vouchsafe a quick delivery and the birth of a healthy baby.

The midwife was getting worried. She had no medical training whatsoever. All she knew about midwifery she had learned the hard way, by practice. She had tried a few simples, such as crushed herbs, and freshly cut raw onions to smell. These remedies had worked with other women in the past; they were of no use now. Her reputation as a midwife was based solely on her having had more successes than failures. While she garnered some credit for good deliveries, her failures were conveniently ascribed to things she could not control: fate, the alignment of planets, the bad karma of the mother, the infant, their ancestors, and their family.

Outside the birthing room, Nethru, Vedu's elder widowed sister, and some of her friends were sitting with anxious looks on their faces. They were chewing *pāna* (betel) leaves and talking in whispers about other deliveries: a few easy and some markedly difficult. It gave them something to do to get their minds off what was happening inside the room. They knew that Vedu's deliveries were difficult, but this one had gone on too long. She was also bleeding. They had prayed for a quick, safe delivery, making promises of *āṅgvaṇa* (vows of obligation) to their *iṣṭa devatā* (favorite gods), *bhūta* (spirit), and *kārṇike devu* (powerful deities). Once in a while the midwife would open the door a crack to report on the lack of progress or to seek a hurried consultation with the women. Finally, the midwife opened the door a crack and motioned two of the more powerfully built of the women to enter the birthing room to help her. The women let out a wail of anguish that rose from their guts, because they knew what she was going to do. She was going to try one last desperate measure—hanging, or *lāmbocē*. In difficult deliveries, when everything else failed, it was customary to hang the woman in labor from the ceiling by her hair. The vertical position of the woman or the pain of her body hanging from her hair, or just the plain wishful, magical thinking (*muṭṭāsa*), of this act was supposed to help deliver the baby. Few women survived such insult to their bodies. Vedu's mother had died under similar circumstances. The midwife wanted the extras to help her support the laboring woman when she passed Vedu's long hair through one of the iron rings attached to the ceiling. Vedu was too weak to stand up even with support. She also knew that she would not survive the hanging, which meant that the baby was as good as dead. Her groans of pain and suffering now became loud cries of despair and prayers for help and relief. The pent-up emotions of the women outside were now let loose in a torrent of loud, long crying and wailing.

At this moment, my grandfather Madhava was passing by the house on his way to the temple. Because of all of the sounds of grief, he thought that someone had died suddenly, so he stopped by to find out. Madhava was rock-solid in a crisis, unflappable and full of plain common sense. His loud, confident, reassuring tone of voice always helped to put heart into people in distress. On being told of the difficult birth, he took charge of the situation. He announced to everyone that things were under control and that there was nothing to worry about. He also sent for a physician to deal with the problem delivery. He sent the women outside the birthing room to boil some water, collect new bandages, or do other chores to put an end to their howling and keep them occupied. He told the midwife that no one was going to hang his sister (*bhaiṇi*) and that she was a fool even to think of it. He gently eased Vedu back on to her pallet. He asked Vedu not to panic; he said that he knew everything would turn out well. The midwife's helpers were to gently massage Vedu's legs, thighs, and belly to ease her pain. He told Vedu that the crisis was over and the time was propitious, *cāṅga veḷu ghaḍi*, for the birth of a healthy baby.

Madhava's calm and collected reassurances, his commonsense actions, and the skill of the physician appeared to turn the crisis around. Vedu finally delivered a healthy baby. She wanted to know whether it was a boy or a girl; she had hoped for a boy. When told it was a girl, Vedu broke down in uncontrollable sobs. Like every Hindu mother, she knew the problems and hardships of marrying off a daughter. Had she undergone all of these troubles and travails to give birth to a mere girl? Madhava again reassured her. He asked Vedu not to grieve at the birth of a daughter. In due course, he said, the girl would make a fine wife for his son Narayana. Thus, on 25 December 1914 my mother was born and betrothed to my father, who was 7 years old.

My Father's Childhood

My father, Narayana, was born on December 8, 1907. This was after *Ājjā* (grandfather) Madhava's return from Bombay in 1904 or so, sick with the plague. In those days, most of the bubonic plague victims died; only his tough constitution must have seen him through. My father, as the firstborn son in a Hindu family, was special. Later, when his three siblings proved to be all girls, all the hopes of the family for its future, along with his responsibilities toward it, were centered on him. He grew up in difficult circumstances because of Madhava's feckless management of his affairs. Madhava could not afford his bad habits—gambling, *bhāṅgi* (pot), and other dissipations—and was slowly and surely sliding into penury and ruin. Working hard to lift himself up from his poverty was not one of his virtues. His various plans for a quick and easy move out of his problems failed. At times, his family was so poor that they could not afford to buy things costing only pennies. Bhavani was a proud woman, born and brought up in the relatively well-to-do family of Ananthayya, a lawyer's clerk who later became a document writer. She was so ashamed at her predicament that she contemplated suicide. Perhaps the thought of her son being brought up by a second wife, *dhākṭi bāila*, and living with her husband's irresponsible ways deterred her from killing herself. She never used to talk about these difficult years in Mulki before they left it for good sometime around April 1923. On being pressed for details, she would just say that my grandfather was a thoroughly irresponsible person with no sense of any obligations to his family.

One of my father's earliest childhood memories is that of a trip to the famous Dharmasthaḷa temple in the district. An account of this journey is interesting because it gives some idea of travel before motor transportation became common in our district. The year was 1915 and my father was 8 years old. Bus service had been started in the South Kanara District in 1914, with one fourteen-passenger bus from Mangalore to Bantwal and back each day. As for the rest of the district, people walked or traveled by *bailā gāḍi* (bullock cart). This was a slow-moving vehicle with two wooden wheels bound by iron rims. It was drawn by two bullocks moving at a leisurely pace, and because it had no springs, it was guaranteed to shake every bone in your body. A dim kerosene hurricane lamp, suspended under the cart driver's seat, provided the only source of light at night. This lamp was supposed to keep away tigers or other wild animals quite common along the road, which passed through virgin forest. My father was accompanied by his parents, Madhava and Bhavani, and a distant relative, Subbakka, a widow. They took with them *bhājjilo phovu* (fried beaten rice), *koclā noṇcẽ* (a type of pickles), and *govā̃ hālvo* (dessert made from wheat). There were of course no restaurants on the way where travelers could get a cup of coffee or tea. Every day, they would travel a few miles, staying overnight with friends or relatives, before continuing. Their first stop was at Kallmaṇḍkur, where we used to own some property, with a GSB (Gauda Sarasvat Brahmana) tenant. Next stop was at Puñjālkaṭṭe, home of Mathura Madhava's niece. Her husband, Govind Bhat, was a priest at the local GSB Krishna temple. On the third day, they reached Dharmasthaḷa, which is about 41 miles (66 km) from Mulki as the crow flies. In Dharmasthaḷa, they stayed with comedian Hāsyagāru Bāppu Bhat, a well-known stage personality. It is interesting to note here the different types of popular entertainment available in the district. There were many plays in which the comedian was quite famous. *Tāḷa maddaḷe*, *harikathā*, *yakṣagāna*, and *gombeyāṭa* (puppetry) were other popular forms of entertainment available in the district (Karanth 1993; 1997; Kamath 1995). The Ganesh *Yakṣagāna Gombeyāṭa* troupe of Kogga Kamath of Uppinakudru, with a tradition extending over four generations of artists, was quite famous. Between 1910 and 1915, there were about thirty such string-puppet troupes in the district. Each of the rich temples in the district used to maintain a *yakṣagāna* troupe that would go on tour part of the year. The cost of maintaining such groups have become prohibitive, leading to their demise. Movies (introduced in the 1920s), radio, and—later—television have replaced these earlier forms of entertainment, whose continued existence appears uncertain. The revival of *yakṣagāna* by noted Kannada author Kota Shivarama Karanth and others, and its school at Mahatma Gandhi Memorial College in Udupi, is a hopeful sign for this art form. The Dharmasthaḷa temple gave the pilgrims rice, lentils, and other commodities to cook their own food according to the rules of ritual purity and caste regulations. The return was equally long, and the whole trip was quite an adventure. My father got smallpox as a boy; he survived the experience and was left with pockmarks on his face and body. During his illness, he amused himself drawing sundry objects and figures, which helped him eventually develop creditable artistic skills. I have been told that some of his drawings of the gods and goddesses of Hindu mythology survived their transport to Udupi. Apparently, they were quite good, though they were relegated to the smoke-filled attic in Ananthayya's house and eventually consigned to flames. I do not ever remember seeing them. Before he left Mulki as a boy of 15, my father once molded out of clay a Gaṇapati and painted it for the Cavati festival. It was good enough to meet all the ritual requirements and used in the religious ceremonies. My father was also quite good at painting with watercolors.

My father grew up in Mulki in a large joint family of temple priests. When he was a little boy, my grandfather Madhava shared the ancestral house with his elder brother, Vasudeva. It is only later that the house was divided, *vāṇṭe jālle*, between the two brothers in about 1916. Perhaps Vasudeva thought that his younger brother was not contributing enough for the upkeep and maintenance of the joint family, and they decided to split their assets. The inherited *paryāya* rights of the family in the temple were kept undivided; the nonperforming brother would be compensated financially from the earnings of the worship. The rooms of the house were divided with the front *jagali* (veranda) held in common. Later, Madhava mortgaged his section of the house to his elder brother, and then sold it to him outright when he could not free it from the mortgage. Madhava and his family left Mulki for good in about April 1923, after having become essentially bankrupt and not knowing where their next meal was going to come from.

Narayana was the first person in the family to get an "English"—a Western—education. Madhava and his elder brother had a basic education of a few years in school followed by many years of training at home in Sanskrit and in the details of *karmāṅga* (priestcraft). They learned mantras in Sanskrit, and also the related procedures for performing worship at the temple from the specialized books of *Āgama śāstra*. They could also read the simple Sanskrit of the epics and translate it into Konkani, our mother tongue, for the laypeople. Such *purāṇa sāṅgcẽ* (recitation of epics), usually commissioned in the rainy season by rich clients, brought additional income to the priests. In addition, they had to learn to conduct the rites-of-passage ceremonies such as birth, initiation (*upanayana*), marriage, and funerals. Vasudeva was considered something of a Sanskrit scholar, a poet, and certainly knew more Sanskrit than Madhava. He composed two devotional poems in Sanskrit, in honor of Lord Narasimha and the Kāla Bhairava, invoked as the Oracle. They are "*Ugra Narasiṁhāṣṭaka*" and the "*Āveśa Kālabhairavāṣṭaka*," respectively. He also had more savvy in business, legal matters, and dealings with the local government bureaucracy than his younger brother did. Both of them could speak and read the local language, Kannada, and speak the local dialect, Tuḷu. Young men in priests' families accompanied their elders to the different ceremonies as assistants and got on-the-job training. Once their elders decided that they knew enough, they could officiate on their own. It is sad that in most cases, what they knew was learned by rote, with little knowledge or understanding of the true import of what they were doing in these ceremonies. They could conduct worship at the temple only after they got married. Hence, young priests got married in their late teens. Because widowers could not officiate in the temple, priests in our families also had to find a new wife after the death of their current spouse if they wanted to continue as a temple priest.

Dayananda (Dayya Mhanthu) was the only son of Vasudeva, Madhava's elder brother. It was decided by his father that he would become a priest. I am not sure whether he completed a high school education. For some reason, maybe because of Madhava's misadventures as a priest and his mismanagement of his resources, it was decided that Narayana was not going to be a priest and would instead get a secular education. The family had to sell the *āsti* (property) that one of our ancestors had bought to pay off its debts to the temple. The reason for giving up the family profession, as succinctly stated by my father in Konkani, was this: One must have rice for the belly (*Poṭṭā śīta poḍkā navẽ*). It is also possible that Ananthayya, his maternal grandfather, could have influenced this choice. The earnings of a priest were inconstant and barely enough to survive on. With an "English" education, one could get a government job, a steady salary with a pension in old age, and some social standing as a government servant, or officer, as they were usually called. Such a job certainly held a better future than the *bhaṭṭa vyāpti* (priesthood) did. This was the way that my grandfather's branch of the family moved into secular professions, away from the gossipy, parochial town of Mulki, into the wide world beyond.

Narayana grew up in the family home in Mulki, living there till June 1922. He was educated at the Mulki Board Elementary School up to the second standard, and at the Mulki Mission Secondary School from the third to the eighth standard, or the third form. He moved to Udupi in June 1922 to join the Christian high school for further studies, to obtain his secondary school–leaving certificate (SSLC). He stayed with his maternal grandparents, Ananthayya and Sri Devi. He was excellent at his studies, always at the top of his class, earning outstanding grades in all subjects. He got a good grounding in English and could speak and write legal documents in that language, in spite of a lack of college education. He very much wanted to go to college but could not afford to do so. The district headquarters at Mangalore was the only place where college education was available. The support that Narayana got from his maternal grandfather, Ananthayya, was half-hearted because he had hopes of training Narayana as an apprentice. Ananthayya had transferred to Narayana an insurance policy worth 1,330 rupees, quite a large sum in those days. He told Narayana that the money could be used for his college education; however, he would have to move to Mangalore with his parents and two sisters and would not be able to come back if things did not work out. One possibility was for them to run a boardinghouse, with Bhavani doing all of the cooking and cleaning, and taking in student boarders. After much discussion, this possibility was considered to be too risky, and Narayana gave up any hope of going to college and decided to apprentice himself to Ananthayya. Later on in life, he had hoped to take correspondence courses to earn a college degree; however, this did not work out for a number of reasons. As is the custom in Brahman families, a horoscope was cast at his birth to predict his future and whether the new baby would have any bad effects on the fortunes of his family. The astrologer is supposed to have predicted a good future with aptitude for a medical education specializing in surgery. However, he was silent about whether money would be available for the child's education, and so were the stars and planets. My father was too poor to afford college or medical school; however, he did show an aptitude for the study and practice of law. He was certainly good at appreciating and learning the fine points of law, with an almost total recall for them and for all manners of forensic transactions. Lawyers used to consult him on complicated legal cases. Some time after finishing high school, he changed his last name to *Bhatji*. As I mentioned elsewhere in this book, in the GSB community, the priests are treated as second-class citizens, the butt of many Konkani jokes, usually centered on their poverty and lack of education. Hence, some Bhats change their names to *Sharma*, a correct Sanskrit designation for a Brahman, or add an honorific such as *-ji*, as in the case of my father. My maternal uncle, Padmanabha, changed his last name to *Sharma*, certainly a more stylish designation. As regards my father, later on in life, he was always called Bhatji, with no mistaking who was being referred to.

My Parents Marry

Madhava had suggested to his cousin Vedu that her daughter Sharada would make a good wife for his son Narayana. This was at Sharada's birth when Narayana was seven and was tantamount to a promise. A promise was one thing; however, the question of whether fate approved of the marriage was an entirely different matter. The one sure way of consulting fate was astrology. Nethru Mhāva accompanied by one of her male relatives came to Udupi to offer Sharada's horoscope for consideration by Madhava and his wife Bhavani.

There is a strict protocol to be followed in all wedding negotiations. Because Nethru was a widow, she could not submit the horoscope; a male relative had to start the negotiations. The bride's family tacitly acknowledges the dominance of the groom's family by making the first move. The favorite astrologers of both families were consulted, and they declared that the horoscopes matched, ensuring much connubial bliss and many children. This was followed by negotiations on dowry, jewelry and saris for the bride, and other material details. All parties in a traditional Hindu wedding, while extolling its virtues in conformity with the codes of law, also participate in some hardheaded bargaining for cash and material assets. With all these matters settled to the satisfaction of both sides, Narayana and Sharada were married in Mulki at the bride's home on February 14, 1929. Narayana was 23 and Sharada was 16. Sharada's married name was Laxmidevi, which was the name of the wife of Lord Narayana in Hindu mythology. There is a complete makeover of the Hindu bride on marriage. She gets a new married name and joins the clan, *gotra*, of her husband. This is the reason girls are not listed in natal family trees. The wedding took place just before the fortunes of the bride's father, Subba Bhat, imploded to next to nothing. (See Chapter 3, "My Maternal Grandparents," for details.) In spite of the impending gloom and doom, the wedding was a grand affair lasting five days. The groom's party came by bus from Udupi. They were entertained royally by the bride's family with daily oil baths (*tellā nhāṇa*), elaborate breakfasts with several dishes, *pejje jevaṇa* (elevenses) at midmorning, lunch with more food, *tiffin* (snacks) at 4 in the afternoon, and dinner at night, followed by more snacks for the really brave and doughty. It is customary to prepare *hāppoḷu, pāppoḍu,* and *vōḍi* (deep-fried crunchy savories), especially for the wedding feasts. A few oversized items, with the name of the bride and the groom pricked into them in Kannada script, were also made just for the married couple. The *hāppoḷu* and *pāppoḍu* with the groom's name are served to the bride, and vice versa. The ceremony of a Hindu wedding lasts only a few hours and can be shortened even further. In the olden days, when travel was difficult, the family get-together was artificially extended to last three, five, or even seven days, to the ultimate ruin of the bride's poor father! The bride's father is always a willing accomplice in these conspicuous expenses that he could not afford, because of his desire to live up to a real or imagined standing in the community. Auxiliary ceremonies involving ceremonial music (*vājjapa*), waving of lights (*ārti*), and benedictions (*śesa bhorcẽ*) were added to the procedure, enabling the attending women to show off their new jewelry and saris, arrange marriages, or indulge in gossip (*pañcādikā*). Till recently, the bride and groom were children married at a very young age. Hence, many games suited to their age, including hide-and-seek, throwing flower bouquets at each other, hunting for a ring in colored water (*vokkuḷa kheḷcẽ*), and others of that type came into vogue (Kudva 1978, Appendix I and II). It is traditional to poke fun at some elders in the family at weddings, breaking the strict protocol of respect for age. The bride's maternal uncle leads the bride into the wedding enclosure and gives her a gift (*uḍgirẽ*). Madhava's elder brother, Vasudeva, did the honors and presented Sharada with a gold sovereign. It is also customary to put a garland of the crisp *vaḍo* round his neck to "honor" him and make him look a trifle ridiculous. Vasudeva was known for his quick temper and did not take kindly to the garland, seeing it as an affront to his dignity. Usually, the groom's party act high and mighty at weddings, in keeping with their dominant status. In the evenings, they would be served a decoction of marijuana (*bhāṅgī pānaka*), to make them look ridiculous under the influence and thus bring them down a notch or two. Because alcohol is forbidden to a Brahmana, pot was an accepted mood-altering substitute to smooth one's way in life. These customs have fallen into abeyance now. These days, Hindu weddings last only for a few hours; the guests get a *tiffin* (snack) and one meal, and then are promptly dispatched on their way. Subba Bhat lived up to the Hindu tradition of the bride's father spending more than he could afford on a daughter's wedding, thus driving himself into debt and penury. The formal entry of the bride into the groom's home, *ghara bharāvaṇi*, was celebrated at our ancestral home in Mulki, which Madhava had left in 1923. At the end of these festivities, the groom's party went back to Ananthayya's home in Udupi. Laxmidevi was quite happy in her new home, with all the privileges of a married Hindu woman, showing off her jewelry, dressed in colorful *sāris*, and wearing flowers in her hair. She used to say that it would have been nice to enjoy all of those perks for a few more years before having any children. However, the happy times were rudely interrupted by my appearance on the scene in the summer of 1930, at her parental home in Mulki. I was of course very welcome as a first-born male child in a Hindu family; however, there was always a tinge of regret for her lost youth in my mother's voice.

New Bride in a Joint Hindu Family

My mother moved in with her husband's family, which had been living in Ananthayya's house since 1923. Here there were three generations of a joint Hindu family under one roof. When I was born, there were four generations living together, under the benevolent despotism of Ananthayya's wife, Sri Devi. Madhava and his wife and children were not happy because they did not have a home of their own. After all, they had been living as guests of Ananthayya and his wife for the preceding six years. My grandmother Bhavani did all the cooking, cleaning, and related household work, as a general-purpose maid.

Sri Devi decided to take it easy and slept most of the time, complaining of various arthritic aches and pains. However, she never let anyone forget who was the real boss. My father did the document writing for Ananthayya, who had assumed a strictly supervisory role. It is true that Ananthayya and his wife had offered Madhava and his family a roof over their head when they had nowhere else to go. Yet they were looking forward to the day when they could afford a home of their own and move out. My father often said, "A meager life of *peja-mīṭa* (rice gruel with salt) in one's own home is better than being a guest in someone else's house."

In the meantime, there was the young bride, my mother, to be trained and molded. This process, sanctioned by years of custom and tradition in a joint Hindu family, is an exercise in dominance and power. The play of power dynamics in a joint Hindu family is discussed in Chapter 1, "Prabhus of Siddhapur," so only a few highlights are repeated here for continuity. The proper training of a Hindu girl to be an ideal wife and mother begins early in her home and never ends. This indoctrination leaves its stamp on most girls for life, killing any initiative and instilling an undue respect for seniority. The young girl's mother and senior women in the family teach her to endure the tyranny of the mother-in-law, not talk back, and to behave with becoming modesty in all her dealings. Any rebellious acts or assertion of rights is considered bad behavior, bound to reflect adversely on the poor girl's upbringing and to dishonor her natal family. In the husband's home, the elder women of the family, joined by younger sisters-in-law and any other woman who can get away with it, form a dominant power coalition that gangs up on the bride to train her properly. The bride's upbringing by her own mother is considered inadequate and is, for all practical purposes, declared null and void. The bride is subordinate with no leverage or power at all. She might complain to her husband, who might or might not listen to her problems. The women in this clique resent their loss of power over their favorite son/brother/nephew and any influence over him by the upstart bride. Their coercion can range from casual insensitive words to physical abuse, though my mother did not experience any of the latter. Birth of a few children (read: boys) adds to the status of the bride as the mother of a new generation, precious to any family. This confers power on her. Finally, when her sons grow up, earn and contribute to the family income, marry and bring home a new bride, the properly trained bride morphs into a tough mother-in-law, prepared to repeat the same cycle of dominance and control over her daughters-in-law. A Hindu joint family, its dominance hierarchy, and the abuse of power inherent to it are facts of life that can never be ignored or papered over with platitudes. There are, of course, exceptions, and kind mothers-in-law who treat the new bride as their own daughter. These must be a rare breed indeed. Most mothers-in-law, however, live up to their formidable reputation in the mythology of a joint Hindu family.

Madhava and Family Move to Their New Home

By 1933, my father had earned and saved enough money to buy a house. However, Madhava's unpaid gambling debts in Mulki could have caused a problem if Narayana had bought a house in his own name. The lenders could have legally possessed the house to satisfy the monies due, simply because Narayana, as Madhava's son, was responsible for the debt. Hence, Ananthayya bought our present house for 3,500 rupees from Narayana's earnings at an auction, and then deeded it to Narayana as a gift, or *dharmaśāsana*. This house is situated opposite Anathayya's in Tenkupet. Madhava and his family moved to our present home on June 2, 1933, at an auspicious time determined by astrologers. My three aunts, Manorama, Mohini, and Sushila, were also part of our family in the move. It is traditional for the woman of the house to light a fire in the new home, boil milk till it overflows, and then drink it with something sweet. This is a bit of sympathetic magic, supposed to ensure plenty and happiness in the new home. This was followed by a Gaṇahoma, or invocation and worship of Śrī Gaṇapati, for good luck and future happiness in the new home. I do not remember any of these events, as I was 3 years old at the time.

The house our family moved into was quite large, with four main sections in the front around a quadrangle, with a second quadrangle and more attachments at the back. Traditional Hindu homes are built around a large open quadrangle; we had two of them in the front and back, with the main part of the house forming the common arm of the two quadrangles. The house faced east, an auspicious direction, and the street in front, which runs north to south, is called Tenkupet, or South Street. This street is so named because it is south of the Śrī Kṛṣṇa temple, the reference point for the topography of Udupi, as its most famous landmark. At the entrance to the house was a two-story building with a sunken passageway (*naḍo*), with veranda (*jagali*), rooms on both sides, and a shop (*āṅgaḍi*) at its north end. A narrow veranda with low wooden railings ran along the front of the house, a good vantage point for observing any public celebrations or festivals. If it was a religious procession, a bronze lamp (*divli*) would be kept on the veranda so that *ārti* could be offered when a palanquin containing an image of a deity passed by. The room to the north of the entry passage was used for storage. It had many Chinese ceramic jars, three to four feet tall, used for pickles of various types. The pickled vegetables were small, tender mangoes, or *āmbuli*; unripe mango, or *āmbo*; tender bamboo shoots, or *kīrlu*; jungle jackfruit, or *pāspoṇosu*; and unripe jackfruit, or *poṇsā sāla*. These jars were dark brown, with dragons rampant on the sides, and must have contained imported confectionary sugar called Chinese sugar. They had close-fitting wooden lids, and it was customary to float a layer of oil on top of the brine to prevent spoilage. After a jar was closed, a piece of cloth folded in several layers was put on it and tied securely at the neck with a stout string to keep the roaches out. I do not know where these jars are now; perhaps they cracked or were thrown out because they were thought to be of no use.

The shop used to be rented as a grocery store. The first tenant did not pay the rent for many years, and my father finally filed a suit against him for the rent. He would have been sent to jail for the debt, but the day before his sentencing, my father withdrew the case, out of pity for the tenant. I always admired my father for this act of kindness and charity. Our second tenant was Mr. Kini, whose grocery did quite well. This was the gentleman whom I mentioned in Chapter 1 ("Prabhus of Siddhapur") who used old U.S. newspapers for packaging groceries—the very newspapers in which I read about the adventures of Li'l Abner and other comic-strip characters.

The veranda on the south side of the entrance was a favorite afternoon napping spot for my grandfather Madhava. With him, this was almost a sacred rite, during which the grandchildren were supposed to make no noise. However, we were a rambunctious lot, with too much unruly excess energy that found an outlet in much noise and laughter. Madhava would finally give up, get up from his nap, and go to a local GSB hotel for his afternoon coffee. He would return with some sweets, such as *halvā* (dessert made from wheat, sugar, and clarified butter) or *mysurpāk* (dessert made with chickpea flour, sugar, and clarified butter), for his grandchildren.

There was a well at the back of the front building that was used for water for the kitchen. The second story of this front building was called *vassarte māḷi,* where menstruating women were segregated from the family for three days to conform to rules of ritual purity. After a bath on the fourth day, they were back among their families. The rules of *anvāḷpaṇa* (ritual purity) used to be observed strictly in our family in those days because once in a while Madhava officiated as a priest in the Mulki temple. We have given up these traditions now, because no one in our family is a working priest.

There was a small cupboard under the steps leading to the second story, where we used to store the kerosene supply for the house. It was bought in tins and pumped out using a small locally made tin pump. We used to suspend erasers, tied to a string, in the kerosene, which was supposed to make them soft and pliable. There was a large bedroom to the south of the passageway and an open veranda in the front. This front part of the house was replaced in the 1940s by a single-story front office for my father, plus an attached bedroom. A new foundation for a grocery shop was put up, but the shop was never built.

The front of the house led to another veranda, running east to west, where for *upanayana* and weddings, a temporary enclosure (*māṇtvi*) used to be erected. This veranda led to the main part of the house, another building with bedrooms, a family shrine (*devākūḍa*), a kitchen and dining area, and a second story (*māḷi*). A small room upstairs was my study and bedroom, where I had some privacy. Next to the main building, running east to west, was another section with an open veranda to the east, right behind the shop and a series of rooms at the back. For many years, we rented this part to a GSB family. Mats made from plaited coconut fronds used to be erected at the borders of open verandas of the house during the monsoon season to prevent rain from getting in. My own feeling is that in those days, we got more heavy rain than what we do now. I have not seen one of these screens in ages.

These four buildings enclosed the front quadrangle of the house, *āṅgaṇa*, at the center of which was a *tulasī*, or holy basil plant, in a *tulasī kāṭṭẽ* (special raised platform for basil) found in almost every Hindu home. Hindu women usually water, apply *kuṅkuma* (scarlet red powder usually applied by women to the *tiḷo*, the auspicious beauty spot on their forehead) to the plant, and circumambulate it, morning and evening, and light a small lamp next to it at night. The holy basil represents a virtuous woman of Hindu mythology, Tulasī. For more on this story and the worship of the holy basil, see Appendix 6, "Feasts and Festivals," Tulasī Vivāha/Pūjā.

At the west end of the building we used to rent out, was our bathroom, which was next to a second well, an open enclosure where maids, *kāmā ceḍũ*, used to wash pots and pans and clothes. Next to the well was the cowshed (*koḍkẽ*) running north to south and enclosing a second *āṅgaṇa* at the back of the house. In that quadrangle, we had a fig (*anjūra*) tree, a tree sorrel (*bimbula*) with bunches of sour *bimbula*, and a curry-leaf (*karbevu*), also known as sweet neem tree. When there were weddings or *upanayana* at our home, professional cooks used to set up their temporary kitchen in the front part of the *koḍkẽ* to prepare food for the communal feasts. When I was in high school, this old *koḍkẽ* was pulled down and a new one with a second-story storage area for hay was put up at right angles to it. In those days, it was difficult to get good milk from vendors, because they usually added water to it. My mother finally gave up the struggle to get good milk, and we bought cows and a she-buffalo. My mother got quite attached to her cattle, so whenever some of them got sick and died, for her it was like losing a member of the family.

Beyond the old cowshed was the backyard (*hittala*). There used to be a small house there, which we used to rent out. It stood empty for many years and was finally pulled down. In the backyard were many coconut and areca-nut palms, watered manually from the well by small irrigation channels leading to each palm. Maintaining them was my grandfather Madhava's hobby and specialty. There were many fruit trees: mango, jackfruit, jungle jackfruit, and starfruit, or carambola. The carambola tree was a favorite spot for the local parrots, who loved the sour fruit. I had hopes of snaring a parrot and keeping it as a pet; however, they were too clever, so I never caught one. This part of the backyard was later bought by my sister Lalitha and her husband after he retired from Calcutta. They dug a well there and built a house. There was a mud wall at the boundary of our property, behind which was a lane, too narrow for regular traffic.

Ours was a joint Hindu family, with Madhava and Bhavani as the nominal heads because they were its elders. My father, Narayana, as the sole breadwinner, however, had the final say in major decisions affecting family finances. He could and did veto some of Madhava's knee-jerk responses to problems. There was some question about the boundary between our property and that of our neighbors to the south. The dispute was over a few inches of land and the exact location of the boundary wall. Madhava wanted to mount a legal challenge, which was vetoed by my father. A civil court case would only enrich the lawyers, waste money that could be gainfully used, and beggar both the litigants. Many years earlier, this had happened to Madhava and his brother Vasudeva, who lost our Kallmaṇḍkur property in payment for the legal expenses of a mindless court case. Madhava never learned from this experience. For him, any dispute was a macho encounter that could be resolved only by the total defeat of the opponent. Because hand-to-hand combat was illegal, the only available venue was a court of law, where a civil suit could be fought at great expense. My father and our neighbor ended up settling the dispute by binding arbitration, which cost nothing.

Goa Trip, 1935: Exiles Visit Their Family Deity

My parents lost a baby boy within a few days of birth because of some infection that had no cure at that time. My sister Lalitha was born in 1934, when I was 4 years old. When she was about a year old, my parents, Lalitha, Madhava, and I went to Goa to visit our Kuladevī Mahālasā temple at Mardol. This was a pilgrimage, in fulfillment of a vow by someone in our family, perhaps during my mother's illness and stay at the local mission hospital. Madhava, as an experienced traveler, was our facilitator on this journey. I remember being awakened very early in the morning, and then going through all of the hustle and bustle before departure. From home we went to Malpe, the local port, to embark on a coastal steamer anchored a few miles away from the shore. We and our luggage were put aboard a wildly pitching open boat for the trip to the steamer. To climb aboard, you had to time your move, attempting to catch the ladder to the steamer at the right moment and hoping for a dry transfer. It was near Christmas, the weather was cold, and we spread our bedding and blankets in the hold of the ship, where it was relatively warm. The bedding and our belongings defined our territory for the duration of trip. Next to us was a group of Muslim men, also bound north, perhaps to Bombay and beyond. From their dress and deportment, it was obvious that they were Muslim. During mealtime, I was fascinated to seeing them eat from a common dish, which is a no-no in a Hindu family. As a child full of curiosity, I was totally mesmerized by what I saw as strange behavior, and I remember staring at them forever, until one of the men kindly offered me the food he was eating with his fingers. Accepting it was of course out of the question, as that represented an even bigger no-no. We had brought some food from home, along with lots of fruit. Before we disembarked at Goa, there was much noise on the docks, with strings of firecrackers going off and other signs of jollity, probably because people were anticipating Christmas.

In Goa, we stayed at the home of the temple priest, where we slept and had our meals. The house had a thatched roof, without even some of the conveniences we were used to at our home in Udupi, which itself was not modern. Fresh, washed banana leaves would be spread on the floor over shallow depressions at each diner's place. The depressions helped to confine the liquids to the limits of the banana leaf and made eating much more manageable, especially for children. It takes some skill and manual dexterity to eat off a flat banana leaf spread on the floor without making a mess of boiled rice and many liquid side dishes. At night, we spread the bedding and blankets we had brought with us in the front veranda of the house. There were a few *bīlã* (holes) in the floor through which *koḷvindūru* (bandicoots, or large feral rats) or snakes could come out and go exploring at night. To prevent any such eventuality, the bedding was placed completely covering any holes. We did not use any mosquito nets. I am amazed that I grew up in India, left India when I was 26, and have been there on visits, without ever having contracted malaria. Must be blind luck!

The old Mahalasa temple of our Kuladevata was at a place called Vernem or Verna. It was destroyed by Captain Diogo Fernand, of the Rachol Fort, on March 7 and then again on March 14, 1567, ostensibly to provide the Portuguese state with its timber and priceless wooden carvings (see Appendix 8, "Goa: A Paradise Lost?"). The stone image of the goddess was saved by the faithful and left in the care of a *gorovu* (cowherd) for safekeeping. The descendants of this caretaker used to greet the newly arrived pilgrims; inquire about their *gotra* (clan), their *paika* (family name), family antecedents, and their present place of residence; and formally announce to the goddess that such-and-such family had returned for a visit from exile. This first visit by the pilgrims was called *dhūḷi bheṭa* (dust visit), because they came to visit the temple as travelers, without first washing the dust from their feet or having had a bath, as is usually done before a temple visit. It was a moving ceremony, reminding the visitors of their past life in Goa, persecutions, exile, the hardships they endured, the faith and allegiance they owed to their family deity, and the thrill of return for a visit. On our last pilgrimage to the temple in 1999, I had hoped to participate in this ceremony with my wife and son. Unfortunately, I found that the ceremony was no longer observed at the temple. The management of the temple had decided that the descendants of the cowherds were not relevant and had gotten rid of them. Thus do we forget history, traditions, and ceremonies and are the poorer for it.

At the Mahalasa temple, newly married couples on their first visit go through a second marriage ceremony. This is conducted at the temple *talẽ* (pond). The couple go through a brief wedding, complete with musical accompaniment (*vājjapa*). A corner of the husband's *āṅgso* (shawl) and the wife's *varla* (end of her *sāri*) are tied together, they circumambulate the pond, and then they visit the temple as newly married couple. I remember seeing my parents remarry in 1935, and my son saw my wife and I remarry on our visit to Goa in 1974. I also remember that the state of art of the musical accompaniments in the temple was atrocious. Whether it was due to the influence of the Portuguese or to a lack of contact and cultural exchange with other parts of India, the music was just terrible. Perhaps those musicians did not know what good traditional music on a *nāgasvaram* (a South Indian oboe-like wind instrument) was supposed to sound like.

Life in a Joint Hindu Family

My childhood was quite happy. As the firstborn son in a Hindu family, I was cherished and spoiled. We were neither rich nor poor; I suppose we could have been classified as lower middle class. I never felt any wants, either for food or clothing. We had a couple of maids for cleaning the house, washing clothes and dishes, and helping my mother with the two cows and the she-buffalo in the cowshed. Ours was a joint Hindu family, with all of the advantages and problems that such an arrangement entailed. The advantages were continuity and stability. Children absorbed family and community traditions as well as religious beliefs by a process of osmosis, without a set program of religious indoctrination. The presence of an older generation that had been through many illnesses and through the major and minor crises of everyday life was reassuring for the younger people. The older generation, with the wealth and power vested in them, maintained a benevolent supervisory position over the whole family. They spoiled the grandchildren, serving as a buffer between them and the stricter disciplinarian parents.

The disadvantages of a joint family were many. Those in the younger generation had to wait for many years before they can assume responsibility for major decisions and become truly mature. Any initiative shown by the young could be stifled, and their ambition could be thwarted by an older generation set in its ways. It is usually the young daughters-in-law who bear the brunt of subordinate status in a joint family; they are ruled by an authoritative mother-in-law. The dynamics of interpersonal push and pull in a joint Hindu family is determined by the power struggle between these two. These are discussed at length in Chapter 1, "Prabhus of Siddhapur," in the context of general pursuit of power by humans. These tensions were there in our family, always just below the surface. As a child, I was never aware of these emotional undercurrents until they burst forth full blown. Looking back on these childhood memories, I see these events as struggle for power between my mother, the daughter-in-law, and my grandmother, *Ānnammā*, as the mother-in-law of the classic joint Hindu family. Because my grandfather Madhava and my maternal grandmother, Vedu, were parallel cousins, Madhava and his wife, Bhavani, were uncle and aunt to my mother. In spite of such close family ties, my mother and grandmother had differences of opinion over trivia, too silly to mention. I guess I was too little to sense these tensions brewing, before they broke out into the open. For me as a child, these were the most painful episodes of my childhood. I used to dread these events. Somehow, they broke out in the open in the evenings, after everyone had had their dinner. My father would be resting in an easy chair (also called a beach chair), and the case for the prosecution would be made by my grandmother and grandfather. My mother would put up a stout defense, the best she could, supplemented by tears. My father would listen impassively because he, poor man, was torn between his duty to his parents and love for his wife. I do not know whether there was any resolution to these quarrels. Perhaps, they allowed each side to blow off steam till the next blowup.

However, they made the early years of my mother's married life unhappy. Her unhappiness, mental tension, and worry perhaps resulted in some psychosomatic problems that she mistook for heart or lung disease. She complained about chest pains, and her self-diagnosis of heart or lung problems led to a dire prognosis of early death. She was convinced that she was going to die young and was worried about the futures of her son and daughter. I must have been 5 or 6 years old at the time, because my sister Lalitha was a baby carried around by my mother. To the north of our house, there was a small school with a garden and play area, separated from our house by a narrow lane. We three went to the school garden so that my mother could talk to me in private. With tears in her eyes, my mother told me about pains in the left side of her chest. She did not expect to live long. She knew that my father would have a second wife, the dread stepmother of Hindu myth and legend, and expected less-than-fair treatment from her for her children, so she wanted me to take good care of my little sister and of myself. After so many years, I still remember this scene in the garden of the little school. This was all too much for a boy of 5 or 6 to handle. I remember how bad I felt, how my eyes were filled with tears, and how inadequate was any comfort I could offer my mother. I am glad that my mother's worries proved to be groundless. She lived to have many more children and to watch them grow to be adults. It was far into the future, that my grandmother, *Ānnammā*, relinquished control over the day-to-day management of the family to my mother. The power struggle between mother-in-law and daughter-in-law is a fact of life in joint Hindu families and is the source of many of its problems. This problem is much attenuated or nonexistent these days for a variety of reasons. Joint families are breaking up, with sons not following their father's trade or profession and moving away from their family home. Holiday visits can be short and sweet, not long enough for the traditional belligerents to draw their line in the sand, prepare their defenses, and plan their tactics before they shout, "Fire!" Women of the younger generation are better educated, earn a substantial part of family income, and are made of sterner stuff than their counterparts in earlier generations. The traditional mother-in-law has learned the new lay of the land, the new power deployment, and has less control over the more assertive modern daughter-in-law. All of these changes are for the better.

My Parents' Beliefs and Customs

My father's beliefs and customs were those of a Hindu of his generation brought up in an orthodox Brahman family of temple priests. The beliefs of his childhood remained essentially unchanged throughout his life. Hinduism also taught him to respect and show tolerance for other religions and beliefs, because Hindus believe that Truth is One, though people call it by different names. Life in a priest's family was circumscribed by additional rules and prohibitions not observed by other Hindus. The diet was strictly vegetarian, with no fish or eggs. Milk and other dairy products could be used in abundance, along with cereals, to provide proteins in the diet. Onions and garlic were prohibited. In addition, there are myriads of customs and usages that are best learned by growing up with them rather than by studying them in a book. After my father's *upanay-*

ana in 1917, his head was close-cropped or shaved except for a tuft of hair (*śeṇḍi*) on the crown of his head. He kept the tuft throughout his life, covered under a black cap. He dressed in a full-length white dhoti worn by Brahmans in a style called *pañcakāsa*. He wore a long, white *jibbā*, or shirt, over a thin muslin undershirt, along with open leather sandals. This dress was cool in hot weather and enabled one to sit on the floor cross-legged. When it rained, the dhoti could be tucked up to the knees so that it did not get wet or muddy. At home he would wear a shorter piece of white cloth round his waist called a *muṇḍa*. He also wore the sacred threads (*jānnuvē*), one as a bachelor and two as a married man. The sacred thread was changed once a year at the thread-changing festival (*suttā punnava*) or on special occasions for purification from ritual pollution. Once in a while he participated in a special purification ceremony called *mantra mudrādhāraṇa*, conducted periodically by the head of Kāśī Maṭha, the guru of the lineage to which we belong. In this ceremony, small, stylized metal representations of the four emblems of Viṣṇu—*śaṅkha*, *cakra*, *gadā*, and *padma*—are heated in embers, and their impressions are left on the arms and chest for men and on the forearms for women and children. As a young man, he used to perform the daily twilight worship, *sandhi*, in the morning, along with the recitation of the Gāyatri. He discontinued this practice in later years because of the pressure of work and lack of time. In his retirement, he started conducting evening worship, which lasted about an hour and consisted of the recitation of *stotra*, or songs of praise of God in Sanskrit and Kannada. These prayers were a great source of comfort for him in his old age. They were part of his religious obligations as an orthodox Hindu, earned him religious merit (puṇya) in this life and a comfortable old age, and would result in a good rebirth after an easy death without any lingering illness.

He believed in astrology, as regards to both its ability to provide unknown details of past events and to its predictive powers. Astrology occupies a peculiar position in the psyche of contemporary Indians irrespective of religion and education. These beliefs, imported from the Babylonians, the Greeks of Alexandria, and others, have become an integral part of Indian culture and Hindu religion. Even many non-Hindus think that there may be some truth in astrology, and they may consult astrologers as a last resort. There were, of course, famous Indian astrologers and astronomers of antiquity who further developed the import from the West and recast it all in Sanskrit, to give it added sanctity and authority. The simple astronomical calculations involved in casting a horoscope and following the planets in the constellations of the zodiac, give it enough of an aura of "science" to impress the believers. Astrology is not a science; it is a matter of belief. There are people who believe in it, and then there are the skeptics who do not. The worship and expiation ceremonies related to the bad influences of the *navagraha* (nine planets), made up of the seven visible planets plus Rāhu and Ketu, have become integral parts of Hindu religion and its rites and ceremonies. These are the ascending and descending nodes where the moon's orbit intersects the plane of the Earth's orbit round the sun. The exact time of birth of a baby is very important for casting its horoscope. The horoscope is closely scrutinized for immediate problems and related expiations, and for contingencies to be expected in the future and their possible outcomes. Astrologers are asked how the child would take to education and studies, the likely profession, acquisition of wealth, prospects for a happy marriage, and children—in short, they are asked to predict the whole life and fortunes of a newborn. The degree of belief in these prognostications varies from person to person. Some believe in frequent consultations with astrologers and will not be involved in important undertakings or business deals without consulting the stars and planets. Others do it pro forma, as a vague nod in the direction of custom and tradition. Some believe that a horoscope may predict a general trend, rather than details, and that hard work and the positive psychological effects of proper expiations can overcome fate. Hence, all fate is not determined by the stars; free will and human effort are very much in effect. The human psyche has problems dealing with the uncertainties of life, so astrology and its predictions provide a measure of comfort because even with all the transactions between the planets that presumably control our fate, humans appear to be in control. The horoscopes of a boy and girl are compared and checked for compatibility of temperament, behavior, character, and so on, before the parents will agree to a marriage. Those rare occasions when astrological predictions turn out to be correct are always remembered, and all of the incorrect predictions are conveniently forgotten and forgiven. Unfortunately, astrology as a belief system has become such an integral part of Hindu religion and customs that anyone not believing in it is accused of being an atheist or a heretic. In his old age, my father prepared a notebook with the details of horoscopes of all members of the family, along with special ceremonies or expiations to be performed at critical times, to ameliorate the baneful influence of the planets.

My father saw astrology as providing a general-purpose database for information on any question troubling people. He implicitly believed that a good astrologer could provide details of what had happened in the past and what will happen in the future. If the predictions were wrong, it meant that the astrologer was not good or knowledgeable. He never questioned whether astrology, by its very nature, could tell anyone anything about the mundane happenings of this world. In this respect, he was very much a traditional, orthodox Hindu. Of course, he was not alone in this implicit belief in the influence of stars and planets in human affairs. Even now in India, people with more education, even in the sciences, still believe in astrology. It is as if they turn off their skepticism when it comes to this ancient belief. Because astrology has become a part of their set of religious beliefs, they consider it sacred and not subject to any scrutiny by common sense or science.

I encountered an example of this when I visited India in 1970s. My parents, my wife, and I went to meet Shilpi Gopal Shenoy in Karkal. He was a self-taught sculptor who had carved many fine pieces in the locally available hard granite. Four granite pillars that he had exquisitely carved in the traditional Hindu style were installed many years ago in the GSB Venkataramana Temple at Karkal. He had also carved many sacred images of Hindu gods for installation in temples. At that time, he and his assistants were working on a monolithic granite statue of Gomateshvara, or Mahavira, a Jain saint, commissioned by the Dharmādhikāri, the Hegde of Dharmasthaḷa, for installation there. The statue was 39 feet (11.9 meters) tall, carved from a single piece of granite and estimated to weigh about 175 tons. I was interested in finding how the sculptor chose the block of granite for carving. He had to make sure that there were no structural faults in the material for it to survive all of the manhandling that it would be subjected to during sculpting and then installation. The sculptor, of course, did not have any tools of modern science, such as ultrasonic testing, to find a block without flaws. My father's prompt answer was that the sculptor consulted an astrologer who would guide him to a spot to locate a suitable block. To him, the planets influenced everything that happens on Earth, and if properly questioned via astrology, they would answer any question put to them. The sculptor, quite an old man at that time, mumbled something and never gave a straight answer, perhaps not wanting to talk about it anyway. I was curious and went to see the mostly finished statue at the granite quarry. This was a big outcropping of granite, quite common in Karkal. It appeared that the sculptor, with plenty of practical experience with granite in that area, appeared to have chosen a spot where the flow of granite was visibly smooth and uninterrupted and thus less likely to contain any faults. I do not know whether the man had consulted an astrologer. He might have, just to reassure everyone that all the proper rites were adhered to and that all bases had been covered. To me, the more practical approach of the sculptor, guided by his experience, makes more sense than appealing to the revelations of planets or stars.

My father was a devotee of the Oracle *darśaṇa*, both at the Mulki temple (see Appendix 7, "The Oracle, or *Darśana Sevā*") and at the temple at Ullala, and other places. The Oracle provided a vehicle for him to convey his current problems, crisis in the family, sickness, and so forth, to a higher power willing to listen to his problems and recommend remedies in the form of *prāyaścitta* (expiations) or adapted standard medical therapies. A pragmatic view of Oracles would call them a form of therapy, where the devotee reports his problems to a higher power, and may be more effective in practice than psychotherapy, depending on one's degree of belief versus skepticism. My father believed in *bhūta* (spirits), *mantravādu* (sorcery and incantations) used against other people, exorcisms, and the whole related belief system that continues to function amongst orthodox Hindus.

My mother's worldview was that of a traditional Hindu girl from an orthodox Brahmana family. She had finished education in the fourth or fifth grade, when her parents decided that she had received all the education she would ever need and kept her at home. My mother could read and understand books in the local language, Kannada, especially those on Hindu mythology or other devotional books. She could not read or understand English. My mother, my grandmother Vedu, and Vedu's elder sister, Nethru Mhava, believed in educating women to enable them to earn a living and be independent of their husband's income, if necessary. My maternal grandfather, Subba, used to beat Vedu once in a while. His five elder brothers used to be more frequent wife beaters, and they also used to verbally abuse their wives, routinely calling them by the *r*-word, which means both "widow" and "whore" (see *rāṇḍa* in the Glossary). These factors made my mother and her elder sister, Tucci Mhava, into ardent feminists who were very supportive of educating their daughters so that they could be financially independent. My mother grew up in comfortable circumstances as the daughter of Subba Bhat, who had a flourishing list of clients, *yajamāna*, for whom he served as the family priest. In addition, he owned property that brought in a yearly income of 150 to 200 *muḍā* of rice, which was quite a substantial amount. After her marriage to my father, she moved to Udupi, where my father lived, about 15 miles north of her birthplace, Mulki. My mother had many pregnancies, resulting in a surviving total of seven boys and six girls. She participated in the usual round of rites, ceremonies, and festivals of a traditional orthodox Hindu home. We did not have any specific religious education corresponding to attending any special classes. Rather, we absorbed religion in the painless osmosis of participating in functions and ceremonies at home, hearing stories of Hindu epics, and observing our elders in action.

My Early Childhood

One of my earliest memories was of my first haircut, or *caulu*. This rite was performed when I was about 3 years old. The barber was *Thomārā* (corruption of *Somavāra*, or Monday, which was perhaps his birthday), our regular barber who used to come to our house when someone needed a haircut or a shave. After my father had had his haircut, I sat in his lap for mine. I was bare-bodied, it was a hot, humid day, and I had a gold chain round my neck with a heart-shaped locket containing some sandalwood paste, *prasādu*, from the Mulki temple for my general protection. I remember vividly the hair clippings sticking to my sweaty body and the morning sun shining on me. We were seated in the veranda parallel and to the north of the house. This was before the present bathroom was built there. Because this was a special occasion, in addition to his regular fee of 4 annas (or one-quarter of a rupee), the barber got some rice, and a couple of coconuts. After a bath, I was taken to the local Śrī Venkaṭaramaṇā temple with the customary offerings of a coconut and five or seven bananas (*nārlu keḷẽ*).

When I was still about the same age, my grandfather Madhava took me swimming in the local temple tank. For some reason, I had a great fascination with water, so he was going to satisfy my curiosity. It was summer, I was bare-bodied, I carried a soapbox, and I was little enough to be carried by my grandfather. On the way, we met an acquaintance, who asked us where we were going, and I remember telling him about the swimming and demonstrating how I was going to pinch my nose to prevent water from going in. I remember the sudden cold of the water later, the water going up my nose despite my pinching it, and my gasping for breath. I have forgotten the rest of this adventure or our trip back home.

A third childhood memory of mine is that of a wedding, most probably that of my aunt Mannakka, taking place at home. In the kitchen, there were piles of sweets ready to be distributed to the guests. I particularly liked licking the sugar syrup hardened on the bottom of a type of sweet, *sāta*. This, of course, was a no-no! While I was busy doing it, my grandfather came into the kitchen to find out what mischief I was up to. His presence interfered with my licking the sugar, and I am supposed to have asked him why was he messing around in the kitchen: "Madhava Bhaṭṭu, *vāsareṇtu kassalyāka gondaḷtā?*" I confess, though I remember licking the sugar off the sweets, that I have forgotten this particular bit of conversation.

The funeral of Haji Abdullaha Sahib (1882–1935), a Muslim notable of Udupi, is another childhood memory. He was a generous philanthropist and a well-liked and respected citizen and was appreciated by the Hindus, Muslims, and Christians to whom he had donated a hospital and many schools and public institutions (Hiriadka and Dundiraj 2001). In 1918 when the price of rice was more than a person with an average income could pay, he imported rice from Rangoon, Burma (now known as Yangon, Myanmar), and sold it to people at cost. The citizens of Udupi remembered his acts of kindness, and during his funeral, a huge throng of people, both Hindu and Muslim, accompanied the coffin to pay their respects. I remember seeing the funeral procession from a grocery shop near our home. Every few steps, people would throw garlands of jasmine, which eventually completely smothered the coffin. I have been told that the coffin was carried by both Hindus and Muslims to honor this pious, generous Muslim who had helped all people irrespective of their religion.

The last memorable incident of my childhood was a visit to our guru, His Holiness Sukrathindra Thirtha, swami of Kāśī Maṭha. My maternal grandfather, Subba Bhat, took my cousin Devaraya and me to see the guru. His holiness wanted to hear a story from one of us. Devaraya was shy and tongue-tied, but I came up with a story I had learned in school. The guru was so pleased that he gave me two apples and a bunch of grapes. In those days, both of those fruits were extremely rare in our district. When we got home, the fruit was divided amongst our large family, each of us getting one slice of apple and one grape.

Our home in Udupi was quite spacious, with two second-story sections, front and back, and much space in the open veranda. During the rainy season, if there was a *samarādhanā* (community feast) in the local GSB temple, food was served on banana leaves (*pāna ghālcê*) to hundreds of people sitting in rows, in all the available space in our home. Volunteers would serve the food and clean up afterward. I remember saying to my folks, "Wouldn't it be nice if all these people could stay and we could eat in their company like this every day?" The childhood self that I remember was a gregarious, confident kid who liked people and company.

My Early Schooling, Grades 1 to 3

I started school when I was 5 years old. At an auspicious time, I went through the formal religious ceremony for *Vidyārambha* (beginning of education; see Appendix 5, "Hindu Rites of Passage"), and was ready to face the world. The municipal girls' school had grades 1 to 8 and was next to the GSB Śrī Venkaṭaramaṇā temple, very close to our home. Though it was called a girls' school, it was coeducational; I was enrolled in it because it was within walking distance from my home. I attended this school for three years from grades 1 to 3. It was essentially, a one-room school with the different grades divided by movable partitions. One long, upstairs room of the present Jogappayya shop, which specializes in dried herbs (*vakdā āṅgaḍi*), was the whole school. The noise level was high, with all the students repeating their lessons after the teachers, and the different grades trying to outdo others in their diligence and earnestness. During summer, when the classrooms were quite hot, a few classes moved to the temple courtyard next door and assembled on the open veranda to the left of temple entrance. Each student had a cloth bag for carrying a slate, its pencil (*kāḍḍi*), and a book or two. I do not think any of us had a rag to wipe the slate; we used our shirtsleeve or shirtfront as an all-purpose slate wiper. I do not remember when we started using paper and pencils; perhaps it was in the third grade. We did not have desks; we sat on low benches and rested the slate on our knees. All of my teachers were women, called *mashterni*. Their names, from grades one to three, were Devi, Nagamma, and Shrimati, who was the youngest and prettiest of the lot. None of them wore the beauty spot (*tīḷo*); they were widows. Teaching was an occupation open to Hindu widows, who could not remarry. For some unknown reason, I had difficulty with the fourth letter of the Kannada alphabet, which we learned in the first grade. In spite of my best efforts, what I wrote on the slate turned out to be a mirror image of its correct form. The teacher was bothered, and so were my parents, who tried all kinds of inducements to correct this problem. Perhaps it was an aberration of some sort in brain–hand coordination; I do not know. In those days, no one knew about such cases; hence, the power structure at school and home thought that the problem was my stubbornness. I remember my mother's desperate attempts and my repeated failures to correct the problem. But somehow I grew out of it. We learned the English alphabet in the second grade, or about age 7. In the same grade, Nagamma *mashterni* brought some candy wrapped in paper one day. She put the package on a low stool at one end of the classroom, and we students assembled in two rows facing each other to form a corridor leading on to the candy. She then blindfolded each student, rotated them clockwise exactly three times, and let them find the candy. There was much shouting, clapping, and other forms of vocal merriment from the class, as the seeker bumped into the rest of the class or went in all random directions. By the time my turn came, I had figured out the system. I rotated counterclockwise thrice, and guided by all the shouting and clapping, I successfully steered my way to the candy. I took home the prize, looking forward to a gigantic feast of candy. Unfortunately, it was strictly rationed, one piece per day over the next few days! Sometime in the second or third grade, the girls' school moved to a big vacant house located in the same street, Tenkupet (South Street), further away from our home. I remember the third grade meeting on the second floor in one big room that we shared with another class. There was a long balcony outside our classroom from which we could look down at the street below. One day, everyone in the classroom, including our teacher, ran to the balcony to look at a funeral procession passing below. A good friend of our teacher's had passed away before her husband as a *suvāsinī* (a married woman whose husband is alive), and I remember the corpse covered with masses of flowers, carried by four men. There was much talk amongst the teachers about the background and virtues of the deceased and about what a pity it was that she had died so young. The girls in the upper grades of the school were a talkative lot whose yak-yakking in class sometimes got out of control. The whole school was sequestered for two extra hours one day as a punishment, which I thought was unfair.

The Christian High School

I transferred to the local Christian high school in 1939 for the fourth grade. This school was founded by the Basel Evangelical Mission (BEM), a German Protestant missionary society in 1896 (Shiri 1985). It was one of the first full high schools in the South Kanara District, offering classes up to the SSLC conferred on a student after he or she passed a government-administered standard examination at about age 16, covering the whole of Madras Presidency. (*Presidency* corresponds to *state*, a geographic and political entity; the usage is a carryover from the rule of the East India Company to that of the British government in 1858.) My father had attended the same school, whose standards of education were considered to be better than the only other alternative available: the education board high school. A few words of explanation are necessary regarding schools run by religious organizations such as BEM or the Jesuits. The teachers were a mix of Christians, Hindus, and Muslims. There was a preference given to teachers belonging to the same Christian denomination as the founders of the school. Most of the students attending these schools are non-Christian, mostly Hindu, and these schools are not free. All students pay the same standard fee, are educated according to a syllabus set by the state, leading to a standard, statewide examination conducted by the education department. They are not free, charity institutions meant for the Christian converts garnered by the missionary effort. Being a Christian or subscribing to the credo of a particular denomination are not requirements for admission to these schools. The requirement that students attend Bible or morals classes once a week constituted the only concession to the Christian orientation of the school.

My father's office was located on the road leading to the high school, and he accompanied me on the morning of my admission to the school. I think it was sometime in July; the monsoons had begun, and the road was wet, the grass was green, and brown muddy water was flowing in the ditches on the side. The school was set in a spacious walled compound of its own, about a mile from my father's office. The school compound was adjacent to the mission hospital founded by the BEM in 1923. The driveway to the school ended in a portico at the entrance where dignitaries arriving by car could alight and be suitably welcomed by the headmaster. There was a garden at the front with crotons and other tropical plants and an exotic palm not native to our district. This palm was a distinguishing feature of the high school that was pointed out to the locals with much admiration and comment as a foretaste of other wonders in store. The headmaster, the Rev. Mark Sanjeeva Rao, was a Sarasvat who had converted to a Protestant faith and was known to my father. After admission, I went to the fourth standard, which I think had two divisions, because all of the students could not be accommodated in one room. The classes were coeducational, with only a few girls who occupied the right-hand front benches facing the teacher. In addition to benches to sit on, the students had desks to put their books and rest their elbows on. The desks with individual compartments for books were a welcome addition compared to the earlier municipal school, where we put our slates and books on our knees. The school was a large, sprawling, two-story building with its own spacious, walled compound. It was built of locally quarried laterite, and it had high ceilings and large windows. There was a large assembly hall on the second floor, usually partitioned into smaller classrooms. The school day began with all of the students and most of the staff members getting together in the assembly room. One of the Christian teachers would read a passage from a Kannada Bible, and then give a short exposition or a sermon. The whole assembly then stood up, and the Christians would pray with the staff member leading, and the rest of us would stand in silence. After the prayer meeting, the students and staff members dispersed to their rooms, and the school day began. The end of each class was marked by the ringing of a large bell hanging from the ceiling, outside the headmaster's office at the entrance to school. The classes ran from 9:30 AM to 12:30 PM and from 1:30 to 4:30 PM, with a lunch break between those two blocks of time. At lunchtime, we walked the couple of miles home, grabbed a bit to eat, and went back to school again. The school was closed for the usual Hindu, Muslim, and Christian religious holidays, along with government public holidays. The school year ended with exams in March or April, and the school was closed for the summer. Heavy monsoon rains with flooding meant special school closings in the July–September monsoon season. During the heavy rains, some students would get wet on purpose so that a kindly teacher would send them home for the day. My father insisted that I wear a mackintosh during the monsoons and a pair of *vhāṇa* (leather sandals) all year round. The raincoat, with its rubber coating, smelled funny, and it was hot and uncomfortable because of the high humidity and warm weather. Besides, it and the *vhāṇa* made me stand out in my class and school, because almost no one wore a raincoat, and all walked barefoot. It was important for me at that age to look like my classmates, and I used to dream up all kinds of excuses for not putting these on. Finally, after some time, my father gave up the struggle with a sigh of resignation.

In my first year at the Christian high school at the end of the monsoons, we got busy preparing for an inspection by some high personage in the state education department. Tables and benches were set up in the open under the mango trees in the school yard, and kids spent many happy hours there preparing bunting for the visit. We had plenty of glue and colored paper to make festive decorations and hang them on long pieces of string. Lessons were suspended for the nonce, and we spent many hours on these arts and crafts projects. Finally, the great day dawned for the visit of this superinspector. The visiting party arrived in a car, accompanied by other dignitaries. We had been instructed to be on our best behavior, to dress nicely, to be silent and attentive. Even the teachers were subdued and solemn. The august personage was a fat gentleman in a Western suit and tie. He walked in the corridors of school with a measured step and a solemn gait, accompanied by the headmaster and the rest of the party. The group would enter a classroom, all of the students and the teacher would stand up till asked to sit down, and the teacher would be suitably obsequious, with a simper on his face. The great man would ask what class it was and would then ask a question pertinent to the subject taught there. If the student chosen at random could answer the question correctly, the teacher and the headmaster breathed a sigh of relief. If not, it was Judgment Day. The year was 1939, and this was the only inspection I remember.

Then there were the war years, and more pressing problems to attend to. When World War II was declared, the German missionaries attached to the high school, mission hospital, and related establishments were declared belligerents and were sent to camps for enemy aliens. I remember a police inspector and a constable coming to our house by car to fetch my father late at night. He had to draw up some legal papers and go through other formalities before the Germans could be sent away. Blackout was imposed at night, and the shades of street lamps were painted black on the outside. There was rationing of food, fuel, and other essential commodities—and various clandestine ways to get hold of them by extralegal means. All prices went up; people grumbled but were powerless to do anything about them. There was a gasoline shortage, and buses were converted to run on charcoal gas generated by a cylindrical contraption fixed to their backs. That is how war came to the small town of Udupi. I remember reading about the end of war in Europe in May 1945. My mother and I, my aunt Tucci Mhāva, all their children, and my cousins Gopalakrishna Bhavaji, and Devaraya formed a large group that went to Sringeri, site of the famous temple built by Śaṅkara. From Udupi, we went by bus to Someshwar, at the foot of the Western Ghats. The road up the hills had many hairpin bends and was considered too narrow for regular buses. We transferred to smaller vans to reach Agumbe, on the Deccan Plateau. Because of the war, there were problems with regular bus service to Sringeri, so my uncle had sent a bullock cart to meet us. Our luggage and the whole group piled into that one cart for our trip to Sringeri. The cart was crowded, jolted every bone in our bodies, and was highly uncomfortable. We traveled overnight on unlit roads through the jungle, talking loudly to bolster our courage. We talked about hungry tigers on the prowl, and our chances of meeting any, on the way. Early the next morning, when we stopped for a light breakfast, the bold headlines in the local Kannada newspaper announced the end of war in Europe.

Fourth grade meant that we had graduated from the slate-and-*kāḍḍi* world of beginners to the notebook-and-pencil world of higher academic status. On the first day, our teacher, Mr. Kunder, asked us to buy only the brand Tip-top pencils for use in class. He was in charge of the school store, which had a monopoly on this particular brand of pencils, and wanted to encourage their sale. Mr. Kunder taught us history and arithmetic. He was a Protestant, a short, muscular, thickset man with a luxuriant walrus mustache, stained from his constant use of snuff. After one of these sessions, accompanied by much auditory excesses, he would wipe the residue with the colorful kerchiefs normally favored by snuff users. Once in a while, he would run out of snuff, absolutely essential for the normal functioning of Mr. Kunder's mind and body, thus precipitating a crisis. An emergency rescue mission would be set in motion. He would give some small change, a couple of annas (1 rupee = 16 annas), to a student and send the child posthaste to his favorite snuff seller a couple of miles from school. I was sent once, with explicit directions for getting to the snuff shop in the hot sun to satisfy Mr. Kunder's addiction. In those days, there was almost no traffic in Udupi, and except for the long walk, the errand provided a welcome break from school.

It was hazardous to sit in one of the front benches in Mr. Kunder's class. Because we were seated alphabetically by surname, that is exactly where I ended up in each class. He would call on me to do a problem in arithmetic or answer a question. I would stand up and do my best, which usually was not enough. A wrong answer resulted in the following action sequence: Mr. Kunder would grab my hair from the front, bend my back, and come down on my back with a loud *thump* with his closed fist, known as delivering a *guddo*. My crew cut did not cramp his style. He would grab the back of my neck in his left fist, bend my back, and bring his fist down on my back in the usual fashion. This particular punishment was Mr. Kunder's specialty; no other teacher used it. I remember one particular incident after all these years. He had put an arithmetic problem on the blackboard and asked me to solve it. I gave the right answer; however, the fist came down on my back anyway. This happened six or seven times in a row before it finally dawned on him, with some promptings from the class, that I had been correct all along. Any apology on his part was out of question. He was the august, infallible teacher, and I was the ignorant pupil approaching his presence to be educated. Physical abuse by teachers was accepted back then as perfectly normal and an essential, helpful part of education. It was part of the process of imparting new knowledge to unruly kids. All of the students in Mr. Kunder's class were in terror of him. Behind his back, they called him Kuṇḍodhara Bhūta, or an ogre, which indeed he was. I was doing poorly in class, and most of my grades were only passing: 35%. Mr. Kunder would write in my notebook: "Your son is doing poorly in class," or something to that effect. I was supposed to show this note to my father and get his signature on it. This ordeal made me a keen student of human nature at a young age. I would wait for my father to finish his evening meal and make sure that he was in a mellow mood before I approached him for his signature. This was hard on me, and even harder on my father! My father was always at the top of his class and was an outstanding student. Here was I, his firstborn, the hope of the family, barely scraping by. He must have wondered, *Where did I go wrong?* For the umpteenth time, my mother would again remind me what a good student my father was, in case I had forgotten. One of my father's classmates was my teacher (I'm not sure of his name now) when I was in fifth or sixth grade, and he always chose me for special attention when reviewing class performance. He would ask me to stand up and then berate me in front of the whole class: "Look at you and your poor grades! I was a classmate of your father's, and he would top the class! Aren't you ashamed of yourself?"

Mr. Kunder's notes to my father and his clenched fist on my back were a nuisance, but I accepted them as part of life. Now that I am older and a bit more cynical, I think that there might have been another reason behind them. Mr. Kunder used to conduct after-school tutorials for a classmate and friend of my mine on the same street where I lived. He would arrive at my friend's home in the evening, would be served coffee and snacks, and then would teach lessons for a couple of hours. This brought him some extra income. It is quite possible that Mr. Kunder thought that my poor performance in class, combined with the physical abuse that he meted out and the notes that he sent home with me, would induce my father to sign me up for extra tuition. He would have had two students instead of one—and double the extra income. Regarding Mr. Kunder's fist on my back, he was the teacher and I was the pupil, and tradition and the school power structure supported the teacher. He had unlimited, unchecked power over me. Power corrupted him, so he abused it. I am thankful that my father did not sign me up for after-school lessons. Perhaps he did not want to spend the extra money or felt that I was too far gone to benefit from it. Anyway, I am glad I had plenty of time to goof around and pursue my own interests.

My years in the fourth and fifth grades brought about another great disappointment for my father. According to him, total mastery of the multiplication tables (*maggi*) up to 20×20, with instant recall, was absolutely essential for acquiring any facility with mathematics. For him, no *maggi* meant no arithmetic or any other mathematics. After finishing his dinner, my father would quiz me on the tables. He would recline in an easy chair, resting with half-closed eyes but quite alert. I would hide in the space behind the chair, to go through this ordeal once more. The singsong recital would begin, my attention would wander, and I would make a mistake and then be interrupted and corrected by my father. Another start would end in a new disaster, a new mistake at a different place. After a few such repeats, my father's severely tried patience would be used up, and more testing would wait for another day. In spite of my best efforts, I never managed to learn the tables. My father tried various bribes, including the promise of a cricket bat if I got at least part of the tables right. This gave me a specific goal to work at, and somehow I managed to get enough things right to earn a bat. It was not a real cricket bat, only a modest imitation cut out of one single plank of wood. However, mastery of the full multiplication table proved to be beyond me. Finally, my father resigned himself to having a dumb son who would never learn his multiplication tables. Year later when I was in graduate school, my father heard rumors that I knew some mathematics. However, I am sure he never believed them, because he knew I had never learned the *maggi*.

There were no overt attempts to proselytize at the Christian high school. The school authorities did depend on the goodwill of the majority Hindus, which they did not want to jeopardize by converting any Hindu students. All students were required to attend a Bible class conducted by our drawing teacher, who would read sections of the Old and New Testaments, creating suitable drawings on the blackboard to illustrate the stories we heard. A student would be called to stand at the front of class and read a story or a section from a thick Kannada Bible. I was called to do this many times; my familiarity with the Bible goes back to those days. Our Bible teacher would take long leaves of absence form time to time, and there were rumors that he was away preaching the Gospel to convert the heathen somewhere in India. We were taught the history of India only up to the fifth grade. In the sixth grade (or first form, according to the English system we copied), histories of both India and England were compulsory. In our classes on Indian history, Mr. Kunder used to derive obvious pleasure from describing the destruction of Hindu temples by Muslim invaders and iconoclasts. He would gloat over the gory details, especially how the Brahman priests were massacred. He would surpass himself in discussing the many raids of Mahmud of Ghazni (971–1030), especially the one on the Somnath Temple in Gujarat in 1026 (Thapar 2002, 425–34). The desecration and destruction of the temple; the breaking of sacred images for the gold, diamonds, and other jewels supposedly hidden in their hollows; and the skewering of the big bellies of fat, lazy Brahmans by Muslim spears and swords would be described in loving detail. I am now convinced that he made up these embellishments, because I have not been able to find them in any history book. Perhaps Mr. Kunder had some anti-Hindu, anti-Brahman bias. Mr. Clare, who used to give us English dictation and conduct Bible classes in the seventh and eighth grades, however, was more explicit. I depend on the recollections of two of my classmates to recall some of his opinions and observations. One of his favorite expressions was "Brahmans are cobras," or, in Kannada, *"Brāhmaṇaru sarpagaḷu"* (personal communication 2007, Kochikar Raghuram Pai). In addition, he would indulge in pejorative comments about specific Hindu gods (personal communication 2008, Udupi Anandraya Shenoy).

Students accepted the periodic spouting of anti-Hindu prejudices with a shrug. It was part of life, the price we had to pay to attend a Christian high school. We never thought of complaining to either the school authorities or anyone else. Even if we had, we might not have gained anything other than a black mark in the teacher's grade book and consequent bad grades! Under the education system of that time, students had no rights and thus accepted whatever school authorities, including teachers, did. In Mr. Clare's dictation classes, each mistake earned the student one blow on the hand with the *edge* of a stout bamboo ruler. His specialty was to aim the blows at the knuckles at the base of fingers on the palm, to cause maximum pain. The trick to coping with this punishment was to take advantage of the fact that our reflexes were quicker than his and move our hands at the last second so that we received the blow on the soft hollow of our palms. I vividly remember his story in Bible class about God's punishment for breaking the Sabbath. One boy, Mr. Clare told us, played cricket on a Sunday and was hit by a fastball right in the middle of his forehead—and died. The moral of the story as I saw it: the God of the Bible does not like cricket.

Mr. Ahmad, a well-built, thick-set man reputed to be an ex-wrestler, was our physical-education teacher. He had taught my father in the 1920s, and just as he did back then, when I was a student he always dressed in the homespun khaddar, with a white Gandhi cap. Physical education was another problem for me, because I have always been ill-coordinated. We assembled in an open shed that was filled with clean white sand from the local beaches, its roof supported by concrete pillars, for the physical-education classes. It was good getting out of the classrooms for these but so very embarrassing to be consistently bad in all sports. When two captains chose team members from the class, I was the last to be picked. No captain ever wanted me on a team, because I was a liability. However, they could not leave me out of the game. Having me on their team was an act of pure charity. In high school, there were minimum standards that students had to meet for various sports, such as the hundred-yard dash, the long jump, and the high jump. The standards were meant for students like me, but I barely managed to scrape by even these minimum levels. I was particularly afraid of the high jump, in which a bamboo pole was positioned horizontally between two upright posts. I was never sure that I could clear the bar, and I was terrified about the real possibility of coming down hard on the bamboo and wreaking havoc on the sensitive parts of my anatomy.

Shri Mukhyaprana Tantri, an orthodox Shivalli Brahmana, taught me Sanskrit in grades 6 through 8. I dropped Sanskrit after three years when I moved to St. Aloysius, because it was not offered there. Hence, my knowledge of Sanskrit is essentially zero.

During my middle-school years, most probably in grades 5 and 6, I came to know Palimar Jayaram Bagilthaya (1922–2008), who worked as a clerk for my father for a few years before moving on to bigger and better things in life. He became the inspector general of police for the State of Karnataka, and then proprietor of the Ajantha group of hotels in Bangalore after retirement from police service. He was a Shivalli Brahman hailing from the village of Palimar. He used to stay at the Palimar Maṭha, one of the eight monastic lineages associated with the Śrī Kṛṣṇa temple established by Dvaita teacher Madhvācārya in Udupi. Dvaita is Dualism. It is a particular Hindu philosophy that emphasizes the difference between the universal God and the individual soul. He would bring monthly issues of a magazine, *Bāla Prapañca* (*Children's World*), published by well-known Kannada author Kota Shivarama Karanth (Inamdar 1973; Karanth 1993). There were articles on various branches of science, including astronomy, physics, and chemistry, that I would eagerly devour. I have been always grateful to Jayaram Bagilthaya for giving me a chance to read this magazine and to Shivarama Karanth for publishing it. Reading it and trying to understand as much of it as I could encouraged my interest in the sciences. This magazine was a refreshing source of science reading in the otherwise dry desert of Udupi. *Encyclopaedia Britannica*, available at the local municipal library, was the only other source of science available to me. When I met Jayaram in retirement in Bangalore during one of my visits, I told him about my gratitude and the part played by *Bāla Prapañca* in my education. Shivarama Karanth visited the State University of New York at Stony Brook in November 1989, giving me an opportunity to thank him also and to talk about the part played by his publication in my early years.

St. Aloysius High School, 1943–1944

In the ninth grade, or the fourth form, I transferred to the high school of St. Aloysius College in Mangalore for the school year 1943–1944. The reason for going to St. Aloysius was the English medium of instruction there, and the hope that it would make life easier for me when I eventually went to college. Forms IV through VI, or grades 9 through 11, constituted the three years of high school, leading on to the SSLC. Each student was issued an individual book, with the same name, bound with canvas and pages of good-quality paper, meant to last a lifetime. A student's academic grades, physical-education benchmarks, and attainments were entered in this book to form a permanent record of progress. I have my father's SSLC book for 1922–1925 and mine for 1943–1946. In my father's day, students were fingerprinted; my generation of students was not. Perhaps the government was not as worried about illegal student substitution in the 1940s.

This high school was a Jesuit institution started in 1880 as an upper secondary school; it morphed into a first-grade college affiliated with Madras University eight years later. It was considered to be the best education institution in the whole district. St Aloysius is famous for its beautiful chapel dedicated to its patron saint, and its frescos and oil-on-canvas paintings. These depict scenes from the Bible, the mighty deeds of Jesuit notables, and the life of St. Aloysius. Brother Antonio Moscheni, an Italian Jesuit, began painting them in 1899 and completed the work two and half years later (Padakannaya 1980). There was a crucifix high on the wall in each class room, in keeping with the Catholic affiliation of the school. Each day began with a prayer. The whole class stood up, the Catholics prayed, and the rest of us were silent and listened. There were no attempts at proselytizing the non-Catholics. Catholic students had to attend their religious exercises while the rest of us had morals lessons. I remember seeing the movie *Blood and Sand* (1941) with Tyrone Power, Linda Darnell, and Rita Hayworth when in Mangalore. This was one of my early exposures to what the West was like. I used to board with my maternal uncle (*boḍu māmu*), Narayana Bhat, my mother's eldest brother. My cousin Devaraya and a number of young men distantly related used to board with my uncle also. Attached to the housing complex where my uncle lived was a second-story room away from his house where all of us slept and studied. A few years earlier, my cousins Gopalakrishna Bhavaji and Vivekaṇṇā (see Chapter 3, "My Maternal Grandparents") had studied for their two-year undergraduate classes at St. Aloysius, and I was following in their footsteps. All of these changes meant extra expenses for my father. However, my father was always generous with money for my education. He had not been able to afford to attend college and hence was most supportive of my education. Though my grades in those days were scraping the bottom, he still had hope that I might get a college education. My mother accompanied me to Mangalore, and I was about 14. We went by bus and by a horse-drawn carriage (*jaṭkā* or *ṭāṇgā*) to my uncle's house in Pentlendpet from the bus station. This was going to be my first stay away from home; I was a trifle apprehensive yet quite excited at the same time. My mother was crying when the time came to say good-bye. I tried my best to show no emotion; however, I could not control a big tear rolling down my cheek. I could not help it. I was quite happy in Mangalore at the St. Aloysius high school. The school was two or three miles from my uncle's house. At the end of the walk, there was quite a steep hill to climb, with hundreds of steps to reach school. I had to do this twice on every school day. According to my SSLC book, I was a scrawny little kid at four feet eight inches, weighing a total of 67 pounds soaking wet. At the end of the year, the consensus was that the distance I had to walk every day was just too much for me and that I should get back to Udupi and the Christian high school. The English medium of instruction at St. Aloysius did not bother me at all, and I actually did quite well in school. At the end of the year, I even won a couple of prizes. I do not remember for what, however; I did not collect them, because they were awarded on the condition that I continue at the same school. What caused this transition from the bottom of the class to the top? I really do not know. It is possible that I studied hard for the first time in my life in Mangalore, instead of goofing off at home. Hence, it was with a renewed confidence that I went home to Udupi and back to the Christian high school.

Back to the Christian High School, 1944–1946

In high school, the quality of teachers was much better than that of teachers of the lower grades, and the treatment of students was more civilized. A.S. Karat was the headmaster (1942–1949) and taught English. In grade 10, or form V, students came to a fork in the road and, following Yogi Berra's advice, took it. They could choose either algebra and geometry or chemistry and biology as optional subjects, depending on whether they planned to become engineers or instead to go into medicine and/or the biological sciences. I wanted to be an astronomer, a profession not opted for by anyone in my class. I did not know how one went about becoming an astronomer. I had some vague ideas that I would have to study mathematics and physics to go into astronomy. Besides, I did not know how my father felt about it or whether he would cast a parental veto, in which case engineering was a possibility. With all of these half-formed ideas floating in my mind, I chose algebra and geometry as optional subjects. These were taught by Udupi Pundalika Jogappa Shenoy (1896–1976), perhaps the best teacher I ever had. He was strict and fair and demanded hard work, and the students learned a lot from him. He taught us English grammar and composition. I learned to write a simple English sentence from him. However, English grammar has remained an arcane mystery to me. Every rule had so many exceptions, which I could never master. Analysis of a sentence into principal and subordinate clauses, determining which words are gerunds or other ornaments of the language, and related exercises in English grammar will always be an esoteric mystery to me. The fact that the same person, Mr. Shenoy, could teach both the rational subjects of algebra and geometry and the highly irrational rules of English grammar always amazed me. B. Padmanabha Rao, who was an excellent teacher, taught chemistry and biology. He was a moderately portly gentleman, always dressed in a dhoti worn in the traditional *pañcakāsa* style. However, it did not cramp his style in class. By the time I reached tenth grade, his demonstration of a frog jumping was famous amongst generations of students and was eagerly anticipated. Mr. Rao would squat on his haunches on the floor to show how a frog's thigh muscles functioned. He was quite agile for his age and physique. It was an amazing feat of physical prowess for a normally sedentary teacher! Karkal Srinivas Rao taught us arithmetic and was also equally good. Unfortunately, he passed away after a brief illness when I was in tenth grade. S.N. Mathias taught geography and history and was a tall, kindly gentleman with a walrus mustache. He had a faraway look in his eyes, as if he was always looking far into the future. He was tolerant of other religions and had a broad-minded outlook on life, without an unkind word to say about anyone. He was headmaster (1949–1957) after I left school in 1946. He came home for a visit in his retirement, and we talked about school days and life in the States. Udupi Ananta Shenoy taught us geography and was a good teacher; we always called him *mashtru*. He sported a paunch, was always dressed in homespun khaddar with a Gandhi cap, and wore a kindly, benevolent smile on his face.

Euclid Sets Me Free

The study of algebra and geometry as taught by Pundalika Shenoy was intellectually a life-transforming experience for me. He was an exceptionally good teacher, and I learned a lot from him. We did not open our textbooks during the first lesson. Instead, he told us about the romance of the life of Srinivasa

Ramanujan (1887–1920), an Indian mathematics prodigy, and his early death at age 33. A physician who attended him in his last days called his death "a tragedy which is too deep for tears" (Kanigel 1991, 331; Bradley 2006). It was a very moving narrative of Ramanujan's struggles to be recognized in the early days, and a sadly short but productive life as a world-class mathematician. The whole class felt proud of his achievements and of the fact that he was an Indian and sad about the unfulfilled promise of his life. Getting a glimpse of the heights of Ramanujan's achievements was a good introduction to the study of mathematics. We studied algebra and the first few books of Euclid (fl. first half of the third century BCE), the Greek mathematician whose book on geometry has been called one of the great successes of world literature, the one textbook that has been in continuous use for the longest time (Sarton 1959, 35–52). Geometry, as taught from Euclid, showed me for the first time what a proof in mathematics was. Starting from a few basic assumptions and limited only by one's own ingenuity and imagination, a person could construct a proof that was, if correct, as good as anyone else's. No dominant authority figure was needed to declare a solution to a problem to be correct; I could prove it to be so. Proofs could be short and sweet, and sometimes I was spellbound by their beauty and simple elegance. This was my awakening, one of the most thrilling, unforgettable experiences of my life. After this revelation, all of the cobwebs of doubt and diffidence were swept away from my mind, the pieces of jigsaw puzzle fell in place, and I was free of the fear of mathematics. Euclid had set me free. I could think for myself, question everything, reject authority, and never accept limits set on my rational thinking by anyone—a power hierarchy or an individual. This was one of my basic rights as a human being, and intellectually I was my own boss. It was a heady feeling of liberation indeed, and I can still recall it with great pleasure.

The basics of one's education and intellectual development are formed in the high school, by about age 16. What was the quality of education that I got in India? On the whole, it was not bad. It had its limitations. We did not study European languages such as French or German, or optional subjects such as music or any instruments to play it with. Mr. Kunder's and Mr. Clare's classes, with the beating and physical abuse, with fear and terror of the teacher, were the low point. I have never understood why humans in different cultures, including India, have thought that fear of physical punishment can be a useful adjunct to education. Even our cousins the chimps can teach their young without beating them (Goodall 1986). Can't humans be equally considerate? The high point of my education was Mr. Shenoy's classes in algebra and geometry. In between, there were many good teachers who taught us what they knew, did not spout their prejudices in class, did not physically abuse us, and for the modest school fees we could afford, taught us a lot. During these years, I developed a love of reading. I was curious, had wide interests, and devoured all the books I could find. It was quite a good start in life.

Teachers and Pupils

Hindus accord great reverence to their teachers. I personally think that teaching is a most noble profession. This respect has now become part of the Indian tradition and of the Eastern societies in general. There is a Sanskrit saying about this: "Parents give a person body and mind, whereas it is a teacher who molds that person into a civilized being." Hence, a teacher deserves the utmost respect, after one's parents. Hindu codes of law declare that a person who contradicts his teacher is guilty of a grave offense and should be excluded from the rites between gods and humans (Doniger and Smith 1991, 59, 3.153). Does this mean that every utterance of one's teachers should be accepted as gospel and that one's critical judgment should be suspended? Unfortunately, some would say yes, but I do not agree. Excessive reverence for one's teachers was a cultural norm and accepted behavior in India when I was growing up; it still continues to be. I do not agree to an abject surrender of one's critical faculties to any person, teacher or not. For example, there is the lecture I received during one of my visits to India from a former teacher of mine after he asked me about my plans for the future. Did I intend to return to India or remain in the United States? I told him that I had plans to settle in the United States permanently, for a number of reasons. This decision did not meet with my teacher's approval, and he proceeded to tell me that I should do otherwise. He subjected me to a long harangue, pointing out the problems of living in a foreign culture and being assimilated there, and how different "they" were from "us." I patiently listened to him. Finally, I told him that his comments represented prejudgment, or prejudice, and were not supported by experience because he had never lived abroad or met any Americans. My teacher got red in the face with anger, extremely upset because I had committed the unpardonable sin of contradicting him! That was the last time we talked. I felt sad about this incident; however, there was nothing I could do about it. My respected teacher refused to recognize the obvious fact that I was no longer the callow youngster he had taught; I had gone through life experiences different from his own and had every right to form my own decisions to lead my life. For most of Indian teachers, their students are kids (*baccā*), and once a *baccā*, always a *baccā*. These teachers are not prepared to acknowledge growth, maturity, and knowledge in their pupils. They do not respect their student's knowledge or ability to use independent judgment; their egos get in the way. Too much reverence for one's teachers and tradition can stifle initiative, enterprise, and originality. The right to question and think for oneself is such a basic human right that nothing should limit it.

A Skeptic Learns to Respect Others' Beliefs

My budding skepticism and incessant questioning of every belief and assumption made me an obnoxious brat, difficult to live with. It is at this juncture that my grandfather Madhava taught me basic tolerance and respect for all beliefs, including the religious. Hinduism believes and respects all religions as containing nuggets of truth. I had been brought up to respect all religions equally. Hinduism does not claim to be the one and only true religion, with all others being false, whatever these terms mean. There have been many instances of Hindu individuals, sects, or groups spouting hate and intolerance regarding other belief systems. However, these are aberrations, a few people or sects pursuing their own agenda for power. Such intolerance is not part of the founding principles or sacred books of what is generally accepted as Hinduism. Madhava taught me these facts in my discussions with him. He was not a Sanskrit scholar like his older brother Vasudeva. However, he had a lot of common sense. I remember asking my grandfather about image worship in Hindu temples. My questions to him: What makes an image in a temple sacred? What confers holiness on a piece of stone or metal? His answer: faith. Faith may be irrational and simpleminded, but everyone needs it in some form to face all the problems of life. A devotee *believes* images in a temple to be sacred as part of faith. If I have no such belief, I need not or should not go to the temple. He said that a person could be an atheist or a doubter and still be a Hindu. As a matter of fact, there was quite a tradition of such skeptics in Hinduism. Nonbelievers deserve the same respect as believers. When people visit a temple, whether they believe in the sacredness of the images or not, they should respect the faith of others who do. Similarly, whether we believe in other religious traditions or not, their places and acts of worship deserve respect simply because believers are fellow human beings. It is not proper for me to judge whether other faiths are true or false; there are many who accept them as true. All people, irrespective of their religious affiliation, have faith and need it to face the problems of life. By a tacit respect for the religious beliefs of others, we assert our common humanity. Respecting other religions is a simple human-to-human transaction that doesn't involve doctrines or theology. If I expect respect for my beliefs, simple reciprocity demands that I respect others' beliefs too. I still remember my grandfather's comments. As I get older and see many instances of religious intolerance and hatred, I am amazed at his very perceptive, humane wisdom. He had much common sense and an abundance of humane concern for others. It is this basic tolerance of other faiths that makes me think of myself as a Hindu.

Growing Pains

From a young age, I had firm convictions about what I wanted do or how to do things. These usually conflicted with the views of my parents, grandparents, and other elders or with the dominance power structure in my family. The result was acts of rebellion on my part and frustrations of different degrees on the parts of my parents and the elders in authority. My earliest recollection of one such rebellion was about my clothes. My mother wanted to save money by buying cloth in bulk and having identical multiples of each item of clothing sewn by a tailor. The result was six or more sets of khaki shorts and corresponding white shirts for everyday wear. In short, it was my uniform. I dearly wanted the clothes to be different, to vary from day to day. I heard my mother's arguments about saving money; however, the message did not sink in because I wasn't earning any and wasn't responsible for paying any expenses. There were other conflicts aplenty, followed by minor skirmishes, losses, gains, and compromises. I suppose these are part of how kids grow up, asserting their independence and trying out their wings. I must have caused quite a bit of anxiety to my parents and frustrations by challenging their authority. These were exacerbated by my very poor performance in school and real anxiety as to whether I would be able to complete my education and have any gainful employment. Growing up is not easy on kids or on their parents. I am grateful to my parents for their patience and for all the love and affection that they showered on me, in spite of my rebellion against authority or their attempts to control me.

An unpleasant memory of my earlier days is my brush with the casual callousness and gross insensitivity to the feelings of the young shown by adults. Some grown-ups would act as if the young had no feelings or that those feelings did not matter, if they had any. Perhaps this attitude is an assertion of the dominance of the older generation over the younger and is very much a part of Asian cultures. These incidents had to do with adults' comments on my personal appearance. Early on, I realized that I was not good-looking or handsome and accepted these facts as part of life. I had come to terms with them and was not overtly bothered by them. I was a short, thin, scrawny kid with a long nose and an ordinary face. It would have been kinder for my relatives and or friends not to comment on or point out these obvious facts. However, this is exactly what they did—and to my face, as if I did not exist. These comments were uncalled for, rude, crude, and unpleasant in the extreme. I was particularly sensitive to these in adolescence, a period of vulnerability when other people's opinions do matter. Recalling these memories, I have wondered whether there was something odd about my family, our friends, the GSB community, or grown-ups in general and their lack of sensitivity to the feelings of the young. Is this part of social conditioning of the young to knock off their sensitive edges, toughen them up, and train them to ignore the opinions of others? Is it because these people had brains that were like cars without brakes that made them blurt out any thought that came to their mind? I have not been able to find answers to all of these questions, even in a most forgiving mood. However, I am sure that these experiences were significant in transforming me into a shy, self-conscious, diffident, introverted person not at ease in the company of others. People wasted their time in gossip, idle chatter, and running down other people, rather than taking a critical look at their own lives. I found comfort in reading a good book and living in a world of introspection and fantasy.

My last two years, June 1944 through April 1946, in the Christian high school in Udupi were quite enjoyable. As described earlier, learning Euclid had been a transforming experience for me, conferring an intellectual power and confidence I had never known before. I was doing quite well in school, earning respectable grades for a change. The next big hurdle was the SSLC examinations, conducted statewide by the government. Unfortunately, a few months before the exams I fell ill with some form of skin infection or dermatitis, *khoroju*, that was affecting much of the town. People blamed the food scarcity and possible adulteration of food during the war years as one of the causes. The usual remedies did not work, and at the height of the infection, my whole body was covered with pus-filled blisters, I was running a fever, and I had a few nights of mild delirium. I was not quite sure whether I would be in shape to appear for the exams. It was traditional for the high school graduating class to have some sort of celebration near the end of the school year, before the final exams. There would be catered coffee and snacks, speeches by the headmaster and the students, and much reminiscing, followed by a group photograph. I was too ill to attend this function, so there is no photograph to show for it. However, as my luck would have it, the skin infection peaked a couple of months before the exams, so I could take the tests. They were conducted at the education board high school, in Udupi, and I felt that I had done quite well on them under the circumstances. St. Aloysius College, Mangalore, was the next logical step, and I knew that I wanted to take mathematics, physics, and chemistry as my main subjects as an undergraduate.

Adolescent Rebellions

Adolescent rebellion can show itself in curious ways. The goal of such exercises is to shake up the status quo or challenge the accepted wisdom. I am convinced that such an attitude in teens—the need to explore new venues of life—must have evolutionary benefits for survival. I refused to accept dominance by others, challenged their thinking, and questioned everything, including the gems of wisdom of my elders. In short, I was a general pain in the neck. My ghost-hunting episode in the summer of 1946 is an example. After the SSLC exam was over, I decided, with my friend and classmate U. Anandraya Shenoy, to investigate the legend of a headless ghost inhabiting the local Hindu crematorium. As two newly minted skeptics, we had to convince ourselves that the ghost did not exist. The background on this alleged phenomenon is as follows: The Hindu crematorium in Udupi is located in what was then an isolated place called Bīḍāguḍḍo. It was a wild wasteland at a slight elevation, on a hillock. In the olden days when it was built, this was a good location for a crematorium because it was on the outskirts of human habitation. The road leading to the crematorium goes past the GSB temple and our home. Funeral processions were thus a common sight, and I grew up observing many of them. We kids used to alert the grown-ups when we saw such a procession passing by the house. They usually knew who the deceased was or would speculate on the person's identity before the local grapevine told them. The crematorium was a walled-in compound with an iron gate, never locked. There was an open shed with a tiled roof supported by pillars, and an elevated parapet that ran on three sides, forming a continuous seat. The cremation proper took place on an elevated *saraḷā mãñco* (iron bedstead) in the center of the compound; the deceased was placed atop it, along with piled wood. A Hindu priest would officiate at the funeral ceremonies, in which the eldest son plays an important part (see Appendix 5, "Hindu Rites of Passage"). People were quite uneasy going to the crematorium because of its association with death and the many ghosts supposedly haunting the place. One local ghost had earned some notoriety. It was supposed to be headless, and therefore sightless, and would walk around swinging its arms, intent on catching the unwary within its reach. The intended prey could run away but would be too scared to escape and would be caught frozen still by fright. The consequences of such an encounter were rather drastic. The ghost would crush to death its prey, whose soul would then became a servitor of the ghost for eternity. Folklore assigns midnight on the new and the full moons as propitious times for ghosts to put in an appearance. Hence, if one wanted to meet a ghost face-to-face, this was the best time. We were convinced that all these were fantasies or delusions induced by self-generated fright, and we were going to prove it. On a full-moon night in summer, the two of us went to the crematorium. We were there till about 3 AM, talking and walking around the place, and there was no ghost. We finally gave up and went home. When news of this night visit to the crematorium got around, the people who heard it were really scared and shuddered at just the thought of it. We were told that what we did was a most foolish and hazardous act. The ghost chose not put in an appearance; otherwise, that would have been an end of us. Of course, the fact that the ghost did not appear on one particular night was not much of a proof for or against its existence. It was enough for a skeptic who did not believe in them anyway. A believer could say that perhaps the ghost was otherwise preoccupied on that particular night, and it was our dumb luck that we did not see it. The moral of this story is that belief is something that is firmly anchored in the human mind, and it is difficult to shake or dislodge it by facts. We learned the hard way that no amount of empirical facts can contradict a firm belief.

As a teenager, and a budding know-it-all, I was highly opinionated, and used to hold forth at length, criticize anything and everything. At this time I started wondering whether I was capable of some self-control and discipline. For a change, I decided to observe total silence, *mouni*, for three weeks. This was partly inspired by the weekly day of silence observed by Mahatma Gandhi. I did not talk, and even tried to suppress my desire to talk, and I read a lot as usual. My long silence must have been a welcome relief for my family and friends. I would go for walks in the evening with my friends to *Ajjarkād*, an open space in Udupi with a small garden maintained by the municipality, and listen to others for a change. At the end of the three weeks, I broke my silence. It was an interesting experiment.

Undergraduate at St. Aloysius College, 1946–1948

I was an undergraduate at St. Aloysius College from June 1946 to 1948. This is a Jesuit college founded in 1880 with three high school classes that has grown into an excellent college, considered the best in the district. When people in the United States hear that I was educated in a Jesuit college yet am not a Roman Catholic, they find it difficult to believe. The Jesuits have a great reputation as puissant evangelizers, so people are amazed that I did not convert. There were no overt attempts at converting anyone when I was in college. A few of the Jesuits who taught me were quite nice and easy to get along with. St. Aloysius was just another college where the non-Catholics paid their fees and got an education in return. Only the Roman Catholics amongst the students had to attend chapel, confession, and other prescribed rituals; the non-Catholics were left to their own devices. The non-Catholics attended what were called morals lessons once a week, on which they were tested at year end.

The weight of religion did not sit heavy on the shoulders of us non-Catholics. The assassination of Mahatma Gandhi on 30 January 1948, was a most tragic event, leading to much soul-searching and introspection. Somehow, as an Indian I felt guilty, so I fasted for a day as an expiation. I was also part of the crowd at the Malpe seashore, when his ashes were immersed in the sea. It is with shame and sorrow that I note that there were some members of my own family in Mangalore whose extreme right-wing Hindu politics made them rejoice at this sad event.

Madhava Educates Me About GSB Cooking

My grandfather had an educated palate, and so did my father. It was a tradition in our family to critique each dish and compliment the cook if it was good, or point out its shortcomings if things were not just right. My grandmother and mother appreciated our comments and compliments, which were well deserved. I believe that such constructive criticism led to a high standard of cooking in our home. It was not a case of any hash slung by the women of the family, however bad, being accepted as the ultimate in good cooking. This is in marked contrast to some other GSB families I have observed where the food, good or bad, is dispatched expeditiously without any comments by the men of the family, who usually eat first. My own appreciation of GSB cooking took time to develop. In my younger years, I never really liked most dishes. I learned to like GSB food in my undergraduate college years just as I was getting ready to leave home for long periods of time. It was during the summer vacations, when my grandfather and I would have lunch together, that he pointed out the subtle balance, taste, texture, consistency, and other markers of good GSB cooking. This was my education in appreciating good food. There is quite a bit of grated coconut used in our cooking to prepare the spice mixture *māsolu*, which is always ground fresh. Coconut is expensive and high in calories. Used in excess, it makes men potbellied, and women zaftig. Powdered spices are never used because with their large surface area, powdered spices taste insipid because of the quick evaporation of the essential oils that give spices their characteristic aroma and taste. In the olden days, depending on the cooked dish and the vegetables used in it, the consistency and texture of the spice mixture used to be different. This was a typical case of a job expanding to fill the slot of time available! There was much free time and labor available from the women of the family, and all these fine distinctions of food preparation were possible. The old subtleties of GSB cooking are not known these days for the simple reason that most people have never tasted them or did not grow up with them. With nuclear families, wives being full-time wage-earners, and the use of modern blenders in the kitchen, spice mixtures are the same for all dishes—one size fits all! During those days, I taught my grandfather how to appreciate a particular GSB dish, *phaṇṇā upkari* of fresh green vegetables (Shenoy 1988, 1999, 2004). This dish is usually made with long beans (*āḷsando*) and snake gourd (*poḍḍāḷẽ*) or ribbed gourd (*ghosāḷẽ*). In our community, these vegetables are usually overcooked so that all their taste and texture are lost, and they taste like mush, not fit for human or beast. I taught my grandmother and mother to cook them for three minutes or less so that they were crunchy and one could taste the freshness of the greens. I was pleasantly surprised to find my grandfather liking this innovation. These dishes are cooked in a *kāili* (wok), with very little oil, some dried hot red peppers, and whole mustard seeds. It is basically a poor man's dish because it entails the use of so little oil and no coconut. Oil and coconut are the most expensive items in our cooking. The whole mustard seeds are cooked in hot oil first, because they need a high temperature to pop. When the crescendo of their popping just reaches its maximum, the red peppers are added. The idea here is to get the capsaicin of the hot peppers in solution in the oil so that the vegetables get a uniform coating of their pungent, smoky taste. After adding the fresh vegetables, the cook engages in some vigorous wrist action with a minimum of cooking. The vegetables should stand up to the cooking with their backbone, virtue, and crunchy texture intact. The liquid that gathers at the bottom of the wok, the essence of the dish (*hummaṇa*), along with the vegetables, should be served on steaming-hot white rice. The taste and texture of the vegetables then come through without any obstructing screen of *māsolu*. In my judgment, this particular class of dishes is the ultimate glory of GSB cooking—simple, basic, nutritious, and tasty.

My Siblings

We are a large family of thirteen siblings: seven males and six females; I am the eldest. My wife Padma and I have one son, Giridhar, an anesthesiologist. Next to me are my two sisters, Lalitha and Kasturi. Lalitha is one of the first female college graduates in our family, with a master's degree in economics. She has two sons: The elder son, Shankar, is a physician practicing in the United Kingdom, and the younger son, Ashok, is a business executive living in Bangalore. Kasturi is an anesthesiologist who practiced in Scotland and now lives in retirement in the United Kingdom. Her elder daughter, Mridul, is in civil service, and the younger, Rekha, is a physician-psychiatrist, and both live in England. My brothers Vasudev, trained as an electrical engineer and now retired, and Raghuvir live in Udupi, along with my brother Suresh, a businessman, and his wife, Shri Laxmi, and my sister, Annapurna. My brother Rathnakar worked as a scientist for the India Defense Ministry, before retirement. One of his daughters, Chaitra, works for IBM India, and her specialty is the design of large computer chips. His other daughter, Sumati, is an architect, and his son, Vedavyasa, is a business executive. My brother Shridhara, a neurologist, and his wife, Suman, live in retirement in Florida. My youngest brother, Sudhir, is a chartered accountant who lives with his wife, Subhalaxmi, and son, Sri Sukrath, in Atlanta. My sister Nandini lives in Atlanta with her husband, Nagesh, and daughter, Neha. My sister Kumuda married Gopalakrishna Bhandary, and they live in Mangalore. He is a businessman and a stockbroker. They have two sons: Avanish, an anesthesiologist, and Ashwin, an architect.

College Studies in Poona

I did reasonably well in the statewide examination that I had to take at the end of the two years of undergraduate studies at St. Aloysius in 1948. The question was: What to do next? I had some vague notions of doing research in physics, following in the footsteps of my cousin, Vivekaṇṇā. He is an organic chemist and the first person in the family to go into research as a profession. He worked at the Indian Institute of Science (IISc.) Bangalore and became a professor and head of the department there. Another choice was to earn a bachelor's degree in physics with two possibilities, engineering or research, depending on how well I did in it. This is what I ended up doing. Narasimha Bappa, my uncle, was a professor of mathematics at Maharashtra Education Society College in Poona, and his younger brother Ramanath Bappa had earned a bachelor of science degree in physics, specializing in radio engineering, and become an employee at the All India Radio. In other words, Ramanath had gotten a government job. A government job meant that a person was set for life, having a steady, well-paying job with a pension at its end; such jobs were therefore considered to be highly desirable. In 1948, I decided to go to Poona for the graduate degree. Travel to Poona was by bus and train. One went by bus over the Western Ghats to a place near Harihar to catch a train to Poona. Train travel was by "intermediate" class, slightly better than third class and less expensive than second class. The train stopped to take in passengers for only a few minutes at Harihar, in which interval one had to fight one's way into the nearly full train compartment. Passengers who were already seated did not help the newcomers; instead, they made their entry as difficult as possible. Once the new passengers were seated, they joined others in the compartment to prevent more people from getting in. This social drama is very similar to new citizens in the United States holding forth on the evils of immigration after they have become citizens and are comfortably settled there!

While in Poona, I learned about the various labels carried by citizens of India, and their abuse in discrimination. These labels are based on caste, language, and region and sometimes on religion. The many labels attached to me included *Brahmana*, *GSB*, *South Indian* or *Madrassi*, and *Kannadiga*. One or more of these labels could be used as a marker for discrimination, overt or covert. Hence, they restrict the range of possibilities open for jobs or admission to schools. In those days, discrimination was muted; later on, it came out in the open with no apologies. Quotas based on caste and reservation of government jobs for some "backward" castes was in vogue in the Mysore state in the south as early as the 1920s, because the Brahmans were seen as monopolizing state jobs (Srinivas 2001, 6; 2002, 646). Assigning quotas for jobs and education became a state policy of social engineering many years later (Pasricha 2006; Guha 2007; Nilekani 2009). In Poona, the locals did not like South Indians, commonly called Madrassis, who were seen as clever, crafty, and after the good jobs that rightfully belonged to Maharashtrians. The Madrassis were good at what they did, hardworking, and frugal. However, they saved their earnings to bring to Maharashtra more of their relatives, who grabbed all of the available jobs. My uncle and aunt asked me not to wear a particular piece of leisure clothing (*muṇḍa*), a favorite of men from the south because it is comfortable in hot weather. My uncle and aunt were afraid to be classified as Madrassis. It is true that we were from South India; however, with our family name, Bhat, we could be mistaken for Maharashtrians, Gujaratis, or even Punjabis. My uncle and his family were fluent in the local language, Marati, and passed themselves off as genuine Maharashtrians. There was also quite a bit of anti-Brahmana feeling in Poona. Jotiba Govindrao Phule (1827–1890) and other social reformers had started the anti-Brahmana movement in the mid-nineteenth century in Poona to redress past wrongs done to non-Brahmana castes and to put an end to exploitation by the priests (O'Hanlon 1985). Later anti-Brahmana sentiments spread to Tamil Nadu, Andhra Pradesh, Kerala, and Karnataka and the rest of South India. I was not really bruised or bloodied by the quota raj (a system of reserving a percentage of jobs for specific castes) of later years, for the simple reason that I never had a regular job in India. I was only an insignificant research student, definitely not a threat to anyone. In those days, jobs in private industry were few. Fixed quotas for seats in educational institutions and government jobs for the lower castes became the norm after the Mandal Commission recommendations were implemented in 1990 (Pasricha 2006; Guha 2007; Nilekani 2009). The question of how to redress past social and economic inequities of the caste system is complicated. There are many people from the upper castes who are poor and politically powerless; some from the lower castes are rich and politically well connected at present. Caste ranks do not go with wealth and power. Universal free education is the best way out of this quagmire of past social injustice to give everyone equal opportunity for the future. The affirmative action of the government to reserve jobs and admissions to schools and colleges should go a long way toward rectifying past wrongs. Affirmative action implies that many other factors in addition to merit have to be considered in jobs or education (see Chapter 1, "Prabhus of Siddhapur," the sections titled "The Hindu Caste System" and "Caste in a Changing World"). However, even in those days, the signs and portents for what lay ahead were obvious. I did not see any future for me in India, with the burden of too many labels, no inherited wealth, and no political influence. Labels from an accident of birth had become primary hooks on which to hang the prejudices of people in power, and they restricted my opportunities for the future. I did not have the temperament to play the fun and games of politics, and jockeying for advantages was distasteful to me. I decided to opt out of the system. When I had an opportunity, I immigrated to the United States. In my new homeland, right now, I have only one label, *Indian immigrant*, written all over my face!

I started attending the Sir Parashurambhau College, on Tilak Road, a school founded in 1916, for my first year of graduate studies in Poona. The classes began early in the morning at 8, which makes a lot of sense in a hot country like India. I had been used to classes starting much later, near 10 AM, in Udupi and Mangalore. Only physics and mathematics were on my syllabus, without other subsidiary subjects such as English or chemistry.

I lived in a three-story hostel right behind the college and ate in one of the student messes (mess halls). From my room, there was a beautiful view of the Parvati Hill temple to the south. There was a small Irani tea shop near the hostel on the college grounds and many more on Tilak Road just outside the compound. I used to go to the tea shop once in a while for a muffin and a cup of tea, which was a real treat. Tea shops like that one are a regular feature of the Bombay and Poona area and are owned and operated by immigrants from Iran—Parsis and others. Near the end of the nineteenth century and in the early twentieth century, when members of the GSB community were particular about food taboos and caste observances, these shops were blamed as the culprits that led caste members down the road of temptation to eat forbidden or ritually polluted food (Conlon 1977, 152). These days all such concerns about food purity have fallen by the wayside and are not very relevant. One day, I decided that I was going to eat an omelet, partly out of curiosity and partly because it was forbidden food. I have almost total recall of this incident, which occurred more because of a desire to break food taboos rather than because of the taste of the omelet.

The weekends were spent in the apartment belonging to my uncle Narasimha Bappa and his wife, Tara Pachchi, on Prabhat Road in an area of Poona called Deccan Gymkhana. I would walk past B.G. Tilak's house, which was quite close to the college, heading north-west. I think this house is a museum now. In this house I once heard a talk by Jiddu Krishnamurti (1895–1986), an author, mystic, philosopher, and public speaker who had a large following; he was so popular that even today, there is the Krishnamurti Foundation of America. Somehow, I could not understand anything of his talk; I have since found that mystics and I operate on different wavelengths and that their thoughts are opaque to me. Tilak Road joined the Sambhaji Bridge over the usually half-dry Mutha River. At the south end of the bridge on the left, there was a small Hanuman temple with an attached wrestling arena, or *akhāḍā*, where one could watch people exercising or wrestling. My uncle's apartment was on the second floor, reached by a flight of stairs on the outside of the building. The stairs led to the kitchen with a balcony, overlooking an open space of the apartment compound. Local peasants from the villages who had come to attend and sell their produce at the weekly fair in town would rest there at midday break to eat their simple lunch, which usually consisted of thick cakes of millet (*bhākri*), some hot green peppers, and a raw onion, washed down with plain water. There was another balcony in my uncle's apartment that overlooked a street running parallel to the riverbank. Under this balcony on the street front were a grocery store, a tea stall, and other shops. On the other side of the river was a Hindu crematorium with smoke coming from it most of the time. Cremation is the final logical and ritual end to all of the vanities of life for Hindus. My uncle, aunt, and their children were quite fluent in the local language, Marati, which is very similar to our mother tongue, Konkani. Marati was the language of instruction in schools, and the kids perhaps knew it better than Konkani.

For some reason, but to my great regret later, I did not try to learn Marati; I wish I had. I transferred to Fergusson College, founded in 1885, for my second year of studies. This college is situated to the north of Deccan Gymkhana and was much closer to my uncle's apartment. There were a number of student hostels and one dining hall with many student messes. Next to it were the bathing facilities. During our India trip in 2004–2005, my wife and I visited both Sir Parashurambhau and Fergusson Colleges and hostels, about fifty years after I had last spent time there. The traffic on the roads had increased out of bounds, there were more people, and both campuses were crowded. The libraries of the colleges where I had spent so many happy hours were in bad shape, with some broken windows and old books piled on the floor. The hostels were poorly maintained, with broken windows patched with cardboard, and a generally bedraggled appearance, compared with my memory of them. It was a sad homecoming. The University of Pune (or Poona) was established in 1948, and its present campus was allocated in 1950. At the completion of my studies at Fergusson College, I had the option of appearing for the final exams given either by the Bombay University or the newer University of Poona; I chose the former. The exam proper was in Bombay. My uncle accompanied me there both for moral support and to help me deal with the logistics of the big city. In May 1950, I passed the bachelor of science degree examination of the Bombay University with first-class honors and distinction in physics and was awarded the Dilip Chhaganlal Kanuga Scholarship and the Rustomjee M. Hirjee Readymoney Prize. After that, I was looking around deciding what to do next when I got a telegram from my uncle Shridhar Bappa, who was the assistant registrar of the Indian Institute of Science, Bangalore: There was an opening in the Raman Research Institute for a research scholarship, which offered me a chance to work under a famous physicist, Sir C.V. Raman.

Raman Research Institute, Bangalore

Sir Chandrasekhara Venkata Raman (1888–1970), a famous Indian physicist popularly known as Raman, was a Fellow of the Royal Society (1924) and won the Nobel Prize in physics in 1930 for the discovery of the Raman effect, and many other honors. His many achievements in the acoustics of musical instruments, light scattering, crystal physics, and other branches of science have been described in two biographies (Venkataraman 1988; Jayaraman 1989). Raman established the institute named after himself in 1948 with a gift of his personal wealth to the Indian Academy of Sciences, founded in 1934. When I graduated in 1950, he was looking for students to work at the institute supported by research scholarships offered by government of India. One day he ran into my uncle Shridhar Bappa and said that he was looking for students. My uncle suggested my name as a possible candidate, and Raman accepted me after an interview. This was a lucky break for me and I eagerly accepted a chance to get involved in physics research and work under a famous physicist. When I joined the institute in 1951, the main building and the machine shop had been built. However, there was no electricity. There was a hostel for students with individual rooms, communal baths, a dining room, and a kitchen. We had a cook and his helper, and the food we got was quite good. The scholarships were 100 rupees ($20) per month for juniors and twice as much for seniors. The pay was quite adequate to take care of our basic needs and even cover the cost of some movies. There were a few optical spectrographs and an X-ray machine, and related equipment. There were about five or six students in the first batch, and A. Jayaraman was Professor Raman's right-hand man who helped him to plan, coordinate programs, and run the institute. The freshly minted graduates who joined the institute were in awe of Raman, who was the professor for all of us. Our side of conversations with him was a series of "yes, sir; no, sir," with very little genuine exchange of ideas or opinions. Or this was so at least in my case. The Indian tradition of reverence for a teacher or guru, Raman's great achievements in physics, and our age differences all conspired to cultivate this feeling of awe, bordering on fear, toward the professor. He had a colorful personality, he had insight into and a passion for physics, and he made many innovative and original contributions to a variety of areas. He was an excellent speaker who could convey his enthusiasm for the subject and highlight its aesthetics. It was indeed a privilege for me to be associated with him and to observe a great physicist at work. Before the institute got electricity, we had much free time on our hands. The professor arranged for us to attend lectures on differential geometry, analytical dynamics, and other graduate courses in mathematics and physics at the Central College of Bangalore. These were extremely useful in our education as physicists and in my course work later on in the United States.

While at the institute, I took up smoking: cigarettes and a pipe. Ever since I had read about Alice's encounter with the hookah-smoking caterpillar, I had been fascinated and wanted to smoke. Though I knew that it was bad for my health, I did it anyway. An act of rebellious, youthful foolishness! I was living in the dorms attached to the institute, and smoking anywhere was a huge no-no. If the professor had found out about it, I would have been kicked out of the institute on the spot! I had to smoke on the sly, brush my teeth and wash my mouth, and indulge in all forms of concealment. I was lucky in not becoming addicted to nicotine, which can be highly addictive. I completely gave up smoking some years later.

I worked under Professor Raman on the optics of heterogeneous media and got a master's degree from the University of Poona in 1954. I stayed at the institute for two more years working on the same subject, without bringing my work to a successful conclusion. In 1956, I applied for a U.S. government grant to study in the United States under the Fulbright Educational Exchange Program. I had to go to New Delhi for an interview; with the professor's letter of recommendation and support, I was selected to participate in the program.

Indian Bureaucracy and Me

After early notification of my selection and impending travel to the United States in June–July of 1956, the days were a whirlwind of activity as I attended to the various preparations for travel abroad. An unending number of bureaucratic details had to be done and approvals had to be obtained from Bombay, Delhi, or Madras. Each of these encounters was an adventure in itself. Every piece of paper was in triplicate with many carbon copies; this was before the advent of photocopiers. Some government official had to certify with an official seal and a signature that each was a "true copy." It is possible that this rule originated before carbon paper was invented; however, no one had bothered to change it afterward! I had to get a certificate of competency in English from a professor at Central College of Bangalore. I never had a regular job in India; I was earning only a student stipend. However, I had to get a tax clearance certificate. The list appeared endless. I have bad memories of Indian bureaucracy, its loops within loops and the sheer delight with which its functionaries applied the arcane minutiae of its rules and regulations. These procedures flattered the ego of every cog in the machine, asserted their dominance, which they indicated by an undecipherable, minute signature. The higher the grade, smaller the signature! I particularly resented obtaining what was known as a "good conduct" certificate from two prominent persons (read: government officials) certifying that my general conduct was above reproach. Why cannot the bureaucrats accept that a person's character is good until proven otherwise? If the police files on an individual are clean, why not accept that as proof of good character? Perhaps this was left over from the British Raj.

It is now customary to blame Indian bureaucracy on the British. This is unfair. It is true that Indians inherited bureaucracy from the British. The question is: What did they do with this inheritance? Did Indians simplify or get rid of it? Did they lovingly nurture it to its present state? Is there an Indian tradition of state bureaucracy? The answers need some elaboration. Kauṭilyā's *Arthaśāstra*, a handbook of statecraft presumably used in the Mauryan Empire (~321–185 BCE), was the oldest in this genre. Its date is uncertain and it is estimated to have been written sometime between the fourth century BCE and the second century CE (Rangarajan 1992, 20). This book is replete with rules, regulations, fines, and punishments for all activities of the citizens of a state—plenty to delight the heart of any modern bureaucrat! Travel within the empire was restricted, and passports were a necessity. India can claim to be one of the first nations to use this bureaucratic document (Rangarajan 1992, 72). With such a noble tradition, the only way to go is up—that is, up to a more elaborate system. The Mogul bureaucracy required that a payment from the royal treasury be processed through ten stages, from its inception to the handing over of money, and approved by various officials scattered over the empire, including the emperor, who had to authorize it twice (Wesson 1967, 287). Modern India has lived up to this challenge and further complicated the inherited bureaucracy in a splendid fashion. The following story, told by Gurcharan Das, confirms that Indian government bureaucracy is as good as ever. In April 1999, a functionary of the Ministry of Steel asked whether officers could use red or green ink in their work. After consulting with six ministries or departments, and after the lapse of about a year, the manual of office procedures was amended to allow only officers above a certain grade to use red or green ink in rare cases (Das 2009, 54–6). Because there are many ambiguities in this decision that cry out for clarification, I am certain that further rulings will appear. Stay tuned. Let me give another example. The wise men of India decreed that one of the worthwhile goals to be pursued in this life is liberation, or *mokṣa*. This is interpreted as escape from the troubles and travails of this life and the cycle of rebirths. Every Hindu or Buddhist is born with a "dossier" of deeds, good and bad, from the past births, popularly called one's karma. This clearly shows that the power of bureaucracy can even breach the life–death barrier! The yearning for liberation is nothing but a heartrending cry of a person caught in the coils of the super bureaucracy of karma, wondering when it will all end. No wonder it was the pious hope of every person to be liberated for good! I have felt this sense of mini-liberation, many a time in the departure lounge of Indian airports, after my latest encounter with local officialdom. The British bureaucratic inheritance has been lovingly nurtured in India to grow to its present monstrous form and complexity. These improvements are entirely due to the Indian creative genius for filigree, ornamentation, and elaboration, almost baroque in its complexity. Such innovations can be very effective in their ability to make life difficult for the common person without official pull or push or influence in high places. I have waited in a long queue only to be told by the official at the counter window that I should have paid a departure tax or something else before getting in this line. The airline management could have put up a sign with this information at the entry to the line; however, they do not. It does not take much imagination to include the departure tax in the price of a plane ticket; however, there is likely some obscure official reason why it just isn't done.

Because all of the various pieces of paper were obtained by mail, one had to plan things well in advance, allowing for a delay of ten to fifteen days. Telephones were highly inefficient in India in 1956 (and continued to be problematic well into the 1970s). A long-distance call to Bombay or Madras had to be booked as many as 24 hours in advance, and finally when you got the other party, the phone connection was bad. A simple telephone call was an adventure in basic communication. There was much shouting of "hullo, hullo" most of the time, and finally one had a garbled connection that made obtaining information during the call highly chancy. In addition, I had to get a passport. In those days, an owner of real estate had to stand surety to guarantee transportation of the remains of the applicant in case of death. I have been very grateful to Jayaraman, my colleague at the institute, who was kind enough to stand surety for me so that I could get a passport. Next, I had to get new clothing for the cold weather in the States, and there were other incidental expenses. Many local banks, including those owned and operated mostly by the GSB, used to advertise loan scholarships for deserving students. These were just bank loans and not real scholarship grants. Because eligibility was based on grades, however, they were called scholarships. I applied for a loan of 1,500 rupees (about $300, with 1 dollar being worth 5 rupees) from one of these banks. The surety for the loan, my father, had good credit, excellent standing in his profession and the community, and owned a house and the property on which it stood. The loan was denied, the stated reason being that the loan officer thought that "it was not necessary for the student to go abroad for further studies." My situation was obviously outside the competence of this gentleman. The bank official was appointing himself an authority on post-graduate education in the United States and deciding that I did not need it. His job was to check the financial worth of my surety for the loan and assess the chances of my paying it back. He controlled the money and had the illusions of power that went with it; I had to live by his pronouncements. My father generously lent me two thousand rupees, for which I have always been grateful. Unfortunately, the heavy clothing I got in Bangalore according to the best local advice was too thick and more suitable for the cold, unheated buildings of the United Kingdom than for the well-heated buildings in the United States. Buying these new clothes was mostly a waste of good, hard-earned money. The moral of these two incidents was: Do not expect any help from anyone; then any random help will always be a rare, pleasant surprise! My parents never asked me to promise to live abroad by the strict norms of Hindu orthodoxy, so long as I was in good health, they were not particularly concerned about what I ate or drank. I have always appreciated their liberal attitude toward life and their not putting too many restrictions on me.

I Leave Home

I must have left home in Udupi sometime in mid-July and flown to Madras to get the U.S. exchange visa. From there I flew to Bombay; both flights were in a DC-3 with a sloping fuselage. The monsoons had begun, and in the gale-force winds the night before I left, the gigantic *aśvattha* tree next to our house had toppled and was blocking the road. The car that was to take me to Bajpe Airport in Mangalore had difficulty getting close to our house to pick me up. This tree had figured prominently in my childhood dreams and nightmares. I had been told that it was inhabited by a gigantic ogre, a *brahmarākṣasa,* who had been observed to stand astride in the middle of the night, with one leg on this tree and another firmly planted on a similar tree, miles away. Such a spectacle was too big for my childhood imagination to comprehend; however, it formed part of my dreams and a few sleepless nights. The practical side of me hoped that in standing astride, the ogre was suitably accoutered for the occasion.

I made sure I had money, passport, ticket and other papers, and then it was time to say good-bye to my family. The moment was too laden with emotion for me and my elders for a formal good-bye. I did not touch their feet, *pāyu dorcẽ*, asking for their blessings and good wishes. I said good-bye all around without these customary formalities. That was the last time I saw my grandfather Madhava Bhat and my grandmother Bhavani.

In Bombay, I stayed for a few days with two of my friends whose hospitality I remember with gratitude. U. Vittala Acharya was senior to me by one year, and his nephew, Ramdas Prabhu, was my classmate at the Christian high school in Udupi. Vittala Acharya was a navigator in Air India at that time, and thanks to him, I got a chance to go into the cockpit of the plane and look with awe at its many dials and controls. The local U.S. consulate had arranged some functions for us, including dinner in a posh restaurant, where I met a fork for the first time. This was followed by a group photo, a copy of which I still have. They also gave us some spending money in foreign currency, which was strictly controlled at that time. Each of us got $5 in currency and $120 in traveler's checks, plus £3 in currency and £10 in traveler's checks. It would be another eight years before I returned home from abroad. In the meantime, my grandparents passed away, my brothers and sisters grew up, and all of us had gotten older and maybe wiser. I had decided to immigrate to the United States and was in the process of getting an immigrant visa.

Both my parents became more religious as time progressed and they got older. This is to be expected in the normal progression of life for most people. In her seventies, my mother was found to be the early stages of Parkinson's disease. Every evening, my mother would light the lamps at the family shrine, as was the duty of an orthodox Hindu woman. All of us asked her to be very careful near open flames while cooking or doing other chores round the house. Unfortunately, one evening when she was lighting the shrine lamps, her sari caught fire. Though the fire was put out immediately and she got only minor burns, we thought it advisable to admit her to the local hospital in Manipal. Though she was healing well and progressing toward a complete recovery, she suffered cardiac arrest on the fourth day and passed away before she could be revived. It was January 22, 1989, and she was 75. After my father retired, he had more time to devote to daily rituals of worship. In his spare time when he was not reading the sacred scriptures such as the *Bhagavadgītā*, the *Rāmāyaṇa*, or the *Mahābhārata*, he filled several notebooks with the invocation of Lord Rama's name: *Śrī Rām, Jaya Rām, Jaya Jaya Rām*. For him, earning merit by invoking Lord Rama's name was a better way of spending his time than engaging in idle gossip or worrying about problems that one could not fix. My father passed away on August 28, 1992, at age 85. I miss my parents and remember their love—and their forbearance during my rebellious teen years. They gave me the best education they could afford and supported my atypical choice of a career. For all this and much more, I will always be grateful. My father was my role model. I always admired how hard he worked at his profession. His singleness of purpose in educating all his children enabled us to hope for a better life.

This brings to my mind another aspect of parental control and children's response to it. Many people note that they felt a sense of freedom and a welcome release from parental authority on the death of their parents. My own feelings on this matter were quite different. When my mother and father passed away, I felt sad especially at the thought that they would not be around to enjoy the joys and sorrows of our lives and that they could not offer their wise counsel or comments on difficult situations in life. As for a sense of freedom or a release from parental authority, I did not feel it for the simple reason that I had never been bound or constrained. I had been free and independent for a long time before they passed away. They were kind enough to acknowledge my independence, to accept and encourage it, many years earlier. I am always grateful to my parents for this act of generosity.

CHAPTER FIVE

Immigrants in a New Country

My Trip Abroad

I flew from Santa Cruz Airport, Bombay, to London via Air India early in the morning on July 22,1956. We left Bombay somewhere around 1 AM and reached Cairo the same morning in time for breakfast. The plane was a four-propeller Super Constellation, relatively slow compared with modern jets. There was a stop in Rome in the afternoon, and then we reached London sometime in the evening of the same day. Our group of about seventeen people from India stayed at the YMCA Indian Student Hostel, 41 Fitzroy Square, in Bloomsbury, near the British Museum. I shared a room with R. Chellia, an economist from Madras and a very nice person. There was a buffet-style cafeteria in the basement, serving breakfast, lunch, and dinner. Everything we saw was strange and new, including lived-in basements. Through the windows of the cafeteria, we could see people walking on the sidewalk outside. We were used to eating dinner between 8 and 9 at night in a hot country like India, but here, dinner was much earlier. London was, of course, the big city about which we had read so much in school. There was plenty to see, and we were looking forward to it with great eagerness. When gathered in the lounge on the ground floor to discuss our plans for the next couple of days, we asked some old-timers amongst the Indian students at the hostel for information and directions. It was obvious from our dress, accents, behavior, and everything associated with us that we were hayseeds from India, out of our country for the first time. These gentlemen, our *deśabandhu* (compatriots), I am sorry to say, were not very helpful. Instead of helping us, they openly ridiculed our English, accents, and manners or lack of them; had a good laugh; and made snide comments amongst themselves at our expense. These big-city sophisticates made fun of us to our faces. This was their way of asserting their superiority and dominance over us, the poor *desi* (country), jungly yokels, fresh out of India. That was lesson 1 for me: Do not expect much help from anyone; manage on your own as best as you can.

The bedroom I shared with Chellia was very cold, in spite of the heavy blanket, quilts, and a fire in the grate. We had to get up at night and feed coins into the gas fire to keep it going. We ate breakfast in a cafeteria that served a version of what it called Indian food that was quite bland and barely palatable. After breakfast, it was time for a bath. I knew that the locals used a tub instead of a shower or pouring water over themselves. However, I was not prepared for just a couple of inches of lukewarm water in the tub, my total allotment for a bath. I guess the wartime shortages and austerities were still in force, so that was all the water that anyone got for a bath.

We had to get used to the customs and mores of the British. We were inundated with "please" and "thank you," which Indians do not use often. In England, there is a superfluous, automatic use of these social courtesies, which was truly amazing to me. In India, we reserve these for momentous occasions such as when one person saves another's life. Anyway, we learned fast.

We went sightseeing at the usual tourist spots: Westminster Abbey, Speakers' Corner in Hyde Park, the British Museum close by to see the Elgin Marbles, and the Rosetta Stone. I signed up for one of the organized tours that went round London on a bus. The bus got caught in a traffic jam that seemed to last for ever. One person on the bus, obviously an American, announced loudly to anyone interested that a "New York cop could have untangled the traffic mess in no time at all." This observation was received with a palpably chilly silence by the local Brits as one more example of a loud-mouthed American in action.

The few days we spent in London went fast, and I think we sailed for New York on July 26 on the RMS *Queen Elizabeth*, of the Cunard Line. Our voyage from Southampton to New York lasted five days; every day we set our watches back by one hour. I think some six of our group were assigned to a table in the dining room, and the bland food served was something of a problem. I had decided that I was going to be a nonvegetarian without any restrictions; proteins to me were just large molecules, irrespective of their source. In the United States, I was not planning on cooking vegetarian; I would eat what the natives did. I had had fish in India, deep-fried and camouflaged with breading. Onboard the ship, the fish was served in all its iridescent, scaly glory, head and tail intact. There I was, looking at the fish—and the fish was looking back at me with what I would call an accusing eye. Perhaps it was my guilty vegetarian conscience working on me. Anyway, I decided to put an end to all of this anthropomorphic nonsense, and I covered the eye with a piece of bread before proceeding further with surgery to remove the skin and bones. Eating was quite an adventure because I was also getting used to the implements at the table.

New York, New York

We landed in New York on Tuesday, July 31, 1956. I do not recall seeing the Statue of Liberty or New York Harbor; I think that we were too busy getting organized with our luggage and immigration documents. After breakfast, our group gathered in a large room, clutching immigration papers, which included a chest X-ray and a physician's report. The U.S. Immigration and Naturalization Service (today known as the U.S. Bureau of Citizenship and Immigration Services) had set up office onboard the ship and processed us through all the formalities. A large van picked us up at the harbor and took us to Hotel Martinique, which no longer exists, sometime late in the afternoon. Three or four of the group were assigned to one room, and all of them decided to explore New York. I was too tired to go out and decided to take a bath and go to bed. Unfortunately, I slipped in the tub and hit my chin on its side, requiring a couple of stitches. I had to go in search of a physician in the neighborhood to get my chin stitched and properly bandaged. While in New York, I tried the automat. This was a clean and efficient coin-operated food-vending establishment. In those days, one could get a slice of cherry pie for a quarter! The next morning, we went to the Institute of International Education in New York, which coordinated the Fulbright Educational Exchange Program for the U.S.–India Educational Foundation. We were to meet the institute people responsible for our program and get our marching orders.

Orientation at Syracuse University

The person in charge of our exchange program at the institute welcomed us round a huge conference table in a bright, sunlit room with big windows. He gave us the details of the next leg of our journey. The institute sent some of us to Syracuse University for a six-week orientation program. The original schedule for this program was from 26 July to 5 September 1956. Because we arrived about a week late, the program was extended by another week into September. At Syracuse University, the group was housed in Haven Hall (which went on to be demolished in 1962 to make room for a new building), a girls' dormitory vacant for the summer. The group was composed of about fifty people from about twenty-five different countries. India was represented by R. Chellia, Vimla Gupta, Saeed Jaffrey, Peetambaran Tampi, and me. It is interesting to note how some characteristics of these national groups stood out enough to be remembered even after so many years. The largest contingent, which numbered seven, was from Japan. Its members functioned in unison as if they had one mind and the same opinions and were synchronized. The most voluble, argumentative group had only two members and was from Greece. They had pronounced left-of-center views, and their mission was to skewer every fat-cat-capitalist person or idea and extol the glories of socialism. We all attended lectures on various aspects of American life—culture, history, and politics—and took several one-day trips to local places of interest. We visited the Oneida Community, including its modern cutlery factory and its former settlement. There was the obligatory baseball game, which was similar to rounder, its supposed ancestor from England, which we had played round a diamond in India. Some authorities question this story of baseball's origin, claiming a pure American lineage from Upstate New York.

To learn more about American life and culture, each student spent a week with an American family that had volunteered to host members of the international group. My hosts were from the small town of Chittenango, New York, near Syracuse, and I will always be grateful to them for their kind hospitality. During my stay, they took me camping near Lake Oneida, which was an interesting, enjoyable experience. We drove to the campground, where we were assigned a concrete platform four to six inches high, with enough area to pitch our tent. Though it rained most of the time, the platform at least kept our stuff dry. We went fishing and caught some pike, which are bony fish. My hosts had entertained students from India earlier, as part of the international exchange program, and knew something of this particular genus. For me, everything was a new experience, and I was drinking it all in. Breakfast with my hosts began with a prayer, which ended with a fervent plea to the Almighty for an early conversion of India to Christianity. Even now with my anthropologist's hat on, I think that this request was rather peculiar. As the only non-Christian at the table, I did not participate in the prayer, maintaining a respectful silence. That my hosts said this prayer every morning has always intrigued me, leading me to many questions ever since. My hosts belonged to some Protestant denomination, but I do not remember which one. They must have been enthusiastic about missionary efforts, hence the prebreakfast request to the Almighty. Yet if they assumed that the natives of India loved their religions as much as they did theirs, how could they have prayed for Indians' conversion? I thought it was rather presumptuous on their part to do so without first asking Indians how they felt about it. The only explanation I have been able to come up with goes something like this: If a friend is sick, we wish her or him a speedy recovery as a matter of course, without asking permission. Some of us might even resort to prayer to bolster our good wishes. For my hosts, the very fact that most Indians were not Christians perhaps implied that they were in a state of compromised spiritual health. Hence, their praying and hoping for India's conversion was a kind, humane gesture in their view, done out of the kindness of their hearts. The fact that such a prayer could be considered crude and rude never entered their minds. I had a good time with my hosts and pitched in with the usual household chores such as washing dishes and working a hand-operated ice cream machine. At the end of a week, I was back in Syracuse, as was the rest of the group. Each of us had stories to tell and experiences to relate about the family visits and about getting used to American life. At the end of the orientation period, I took a train to Columbus, Ohio, my next stop.

Ohio State University

Ohio State University (OSU), founded in 1870 as a land-grant university, had about 20,000 students when I joined in 1956. After being admitted for the fall semester, all of the foreign students gathered in a huge hall to get a general introduction to university life. Students for whom English was a second language had to take an English competency test. Quite of a few of the students from India were outraged at this requirement. They claimed fluency in British English, which they thought should be good enough for the locals. With such an inflated idea of their knowledge of English, they did not bother to look at the study material or the test requirements. Some failed the test and had to attend remedial classes in English, and then had to take the same test again. My attitude is to treat all exams as a necessary evil to be taken seriously. I went through all of the reading material given, and I passed the test the first time.

Football at OSU was not just a collegiate sport; it was *the* religion, with all of the attendant rituals. Out of curiosity, I bought a season ticket the first year to find out what all of the fuss was about. Attendance at a couple of games left me totally unmoved. All I could make out of the action was that there were two groups of huge men who looked like gorillas in armor, and they fought for the possession of one football. Somehow all of the nuances of the game were lost on me. I decided that attending games was a waste of time, so I gave away my ticket to the first person who asked for it. The OSU Buckeyes were almost professional football players masquerading as students, according to some critics. The weekly highlight of the religious observance was the Saturday-afternoon football game, in which the powerhouse Buckeyes usually annihilated any opposing team, to no one's surprise. Every OSU victory was celebrated by the ringing of the Victory Bell (a gift of the classes of 1943, 1944, and 1954), weighing 2,420 pounds and residing 150 feet from the ground on the ramparts of the southeast tower of the OSU stadium, to announce to the faithful another triumph of good over evil. The believers claimed that on a clear day, the bell could be heard five miles away. The whole university, including all of its libraries, closed down for Saturday-afternoon home games. When a few of us requested that the university's main library be kept open on Saturday afternoons, this "heretical depravity" caused quite a stir. The university did open the library, but this grave anomaly was not publicized. The Buckeyes' archenemy was another football powerhouse—the University of Michigan Wolverines, at Ann Arbor, Michigan. The OSU–Michigan game, which usually ended the football season, was a drama of cosmic proportions—the ultimate battle between good and evil. Over the years, this game had acquired its own mythology, saga, and portion of the faithful. Presiding over all of these observances was the head football coach, Wayne Woodrow "Woody" Hayes (1913–1987), now of blessed memory, a cult hero elevated to the semidivine status of guru by university alumni and the residents of Columbus. For most of the alumni, these games were the most important things that ever happened to them during their university years. Any other skills or knowledge they picked up was incidental or unintentional. I learned this from a letter I got from the OSU Alumni Association Club of New York City inviting me, as an alumnus, to attend one of their collegial meetings where movies of past Buckeye victories were to be shown, and of course they would all end with the joyous ringing of the Victory Bell and the singing of the Buckeyes' fight song. These alumni wanted to savor every moment of past football victories, once more with feeling. It was truly an amazing bit of juvenile nostalgia. Unfortunately, as a nonbeliever in all rituals, I had to pass up this happy occasion.

The River Road Dorms were a group of eleven temporary buildings erected to house the huge numbers of veterans returning to the university after World War II. One building was occupied by graduate and professional-school students only. The showers and toilet facilities were common and open to all, with no privacy. Quite a few students from India saw this as a problem and found other accommodations. Attached to the dorms was a buffet-style cafeteria, where the food was basic Midwestern. Buses ran between the dorms and the university every few minutes on school days and holidays. Most of the bus drivers were students working part time while studying at the university, an arrangement that was new to me. In India, if you could not afford school fees, you did not attend school. Some of the bus drivers were blacks who made snide remarks about us Indian students and called us epithets such as "snake charmers." Blacks were lower than whites in the dominance hierarchy of American society, but they felt superior to us Indians, perhaps seeing us as fresh out of the trees of Indian jungles because our lack of sophistication and polish was so very obvious. Thus does human ego compensate for its inferior status by feeling superior to someone else with even less standing.

Racial Discrimination, Old and New

This leads to the question of whether I experienced overt discrimination in the United States from anyone other than the university bus drivers. After all, my ethnic origin is written all over my face, giving me an obvious label: *alien.* The answer to this question involves some discussion, a few comments, and a history of how immigrants from India were treated in the United States. Unfortunately, that history is a story of racist laws and practices in the United States and Canada, aided by the British, who did not protest when racial prejudice was practiced against their Indian subjects or offer them any help. The British were as racist as the Canadians or Americans and did not see any problems to worry about. Discrimination against aliens occurs in all countries and cultures. Usually, it lies just below the surface, waiting to sprout when conditions are just right: when resources are scarce, such as jobs, food, land, and mates; when someone appears who can be readily identified as an "other" because of ethnic characteristics; and when there is the feeling that these outsiders are depriving "us" of some of these scarce resources.

In 1907, worry about jobs and racial hatred of Chinese, Indians, Japanese, and Koreans set off riots among Americans in Bellingham, Washington, and among Canadians in Vancouver, British Columbia (Jensen 1988). Americans and Canadians declared that their respective countries belonged to the whites and would continue to do so. Americans formed organizations named Exclusionary Leagues to keep out Asians on the West Coast and Southern Europeans on the East Coast. While unruly mobs attacked Asians, beat them up, and burned their dwellings and property to run them out of town, local police and civil administrations looked on, doing very little to protect them because they sympathized with the mobs. Asian immigrants were not allowed to land or were sent back because they did not meet ad hoc regulations concerning literacy, medical conditions, personal finances, directness of voyage route, or anything else dreamed up by immigration authorities on the spot. The British, who could be eloquent about the Empire and the benefits that it conferred on Indians when convenient, did nothing to defend the rights of Indian immigrants, who were citizens of the Empire. The British sympathized with the "whites only" ideologues, both American and Canadian. Exclusionary laws against Asian immigrants were enacted against the Chinese (1904), against Indians (1917), and against others. To those Asians who were already in the country, naturalization or becoming a U.S. citizen legally was another hurdle. Congress had passed a law in 1790 authorizing certain courts to naturalize "free white persons," without giving a legal definition of *white.* Whether an applicant for citizenship was white or not was decided by a local judge, court clerk, or the U.S. Immigration and Naturalization Service, and the criteria varied from case to case. In 1920, the application for citizenship of Bhagat Singh Thind, a veteran of the U.S. Army, was refused by the immigration service because he was not white. This case finally ended up in the U.S. Supreme Court, which unanimously upheld the denial in 1923. The court opined that the meaning of the "free white person" of the statute was to be interpreted not according to science or anthropology but with the understanding of "the common man." The court was criticized for its creation of a legal fiction called "the common man"; however, its decision was the law of the land (Jensen 1988).

The human consequences of this court decision were far-reaching. The government decided to apply the Thind decision retroactively and denaturalize people who had been granted citizenship. They were accused of fraud in their citizenship applications, though they had committed none. It was a case of an earlier prevailing judicial interpretation of law by state functionaries that was declared wrong by the U.S. Supreme Court. Once Indians were deprived of their citizenship, under the 1920 Alien Land Law, they could not own land. The California attorney general instituted legal proceedings to revoke Indian purchases of land and to forbid them to farm on leased or contracted land. Indians in California, by hard work, had reclaimed extensive land that no one else wanted because it was agriculturally marginal or a desert. The local dominant whites wanted this newly fertile land, and they were going to get it. The Asiatic Exclusion League pointed out that Indians owned over 2,000 acres of this reclaimed land and had leased another 86,000 acres of the most productive land in the state (Jensen 1988, 258). The power structure of the state wanted to exploit cheap Indian labor as farm workers and did not want them to profit from owning or cultivating their farms or by leasing them. Indian applications for licenses to marry white women were denied. The legalized land grab and other harassments of Indians are examples of the perversion of justice motivated by racism. Appeals to the British government to fight the injustices done to the citizens of the Empire brought no help. The British ambassador only requested an extension of the deadline given to Indians to liquidate their land holdings. Tit-for-tat proposals for heavy taxes on American-owned land in India were squelched by the British colonial rulers. Some Californians saw the injustice of these forced sales of property and helped Indians by assuming legal titles to the properties or by forming dummy landholding entities. A few Indians with children born in the United States transferred land titles to their children, who were citizens by birth. To save their property, some Indians married Mexican women who were citizens. It was only in 1946 that the U.S. Congress passed a law granting naturalization and an immigration quota for Indians (Jensen 1988).

All of this was history when I entered the United States in 1956. As an exchange student expected to learn the American way of life and someone who was not after a union job, real estate, or the favors of American women, I was not seen as a threat. American society had progressed far from the old unjust laws against Asians, and because many American soldiers had traveled abroad and seen the world, there was the widespread sense that the United States was a nation of immigrants—white, yellow, brown, and black (Jensen 1988). It is fair to say that I have not experienced any overt discrimination during more than fifty years of my life in the United States, first as an immigrant and then as a citizen. The promotions and salary increases that I got were mostly in keeping with my competence on the job. I am not saying that there is no discrimination in the United States; it is alive and well. It is quite possible, however, that the academic and research communities of the Northeast and Midwest I moved in were not representative of the whole country or that I was not sensitized enough to feel discriminated against. When I was working at Brookhaven National Laboratory, I do remember hearing a few complaints of "too many Indians and Chinese" in some departments; that was about it. I have always been pleasantly surprised and grateful for the basic fairness, kindness, humanity, openness, and lack of discrimination or xenophobia of the average non-Indian Americans whom I have met. Though all societies have stratification and ranks, American society is less hierarchical than others, such as those in Great Britain or India. In the last chapter, I mentioned the many labels I carried in India and how some of them were used to discriminate on the basis of caste, language, or regional origin. Genetic inclination to cooperate with the members of the tribe implies a tendency to note and mark individuals outside the tribe as the "other." Cooperation with the in-group and discrimination against the out-group are two sides of the same genetic coin, and all of us are heirs to this inheritance. I became a naturalized U.S. citizen on October 5, 1973, and my wife was naturalized on June 2, 1987.

Graduate School at Ohio State University

Most of my friends were Korean War veterans who were in graduate school at the end of their military service. They were a highly irreverent lot, used to questioning most accepted norms of life and marching to a different drummer. One or two of them had cars, which enabled us to go to the only Mexican restaurant in the whole of Columbus, at least once a month. I would gorge on their green sauce made with hot green peppers, finishing up a whole bowl. There was a Chinese restaurant very near the campus whose fried rice, properly doctored with hot Tabasco sauce, was palatable. I was a regular customer there, and the proprietor would charge me an extra quarter for the sauce because I used to empty nearly a whole bottle at one sitting. In those days in Columbus, yoghurt was considered quite exotic and foreign and was not easily available. However, I did find some excellent homemade plain yoghurt close by. Near the university was a Lebanese restaurant. When I asked the owner, who was working behind the counter, whether he had any *labān* (yoghurt), he almost cried with joy! He often prepared some for himself, but his customers had never requested it. I became a regular customer there. While being weaned from the spicy foods I grew up with, I was learning to appreciate the local bland foods. For my first Thanksgiving that year, many American families invited all the new foreign students at OSU to celebrate with them. I was quite nervous about the possibility that I would use the wrong fork or spoon and would be an all-around sorry example of a student from India. But after a few years in the States, I just stopped worrying about such trivial things.

Two incidents in Columbus stand out among my memories of OSU. First, author, humorist, and cartoonist James Thurber (1894–1961), an OSU alumnus, visited the campus and gave a talk in the open air to a huge group of students and faculty. Second, recording artist E. Power Biggs (1906–1977) gave an organ concert in one of the local Protestant churches. The church organ had been refurbished, and Biggs was invited to inaugurate it. When we entered the church, my friends were warning each other not to get too close to the sanctuary, lest they precipitate some signs and portents of divine displeasure! Being a non-Christian, I had no such concerns. That day we heard some glorious Bach, Buxtehude, and other baroque organ music.

While living at the River Road Dorms, I was dragged into giving a talk on Hinduism at a local Protestant church attached to the university and serving its students. This was a most curious incident. The man who organized this presentation was a Korean acquaintance of mine who was a member of the congregation. I also induced a Ceylonese student to talk about Buddhism. My understanding was that the group wanted to know about Hinduism and Buddhism. Instead, this group had its own agenda to convince everyone of the superiority of its religion. At the end of our talks, the pastor of the church talked about his beliefs and ended by declaring that the earlier presentations and his summing up *proved* that his particular branch of Christianity was the most superior religion! I was most surprised at this conclusion, especially at the sheer gall of such conceit. I had been brought up to respect all religions as equal, and the question of one being better than another or one religion being the best of the whole lot had never entered my mind. We did not have a chance to reply to the pastor, who closed the proceedings after his pronouncements. After this unsettling experience, I have always steered clear of such "true believers." I am convinced that any exchange of views on religious beliefs with such people is a waste of time. I learned the hard way why it is best to avoid arguing about religion and politics.

After I had lived for a couple of years in the River Road Dorms, the university decided to pull them down to replace them with new buildings. About six of us students who hung around together decided to share a house with a kitchen to reduce food costs. We looked around and found an old house, with two floors, a kitchen, and a backyard, at 150 West Frambes Avenue, next door to the university. A proper WASP (white Anglo-Saxon Protestant) in the group was our representative to negotiate the rent and sign the lease. The rent was reasonable; however, the landlady wanted to know more about us, our ethnicities, and our habits. She wanted to know whether there was anyone from India. Apparently, she had heard that Indian students were not clean. Our spokesperson assured her that I was as clean as the next person. Next, she asked whether there were any blacks. Sure enough, one of us was black. At this she gave up and dared not ask for any more ethnic details. She told the WASP that if he wanted share a house with such a group, it was his problem, and she would not have anything more to say. Our friend assured her that all of us were habitually clean and that we would take good care of her house and pay the rent on time. I lived there for the next two years, till I graduated and left Columbus in December 1961. That old house was pulled down after the university bought the property and built new graduate-student housing there. While I was living in the house, my friends introduced me to Western classical music. One of them had a good hi-fi system and a huge collection of records, with a heavy emphasis on baroque music. Friday evenings were devoted to music and my musical education.

I registered as a graduate student in the physics department with Professor M.L. Pool, an experimental nuclear physicist. This change of specialization from optics to nuclear spectroscopy was deliberate, because I wanted to change fields and hoped to learn new things. I was lucky in the choice of my doctoral thesis adviser. He was a kindly man who believed in getting his graduate students out of graduate school as expeditiously as possible, through course work, exams, and a thesis, and searching for a job in the real world. He used to call the doctorate a union card, which indeed what it is. He did not believe in abusing graduate students as cheap conscripted labor while their thesis was awaiting completion. Unfortunately, however, such abuse was the standard operating procedure under a few faculty members at the university. Professor Pool was an easy man to talk to, and so was his right-hand man, Russell Sullivan. I learned a lot from them and other graduate students, especially the practical aspects of electronics applied to nuclear physics. Funds for new equipment were limited; hence, graduate students built their own apparatus. This hands-on experience in building amplifiers and low-noise preamplifiers from scratch, including doing the layout, doing the breadboarding, making circuit boards, and finally checking them out and fixing them was invaluable for me as an experimental physicist. I cleared all of the hurdles to getting my "union card" and graduated in August 1961. The biggest hurdle was typing my dissertation with my index finger to meet the stringent requirements and get the approval of the eagle-eyed inspector at the graduate school. All degree candidates were scared of her because she was known to throw back a dissertation if she noticed even the smallest deviation from her strict guidelines. I did not have the $100 or so needed to pay a professional typist to get the job done right, so I did it myself (Bhat 1961). The results of the dissertation were later published jointly with my thesis advisor in a professional journal (Bhat and Pool 1962). Professor K. Narahari Rao, a well-known optical and infrared spectroscopist in the physics department, helped me a lot in various ways. It was he who suggested that I should apply for a postdoctoral fellowship from the National Research Council Canada (NRC); he was kind enough to write a letter of recommendation.

Atomic Energy of Canada Limited

I was an NRC postdoctoral fellow for about two years, from December 1961 to January 1964 at the Chalk River Laboratories (CRL) of the Atomic Energy of Canada Limited (AECL) at Chalk River, Ontario, Canada. These facilities are the only establishments in the essentially rural community in Renfrew County, about 182 kilometers northwest of Ottawa. Most of the laboratory personnel who worked at the CRL lived in the community of Deep River, about 18 kilometers away. The CRL provided bus service between the two villages. The unmarried AECL staff members lived at the New Staff Hotel in Deep River. It was a five-story building with its own cafeteria and recreational facilities, and it was close to the center of social activities in town. In those days, the total population of Deep River was about 2,000, essentially all of the people who worked at Chalk River. It was a one-company town. The winters there were about six months long, and both of the rural communities were quite isolated. It was a good place to enjoy nature for an outdoorsy type with interests in hiking, fishing, boating, swimming, and similar activities. For staff members not terribly interested in these activities, and for family members whose interests were not focused on research, life in Deep River was hard. There was quite a bit of alcohol abuse, and the long, cold winters were conducive to producing large families. I worked at the fast-chopper facility, a joint project of the Brookhaven National Laboratory (BNL), in Upton, New York, and the AECL. This joint project had been initiated by Donald J. Hughes (1915–1960), a well-known physicist, of Brookhaven National Laboratory. The neutrons produced by the National Research Universal, a 200-megawatt thermal reactor that began operating in 1957, were pulsed by the fast-chopper for use in our experiments.

After Hughes died, Harry Palevsky (1919–1990) replaced him as the head of the neutron physics group at BNL, with Robert E. Chrien and John A. Moore as the physicists from BNL. P.P. Singh was an NRC postdoc at CRL, and I was his replacement because he was going to Indiana University to join its physics faculty. Work with the chopper group facilitated my transfer to BNL on Long Island in 1964, at the end of my fellowship at CRL.

Brookhaven National Laboratory, Upton, New York

I joined Harry Palevsky's fast-chopper group in the physics department at BNL in March 1964 as a postdoc to work at the Brookhaven Graphite Research Reactor. BNL, funded by the Department of Energy, was founded in 1947 and has a history of many significant contributions to science (Crease 1999). The fast-chopper group at the graphite reactor was founded by Donald J. Hughes. It measured neutron resonances and neutron cross-sections, so essential to the applied uses of nuclear physics such as nuclear reactors or weapons. To compile, evaluate, and publish these data, the Brookhaven Neutron Cross Section Compilation Group, popularly known as the Sigma Center (and now known as the U.S. National Nuclear Data Center), was established in 1952. *BNL-325*, popularly called the *Barn Book* and first published in 1955, was the Sigma Center's most famous publication. It became a much-used source of cross-section data worldwide and has gone through many editions since. After the death of Hughes, these activities were moved to BNL's Department of Nuclear Engineering. A new fast-chopper was being designed and tested at that time, under the leadership of Robert E. Chrien, for installation at the High-Flux Beam Reactor, which went critical in 1965. The new fast-chopper was designed for studying neutron capture gamma rays and associated physics. It was used for many years—1967 to 1979—and resulted in many publications before it was retired.

In June 1967, my appointment in the physics department came to an end, and I went home to India for a three-month vacation. I was looking for a job, but it was not clear where I would be going next. In August 1967 I married Varada at Moodabidri, South Kanara District. She belongs to the Hegde family of Maroor, near Karkal. It was a traditional Hindu wedding with overtones of Gauda Sarasvat Brahmana (GSB) customs. My uncle Kaṭapāḍi Śrīpati Bhat was the officiating priest. After a Hindu wedding, there is a complete makeover of the bride; she gets a new name, clan (*gotra*), family deity, traditions, and so on. My wife's married name is Padma, after my paternal grandmother. Because my grandmother had died before her husband, making her a *suvāsinī*, her name was considered auspicious. My wife Padma came to the United States on an immigrant visa in August 1968. We rented a house in the town of Center Moriches, living there for six years. Our son Giridhar was born there in 1971.

We built a house in the town of Miller Place and moved into it on February 15, 1974. At that time, the Miller Place school district was supposed to be better than average, so it was the main factor in our choosing to live there. Giridhar graduated from Miller Place High School in June 1989, with many prizes and scholarships. He was the class valedictorian and was elected to the National Honor Society. He wanted to be a physician and directed his studies toward the life sciences. He graduated from Yale in 1993 with a bachelor of science degree in biochemistry, spent a couple of years in doing research on protein structure there, and earned an MD from the University of Pennsylvania in 1999. He practices anesthesiology in New Jersey.

After I became a citizen, I was able to act as sponsor for my brothers Shreedhara (Shiddha) and Sudhir so that they could emigrate to the United States. When they arrived, I advised them to stop following the Indian practice of addressing one's superiors as madam or sir. I asked them to stand up straight, never be obsequious, look the other person squarely in the eye, and treat her or him as an equal. You are as much of a person as the other, I told them. This advice, they claim, has been useful. Shiddha is a neurologist who got most of his medical education in India, with two medical degrees in internal medicine and neurology, plus postdoctoral training. In looking for a teaching position in India, he found that the power structure of medical schools was putting too many restrictions on any private practice and paying low salaries. My advice to him was to bid good-bye to Indian bureaucracy and start a new life in the United States. He has not regretted this change of venue. He had to repeat his residency in the United States to meet the requirements of the American Medical Association (AMA). There are two perspectives on such requirements for graduates of medical schools outside the United States. The AMA, exercising its dominance as most human organizations do, sees them as necessary to maintain the high standards of U.S. medical care. International physicians see them as exclusionary rules, some humiliating, others tiresome, intended to keep most such physicians out of the country.

In September 1967, I moved to BNL's newly formed National Nuclear Cross Section Center (NNCSC), whose director was Sol Pearlstein (1930–2003). My experimental background with the fast-chopper and neutron physics proved to be useful in the data-evaluation work at the NNCSC. Initially I was involved with the evaluation of neutron cross-sections, writing of associated computer codes, and participating in the Cross Section Evaluation Working Group. In 1977 the NNCSC was renamed the National Nuclear Data Center (NNDC) to reflect the additional responsibilities assigned to the group by the U.S. Department of Energy: to evaluate nuclear structure and decay data, publish the journal *Nuclear Data Sheets*, and coordinate this work nationally and internationally. Evaluation of nuclear structure data took me back into the nuclear spectroscopy I had done as a graduate student. I was in charge of the nuclear structure data evaluation group for many years. During my years at the NNDC, I attended many meetings of the nuclear structure and/or cross-section data evaluators at other data centers in the United States and abroad. I was promoted to the position of senior scientist in July 1978, a position I held till my retirement from BNL on January 3, 2000.

Life in Retirement

The work I had been doing at the NNDC, nuclear structure data evaluation, and managing the data evaluation group had become somewhat routine. I felt that instead of coasting along, I needed change. Retirement was a change, yes, but I wondered what was I going to do. But I had many interests and soon realized that I knew the things I wanted to work on. The most important was writing this book. I had some vague ideas about writing a narrative of my family's life in India and the stories of our past. Immigrating to the United States was a big step and more or less a break with our life in India. If I did not put these memories down on paper, they would be lost forever. This had happened in the earlier migrations of our community, and I did not want a repeat of that mistake. My son, Giridhar, born and brought up in the United States, had shown great interest in our past, and retirement was an opportunity for me to tell about our past in this book. Because of all of that, this family book became project number 1.

I had also heard about the Round Table (RT) at the State University of New York (SUNY) at Stony Brook from Sol Pearlstein, the former head of the NNDC and my good friend. He had joined the RT and spoke highly of its workshops and the opportunities to explore new venues of knowledge that it offered. These activities at least kept the old neurons firing, so participating as a member of the RT became project number 2 for retirement. The RT, a peer learning group for retired adults, was formed in October 1988 as part of continuing education at SUNY at Stony Brook. Classes on various subjects, called workshops, are conducted by members to an interested audience composed of the rest of the group. All members participate in the project as equals—hence the name Round Table. It was renamed the Osher Lifelong Learning Institute in 2007 in recognition of a generous grant from the Bernard Osher Foundation. The group has flourished: As I wrote this, it had 739 members. It offered 63 workshops for the spring 2009 semester. I joined the RT in the spring 2001 semester and have been a member ever since. I have participated in many of these workshops and found them all to be very interesting.

However, two workshops on Buddhism and yoga deserve special mention. I attended The Psychology of Buddhism and The Psychology of Yoga, both conducted by my friend Marvin Levine. Marvin was a professor in the

Department of Psychology at SUNY at Stony Brook from 1965 until he retired in 1990. He has long been interested in the Buddhist and Hindu views of life and is a longtime practitioner of yoga and the author of *The Positive Psychology of Buddhism and Yoga* (Levine 2000). Before I took those courses, I had only a very superficial knowledge of Buddhism. Attending them gave me an opportunity to study and practice aspects of Buddhism in some depth. This experience was very significant for my mental and emotional development. I have been always intrigued by two things about Buddhism: insight meditation, also called Vipassana, as a tool for self-transformation, and the doctrine of *Anattā* (no-self) as a matter of belief. The doctrine of no-self appears to have been borrowed from the materialist or the world-directed philosophers, the *Lokāyata*, by the Buddha, and transformed in a characteristic way as a centerpiece of his teachings. Exploring this idea of no-self, from the sixth century BCE, in the context of new experimental knowledge in neurology and related sciences proved to be very helpful for my understanding of Buddhism.

Insight, or Vipassana, Meditation

Insight meditation is mindfulness, or attentive awareness of mental concentration, used to examine the nature of ideas or objects as they are. I was interested in this type of meditation shorn of its religious or mystical overlays and purely as an exercise in self-examination and transformation. I see it as a form of objective, moment-by-moment, nonjudgmental self-introspection. It is the sort of examination without which life is not worth living, to paraphrase Socrates (Tredennick and Tarrant 1954). This is the basic approach to insight meditation with a minimum of mystery and mysticism, which is acceptable to me as a skeptic. I wanted to try it out and see how it worked in practice with an open mind. Insight meditation is a vast subject, with a tradition going back to the Buddha and an extensive literature contributed by people who spent their lives practicing and exploring it. As a beginner, I found the book *Mindfulness in Plain English*, written by the Venerable Henepola Gunaratana, a Buddhist monk in the Theravada tradition, extremely useful (Gunaratana 1992). This book discusses the basics of insight meditation and has directions for its practice for a beginner. I also got some tapes from the Bhāvanā Society in West Virginia (http://www.bhavanasociety.org/), a monastery and meditation center founded by Gunaratana. He and his colleagues recorded these tapes for beginners in meditation, giving explicit instructions on how to meditate. I started meditating for about an hour every day beginning sometime in 2002. I also started selective reading of the vast literature on the subject, paying particular attention to books that had more practical guidance for meditation and less to those that had esoteric speculations about it. Both the tapes and the books I read were extremely useful to me in fixing the cultural context and the thinking behind insight meditation, which is such an important part of Buddha's original teaching. Attentive awareness and focus on one particular object at a time, instead of multitasking or flitting from one topic to another, had immediate beneficial effects for me. I had been troubled for many years, beginning in my adolescence, with obsessive bad thoughts with a touch of scrupulosity. Scrupulosity is an excessive, obsessive concern with one's failings, real or imagined, in the context of religious strictures: the many do's and don'ts (Baer 2000, 2002; Rapoport 1991). For the first time in my life, I was able to control the bad thoughts and eventually eliminate them entirely from my consciousness—by practicing mindfulness. This sense of liberation from the convolutions of my own mind was the most beneficial effect of insight meditation for me. This was the self-transformation that I had hoped to achieve through insight meditation. The sense of freedom and joy that I felt because of this has remained with me ever since. Mindfulness practiced in the mundane things of everyday life can also enrich these activities immensely. Exercising on a treadmill or a stepper, eating an apple or tasting a simple meal—these acquire a depth of experience never sensed before if done mindfully and not by rote. It pays immense dividends not to put one's mind on autopilot and coast along. Multitasking can be a terrible waste of time, though its avowed purpose is to use time more efficiently. Being an active, interested, mindful participant in one's life with moment-to-moment awareness is certainly more rewarding than coasting. I found the meditation experience interesting enough to explore it further, so I signed up for retreats at two Buddhist meditation centers.

Meditation Retreat at Insight Meditation Society

The nine-day meditation retreat, from August 30 to September 8, 2002, at the Insight Meditation Society (IMS; http://dharma.org/ims) in Barre, Massachusetts, was my first encounter with a professionally organized retreat. This was a retreat meant for beginners with some meditation experience. Ruth Denison, a pioneer meditation teacher, was in charge of the course. She has been a practitioner of Vipassana meditation since the early 1960s, after obtaining training in Burma (now Myanmar) in the tradition of Sayagyi U Ba Khin, and has led many retreats since 1974. She has her own desert Vipassana center, Dhamma Dena, at Joshua Tree, California. At the retreat I attended, there must have been thirty to forty attendees; they were called yogis. There was a nominal charge for the course to cover boarding and lodging. In addition, each yogi was expected to volunteer for a "yogi job"; mine was to wash teapots at 5:45 PM every day. Each yogi was assigned a comfortable private room with a bed, desk, and cupboard, with communal showers and toilet facilities on each floor. A typical day lasted from 5 AM to 10 PM, with breakfast and lunch as the two main meals of the day, plus a light snack in the evening. The food was ovo-lacto vegetarian, which means that it included dairy products and eggs, and was prepared with an eye to good nutrition. After registration and orientation, the yogis observed what is called noble silence to quiet the mind and body. Reading, writing, journal entries of any kind, sending or receiving mail, making telephone calls, or talking with other yogis was forbidden, to encourage introspection and still the mind. We formally began the retreat on the evening of the first day by reciting the Three Refuges: in the Buddha; his teachings, the Dhamma; and the monastic order, the Saṅgha. The yogis volunteered to live by the Five Precepts: to not harm any sentient being, to not to take what is not freely given, to abstain from sex, to observe noble silence, and to abstain from alcohol, drugs, or any other intoxicants. All participants ate, meditated, and listened to talks together as a group. The teacher's discourse on a chosen topic was followed by meditation, with alternate periods of sitting and walking meditation on the premises or outside, on the surrounding grounds. Small groups of a few yogis met with the teacher once or twice, with questions or request for clarification of parts of her talks. Denison's teaching was eclectic. She combined what may be called standard Vipassana with other types of meditation she has practiced, resulting in a course that was quite interesting, wide-ranging, and informative. The retreat reinforced my meditation experience and confirmed that what I had been doing was the proper way to go about it. It also gave me a chance to seek clarification on a few points from an experienced teacher.

Meditation Course at Vipassana Meditation Center

Next I attended a ten-day meditation course at the Vipassana Meditation Center *Dhamma Dharā* (VMC) in Shelburne, Massachusetts (http://www.dhara.dhamma.org/ns/index.shtml), October 1 through 12, 2003. This organization offers courses in Vipassana meditation, as taught by S.N. Goenka, a householder teacher and his assistants, in the tradition of Sayagyi U Ba Khin. Details of this method are described in *The Art of Living: Vipassana Meditation, as Taught by S.N. Goenka* (Hart 1987). Goenka has founded and maintains and directs many meditation centers all over the world to meet the demand to learn Vipassana. The 2003 meditation course offered a different experience from that offered by the IMS retreat: The course was more rigorous, with a stricter code of discipline, and made greater demands on the students. Complete segregation of the sexes, even among married couples, was observed. Men and women lived, ate, entered the common meditation hall, and meditated separately, and there was no physical contact between people of the same or opposite sex. Though Goenka was somewhere in India at the time, it was obvious that he exercised tight control over the contents and conduct of the course at the VMC, to ensure their conformity with the tradition of his lineage. Leslie Jennings, the assistant teacher in charge of the course, and her helpers had been trained and approved by him. Teacher's discourse, held every night from 7 to 8:15 PM in the meditation hall, was a video by Goenka discussing the tradition and philosophy of Vipassana. Audiotapes of Buddhist chants by Goenka, who has a beautiful, commanding voice, were played as part of instruction. Students declared their willingness to comply fully with the teachers' guidance and instructions, observe course discipline, and meditate exactly as instructed without any additions or deletions. A typical day began at 4 AM and ended at 9:30 PM when the students retired to bed with lights out. We meditated for a total of about 11 hours each day, with a few sessions in the privacy of a cubicle or sleeping space assigned to us and the rest in a common meditation hall.

At the registration desk, each student filled in a form with personal information, including previous meditation experience, type of practice, and its duration. We also surrendered our cell phones and other personal belongings and promised not to contact relatives or friends on the outside. The course began in the evening of arrival day with the recitation of the Three Refuges and our voluntarily agreeing to abide by the Five Precepts. Students taking the course for a second time were expected to follow three additional precepts: to abstain from eating after midday, to abstain from sensual entertainment and bodily decoration, and to abstain from using high or luxurious beds. They were also assigned daily housekeeping jobs at the VMC, including cleaning toilets and bathrooms. First-time students did not have to do these odd jobs. We maintained the noble silence of body, speech, and mind, for the duration of the course, to cultivate a sense of isolation. We could of course talk with the instructors at any time about specific questions. Any other religious rituals or objects, physical exercises (including yoga), and use of objects of veneration were forbidden. Reading or writing, taking down notes, and listening to music were not allowed. Breakfast and lunch, with strictly vegetarian food, were the two main meals of the day. Lunch was always over by noon, to conform to one of the Buddhist monastic rules. The evening meal was an apple or a banana with some tea. All of these meals were eaten in contemplative silence without idle chatter. Most of us meditated on the floor of the meditation hall, on a square mat with a round cushion on it, keeping our spine erect and maintaining a full or half-lotus posture. Because sciatica was bothering me, the teacher gave me special permission to use a chair. The teacher sat on a raised platform facing the students. One of her two assistants summoned four or five of us to meet with her every few days to monitor our progress. Meditation mats were spread on the floor next to her raised platform, and she asked us how we were progressing and answered any questions. There was also a circular shrine away from the communal meditation hall, with a central image of the Buddha, and individual private meditation rooms radiating from it like sections of a pie. One of these rooms could be reserved for a specific period for a private meditation session. I tried it once, and it was a very quiet, peaceful, undisturbed experience.

A teaching situation by its very nature makes the dominance of the teacher over the pupil very obvious; however, it was more evident at VMC than at IMS. This dominance was made very clear in many ways, big and small. Our teacher's seat was elevated more than the students' seats, and we had to get her permission for any deviations from the norms of sitting, meditating, and so on. I believe that transfer of knowledge or teaching is possible under circumstances of true equality between teacher and pupil. However, such collegiality is rare. I was a trifle surprised and somewhat amused to find human dominance and hierarchy in a Buddhist monastic setting, once again proving the presence of the primacy drive in all human activities. My one problem during the course was insomnia, brought about, most probably, by ten to eleven hours of meditation every day. At night I was wide awake and could not sleep. The teacher noted that about 80% of her students had the same reaction. I had to sleep in my cubicle for about an hour, during the morning meditation period (9–11 AM), to keep functioning. However, even with so little sleep, I was quite alert and awake during the meditation sessions for the rest of the day. The whole 10-day course at the VMC was free. Both first-time students and repeat attendees could make a donation at the end of the course that was based on their means. After the course was over, I wrote a letter to Goenka, addressed to his operations center in India, requesting answers to some questions about Vipassana that the teacher at VMC could not or did not answer. I am not sure whether he got the letter, because I never got a reply.

A short time after the course at VMC, I stopped meditating. I felt that the incremental progress I made was not worth the time I spent on it every day. This was a personal decision; however, the benefits I got from this experience were substantial. The habit of mindfulness that I learned during the practice of meditation has remained with me as a useful adjunct. I do not multitask; I try to do one thing at a time with total and complete attention. I learned a few things about myself from these meditation retreats. I am certain that I could never be a joiner, one who is part of a monastery or a religious or political group and who lives by someone else's rules. I am a skeptic who questions everything and finds few convincing answers. I could never accept another person as a master or guide; that would be abdicating my right to think. I think for myself and march to my own drumbeat.

The Buddhist Doctrine of *Anattā* (No-Self) and Indian Materialists

Indian speculations about the nature of the human soul or sense of self cover a wide spectrum of opinions. The vast mansion of Indian thought has always had room for diverse assertions on life in this world and the hereafter and has fostered many schools of thought. These varieties of ideas or doctrines of philosophy were called viewpoints, perspectives, or *darśanas*. The sixth century BCE was a time of great intellectual ferment, and there is documentation of the different creeds in vogue at that time. These are the orthodox schools that espoused Vedic sacrifices and rituals or encouraged as an alternate the study of the Upaniṣadic philosophy, considered to be the culmination of Vedic thought. Both of these schools believed the soul, self, or *ātman* to be immortal. This belief was called the eternalist view by the Buddhists, who were one of their critics. Performance of proper Vedic sacrifices earned merit in the hereafter with a promise of an exalted life for a specified period of time in Indra's heaven. The Upaniṣads speculated about the supreme being, Brahman, the all-pervading universal spirit, the nature of self, ātman, the relationship between these, and how to achieve liberation from the cycle of birth and death through the path of knowledge. The three main heterodox creeds were Buddhism, Jainism, and the materialists (the world-directed, or Lokāyata or Cārvāka). The heterodox schools rejected the Vedas as the ultimate authority and source of valid knowledge. The Buddhists lived by the teachings of Siddhārtha Gautama (or in Pali, Siddhattha Gotama; 563–483 BCE), called the Buddha or Awakened One, after his enlightenment (Schumann 1989; Gethin 1998; Eliade 1987). Followers of Vardhamāna, a contemporary of the Buddha, was called Mahāvīra (Great Hero) or Jina (Victorious), after whom his followers are called Jains; his teachings are called Jainism (Dundas 2002).

There is an ancient tradition of materialism in the doctrines of India, going back all the way to the Vedas, Upaniṣads, and the Epics (Dasgupta 1965, 3:512; Radhakrishnan and Moore 1989; Mittal 1974; Basham 1982, 1987; King 1999; Sen 2005; Cowell and Gough 2007). The spokespersons for the materialists may have been many; however, Bṛhaspati (ca. sixth century BCE) and his student Cārvāka are the best known. There is some controversy as to whether Cārvāka was a real person. *Bṛhaspati-sūtra* (~600 BCE), the earliest work on materialism, is lost; however, we know quite a lot about Bṛhaspati's teachings from other materialists or their detractors (Radhakrishnan and Moore 1989; Dasgupta 1965, 1:78; 3:512; King 1999; Sen 2005; Cowell and Gough 2007, 2–11). The materialist philosophy and its followers were known under various names: atheist, denier, or unbeliever (*nāstika*); heretic (*pāṣaṇḍa*); sophist or logician (*haituka*); world-directed (Lokāyata); Cārvāka (a follower of the philosophy of Cārvāka) (Matilal 1987). In the twentieth century, this materialistic school was recast as one of the earliest examples of naturalism or humanism in ancient India (Hiorth 1996). The new names *naturalist* and *humanist* sound better and are less pejorative than the old names: *atheist, denier, unbeliever,* and *heretic.*

What do we know about the worldview or viewpoint of the materialists or humanists? Their thinking covered a wide spectrum; there were heights of bold, revolutionary speculations side by side with low ad hominem attacks on the character, moral worth, and manliness of their opponents. The materialists questioned everything: rites and rituals and their efficacy; the afterlife; and the pious, wishful thinking of the faithful associated with it. First and foremost, the materialists were quite voluble in rejecting the ultimate, supreme authority of the Vedas, which automatically made them atheists, deniers, or unbelievers; or those outside the mainstream of society. They declared the Vedas to be tainted by three defects: lies, self-contradiction, and tautologies. The Vedas were portrayed as the incoherent mutterings of questionable characters who could not find a better way of making an honest living because of a lack of initiative or common sense. The quarrels between the Vedic scholars showed them to be imposters, each group extolling the virtues of their own practices such as sacrifices or the path of actions or contemplation as an alternate path of knowledge.

Sacrifices to the gods and oblations to the Manes (the spirits of the dead) were fruitless and a waste of time and energy; their only purpose was to provide a livelihood for priests. Death and the dissolution of the body is the only liberation one can expect in this life. Perception is the only valid source of knowledge; what is not seen does not exist. They even rejected inference as leading to knowledge. Hence, there is only this world and no hereafter, no heaven or hell, which are mere inventions of desperate fools and rogues. The ultimate principles out of which everything else is made are the four elements: earth, water, fire, and air. Consciousness is made of these elements and will disappear at death, when it is resolved into its constituents. Soul is only body enlivened by intelligence; it ceases to exist when the body dies. This belief came to be called the annihilationist view by the Buddhists. Intelligence or consciousness can originate from a proper combination of the right constituents of the four elements; there is nothing else other than these atomic arrangements and recombinations. Examples are the red color of masticated betel leaf, produced from its colorless constituents, such as the areca nut and slaked lime, or the inebriation from fermented fruit juice or molasses. God, religion, freedom, and immortality are postulates and mere illusion. Nature is indifferent to what is good or evil to humans, and past events do not support a benevolent divine providence. Pleasure and pain are facts of life, and happiness lies in pursuit of the first and in avoidance of the second. Penances are for fools who are stupid enough to observe them. Enjoyment of sensual pleasures is the only worthwhile end of human beings. Virtue and vice do not qualify as absolute values but are mere social conventions.

We know the names of a few of these materialists who preached all or some of these beliefs, along with their antinomian teachings. Jābāli, a Brahman skeptic and an advisor to King Daśaratha in the *Rāmāyaṇa*, told Lord Rāma that there is no life after death; hence offerings to the Manes are a waste of food and are not needed. In this world, the only reality is that which is directly perceived by the senses, and nothing else. It is futile trying to earn merit in the next world at the expense of pleasures in this world, Jābāli said, and asked Lord Rāma not to go into exile (Walker 1968, 1:500; Dasgupta 1965, 3:530; Sen 2005). Sañjaya Belātthiputa (d. 480 BCE), a *nāstika* (a skeptic and agnostic), condemned attempts to speculate about the hereafter as a waste of time and effort (Walker 1968, 2:348). Ajita Keśakambalī ("Ajita of the hair blanket") was another nihilist who had similar views (Walker 1968, 1:19–22; 2:348; Dasgupta 1965, 3:521). Bharadvāja, in the *Mahābhārata*, asserted that life functions can be explained by solely physical and physiological means and that the assumption of the existence of a soul is unnecessary (Dasgupta 1965, 3:530). While belief in an eternal soul in the Vedic and Upaniṣadic tradition and its total denial by the materialistic Lokāyata teachings were the two extremes, there were quite a few who accepted some beliefs of both. These middle-grounders were well versed in the Vedas, performed sacrifices and other rituals, and led exemplary lives of upright virtue, yet did not believe in the next world or the hereafter (Dasgupta 1965, 3:530). Such skeptics and their beliefs are mentioned in the Upaniṣads, and their teachings were well known to the orthodox, at least in the early days. Kauṭilyā groups the Sāṅkhya, Yoga, and the Lokāyata teachings together as logical sciences, without any pejorative names such as *atheist* or *materialist*, which the Lokāyata acquired later on. As already mentioned, the teachings of Bṛhaspati are lost, and the *Tattvopaplavasiṁha* ("Dogma Assailing Lion") of Jayarāśi Bhaṭṭa (fl. seventh century CE) is the only surviving book of the *nāstika*. This is essentially a treatise on logic that refutes and attacks the teachings of other schools of philosophy (Radhakrishnan and Moore 1989, 236–246; Walker 1968, 1:503). These heterodox schools of thought did not die out completely; they are mentioned a few times at later dates. During Akbar's reign (1556–1605) and his discussions with followers of various religions, Cārvāka were represented (Sen 2005, 288–9).

The materialists appear to have survived for quite some time, especially in South India, as attested by documentary evidence from at least two independent sources in the seventeenth century. The Rev. Abraham Roger was a Dutch pastor at their settlement at Pulicat, a few miles north of Madras (Chennai), (Map 1) from 1632 to 1642. To get authentic information about Hinduism, he enlisted the help of a Brahmana, Padmanābha. The result of these enquiries was posthumously published in the Netherlands in 1651 and is a record of the Hindu society in Pulicat. Roger's informant told him that the Cārvāka and Pāṣaṇḍa were two of the six sects of Brahmana living in Pulicat, with the Vaiṣṇava, Śaiva, Śākta, and Smārta being the remaining four (Lach and Van Kley 1993, 3:1029–57). It is further stated that the Cārvāka believe that this life is all there is, without any transmigration of souls or afterlife. In spite of such beliefs, they lead exemplary, socially upright lives. Similarly, the Pāṣaṇḍa, who denied all Hindu doctrines, including an afterlife, were concerned only with their present lives and their immediate welfare (Lach and Van Kley 1993, 3:1035). Dr. John Fryer (ca. 1650–1733), a young physician who was a graduate of the University of Cambridge, was employed by the East India Company to attend to its servants in the East. An account of his travels in India from 1672 to 1681, published in London in 1698, mentions atheists (Pāṣaṇḍa) who attribute everything that happens to chance, as part of Hindu society (Lach and Van Kley 1993, 3:874). It is quite possible that such heterodox sects might have existed in other parts of India for a long time, well into the present; they are indicative of the general tolerance of Hinduism and its acceptance of dissent.

It is evident from the preceding discussion that these ideas about "no-soul" or "no-self" predate the Buddha and were in the air when he was exploring various venues of thought during his wandering years before achieving enlightenment. It is also fair to say that he must have borrowed this insight from an earlier materialistic tradition. However, he recast it to fit within the framework of the rest of his teachings. Buddha taught that a human being was made up of five aggregates: the physical body, sensations, perceptions, mental formations or volitions, and consciousness, and nothing else, such as a soul or a self that was eternal (Rahula 1974; Collins 1987; Gethin 1998). This teaching is known as the doctrine of no-self in Buddhism. However, in making this assertion as part of his teaching, the Buddha added qualifiers to make the distinctions between Buddhist no-self and earlier ideas. Buddha had to stress these distinctions to make his doctrine of no-soul part of his teachings on rebirth, ethics and morality, and the whole superstructure of the new religion of Buddhism. Buddha remained silent when Vacchagotta, a wandering philosopher who always approached Buddha with questions and who was known by his last name or clan (Vatsa *gotra*), asked, "Is there a self?" Buddha's answer again was silence when Vacchagotta asked, "Is there no self?" Later, Buddha explained his response to his disciple Ananda. Answering yes to the first question would have implied that the Buddha was agreeing with the Vedic or

Upaniṣadic eternalists who maintained that soul was eternal; answering no to the second question would have meant that he was with the annihilationists who taught that the soul ceased to exist with death (Bodhi 2000, 1393–4). Buddha wanted to emphasize that his doctrine, which said that all phenomena are nonself, conformed to a middle way between these two extremes (Rahula 1974, 20–34; Gethin 1998, 133–62; Schumann 1993, 85–6). An explanation of the doctrine of no-self in the *Milindapañha* ("Questions of Milinda," c. first century BCE) helps to clarify it further. This Buddhist work describes a question-and-answer session between Indo-Greek King Menander (c. 150–135 BCE), or King Milinda in Pali, and a Buddhist sage, Nagasena (most probably fictional) (Conze 1959, 147–9; Thapar 2002, 215). Nagasena points out that the label chariot can only be applied to a particular configuration of all of the parts of a chariot (the pole, axle, wheels, framework, flagpole, etc.), and not to any one of them individually. The chariot is not an entity that exists independently of a particular assembly of its parts. Similarly, the five aggregates together form a person with a name and form. Such a person does not have a permanent self independent of its constituent parts.

Sense of Self and Conscious Will Versus Empirical Evidence

Buddhism and its teaching of no-self can lead one to ask: What is the empirical evidence regarding the idea of no-soul/no-self in Hindu materialism or Buddha's teaching? The intuitive assertions of no-soul/no-self are well and good; however, are they supported by any experimental data? Can the empirical data tell us anything, either to assert or deny such belief? What is the relevance of such data to these assertions? At about this time I read two interesting books: *The User Illusion*, by Tor Nørretranders, and *The Illusion of Conscious Will*, by Daniel M. Wegner (Nørretranders 1998; Wegner 2002). The first author is one of Denmark's leading science writers, and his book, published in Danish in 1991, was translated by Jonathan Sydenham. The second author is an experimental psychologist and a professor in the Department of Psychology at Harvard University. After reading these and related books, I decided to give a talk, "The Brain and Its User Illusions," to interested members of the RT in September 2004. The aims of this talk were several. First, I wanted to organize the material for clarifying the issues and to think through the subject in presenting it in a coherent manner. Second, I wanted to present the available experimental data in the context of the questions: Is sense of self (I-me-mine) a user illusion? Is conscious will a user illusion? This talk was not meant to prove or convince anyone that the answers to these questions were either a yes or a no. Such answers depend on available experimental data, and how you interpret them. Thus, reason, logic, emotion, and belief all play a part. Or in other words, the conclusions could depend on science and opinion. Science is subject to experimental verification, whereas opinion is accepted on faith and belief. Both the sense of self and conscious will are major concepts intimately tied with a person's ego and deeply held religious beliefs. Hence, the same empirical evidence can elicit entirely different responses from different people. I wanted the members of the audience to listen to the evidence and find the answers for themselves.

User Illusion

What is a user illusion? This new term was coined by Alan C. Kay, a member of the XEROX Palo Alto Research Center (PARC), in the 1970s in the context of improvements in the computer-user interface (Hiltzik 1999; Nørretranders 1998, 290). Kay was working on software designed to introduce children to computers as painlessly as possible. Earlier tradition in programming computers expected a user to remember and employ a large number of machine commands in writing a program. This constraint was quite demanding and made programming and applications more complicated than they really were. Kay wanted the built-in computer system to deal with all such messy details and present an interface that was compatible with the user's limitations, expectations, and convenience; in his case, 10- to 12-year-old children. This is when he and his colleagues hit on the concept of the user illusion (Kay 1984, 54). User illusion is a narrative or a myth cobbled together by the user to explain what a computer's operating system does and guess as to what it might do next. The following two examples should make this term clear. Suppose one wants to write a letter on a computer. The word processor presents on the monitor what looks like a blank sheet of paper. The letter is typed in the usual format with a letterhead, date, recipient's address, salutation, the text, and the closing, and saved as a file. It can then be printed to get a hard copy that is a replica of the computer display that can be mailed. The saved file corresponding to the letter is a series of binary digits: 0's and 1's; there is nothing in the computer that is an image of the hard copy. The letter in the correct format with the appearance of a typed sheet of paper is only a user illusion created by the operating system of the computer. The user illusion is the picture of the computer system, its response and how it behaves, that is in the user's mind; it has nothing to do with the reality inside a computer! To enhance the user illusion and make it more effective, it helps to have the monitor display an accurate representation of the user illusion. In the preceding example, the computer display shows a sheet of paper with the typed letter on it. The illusion should be user friendly and function as an active extension of the user to complete specific tasks by means of menus or icons.

The user-friendly interface requires input compatible with the abilities of a typical user, such as being able to type from a keyboard, and no programming skills. Other user illusions, made to order, are also possible. Garry Kasparov, a chess grandmaster, lost to IBM Deep Blue in the much-publicized man-versus-machine six-game chess contest in May 1997 (Pandolfini 1997, Hsu 2002). Deep Blue was a specially designed computer with very sophisticated programming and hardware that defeated Kasparov 3.5 to 2.5 with two wins to one and three draws. The grandmaster and his ego could never accept the fact that a mere aggregate of transistors, resistors, and wires could get the better of a human named Kasparov. Kasparov saw nearly human deep intelligence and creative originality in the computer's chess moves, especially in the second game, and suspected human intervention during the game, against rules. He firmly believed that opponents had cheated and secretly used the services of a human grandmaster to defeat him. That was Kasparov's face-saving user illusion. The truth was that the Deep Blue team never cheated. User illusion is a connected narrative, a story, or a myth that describes the user's interaction with the computer. The reality behind it could be something else.

The Human Brain and Its User Illusions

What do user illusions have to do with human consciousness or conscious free will? Nørretranders wrote that our "consciousness is our user illusion for ourselves and the world," or, in other words, "I am my user illusion of myself" (Nørretranders 1998, 292). This metaphor for consciousness or sense of self, coined by Nørretranders, would be shown to be apt and fitting in more than one way. Our consciousness is a user-friendly interface with ourselves and others. A sense of self is part of this package, because humans posit an agent behind every purposeful action. The experience of conscious will can also be seen to be a user illusion for several reasons, including the time sequence of events leading on to voluntary movements by humans (Libet et al. 1983; Cotterill 1990; Libet 1993; Hall 2010).

Conscious amd Nonconscious Parts of the Brain

It is estimated by neurologists that the human brain receives a huge amount of data from the rest of the body every second. The amount of input data is measured in bits (binary digits) per second, or bps. The data from all of the neural receptors in a human body are estimated to be about a few billion bps. The human consciousness, however, is not aware of all of these data flooding the brain. Various experiments have estimated the capacity of human consciousness to process sensory data to be between about 16 and 45 bps (Nørretranders 1998, 138). These numbers can be seen to be reasonable by the following familiar example. There are 24 frames per second projected in a movie, and 25 or 30 frames per second shown in TV transmissions to create the illusion of continuous motion. Data input into the consciousness at these rates or faster blur into each other, so the estimate of the capacity of human consciousness to handle such data appears reasonable. The human consciousness is not aware of a huge amount of data processing that goes on continuously in the nonconscious brain. It is only one in a billion bits of the data reaching the brain that is fed into consciousness so that we become aware of it. Our consciousness, with its low capacity for data processing, appears to be the friendly interface with the nonconscious part of the brain that processes the rest of the extensive input data.

There are at least two circumstances that encourage humans to form the idea of a sense of self or a soul. The first are the minutiae of individual survival and the second originate from a communal life in a tribe. Evolution selectively chose the high-priority information that was needed for consciousness, the bare essential for survival and reproduction. All of the rest of information not immediately needed was relegated to the nonconscious part of the brain. To run away from a predator or fight it, to chase prey when hungry, to find a mate—all of these actions were needed for survival. All such purposeful actions on the part of every individual could have led to a sense of self, because human brains look for an agent behind every purposeful action. This must be the origin of an individual self or soul as part of consciousness. In early humans, cooperation with other individuals and communal life in a group also increased chances of survival or conferred the benefit of reproductive fitness. Reproductive fitness is defined as the capacity to contribute offspring to future generations. Hence, social skills also became part of the repertory of consciousness of each individual, with the awareness of "me" versus "other." These include the ability to read the minds of other members of the tribe from their facial expressions, body language, and, of course, speech. Each person in the tribe posits that other members think more or less like him- or herself and has a similar sense of self or soul. Each person has certain rights and privileges and an accepted standing in the group hierarchy. This is also accompanied by other knowledge necessary for the smooth functioning of the interpersonal relations. Each member contributes the skills of a hunter, food gatherer, and warrior, while conforming to the mores of the tribe. This conformity bestows on each individual a communal self entitled to help, protection, and other survival advantages from the tribe. The price paid by each individual is the sacrifice of some personal liberties to the leaders of the tribe, who presumably act for the good of the group. This appears to be the origin of the self identified with individual ego, or the sense of self that is part of the friendly user interface called consciousness. Social skills demand an ability to think through possible responses to individual actions from other group members, before carrying them out. This understanding of the actions of other members of a communal group appear to be mediated by mirror neurons (Rizzolatti and Craighero 2004). These mirror neurons could also help primates to learn new survival skills by imitation. These social skills could have morphed into our sense of fairness, equity, and morality (de Waal 2005, 2006). Each primate developed awareness, both of itself and of others, which could be used to cooperate with other group members. This awareness of other members of a social group and problems of getting along with them must have been the origin of individual rights and responsibilities, accountability for one's actions, and individual morality as a practical tool for lessening friction and promoting cohesion and cooperation within a group. Such awareness could also be used occasionally to deceive deliberately to obtain food and sex. Our cousins the chimps appear to be quite good at such intentional deception, and so are we (de Waal 1997, 35–6, 38–9; 1998, 34–6, 62–3). Cheating, without being caught, at least once in a while, does confer a few survival advantages, and all primates cheat. It is a sure sign of self-awareness, as well as of the ability to put oneself in the position of another member of the group and know how that member would think or respond to a particular situation.

Consciousness is aware of the external world only through the preprocessed and interpreted data from the nonconscious part of the brain; it is never aware of the primary or basic input data. Like the computer user in the earlier example of a letter written on a computer, the consciousness never senses the 0's and 1's; it senses only the words of the letter. Studies on patients with split-brain surgery, discussed later in this chapter, show that consciousness creates a coherent narrative of the mind and behavior of a person, even supplying missing parts where necessary. The sense of self, part of the user-friendly interface called the consciousness, also helps each individual to live as part of a group that practices cooperation enlivened with competition. Such a group must have conferred benefits of reproductive fitness and strengthen the sense of self as part of evolution. This is the user illusion of the sense of self. To recall Nagasena's analogy of the chariot mentioned earlier, the complete sense of self can only be associated with a properly functioning brain and body. If their full functioning is compromised in anyway, as in dementia or other diseases, the normal sense of self will be adversely affected.

Some Consequences of User Illusion of Self

One immediate consequence of the user illusion of self is to ascribe to it a reality or assume the usual ghost in the machine. This is only the first step in making a number of assumptions, all based on faith and belief, and none supported by experimental data about the self or an individual soul. These assumptions, most of them wishful thinking, are part of the support system of a person's favorite religion, politics, or related belief system. Individual ego, when confronted with the realities of life, such as an uncertain and fear-provoking future and the utter powerlessness and lack of control by the individual, lead naturally, for the individual or the tribe, to positing the hypothesis of an all-powerful deity of superlative attributes who is on the side of the individual or the tribe and acts as its protector. This is a type of power coalition that could be warm and comforting in an uncertain life. The continuity of life after death, the immortality of the soul, and reward–punishment systems in heaven and hell all came to be accepted as part of the belief system of religions. In the fertile field of reassurances about the hereafter, religious professionals found an ideal situation in which to assert their dominance. They claimed special privileges and status because of their supposed ability to mediate between the individual and the tribal deity and the certainty of reassurances about the hereafter they provided. Dominance and exploitation by religious professionals is the price believers have to pay for the comfort and assurances they get in return. Hence, the birth of human ego or sense of self had many consequences—some expected, others not foreseen.

Models of Self

At present, no one understands how signals fed into the brain become consciousness, the sense of self, the I-me-mine, that all of us are familiar with (Koch 2004; Gazzaniga 2008). Because such understanding is far in the future, tentative steps have been taken to form models of a person's different types of self, as discussed in the following sections.

Genetic Self

The genetic self, or a person's genome, is inherited from one's parents at conception. The genome and the environment together determine the trajectory of a person's life, including the onset of various diseases and debilitating circumstances of later life. A newborn weighs about 7 to 10 pounds, whereas an adult might weigh about 150 pounds. To get to adult size, that baby undergoes a growth of about 15-fold. Hence, in an adult, most body cells that were present in babyhood have been replaced by new cells, except for neurons, which undergo changes, new growth, and pruning as life progresses. Under these circumstances, why do we say that the baby and the adult are the same person? Problems of identity, change, and continuity raised by this question have an ancient pedigree and came to be called the "ship of Theseus paradox." Theseus, who later became king of Athens, had used a thirty-oar ship during his voyage to Crete to kill the Minotaur and free the Athenian maidens and youths sent as tribute to Minos, king of Crete. Plutarch mentions that this ship was preserved in Athens and could be seen as late as during the lifetime of Demetrius of Phalerum (ca. 345–283 BCE), an Athenian scholar, statesman, orator, founder, and first librarian of the great library of Alexandria (Clough 2001, 1:13–4; Seyffert 1956). The decayed planks of the ship were replaced one by one, till all the planks were new. Local philosophers questioned whether the ship made of new planks could still be called a ship of Theseus. If the old planks were assembled to form another ship, which ship had a better claim to being called a ship of Theseus? The ship of Theseus paradox has long been discussed as a problem in philosophy (Audi 1999; Olin 2003; Sorensen 2003). New and interesting perspectives on these old problems are possible from the viewpoint of modern genetics (Danchin 2002). It is the genetic self or the genome of a person that retains the identity of a person throughout life.

Legal or Physical Self

After birth, one acquires a physical or legal self, with name, birth certificate, Social Security number, passport, citizenship papers, fingerprints, retinal scan, and so on. This confers legal privileges as well as responsibilities that are backed by society, as set forth in the constitution of the nation that claims the person as a citizen. Such rights are now generally accepted as human rights, especially after their approval and acceptance by members of the United Nations.

Damasio's Models of Self

Damasio is a physician who has worked with patients with neurological problems. To explain the results of his research on the human brain, he has postulated different types of consciousness and corresponding kinds of self (Damasio 1994; 1999; 2003). In a healthy brain, these layers of consciousness or types of self work in partnership, resulting in a total functioning normal individual. If parts of the brain are compromised by disease, accidents, or surgery, these models are used to explain the observed symptoms. Such models, it is good to remember, represent the currently available data, and future observations could change the picture. A detailed discussion of such these models including what parts of the human brain are or presumed to be involved, is found in Damasio's books. Here, I touch only on the highlights as he described them. At the root of this scheme is the nonconscious protoself made up of a continuous, real-time representation of the state of the human body. This feeds into a core consciousness with a core self that contains a transient but conscious reference to individual organs of the body, with a strong involvement of the genetic self or the genome. Damasio believes that the core self undergoes minimal changes during the lifetime of the organism. The core consciousness supports the autobiographical consciousness and the autobiographical self made up of current memories as well as reactivation of past ones. It is reasonable to assume that the core and autobiographical consciousnesses together give rise to the feeling of a self or soul in the body, sometimes called the ghost in the machine. This expression was introduced by Gilbert Ryle (1900–1976), a philosopher who called it the dogma of the Ghost in the Machine, which he proved to be entirely false because it was a category mistake (Ryle 1949, 18). These ideas have been further pursued by Rodney Cotterill, to deny such an entity, in his book: *No Ghost in the Machine* (Cotterill 1990). However, it is difficult to exorcise the ghost and cast it away, because humans like to postulate an agent behind every action that seems purposeful. Such an agent is the ghost in another guise. It is good to recall that the apparently purposeful coiling and uncoiling of the toy Slinky as it moves down, or "walks" down, some stairs has no agent other than the laws of physics controlling it (Hood 2009, 114).

What do the empirical data tell us about the sense of self and its development in the course of human life? The earliest detection of sense of self in a baby is supposed to be at about age 2, with the birth of empathy. Crying by another human can elicit a sympathetic response from a baby. Perhaps it represents the earliest sign of separation of one's self from the other (de Waal 2005, 185). It is generally accepted that a person's earliest memories begin at about age 3, which may be considered the beginning of the autobiographical consciousness and self. As a baby grows, it acquires an extended consciousness, with a demarcation of self and others, the birth of taboos, do's and don'ts. It is generally considered that the sense of self is fully formed in the first decade of life, when the brain pathways are fully insulated by myelin. However, the full growth of the neural network, with all its checks and balances, may not be in place till the third decade of life. Along the way, a person acquires a social self with social consciousness, as a responsible member of society. The growth of these different stages of consciousness and corresponding sense of self, or its "outfolding," appears analogous to the blooming of a flower in the morning sun. The fully formed sense of self can be compromised by accidents, dementia caused by normal aging, or diseases such as Alzheimer's. This is also accompanied by the progressive structural deterioration of the brain and a gradual "infolding" of the sense of self. In severe dementia, there appears to be a slow withdrawing of the person, accompanied by a gradual diminution of social interactions and social self; isolation from family members with the loss of extended self and taboos; failure to recognize family, friends, and the loss of autobiographical self; followed by the loss of core self, and with it, the sense of self. The poignant question "Who am I?" may be the last cry for help from a person drowning in the bottomless whirlpool of dementia and the dissolution of sense of self (Damasio 1999, 209). One sad fact of dementia is that the sense of self can vanish while a person is alive and functioning in a much diminished way. It is truly a living death. Is this proof, as Crick suggested, that the humans are nothing but an aggregate of neurons (Crick 1995, 1)? Or, as LeDoux, a neuroscientist, would have it: "You are your synapses" (LeDoux 2002, ix). Synapses are the spaces between brain cells in which information is transmitted by chemical means with neurotransmitters. Such evidence may not be considered a proof that convinces everyone; however, it is highly suggestive of the conclusion that without a normally functioning brain, there is no complete sense of self, no person. The eyes of a severely demented person tell it all: they are blank, there is no sense of a person behind them, and they show no response to their surroundings.

Ramachandran's Characteristics of Self

V.S. Ramachandran, a neuroscientist, has defined the human self in terms of five characteristics: continuity, or an unbroken narrative of one's life; unity of self experienced as one person; ownership of the body in which the self resides as a free agent in charge of one's actions; and self-awareness (Ramachandran 2004, 96–98). It is also pointed out by him that each or some of these attributes of self can disappear if the corresponding parts of the brain are compromised by disease, accidents, or surgery. Again, these facts prove that the sense of self, with its complete set of attributes, cannot exist without a fully functioning, healthy brain.

Additional Observations on Self

In a few patients with epilepsy that cannot be treated by other means, the thick bundle of nerves connecting the right and left hemispheres of the brain is cut surgically. This effectively isolates the two hemispheres of the brain, with the result that each is not aware of what the other does. This procedure is called split-brain surgery and has enabled neurologists such as Sperry, Gazzaniga, and LeDoux to study the specialization of the two hemispheres of the human brain (Gazzaniga 2008). In most right-handed people, the left hemisphere is dominant, specializing in language, speech, and intelligent behavior, while the right is good in such tasks as upright face recognition, focusing attention, and making perceptual distinctions. Researchers also found a module in the left brain that formed a narrative of the actions of the disconnected right brain, about which it had no direct information. This left-brain module has been called an interpreter because it forms a connected narrative, story, or a myth out of the information it knows on the behavior of the disconnected right half (Gazzaniga 2008). The interpreter is assumed to play a key role in the formation of the sense of self, including its unity as the undivided self of one person, by binding together all of the information that it receives from the different modules of the brain. This again justifies calling the sense of self a user illusion or an artifact of the brain. It is also possible that the interpreter module plays a significant part in the interplay between reason and belief in making decisions. A person's gut feeling could be the conclusion arrived at by the much larger number of neurons participating as the nonconscious part of the brain, compared with the logical consciousness. A gut-feeling conviction may not be always supported by conscious, objective, known empirical data and reason. Having arrived at a decision, a person could be just finding logical arguments in support of such a conclusion by the astute use of the interpreter. Damasio has pointed out the important role of emotions in human decision making (Damasio 1994, 127–201). Perhaps there is quite a bit of overlap between one's gut feelings and emotions, and the so-called reasoning or logic behind decisions may be just a veneer that hides the real decider.

Newberg and colleagues compared the brain images of people practicing intense meditation or prayer with their baseline brain images at rest (Newberg, D'Aquili, and Rause 2001). They observed that during these rituals, the brain activity in the left orientation association area showed a marked decrease compared with the right side. These changes were accompanied by a decrease or dissolution of the sense of self and an increased feeling of unity or identification with the universe at large, or the object of meditation or prayer. In the Tibetan Buddhist and in the Franciscan traditions investigated here, the aim of meditation or prayer is exactly that. It is to overcome the limits of one's ego and achieve a sense of identity with the object of one's devotions. This feeling of the suspension of the sense of self is ascribed to a decrease in the sensory input to the orientation association area of the brain brought about by meditation or prayer (Newberg, D'Aquili, and Rause 2001, 113–23). Whether this model is correct or not, and despite whether it has to be changed to explain newer, later data, the fact remains that the boundaries between the self and other can be made to disappear under the voluntary control of the practitioner. This fact once again shows that the sense of self is an artifact, a user illusion, of a normally functioning brain and nothing more. On the other hand, a person can say that there is more to one's sense of self than what is observed by laboratory experiments—it is the immortal soul! However, if such an entity is above and beyond experimental observations and the testing of hypotheses, its very nature would be a matter of opinion and not of science.

There are various additional observations on how consciousness and sense of self can be modified by external agents. Since they first appeared on Earth, humans have been experimenting with altered states of consciousness, out of curiosity, for variety, for recreation, or in search of a supranatural experience in a religious rite. The methods used to attain such altered states of consciousness are various, attesting to human originality: Fasting, exposure to the elements, sensory deprivation, and self-mortification are some of the methods that different cultures have tried. Repetitive visual or auditory input and physical movements such as dancing and whirling have also been effective in altering consciousness. Neuropathology of various sorts—epilepsy, with or without temporal lobe focus; any number of conditions that could lead to the occurrence of temporal lobe transients; viral infections; other diseases, including lesions and atrophy of parts of the brain; brain surgery—can result in marked changes in personality and behavior. Trauma sustained through warfare, accidents, or sports injuries can also cause problems. Drugs similar in chemical structure to neurotransmitters have been used since prehistory for recreation or as part of religious rituals. Electrical and magnetic stimulation of the brain can cause intense emotions, including "mystical experiences," memory recall, and the sense that there is a supranatural presence, and reproduce "out-of-body" or "near death" experiences (Della Sala 1999; Persinger 1987). Damasio has pointed out the important part played by emotions and feelings in the formation of the sense of self (Damasio 1999). Our sense of self can also be adversely affected by a loss of place in a dominance hierarchy (de Waal 2005, 50–1). Chimps or humans who lose alpha status become mere hollow shells of their former selves. This is one of the strictly social conditions that affect our self-image. Sudden loss of wealth, bereavement, and learning of a fatal illness and impending death are other factors that can have similar adverse effects. Mental problems such as depression and bipolar disorder can result in much compromised states of self or even, in severe cases, lead to suicide (Solomon 2001; Torrey and Knable 2002; Jamison 1995; 1999).

Empirical Data and the Self

What do all these empirical data amount to? It depends on how we interpret them, how much weight we give to such interpretation, or our temperament. Empirical data on the mind–body connection, and how mental states can be influenced by external chemical or physical agents and by the condition of the body, are suggestive of a proposition that the user illusion of self is determined by the brain. This interpretation is also supported by observations about cases of severe dementia and the progressive loss of all human attributes, including intelligent speech, memory, and the sense of self. The strongest case that empirical data can make in support of the idea that the self is nothing but a by-product of a healthy, normally functioning brain is the disappearance of an individual's identity in dementia. For materialists or skeptics, these data are significant, merely confirming their belief that the mind and consciousness are nothing more than neural states of the brain that can be explained by natural laws. As yet, there are no reductionist explanations of how consciousness originates from sensations; however, some will be formulated, most probably by the twenty-second century, to confirm the convictions of those who have been saying, "There is no ghost in the machine." Such a conclusion is in consonance with the teachings of the Hindu materialists or humanists: Bṛhaspati and his school and the no-self doctrine of the Buddha. These intuitive speculations, put forth in the sixth century BCE, are truly revolutionary. However, it is good to remember that these no-self doctrines are opinions or beliefs, just as are doctrines that assert that there is a self or a soul. Believers in some religious traditions assert that in addition to the human attributes derived from a normally functioning brain, each person has an immortal, nonmaterial, supranatural soul or spiritual essence, completely independent of the brain. Such a soul by its very definition will be beyond the reach of experimental observations and cannot be studied by science. No one has yet invented an experimental device, a soul-detector, to detect a soul or measure its properties. Without such experimental data, any proposition about a soul's existence will remain empirically undecidable and will be strictly a matter of belief, faith, or opinion. The lack of experimental data severely limits how much we know or can talk about souls in general, and we can only reasonably side with the agnostic who says, "I do not know."

Interactions of a Nonmaterial Soul with a Material Body

The hypothesis of a supranatural soul raises two interesting questions that have not been answered to everyone's satisfaction. The first is a mechanism for the interaction of the nonmaterial soul with a material brain and body. Most religions declare such a mechanism to a mystery, known only to God. The second is the process by which this essence gets associated with moral responsibility for actions performed by the body, mind, and its "soul." The moral responsibility in this world is supposed to result in punishments for various lengths of time and degrees of severity in each religion's version of hell. These accounts never explain how the nonmaterial soul can experience pain or pleasure in the hereafter, where there are no sensory neurons or a brain to experience these states. Such an extrapolation from a material world to a nonmaterial situation appears to be totally meaningless. Again, the answer to the details of such a process is that it is a mystery. It is in this context that various religions have erected their own superstructure of ethics, theology, and the use or abuse of such social-control mechanisms as shame, sin, guilt, merit, and expiation. These assertions, by their very nature, are beyond experimental verification or the scrutiny of truth-in-advertising laws. One immediate consequence of such faith is the tacit acceptance of the dominance hierarchy of the religion professionals and their claims to being privy to all of these special communications from their favorite god. A skeptic can even hazard the theory that the whole superstructure of religions involving heaven and hell, reward and punishment, promises of an immortal life as opposed to eternal damnation, and related ideas is preached by these worthies so that they can gain dominance and power over the believing faithful. It is the extension of the primacy drive into a new dimension of the supranatural. In short, this is a package deal of all religions, where faith demands that the believer accept the totality of theology, eschatology, special privileges, promises for the hereafter, and the dominance of the religious elite in the here and now. It is pursuit of power by other means.

Conscious Will as a User Illusion

It is tacitly accepted by some that individual conscious will is free of any constraints. As such, every individual is morally or legally responsible for her or his actions. The consequences of this assumption have been discussed over ages by philosophers, legal and religious scholars. How free is conscious will in the context of our present knowledge on the subject? In real life, it is found that there are a number of subtle, hidden constraints on free will that perturb its freedom. These lead us to conclude that conscious will is not as free as it is said to be or a few would like it to be.

Determinism and Free Will

Determinism and free will are contradictory; this is an old problem much debated by philosophers. Max Born, a physicist, said that if one believes in strict determinism, free will is an illusion. Put another way, a belief in free will implies that the deterministic laws of nature are a futile exercise (Born 1968, 107). (Objects in the everyday world of human experience are large compared with atomic dimensions; hence, quantum indeterminism is not relevant here.) As has been pointed out by Wegner, free will and determinism are not exact opposites because they belong to different categories. Free will is a feeling, whereas determinism is a process, and it is not possible to balance the first against the second (Wegner 2002, 322). However, is it possible for determinism to influence decisions of free will in ways that are not obvious? What do empirical data tell us about this question? Computer games designed to study decision-making processes at the Center for Neural Sciences at New York University, under Paul W. Glimcher, were able to predict with 90% success choices made by individuals (Hall 2010, 87). It is quite possible that such deterministic predictability of outcome could depend on types of experiments or other variables. This needs further study; stay tuned.

Conscious versus Nonconscious Brain

It was pointed out earlier that the conscious brain has a data-processing capacity that is small compared to the much larger (by several orders of magnitude) data-processing ability of the nonconscious part. The fact that the nonconscious brain is involved in decisions was first shown by the neurologic experiments of Libet discussed later in this section. These experiments showed that the nonconscious brain decides a fraction of a second before the conscious brain is aware of it to carry out a self-initiated voluntary movement. Recent work by John-Dylan Haynes and coworkers at the Max Planck Institute for Human Cognitive and Brain Sciences, Leipzig, has shown that in some cases, this interval could be as large as 10 seconds (Hall 2010, 91). Solutions to complex problems that baffle the conscious brain appear suddenly out of the blue, presumably solved by the nonconscious part of the brain.

Genetic Effects on Decisions

Individual differences in making decisions may be due to genetics. Some individuals are decisive, whereas others procrastinate; there are risk-takers and thrill-seekers, whereas there are others who cannot live with such excitement; some seek novelty and yet others are quite satisfied with tradition and routine; a few are at peace with their decisions and subsequent actions, yet others go back and dwell on the pros and cons forever. The list can go on and on. Because some of these characteristics run in families, they must have a strong genetic component, not completely understood now.

Tribal Mores, Norms of Behavior, and Group Status

Tribal mores, accepted norms of social behavior including codes of morality and personal responsibility, can severely restrict decisions. Associated with these ideas is the status of the individual in the power hierarchy of the tribe. There will be a great reluctance to decide on anything that will jeopardize the high status of an individual, or what other members of the tribe think of the person. If, however, the decision that can enhance individual status in a hierarchy, it will be acceptable. The primacy drive can influence decisions in subtle ways.

Causal Connection Between Mind and Body

The experience of conscious will occurs when a human mind decides on an action and then the body performs it. The mind wanting to do something and the body then doing it, both governed by the conscious mind, are entirely distinct, and confusing them leads to the illusion of conscious will (Wegner 2002, 3). As has been pointed out by Wegner, the feeling of conscious will is very much dependent on the causal connection between the mind and body; hence it is an illusion, as is explained in the following paragraphs. Hence, the feeling that the conscious brain of a person wills an action is an illusion. Both these aspects of the experience of conscious will need some explanation. An action can be preceded by two choices of the human *mind*: wanting to do it or not wanting to do it. This can be followed by two actions of the *body*: do or not do. A successive happening of these two can result in four choices as follows:

1. The mind wants to act, and the body does it.
2. The mind does not want to act, and the body does nothing.
3. The mind is not conscious of acting, in spite of which an action occurs.
4. The mind thinks it is acting, yet the body is not an active agent of influence.

These four possibilities are best represented by a 2 × 2 square (Wegner 2002, 8). The experience of conscious will is strongest in the first two cases, where the mind and the body are in consonance; it is not as strong in the remaining two, where they are not. This is one of the reasons conscious will is an illusion. Psychologists call the situation automatism when the mind is not aware of an action and thus does not feel will and yet the body acts. Examples of these are automatic writing, use of the Ouija board, and many others discussed by Wegner (Wegner 2002, 99–144). The last case is called illusion of control, when a physical agent does not cause an action, but the mind thinks that it does. Here are some examples of illusion of control: A rare event occurs, such as the pitching of a perfect baseball game, and the pitcher expects that it will happen again if only he or she wears the same clothes. The clothes may never be laundered again so as not to wash away their "magic," which is expected to compel the rare event to happen again. A gambler wins big after talking to the dice or doing any other similar ritual and thinks that he or she could make it happen again if only the "magic" ritual is repeated. Thus, the circumstances of the mind wanting and the body performing an action influence the feeling of conscious will, pointing to it as an illusion.

Libet's Neurologic Data

In 1965, Kornhuber and Deecke observed that electrodes attached to the scalp of a person recorded cerebral activity that preceded any physical action performed. They called this the buildup of electrical activity in the brain, the readiness potential (RP), indicative of the motor area of the brain preparing for action (Nørretranders 1998; Wegner 2002). Libet and his group measured the duration of the sequence of events, including the RP, before the occurrence of some voluntary movement by the person under study. The movement was self-initiated and acted on by the person under her or his volition and not on an external command. The RP was found to occur about 550 milliseconds (1 millisecond = .001 second), before the act in most cases, and by as much as 1,050 milliseconds for complex movements that needed preplanning. The study participant's awareness of wanting to move happened after the onset of RP—200 milliseconds before the action (Libet et al. 1983; Libet 1993). These measurements have been repeated and confirmed independently. Thus, before the conscious brain is aware of wanting to act, the nonconscious brain has already begun the action. This experimental result has to be accepted as a fact of life, in spite of the problem of moral responsibility for our actions that it creates. Libet has emphasized that though the intent to act arises without the awareness of consciousness, human free will can exercise a veto, thus making a moral choice (Libet 1993, 278–9). This result is a consequence of evolution, which decided that it is more efficient for the nonconscious brain to act before the conscious part is aware of it. Thus, conscious free will is an illusion in more than one way. First, the degree of experiencing free will can vary with circumstances, and second, the ego of an individual might feel that it initiates an action, but the nonconscious brain has already started it. All of these circumstances indicate that conscious will is a type of user illusion. If this assertion creates a moral problem, it is time for theologians to retool their moral controls and perhaps find new answers to their problem.

This study, in preparation for the 2004 talk that I gave on the sense of self and the conscious will as user illusions, and later thinking on these problems, has been quite helpful to me. This part of my education has continued to occupy my mind and has been crucial in forming my worldview and in helping me separate the empirically known from the merely speculative.

Our Travels in Retirement

During my working years, my wife and I had dreamed of traveling not for business but for pleasure, out of curiosity. Travel became an important item on our agenda in retirement for fun and as a form of anthropological exploration. We wanted to see a few countries before we got too old to travel. Long plane trips are problems that get worse with age and declining service on planes in general. The security measures instituted after the terrorist attacks of September 11, 2001, are a necessary nuisance to protect the innocent public. It is amusing to note that these measures are an example of applied myth and ritual theory espoused by some anthropologists (Segal 1998). The rituals we are all familiar with make us remove our shoes, belts, coins, metal objects, and so forth, motivated by the fervently held myth that doing so will prevent the bad guys from carrying out their nefarious plans.

Australia, New Zealand, and Fiji

Our first trip was to Australia, New Zealand, and Fiji in January–February 2002, for about 29 days. We were part of a large group of retired Americans, and the trip was organized by a professional tour group. We found the Australians to be open, hospitable, straightforward people, without any of the British or European delusions of cultural superiority. In Australia we went up in a hot air balloon, early in the morning one day. It was quite an experience to see kangaroos and other animals from the air! The balloon landed in a field, and some of us stepped into the plentiful cow patties lying around and concealed by the tall grass. From the sublime to the ridiculous! The New Zealanders were equally open and hospitable. On our way to Queensland, we flew over the Tasman Glacier and had lunch at the Mt. Cook National Park, where there was a spectacular view of the mountains. We visited a Maori village to enjoy a staged ceremony of welcome by their local chief, with an elected "chief" from our group. They put on a Maori dance and other tribal ceremonies, followed by a *hangi* feast cooked in the traditional way in a pit, with the raw food overlaid with embers. Maoris have been able to survive and keep their culture alive and are much better off compared to other native peoples. This is because they fought the British settlers to a standstill, forcing them to negotiate the Treaty of Waitangi (1840), which granted the Maori British citizenship and land rights. They survive today because they fought for their rights. Violence does pay dividends, and sometimes it is the only way to prevail. Otherwise, people will walk all over you. Unfortunately, this was the sad fate of Native Americans and of Australian Aborigines. Fiji looked very much like the South Kanara District with its coconut, jackfruit, breadfruit, mango, and other trees; tropical flowers; and the hot, humid weather. We stayed at the Warwick Fiji Hotel Korolevu, which was in a bubble totally separate from the rest of the island. The locals entered the bubble to work at the hotel and left it to go home at night. I had hopes of seeing Suva, the capital, and of trying some local restaurants. This proved to be impossible. The roads were bad; there was no transportation other than what was provided by the tour group. Local Fijians were employed in the gift shops in the hotel, as waiters, and as hotel staff members. In the evening, some of them put on their tribal regalia and took part in a ceremony of lighting flaming torches fixed to strategic locations on the hotel grounds, accompanied by much drumming. The hotel guests would relax with their drinks while the natives ran around, doing their stuff. It was colonialism and the flaunting of the might of the ruling class at its worst! I felt ashamed and embarrassed to be part of the dominance hierarchy of the *sahib lok*, or the ruling elite of the Raj. Among the hotel staff members, there were some people of Indian origin. These were the descendants of indentured labor from India recruited to work in the sugar cane fields owned by British settlers. The story of Indian migrations to Fiji and the rest of the Pacific region has been told recently (Hajratwala 2009). We could see some of the rusting sugarcane factories by the wayside; I do not know whether they are still functioning or not. The native Fijians and the descendants of the Indian indentured laborers do not get along well; they fight for dominance. The Fijians resent the Indians as interlopers, though they were all born in Fiji and have lived there for many generations. For the native Fijians and Indians, the only source of livelihood appears to be the tourist trade, any remaining sugar-cane industry, and some agriculture. There is one university, and a few schools, and little else. The pace of life is very slow and languid, as is the local greeting of "Boola, boola!" On the whole, Fiji was very depressing. I could not see any future for the Fijians or the Indians on the island.

Japan

A seventeen-day trip to Japan in August/September 2005 was our next adventure. Japan is beautiful and clean, with its exquisite landscape and gardens. We learned that children are taught civic responsibility when quite young and learn to clean up after themselves and not litter. There was no rubbish or garbage even on the sides of railway tracks! Tour buses had trash bags in front of every seat; and we learned to dispose of our trash properly. We stayed for three days in Tokyo before venturing further. Our stay in Tokyo was memorable because of my encounters with The Thing. The Thing was an automated, electronically controlled toilet seat with a personality of its own. It was an example of the Japanese love of electrical gadgets gone mad! Apparently this was an American invention later bought by the Japanese, because it did not sell well in the United States. Attached to the toilet seat or the throne was a thick cable ending up in a control panel, about eighteen inches long, with some ten to twelve dials. I never learned how to use all these dials or how to turn off the damned Thing. Its eternal vigilance was most unpleasant. I got a feeling that Big Brother was watching my every move. I am sorry if I sound paranoid about it. The Thing would sense when a person sat on or got off the throne and automatically flush, causing much noise in the middle of the night and waking up my wife. In short, one could not sneak up on The Thing or surprise it. The actions of The Thing were so purposeful that it was easy to ascribe diabolical cunning mixed with a depraved trickster soul to it. The Throne was heated, a few times too much, making it truly a hot seat. My wife experienced this problem in one of the bathrooms in the hotel lobby. Someone must have left the temperature control on maximum, because she jumped off the seat with a scream. I have photos of The Thing to prove that it was real and not a paranoid delusion.

When in Tokyo, we visited Kamakura to see the bronze image of the Buddha, Daibutsu. We saw the early morning auction of fresh-frozen tuna in the Tsukiji Fish Market, and then ate a breakfast of hot soup and fresh sushi. Though I have tried the sushi a few times out of curiosity, my wife and I are not great fans of raw fish. In Hakone, we stayed at a Japanese-style hotel. The rooms had tatami mats on the floors, and the bathrooms were Japanese style. We put on kimonos before sitting down to an elaborate Japanese-style feast with many dishes, each exquisitely assembled to please the eye and a work of art in itself. Mineral water from the local hot springs was channeled into separate baths for men and women, which we enjoyed a lot. We traveled by the Shinkansen, known as the bullet train, part of the way. Passengers are told where to stand on the platform, and the train stops exactly in front of you so that you can access your reserved seat with a minimum of trouble. Amazing! In Kanazawa, our group attended a tea ceremony in the famous Kenrokuen Garden. A powerful typhoon was expected in the area at the time, and it was truly amazing to see how trees, some very old, were prepared to withstand the high winds. Vulnerable tree branches were wrapped in quilted padding before being propped up by sturdy wooden supports to prevent any breakage. The keepers of the grounds must have put in quite a bit of work to protect those old trees. The Japanese gardens are beautiful because of the enormous amount of human effort that goes into keeping them that way. Kyoto was wonderful, with its treasures of old Japan. The high point of our trip was a visit to the Koryu-ji Temple to see the wooden image of Miroku Bosatsu (Maitreya Bodhisattva, or Buddha of the Future) in the museum behind the temple. This seventh-century wooden image was brought from Korea along with Buddhist scriptures to introduce Buddhism into Japan. Because of its age, the image is no longer used in daily worship and is kept in a museum. An introspective Buddha with an enigmatic smile proclaims *śūnyatā* (emptiness) with the tips of the thumb and the third finger of his right hand touching. It is one of the most beautiful sculptures I have ever seen. A visit with a Japanese family was part of our itinerary. Our hosts were Mr. and Mrs. Nobuo Mizuguchi; he is a retired aeronautic engineer, and she is a homemaker. They had traveled widely through China, the United States, and Europe. They had also invited two women, friends of our hostess. Their English was much better than our

Japanese, and we had a delightful visit. When they learned that I was retired, one of the women asked Padma whether I was a "low-maintenance" husband. This requires some explanation. Retired husbands in Japanese folklore have acquired some notoriety and are called *nureochiba* (wet leaves), which stick to the pavement and are difficult to scrape off. With nothing to do in retirement, they offer to help around the home, are difficult to get out of the kitchen, and are a general pain in the neck. Because I minded my own work, Padma assured her that I was indeed low maintenance. Our hostess was a teacher of the Japanese tea ceremony, and she served us tea as honored guests. Then she showed Padma the basic steps of the tea ceremony. Padma did the honors and served tea to our hostess, and she did it quite well. I have photos to prove it.

St. Petersburg and Scandinavia

A Scandinavian odyssey was our next trip. In a span of twenty-three days in July–August 2006, my wife and I visited St. Petersburg and the Scandinavian countries, including Iceland. We were part of a group of about 45 people, all retirees. The four days in St. Petersburg, with visits to the State Hermitage Museum, Petrodvorets Palace and Gardens with thousands of fountains and waterworks, cathedrals, and other places of interest, were memorable. In my brush with mineralogy, I had seen pictures of huge vases and whole rooms decorated with the dark green mineral malachite in Russia, and this was my chance to see them in person and admire them. They were beautiful and very impressive, and so was the newly restored Amber Room in Catherine Palace in Pushkin. The luxury of the dominance hierarchy of royalty, nobility, and the rich seemed obscene compared with what must have been the life of Russian serfs. No wonder the peasants revolted, precipitating a revolution in 1917!

Though we stayed at a hotel sporting many stars after its name, the comfort and convenience of guests were not part of management's game plan. In addition, the staff members still lived in a worker's paradise, much more concerned about their perks and privileges than with the needs of hotel guests. Any special requests were answered by a curt no or "Not done that way." If by some chance the hotel guests enjoyed a little convenience, it was strictly unintentional.

We next went to Helsinki, Finland, and Copenhagen, Denmark. The hotel in Copenhagen was a converted warehouse; massive ancient wooden beams meant to support high floor loading were everywhere. A visit to Kronborg Castle, home of Hamlet, set on the cliffs of Elsinore, was obligatory. In Copenhagen, we boarded an overnight ship bound for Oslo. Padma gets seasick very easily and was worried; however, the sea was smooth as a millpond. Norway and its fjords were beautiful. We saw the famous Viking longboats dating back to 800 CE in the Viking Ship Museum in Oslo. We visited the Kon-Tiki Museum and saw the balsa raft *Kon-Tiki*, built in 1947, and the papyrus boat *RA II* of 1970, both famous from the Thor Heyerdahl expeditions. Our next stop was in Eidfjord, where our room had a magnificent view of the fjord that changed with the light of the day. In Stockholm, Sweden, we visited the Vasa Museum, which houses a fully salvaged and restored seventeenth-century warship, the *Vasa*.

On this vacation, we were surprised at the amazingly hard-nosed we-do-not-trust-you stance of the hotels; I had never seen such a brazen attitude in all my years of travel. We could not make an international telephone call or open the minibar in the room without giving a credit-card number. The minibars were stocked so full that they had no room even for a small carton of milk. If a guest at the hotel in Copenhagen used the minibar to keep a personal item cool, the charge was 40 kroner (then approximately $6.60). Just as in Russia, the hotels in Denmark did not appear to be concerned with the convenience of their guests.

On our way home, we visited Iceland and its barren, almost lunar landscape. A dip in the Blue Lagoon, a blue-tinged geothermal pool of hot mineral water in Reykjavik, brought us close to the hot interior of Mother Earth. The waterfalls at Gullfoss, and the periodically spouting hot springs, including the Great Geysir, were spectacular. To get a good picture of the geyser without getting my camera wet, I had to watch for wind directions and place myself accordingly. We drove to a glacier in a car with special wheels to see more of the same desolate landscape.

Turkey, Greece, and London

In September 2007, we went to Turkey and the Greek Islands and mainland, and then stopped by London on the way back for five days. We spent four days in Istanbul, and visited the usual tourist spots: the Spice Market, Topkapi Palace, various mosques, the Aya Sofya, the Hippodrome, the Obelisk of Theodosius, the bronze Serpentine Column, and the Column of Constantine. At night, we dined at a nightclub, the Turkish Delight, while we watched belly dancers. Tourists there from different countries sat at tables complete with their own national flags. Turkish food is interesting but heavy on meat.

We wanted to try a genuine Turkish bath, and the charges at the Çemberlitaş Hamami, built in 1583 by the famous architect Sinan (~1490–1588), looked reasonable. This bath had separate facilities for men and women, and Padma, with another woman from our group, accompanied me. On checking in, each person gets a sliver of soap, a new pair of disposable rough gloves for cleaning, a metal bowl for pouring water, and a towel with a key to a cubicle for storing belongings. After undressing, you place the towel round your waist and then enter a steam room with an octagonal heated marble platform with many water taps on the wall surrounding it. After you pour the warm water over yourself a few times, you lie on the hot platform, where the inverted bowl acts as a pillow. With all of the heat and humidity, you perspire and all of the pores in your skin open. After a while, an attendant enters with a bucket, works up lots of lather, and starts working on you with soap and gloves to do a thorough job of cleaning. You next move to a different room to sit under one of the cold taps for more washing of your head and body. You can then shower alone as a finale in a different room. You end by tipping the attendant and sipping hot tea while a sense of cleanliness and general well-being pervade you. Padma and her friend had an experience in the women's part of the bath that was equally delightful as mine.

We then flew to Athens. I had been to Greece in January 1964 for a few days to visit places of archaeological interest after leaving Canada and on my way home to India. This was my second visit after more than forty years. After a day in Athens and a visit to the Acropolis and the Parthenon, we boarded a ship for a four-day cruise among some of the Greek Islands: Mykonos, Patmos, Rhodes, Crete, Santorini, and back to the Piraeus in Attica. We also visited Kusadasi and Ephesus in Turkey as part of the cruise. The weather was great, and we really enjoyed the wine-dark Aegean. On the mainland, we went to Olympia, Nauplia, Mycenae, Epidaurus, Arachova, Delphi, Kalambaka, and back to Athens. At the sanctuary of Asclepios in Epidaurus and the attached theater with its wonderful acoustics, our group stood in the center of the orchestra and sang "When the Saints Go Marching In," led by Robert Long, a nuclear engineer from Albuquerque, New Mexico. The song sounded amazingly good and was heartily applauded by the other tourists in the auditorium. The ancient monasteries of Meteora, built on almost inaccessible outcroppings of rock to escape persecution, and their frescoes are unique examples of Greek Orthodox monastic life. We spent almost a whole day exploring the ancient Agora of Athens and tried hard to locate the prison where Socrates was held before his execution. Unfortunately, we could not find it, and local guides were not particularly helpful. Perhaps its location is only a guess. The National Archaeological Museum of Athens had a memorable special exhibition on Praxiteles (b. ~390 BCE), in addition to all its other treasures. I was particularly happy to see the Antikythera mechanism. This unique device was discovered in 1900 by some Greek sponge divers on the shores of the island of Antikythera, which lies in the shipping channel between mainland Greece and Crete. It was part of a marine wreck believed to have occurred at some point between 80 and 60 BCE. At first sight, the object looks like a congealed mass of corroded green metal with sea encrustations. However, recent work by astronomers, archaeologists, chemists, and physicists using high-resolution X-ray tomography, combined with reconstructions, has revealed this to be the remains of a sophisticated 2,000-year-old analog computer, or a lunar–solar calendar and eclipse predictor (Marchant 2009; Freeth et al 2006). This mechanism was made from more than thirty interlocking bronze, notched gear wheels, each about 2 millimeters thick, with Greek inscriptions serving as directions for use. It was mounted on a wooden frame and was about 12.4 × 7.5 × 3.9 inches. Most probably, it was constructed sometime between 150 and 100 BCE in Rhodes. This is an amazing piece of technical achievement on the part of ancient Greeks, attesting to their manual dexterity and technical sophistication.

The Greek love of an elaborate lunch followed by a leisurely siesta, with the result that shops are closed during most of the day, makes life very difficult for tourists. Such a lunch played a crucial role in the capture of Athens by the tyrant Pisistratus in 546 BCE: The Athenians, who had marched toward Marathon to fight Pisistratus, were either having lunch or sleeping off its aftereffects when he appeared on the scene. They did not fight the invading forces, failing utterly in their mission (de Sélincourt 1962, 115). People easily forget their past and do not learn from it. The Greeks appear to love their midday custom and intend to maintain it.

We visited London briefly because Padma had never been there and we wanted to meet my sister Kasturi; her daughters, Mridul and Rekha; and their families. Kasturi is a physician who worked as an anesthesiologist in Scotland; she is retired and lives in London suburbs. Her elder daughter Mridul, is in civil service, and the younger daughter Rekha, is a physician-psychiatrist. We stayed at the Tavistock Hotel; right in front of it is a park with a seated bronze statue of Mahatma Gandhi. We saw all the tourist sights, including the British Museum, which had a special exhibit on Qin (Ch'in) Shi Huangdi (221–210 BCE), the first Qin emperor of China, and the terracotta army guarding his grave mound. The Chinese at that time had solved the problem of mass production of identical weapons with interchangeable parts and had the very sophisticated technology needed for it. They had even standardized agricultural implements and the width of axles for carts! We attended an excellent matinee performance of *Love's Labour's Lost* at Shakespeare's Globe Theatre. The seats in the middle gallery were good; however, it was too bloody cold for September, and we wished we had warmer clothes. At the end of the play, the pipe and tabor struck up a lively tune, heralding revelries to come. The cast broke into a bold, lusty, stomping, romp of much merriment. Perhaps the scantily though fetchingly clad women on the stage were trying to keep warm!

Israel, Egypt, and Jordan

We traveled to Israel, Egypt, and Jordan next, staying from 25 October through 20 November in 2009. We spent six days in Israel, fifteen days in Egypt, and another six days in Jordan. On the whole, this trip was enjoyable. We ate all the vegetables, fruits, and salads without the gastrointestinal problems popularly called Pharaoh's revenge. Our interest in Israel was entirely cultural and historical, without any religious overtones, though religions—Judaism, Christianity, and Islam—are very much a presence there. The Israeli–Palestinian problems are also evident to any person visiting there, even a casual tourist. The wall of separation on the West Bank, the control and checkpoints for the Palestinians, and the difference in the appearance of Jewish versus Palestinian houses and villages are all facts of life. Our Israeli tour guide, a resident of Jerusalem, was quite open in discussing both sides of these problems. These are complex issues of power and dominance built on deeply held beliefs in the ancient mythology of Jewish and Palestinian sacred texts, colliding with the present-day realities of life. They also point out the hazards of strongly held belief in mythologies as real-life events. I was surprised to find our tour guide talking about Herod the Great as a non-Jew. On my pointing out the forced conversion to Judaism of his grandfather, Herod Antipater I, and fellow Idumeans under John Hyrcanus (135–104 BCE), she grandly declared that Herod's mother was not really Jewish (Schalit 2007; Stern 2007). I suppose these questions of who is "genuinely" Jewish will always be with us. We could see only a limited number of places and things in Jerusalem and Israel in the six days that we were there. Because of some riots, we could not go to the Dome of the Rock or its surroundings; perhaps as non-Muslims, our group could not enter the place anyway. The Holocaust museum Yad Vashem, the Via Dolorosa and related churches, the Shrine of the Book housing the Dead Sea Scrolls, and other places of historical interest were memorable. We took the cable-car ride to Masada and saw the Qumran caves and the ruins of the place that housed the Qumran community; we also saw Caesarea, built by Herod. Floating in the Dead Sea was quite an experience, both in Israel and later in Jordan. In Jordan, as Padma and I were getting out of the Dead Sea and chatting in Konkani, we were recognized as fellow Konkanis by a few GSB tourists who were from Udupi.

We spent a week in Cairo and the neighboring areas before moving on to the boat *MS River Anuket* on the Nile. We were put up at the Mariott Hotel, a former palace with the best of modern facilities. I was in Cairo for about 24 hours in 1964, having missed the connecting flight from Greece to India; hence, this was my second visit to the Pyramids, the Sphinx, and the Museum of Egyptian Antiquities. The food at the Mariott and on the boat was tasty. The high points of the boat cruise were the Aswan High Dam and the recently transposed temple of Abu Simbel high above the waters of the Nile.

In Old Cairo, we visited the Ben Ezra Synagogue, famous for the discovery of its Geniza documents, a huge number of Jewish manuscripts or fragments of manuscripts, sacred and secular, spanning nearly a thousand years, from the ninth to the nineteenth century CE (Khan and Ben-Sasson 2007; Ghosh 1992). The present building is a restoration completed in 1997. The original synagogue was built in 882 CE in an area called Fustat, now Old Cairo, and had Rabbi Moses ben Maimon (Maimonides, 1135–1204 CE), among other notables, as a member of the congregation. The Geniza was a repository of various documents that could not be destroyed because they had God's name on them and had to be disposed of according to prescribed rituals. The business letters, marriage settlements, and other secular documents tell the stories of many ordinary Jewish people—their lives and loves, sweet and bitter. The story of Abraham Ben Yijū, a Tunisian merchant, industrialist, scholar, and poet has been found at the Geniza (Goitein 1971, 20; 1973, 1978). The story of this Jewish merchant who lived for seventeen or eighteen years, from about 1130 to 1148 CE, at Mangalore in the South Kanara District (Map 1), has been extracted by Amitav Ghosh in his book, *In an Antique Land* (Ghosh 1992). Ghosh learned to read Judeo-Arabic, a colloquial dialect of medieval Arabic written in Hebrew script, to unravel this story from Ben Yijū's business letters. He followed the trail of the letters in the many libraries in which they are dispersed now. A bare outline of his story is given here; a full account is told by Ghosh and others (Goitein 1971, 1973, 1978; Gordon 2008). Ben Yijū was born in Mahdia, Tunisia, to a rabbi. As a merchant, he moved to Fustat (Old Cairo), to Aden (in Yemen), and then to Mangalore. He was a cultured man—a calligrapher, scholar, and poet—and a man of refined tastes. A public document has survived that is dated Monday, 17 October 1132; it is an instrument of manumission in which he sets free his slave, a Nayar woman, Ashū, has survived and is now preserved in St. Petersburg (Goitein 1971, 20). Some three years later, they have a son Surūr (Joy) and then a daughter, Sitt al-Dār (Mistress of the House). There is mention of a Nayar brother-in-law. Nayar women had property rights from matrilinear descent observed in their high-status warrior community and much greater autonomy compared to other Hindu women. Did Ashū convert to Judaism? Did they marry? Was the marriage Halakic? The letters inspire many questions but provide no answers. Most probably Ashū did not convert, or perhaps there was no marriage, just a working arrangement between the two. How do we know this? Letters from Ben Yijū's friends greet his son and daughter and even his slave or servant, Bomma, by name, whereas they are silent about Ashū. Even Ben Yijū's letters do not mention her by name. She appears to be in a curiously anomalous position, tacitly treated as an "other." Perhaps this liaison did not meet the standards of propriety of his friends and family; we can only guess. Ben Yijū's jolly urge to propagate the species triumphs over tribal and religious strictures, and he prospers in Mangalore with his trade and a bronze factory and becomes quite rich. Bomma, a local who was a slave or servant to Ben Yijū, is another prominent actor in this drama. He is sent to Aden as Ben Yijū's business agent, gets drunk a few times, and has his share of adventures. Ben Yijū decides to fold his tent and leave India permanently in about 1138–1139 and move to Egypt. Strong family bonds and changed circumstances of his two brothers living in the Mediterranean countries force his departure. He is also anxious to find mates for his children from among his own people. He leaves behind his companion, Ashū, and, accompanied by his son, daughter, and Bomma, moves to Aden. In a letter dated September 11, 1149, from Aden, he mentions his search for mates for his children from among their cousins and also offers his wealth to his brothers in their straitened circumstances. Ben Yijū told his brothers that the wealth he had acquired should be enough for his family as well as theirs, and being a pious Jew, he invoked God to make that wish come true (Goitein 1973, 203). During his three-year stay in Aden, his firstborn son, Surūr, dies, and his younger brother defrauds him of a large sum of money. Leaving behind these adversities, he moves to Egypt, where in the summer of 1156, his daughter marries her cousin, Peraḥyā ben Joseph, son of his elder brother, who becomes a judge in a rabbinical court. A detailed list of her trousseau is preserved in the State Library of St. Petersburg (Goitein 1973, 202, 327). Ben Yijū fades away from recorded history after his daughter's wedding; there is no mention of his death in any surviving documents. He is one example of the many merchants of Jewish, Arabic, and other ethnicities involved in the millennia-old trade between the Mediterranean countries and the west coast of India.

A visit to the new Bibliotheca Alexandrina, built near the site of the famous ancient Library of Alexandria, was memorable. The library and an astronomy observatory were part of the Museion, or museum, dedicated to all the Muses, and a center for learning and research. In the foyer of the building is a marble statue of Demetrius of Phalerum, perhaps the first founder of the library under the Ptolemies (Seyffert 1956). It would be most fitting to have there a statue of Hypatia (ca. 335–415 CE), daughter of Theon, a mathematician who taught at the library (Dzielska 1995). Hypatia was an astronomer, mathematician, and philosopher who taught philosophy and mathematics at the library and in her home. Unfortunately, she was a victim of the power struggle between the civil authority of Orestes, the prefect of Egypt, and the religious faction of Cyril,

Bishop of Alexandria (and later St. Cyril, Father and Doctor of the Church), who represented the new power of Christianity, flexing its muscles. Orestes was a moderate Christian who, as the civil governor, wished to treat all the citizens of Alexandria, Jews, Christians of different sects, and followers of the old religions, Greek and Egyptian, equitably. Cyril of Alexandria had succeeded his uncle as the bishop and had also inherited control over a militia of several hundred armed monks. Cyril believed in a proactive muscular Christianity backed by local Christians and the militia. Hence, he was not a detached spectator of the political power struggle with the prefect and was actually in the thick of it. Provoked by an earlier attack by Jews on Christians, and alarmed by the threat of their proselytizing, he expelled Jews from Alexandria and confiscated their property. He destroyed the churches of the Novatians, another Christian heretic sect, and expropriated their wealth (Burghardt 2003). There is a difference of opinion about the extent of Cyril's involvement in Hypatia's death. Some opine that Hypatia was brutally murdered by a Christian mob of men employed by Cyril (Dzielska 1995, 102–5; Deakin 2007), while a dissenting opinion holds that this charge is unfounded (Burghardt 2003). Though Cyril might not have participated directly in Hypatia's lynching, he was most probably responsible for inciting the passions of the Christian zealots who did the dirty deed. What is certain is that Hypatia was one of the early martyrs to Christian intolerance against the pagan Greeks and their culture. The meek, lowly, docile Christians of yesteryear had become dominant, intolerant, aggressive wielders of power, which corrupted them. The primacy drive triumphed once again!

The final leg of our trip was to Amman, Jordan, the Dead Sea, Jerash (a well-preserved Greco-Roman city), and of course the façade of the Treasury in Petra. We walked from our hotel to the Treasury on a chilly, overcast day, perhaps going over an ancient caravan trade route. I am sorry to state that all the publicity and hype about the Treasury did not live up to the reality. I am glad to have seen it; however, it was not the mind-blowing experience I had expected. Our tour of Wadi Rum, with its strange and beautiful rock formations, including the aggregate of high cliffs called the Seven Pillars of Wisdom, made famous by Lawrence of Arabia, was certainly much more impressive. These short trips to different countries, cultures, and civilizations give us the smallest taste of their life. The residual memories of these trips depend on a number of factors, including the hotels, food, transportation, and our day-to-day guides—the trip leaders provided by the tour organizers. Our best tour experience was in Egypt, followed by Jordan and Israel. The trip leader in Jordan was certainly unique among all of the tour guides we met in all of the earlier five tours with the same tour outfit. We came to know him better than the others, he was more empathetic than the others, and if the tour had lasted longer, he would certainly have inducted the whole group into his Bedouin tribe!

Konkani Sammelana

Every two years during the July Fourth weekend, the Konkani speakers in the United States and Canada have a gathering, or *sammelana*. We have attended the past three meetings in Anaheim, California (meeting 5, 2004); Hamilton, Ontario (meeting 6, 2006); and Santa Clara, California (meeting 7, 2008). We did not attend the earlier four meetings of this series. About 1,500 to 2,000 people attend these events, which last for about three days and are filled with many Konkani cultural happenings, including seminars and lectures, classical and modern dancing, concerts, plays and comedy skits, and other celebrations. There is a separate youth program with events that suit the tastes and mores of the young who were born in the United States and Canada, to acquaint them with Konkani traditions from back home. CDs are available so that we can enjoy the amazing range of artistic talents of the Konkani community exhibited at these meetings. Konkani food from the west coast of India is served, with the active cooperation of local caterers whose staff members are trained to make these special regional dishes. Above all, there are meetings with friends and relatives and catching up on the latest happenings in the community. The logistics of these events are truly staggering, and yet these events have been extremely well organized through the year-long hard work of local organizing committees. The Konkanis can work wonders when they cooperate and strive together.

Closing Thoughts

This is the end of the story of my family. It is my version of events as I saw or heard about them. To the members of my family who have a different narrative, I invite them to write it down. Be bold, hold forth, and tell your own story. I would be interested in listening to it. Writing this book has been an interesting experience. Recalling the past, reliving the incidents I remember, and experiencing the self-examination and introspection that writing involves have been helpful in coming to terms with myself and my past. I recommend it to everyone as a useful exercise in perceptive living. In the meantime, I keep active, eat and drink in moderation, and exercise to keep fit. My curiosity remains unabated; to satisfy it, I try to learn new things. The thrill of understanding new ideas and melding them with the old mind-set is still there; it is its own reward. The passing drama of life has not lost its fascination to me. I see and delight in it. I detest dominance of one person by another and the exploitation that follows from it, and speak out against both where ever I find these. The abuse of tools of social control such as guilt, shame, and sin, to manipulate and use others is equally wicked. These in excess are an existential threat to a life of sanity, moderation, and compassion and should be used sparingly, if at all. Dominance and abuse of tools of social control by some hierarchies are abhorrent because they can also involve bondage, either physical or mental. My wife and I travel a little, as much as our aging bodies will allow. My genes along with the environment are in control of the trajectory of my life. I anticipate with equanimity the final dissolution and extinction (*nirvāṇam*) of the illusion of my sense of self in the rising tide of entropy.

In the summer of 1998, the Center for India Studies at SUNY at Stony Brook organized a series of lectures called "Discovering India: A Children's Odyssey." These were meant to introduce 8- to 14-year-olds to the various aspects of India's culture and civilization in a number of one-hour talks. I volunteered to cover India's contribution to the sciences and mathematics in two lectures. In preparing for these talks, I came across a poem by Rabindranath Tagore (1861–1941), whose many contributions to Bengali literature are well known and who was awarded the Nobel Prize for literature in 1913 (Dutta and Robinson 1996). This intriguing poem was written in 1896 and was given a Bengali title: "*Tattwagnanhin.*" A Sanskrit equivalent would be "*Tatvajñānahīna.*" It has been translated many times, and I have seen at least six different versions, in anthologies of Tagore's poems or on the Web. In one recent collection, the poem's title is translated "Unphilosophical" (Chaudhuri 2004, 120, 391). I would rather call it "The Agnostic." An agnostic readily admits that there are areas of knowledge that are not known. *Agnostic* and *agnosticism* were words coined in 1869 by Thomas Henry Huxley (1825–1895), English biologist, to stake out his intellectual position on the limits and validity of knowledge (Lightman 1987). Agnostic is a person who claims that *gnosis*, or esoteric knowledge of spiritual matters, is unknown or unknowable. There is no knowledge beyond the material phenomena which are observed and understood. In the Hindu tradition, agnosticism has an ancient lineage going back to the *Ṛgveda* (ca. 1500 BCE). The *Nāsadīya Sūkta* (*ṚV* 10.129; O'Flaherty 1981, 25), a creation hymn, is full of questions on the origin and creation of the cosmos—who, what, where, whence, and how. The intent of this hymn is to provoke thought, not provide answers. The Vedic poet speculates that perhaps only the creator can answer these questions, and wonders whether even he can. Then there is another creation hymn, "The Unknown God," (*ṚV* 10.121; O'Flaherty 1981, 26) in which an agnostic poet sings a refrain wondering: "Who is the God whom we should worship with the oblation?" Agnosticism accepts these limits on knowledge, which are also implied in the poem. This poem was part of a Bengali book of popular science essays on atoms, the stars, the sun, and the planets by Tagore, published in 1937. A translation of this book by Ms. Indu Dutt contains this poem without a title (Tagore 1969). I distributed copies of this poem to illustrate to my young audience at SUNY at Stony Brook the two distinct methods of exploring the universe: philosophical inquiry and scientific investigation, each of which leads to entirely different results from the other. Meditation on the universe with eyes closed is a type of philosophical inquiry that leads to opinions. Observing the universe with eyes open and with a hunger for new information, combined with experiments that suggest new hypotheses or refute them, is scientific investigation, which results in understanding. Tagore's graphic imagery of the philosopher who is focused on the realm of thought and detached from the world versus the scientist who is very much engaged with it are unforgettable. I wanted my audience to carry these images in their minds, whether they understood the differences between these two modes of inquiry or not. I had no way to judge how much of this message got through.

Here is the poem as translated by Indu Dutt, with its original title:

The Agnostic

Whoever wishes,
May he sit in meditation
With eyes closed
To verify if the universe be true or false.

I, in the meanwhile,
Shall sit with insatiate eyes
To see the universe
While the light lasts.

APPENDIX ONE

The Cast

The cast of this story, mostly family members, is listed here in case the reader has problems placing any person in the proper context. Names of the main actors in the story narrated in Chapters 1 to 5 are given; some auxiliary names are left out. For names, every attempt has been made to have a one-to-one correspondence with the family narrative and the genealogy charts in Appendix 2, "Family Genealogy." Dates are given if known; a few individuals requested that no dates should be given for their immediate family. Professions are listed as additional distinguishing markers. The numbers in parenthesis are from a genealogy chart, reproduced with updates as Chart 2, "Descendants of Narasimha Bhat," in Appendix 2. These numbers are helpful in distinguishing amongst individuals with the same name but belonging to different generations. Birth names and married names of women are indicated where known.

The following abbreviations are used: aka = also known as; b/n = birth name; b/o = brother of; d/o = daughter of; f/o = father of; h/o = husband of; m/n = married name; m/o = mother of; s/o = son of; w/o = wife of.

Ammanni: w/o Ganapathi Bhat (#92), m/o Vasudeva Bhat (#102) and Madhava Bhat (#103). Homemaker.

Ananthayya Prabhu: (1872–1947), s/o Venkataramana Prabhu, adopted f/o Shridhar Prabhu, h/o Sri Devi. Document writer.

Annapurna: (b/n) Nayak (m/n) (1958–), d/o Narayana Bhatji (#119) and Laxmidevi aka Sharada, w/o Prabhakar Nayak. Homemaker.

Appi: (b/n), aka Sarasvathi (m/n), aka Bappamma (1899–1980), d/o Ananthayya Prabhu and Sri Devi, w/o Manjeshwar Narayana Bhat. Homemaker.

Ashok Kamath: (1971–), s/o Lalitha and Gopalakrishna Kamath, h/o Chaya Kamath. Businessperson.

Ashwin Bhandary: (1977–) s/o Kumuda and Gopalakrishna Bhandary, h/o Sri Vidya. Architect.
Avanish Bhandary: (1973–) s/o Kumuda and Gopalakrishna Bhandary, h/o Sri Kala. Physician/anesthesiologist.

Baba Bhat: aka Babanna, s/o Majoor Bhat, h/o Sundari, son-in-law of Subraya (aka Subba) Bhat.
Bantwal Govind Bhat: h/o Mathura, aka Sitabai. Priest.
Bhavani: (b/n) aka Padmavathi (m/n) (1891–1958), d/o Ananthayya Prabhu and Sri Devi, w/o Madhava Bhat (#103), my paternal grandmother. Homemaker.

Chaitra Bhat: (b/n) (1973–) d/o Rathnakar (aka Madhavaraya) Bhat (#140) and Jai Bhavani. Electronics engineer, IBM.

Dasappa Kamath: f/o Sri Devi, father-in-law of Ananthayya Prabhu.
Dayananda Bhat: (#118) aka Dayya Mhanthu, s/o Vasudeva Bhat (#102), who assembled the clan Atri genealogy chart included in Appendix 2. Priest.
Devaraya Bhat: (1929–2007) s/o Narayana Bhat aka Hodu Mamu and Sulochana, h/o Indira. Businessperson.

Ganapathi Bhat: (#92) s/o Narasimha Bhat (#83), h/o Ammanni, f/o Vasudeva Bhat (#102) and Madhava Bhat (#103). Priest.
Giridhar Bhat: (#145) (1971–) s/o Radhakrishna Bhat (#138) and Padma (aka Varada). Physician/anesthesiologist.
Gokulananda Sharma: aka Gokulanna, s/o Tulasi (aka Tucci Mhava) and Taranath Krishna Bhatt, h/o Pratibha (aka Vasanthi). Professor Emeritus, Engineering Science and Mechanics, Pennsylvania State University, University Park, Pennsylvania, United States.
Gopalakrishna Bhandary: (1939–) h/o Kumuda, f/o Avanish and Ashwin Bhandary. Businessperson.
Gopalakrishna Bhat: aka Gopalakrishna Bhavaji (1923–2004), s/o Narayana Bhat (aka Hodu Mamu) and Sulochana, h/o Maya. Chemical engineer.

Haradi Vasudeva Pai: Ananthayya Prabhu's second employer. Lawyer.

Kanaka Mai: second w/o Kumble Subraya Prabhu, employer of Ananthayya Prabhu. Homemaker.

Kasturi: (b/n) Hegde (m/n) (1936–), d/o Narayana Bhatji (#119) and Laxmidevi (aka Sharada), w/o Taranath Hegde. Physician/anesthesiologist.
Katapadi Sripathi Bhat: aka Katapadi Mamu (1910–1995), s/o Upendra Bhat, h/o Manorama (aka Mannakka). Priest.
Kitti Mai: first w/o Kumble Subraya Prabhu, employer of Ananthayya Prabhu. Homemaker.
Krishna Bhat: (#93) aka Kuttani, s/o Narasimha Bhat (#83), f/o Nethravathi, Mathura, and Vedavathi. Priest.
Kumble Subraya Prabhu: aka Kumble Subrayu, Ananthayya Prabhu's first employer (not related). Lawyer.
Kumuda: (b/n) Bhandary (m/n) (1948–), d/o Narayana Bhatji (#119) and Laxmidevi (aka Sharada), w/o Gopalakrishna Bhandary. Homemaker.

Lalitha: (b/n) Kamath (m/n) (1934–), d/o Narayana Bhatji (#119) and Laxmidevi (aka Sharada), w/o Gopalakrishna Kamath. Homemaker.

Madhava Bhat: (#103) aka Ajjo (1884–1959), s/o Ganapathi Bhat (#92) and Ammanni, h/o Bhavani (aka Padmavathi), and my paternal grandfather. Priest.
Majoor Bhat: f/o Baba Bhat. Tax official.
Manjeshwar Narayana Bhat: aka Puttur Ajjo (1886–1962), h/o Appi, aka Sarasvathi, f/o Narasimha Bhat (aka Narasimha Bappa). Teacher.
Manjeshwar Shridhar Bhat: (1914–1989) s/o Manjeshwar Narayana Bhat and Appi (aka Sarasvathi), adopted s/o Ananthayya Prabhu and Sri Devi. Lawyer; Registrar, Indian Institute of Science, Bangalore, India.
Manorama: (b/n) aka Mannakka (1921–2002), d/o Madhava Bhat (#103) and Padmavathi (aka Bhavani), w/o Katapadi Sripathi Bhat (aka Katapadi Mamu). Homemaker.
Mathura: aka Sitabai, d/o Krishna Bhat (#93; aka Kuttani), w/o Bantwal Govind Bhat. Homemaker.
Mohini: (b/n) aka Mohiniakka (1922–2010), d/o Madhava Bhat (#103) and Padmavathi (aka Bhavani), w/o Anantha (aka Aithu) Bhat. Homemaker.
Mridul Tansley: (1967–) d/o Kasturi and Taranath Hegde, w/o Phillip Tansley. Civil service, United Kingdom.

Nagesh Rao: (1952–) h/o Nandini Rao, f/o Neha Rao. Computer engineer.
Nandini: (b/n) (1956–) d/o Narayana Bhatji (#119) and Laxmidevi (aka Sharada), w/o Nagesh Rao. Bank employee.

Narasimha Bhat: (#1) progenitor of our family of clan Atri in Mulki. Priest.

Narasimha Bhat: aka Narasimha Bappa (1912–1991), s/o Manjeshwar Narayana Bhat and Sarasvathi, h/o Tara (aka Tara Pachchi). Principal and Professor Emeritus, Mathematics, Maharashtra Education Society (MES) College, Pune, India.

Narayana Bhat: aka Hodu Mamu (1902–1980), s/o Subraya (aka Subba) Bhat and Vedavathi. Priest.

Narayana Bhatji: (#119) (1907–1992) s/o Madhava Bhat (#103) and Padmavathi (aka Bhavani), h/o Laxmidevi (aka Sharada), and my father. Document writer.

Neha Rao: (1987–) d/o Nandini and Nagesh Rao. Pharmacist.

Nethravathi: aka Nethru Mhava (1880–1946), d/o Krishna Bhat (#93; aka Kuttani), w/o Padubidri Srinivasa Shenoy. Homemaker.

Padma: (m/n) aka Varada (b/n) (1936–), d/o Maroor Vitala Hegde and Indira, w/o Radhakrishna Bhat (#138), m/o Giridhar Bhat (#145). Homemaker.

Padmanabha Sharma: aka Panni Maamu (1912–1963), s/o Subraya (aka Subba) Bhat and Vedavathi, h/o Anasuya (aka Rohini). Dentist.

Padubidri Srinivas Shenoy: h/o Nethravathi (aka Nethru Mhava). Businessperson.

Panduranga Bhat: aka Pandu, f/o Narayana, Krishna, Srinivasa, Ramachandra, Padmanabha, and Subraya (aka Subba) Bhat. Priest.

Panduranga Sharma: (1945–) s/o Padmanabha Sharma (aka Panni Maamu) and Anasuya (aka Rohini), h/o Lakshmi. Computer engineer.

Premananda Bhat: aka Premanandu (1934–), s/o Sarasvathi aka Appi (aka Bappamma) and Manjeshwar Narayana Bhat, h/o Malathi. Defense Department.

Pushpa: (b/n) Bhat (1951–), d/o Narayana Bhatji (#119) and Laxmidevi (aka Sharada), w/o Subhas Bhat. Bank employee.

Radhakrishna Bhat: (#138) (1930–) s/o Narayana Bhatji (#119) and Laxmidevi (aka Sharada), h/o Padma (aka Varada), f/o Giridhar Bhat (#145); the author. Nuclear physicist.

Raghuvir Bhat: (#142) (1946–) s/o Narayana Bhatji (#119) and Laxmidevi (aka Sharada).

Ramanath Bhat: aka Ramanath Bappa (1924–), s/o Sarasvathi (aka Appi, Bappamma) and Manjeshwar Narayana Bhat, h/o Prema Bhat. Electronics engineer (retired), All India Radio.

Rathna: (b/n) aka Rathna Akka, aka Sharada Kini (m/n) (1921–1989), d/o Appi (aka Sarasvathi, Bappamma) and Manjeshwar Narayana Bhat, w/o Vasudeva Kini. Homemaker.

Rathnakar Bhat: (#140) aka Madhavaraya (1941–), s/o Narayana Bhatji (#119) and Laxmidevi (aka Sharada), h/o Jai Bhavani (aka Sharada). Scientist.

Rekha Wooton: (1975–) d/o Kasturi and Taranath Hegde, w/o Alexander Wooton. Physician and psychiatrist.

Seetharam Prabhu: (1900–1916) s/o Ananthayya Prabhu and Sri Devi.

Shankar Kamath: (1969–) s/o Lalitha and Gopalakrishna Kamath, h/o Rakhee, f/o Siddhartha. Physician specializing in internal medicine.

Sharada: (b/n) aka Laxmidevi (m/n) (1914–1989), d/o Subraya Bhat and Vedavathi, w/o Narayana Bhatji (#119), and my mother. Homemaker.

Shreedhara Bhat: (#141) aka Shiddha (1943–), s/o Narayana Bhatji (#119) and Laxmidevi (aka Sharada), h/o Suman. Physician specializing in neurology and internal medicine.

Shridhar Prabhu: aka Shridhar Bappa (1914–1989), adopted s/o Ananthayya Prabhu and Sri Devi, h/o Srimathi (m/n) (aka Pacci, Rathni; b/n). Lawyer; Registrar, Indian Institute of Science, Bangalore, India.

Soira Vittala Bhat: progenitor of my maternal family of clan Vatsa; built Vittala Gudi in Mulki. Priest.

Sri Devi: aka Hodemma, aka Shirdevi (1872–1936), d/o Dasappa Kamath, w/o Ananthayya Prabhu. Homemaker.

Sri Laxmi: (m/n) aka Dakshayani (b/n) (1955–), w/o Suresh Bhat (#143). Homemaker.

Sri Sukrath Bhat: (1998–) s/o Sudhir Bhat (#144) and Subhalaxmi (m/n) (aka Sheethal; b/n).

Srimathi (m/n) Prabhu: aka Rathni (b/n), Pacci (1919–1986), d/o V.D. Kamath, w/o Shridhar Prabhu. Homemaker.

Srinivasa Ganapathi Bhat: (#145C) s/o Ganapathi Bhat (#133); the only practicing priest left in our family. Priest.

Srinivasa Shridhara Prabhu: (1938–) s/o Shridhara Prabhu (aka Shridhar Bappa) and Srimathi, h/o Jayanthi. Professor Emeritus, Electrical Engineering, Indian Institute of Technology Kanpur, India.

Subhalaxmi: (m/n) aka Sheethal (b/n) (1966–), w/o Sudhir Bhat (#144). Homemaker.

Subraya Bhat: aka Subba (1859–1948), s/o Panduranga Bhat, h/o Vedavathi (aka Vedu, Ammi), my maternal grandfather. Priest.

Sudhir Bhat: (#144) (1961–) s/o Narayana Bhatji (#119) and Laxmidevi aka Sharada, h/o Subhalaxmi (aka Sheethal). Chartered accountant.

Suman Bhat: aka Vatsala (1947–), d/o Pundalika and Mukta Shenoy, w/o Shreedhara Bhat (#141; aka Shiddha). Homemaker.

Sumathi: (b/n) Bhat (1975–), d/o Rathnakar (aka Madhavaraya) Bhat (#140) and Jai Bhavani. Architect.

Sundari Bhat: d/o Subraya (aka Subba) Bhat and his first wife, w/o Baba Bhat. Homemaker.

Suresh Bhat: (#143) (1953–) s/o Narayana Bhatji (#119) and Laxmidevi (aka Sharada), h/o Sri Laxmi (aka Dakshayani). Businessperson.

Sushila aka Sushilakka: (1925–1999) d/o Madhava Bhat (#103) and Padmavathi (aka Bhavani), w/o Karkal Keshava Joishy. Homemaker.

Tara Bhat: aka Tara Pachchi (1920–1990), w/o Narasimha Bhat (aka Narsimha Bappa). Homemaker.

Taranath Krishna Bhatt: aka Mhanthu (1902–1987), h/o Tulasi (aka Tucci Mhava). Physician.

Tulasi: aka Tucci Mhava (1905–1983), d/o Subraya (aka Subba) Bhat and Vedavathi, w/o Taranath Krishna Bhatt. Homemaker.

Vasanth Sharma: (1942–) s/o Padmanabha Sharma (aka Panni Maamu) and Anasuya (aka Rohini). Computer engineer.

Vasudeva Bhat: (#102) s/o Ganapathi Bhat (#92) and Ammanni, f/o Dayananda Bhat (#118) and b/o Madhava Bhat (#103). Priest.

Vasudeva Bhat: (#139) (1939–) s/o Narayana Bhatji (#119) and Laxmidevi (aka Sharada). Electrical engineer.

Vasudeva Kini: (1918–2009) h/o Rathna ([b/n] aka Rathnakka, Sharada [m/n]). Businessperson.

Vasudeva Taranath Sharma: aka Vasudevu or VTS, s/o Tulasi (aka Tucci Mhava) and Taranath Krishna Bhatt, h/o Arundathi. Businessperson.

V.D. Kamath: f/o Srimathi (aka Rathni), father-in-law of Shridhar Prabhu. Engineer.

Vedavathi: aka Vedu (aka Ammi) (1883–1972), d/o Krishna Bhat (#93; aka Kuttani), w/o Subraya (aka Subba Bhat), and my maternal grandmother. Homemaker.

Vedavyasa Bhat: (1979–) s/o Madhavaraya (aka Rathnakar) Bhat (#140) and Jai Bhavani. Businessperson.

Venkataramana Prabhu: f/o Ananthayya Prabhu. Priest, Haridasa, Nagapathri.

Vilasini Prabhu: aka Villa, d/o Tulasi (aka Tucci Mhava) and Taranath Krishna Bhatt, w/o N. M. Prabhu. Obstetrician-gynecologist.
Vittal Bhat: (#91) s/o Narasimha Bhat (#83), b/o Ganapathi Bhat (#92) and Krishna Bhat (#93). Priest.
Vivekananda Bhatt: aka Vivekanna, s/o Tulasi (aka Tucci Mhava) and Taranath Krishna Bhatt, h/o Maitreyi (aka Sarojini). Professor Emeritus, Organic Chemistry, Indian Institute of Science, Bangalore, India.

Yeshvant Bhat: aka Yeshvanthu (1932–2009), s/o Sarasvathi Bhat (aka Appi, Bappamma) and Manjeshwar Narayana Bhat, h/o Meera Bhat. Electronics engineer.

APPENDIX TWO

Family Genealogy

Genealogy Charts

Three genealogy charts are attached to the end of this appendix:

- Chart 1: Descendants of Venkataramana Prabhu (narrative in Chapter 1, "Prabhus of Siddhapur")
- Chart 2: Descendants of Narasimha Bhat (story in Chapter 2, "My Paternal Grandparents")
- Chart 3: Descendants of Panduranga Bhat (details in Chapter 3, "My Maternal Grandparents")

These charts were assembled using a computer program called Family Tree Maker (Pedersen 2010). The charts are not complete or up to date for a number of reasons, including the fact that I had difficulty in obtaining input data. I hope that someone in our family will update them in the future.

The charts are easy to interpret once their structure is understood. The number preceding each name or to its left denotes the generation of the person, starting with the progenitor of the chart as generation 1. A spouse is shown immediately under the name of a person with a plus sign (+) and with the same generation number as the partner. Children are shown in a vertical column, indented to the right with respect to their parents and with a generation number one more than that of their parents. Dates pertaining to a person are shown immediately after a name. A few people requested that no dates should be shown after their names. Because a complete date of birth could be used in identity theft, only birth years are shown, except for the deceased.

Chart 1: Descendants of Venkataramana Prabhu
These are the maternal ancestors of my father who were originally from Siddhapur in the northern part of the old South Kanara District. The current head of the family is Srinivasa Shridhara Prabhu, who retired in 1998 as professor of electrical engineering and dean of faculty affairs from the Indian Institute of Technology, Kanpur.

Chart 2: Descendants of Narasimha Bhat
Narasimha Bhat is the progenitor of our family in Mulki on the paternal side. He was the Atri *gotra* (clan) priest brought from Kochin to officiate in the Mulki temple. There is an oral tradition in our family that during our life in Kochin and maybe earlier, our family name was either Nayak or Pai. I have heard both family names mentioned; I am not sure which is correct. These are *laukika* (secular) surnames indicating a family profession different from that of priest. It is possible that our family lost everything that they possessed during the exile from Goa and had to start from scratch to survive. Narasimha Bhat must have been quite well versed in Sanskrit and the traditional rites and rituals to morph into a newly minted priest. Information about our earlier life in Goa or Kochin is lost; the memory banks were wiped clean in the upheavals of exile and the later migration to Mulki. My brother Sudhir tells me that a branch of our family (i.e., same *gotra*) still lives in Kochin; I have not tried to contact them. Most probably, the flight of the family from Goa was in the 1560s during the height of religious persecution by the Portuguese. This is strictly conjecture, not supported by any records. There are a few community traditions that the exiles, including our family, sailed down to Kochin in small coastal trading sailboats, *macvo*. We do not know anything else about Narasimha Bhat or his family. However, we can try to estimate his date of birth as follows. My father, Narayana, born in 1907, is the fourteenth generation after him. If we assign 20 years as the interval between generations, we get an estimate of about 1650 CE for the date of birth of Narasimha. This date could be off by as much as 100 years. Again, I stress that this is only an estimate based on all the assumptions listed here. A generation interval of 20 years appears reasonable because professional priests used to marry young, because only married men could conduct worship in a temple. When he moved to Mulki, his house (hut?) was on the temple grounds on the present *bhojana śālā* (dining hall), to the south of the temple.

The data for this chart are from a family tree assembled by my uncle Dayya Mhanthu (Dayananda Bhat, #118), copied by my father, Narayana Bhatji (#119), and mailed to me in August 1977. The numbers preceding a name indicate generations after Narasimha Bhat, who is assigned to generation 1. Numbers in parentheses after names are from the family chart and do not have any significance. They help to separate people with the same name in different generations. I know nothing about the original sources used by my uncle to establish this genealogy. My inquiries about these sources to his children and grandchildren were not fruitful. The chart begins with the family progenitor, Narasimha Bhat (#1) and ends in the seventeenth generation after him. There are no dates, and children who did not attain maturity are left out. Names of wives are not given, though they assume the husband's *gotra* on marriage. Daughters were left out because they married outside the parental *gotra* and assumed their husbands' *gotras*. In short, the chart is incomplete and is that of a patriarchal family, in which only males matter. I have a feeling that this chart was assembled for the specific purpose of settling questions of inheritance rights for the cycle of worship, *paryāya*, in the local temple. It was not meant to convey other relevant information about the family. The chart was assembled perhaps in the 1960s and has been updated only partially. There is only one professional priest, Srinivas Ganapati Bhat (#145C), left in the family; the rest are in other professions.

In writing this book, I have used information assembled by my father, Narayana Bhatji, in a notebook (Bhatji n.d.), supplemented by tape-recorded interviews (Bhatji 1983; 1990). Letters between my brother Shreedhara Bhat (#141, aka Shiddha) and me have been another useful source of information. I have also used a tape-recorded interview with my cousin Villa (Prabhu 2005).

Chart 3: Descendants of Panduranga Bhat

The third chart shows the descendants of Panduranga Bhat, my maternal great-grandfather belonging to the Vatsa *gotra* and a descendant of Soira Vittala Bhat, who is supposed to have migrated to Mulki in the thirteenth or fourteenth century and built a small temple, Vittala Gudi or Mulki Mata, in a hut (see Chapter 2: "My Paternal Grandparents" and Chapter 3: "My Maternal Grandparents"). Unfortunately we do not have any information on Soira Bhat or his progeny, and there are blanks in the chart corresponding to many missing generations. This chart begins with Panduranga Bhat and ends with the current members of the family. There are no practicing priests in my maternal family now.

The Legend of Bikkayya Bhat

The legend of Bikkayya Bhat (#76 in the second chart) is a curious incident in the story of our family that strains belief. The story has *bhūta* (spirits), their fatal influence, astrology, sorcery, and related belief systems with supernatural beings as active participants in human affairs. I have included this story here to give a flavor of the times, including the beliefs prevalent circa 1830 in the village of Mulki in an orthodox family of Hindu priests. It is up to the reader to decide how much of this story can be believed.

Bikka, as he was called, was the son of Baba (#72), who also had two younger sons, Vittal (#77) and Rama (#78). He belonged to the tenth generation after Narasimha; using the same method of estimation as already described, we can calculate the year of his birth as being about 1830. Bikka was a Sanskrit scholar, an astrologer, and a sorcerer, or *mantravādi*. Dabbling in sorcery by a Brahman is usually frowned on because it could lead to unforeseen consequences, usually harmful to the person and his family. However, the small fees that Bikka garnered from these activities were a useful supplement to his earnings from the temple and the services that he provided as a priest. It is believed that the bad effects of practicing sorcery can be counteracted by performing specific rites prescribed by custom. He had a young son who was a rising Sanskrit scholar and an astrologer and who was expected to surpass his father in learning and scholarship. Bikka also had a violent temper bordering on the uncontrollable. Self-control and moderation were not among his virtues. The son ended up becoming the unwitting victim to this flaw in his father's character.

Bhūta worship is quite common in the part of the Karnataka state I come from, but it needs some explanation (Upadhyaya 1996; Upadhyaya and Upadhyaya 2002; Navada and Fernandes 2008). It is of great antiquity and could even pre-date the spread of orthodox Hinduism. At present it is on the fringe of Hinduism. *Bhūta* refers to spirit in general and could encompass any of the following: chthonic, totemic, or animistic deities worshiped since olden days and whose origins have been forgotten; some of these deities that are now identified with Hindu incarnations and have become part of mainline Hindu tradition and more "respectable"; or the spirits of warriors who distinguished themselves in local battles and who were famous enough to be remembered and deemed worthy of veneration. In general they are considered to be subsidiary to the deities worshipped in temples of traditional Hinduism. Once a year, on an auspicious day determined by an astrologer, the spirit is worshipped at a special ceremony with a sacrifice of a cock, goat, or a buffalo and libations of locally brewed toddy made from fermented coconut sap. These are "non-Sanskritized" rituals in which Brahmans do not participate. Animals sacrificed to the spirit are garlanded with red flowers, daubed with red coloring, or draped in red cloth as part of the ceremony. Hence, people are warned not to cross the line of sight of the spirit wearing red flowers or garments lest the spirit mistake such a person as an intended sacrifice and inadvertently cause some harm. Noon and sunset are also considered to be times when the influence of the spirit is especially strong and people are particularly susceptible to its baneful effects. Because alcoholic beverages and animal sacrifices are not usually part of worship in a Hindu temple, the officiating priest is a non-Brahman and belongs to one of the castes of local cultivators. As part of this ceremony, a person "possessed" by the spirit acts as the medium for an oracle. Again, this medium is a non-Brahman, a hereditary practitioner belonging to a caste of cultivators, or toddy tappers. He answers questions posed by the devotees regarding any problems such as illness in the family, litigation, planned activities, and missing people or material things and suggests remedies or solutions that could involve offerings for the spirit or some other temple. Such a person mediating between the spirit and its devotees is called a *darśaṇā pātri*, or medium for the oracle. If the spirit is angered by some act of omission or commission by its devotees, it tells them details of the act as well as its *prāyaścitta*, or expiation. This worship is done at a *bhūtasthāna*, which is usually a structure containing a representation of the spirit, which could be a simple stone or an image of stone or metal. Some of these places of worship are in fields of cultivation, and the owner of the field is expected to bear the expenses of the yearly worship. Thus the owner and his family "inherit" the spirit and the obligation for its worship along with the title to the property.

According to the family legend, Bikka and one of these spirits crossed paths under these circumstances. On special occasions as part of the religious ceremonies performed at home, Hindus invite Brahmans and their wives to an elaborate feast, usually at noon. Gifts, prescribed by religious custom and traditions, are also given. One day, Bikka's sister-in-law was invited to one of these feasts, and apparently she had a red (auspicious color) sari on, and she wore some *ābbālẽ* (red flowers), which were in season, in her hair. On her way to or from the feast, this woman passed in front of the spirit's place at noon. On reaching home, she complained of not feeling well and took to her bed with a high fever. She died within a day or two. The sudden death of this otherwise healthy person was naturally ascribed to the *dṛṣṭi* (evil eye) of the spirit and the fact that she was wearing a red sari and flowers when she was passing in front of the spirit's place. This suspicion was further confirmed by astrology, to the satisfaction of all concerned. Bikka, who was the local expert in incantations and astrology, felt that he had to do something to fix this problem. At the next yearly ceremony of sacrifice for the spirit, he chose the time of worship and also used some incantations to keep the spirit from ever again being able to look straight out horizontally and thus harm any other living creature. As proof that his incantations worked, it was noticed that the medium for the oracle of the spirit could not lift his gaze and looked only at the ground during the ceremony. In addition, one of the first questions the oracle asked was: "How fares Bikka Bhat's family?" Was this a threat? Did the spirit seek revenge because of what Bikka had done to it? There were many questions in the legend, but no answers.

One day at noon, Bikka was hungry and cross when he returned home from his ablutions and worship at the temple. At the entrance to his home, he saw his young daughter-in-law sitting in the passageway and combing her long black hair. In traditional Hindu families, this part of the personal toilet is usually done in the privacy of one's room, certainly not in front of one's father-in-law or elders. Bikka construed this as an act of disrespect, an affront to his dignity, and his anger flared. He told his daughter-in-law: "*Rāṇḍe* ("widow," "slut," "whore"), go in and finish your toilet in your room." She was a spirited young woman with a sharp tongue and supposedly replied: "I am not what you call me. She"—meaning her mother-in-law—"is in the kitchen." To understand the full import of this exchange, I have to digress and explain Hindu mores. The *r*-word is rude and thus never used in polite conversation, and certainly *never* used with reference to a woman whose husband is living. A widow's life in Hindu society is abominable, a living hell; hence this word is charged with more emotion than is carried by its literal meaning. If the daughter-in-law had kept her mouth shut and meekly accepted his rebuke, Bikka would have calmed down. But a tart reply challenging his authority, casting aspersions on his wife's virtue and questioning his own longevity, was more than he could bear. He went out in a great wrath to summon whatever evil forces he controlled by his incantations. He performed death-dealing rites, killing his only son. He cut his nose to spite his face. Any remorse Bikka felt came too late. At the son's funeral pyre, he piled all his manuscripts (*taḷti pustakã*) on sorcery, and burned them. He did not want anyone else in the family to practice sorcery in the future. However, when he came home, he lit a *poṇti* (a small oil lamp), went in search of his grieving daughter-in-law, and asked her: "Who is the *rāṇḍa* now?

That is the dark, tragic legend of Bikkayya Bhat. Was it the revenge of the spirit for Bikka's sorcery to restrict its sight? Did the spirit use Bikka's great weakness, his uncontrollable anger, to retaliate? The reader may wonder: Is it possible for a spirit to kill a woman? Or did she die of sunstroke? Was it a fast-moving bacterial or viral attack? Is it possible to kill a man with incantations?

A certain amount of skepticism is in order in considering these questions. However, what is relevant is what *they*, the people involved in the story, believed and not whether these incidents can bear the careful evidentiary scrutiny of a more skeptical age. The magical "pointing" death of a person brought about by a witch doctor, prevalent among the Australian aborigines and in other cultures and documented by anthropologists, is of interest here (Montagu 1967, 36; Wegner 2002, 288). If a person wants to kill an enemy, a specially prepared "pointing" stick or bone is prepared and a spell is cast by pointing the stick at the intended victim. The efficacy of the spell depends on the firm belief of the object of this curse that he or she is going to die unless there is magic to counteract the spell's fatal effects. The same curse may bounce off a nonbeliever, leaving nary a dent. After the death of Bikka's son, the family lost many children, especially boys, who died young. There was talk of a family curse that had to be removed. At the time, one of the gurus of *Kāśi Maṭh* blessed the head of the family and his wife, *mātyāri hātu kāṇu*, to remove any curse and ensure an abundance of healthy children. The guru also gave him an image of Santāna Gopāla, which shows Lord Kṛṣṇa holding a baby in his arms, to be worshipped in the family shrine in perpetuity. This image, worshipped daily, is still in the family shrine of our ancestral home in Mulki.

CHART 1. Descendants of Venkataramana Prabhu

..... 1 Venkataramana Prabhu

..... + Padmavathi Prabhu

.... 2 Ananthayya Prabhu aka Hodajjo b: 03 Jan 1872 in Siddhapur, d: 1947 in Udupi

.... + Sri Devi Prabhu aka Hodemma aka Shirdevi b: 1872, d: Aug 1936 in Udupi

.... 3 Padmavathi Bhat aka Bhavani aka Annamma b: 15 Aug 1891 in Udupi, d: 25 Dec 1958 in Udupi

.... + Madhava Bhat (#103) aka Ajjo b: 22 Jan 1884, m: 1902, d: 13 Jun 1959 in Udupi

.... 4 Narayana Bhatji (#119) b: 08 Dec 1907 in Udupi, d: 28 Aug 1992 in Udupi

.... + Laxmidevi Bhatji aka Sharada b: 25 Dec 1914 in Mulki, m: 14 Feb 1929 in Mulki, d: 22 Jan 1989 in Udupi

.... 5 Radhakrishna Bhat (#138) b: 1930 in Mulki

.... + Padma Bhat aka Varada b: 1936 in Karkal, m: 20 Aug 1967 in Moodabidri

.... 6 Giridhar Bhat (#145) b: 1971 in Port Jefferson, NY

.... 5 Lalitha Kamath b: 1934 in Udupi

.... + Hosadurg Gopalakrishna Kamath b: 17 Apr 1924, m: 08 Dec 1965, d: 17 Jan 2007 in Udupi

.... 6 Shankar Kamath b: 1969 in Udupi

.... + Rakhee Kamath b: 1971

.... 7 Siddhartha Kamath b: 2004

.... 6 Ashok Kamath b: 1971 in Udupi

.... + Chaya Kamath b: 1972

.... 5 Kasturi Hegde b: 1936 in Udupi

.... + Taranath Hegde b: 15 May 1938, m: 26 Jun 1966 in Bangalore, d: 30 Jan 1994

.... 6 Mridul Tansley b: 1967

.... + Brian Brivati b: 1966

.... 7 Maximillian Krishna Brivati b: 1999

CHART 1. (*cont'd*)

.... 7 Hannah Indra Brivati b: 2000
.... + Phillip Tansley
.... 7 Irene Tansley b: 2010
.... 6 Rekha Wooton b: 1975
.... + Alexander Wooton
.... 7 Noah Taran Wooton b: 2009
.... 5 Vasudeva Bhat (#139) b: 1939 in Udupi
.... 5 Madhavaraya aka Rathnakar Bhat (#140) b: 1941 in Udupi
.... + Jai Bhavani Bhat aka Sharada b: 1949, m: 02 Mar 1972
.... 6 Chaitra Bhat b: 1973
.... 6 Sumathi Bhat b: 1975
.... 6 Vedavyasa Bhat b: 1979
.... 5 Shreedhara Bhat (#141) aka Shiddha b: 1943 in Udupi
.... + Suman Bhat aka Vatsala b: 1947, m: 29 Nov 1972
.... 5 Raghuvir Bhat (#142) b: 1946 in Udupi
.... 5 Kumuda Bhandary b: 1948 in Udupi
.... + Gopalakrishna Bhandary b: 1939, m: 30 Jan 1972
.... 6 Avanish Bhandary b: 1973
.... + Sri Kala Bhandary
.... 7 Sai Dhruva Bhandary b: 2008
.... 6 Ashwin Bhandary b: 1977
.... + Sri Vidya Bhandary
.... 5 Pushpa Bhat b: 1951 in Udupi
.... + Subhas Bhat b: 02 Jan 1951, m: 22 May 1985, d: 21 Aug 2011
.... 5 Suresh Bhat (#143) b: 1953 in Udupi

(*continued*)

CHART 1. Descendants of Venkataramana Prabhu (*cont'd*)

.... + Sri Laxmi Bhat aka Dakshayani b: 1955, m: 09 Jul 1992
.... 5 Nandini Rao b: 1956 in Udupi
.... + Nagesh Rao b: 1952, m: 09 Aug 1981
.... 6 Neha Rao b: 1987
.... 5 Annapurna Nayak b: 1958 in Udupi
.... + Prabhakar Nayak m: 06 May 1992
.... 6 Jagannatha Nayak b: 1994
.... 5 Sudhir Bhat (#144) b: 1961 in Udupi
.... + Subhalaxmi Bhat aka Sheethal b: 1966 in Udupi
.... 6 Sri Sukrath Bhat b: 1998 in Chattanooga, TN
.... 4 Manorama Bhat aka Mannakka b: 23 May 1921 in Udupi, d: 18 Aug 2002 in Bangalore
.... + Katapadi Sripathi Bhat aka Katapadi Mamu b: 29 Mar 1910, d: 06 Aug 1995
.... 5 Padmanabha Bhat b: 02 Nov 1936 in Udupi, d: 12 Dec 2000
.... + Vathsala Bhat
.... 6 Chandrika Prabhu
.... + Prakash Prabhu
.... 7 Gaurav Prabhu
.... 6 Harish Bhat
.... + Pallavi Bhat
.... 7 Adi Bhat
.... 5 Chandramathi Kamath
.... + Annapa Kamath
.... 6 Sudhakar Kamath
.... + Meera Kamath
.... 7 Rahul Kamath

CHART 1. ***(cont'd)***

.... 7 Meghan Kamath
.... 6 Praveen Kamath
.... + Shanthi Kamath
.... 7 Nayna Kamath
.... 7 Neil Kamath
.... 6 Govindaraja Kamath
.... + Vinaya Kamath
.... 7 Sonali Kamath
.... 7 Mona Kamath
.... 5 Ramanath Bhat d: Deceased
.... + Sulatha Bhat
.... 6 Prakash Bhat
.... 6 Prashant Bhat
.... 5 Sumathi Shenoy
.... + Gokuldas Shenoy d: Deceased
.... 6 Gurudas Shenoy
.... + Amitha Shenoy
.... 7 Rakhi Shenoy
.... 6 Rekha Betigere
.... + Sandeep Betigere
.... 7 Sharanya Betigere
.... 7 Neel Betigere
.... 5 Sathyanath Bhat
.... + Savitha Bhat
.... 6 Soumya Pai

(continued)

CHART 1. Descendants of Venkataramana Prabhu (*cont'd*)

.... + Anil Pai
.... 6 Shubha Rao
.... + Aloke Rao
.... 5 Taramathi Shenoy
.... + Ramesh Shenoy
.... 6 Ravindra Shenoy
.... + Preethi Shenoy
.... 4 Mohini Bhat aka Mohiniakka b: 29 Oct 1922 in Udupi, d: 14 Aug 2010
.... + Anantha aka Aithu Bhat b: 1911, d: 1961
.... 5 Surendra Bhat b: 1939 in Udupi
.... + Nirupama Bhat b: 1947
.... 6 Harish Bhat b: 1972
.... + Rama Bhat
.... 7 Mahima Bhat b: 2006
.... 6 Nagaraj Bhat b: 1973
.... + Vidya Bhat
.... 6 Yoginibai Rao b: 1977
.... + Premachandra Rao
.... 7 Suraj Rao
.... 7 Samartha Rao
.... 5 Vijayendra Bhat b: 1943
.... + Laxmi Bhat
.... 5 Radhabai Rao b: 1945
.... + Anantha Rao
.... 5 Rajendra Bhat b: 1947
.... + Rekha Bhat

CHART 1. (*cont'd*)

.... 5 Gangadhara Bhat b: 1949
.... + Gayathri Bhat
.... 6 Ananda Bhat
.... 5 Mathurabai Kamath b: 1951
.... + Laxmana Kamath
.... 5 Jagadisha Bhat b: 1953
.... + Jyothi Bhat
.... 5 Veenabai Pai b: 1955
.... + Prakash Pai
.... 5 Malathibai Prabhu b: 1957
.... + Pundalika Prabhu
.... 5 Yogisha Bhat b: 1960
.... 4 Sushila Joishy aka Sushilakka b: 21 Sep 1925, d: 15 Jun 1999
.... + Karkal Keshava Joishy b: 18 Feb 1913, d: 16 Nov 1989
.... 5 Vittaldas aka Prabhakar Joishy d: Deceased
.... + Nalini Joishy
.... 6 Rashmi Joishy
.... 5 Suresh Joishy
.... + Muktha Joishy
.... 6 Mahima Joishy
.... 6 Mahant Joishy
.... + Naina Joishy
.... 5 Geetha Pai
.... + Shivram Pai

(*continued*)

.... 6 Sushanth Pai
.... + Anuradha Pai
.... 7 Nivedh Pai
.... 6 Subhiksha Shenoy
.... + Vinod Shenoy
.... 7 Divakar Shenoy
.... 5 Anandram Joishy d: Deceased
.... + Indumathi Joishy
.... 6 Prathima Joishy
.... 3 Sarasvathi Bhat aka Appi aka Bappamma b: 29 Jun 1899 in Udupi, d: 30 Jan 1980 in Pune
.... + Manjeshwar Narayana Bhat aka Puttur Ajjo b: 22 Jun 1886, d: 17 Nov 1962
.... 4 Narasimha Bhat aka Narasimha Bappa b: 12 Jul 1912 in Udupi, d: 15 Nov 1991 in Pune
.... + Tara Bhat aka Tara Pachchi b: 22 Jan 1920, m: 10 Feb 1936 in Mangalore, d: 29 Sep 1990 in Pune
.... 5 Vasanti Bhat-Nayak b: 10 Jun 1937 in Mangalore, d: 12 Feb 2009 in Mumbai
.... + Narasimha Nayak b: 1930, m: 14 Nov 1971
.... 6 Poornima Nayak b: 1973
.... 6 Rajgopal Nayak b: 1976
.... + Sunita Nayak
.... 7 Radhika Nayak
.... 5 Satyendra Bhat b: 1940
.... + Vijayalakshmi Bhat
.... 6 Gurudatt Bhat b: 1970
.... + Rashmi Bhat b: 1974, m: 23 Aug 1997

CHART 1. *(cont'd)*

.... 6 Naveenachandra Bhat b: 1974
.... + Jyoti Bhat b: 1974
.... 7 Shruti b: 2002
.... 5 Varadraj Bhat b: 1946
.... + Sheila Bhat b: 1950, m: 16 Apr 1975
.... 6 Ajoy Bhat b: 1976
.... 6 Nisha b: 1979
.... 5 Sudha Shenoy b: 1947
.... + Gopala Shenoy m: 18 Feb 1979
.... 6 Swatee Shetye (Shenoy) b: 1979
.... 6 Urmila Shenoy b: 1981
.... 5 Usha Hegde(Kadekar) b: 1949
.... + Satish Hegde(Kadekar) b: 1948, m: 02 Nov 1981
.... 6 Prasad Hegde(Kadekar) b: 1982
.... 6 Sailee Hegde
.... 5 Ganesh Bhat b: 1953
.... + Snehal Bhat b: 1954, m: 01 May 1979
.... 6 Chetan Bhat b: 1980
.... 6 Gauri b: 1982
.... 4 Sharada Kini aka Rathna aka Rathnakka b: 29 Dec 1921 in Udupi, d: 16 Sep 1989 in Katapadi
.... + Vasudeva Kini b: 07 Feb 1918, d: 18 Apr 2009
.... 4 Ramanath Bhat aka Ramanath Bappa b: 1924 in Puttur
.... + Prema Bhat b: 1932, m: 15 May 1949 in Udupi
.... 5 Sandhya Pai aka Kusuma b: 28 Dec 1950, d: 11 Jun 2011
.... + Ramakrishna Pai b: 1946

(continued)

.... 6 Aparna Pai
.... + Muralidhar
.... 6 Alka Pai
.... 6 Amita Pai
.... 5 Rajendra Bhat b: 1953
.... + Anita Bhat b: 1958
.... 6 Supriya Bhat b: 1984
.... 6 Vijaya Bhat b: 1987
.... 5 Radhika Mallya aka Vijaya b: 1957
.... + Ramanand Mallya
.... 6 Reshma Mallya
.... 5 Sudhakar Ramanath Bhat b: 1961
.... + Sangeetha Bhat
.... 4 Yeshvant Bhat aka Yeshvantu b: 06 Apr 1932, d: 16 Jul 2009
.... + Meera Bhat b: 06 Jul 1937, d: 19 Oct 2003
.... 5 Usha Bhat b: 1957
.... + Umesh Bhat
.... 6 Nithin Bhat
.... 5 Ravindra Bhat b: 1961
.... + Rekha Bhat
.... 6 Deepali Bhat b: 1992
.... 6 Deeksha Bhat
.... 5 Geeta Kudva b: 1965
.... + Rajagopal Kudva
.... 6 Niyatee Kudva b: 1992
.... 4 Premananda Bhat aka Premanandu b: 1934
.... + Malathi Bhat

CHART 1. *(cont'd)*

.... 5 Vinaya Hegde
.... + Ramachandra Hegde b: 1959
.... 5 Jayalaxmi Rao
.... + Srinivasa Rao
.... 6 Anindita Rao
.... 6 Aditya Rao
.... 5 Manjunath Bhat
.... + Sadhana Bhat
.... 6 Prakriti Bhat
.... 3 Seetharam Prabhu b: 1900 in Udupi, d: 1916 in Udupi
.... 3 Shridhar Prabhu aka Shridhar Bappa (adopted) b: 29 Dec 1914 in Udupi, d: 28 Oct 1989 in Bangalore
.... + Srimathi Prabhu aka Pacci aka Rathni b: 14 Apr 1919, m: 1935, d: 12 Jan 1986
.... 4 Rama Prabhu b: 09 Apr 1936, d: Deceased
.... 4 Srinivasa Shridhara Prabhu b: 1938
.... + Jayanthi Prabhu b: 1939, m: 20 May 1965
.... 5 Ravindra Prabhu b: 1972 in Mangalore
.... 5 Vinayaka Prabhu b: 1977 in Mangalore
.... 4 Svarnalatha Rao b: 1940
.... + A.V. Ramachandra Rao
.... 4 Chitra b: 1945
.... + Venugopal
.... 4 Jayanthi Hari Dass b: 1959
.... + N. D. Hari Dass
.... 5 Shantala Hari Dass

CHART 2. Descendants of Narasimha Bhat

..... 1 Narasimha Bhat (#1)
.... 2 Bhagana Bhat (#2)
.... 3 Santhayya Bhat (#3)
.... 4 Venkatesh Bhat (#4)
.... 5 Baba Bhat (#7)
.... 6 Keshava Bhat (#11)
.... 7 Narasimha Bhat (adopted; #15)
.... 8 Raya Bhat (#20)
.... 8 Rama Bhat (#21)
.... 9 Narasimha Bhat (#30)
.... 9 Baba Bhat (#31)
.... 8 Vithapa Bhat (#22)
.... 8 Lakshmana Bhat (#23)
.... 6 Charda Bhat (#12)
.... 7 Ramachandra Bhat (#16)
.... 7 Narna Bhat (#17)
.... 8 Charda Bhat (#24)
.... 7 Bhabhat (#18)
.... 6 Chidki Krishna Bhat (#13)
.... 7 Venkatesh aka Annu Bhat (#25)
.... 8 Anantha Bhat (#32)
.... 8 Padmanabha Bhat (#33)
.... 9 Krishna aka Srinivas Bhat (#38)
.... 10 Anantha Bhat (#49)
.... 10 Thimmarsa Bhat (#50)
.... 11 Radhakrishna Bhat (#58)

CHART 2. (*cont'd*)

.... 11 Taranath Bhat (#59)
.... 11 Devadas Bhat (#60)
.... 11 Rohidas Bhat (#61)
.... 11 Divakara Bhat (#62)
.... 11 Satish Bhat (#63)
.... 11 Viveka Bhat (#64)
.... 9 Manjunath Bhat (#39)
.... 9 Narayana Bhat (#40)
.... 10 Dayananda Bhat (#51)
.... 10 Anandaraya Bhat (#52)
.... 10 Vedavyasa Bhat (#53)
.... 10 Upendra Bhat (#54)
.... 9 Venkatesh aka Annu Bhat (#41)
.... 10 Gopala Bhat (#55)
.... 10 Baba Bhat (#56)
.... 10 Achutha Bhat (#57)
.... 7 Madhava Bhat (#26)
.... 8 Marthu Bhat (#34)
.... 8 Purushothama Bhat (#35)
.... 9 Keshava Bhat (#42)
.... 9 Manju Bhat (#43)
.... 9 Devadas Bhat (#44)
.... 9 Gopi Bhat (#45)
.... 9 Haridas Bhat (#46)
.... 5 Kelladi Madhava Bhat (#8)

(*continued*)

CHART 2. Descendants of Narasimha Bhat (*cont'd*)

.... 5 Thimmarsa Bhat (#9)
.... 5 Kari Narasimha Bhat (#10)
.... 6 Vittal Bhat (#14)
.... 7 Manja Bhat (#19)
.... 8 Narayana Bhat (#27)
.... 8 Srinivas Bhat (#28)
.... 8 Narasimha Bhat (#29)
.... 9 Chardappa Bhat (#36)
.... 10 Narasimha Bhat (#47)
.... 9 Vamana Bhat (#37)
.... 10 Srinivas Bhat (#48)
.... 4 Srinivasa Bhat (#5)
.... 5 Baba Bhat (#65)
.... 6 Ananthacharya (#66)
.... 7 Ramachandra Bhat (#67)
.... 8 Narasimha Bhat (#68)
.... 9 Rama Bhat (#71)
.... 9 Baba Bhat (#72)
.... 10 Bikkayya Bhat (#76)
.... 10 Vittal Bhat (#77)
.... 11 Baba Bhat (#82)
.... 10 Rama Bhat (#78)
.... 11 Narasimha Bhat (#83)
.... 12 Vittal Bhat (#91)
.... 12 Ganapathi Bhat (#92)
.... + Ammanni

.... 13 Vasudeva Bhat (#102)
.... 14 Dayananda Bhat (#118) aka Dayya Mhanthu
.... + Narayani Bhat aka Sharada
.... 15 Sumithra Kamath
.... + Venkatesha Kamath
.... 16 Geetha Kamath
.... 16 Gopinatha Kamath
.... 16 Ganesha Kamath
.... 16 Parvathi Kamath
.... 16 Rama Kamath
.... 16 Muktha Kamath
.... 16 Chitra Kamath
.... 16 Nirmala Kamath
.... 15 Vittala Bhat (#132)
.... + Rukmini Bhat aka Tara
.... 16 Nirmala Bhat
.... 16 Jagadeesha Bhat (#145A)
.... 15 Ganapathi Bhat (#133)
.... + Shantha Bhat aka Lilavathi
.... 16 Gopalakrishna Bhat (#145B)
.... + Geetha Bhat aka Chandrika
.... 17 Vignesha Bhat
.... 16 Srinivasa Ganapathi Bhat (#145C)
.... + Svathi Bhat aka Mallika
.... 17 Ananda Bhat aka Dayananda

(*continued*)

.... 17 Pallavi Bhat
.... 16 Sitha Shenoy
.... + Viveka Shenoy
.... 17 Vandana Shenoy
.... 16 Achutha Bhat (#145D)
.... + Akshatha Bhat aka Vijaya
.... 17 Ankitha Bhat
.... 15 Anantha Bhat (#134)
.... + Sunanda Bhat
.... 15 Venkatesha Bhat (#135)
.... + Padmaja Bhat aka Bharathi
.... 16 Harish Bhat (#145E)
.... + Anita Bhat
.... 16 Radhika Bhat
.... + Aravinda Bhat
.... 17 Arjuna Bhat
.... 16 Rupa Bhat
.... 15 Shobha Bhat aka Sulochana
.... + Shridhar Bhat b: 29 Nov 1936 in Mulki, d: 16 Feb 2009
.... 16 Anupama Bhat
.... 16 Udaya Bhat
.... + Deepa Bhat
.... 17 Adithya Bhat
.... 17 Siddhartha Bhat

.... 16 Prathibha D'Souza
.... + William D'Souza
.... 17 Nikita D'Souza
.... 15 Narasimha Bhat (#136)
.... + Laxmidevi Bhat aka Vijayalaxmi
.... 16 Sudha Bhat
.... + Radhesha Bhat
.... 16 Sumathi Bhat
.... 15 Ramachandra Bhat (#137)
.... 13 Madhava Bhat (#103) aka Ajjo b: 22 Jan 1884, d: 13 Jun 1959 in Udupi
.... + Padmavathi Bhat aka Bhavani aka Annamma b: 15 Aug 1891 in Udupi, m: 1902, d: 25 Dec 1958 in Udupi
.... 14 Narayana Bhatji (#119) b: 08 Dec 1907 in Udupi, d: 28 Aug 1992 in Udupi
.... + Laxmidevi Bhatji aka Sharada b: 25 Dec 1914 in Mulki, m: 14 Feb 1929 in Mulki, d: 22 Jan 1989 in Udupi
.... 15 Radhakrishna Bhat (#138) b: 1930 in Mulki
.... + Padma Bhat aka Varada b: 1936 in Karkal, m: 20 Aug 1967 in Moodabidri
.... 16 Giridhar Bhat (#145) b: 1971 in Port Jefferson, NY

(*continued*)

.... 15 Lalitha Kamath b: 1934 in Udupi
.... + Hosadurg Gopalakrishna Kamath b: 17 Apr 1924, m: 08 Dec 1965, d: 17 Jan 2007 in Udupi
.... 16 Shankar Kamath b: 1969 in Udupi
.... + Rakhee Kamath b: 1971
.... 17 Siddhartha Kamath b: 2004
.... 16 Ashok Kamath b: 1971 in Udupi
.... + Chaya Kamath b: 1972
.... 15 Kasturi Hegde b: 1936 in Udupi
.... + Taranath Hegde b: 15 May 1938, m: 26 Jun 1966 in Bangalore, d: 30 Jan 1994
.... 16 Mridul Tansley b: 1967
.... + Brian Brivati b: 1966
.... 17 Maximillian Krishna Brivati b: 1999
.... 17 Hannah Indra Brivati b: 2000
.... + Phillip Tansley
.... 17 Irene Tansley b: 2010
.... 16 Rekha Wooton b: 1975
.... + Alexander Wooton
.... 17 Noah Taran Wooton b: 2009
.... 15 Vasudeva Bhat (#139) b: 1939 in Udupi
.... 15 Madhavaraya aka Rathnakar Bhat (#140) b: 1941 in Udupi
.... + Jai Bhavani Bhat aka Sharada b: 1949, m: 02 Mar 1972

.... 16 Chaitra Bhat b: 1973
.... 16 Sumathi Bhat b: 1975
.... 16 Vedavyasa Bhat b: 1979
.... 15 Shreedhara Bhat (#141) aka Shiddha b: 1943 in Udupi
.... + Suman Bhat aka Vatsala b: 1947, m: 29 Nov 1972
.... 15 Raghuvir Bhat (#142) b: 1946 in Udupi
.... 15 Kumuda Bhandary b: 1948 in Udupi
.... + Gopalakrishna Bhandary b: 1939, m: 30 Jan 1972
.... 16 Avanish Bhandary b: 1973
.... + Sri Kala Bhandary
.... 17 Sai Dhruva Bhandary b: 2008
.... 16 Ashwin Bhandary b: 1977
.... + Sri Vidya Bhandary
.... 15 Pushpa Bhat b: 1951 in Udupi
.... + Subhas Bhat b: 02 Jan 1951, m: 22 May 1985, d: 21 Aug 2011
.... 15 Suresh Bhat (#143) b: 1953 in Udupi
.... + Sri Laxmi Bhat aka Dakshayani b: 1955, m: 09 Jul 1992
.... 15 Nandini Rao b: 1956 in Udupi
.... + Nagesh Rao b: 1952, m: 09 Aug 1981
.... 16 Neha Rao b: 1987

(*continued*)

CHART 2. Descendants of Narasimha Bhat (*cont'd*)

.... 15 Annapurna Nayak b: 1958 in Udupi
.... + Prabhakar Nayak m: 06 May 1992
.... 16 Jagannatha Nayak b: 1994
.... 15 Sudhir Bhat (#144) b: 1961 in Udupi
.... + Subhalaxmi Bhat aka Sheethal b: 1966 in Udupi
.... 16 Sri Sukrath Bhat b: 1998 in Chattanooga, TN
.... 14 Manorama Bhat aka Mannakka b: 23 May 1921 in Udupi, d: 18 Aug 2002 in Bangalore
.... + Katapadi Sripathi Bhat aka Katapadi Mamu b: 29 Mar 1910, d: 06 Aug 1995
.... 15 Padmanabha Bhat b: 02 Nov 1936 in Udupi, d: 12 Dec 2000
.... + Vathsala Bhat
.... 16 Chandrika Prabhu
.... + Prakash Prabhu
.... 17 Gaurav Prabhu
.... 16 Harish Bhat
.... + Pallavi Bhat
.... 17 Adi Bhat
.... 15 Chandramathi Kamath
.... + Annapa Kamath
.... 16 Sudhakar Kamath
.... + Meera Kamath
.... 17 Rahul Kamath

CHART 2. ***(cont'd)***

.... 17 Meghan Kamath
.... 16 Praveen Kamath
.... + Shanthi Kamath
.... 17 Nayna Kamath
.... 17 Neil Kamath
.... 16 Govindaraja Kamath
.... + Vinaya Kamath
.... 17 Sonali Kamath
.... 17 Mona Kamath
.... 15 Ramanath Bhat d: Deceased
.... + Sulatha Bhat
.... 16 Prakash Bhat
.... 16 Prashant Bhat
.... 15 Sumathi Shenoy
.... + Gokuldas Shenoy d: Deceased
.... 16 Gurudas Shenoy
.... + Amitha Shenoy
.... 17 Rakhi Shenoy
.... 16 Rekha Betigere
.... + Sandeep Betigere
.... 17 Sharanya Betigere
.... 17 Neel Betigere
.... 15 Sathyanath Bhat
.... + Savitha Bhat
.... 16 Soumya Pai
.... + Anil Pai

(continued)

CHART 2. Descendants of Narasimha Bhat (*cont'd*)

.... 16 Shubha Rao
.... + Aloke Rao
.... 15 Taramathi Shenoy
.... + Ramesh Shenoy
.... 16 Ravindra Shenoy
.... + Preethi Shenoy
.... 14 Mohini Bhat aka Mohiniakka b: 29 Oct 1922 in Udupi, d: 14 Aug 2010
.... + Anantha aka Aithu Bhat b: 1911, d: 1961
.... 15 Surendra Bhat b: 1939 in Udupi
.... + Nirupama Bhat b: 1947
.... 16 Harish Bhat b: 1972
.... + Rama Bhat
.... 17 Mahima Bhat b: 2006
.... 16 Nagaraj Bhat b: 1973
.... + Vidya Bhat
.... 16 Yoginibai Rao b: 1977
.... + Premachandra Rao
.... 17 Suraj Rao
.... 17 Samartha Rao
.... 15 Vijayendra Bhat b: 1943
.... + Laxmi Bhat
.... 15 Radhabai Rao b: 1945
.... + Anantha Rao
.... 15 Rajendra Bhat b: 1947
.... + Rekha Bhat

CHART 2. (*cont'd*)

.... 15 Gangadhara Bhat b: 1949
.... + Gayathri Bhat
.... 16 Ananda Bhat
.... 15 Mathurabai Kamath b: 1951
.... + Laxmana Kamath
.... 15 Jagadisha Bhat b: 1953
.... + Jyothi Bhat
.... 15 Veenabai Pai b: 1955
.... + Prakash Pai
.... 15 Malathibai Prabhu b: 1957
.... + Pundalika Prabhu
.... 15 Yogisha Bhat b: 1960
.... 14 Sushila Joishy aka Sushilakka b: 21 Sep 1925, d: 15 Jun 1999
.... + Karkal Keshava Joishy b: 18 Feb 1913, d: 16 Nov 1989
.... 15 Vittaldas aka Prabhakar Joishy d: Deceased
.... + Nalini Joishy
.... 16 Rashmi Joishy
.... 15 Suresh Joishy
.... + Muktha Joishy
.... 16 Mahima Joishy
.... 16 Mahant Joishy
.... + Naina Joishy

(*continued*)

CHART 2. Descendants of Narasimha Bhat (*cont'd*)

.... 15 Geetha Pai
.... + Shivram Pai
.... 16 Sushanth Pai
.... + Anuradha Pai
.... 17 Nivedh Pai
.... 16 Subhiksha Shenoy
.... + Vinod Shenoy
.... 17 Divakar Shenoy
.... 15 Anandram Joishy d: Deceased
.... + Indumathi Joishy
.... 16 Prathima Joishy
.... 12 Krishna Bhat (#93) aka Kuttani Bhat
.... + Tulasi Bhat
.... 13 Nethravathi Shenoy aka Nethru Mhava b: 1880, d: 1946
.... + Padubidri Srinivas Shenoy d: Deceased
.... 13 Mathura Bhat aka Sitabai
.... + Bantwal Govind Bhat d: Deceased
.... 14 Ananda Bhat d: Deceased
.... + Padmavati Bhat d: Deceased
.... 15 Ganesh Bhat
.... 14 Vasudeva Bhat d: Deceased
.... + Satyavati Bhat d: Deceased
.... 15 Radhakrishna Bhat
.... + Anuradha Bhat

CHART 2. *(cont'd)*

.... 14 Anantha aka Aithu Bhat b: 1911, d: 1961
.... + Mohini Bhat aka Mohiniakka b: 29 Oct 1922 in Udupi, d: 14 Aug 2010
.... 15 Surendra Bhat b: 1939 in Udupi
.... + Nirupama Bhat b: 1947
.... 16 Harish Bhat b: 1972
.... + Rama Bhat
.... 17 Mahima Bhat b: 2006
.... 16 Nagaraj Bhat b: 1973
.... + Vidya Bhat
.... 16 Yoginibai Rao b: 1977
.... + Premachandra Rao
.... 17 Suraj Rao
.... 17 Samartha Rao
.... 15 Vijayendra Bhat b: 1943
.... + Laxmi Bhat
.... 15 Radhabai Rao b: 1945
.... + Anantha Rao
.... 15 Rajendra Bhat b: 1947
.... + Rekha Bhat
.... 15 Gangadhara Bhat b: 1949
.... + Gayathri Bhat
.... 16 Ananda Bhat
.... 15 Mathurabai Kamath b: 1951
.... + Laxmana Kamath

(continued)

.... 15 Jagadisha Bhat b: 1953
.... + Jyothi Bhat
.... 15 Veenabai Pai b: 1955
.... + Prakash Pai
.... 15 Malathibai Prabhu b: 1957
.... + Pundalika Prabhu
.... 15 Yogisha Bhat b: 1960
.... 14 Shuka Bhat d: Deceased
.... 14 Vaikunta Bhat d: Deceased
.... + Shrimati Bhat
.... 15 Gitabai Kini
.... + K. S. Kini
.... 15 Srashta aka Sucharita Nayak
.... + K. R. Nayak d: Deceased
.... 15 Laxminarayana Bhat
.... + Shalini Bhat
.... 15 Rajaram Bhat d: Deceased
.... 13 Vedavathi Bhat aka Vedu aka Ammi b: 1883 in Mulki, d: Oct 1972 in Bangalore
.... + Subraya Bhat aka Subba Bhat b: 1859 in Mulki, d: 1948 in Mulki
.... 14 Narayana Bhat aka Hodu Mamu b: 13 Nov 1902 in Mulki, d: 23 Dec 1980 in Mulki
.... + Laxmidevi Bhat aka Sulochana d: Deceased
.... 15 Gopalakrishna Bhat aka Gopalakrishna Bhavaji b: 13 Sep 1923 in Karkal, d: 22 May 2004 in Bangalore

CHART 2. (*cont'd*)

.... + Maya Bhat d: Deceased
.... 16 Madankumar Bhat b: 1953 in Mangalore, d: 12 Feb 1989 in Bangalore
.... + Mala Bhat
.... 17 Meena Bhat
.... 17 Mahesh Madan Bhat
.... + Padmaja Bhat
.... 18 Akshata Bhat
.... 18 Agasthya Bhat
.... 15 Devaraya Bhat b: 22 Oct 1929 in Mulki, d: 05 Aug 2007
.... + Indira Bhat
.... + Ramabai Bhat aka Mai b: 15 Feb 1917, d: 21 Oct 1990 in Mulki
.... 15 Shridhar Bhat b: 29 Nov 1936 in Mulki, d: 16 Feb 2009
.... + Shobha Bhat aka Sulochana
.... 16 Anupama Bhat
.... 16 Udaya Bhat
.... + Deepa Bhat
.... 17 Adithya Bhat
.... 17 Siddhartha Bhat
.... 16 Prathibha D'Souza
.... + William D'Souza

(*continued*)

CHART 2. Descendants of Narasimha Bhat (*cont'd*)

.... 17 Nikita D'Souza
.... 15 Jayadeva Bhat b: 1947 in Mulki
.... + Jayashree Bhat aka Sumathi
.... 14 Tulasi Bhatt aka Tucci Mhava b: 1905 in Mulki, d: 13 Dec 1983 in Bangalore
.... + Taranath Krishna Bhatt aka Mhanthu b: 1902, m: 1919, d: 25 Dec 1987 in Bangalore
.... 15 Vivekananda Bhatt aka Vivekanna
.... + Maitreyi Bhatt aka Sarojini b: 17 Oct 1933, d: Deceased
.... 16 Siddhartha Bhatt
.... + Vidya Bhatt
.... 17 Rahul Bhatt
.... 17 Atul Bhatt
.... 16 Patanjali Bhatt
.... + Jyothi Rau
.... 17 Sujaya Bhatt
.... 17 Sharmila Bhatt
.... 16 Chandrasmitha Kamath
.... + Hemanta Kamath d: Deceased
.... 17 Nalin Kamath
.... 16 Divyavadana Bhandary
.... + Bhandary
.... 17 Maya Bhandary
.... 15 Gokulananda Sharma aka Gokulanna
.... + Pratibha Sharma aka Vasanthi d: Deceased

CHART 2. (*cont'd*)

.... 16 Yashodhara Sharma Koehler
.... + Warren Reed Koehler
.... 16 Malavika Sharma Judd
.... + Todd Michael Judd
.... 17 Kiran Gokul Judd
.... 17 Janak Kailesh Judd
.... 15 Vilasini Prabhu aka Villa
.... + N. M. Prabhu d: Deceased
.... 16 Vasudeva Prabhu
.... + Amrutha Prabhu
.... 17 Aparajita Prabhu
.... 17 Vijayanthi Prabhu
.... 16 Shailesha Prabhu
.... + Sheethala Prabhu
.... 17 Prithvi Prabhu
.... 15 Vasudeva Taranath Sharma aka VTS
.... + Arundathi Sharma
.... 16 Raguvendra Bhatt
.... + Divya Bhatt
.... 17 Sarvajit Bhatt
.... 16 Pradyumna Bhatt
.... + Shalini Bhatt
.... 17 Anirudha Bhatt
.... 15 Ramakrishna Taranath Bhatt
.... + Mathura Bhatt aka Pramoda

(*continued*)

.... 16 Dhananjaya Bhatt
.... 16 Sumanta Bhatt
.... 14 Padmanabha Sharma aka Panni Maamu b: 25 Sep 1912 in Mulki, d: Dec 1963 in Manipal
.... + Anasuya Sharma aka Rohini b: 31 Jul 1922 in Udupi, d: 06 Feb 2000 in Udupi
.... 15 Vasanth Sharma b: 1942 in Udupi
.... 15 Saudamini Sharma b: 1944 in Mulki
.... 15 Panduranga Sharma b: 1945 in Mulki
.... + Lakshmi m: 20 Dec 1982
.... 15 Sudhakar Sharma b: 22 May 1951 in Mulki, d: 07 Nov 2006 in Udupi
.... 14 Laxmidevi Bhatji aka Sharada b: 25 Dec 1914 in Mulki, d: 22 Jan 1989 in Udupi
.... + Narayana Bhatji (#119) b: 08 Dec 1907 in Udupi, m: 14 Feb 1929 in Mulki, d: 28 Aug 1992 in Udupi
.... 15 Radhakrishna Bhat (#138) b: 1930 in Mulki
.... + Padma Bhat aka Varada b: 1936 in Karkal, m: 20 Aug 1967 in Moodabidri
.... 16 Giridhar Bhat (#145) b: 1971 in Port Jefferson, NY
.... 15 Lalitha Kamath b: 1934 in Udupi
.... + Hosadurg Gopalakrishna Kamath b: 17 Apr 1924, m: 08 Dec 1965, d: 17 Jan 2007 in Udupi

CHART 2. (*cont'd*)

.... 16 Shankar Kamath b: 1969 in Udupi
.... + Rakhee Kamath b: 1971
.... 17 Siddhartha Kamath b: 2004
.... 16 Ashok Kamath b: 1971 in Udupi
.... + Chaya Kamath b: 1972
.... 15 Kasturi Hegde b: 1936 in Udupi
.... + Taranath Hegde b: 15 May 1938, m: 26 Jun 1966 in Bangalore, d: 30 Jan 1994
.... 16 Mridul Tansley b: 1967
.... + Brian Brivati b: 1966
.... 17 Maximillian Krishna Brivati b: 1999
.... 17 Hannah Indra Brivati b: 2000
.... + Phillip Tansley
.... 17 Irene Tansley b: 2010
.... 16 Rekha Wooton b: 1975
.... + Alexander Wooton
.... 17 Noah Taran Wooton b: 2009
.... 15 Vasudeva Bhat (#139) b: 1939 in Udupi
.... 15 Madhavaraya aka Rathnakar Bhat (#140) b: 1941 in Udupi
.... + Jai Bhavani Bhat aka Sharada b: 1949, m: 02 Mar 1972
.... 16 Chaitra Bhat b: 1973
.... 16 Sumathi Bhat b: 1975
.... 16 Vedavyasa Bhat b: 1979

(*continued*)

CHART 2. Descendants of Narasimha Bhat (*cont'd*)

.... 15 Shreedhara Bhat (#141) aka Shiddha b: 1943 in Udupi
.... + Suman Bhat aka Vatsala b: 1947, m: 29 Nov 1972
.... 15 Raghuvir Bhat (#142) b: 1946 in Udupi
.... 15 Kumuda Bhandary b: 1948 in Udupi
.... + Gopalakrishna Bhandary b: 1939, m: 30 Jan 1972
.... 16 Avanish Bhandary b: 1973
.... + Sri Kala Bhandary
.... 17 Sai Dhruva Bhandary b: 2008
.... 16 Ashwin Bhandary b: 1977
.... + Sri Vidya Bhandary
.... 15 Pushpa Bhat b: 1951 in Udupi
.... + Subhas Bhat b: 02 Jan 1951, m: 22 May 1985, d: 21 Aug 2011
.... 15 Suresh Bhat (#143) b: 1953 in Udupi
.... + Sri Laxmi Bhat aka Dakshayani b: 1955, m: 09 Jul 1992
.... 15 Nandini Rao b: 1956 in Udupi
.... + Nagesh Rao b: 1952, m: 09 Aug 1981
.... 16 Neha Rao b: 1987
.... 15 Annapurna Nayak b: 1958 in Udupi
.... + Prabhakar Nayak m: 06 May 1992
.... 16 Jagannatha Nayak b: 1994
.... 15 Sudhir Bhat (#144) b: 1961 in Udupi

CHART 2. *(cont'd)*

.... + Subhalaxmi Bhat aka Sheethal b: 1966 in Udupi
.... 16 Sri Sukrath Bhat b: 1998 in Chattanooga, TN
.... 11 Srinivas Bhat (#84)
.... 12 Baba Bhat (#94)
.... 13 Anantha Bhat (#104)
.... 14 Achutha Bhat (#120)
.... 9 Santha Bhat (#73)
...... 10 Anantha Bhat (#79)
.. 8 Baba Bhat (#69)
.... 9 Ramachandra Bhat (#74)
...... 10 Krishna Bhat (#80)
.... 11 Narasimha Bhat (#85)
.... 12 Srinivas Bhat (#95)
.... 12 Ramachandra Bhat (#96)
.... 13 Narasimha Bhat (#105)
.... 13 Krishnaraya Bhat (#106)
.... 14 Ramachandra Bhat (#121)
.... 14 Manjunatha Bhat (#122)
.... 14 Anantha Bhat (#123)
.... 11 Puthu Bhat (#86)
.... 12 Venkataramana Bhat (#97)
.... 13 Ramakrishna Bhat (#107)
.... 13 Gopala Bhat (#108)

(continued)

CHART 2. Descendants of Narasimha Bhat (*cont'd*)

.... 11 Achchu Bhat (#87)
.... 12 Madhava Bhat (#98)
.... 13 Vamana Bhat (#109)
.... 14 Anantha Padmanabha Bhat (#124)
.... 13 Janardhana Bhat (#110)
.... 14 Narayana Bhat (#125)
.... 14 Ramanatha Bhat (#126)
.... 14 Vasudeva Bhat (#127)
.... 11 Anantha Bhat (#88)
.... 8 Charda Bhat (#70)
.... 9 Pattu Bhat (#75)
.... 10 Santha Bhat (#81)
.... 11 Lakshmana Bhat (#89)
.... 11 Annu Bhat (#90)
.... 12 Padmanabha Bhat (#99)
.... 13 Govinda Bhat (#111)
.... 13 Nagesh Bhat (#112)
.... 13 Sanjiva Bhat (#113)
.... 12 Mukunda Bhat (#100)
.... 13 Narayana Bhat (#114)
.... 14 Mukunda Bhat (#128)
.... 14 Sadashiva Bhat (#129)
.... 14 Panduranga Bhat (#130)
.... 13 Sarvothama Bhat (#115)
.... 13 Chardappa Bhat (#116)
.... 13 Annu Bhat (#117)

CHART 2. (*cont'd*)

.... 14 Ananda Bhat (#131)
.... 12 Narayana Bhat (#101)
.... 4 Govinda Bhat (#6)
.... 5 Mala Bhat (#146)
.... 6 Rama Bhat (#148)
.... 7 Narasimha Bhat (#151)
.... 8 Krishna Bhat (#157)
.... 9 Raya Bhat (#162)
.... 10 Krishna Bhat (#173)
.... 11 Ramaraya Bhat (#188)
.... 12 Gopalakrishna Bhat (#208)
.... 12 Vittal Bhat (#209)
.... 11 Kamalaksha Bhat (#189)
.... 11 Narasimha Bhat (#190)
.... 7 Annu Bhat (#152)
.... 7 Venkatesh Bhat (#153)
.... 6 Krishna Bhat (#149)
.... 7 Madhava Bhat (#154)
.... 8 Narayana Bhat (#158)
.... 9 Venkatesh Bhat (#163)
.... 10 Padmanabha Bhat (#174)
.... 10 Sarvothama Bhat (#175)
.... 11 Ramana Bhat (#191)
.... 11 Narasimha Bhat (#192)
.... 10 Vaman Bhat (#176)

(*continued*)

CHART 2. Descendants of Narasimha Bhat (*cont'd*)

.... 11 Padmanabha Bhat (#193)
.... 11 Rama Bhat (#194)
.... 9 Narasimha Bhat (#164)
.... 10 Lakshmana Bhat (#177)
.... 10 Narayana Bhat (#178)
.... 9 Vittappa Bhat (#165)
.... 10 Vedavyasa Bhat (#179)
.... 11 Vittappa Bhat (#195)
.... 11 Sitarama Bhat (#196)
.... 9 Subraya Bhat (#166)
.... 9 Raya Bhat (#167)
.... 9 Madhava Bhat (#168)
.... 9 Vedavyasa Bhat (#169)
.... 9 Shridhar Bhat (#170)
.... 10 Raya Bhat (#180)
.... 10 Vaikunta Bhat (#181)
.... 11 Achutha Bhat (#197)
.... 11 Ganapathi Bhat (#198)
.... 8 Anantha Bhat (#159)
.... 9 Subraya Bhat (adopted; #171)
.... 10 Anantha Bhat (#182)
.... 11 Kodanda Bhat (#199)
.... 10 Gopal Bhat (#183)
.... 11 Narasimha Bhat (#204)
.... 11 Subraya Bhat (#205)
.... 11 Ramana Bhat (#206)

CHART 2. *(cont'd)*

.... 11 Narayana Bhat (#207)
.... 8 Keshava Bhat (#160)
.... 9 Krishna Bhat (#172)
.... 10 Vasudeva Bhat (#184)
.... 10 Keshava Bhat (#185)
.... 11 Vasudeva Bhat (#200)
.... 10 Srinivasa Bhat (#186)
.... 10 Mukunda Bhat (#187)
.... 11 Krishna Bhat (#201)
.... 11 Hari Bhat (#202)
.... 11 Govinda Bhat (#203)
.... 7 Annu Bhat (#155)
.... 8 Anantha Bhat (#161)
.... 5 Javara Bhat (#147)
.... 6 Manjayya Bhat (#150)
.... 7 Bikki Bhat (#156)

CHART 3. Descendants of Panduranga Bhat

..... 1 Panduranga Bhat
.... 2 Narayana Bhat
.... 2 Krishna Bhat
.... 2 Srinivasa Bhat
.... 2 Ramachandra Bhat
.... 2 Padmanabha Bhat
.... 2 Subraya Bhat aka Subba Bhat b: 1859 in Mulki, d: 1948 in Mulki
.... + First wife: Name not known d: Deceased
.... 3 Sundari Bhat
.... + Baba Bhat
.... + Vedavathi Bhat aka Vedu aka Ammi b: 1883 in Mulki, d: Oct 1972 in Bangalore
.... 3 Narayana Bhat aka Hodu Mamu b: 13 Nov 1902 in Mulki, d: 23 Dec 1980 in Mulki
.... + Laxmidevi Bhat aka Sulochana d: Deceased
.... 4 Gopalakrishna Bhat aka Gopalakrishna Bhavaji b: 13 Sep 1923 in Karkal, d: 22 May 2004 in Bangalore
.... + Maya Bhat d: Deceased
.... 5 Madankumar Bhat b: 1953 in Mangalore, d: 12 Feb 1989 in Bangalore
.... + Mala Bhat
.... 6 Meena Bhat
.... 6 Mahesh Madan Bhat
.... + Padmaja Bhat
.... 7 Akshata Bhat
.... 7 Agasthya Bhat
.... 4 Devaraya Bhat b: 22 Oct 1929 in Mulki, d: 05 Aug 2007
.... + Indira Bhat
.... + Ramabai Bhat aka Mai b: 15 Feb 1917, d: 21 Oct 1990 in Mulki

CHART 3. (*cont'd*)

.... 4 Shridhar Bhat b: 29 Nov 1936 in Mulki, d: 16 Feb 2009
.... + Shobha Bhat aka Sulochana
.... 5 Anupama Bhat
.... 5 Udaya Bhat
.... + Deepa Bhat
.... 6 Adithya Bhat
.... 6 Siddhartha Bhat
.... 5 Prathibha D'Souza
.... + William D'Souza
.... 6 Nikita D'Souza
.... 4 Jayadeva Bhat b: 1947 in Mulki
.... + Jayashree Bhat aka Sumathi
.... 3 Tulasi Bhatt aka Tucci Mhava b: 1905 in Mulki, d: 13 Dec 1983 in Bangalore
.... + Taranath Krishna Bhatt aka Mhanthu b: 1902, m: 1919, d: 25 Dec 1987 in Bangalore
.... 4 Vivekananda Bhatt aka Vivekanna
.... + Maitreyi Bhatt aka Sarojini b: 17 Oct 1933, d: Deceased
.... 5 Siddhartha Bhatt
.... + Vidya Bhatt
.... 6 Rahul Bhatt
.... 6 Atul Bhatt
.... 5 Patanjali Bhatt
.... + Jyothi Rau
.... 6 Sujaya Bhatt
.... 6 Sharmila Bhatt
.... 5 Chandrasmitha Kamath

(*continued*)

CHART 3. Descendants of Panduranga Bhat (*cont'd*)

.... + Hemanta Kamath d: Deceased
.... 6 Nalin Kamath
.... 5 Divyavadana Bhandary
.... + Bhandary
.... 6 Maya Bhandary
.... 4 Gokulananda Sharma aka Gokulanna
.... + Pratibha Sharma aka Vasanthi d: Deceased
.... 5 Yashodhara Sharma Koehler
.... + Warren Reed Koehler
.... 5 Malavika Sharma Judd
.... + Todd Michael Judd
.... 6 Kiran Gokul Judd
.... 6 Janak Kailesh Judd
.... 4 Vilasini Prabhu aka Villa
.... + N. M. Prabhu d: Deceased
.... 5 Vasudeva Prabhu
.... + Amrutha Prabhu
.... 6 Aparajita Prabhu
.... 6 Vijayanthi Prabhu
.... 5 Shailesha Prabhu
.... + Sheethala Prabhu
.... 6 Prithvi Prabhu
.... 4 Vasudeva Taranath Sharma aka VTS
.... + Arundathi Sharma
.... 5 Raguvendra Bhatt
.... + Divya Bhatt

CHART 3. (*cont'd*)

.... 6 Sarvajit Bhatt
.... 5 Pradyumna Bhatt
.... + Shalini Bhatt
.... 6 Anirudha Bhatt
.... 4 Ramakrishna Taranath Bhatt
.... + Mathura Bhatt aka Pramoda
.... 5 Dhananjaya Bhatt
.... 5 Sumanta Bhatt
.... 3 Padmanabha Sharma aka Panni Maamu b: 25 Sep 1912 in Mulki, d: Dec 1963 in Manipal
.... + Anasuya Sharma aka Rohini b: 31 Jul 1922 in Udupi, d: 06 Feb 2000 in Udupi
.... 4 Vasanth Sharma b: 1942 in Udupi
.... 4 Saudamini Sharma b: 1944 in Mulki
.... 4 Panduranga Sharma b: 1945 in Mulki
.... + Lakshmi m: 20 Dec 1982
.... 4 Sudhakar Sharma b: 22 May 1951 in Mulki, d: 07 Nov 2006 in Udupi
.... 3 Laxmidevi Bhatji aka Sharada b: 25 Dec 1914 in Mulki, d: 22 Jan 1989 in Udupi
.... + Narayana Bhatji (#119) b: 08 Dec 1907 in Udupi, m: 14 Feb 1929 in Mulki, d: 28 Aug 1992 in Udupi
.... 4 Radhakrishna Bhat (#138) b: 1930 in Mulki
.... + Padma Bhat aka Varada b: 1936 in Karkal, m: 20 Aug 1967 in Moodabidri
.... 5 Giridhar Bhat (#145) b: 1971 in Port Jefferson, NY
.... 4 Lalitha Kamath b: 1934 in Udupi
.... + Hosadurg Gopalakrishna Kamath b: 17 Apr 1924, m: 08 Dec 1965, d: 17 Jan 2007 in Udupi
.... 5 Shankar Kamath b: 1969 in Udupi

(*continued*)

CHART 3. Descendants of Panduranga Bhat (*cont'd*)

.... + Rakhee Kamath b: 1971
.... 6 Siddhartha Kamath b: 2004
.... 5 Ashok Kamath b: 1971 in Udupi
.... + Chaya Kamath b: 1972
.... 4 Kasturi Hegde b: 1936 in Udupi
.... + Taranath Hegde b: 15 May 1938, m: 26 Jun 1966 in Bangalore, d: 30 Jan 1994
.... 5 Mridul Tansley b: 1967
.... + Brian Brivati b: 1966
.... 6 Maximillian Krishna Brivati b: 1999
.... 6 Hannah Indra Brivati b: 2000
.... + Phillip Tansley
.... 6 Irene Tansley b: 2010
.... 5 Rekha Wooton b: 1975
.... + Alexander Wooton
.... 6 Noah Taran Wooton b: 2009
.... 4 Vasudeva Bhat (#139) b: 1939 in Udupi
.... 4 Madhavaraya aka Rathnakar Bhat (#140) b: 1941 in Udupi
.... + Jai Bhavani Bhat aka Sharada b: 1949, m: 02 Mar 1972
.... 5 Chaitra Bhat b: 1973
.... 5 Sumathi Bhat b: 1975
.... 5 Vedavyasa Bhat b: 1979
.... 4 Shreedhara Bhat (#141) aka Shiddha b: 1943 in Udupi
.... + Suman Bhat aka Vatsala b: 1947, m: 29 Nov 1972
.... 4 Raghuvir Bhat (#142) b: 1946 in Udupi
.... 4 Kumuda Bhandary b: 1948 in Udupi
.... + Gopalakrishna Bhandary b: 1939, m: 30 Jan 1972

CHART 3. (*cont'd*)

.... 5 Avanish Bhandary b: 1973
.... + Sri Kala Bhandary
.... 6 Sai Dhruva Bhandary b: 2008
.... 5 Ashwin Bhandary b: 1977
.... + Sri Vidya Bhandary
.... 4 Pushpa Bhat b: 1951 in Udupi
.... + Subhas Bhat b: 02 Jan 1951, m: 22 May 1985, d: 21 Aug 2011
.... 4 Suresh Bhat (#143) b: 1953 in Udupi
.... + Sri Laxmi Bhat aka Dakshayani b: 1955, m: 09 Jul 1992
.... 4 Nandini Rao b: 1956 in Udupi
.... + Nagesh Rao b: 1952, m: 09 Aug 1981
.... 5 Neha Rao b: 1987
.... 4 Annapurna Nayak b: 1958 in Udupi
.... + Prabhakar Nayak m: 06 May 1992
.... 5 Jagannatha Nayak b: 1994
.... 4 Sudhir Bhat (#144) b: 1961 in Udupi
.... + Subhalaxmi Bhat aka Sheethal b: 1966 in Udupi
.... 5 Sri Sukrath Bhat b: 1998 in Chattanooga, TN

APPENDIX THREE

Atri Gotra, or Clan *Atri*

Origins of *Gotra*

What is a *gotra*? In answer, we have to talk about our ancestors and the past. A *gotra* is an exogamous unit of a patriarchal society meant to prevent inbreeding. It is best translated as "clan" and is usually named after its progenitor. For example, Atri, a mythic, semi-divine Vedic sage, was the progenitor of clan Atri, or Atri *gotra*, which is my family's clan. In theory at least, a *gotra* denotes all people who claim descent from an unbroken male line from this ancestor (Kane 1974, 2:484). Of course, no one has a family tree, birth certificate, or other record of such a relationship, for the simple reason that this progenitor lived in a mythic past, at the dawn of time, perhaps even before the invention of writing. Besides, my clan's ancestors were not good at keeping and maintaining written records, and any such records would have been lost during our many migrations. Genetics tells us that the Y chromosome transmits the genetic information of an individual from father to son, strictly along the male line. It would be interesting to do a Y-chromosome analysis of males of the same *gotra* and of the different *gotras*, and then compare them. Such field data should throw interesting light on the various claims of descent from a common ancestor. Are they real or myths—perhaps based on a primacy conceit? Most people would like to think of this progenitor as a real historical person; however, these accounts have a strong air of myth and legend about them.

Consider the *gotra* another label attached to every person, just like a given name. For our family, the *gotra* name is Ātreya and Ātreyī, for men and for women, respectively. It means a male or female descendant of Atri, collectively called Atris in this account. As a matter of fact, the *gotra* name was the family name for thousands of years, before it was replaced by modern conventions (see the section "Conventions for Names"). Amongst Hindus, the memory of individuals' *gotras* has been kept alive mostly amongst the priests, the Brahmans. The warriors and merchants usually adopted the *gotra* of their family priest, even in the olden days. A *gotra* is divided into a few subgroups, each of which has its own *pravara* (group of distinguished ancestors). The relationship between a *gotra* and *pravara* is best defined as follows: "*Gotra* (progenitor) is the latest ancestor or one of the latest ancestors of a person by whose name his family has been known for generations; while *pravara* is constituted by the sages or the remotest ancestor alone" (Kane 1974, 2:497). One can think of the *pravara* sages as the most distinguished members of the clan, noted for their poetic contributions to the *Ṛgveda*, or other mighty deeds. This list can contain one, two, three or five people, never four. The exogamy applies to the *gotra–pravara* combination, thus introducing a second layer of *pravara* exclusion. The rules of exogamy can be quite complicated, and books have been written on the subject (Brough 1953). It is possible that the *gotras* having a common *pravara* sage were the same, before splitting off into independent groups. Thus the *gotra* and *pravara* form the "coordinates" that position a person within Hindu society, especially in the context of religious rites. For the Atri *gotra*, the *pravara* list has three sages: Ātreya, Ārcanānasa, and Śyāvāśva. This list of clan personages is recalled at all religious functions and other rituals. Thus the *upanayana mekhalā* (initiation girdle) has as many knots as there are *pravara* sages; the same number of tufts of hair were left on a boy's head at the *caula* (first haircut) ceremony. In some cases, in the Vedic age, one could guess a man's clan affiliation just by looking at him because the way a man wore his hair was particular to his clan: "The Vāsiṣṭhas wear a braid on the right side, the Ātreyas a three-fold braid, the Aṅgirasas a five-fold top-knot, the Bhṛgus are shaven, the rest wear a crest." (Rahurkar 1964, 75). Lists of the different *gotras* and *pravaras* are available in the literature (Brough 1953; Kane 1974, 2:1263–6; Rahurkar 1964, 73).

How does one know the family *gotra*? It is a bit of information handed down in the family from father to son and is part of the family tradition. There is no membership card or a certificate attesting to this fact. At Hindu religious functions, the officiating priest asks for the *gotra* of the person, *yajamāna*, on whose behalf the rites are conducted and recites it as part of the proceedings. The Vedic tradition was for one of the officiating priests to trace the descent of the *yajamāna* forward from the founding ancestor while a second priest traced the chain of relationship backward. This is called the recitation of *ārṣeya* (sacred descent) and is meant to authenticate the credentials of the person for establishing the sacred fire and then performing the ceremony. The forward and reverse recitations were useful mnemonic devices in an age before writing became common. This recitation to Agni, a Vedic god, recalls all the ancestors who established the sacred fire for Vedic rituals in the past, attesting to one's right to do the same. Hindu society being patriarchal, *gotra* membership is passed down in the male line. Girls belong to the father's *gotra* before marriage; they assume their husband's *gotra* upon marriage. The bride's new *gotra* is used for the first time in the sacrifice offered by the couple as part of the wedding ceremonies. Along with many other aspects of religion and its rites and rituals, there is much less emphasis on *gotra* today. Many people do not even know their *gotra* or care about it.

In Sanskrit, *gotra* also means "cow pen." Cattle were the most prized possession of the Ārya (noble). *Ārya* was a designation made by the free people of the Vedic age who spoke Indo-European languages; those whom they subjugated, slaves, were *dāsas*. Certain families who used to pen their cattle at night in a common enclosure came to be considered as related or belonged to the same *gotra*. These cattle were also branded with common marks to identify them as clan property to discourage others from stealing them (Kosambi 1950). Stealing cattle belonging to a different clan was a minor sport amongst these tribes, especially amongst young men brimming with energy and mischief. These raids usually led to counterattacks and minor skirmishes; hence, the word *gaviṣṭi* means both "wishing for cattle" and "desiring a fight." Thus the family bonds were further strengthened by having to defend their cattle against common enemies.

How many *gotras* are there? It depends on who is counting. There are supposed to be eight original *gotras*, one for each of the *Saptarṣis* (seven sages), plus Agastya. These founding fathers of the *gotras*, called the *gotrakāra Ṛṣi* (clan-making sages), are Viśvāmitra, Jamadagni, Bharadvāja, Gautama, Atri, Vasiṣṭha, Kaśyapa, and Agastya. Over the ages, new *gotras* were added for various reasons; at present, there are thousands of them. However, the total number of *pravara* is 49 (Kane 1974, 2:484). In practice, the *gotra–pravara* system has blossomed into one of great complexity and quite a bit of controversy. Books devoted to this one topic have been written to bring some order to the confusion; for example, there is The *Gotra-Pravara-Mañjarī* of *Puruṣottama-Paṇḍita*, translated as *The Early Brahmanical System of Gotra and Pravara*, with commentary, by John Brough (Brough 1953, 1955). Some of the speculations on the origin of these *gotras* by Damodar Dharmananda Kosambi are also interesting (Kosambi 1950; 1951; 1953; Brough 1953). Kosambi notes that a few *gotra* names, such as Kaśyapa (tortoise) and Kuśika (owl), were derived from the clan totems of pre-Aryan indigenous people. He further proposes that the priests of these people were inducted into the Vedic religion and became part of its *gotra* system (Kosambi 1950, 28–9). Mixing of the customs, traditions, and the peoples of the dominant and subservient groups must have been quite common, especially because dominance implies sexual exploitation. Diffusion across the boundaries of dissimilar groups is a physical fact that cannot be denied. Hence, the "purity" of any group, whatever it means, is a bit of wishful thinking or a myth. At present, amongst the Sarasvats, twenty-one *gotras* are recognized as canonical (Kosambi 1953, 206).

The Vedic Age and the River Sarasvatī

A few comments on the Vedic age are in order before we proceed further. The time and the space coordinates for the events of the Vedic age are educated guesses and nothing more; there are no reliable records on this vital information. Romila Thapar, a historian, assigns ~1500–500 BCE for the composition and compilation of the main body of the Vedic corpus (Thapar 2002, xiii). Wendy Doniger, a Sanskrit scholar, estimates ~1700–1500 BCE for the composition of hymns of the *Ṛgveda*, with the Vedic age ending in ~300 BCE with the compilation of *Gṛhyasūtras* (Doniger 2009, 85–198). Rajesh Kochhar, an astrophysicist, assigns a time frame from after ~1700 to ~900 BCE to the composition of the hymns, which he thinks occurred before the Indo-Europeans crossed into India (Kochhar 2004, 220–2). Information on where these activities took place is also vague. Archeological data pertinent to this early period of Indian history extends from the highlands of Iran, Afghanistan, Pakistan, and the Punjab (Fairservis 1975; Allchin and Allchin 1996; Chakrabarti 1999; Kochhar 2004). The linguistic and other relevant data on the problem have also been extensively discussed (Bryant 2001; Kochhar 2004). A related question that comes up in this context is this: Were the people who spoke Indo-European and called themselves Ārya indigenous, or did they originate outside India? Current knowledge of archeological and linguistic research favors a theory of gradual migration of the nomadic Indo-European speakers from Iran and Afghanistan to the plains of Punjab and further east into India (Thapar 2002, 105–6; Kochhar 2004). Archeological, linguistic, and other data strongly indicate that the homeland of these tribes was somewhere in the Caspian Sea–Black Sea region, from which they spread into lands east and west (Bryant 2001; Anthony 2007). India is not the home of the wild horse, and there has been a paucity of horse bones found in archeological digs there, whereas the Vedic society was very much involved with the horse (Bryant 2001, 115). At the time of the composition of the Vedic Brāhmaṇa literature, it had become difficult to obtain *soma*, a plant that grew in the mountains and was used to prepare a sacred drink (Kochhar 2004, 199). Both of these facts lead one to conclude that most probably the composition of the *Ṛgveda* occurred outside India (Kochhar 2004, 199). There are alternate proposals assigning India as the homeland of the Indo-European tribes that question their foreign origin and subsequent migration into the Punjab (Radhakrishna and Merh 2002). Archeological, linguistic, and other data do not support this conjecture.

The location of the river Sarasvatī ("flowing one"), which plays such an important part in the Vedic age, has intrigued scholars since the beginning of Vedic studies. Geologist Richard Oldham raised the question of its location in 1886 and 1893, and studies on this problem have continued into recent years using modern measurement techniques such as satellite imaging (Radhakrishna and Merh 2002, 81, 89; Kochhar 2004, 118; Danino 2010). The mighty Sarasvatī of the *Ṛgveda* no longer exists as a river in India; geological, tectonic, climate, and other changes could have modified it. One hypothesis identifies it with the present river Ghaggar, which runs dry in the desert of Rajastan. The ancient channel of a big river identified with Sarasvatī has been traced using a variety of techniques: geological, geomorphological, pollen and spores analysis, and satellite imagery. Archeological explorations of many sites along its ancient bank are also discussed in the references just cited. However, Kochhar identifies the Sarasvatī with the Helmand, the Dṛṣadvatī with the Arghandab, the Āpayā with the Tarnak, and the Ārjīkīyā with the Arghastan, forming parts of the Helmand–Arghandab river system in Afghanistan, in support of his thesis that most of the Ṛgvedic hymns were composed on the banks of these rivers (Kochhar 2004, 131, 222). It is also possible that the Vedic people carried their names for some of these rivers with them in their eastward migrations and selectively bestowed them on the most appropriate candidates that they found (Kochhar 2004, 140). These hypotheses have been challenged by alternate proposals (Danino 2010, 260–5). It is earnestly hoped that someone will be able to untangle all of the available data and identify the "real" Sarasvatī, at least to the satisfaction and general approval of all of the experts on the subject. In view of the available data on the identification of the Sarasvatī, this is one of those problems guaranteed to keep scholars busy for some time. The Gauda Sarasvat Brahmana (GSB) community gets its name from an eponymous ancestor, Ṛṣi Sārasvat, "son of the river," on whose banks he lived in the Vedic age (Dowson 1968, 283). The banks of this river, whereever it was, served as the starting point of the later dispersal and migrations of the GSB.

Conventions for Names

Conventions for Hindu names have changed over the ages. This is a complicated subject with many variations: Some are the dictates of religious texts, others are the product of human originality and invention, borrowed local customs, or changes in living conditions. These details may be found in P.V. Kane's *History of Dharmaśāstra (Ancient and Medieval Religious and Civil Law)*; I mention only the highlights here (Kane 1974, 2:238–54). In the Vedic age, it was customary for a person to have three names: a given name, a patronymic, and a third clan name, as in Śvetaketu Āruṇeya ("son of Āruṇi") Gautama.

There were complicated rules for choosing the first name, both for boys and girls, its initial letter, the number of syllables, and so on. Sometimes it was determined by the *nakṣatra* (asterism) under which the baby was born. The author of Arthaśāstra was Viṣṇugupta (given name) Cāṇakya (patronymic, "son of Caṇaka") Kauṭilya (of Kuṭila *gotra*) (Rangarajan 1992; Kosambi 1951). A slightly different version of the origin of this name holds that Cāṇakya was born of a Brahmana called Caṇin who resided in Caṇaka, a village in the Golla District. His paternal grandfather and other ancestors must have been called Caṇaka, after the village, and he got his patronymic from this name (Kane 1990, 1:167). Performing a Vedic sacrifice involved huge expenses, and if a person could claim a successful completion of one, it was quite a big achievement. Such a person wanted this event to become part of his family's history and its claim for distinction. This was the fourth name, the *somayājī*, acquired later on in life by performing a sacrifice (a *somayāga*). An ancestor of Atul Behari Vajapayee, a former prime minister of India, must have performed the Vājapeya ("drink of strength") sacrifice and wanted everyone, including his descendants, to remember it. This was a very expensive sacrifice in which the number 17 played a predominant role. It was a 17-day-long sacrifice in which 17 cups of *surā* (wine) and *soma* (a mood-altering sacred drink) were offered, a race of 17 chariots took place, 17 drums arranged near the sacrificial altar were beaten, and so forth (Kane 1974; 2: 1206–14). No wonder this doughty ancestor wanted the event remembered forever as his family name! People could also be known by their given name and country or locality, such as in the name Janaka (given name) Vaideha ("of Videha"). Adding the name of the place of birth or origin is now a South Indian custom. Though the use of a patronymic was the norm, as could be expected in a patriarchal society, use of a matronymic, or the *gotra* of the maternal grandfather, is also known in a few cases. Prahlāda (given name) Kāyādhava (matronymic, "son of Kayādhū, wife of Hiraṇyakaśipu") and Mahidāsa (given name) Aitareya (matronymic, "son of Itarā") are examples. Kosambi thinks that use of matronymics is a non-Ārya custom, adopted from the indigenous people. In the lineage of pupils at the conclusion of the Bṛhadāraṇyaka Upaniṣad, they are all designated by their matronymics. The question is why? Did all the student/teachers of this particular Upaniṣad belong to the pre-Aryan matrilineal society? This is an interesting situation that has never been fully explained, as far as I know. There are a few cases known in which the person used a patronymic followed by a matronymic. Thus we have Purumīḍha or Purumīḷha (given name) Vaidadaśvī (patronymic, "son of Vidadaśva") Māheya (matronymic, son of "Mahī Ārcanāna"). I suppose it all depends on how well known one's parents were or how high the father or mother or both were on the local social ladder of a dominance hierarchy. The primacy conceit triumphs again! Use of the *gotra* name as part of one's full name seems to have continued on through the twelfth or thirteenth century CE, as can be seen from the examples that follow. This custom is no longer observed generally; one's *gotra* name is recalled only as an *ārṣeya* recitation.

In the GSB community in Goa, the family profession, rather than the *gotra* name, came to be adopted as the family name. Each Goan village must have had either a single or very few people filling a particular professional niche, and thus they could be easily and uniquely identified in the village. Hence, their job titles became labels or family names. Bhaṭṭa literally means "a learned Brāhmaṇa" and is similar to the academic title "doctor," usually awarded at the end of a lengthy period of study. It could be added at the beginning of the name, as in Bhaṭṭa Nārāyaṇa, or at the end of the name, as in Nārāyaṇa Bhaṭṭa, from which usage it became a family name. Nāyak, meaning "leader" or "commander," is a military title; Śānabhāga, Śānabhoga, or its shortened form, Śeṇoy, means "village clerk," and so on it goes. The etymology of Pai is uncertain; there is no one accepted explanation of its origin. A few of us use the locality, the name of the ancestral village, or the location of family property as part of our name. This is a South Indian custom. Our family has been living in Mulki, which is short for Mūlikāpuram ("town of medicinal herbs"), for many generations, and we add it to our names. A few of us add a patronymic also. These days, some people adopt the name of their "native place" (i.e., ancestral village), as their last name. Such variations are endless.

Women use their father's *gotra* till marriage; after the wedding, they take their husband's *gotra*. It is customary to change the bride's given name as part of the wedding, because marriage was once considered a complete makeover of the bride. The new name would be that of a person from the husband's family who had died as a *suvāsinī* (married woman whose husband is alive); that is, a woman who had died before her husband. This person's name was considered auspicious, and the bride would be named after her with the pious hope that she in her turn would never become a widow.

Ṛgveda and the Family Books

The Hindu tradition declares the Vedas to be eternal and of divine origin, or *apauruṣeya* (not crafted by humans). The inspired poets or sages, the singers of the sacred *sūktas* (hymns), are the *ṛṣis* (seers) who "saw" the Vedic hymns. In effect, they responded to these eternal verities and expressed them as the words of the Vedas, like a radio or TV receiver that senses electromagnetic signals and provides audio and video output. "The implication of this interpretation obviously is that the Veda is eternal that it has not been created by any agency, and that the only thing for which the *ṛṣis* may claim credit is that they 'discovered' it and brought it to the notice of posterity" (Rahurkar 1964).

The *Ṛgveda* is divided into ten *maṇḍalas* (rounds or books). The divisions and editing of the Veda were formalized by Veda Vyāsa ("compiler"), also known as Kṛṣṇa Dvaipāyana, the son of the sage Parāśara and the fisherwoman Satyavatī. Of these, six books are considered to be the oldest core or nucleus of the *Ṛgveda* and are called the family books. Each book contains the hymns composed mostly by one family of *ṛṣis*. Those sages and books are Gṛatsamada (book 2), Viśvāmitra (book 3), Vāmadeva and the family of Gotamas (book 4), Atri (book 5), Bharadvāja (book 6), and Vasiṣṭha (book 7). There are a few hymns in the Atri family book that were composed by people not belonging to the family, and the story of Apālā Ātreyī is given in book 8. Most of the hymns in book 8 are by the Kaṇvas, though it is not called a family book as such. It appears that the Atris and Kaṇvas were on friendly terms, and many hymns by the Ātreyas are in book 8. In general, the Atris seem to have been a friendly lot, being on good terms with people of other *gotras*, because they are mentioned in favorable terms in books other than their family book (Kosambi 1950; Rahurkar 1964). There are a few versions of the table of contents, or index, of the *Ṛgveda*, called Anukramaṇī or Sarvānukramaṇī, that keep track of the number of hymns, authors, god or gods worshipped, meter, and many other details. There are a total of 1,028 hymns, of which 11 hymns together are called *vālakhilya sūktas* (apocryphal hymns: *ṚV* 8.49–59). As regards the number of Vedic seers, there is a problem in noting an exact number. One name could correspond to many people, or conversely, a few names might denote the same person. Hence, all numbers of the authors of hymns should have a qualifier: "about." According to one index, there are about 407 seers of the *Ṛgveda* (Rahurkar 1964, 303). As regards *ṛṣikās* (female seers), this number depends on one's criteria for inclusion in the list. One list of women who composed Vedic hymns has 16 women (Sarasvati and Vidyalankara 1977, 1:219); their names are given in Appendix 5, "Hindu Rites of Passage." Another more recent list has 27 names neatly divided into three groups of 9 each (Harshananda 2008, 3:117). However, this augmented list could have problems because it includes nonhumans such as the Vedic female dog Saramā. In the Atri maṇḍala, there are 87 hymns, and the total number of seers who contributed to the Ṛgveda is about 42, including 2 women. These hymns can be categorized as follows: to Agni, 27; to Indra, 8; to Agni, Indra, and other gods, 6; to other gods, 46. As regards the literary quality of the book of Atris, one expert in Vedic literature offers the following comments:

> . . . we find that the Atris are no mean poets and that many of the hymns in the fifth *maṇḍala* make a very impressive reading. The principal literary contribution of the Atris is in the form of what may be called lyrics of Nature. In these,

the Atris have dealt with the two aspects of Nature, namely, the *saumya* (i.e., the serene) and the *ghora* (i.e., the terrible or awe-inspiring). The Uṣas-hymns (hymns to Dawn) for instance, belong to the former type. These are, indeed, the pearls of lyric poetry which appeal to us as greatly through their fine comprehension of the beauties of Nature as through their flowery language. [Rahurkar 1964, 85]

Uṣas hymns (*ṚV* 5.79–5.80) describe the dawn. The Vedic poet sings:

Dawn, Child of Heaven, radiant in garments of changing tints, lovely in peerless beauty, you gleam in splendor, your limbs bright with bathing in the dews of heaven, standing erect in a swift chariot, to receive our homage and worship.

One of the perplexing questions that bedevil the reader of these lines is this: Are Atri and his clan mythical, or were they real historical people? Whatever we know about the Atris, and other clans of the Āryas, is extracted from the Vedas and the auxiliary literature associated with them. Arthur Anthony Macdonell and Arthur Berriedale Keith (1995, 1:17) declare that the Atris were not historical people, though the fifth maṇḍala of the *Ṛgveda* is correctly attributed to them. This opinion is rather curious if one does not accept the spontaneous origin of the fifth book of the *Ṛgveda.* Whether available data are good enough to decide the historical reality of the Atris is a matter of opinion. I feel that the Atris were real historical people, with an accretion of myths built around them at a later date. What follows here are the reasons in support of my belief. Amongst the Vedic people, the Atris seem to have been identified as a clan or a group with their own set of family hymns, distinct enough to be assigned a "family book" in the *Ṛgveda.* They or events in which they participated are mentioned in other books of the Veda by their contemporaries. "The Atris have one peculiarity which distinguishes them from the other particular families of Ṛgvedic seers; they alone are mentioned often outside their own book" (Kosambi 1950, 29). The Atris were beneficiaries of gifts from historical kings or tribal chiefs. The hymns of the Veda ascribed to them could not have appeared out of the blue. It is highly unlikely that some anonymous poet composed them and assigned them to mythical people, because there was such great honor and status associated with being a singer of Vedic hymns that personal ego would have prevented such acts of poetic generosity and transfer of authorship. In dismissing the Atris as myths who cannot claim any historical reality, one should not create a new myth of spontaneous generation of Vedic hymns or dismiss events mentioned by Vedic contemporaries as just stories. There must be a core of real historical events behind them. The problem for us is to separate the real from the imagined. I hope it can be done by eliminating the miraculous from the plausible and accepting the residue with a healthy dose of skepticism.

It is a fact that the Atris called themselves a distinct tribe or a clan, one that appears to have enjoyed royal patronage as priests of the *pañcajanāḥ* (five tribes): Puru, Anu, Druhyu, Turvaśa, and Yadu, who were amongst the first Vedic people on the scene (Rahurkar 1964, 70). We can glean some historical information from Vedic hymns called the *dānastuti* (eulogy of gift). These particular hymns were thank-you notes to donors, with hopes for similar generosity in the future. Some of the kings or tribal chiefs eulogized by the Atris are Traivṛṣṇa Tryaruṇa; Trasadasyu, son of Purukutsa; Aśvameda Bhārata; Ṛṇañcaya, king of the Ruśamas; and Ūrjavya. We find that the Atris are mentioned in the hymns and the family books of the *Ṛgveda*, especially those of the Priyamedhas, the Kaṇvas, the Gotamas, Āṅgirasas, and the Kākṣivats. The Atris and Kaṇvas appear to have been one family in earlier days and to have been on amicable terms even after they separated. In short, the Atris were a friendly lot who got along well with other groups or tribes. We can also find the names of some of the rivers on whose banks they offered the various sacrifices: Paruṣṇī = Irāvatī = modern Ravi; Kubhā = Kabul River; Yamuna (Kochhar 2004). The Brahmanical tradition considers the Atris to have been one of the principal contributors to the cult of the sacrificial fire, Agni; the rites of *śrāddha* (ancestor worship); *soma* worship; and many hymns of the *Ṛgveda*.

Soma Pavamāna

Soma Pavamāna (*Soma* the clear-flowing, or self-purifying) is the deity who is praised, and worshipped in the ninth book of the *Ṛgveda*. The 114 hymns in this book are addressed to Soma and sing his praises. The plant, and the juice extracted from it, were all deified in Vedic rites under this name. The Vedic people identified themselves as *soma* pressers to distinguish themselves from others—the nonpressers. This fact is an indication of the importance attached to these rites by the Vedic people. *Haoma*, a cognate of *soma*, occurs in the Avesta, the sacred book of the Zoroastrians, the Parsis of India (Brough 1971; Boyce 1987, 1989). Linguists have established close similarities in the language of the *Ṛgveda* and the Avesta. There were also cultural contacts between the Vedic and the Avestan people at one time before their separation, giving rise to common or similar belief and ritual systems. What is *soma/haoma*? Trying to answer this question has given rise to much scholarly controversy.

Soma was a drink used in the sacred rituals of the Vedic people. It was supposed to confer feelings of immense power; intimations of immortality, ecstasy, poetic inspiration; and above all, communion with the holy and the gods for the people who drank it as part of the Vedic sacrificial ceremonies (O'Flaherty 1981; Kane 1974, 2:976–1255; Mallory 1997a; Mallory 1997b; Kochhar 2004, 99; Letcher 2008). A description of the *soma* plant, the preparation of the sacred drink and its offering, and the rites, rituals, and the mythology behind these is available in Vedic literature (Hillebrandt 1999, 1:121–332). The drink kept the Vedic poets alert and awake and inspired them to heights of poetic fancy (Falk 1989, 79–80). The Vedic gods, especially Indra, who was very fond of *soma*, were invited to drink it, and the officiating priests consumed it as part of the rites. It was obtained by crushing some plant or plant product between stones; filtering the juice through wool; and mixing it with milk, curds, water, barley, honey, or clarified butter (ghee). It was drunk as part of a sacred ritual after offering it to the gods. There were usually three pressings, at morning, midday, and the evening. It could not have been alcoholic, because there was not enough time for sugar fermentation to produce alcohol. The juice of the plant, used as a sacred drink, was never mixed with cannabis or poppies (Kochhar 2004, 102). What little we know about the plant comes from incidental references in ritual texts, which are *not* field guides to botany. Hence, perhaps we will never know what it is; we can only make an educated guess. *Soma* had become rare and unobtainable even in the age of the *Brāhmaṇas* (~800 BCE), and substitutes were recommended (Kane 1974, 2:1202; Kochhar 2004, 98–112). The identity of this plant had always been a conundrum for scholars studying the Vedic texts and commenting on it and life in the Vedic age. The fertile imaginations of the scholars and the few vague clues to its identity gave rise to a number of suggestions in the early years of Vedic study, which rose to more than 100 in the twentieth century (Wasson 1968, 95–147; Smith 1972, 481; Letcher 2008, 143).

Is Soma *a Species of the Genus* Ephedra*?*

One candidate plant for *soma* is any one of about forty species of the genus *Ephedra* growing across Eurasia and used by the Indo-European tribes in preparation of their sacred drink (Mallory 1997b). These plants contain the active chemicals ephedrine and pseudoephedrine, with the amount depending on the species, region of growth, mode of storage, and other particulars. These chemical compounds are stimulants: They keep a person alert and awake; stimulate the brain; increase the heart rate; constrict blood vessels, leading to higher blood pressure; increase metabolism, resulting in an increase in body heat; and expand bronchial tubes, making breathing easier. Excessive use of these chemicals could result in serious adverse drug reactions: high blood pressure, irritability, nervousness, dizziness, trembling, irregular and fast heartbeat, seizures, heart attack, stroke, or death (Wikipedia. "Ephedra," http://en.wikipedia.org/

wiki/Ephedra, accessed 17 December 2010). Archeological excavations on the banks of the Murghab and Amu Rivers south of the Aral Sea have yielded further evidence in support of the use of the Ephedra for ritualistic purposes by the cultures of the late Bronze Age (c. 2200–1700 BCE) (Mallory 1997a, 1997b; Kochhar 2004, 168–9). At a site in the Murghab Delta, with a calibrated radiocarbon date of 1745 BCE, an analysis of organic residue in ritual vessels in a presumed cultic center showed microscopic twigs of *Ephedra* as well as traces of poppy. Traces of poppy were also found in a stone mortar and pestle found along with these vessels (Kochhar 2004, 169). At another archeological site with a radiocarbon date of 1887 BCE, traces of *Ephedra*, poppy, and cannabis were found in the residue of ritualistic vessels (Kochhar 2004, 169). These data, if confirmed by other independent investigators, would be the strongest evidence for *Ephedra* forming perhaps a main constituent of the sacred drink of these Indo-European tribes. Other additives such as the poppy or cannabis, if confirmed, could be local variations. It has been suggested that the ritual of a sacred drink originated in these cultural centers and moved southward into the historical homelands of the Indo-Iranians (Mallory 1997a; 1997b). The Parsis of India, heirs to the traditions of the Avesta, use in their ceremonies imported *Ephedra procera*, native to the Harirud Valley of Afghanistan (Stein 1931; Boyce 1987, 1989; Falk 1989, 86). The plants are now usually imported from the mountainous regions of Iran or Afghanistan by the Parsis of India. The Namboodri Brahmans of Kerala have continued the tradition of Vedic sacrifices into modern times. Frits Staal, a Vedic scholar, accompanied them on their *soma*-acquisition trip, collected a few specimens of the plant, and had them identified as *Ephedra vulgaris* (Staal 1975, 203). These two examples are interesting, and if it is *assumed* that the identity of the plant has been transmitted in these two traditions unchanged, with no substitutes used, then *soma* is a species of genus *Ephedra*. However, this modern usage of *Ephedra* does not conclusively prove the identity of *soma*, because of possible use of substitutes at a later date. Harry Falk and Rajesh Kochhar list all the physical characteristics of *soma/haoma* described in the Vedic and Avestan texts that support their identifying the plant as *Ephedra* (Falk 1989, 85–7; Kochhar 2004, 98–112): the growth habit of the plant, which could be as high as six feet; the yellowish to bluish green color of the twigs; the leafless stems of the bush; its growth in mountainous regions; the astringent or sharp taste of the plant; a pleasant pine-like aroma; the fact that consuming the plant discourages sleep; and adverse reactions such as heart palpitations that occur when it is imbibed in excess. Kochhar concludes that if *soma* is identified with *Ephedra* and the Ṛgvedic people are assumed to have lived or passed through the Hindu Kush region where this plant grows plentifully, it provides a consistent answer to the *soma* conundrum (Kochhar 2004, 112).

Is Soma Amanita muscaria*?*

The identification of *soma* with the mushroom *Amanita muscaria*, commonly called fly agaric, by Robert Gordon Wasson (1898–1986) caused quite a stir in the 1960s. Wasson, an international banker and amateur mycologist and anthropologist, investigated, ingested, waxed enthusiastic about, and wrote about psychotropic mushrooms and their use in Mexican and Native American folk religions. Later he proposed the use of similar mushrooms in the religious Eleusinian Mysteries in ancient Greece, and investigated the use of *A. muscaria* in Siberian shamanism. These mushrooms are also called sacred, magic, or psychedelic because of their peculiar consciousness-altering properties. To do full justice to the wide use of such mushrooms in religious rites, Wasson and his colleagues later coined a new word: *entheogen* (god generated within) to replace the word hallucinogen (Wasson et al, 1986, 30; Riedlinger 1997, 225). Wasson saw the birth of religions as coinciding with the beginning of the Age of Entheogens, in which humans felt the mysterious and the sacred in the immediacy of mind-altering experiences brought on by eating the sacred mushrooms or ingesting similar naturally occurring substances such as ergot (Wasson et al 1986, 78). Ergot is a type of fungus that infests rye, wheat, barley, and similar grasses and is psychotropic. He must be credited with bringing these secret religious practices to the attention of general public in a now famous *Life* magazine article of May 13, 1957, and later publications (Wasson et al 1986; Riedlinger 1997, 257). The *Life* article is credited with the birth of the psychedelic revolution of the 1960s (Riedlinger 1997, 8). Many of the people involved in this new age of expanded consciousness, including Timothy Leary, acknowledged Wasson as their spiritual guide, or guru. It is not clear whether Wasson had any benevolent guru-like feelings toward his self-appointed disciples. He did not approve of their less-than-reverential attitude toward the sacred mushrooms or their frankly hedonistic enjoyment of these and other consciousness-altering chemicals. He became a zealous psychotropic mushroom missionary and an amateur anthropologist, seeing mushrooms as important cultural agents in certain religious practices all over the world (Wasson et al 1986, 17–81, 117–39). A few of his critics have accused Wasson of finding the sacred or magic mushrooms wherever he looked, with some justification (Wasson et al 1978, 12; Riedlinger 1997, 65).

One result of his insights was the book *Soma: Divine Mushroom of Immortality* (Wasson 1968; 1979). In proposing that the Vedic *soma* was the hallucinogenic mushroom *A. muscaria*, or fly agaric, he bolstered his case with translations of the *Ṛgveda* by Wendy Doniger O'Flaherty, a Sanskrit and Vedic scholar. As part of his thesis, Wasson tried to establish parallels between Siberian shamanic practices of eating the fly agaric and the Vedic text. In Siberia, the effects of the hallucinogenic agent in the mushroom were experienced twice: first by eating the mushroom and second by drinking the urine of those who had eaten it. The active psychotropic chemical was excreted in the urine and was potent enough to bring about the desired effects a second time. The Vedic texts, especially those dealing with sacrificial rites, give a very detailed description of the procedures of such rites, and as noted by Sanskrit scholar Daniel H.H. Ingalls, the Vedic people were not particularly embarrassed to talk about natural bodily functions (Ingalls 1971, 190). However, there is no explicit mention of urine drinking in any form in the Vedic text, or the eating of mushrooms, both of which are prohibited to priests. Wasson tried his best to make a case for two forms of *soma* in the Vedas, the fresh juice and the recycled *soma*-laden urine. The scholarly reaction to Wasson's thesis was divided. A few were convinced, and others put forth strenuous objections. A twenty-page review of the book by Huston Smith, professor of philosophy at MIT, was in general favorable (Smith 1972). Smith felt that by identifying *soma* with fly agaric, Wasson had solved the puzzle of its identity. A majority of scholars polled by Smith agreed with this conclusion, with a few dissents or assents with qualifications. Ingalls (1916–1999), Wales professor of Sanskrit at Harvard University and a Vedic scholar, agreed with Wasson's identifying of *soma* as fly agaric. However, he could find no evidence for the drinking of recycled soma urine in the *Ṛgveda* (Ingalls 1971, 188). The use and abuse of hallucinogens, natural or synthetic, were very much in fashion in the 1960s and 1970s and could have influenced these scholarly judgments declaring that *soma* is *A. muscaria.*

Dissents were summarized by John Brough, a Vedic scholar from the University of Cambridge, in his thirty-two-page review of Wasson's book (Brough 1971). This criticism was answered by Wasson in a fifty-page article (Wasson 1972, 1990). When authors wax prolix in learned publications and there is a copious flow of scholarly ink, one can be sure that there are many unanswered questions that can never be easily settled. This is very true here, and all the objections that were raised by Brough and others have not been answered satisfactorily by Wasson. There is the problem of the difficulty of translation of the Vedic text. The poetic language of the verses, full of metaphors, some clear and others opaque, has different layers of interpretation and understanding, resulting in no single authoritative translation. Multiplicity of meanings of Vedic hymns results in many possible choices, and one can always find a reading that supports one's favorite theory. Was the *soma* a stimulant or a hallucinogen? The answer very much depends on a subjective reading of the Vedic text. Or the answer is a conjecture, an educated guess, or an opinion. Some scholars support the idea of the *soma* as a stimulant (Brough 1971; Falk 1989;

Kochhar 2004); others think it was a hallucinogen (Wasson 1968; Ingalls 1971; Smith 1972). Are the *soma* hymns the poetic joy of people experiencing the exhilaration of a stimulant, or instead the result of their hallucinating under its influence? Poetic texts can be deceptive in providing an answer. One example is the *Labasūkta* (Quail hymn, *ṚV* 10.119), in which Agni, or Indra in the form of a bird (quail), has drunk the *soma* and, under its influence, praises himself as one who has attained gigantic proportions (O'Flaherty 1981, 131). For the advocates of *soma* as a hallucinogen, this hymn is proof that the person who drank it is hallucinating, on a "trip." Others see such an interpretation of the hymn as wrong because they see only the Vedic gods pervading space, one of their defining characteristics (Falk 1989, 78–9). The use of Vedic or Avestan texts for a forensic investigation of the chemical nature of the source of poetic inspiration is a novel and interesting idea. Whether the answers it provides are believable is an open question. An example is a quote from an anonymous Chinese poet waxing ecstatic over several cups of nothing stronger than tea, to make the point that hallucinogens need not be the only source of poetic rapture (Letcher 2008, 153–4). The botanical identification of the plant depends partly on whether it is considered a stimulant or a hallucinogen. Those who support *soma* as fly agaric, a hallucinogen, look for evidence to support this assumption. Others see *soma* only as a stimulant and hunt for clues that support this thesis. Data from the Siberian, Chinese, and other cultures on mushroom-eating, urine-drinking, and related shamanic practices are interesting; however, they are not particularly relevant to the quest to establish the Vedic identity of *soma* (Brough 1971, 332–3). Then there is the elaborate preparation of the drink. The question has been raised: Why go through with it when they could have just eaten the mushroom? Wasson pointed out recent chemical and pharmacological research, which has discovered that by drying the mushroom and reconstituting it by steeping it in water increases the potency of its psychotropic effects (Wasson 1972). Close parallels between Siberian shamanic practices and Vedic rites appear to be highly improbable; the two cultures were separated by thousands of miles and had no known contact. There are also the bad effects of fly agaric "trips," because of which the mushrooms are not very popular even with Siberian shamans (Letcher 2008, 149). Hence, the euphoria of the Vedic text about the good effects of *soma* appears misplaced. Wasson's own experience of eating fly agaric was not what he had expected:

> In 1965 and again in 1966 we tried out the fly-agarics repeatedly on ourselves. The results were disappointing. We ate them raw, on empty stomachs. We drank the juice, on empty stomachs. We mixed the juice with milk, and drank the

> mixture, always on empty stomachs. We felt nauseated and some of us threw up. We felt disposed to sleep, and fell into a deep slumber from which shouts could not rouse us, lying like logs, not snoring, dead to the outside world. When in this state, I once had vivid dreams, but nothing like what happened when I took the Psilocybe mushrooms in Mexico, where I did not sleep at all. [Wasson 1968, 75]

Wasson and colleagues did not experience any entheogenic epiphanies after eating fly agaric; instead, they fell asleep. Did the disappointing experience give rise to any doubts in Wasson about equating *soma* with fly agaric? Apparently not. Wasson seems to have completely neglected these experimental data of his personal experience with the mushroom. It did not cramp his style in trumpeting *soma* as fly agaric or his missionary zeal for magic mushrooms as entheogens. Fly agaric, being a depressant, puts people to sleep, making it not the right prescription for preparing for battle, whereas the ephedrine in *Ephedra* is a powerful stimulant that could have been ingested as a drink by Indra and other warriors preparing for a fight (Brough 1971, 361). All of these objections to Wasson's thesis are discussed in a new book on mushrooms (Letcher 2008, 142–55). Some disturbing facts that Letcher discovered in going through Wasson's archives have raised questions about Wasson's scholarly credentials. Wasson, in his enthusiasm to prove his case, appears to have "encouraged photographer Allan Richardson to 'tinker' with the photos to make them more persuasive, [which] suggests that he was less than confident about the strength of this opening argument himself" (Letcher 2008, 145). In short, the objective facts that the photos were supposed to show in the book on soma were "doctored" or "similarly cropped and treated so that they would emphasize the chosen qualities" (Letcher 2008, 145). All of this "photographic jiggery-pokery," as Letcher calls it, calls into question Wasson's scholarly objectivity and gives a bad odor to his work. Wasson's identification of *soma* is not as conclusive as he thought it was. The optimism of Wasson's friends, fans, admirers, and amen corner, who feel that the identity of *soma* as *A. muscaria* has been settled for good (Riedlinger 1997), is in my opinion premature. The identity of *soma/haoma* is a problem that does not have a clear-cut answer. Scholars are faced with for-or-against arguments for their favorite hypothesis. Ultimately it is a question of judgment for each person, or a matter of opinion. Each person has to decide whether these pros and cons amount to the certainty of identification. Experts have their favorite choice for *soma/haoma*; the leading candidates are a species of *Ephedra* or *Amanita muscaria*, with some other plants in the race too. There is an abundance of subjective opinions and a dearth of objective data on this problem. Under these circumstances, it is not possible to know with certainty what *soma/haoma* is. To summarize, the identity of *soma/haoma* remains unproven. Because of the paucity of clues in the Vedic and Avestan texts, most likely it will remain so.

Some Notables of Clan Atri

The following is a more or less chronological list of some members of clan Atri, along with what little we know about them. Most of the narrative that follows refers to the Vedic people, except for a few members of the clan who appeared at the transition to the early and later historic period. This transition is obvious from the context. The Vedas are liturgical texts and were not meant to be historical documents. Any historical information that we can extract from them is incidental to the main ritual and liturgical nature of the Vedic hymns. Hence, the probable dates of the people or narratives mentioned earlier are conjectures. These dates are highly uncertain and are scholarly guesses because of the dearth of good input data available to extract them. This information may be found in the writings of V.G. Rahurkar, Kochhar, Edwin Bryant, and David W. Anthony, already cited. We know some of them as authors or seers of Vedic hymns; others are known from the part they played in Hindu literature or traditions. This is a sample of the clan members and is meant to give a flavor of the times they lived in and of their worldview, prejudices, and perhaps what motivated them. These people are treated as ordinary human beings who lived and loved as such and did what other ordinary humans do. This cast of characters has been chosen with one simple criterion: There is an interesting story attached to each name. These are their myths and legends, their words and deeds. I hope that these stories have fleshed them out to live again for a few fleeting moments in our memories. The list begins in the Vedic age and ends in historical times. The information that I have provided about these ancestors is fragmentary, selective, incomplete, and I wish that we knew more about them. It is quite possible that in some cases, the actual names of the composers had been forgotten by the time the *Ṛgveda* was assembled. Instead of the author being noted as unknown, certain words in the hymns came to designate its author. There are also other names, which appear to be of doubtful authenticity for various reasons. These problems have been analyzed and discussed in a recent monograph on Ṛgvedic names by Manfred Mayrhofer (Mayrhofer 2003). If the meaning of a name is readily available, it is provided here to supplement other information on the Vedic seer.

Atri Bhauma

Atri Bhauma, the progenitor of Clan Atri, is the mind-born son of Brahma or Prajāpati. Atri means "eater" or "devourer," and Bhauma, "of the earth." I have not been able to find the origin of the legend as to how he acquired this epithet. The dictionary defines *Bhauma* as another name for *Atri*, without explaining why (Apte 1998). He is the author or seer of many hymns to Agni (*ṚV* [*Ṛgveda*] 5.27), Indra (*ṚV* 5.37–9), Indra and Sūrya (*ṚV* 5.40), Indra and Agni (*ṚV* 5.86), Viśve Devās (*ṚV* 5.41), Viśve Devās and Rudra (*ṚV* 5.42–3), the Aśvins ("possessed of horses"; *ṚV* 5.76–7), Parjanya (*ṚV* 5.83), the Earth (*ṚV* 5.84), and Varuṇa (*ṚV* 5.85).

Anasūyā ("without spite") was Atri's wife, famous as a *pativratā* (woman devoted to her husband). Brahmā, Viṣṇu, and Śiva once wanted to put her virtue to a test. While Atri was away, they went to his dwelling and requested hospitality from Anasūyā, with the proviso that they should be served a meal while she was naked. The dictates of hospitality constrained her to accede to the guests' smallest wish; however, Anasūyā was not fazed. She sprinkled the guests with some consecrated water from Atri's *kamaṇḍalu* (water pot), and by the power of her virtue, she transformed them into babies. She then nursed them while nude to fulfill the obligations of hospitality. Brahmā, Viṣṇu, and Śiva were mightily pleased with Anasūyā and asked her to request a boon from each of them. She wished each of them to be born as a son to her and Atri. Her wish was fulfilled, and the couple had three sons: Soma, Datta, and Durvāsas, born with the essence of Brahmā, Viṣṇu, and Śiva, respectively. Atri and Anasūyā later had two more children, a son Aryaman ("nobility") and a daughter Analā ("purity").

The hymn to Indra and Sūrya ("sun"; *ṚV* 5.40), by Atri, is traditionally considered the family hymn of the Atris. What is a family hymn? "These family-hymns record some unusual exploit of the early ancestor or rather the founder of the family, an exploit which is normally described as having been performed with the help of Indra and which is considered to be bringing special glory and credit to the whole family" (Rahurkar 1964). What was the heroic challenge Atri had to face? Atri rescued the sun from the clutches of Svarbhānu the Asura ("anti-god"), who had pierced the sun with darkness (O'Flaherty 1981, 187; Jamison 1991, 235). The gods appeal to Atri to rescue the sun. Atri rallied round, offered *soma* to fortify the sun and himself, and on the fourth incantation freed the sun from the clutches of the evil demon. Svarbhānu in later Hindu mythology represents Rāhu ("the seizure"), the ascending node of the moon's orbit; the descending node is called Ketu ("the comet" or "tail").[1] What the hymn describes is a solar eclipse and Atri's magic in rescuing the sun. The

[1]The ascending node is the point of intersection of the moon's orbit with the ecliptic, going from south to north. The ecliptic is the plane of earth's orbit round the sun. The moon has to be close to one of these nodes for an eclipse to occur. That is the reason why an eclipse is called a *grahaṇa* (grasping) of the sun or moon by Rāhu or Ketu.

gods and men were grateful to Atri for rescuing the sun. This doughty deed would be remembered forever at *soma* sacrifices by a special *dakṣiṇā* (ritual gift), called *atrihiraṇya* ("Atri gold"), given to a descendant of Atri at the mid-day pressing of *soma* (Jamison 1991, 185–7). In Hindu tradition, the sun is represented by gold, hence the ritual gift of gold. If only Atri had bothered to record the time, totality, and approximate location of this adventure, we could have dated the event and the Vedic age by eclipse calculations. Alas for posterity, Atri's priorities were different.

Atri was confined for a time in a glowing, hot cleft or hole in the ground, by his enemies the Asura. He prayed to the Aśvins; they answered his prayers and released him from the prison (*ṚV* 1.116.8 and 1.117.3). Some scholars have confused this adventure with that of Saptavadhri Ātreya, whose tale is told in a later section in this appendix; others think that they are different people (Rahurkar 1964).

Rāma ("charming"), the seventh incarnation of Viṣṇu, born the son of Daśaratha ("possessing ten chariots"), accompanied by his wife Sītā ("the furrow," where she was found as a baby), and brother Lakṣmaṇa ("endowed with lucky signs"), were entertained at the hermitage of Atri and Anasūyā, near Citrakūṭa, when they went into exile. Anasūyā blessed Sītā and gave her some ornaments and an unguent to keep her young and beautiful forever.

Atri initiated many new Agni and *soma* rituals, thus making significant contributions to the corpus of Vedic sacrifices. Perhaps his most important innovation was the introduction of *śrāddha* (offerings to the Manes, or deceased ancestors) (Rigopoulos 1998, 47). These offerings are made with much *śraddhā* (faith) that they will eventually reach the ancestors, and thus they are called *śrāddha* (Kane 1973, 4:351–2). Atri is supposed to have instructed Nimi, son of Datta, to perform the first *śrāddha* for his son. The introduction of this ritual was to have important and long-lasting consequences in Hindu society. Every Hindu owes a threefold debt at birth: to the gods, the sages, and his or her ancestors. The debt to ancestors is repaid only by begetting a son who will perform *śrāddha* for his ancestors. Only a son could perform this ritual for his father and ancestors; hence, having a son became very important. Could a wife or a daughter perform this ritual for the dead husband or father? The answer is complicated, because some authorities on Hindu traditions allow it under very special circumstances, whereas others do not (Kane 1973, 4:259). Thus a son became an all-important conduit for the welfare of a man and his ancestors in the hereafter. A wife who gave birth only to girls was at a great disadvantage in Hindu society. Codes of law supported a man marrying again in the hope of begetting a son. Girls became second-class children and were discriminated against. Lawgivers decreed that a child who can perform *śrāddha* should inherit a man's estate; therefore, wives and daughters who could not perform this ritual did not inherit their husband's or father's estate, according to the most widely used code of laws, the Mitākṣarā. Almost all of the inequities and injustices meted out to girls in Hindu society can be ultimately traced to the importance attributed to this ritual. It is an example of the law of unintended consequences. Did Atri really originate this tradition? It is possible; there is this indirect evidence: Atri gave his only son for adoption by another sage, Aurva, son of Urva and grandson of Bhṛgu (Kane 1974, 2:8; Kane 1973, 3:662–3). This could not have happened if *śrāddha* had been part of accepted practice. Hence, it is possible that Atri instituted this ritual after this adoption had taken place. There are three other candidates for the title of originator of *śrāddha*: Jamadagni, Manu, and the Varāha incarnation of Viṣṇu (Rahurkar 1964, 215; Kane 1973, 4:349).

The highest point of Mt. Abu, in Rajasthan, is called Guru Śikhar ("Guru's Peak"; it is 1,721 meters/5,647 feet high). On this peak is a small temple dedicated to either Atri or his son Dattātreya; there are conflicting descriptions of the principal deity.

Soma Ātreya

Soma was born from the essence of Brahmā, according to the legend of his birth already mentioned here. Later on, he came to be identified with Earth's satellite, the Moon, and called Candra. He also represented the deified ambrosia of the gods, the plant and its extract, Soma Pavamāna. He was the source of this divine drink for the gods, and making sure that they got an abundance of it was his responsibility. The divine marriage of Soma and Sūryā, daughter of Sūrya, the Sun, as described in *ṚV* 10.85, is considered a model for all later Hindu weddings (O'Flaherty 1981, 267). Many of the verses from this hymn are recited at Hindu weddings as part of the ceremonies. It describes the groom's party arriving at the bride's home for the wedding and then departing for the husband's home with the new bride. The verses implore the gods: "Generous Indra, give this woman fine sons and the good fortune of her husband's love. Place ten sons in her and make her husband the eleventh" (O'Flaherty 1981, 271, 10.85.45).

See Appendix 5, "Hindu Rites of Passage," for other details of Hindu weddings.

Dakṣa ("ritual skill") had 27 daughters, the *nakṣatra* ("asterism"), also called the lunar mansions. Soma married all of them with the promise that he would be equally fond of all of them. However, he particularly liked the beautiful Rohiṇī ("the red one") and paid more attention to her, provoking the jealousy of her sisters, who complained to their father. Dakṣa cursed Soma for reneging on his promise; he would be struck down with consumption. His wives had not expected such an extreme punishment from their father and begged him to withdraw his curse. A powerful curse, once uttered, could not be withdrawn, said Dakṣa. However, he could attenuate it; the Moon would progressively wane to nothing at each new Moon and would be restored to his full glory at each full Moon. Another legend has it that at the new Moon, the gods have drunk their fill of *soma*, shrinking the Moon to nothing, and the Moon slowly regains in size when it is filled up again. Soma performed the *rāja-sūya* ("royal sacrifice"), as a result of which he became mighty with unlimited power. Power corrupted him; he became arrogant and licentious and abducted Tārā ("star"), wife of Bṛhaspati ("lord of sacred speech"), the teacher of the gods. Soma even ignored a direct command from Brahmā to give her up. There was a big battle, and everyone who was anybody got involved. Finally, Soma was forced to liberate his victim. However, Tārā was pregnant with Soma's baby. She gave birth to Budha, the planet Mercury. Soma (Candra), Budha, and Budha's descendants form the Lunar Dynasty of Hindu *purāṇas* ("ancient tales"). Yādavas, with Balarāma; Kṛṣṇa; the good Pāṇḍavas; and the bad Kauravas all belong to the lineage of the Lunar Dynasty. Their genealogy, adventures, and good and bad deeds, and the moral lessons to be derived from them, are to be found in the epics, Mahābhārata and Bhāgavata, and in other works of Hindu tradition (O'Flaherty 1975; Bhattacharji 1988). See the genealogical chart in the Mahābhārata of van Buitenen (volume 1, p. 13), for the family tree of Atri and his descendants (van Buitenen 1973, 1:12–13). I will not deal with the lives of any of these mighty heroes here; they have been amply described in the books listed in the Bibliography.

Datta Ātreya, or Dattātreya

Some legends of the birth of Datta ("given, presented") Ātreya, or Dattātreya, describe him as the representation of the essence of Viṣṇu only, whereas other myths say that his birth was the comingling of the essences of Brahmā, Viṣṇu, and Śiva. These days, Dattātreya is worshipped as representing the Hindu Trinity. His iconic representations show either one face with two arms or three heads with six arms. He is shown as a mendicant or a yogi, accompanied by four dogs standing for the four Vedas and Kāmadhenu ("wish-fulfilling cow"). The center of his worship used to be Maharashtra; however, it has now spread to other parts of India: Karnataka, Andhra Pradesh, Kerala, Tamil Nadu, Gujarat, and Nepal (Rigopoulos 1998). Worship of Dattātreya is multifaceted. The deity has a large cross-section of devotees, covering the whole spectrum of economic classes and a wide variety of ritual traditions and social statuses. Under a general umbrella of *advaita* ("nondual") philosophical convictions, one finds Brahmanical ritual orthodoxy, antinomian Tantrism, the world-renouncing Yoga, Vaiṣṇava *bhakti* ("faith"), Śaiva asceticism, Śāktism (worship of deified energy Śaktī represented as a goddess such as Durgā), and

Devī worship. This syncretism extends even to popular Sufism of Islam and to Jainism. The Bābā Buḍān Hills, named after the Sufi saint Bābā Buḍān, are situated northwest of Mysore and are believed to have been the hermitage of Datta Ātreya. This otherworldly Sufi saint, mentioned earlier, conferred on all humanity the boon of coffee by smuggling (or liberating) some viable beans out of Yemen. This was in a good cause, because the saint had developed a fondness for coffee, which he needed to keep him awake during his meditations. The details of the Datta cult and its centers of worship are to be found in *Dattātreya, The Immortal Guru, Yogin, and Avatāra*, by Antonio Rigopoulos (Rigopoulos 1998).

Durvāsas Ātreya

Durvāsas ("ill-clothed") Ātreya was one of the sons of Atri Bhauma, the progenitor of clan Atri. According to legend, he was born from the essence of Śiva and inherited his angry nature. He is notorious in the Hindu tradition for his irascible temper, which got many humans, gods, demons, and others into trouble. He described himself as one "whose nature is stranger to remorse" (Dowson 1968). He is supposed to have taken a vow of being *unmatta* ("intoxicated"), elevated, frantic, abnormal, mad, or all of these. His specialty was cursing people on the slightest provocation. With each curse, he lost part of the merit gained by austerities. He would then undertake more austerities to "recharge his batteries," as it were, so that he could curse some more! He cursed poor Śakuntala for not showing him the proper respect due to an honored guest, and as a result, Duṣyanta, her lover, would not acknowledge her as his wife. He could be quite human when he was pleased, as he was, for example, with Kuntī, who was given a boon by which she could have a child by any god she wished to invoke. That is how Kuntī gave birth to Karṇa, Yudhiṣṭhira, Bhīma, and Arjuna. When Kṛṣṇa did not meet Durvāsa's standards of hospitality, he cursed Kṛṣṇa and predicted his end and that of the Yādava lineage. Durvāsas once gave a garland of fragrant flowers to Indra. Instead of treating it as a precious gift from an august personage, Indra casually draped it on the head of his elephant. The garland slipped, fell to the ground, and was trampled by the elephant. Durvāsas was beside himself with anger; he cursed Indra and foretold the subversion of Indra's sovereignty over the three worlds by the Asuras. The tales of his behavior go on and on. In short, Durvāsas was a curious character who was not in harmony with himself, his acquaintances, or his surroundings. He forgot nothing and never forgave.

Śyāvāśva Ātreya

Śyāvāśva composed twelve hymns in book 5 of the *Ṛgveda* and contributed to parts of one hymn each in books 8 and 9; he is most probably named after the *pravara ṛṣi.* (prominent ancestral seer) for clan Atri and is not the *pravara ṛṣi* himself. He was the son of Arcanānasa Ātreya and the grandson of Atri Sāṁkhya, both composers of Vedic hymns (Rahurkar 1964). Śyāvāśva literally means "dark brown or bay horse." Owning a bay horse—was it unique enough to become an epithet? The word *aśva* can also mean "pervader" and is used as a symbol for luminous deities in Vedic literature (Daniélou 1964, 128). This illustrates the difficulty of giving a simple meaning to a name in the Vedas! Śyāvāśva's compositions are hymns to the Maruts ("storm gods"; *ṚV* 5.52–60); the *dānastuti* ("gift hymn") to the Maruts, Śaśīyasī Tarantamahiṣī, Purumīḍha Vaidadaśvī, and Rathavīti Dārbhya (*ṚV* 5.61); and the hymns to Savitṛ (*ṚV* 5.81–2).

Arcanānasa and Śyāvāśva were officiating at a sacrifice for the king, Rathvīti Dārbhya. During these ceremonies, Arcanānasa saw Rathavīti's beautiful daughter and asked for her hand in marriage for his son. King Rathavīti was agreeable to the marriage proposal; however, his wife was not. The queen was a bit of a snob, and she felt that a mere priest who had no Vedic verses to his credit was not good enough for her daughter. She declared that her daughter would marry only a *ṛṣi* of Vedic hymns, and none less. Poor Śyāvāśva was in a tough spot! On their way back, Arcanānasa and Śyāvāśva were honored by gifts from Śaśīyasī, chief queen of Taranta, or Tarantamahiṣī, and Purumīḍha. Śyāvāśva was also fortunate enough to meet the Maruts, composed hymns praising them, and thus became a *ṛṣi.* The result was the hymn *ṚV* 5.61, which praises the Maruts who inspired him and thanks his patrons, Śaśīyasī, Purumīḍha, and his future father-in-law, Rathavīti, for their generosity. He later married Rathavīti's daughter with the queen's blessings (Rahurkar 1964; Sarasvati and Vidyalankara 1977). The queen could now claim a *ṛṣi* for a son-in-law and hold her head high as his proud mother-in-law.

Saptavadhri Ātreya

A few scholars have identified Saptavadhri Ātreya with Atri, the progenitor of the clan. However, as pointed out by Rahurkar, the Vedic Index identifies him as an Ātreya, or a descendant of Atri, and not the progenitor himself (Rahurkar 1964, 82). I follow this assignment. Saptavadhri, or "seven times emasculated," must be a metaphor referring to his long separation from his wife because of the evil machinations of his enemies, and not a description of any drastic changes to his anatomy. His subsequent rescue by the Aśvins is narrated in *ṚV* 5.78 (O'Flaherty 1981; Jamison 1991, 235).

The hymn implores the Aśvins, to rescue Saptavadhri, who had been imprisoned in a hot pit, away from his wife, by his enemies the Asuras, the anti-gods or bad guys. Because the Aśvins were physicians who released Saptavadhri from a confined space, parts of this hymn were recited in the olden days as sympathetic magic for the safe delivery of a baby.

Atri Sāṁkhya Ātreya

Atri Sāṁkhya Ātreya is the son of Saṁkhya Ātreya, and the seer of the hymn to the Aśvins (*ṚV* 10.143). He is the father of Arcanānasa Ātreya, Apālā Ātreyī, and many other hymn makers, and the grandfather of Śyāvāśva Ātryea. Many of his sons and his daughter Apālā grew up to be the seers of the Vedic hymns. He must have been bald, because his daughter prayed Indra to give him a full head of hair.

Apālā Ātreyī

Apālā Ātreyī is the daughter of Atri Sāṁkhya (*ṚV* 10.143) and the youngest sister of Vasuśruta (*ṚV* 5.3–6), Pratibhānu (*ṚV* 5.48), Viśvasāman (*ṚV* 5.22), Vasūyu (*ṚV* 5.25–6), Sutaṁbhara (*ṚV* 5.44), Gopavana (*ṚV* 8.73–4), Paura (*ṚV* 5.73–4), and Arcanānas (*ṚV* 5.63–4, 8.42 [Rahurkar 1964, 285]). With such a large number of Vedic poets, theirs was an abundantly talented family!

Her name has been interpreted as "boundless" (Jamison 1991, 149–73) or "maiden," meaning without a protector or a husband (Sarasvati and Vidyalankara 1977). She is the *ṛṣikā* of the hymn to Indra, *ṚV* 8.91, named after her. This has been the subject of much scholarly commentary, with etymological, grammatical, and textual analyses of the hymn that differ slightly in details (O'Flaherty 1981; Schmidt 1987; Jamison 1991). However, behind the screen of this learned discourse, there is the following simple story of her adventures as narrated in the hymn, a version that mainly follows Hanns-Peter Schmidt (1987):

Apālā is a maiden who is worried about the blemishes on her skin, which could make her less than attractive to prospective suitors. Perhaps she is a teenager bothered by her pimples? On her way to a river, she sees some *soma*, which gives her the bright idea of offering it to Indra and asking for boons in return. Will Indra oblige? She will soon find out. She chews the *soma* and invites Indra to partake of its juice from her mouth to the traditional ritual accompaniment of fried grain, gruel, cakes, and songs of praise. Indra accepts her invitation and drinks *soma* from her mouth. He grants her three boons of fertility: vouchsafing for the growth of hair on her father's bald head, crops in his barren fields, and hair on her nether belly. He cures the blemishes on her skin thrice, transferring her affliction first to a hedgehog, then to a monitor lizard, and last to a chameleon, leaving her with a glowing skin fit to be fondled.

Viśvavārā Ātreyī

Viśvavārā Ātreyī is the second female composer in the family book of the Atris. Her hymn is to Agni (*ṚV* 5.28), and she prays for conjugal happiness and security in life. The seer of this hymn had some skin disease that did not make her attractive to her husband. She prayed to Agni for a cure, which was granted, restoring her to a state of married bliss. It is a tradition to recite the last two stanzas of this hymn during the kindling of the sacred fire with araṇi (sticks of wood rubbed against each other to kindle a fire), for the new-Moon and full-Moon sacrifices (Rahurkar 1964, 68).

We do not know the real name of the author of this hymn. Viśvavārā is a name made up from a word picked from the text. Several variations of this word are to be found in the different books of the *Ṛgveda*, and thus it is not a proper name (Sarasvati and Vidyalankara 1977, 6:1900–1).

The text of the hymn clearly indicates a woman offering oblations to the sacred fire and thus discharging the offices of a sacrificial priest (Sarasvati and Vidyalankara 1977, 6:1900–1). However, an account of a Vedic ritual conducted in 1981 near Poona shows the wife touching the arm of her husband, who is offering oblations, with a long blade of *kuśa* grass (Leslie, 1992, 31). That was the extent of her involvement in the ceremonies. Why this drastic change or marginalization of women as participants in Vedic rituals? In the Vedic age, a wife could and did offer oblations in household fires during her husband's absence. At later times, women were even forbidden to utter Vedic mantras; these were considered too sacred for the lips of a woman! The possible reasons for this change are many; I will try to enumerate (Altekar 1999, 343–8) them.

Food offerings to the Manes, *śrāddha*, became very important in the post-Vedic period, and only a son could perform this rite. This act came to be known as discharging a person's debt to ancestors; hence, begetting a son was quite important, as mentioned earlier. The result was that daughters became second-class children without inheritance rights, as discussed in an earlier section on Atri. The process of unequal treatment of women had begun, and it was a slippery slope from there.

Vedic ceremonies could be performed only by a married couple acting together as a unit. In order for the wife to be allowed to discharge her obligations, she went through *upanayana* (the initiation ceremony) as a girl, she was educated, and she could recite the necessary Vedic hymns and mantras correctly with proper enunciation. Because they had only a few years of education, girls usually married when they were 16 or 17 years old (Altekar 1999). At a later time, the ceremonies became more complex, requiring many years of training and study, pushing the age of marriage to 22 to 24 years to achieve some competency in rituals. This resulted in only a few committed girls getting the necessary education and training, with most others choosing to obtain only a little or no education. With the conquest of the indigenous people by the free Ārya, *dāsas* (slaves) became quite common. This system was bad for both: Unlimited power corrupted the master, and slavery was harsh and cruel for the *dāsa*. The social consequences of slavery were many and long-lasting. There was the influx of large number of servile peoples, both inside the house as part of the family and outside in the fields as slaves or serfs. Men married many conquered women who did not speak Sanskrit; *dāsī*, who were not educated, could not pronounce Sanskrit and therefore could not participate in rituals. Polygamy and casual concubinage, as exercises of power over servile women, became the norm. Children grew up in a polyglot family, their mother tongue was not Sanskrit, and they could not understand it. Labor was cheap, and the women of the family became merely additional helpers round the house, along with the *dāsī*. The *dharmapatnī* (legal wife) lost her privileged position and gradually ceased to be an equal participant in household Vedic ceremonies, or *sahadharmiṇī*. This resulted in fewer and fewer women getting an education and thus lacking the ability to speak and understand Sanskrit. The economic status of women must have also deteriorated in society's transition from a nomadic to a settled agricultural economy. All these changes were gradual, cumulative, and irreversible. These factors resulted in girls' not getting an education, becoming completely dependent on the males of the family, and marrying early. The overt and covert misogyny of a patriarchal society that ascribes all virtues to males, and most human failings to women, also contributed to this sorry state of affairs. The authors of the codes of law decreed that a wife should revere her husband as a god on earth, even if he was morally despicable (Altekar 1999, 348). Such pronouncements by the authors of codes of law indicate that these men had lost their moral compass and that the women had lost claim to any semblance of human rights. Any person could abuse the system of sacred literature by appropriate interpolations inserted in them to sanctify personal prejudices. Women became dumb, docile, much-exploited childbearing devices living a life of drudgery and servitude. They were further constrained by the hard taskmaster of their conscience in trying to live up to impossible ideals set up by a patriarchal society. Another factor contributed to the loss of rights by women in Hindu society: The number of restrictions put on Hindu women came to be seen as providing Hindu society with commensurately higher ranking in the social hierarchy. Thus, communities that prohibited remarriage of widows came to be considered superior to those that allowed it. The ranks and status of each *jāti* (birth group) was, in other words, built on the backs of its women. Once this curious belief came to be accepted, there was no limit to the number of acts forbidden to women by the patriarchs. They were quite creative and introduced any number of rules and regulations applicable only to women. The *jāti* that could not afford the luxury of such restrictions because of economic or any other reasons was pushed lower on the scale of respectability. The virus of primacy conceit does indeed work in devious and curious ways.

Prabhākara Ātreya

Prabhākara Ātreya is the earliest historical person amongst the Ātreyas (Pargiter 1997, 228). He married the ten daughters of the Paurava king, Bhadrāśva, or Raudrāśva, and his queen Ghṛtācī. He had ten sons called Svastyātreyas, and from him the Ātreya *gotras* are descended.

Punarvasu Ātreya

Punarvasu ("the two that give wealth again") is the name of the seventh lunar mansion, or *nakṣatra*, the alpha and beta Geminorum, or the bright stars Castor and Pollux (Macdonell and Keith 1995, 1:416). It was also the name of a renowned physician who taught medicine at the University of Takṣaśilā (Taxila, near Islamabad in modern Pakistan), capital of Gandhāra, or Gāndhāra[2] (Dowson 1968 105; Walker 1968, 1:369; Finegan 1989). Punarvasu Ātreya (sixth century BCE) was a contemporary of Suśruta, the famous surgeon who taught at the University of Kāśī, and the Buddha (Sarton 1927; Dasgupta 1965, 2:273–436; 3:277–395; Kutumbiah 1962; Chattopadhyaya 1982, 1986–1991; Ninivaggi 2008). We learn about the university, its curriculum, and the students from the Buddhist Jātakas (Mookerji 2003; Schumann 1989). The medium of instruction was Sanskrit, and the subjects taught were based on Hindu culture. The university, because of its fame as a great center of learning, attracted students from all parts of India. Princes, nobles, merchants, tailors, fishermen, rich and poor formed the student body. Those who could afford to paid the fees charged; others provided services to their teachers in lieu of money. Pasenadi (Prasenajit in Sanskrit), prince and later king of Kosala; the dreaded highway robber Aṅgulimāla ("finger-necklace"); and Kauṭilya, the author of the Arthaśāstra and chief minister of the first two Mauryan emperors (c. 321–268 BCE), Chandragupta and Bindusara, were some of the famous alumni of the university. Pasenadi was a philosopher-king who had many discussions with the Buddha on philosophical and ethical questions. Aṅgulimāla was the son of the Brahman Gagga, a court official. In spite of his university education, Aṅgulimāla chose a life of crime, sporting a macabre, gruesome trophy of the fingers of the people he had murdered. The Buddha met him alone and persuaded him to give up a life of crime and become a monk. Kauṭilya, the author of *Arthaśāstra* ("science of material gain"), a guidebook on statecraft, instructed a king on how to acquire and maintain power by any means, foul or fair. Jīvaka Komārabhacca of Rājagṛaha, who was a personal physician of the Buddha and his order, had studied medicine under Ātreya for 7 years. The

[2]The country between the lower Kabul valley and the upper Indus, straddling the present Afghanistan–Pakistan border.

university was famous for its religious studies as well as its secular curriculum, including medicine. The religious subjects studied were the Vedas, the Vedāngas (branches of knowledge auxiliary to Vedic studies), philosophy, and rituals including magic; secular subjects included medicine, music, law and politics, elephant training, and military sciences such as fencing and archery. Ātreya had six disciples who became quite famous physicians and who wrote treatises on medicine, now mostly lost (Kutumbiah 1962; Sarmah 1991, 275): Agniveśa, Bhela (or Bheḍa), Jātukarṇa, Parāśara, Hārita, and Kṣīrapāṇi (or Kṣarapāṇi). *Caraka Saṁhitā*, written many years later by Caraka, who was in the lineage of the students of Agniveśa, passed on the teachings of Ātreya, as embodied in Agniveśa and other Saṁhitās, of Ātreya's students (Valiathan 2003). This system of medicine is now known as the Ātreya-Caraka tradition. It is possible that the science of medicine, or Āyurveda of the Āterya-Caraka tradition, grew out of the Atharva Veda, because it identified medicine with the fourth Veda. This connection is supported by the fact that therapy consisted of extensive use of herbs supplemented by magical amulets and incantations, or mantras. The herbs might have cured, and the amulets and magic words might have convinced the patient that supernatural help was on the way. Herbs were supposed to cure diseases caused by unwholesome diet and other bad habits. Health problems resulting from past sins and transgressions of the moral code were treated with amulets and incantations. Was this an early example of the mind–body connection in healing? Perhaps it was. This interaction between the religious and philosophical beliefs of the Ātreya-Caraka tradition and its practice of medicine gives us insights into the state of the medical arts in those days (Weiss 1980; Valiathan 2003). In the Atharva Veda, there is a section about wandering physicians, *cāraṇa vaidya śākha*, or itinerant medical practitioners, who would travel from place to place and provide services to their patients. It is interesting to note that the name Caraka literally means "wanderer," and it is possible that he belonged to a fraternity or guild of wandering physicians.

Gautama Ātreya, Bhikṣu Ātreya, and Ātreya

Gautama Ātreya, Bhikṣu Ātreya, and Ātreya are mentioned in the list of sages who assembled in olden days, at an unknown date, to discover the causes of diseases and their remedies. Their works on medicine have not survived. Kṛṣṇa Ātreya is mentioned in the *Mahābhārata* as one of the founders of the science of medicine (Dasgupta 1965, 2:276; Chattopadhyaya 1982, 1986–1991). Cakrapāṇidatta (~1060 CE), one of the commentators on medicine and author of *Āyurvedadīpikā*, says that Kṛṣṇa Ātreya and Ātreya are two authorities on medicine who are different from the great teacher Punarvasu Ātreya of the Caraka Saṁhitā.

Brahmanandin Ātreya

Brahmanandin Ātreya (eleventh century CE?), wrote a commentary on the Chāndogya Upaniṣad and lived earlier than the Rāmānuja, who quotes him as a revered precursor (Dasgupta 1965, 3:106–7).

Praṇatārtihara Ātreya

Praṇatārtihara Ātreya, also called Praṇatārtihara Pillan, was a prominent disciple of the great Rāmānuja (1017–1137), founder of the Viśiṣṭādvaita school of Vedānta. There are quite a few Ātreyas involved here, and some of them with multiple names, or the same name: Rāmānuja (Dasgupta 1965, 3:105). I have done my best to untangle the multiple strands of information available here. Dasgupta assigns them Ātreya *gotra*; perhaps he means their *gotra* name is Ātreya, or a male descendant of the sage Atri (Dasgupta 1965, 3:109–10).

Varadarāja Ātreya

Also known as Uḍāli, Varadarāja Ātreya (twelfth century CE) was the author of *Vivekatilaka*, a commentary on the Rāmāyaṇa. He lived later than the Rāmānuja and is cited in the *Īḍu*, the great thirteenth-century commentary on the Tiruvāymoḷi, a devotional poem in Tamil (Sastri 1966, 343).

Rāmānuja Ātreya

Rāmānuja Ātreya is also known as Rāmānuja Pillan or Padmanābhārya, son of Praṇatārtihara Ātreya, disciple of Naḍaḍur Amaal of the lineage of Vātsya Varada, also known as Varadaviṣṇu Miśra, son of Devarāja, brother-in-law of the Rāmānuja (Dasgupta 1965, 3:110).

Rāmānuja Ātreya, or Rāmānujācārya II

Rāmānuja Ātreya (born in 1220), also known as Rāmānujācārya II, Śrī Rāmānuja Pillan, author of *Nyāya-kuliśa, Divya-sūri-prabhāva-dīpikā, Sarva-darśana-śiromaṇi,* and *Mokṣa-siddhi*, books on Hindu philosophy, was a disciple of Kidambi Rāmānuja (Sastri 1966, 356; Dasgupta 1965, 3:118).

Varada Ātreya

Varada Ātreya wrote *Rahasya-traya-sāra-vyākhyā*, a commentary on Veṅkaṭnātha's *Rahasya-trya-sāra*, a book on philosophy (Dasgupta 1965, 3:132).

Vasanta Madhava and His Sons, Narahari, Bachanna (Bhaskara), and Mallappa, All Ātreyas

Madhava Mantri (*Amātya*, or minister) drove Muslims out of Goa and conquered it for King Bukka I (1344–77) of Vijayanagara in 1366 (Kudva 1978, 35–

40; Gune 1979, 1:128). As a reward for their bravery in the fight, he appointed Vasant Madhava and Mayi Shenai Wagle as administrators in Goa. Vasant Madhava administered thirty-six *mahals* (districts) of Chandragutti (Malnad) as the *pradhāna* (chief minister) of Vijayanagar, and a stone inscription from 1379 commemorates 13 years of this service. He finally rose to be the *pradhāna* of Harihara II (1377–1404) and was called by the title *gove pura varadhishvara* ("princely lord of the City of Goa"). Vasant Madhava was recalled from Goa in 1391 and promoted to be the ruler of Banavasi. A stone inscription from 1396 records his *gotra* as Atri and mentions his two surviving sons, Bachanna and Mallappa.

Narahari succeeded his father Vasant Madhava as the viceroy of Goa in April 1391 and ruled till his death in 1395. He is described as a devotee and patron of learning.

Bachanna Wodeyar succeeded Narahari in 1395. An inscription of 1396 describes his exploits in extending the kingdom of Goa-Gutti on all sides and in the capture of the Bahmani fortress of Rangini, fifty-five miles south of Kolhapur, with all of its dependencies. He extended the boundaries of the Goa-Chandragutti province under Vijayanagar to the modern Belgaum and part of Kolhapur District. Bachanna continued in the viceroyalty of Goa till 1406. A copperplate inscription from 1407 in Bilimili, in the Uppinangadi taluk of South Kanara District, notes that he was the administrator of Mangalur-rajya.

Mallappa Wodeyar was the administrator of Barkur-rajya in Tuluva *desha* (country), according to a stone inscription of 1389–1390 at Mangalkeri, near Barkur in the Udupi taluk of South Kanara District.

This is an incomplete description of some notable members of clan Atri. It leaves out some of the poets of the Atri family book of the *Ṛgveda* and quite a few of the clan members from more recent times who left no liturgical or historical records.

APPENDIX FOUR

Kinship Terms in Konkani

There is no one "standard" Konkani, and its accent, usage, and vocabulary vary with the region where it is used. Konkani has absorbed words from many of the local languages, such as Marathi, Kannada, and Malayalam, with the result that the Konkani of Goa, of North and South Kanara Districts, and of the Kochin region differ from one another. The Konkani of the Gauda Sarasvat Brahmana (GSB) community of the South Kanara District is different from that of the Roman Catholics of the same region. I do not have the knowledge or the expertise to cover all the regional variations of the kinship terms in Konkani. The compilation given here is therefore a small subset limited to GSB usage in the South Kanara District. It has been assembled with help from my immediate family and from the references cited. The origins of some Konkani terms from Sanskrit are obvious from their close similarity; wherever possible, similar-sounding Sanskrit words are given. Other Sanskrit terms are given, where available, for completeness. Some terms might have been borrowed or adopted from local usage, or are of obscure origin. In a few cases of unfamiliar terms, I have indicated the source explicitly.

Much background information on Indian kinship terms is to be found in *Kinship Organization in India* by Irawati Karve, who has discussed kinship usages from the Vedas, Brāhmaṇas, to the historical age and modern times, and compared them in Sanskrit and other Indian languages, not including Konkani (Karve 1965). Victor D'Souza has a table of kinship terms of Navayats, a Konkani-speaking Muslim community of the west coast of India, in *The Navayats of Kanara: A Study in Culture Contact* (D'Souza 1955). Both these sources are worth reading for kinship term usages and their evolution in India. Other good sources are dictionaries and similar compilations, of which the following are very useful: *The Student's English–Sanskrit Dictionary*

(Apte 1884), The *Practical Sanskrit–English Dictionary* (Apte 1998), *A Higher Konkani Grammar* (Janardhan 1991), *A Practical Konkani–English Encyclopaedic Dictionary* (Janardhan 1999), and *English–Sanskrit Dictionary* (Monier-Williams 1976).

A few kinship terms do not exist in some languages. An example is the terms for the in-laws of one's son or daughter—*veyu* or *veṇi* in Konkani—which are not used in English (Table 3). My copyeditor, Katharine O'Moore-Klopf, pointed out this interesting fact. The question is: why? I suggest the following hypothesis: Kinship terms exist only if they are needed in negotiating the power dynamics inside a family or between families. If a person designated by a kinship term has no power to negotiate with, that person will not merit a term. It is that brutally simple. Why did *veyu* and *veṇi* become important amongst the GSB and Hindus and not so significant in a Western context? In a traditional Hindu family, a son brings his new bride to his parents' home. At the head of this family are his parents, who preside over a joint family made up of his married brothers and their families, unmarried brothers and sisters, and other dependents. The newly married young man is just one amongst many of his brothers with no significant power. His parents are the center of power and will be on a par with his parents-in-law in any interfamily negotiations. Hence, the in-laws merit a well-defined niche and a special name in the power hierarchy. These days, a young man finds a job away from home and establishes his own family, with himself and his wife as heads. These modern families are very similar to Western families in which the people in charge are the breadwinners—the husband and wife. The parents or parents-in-law have little authority and are not very relevant to the day-to-day functioning of their children's families or their lives. The corresponding Konkani kinship terms are slowly becoming obsolete, and some younger people even do not know them. It is quite possible that these names will disappear in the sinkholes of memory in a few generations. Kinship terms should be looked at as an end-product of many social factors: the rights and obligations of individuals, the laws of inheritance of wealth or power by children, their earnings, and the corresponding acquisition of power and its use in the pecking order within a family. If the interpersonal power dynamics changes, so will the relevance of the corresponding kinship terms.

Explanation of Tables

The definitions, abbreviations, and conventions used here are customary in anthropology (Hicks and Gwynne, 1994). Every attempt has been made to include in each table all the information needed to facilitate its use.

Ego, or *I*, is the person from whose perspective the kinship terms are defined. Thus it is understood that in all the kinship terms, ego is assigned the first place, though it may not be shown explicitly. Some kinship terms that depend on whether the ego is a man or woman are shown explicitly for these two cases.

The abbreviations for the kinship terms of the first degree in Table 1 are the first letters of the corresponding words in English, except for *sister*, which is indicated by the letter *Z* in conformity with usage in anthropology.

The kinship terms of the second and third degrees in Tables 2 and 3, respectively, are compounded from the letters of the basic terms and should be read from left to right. Thus in Table 3, *WZS* means "wife's sister's son." There are a few fourth-degree kinship terms in Table 3 because it was decided not worth having a separate table for them.

Other relationships and relational terms that did not fit into any of the above categories are given in Table 4.

Qualifiers such as *E* (elder) and *Y* (younger) are given in parentheses immediately to the right of the kinship term modified. Thus *B(E)* and *B(Y)* refer to ego's brothers, elder to and younger than ego. *FB(E)* and *FB(Y)* refer to ego's father's brothers, elder to and younger than ego's father.

Children of siblings of the same sex are parallel cousins. Parallel-cousin marriages are prohibited in the GSB and in other Hindu communities. Hence, we find the peculiar designations of cousin-brother and cousin-sister in Indian groups that follow such a custom.

Children of siblings of opposite sex are cross-cousins. Cross-cousin marriages are allowed amongst the GSB. This has led to the custom of a boy calling his female cross-cousin his *hakkā bāila* (rightful wife) and a girl calling her male cross-cousin her *hakkā bāmmuṇu* (rightful husband) in banter, especially when the chances of their getting married are remote because of age differences or other circumstances. Cross-cousin marriages are called *māvḷo bhācci soirika* (uncle–niece marriage). Perhaps in the past, actual uncle–niece marriages were customary, though now it is the cross-cousins who wed. In the olden days when the bride was a child, a maternal uncle used to carry her into the wedding enclosure *(māṇṭvi)*. Nowadays, an adult bride is usually led into the wedding enclosure by a maternal uncle, though a few foolhardy uncles try to show off their weight-lifting prowess. This ceremony may be the maternal uncle "signing off" on his traditional right and may be the last remnant of an uncle–niece marriage of yesteryear.

TABLE 1. Kinship Terms of the First Degree		
KINSHIP	KONKANI	SANSKRIT
AC (adopted child)	*Posko cerḍũ* (sing.); *poskī̃ cerḍūvā̃* (pl.)	*Poṣya bāla, poṣya śiśu*
AD (adopted daughter)	*Poski dhūva*	*Poṣya duhitṛa*
AS (adopted son)	*Posko pūtu*	*Poṣya putra*
B (brother)	*Bhāvu*	*Bhrātṛa, sahodara*
B(E)	*Hōḍu bhāvu*; *aṇṇā*, or given name as a prefix to *aṇṇā*	*Agraja* (EB)
B(Y)	*Dhāklo bhāvu*, usually called by name	*Avaraja, anuja* (YB)
B, step-,	*Aṇṇā* or *bhāvu* with a qualifier: *hoḷḷiyelo, dhākliyelo*, or *dhākṭiyelo*	*Vaimātṛaka, vimātṛaja*
C (child)	*Cerḍũ* (sing.); *cerḍūvā̃* (pl.)	*Cārudarśan* ("lovely to behold")[1]
D (daughter)	*Dhūva*	*Duhitṛa* ("one who milks"), *nandanā, tanayā, sutā*
D, step-,	*Dhūva* with a qualifier: *hoḷḷiyeli, dhākliyeli*, or *dhākṭiyeli*	*Sapatnisutā*
Ego, or I	*Hā̃vā̃*	*Aham*
F (father)	*Ānu*,[2] *bāppusu*	*Pitṛ, tāta*
H (husband)	*Bāmmuṇu*,[3] *yajmānu* (archaic and formal), *tānni* (old-fashioned), *to* (modern and egalitarian), *bāmmṇā* (heard rarely)[4]	*Brāhmaṇa, pati, bhartṛa, āryaputra* (usual form of address in Sanskrit drama)
M (Mother)	*Āmmā, āvsu*	*Ambā, akkā, mātṛ, ambālikā, ambāyu*
M, co-; M, step-,	*Māvśi*	*Vimātṛa, samātṛa*
S (son)	*Pūtu*	*Putra, sūnu, nandana, tanaya*
S, step-,	*Pūtu* with a qualifier; *hoḷḷiyelo, dhākliyelo*, or *dhākṭiyelo*	*Sapatnīsuta, vimātṛaja*
Twins	*Javaḷi*[5] *cerḍūvā̃, avaḷi-javaḷi*[6] *cerḍūvā̃*	*Yugalam, yamalam bāla*
W (wife)	*Bāila*,[7] *gharā yajmāni* (archaic and formal), *whaigo* (usual), *bāile* (heard rarely), or called by name	*Bhāryā, patnī, jāyā, sahadharmiṇī*

(*continued*)

TABLE 1. (*cont'd*)

Kinship	Konkani	Sanskrit
W, senior	*Mhālgaḍi* or *hoḷḷi bāila*	*Jyeṣṭa bhāryā*
W, junior	*Dhākli bāila*	*Sapatnī* (co-wife)
W, first	*Surve bāila*	*Prathama bhāryā*
W, second	*Dhākṭi* or *donni bāila*	*Dvitīyaka bhāryā*
Z (sister)	*Ākkā, bhaiṇi*, or called by name	*Bhaginī, svasṛa, sodarā*
Z (E)	*Ākkā, hōḍi bhaiṇi*	*Agrajā* (EZ)
Z (Y)	*Dhākli bhaiṇi*, or called by name	*Avarajā* (YZ)
Z, step-,	*Ākkā* or name with qualifier: *hoḷḷiyeli, dhākliyeli*, or *dhākṭiyeli*	*Vaimātrī, vaimātreyī*

The abbreviations for the kinship terms of the first degree are the first letters of the corresponding words in English except for *sister*, which is indicated by the letter Z. E = elder; Y = younger; B(E) = EB = elder brother; B(Y) = YB = younger brother; Z(E) = EZ = elder sister; Z(Y) = YZ = younger sister. sing. = singular; pl. = plural.

[1] Janardhan (1999, 121).

[2] This term might have been borrowed from Kannada speakers, some of whom use *aṇṇā* for "father." Janardhan thinks that the usage might have originated from *aṇṇā*, for "elder brother," used to address a young father so as not to make him feel too old. However, this explanation is not convincing because a person feeling embarrassed about his age or wishing to appear younger than his years is a Western rather than an Asian conceit.

[3] *Koṅkaṇized Brāhmaṇa.* This form of address is strange and unnecessary if a Brahmana woman has married into a family of the same caste. However, it makes sense if the bride is a non-Brahmana who might have taken pride in such a socially upscale marriage. There is a legend that when the GSB moved to Goa from Bengal or other places, many women of the community died on the way because of hardships of the journey. The men had to find brides from the local Konkani-speaking community, whose language and customs were adopted by the new immigrants. These brides became the mothers, *āmmās*, of the community, bestowing their mother tongue (*āmmāci geli* or *āmcigeli bhāsa*) Konkani, on the GSB community. Some people who want to keep the legend of caste purity alive deny this story.

[4] In the olden days, a wife was forbidden to call her husband by name.

[5] From Kannada (Kittel 1968, 2:681).

[6] From Kannada (Kittel 1968, 1:123).

[7] *Bāila* could have been derived either from the Sanskrit *bhāryā* or from the Konkani *bhāili*, for "outsider." This could mean either belonging to a *gotra* or clan other than that of the husband, as is normal, or an outsider from the community if the bride was a non-Brahmana. This comment and comment 3 make sense if marriages with brides from outside the community did indeed take place. Some people who believe in the legend of caste purity deny this story.

TABLE 2. Kinship Terms of the Second Degree		
KINSHIP	KONKANI	SANSKRIT
BD	*Dhuvḍi* (man speaking)	*Bhrātrīyā*
BD	*Bhācci* (woman speaking)	*Bhrātṛaputrī*
BS	*Puttaṇyo* (man speaking)	*Bhrātṛavya*
BS	*Bhācco* (woman speaking)	*Bhrātṛaputra*
B(E)W	*Bhāvaja* (general term); called *vhanni*	*Bhrātṛajāyā*
B(Y)W	Called by name	*Bhrātṛa vadhu*
DH	*Jāvāyī*	*Jāmātṛa*
FB(E)	*Mhāntu*	*Pitṛavya, tātagu*
FB(Y)	*Bāppā*	*Tātatulya*
FF	*Ājjo*	*Āryaka, pitāmaha*
FM	*Ājji, ānnama* (if father is single son); *bāppamā* (if father has brothers)	*Āryakā, pitāmahī, pitṛaprasū, pitṛasū*
FZ	*Māvaḷnī* (general term), called *ākkā*	*Pitṛasvasṛa*
HB(E)	*Bhāyyo*	*Bhrātṛaśvaśura* (E)
HB(Y)	*Deru*	*Devara* (E or Y), *devṛa* (Y)
HF = WF	*Māvū*	*Ārya, śvaśura*
HM = WM	*Māyī̃*	*Āryā, śvaśrū*
HZ	*Naṇanda* (general term); also called *vhanni*	*Nanandṛa* ("giver of joy"[1])
MB(E)	*Hōḍu māmu*	*Māma, māmaka*
MB(Y)	*Sānu māmu* or by uncle's given name as a prefix to *māmu*	*Mātulaka, mātula*
MF	*Ājjo*	*Āryaka, mātāmaha*
MM	*Ājji, āmmammā* (if no sons), *māmmammā* (if has sons)	*Āryakā, mātāmahī*
MZ(E)	*Mhāva*	*Mahā akkā, mahakā* (?)
MZ(Y)	*Pācci*	*Mātṛasvasṛa*
SD = DD	*Nāti*	*Naptrī*
SS = DS	*Nāttu*	*Naptṛa*
SW	*Sūna*	*Snuṣā*
WB	*Mevṇo*; called *bhāvāji* or by name if younger	*Śyāla, śyālaka*

(*continued*)

TABLE 2. (*cont'd*)

Kinship	Konkani	Sanskrit
WZ(E)	*Mevṇi*	*Śyālakī, śyālikā*
WZ(Y)	*Mevṇi*	*Śyālakī, śyālikā*
ZD	*Bhācci* (man speaking)	*Bhāgineyī, svasrīyā*
ZD	*Dhuvḍi* (woman speaking)	*Svasreyī*
ZH	*Mevṇo*, also called *bhāvāji*	*Bhaginīpati*
ZS	*Bhācco* (man speaking)	*Bhāginīya, bhāgineya*
ZS	*Puttaṇyo* (woman speaking)	*Bhāgineya, bhāginīya*

Kinship terms of the second degree are formed by linking together in a chain the letters of the basic terms and should be read from left to right. For example, WB = wife's brother; E = elder; Y = younger.

[1] A probable euphemism in view of the usually strained relations amongst the sisters-in-law.

TABLE 3. Kinship Terms of the Third Degree

Kinship	Konkani	Sanskrit
FBD	*Bhaiṇi* (cousin-sister), *ākkā* if E	*Bhaginī*
FBS	*Bhāvu* (cousin-brother), *aṇṇā* if E	*Bhrātṛa*
FB(E)W	*Mhāva*	*Pitṛavya jāyā*
FB(Y)W	*Pācci*	
FFF = FMF	*Pijjo, paṇājjo, hōḍājjo*	*Prapitāmaha*
MFF = MMF	*Pijjo, paṇājjo, hōḍājjo*	*Pra-mātāmaha*
FFM = FMM = MFM = MMM	*Pijji, paṇājji, hōḍāmmā*	FFM = *Prapitāmahī*; MFM = MMM = *Pramātāmahī*
FZD	*Hakkā bāila* (man speaking); *ākkā* (if E); call by name if Y (woman speaking)	*Paitṛaṣvaseyī, paitṛaṣvasreyī*
FZH	*Māmu*	*Pitṛasvaṣrapati*
FZS	*Bhāvāji, hakkā bāmmuṇu* (woman speaking); *bhāvāji* (man speaking)	*Paitṛaṣvaseya, paitṛaṣvasrīya*
HBD	*Dhuvḍi*	*Devaraputrī*
HBS	*Puttaṇyo*	*Devaraputra*
HB(E)W	*Bhāyyā bāila, mhālgaḍi jāva, hōḍi jāva, ākkā*	*Yātṛa*

(*continued*)

TABLE 3. Kinship Terms of the Third Degree (*cont'd*)

Kinship	Konkani	Sanskrit
HB(Y)W	*Derā bāila, dhākli jāva*, or called by name	
HFB = WFB; HMZH = WMZH	*Phāgra māvũ*	*Phalgu māma* ("secondary uncle")
HFBW = WFBW; HMZ = WMZ	*Phāgra māyī̃*	*Phalgu māmī* ("secondary aunt")
HZD	*Bhācci, hakkā sūna*	
HZH	*Bhāvāji*	*Nanāndṛapati*
HZS	*Bhācco, hakkā jāvāyī*	*Nānāndra*
MBD	*Hakkā bāila* (man speaking), *vhanni* (woman speaking)	*Mātuleyī*
MBS	*Bhāvāji, hakkā bāmmuṇu* (woman speaking), *bhāvāji* (man speaking)	*Mātuleya*
MBW	*Māyī̃*	*Māmī, mātulānī*
MZD	*Bhaiṇi, ākkā* (if older); called by name if younger	*Mātṛasvaseyī*
MZ(E)H	*Mhāntu*	*Mātṛasvasṛapati*
MZ(Y)H	*Bāppā*	
MZ(E)S	*Aṇṇā* (if older)	*Mātṛasvaseya*
MZ(Y)S	Called by name if younger	
SSD = DSD = SDD = DDD	*Poṇtri*	*Pranaptṛī*
SSS = DSS = SDS = DDS	*Poṇtro*	*Pranaptṛa*
SWF = DHF	*Veyu*	*Vaivāhika*
SWM = DHM	*Veṇi*	*Vaivāhikā*
WBD	*Bhācci, hakkā sūna*	
WBS	*Bhācco, hakkā jāvāyī*	
WBW	*Mevṇyā bāila, bhāvāji baila*	
WZD	*Dhuvḍi*	
WZH	*Sāḍḍu*	*Nanāndṛapati*
WZS	*Puttaṇyo*	

Kinship terms in this table are compounded from the letters of the basic terms and should be read from left to right. For example, WZS = wife's sister's son; E = elder; Y = younger.

TABLE 4. Other Relationships and Curiosities		
Relationship	Konkani	Sanskrit
Aunt	*Māyī*[1]	*Māmī, mātulī, mātulānī*
Boy attendant for the groom	*Dheḍḍo*[2]	
Bride	*Vhakkala*	*Vadhū*
Bride's garland	*Vhakkleli phullā māḷā*	*Vadhūsraj* (bride's garland put by the groom)
Bridegroom	*Vharetu*	*Vara*
Bridegroom's garland	*Vharetāli phullā māḷā*	*Varasraj* (bridegroom's garland put by the bride)
Bride's procession	*Chellye kārālē vharaṇa*	*Vadhū yāna, vadhūpakṣa yāna*
Bridegroom's procession	*Chellyā kārālē vharaṇa*	*Vara yāna, varapakṣa yāna, varayātrā, varaprasthānam*
Bridegroom's Kāśī journey	*Kāśī yātrā*[3]	*Varanimantraṇam*
Bride's entry into husband's home	*Ghara bharāvaṇa*	*Vadhūgrahapraveśa, vadhūpraveśa*
Cousin	*Bhāvāji*[4]	
Girl attendant for the bride	*Dheḍḍi*[5]	
Guest (female)	*Soiri* (sing.), *soiriṇi*	*Sviya* (one's own)
Guest (male)	*Soiro* (sing.)	
Guests	*Soirī* (pl.)	
Hospitality	*Sammānu*	*Atithi satkāra*
Husband's house	*Bāmmaṇā tancē ghara*	
Mistress (extramarital)	*Rābbonu ghetili, dovornu ghetili, ceḍi* (pejorative)	*Ceḍī*[6]
Newly wed couple	*Navē vharā*	*Vadhūvaram*
Parent's house (woman speaking)	*Kuḷāra*	*Kula āgāra*
Priest	*Bhaṭṭu, bhaṭṭu māmu*	*Bhaṭṭa* (title of a learned *Brāhmaṇa*)
Priest's wife	*Bhaṭṭiṇi, bhaṭṭiṇi māyī*	*Bhaṭṭinī* (wife of a learned *Brāhmaṇa*)

(*continued*)

TABLE 4. Other Relationships and Curiosities (*cont'd*)		
RELATIONSHIP	KONKANI	SANSKRIT
Uncle	*Māmu*[7]	*Māma*
Wedding	*Soirika, vhārdika*	*Svīkaraṇa, svīkāra, varadīkṣā*
Wedding procession	*Vhārdike vharaṇa*	*Vara yāna*
Widow	*Vidhavā, bāmmuṇu nāttili*	*Vidhavā*
Woman whose husband is alive	*Ayyapaṇa bāila maniṣī, savvāśini*	*Suvāsinī, bhartṛamatī*

sing. = singular; pl. = plural.

[1] General form of address for any woman older than ego.

[2] Apparently, this usage is confined to Karnataka. It may have been derived from the Konkani *dēḍa*, for "one and a half," referring to the groom and the boy and to the bride and the girl. In the olden days, the groom and the bride themselves were children; however, they were not supposed to talk to each other during the wedding, which lasted seven or more days. The boy attendant was called a *hoḷō*, a jester or go-between, and the girl attendant was called a *hoḷī*, a female jester or go-between; they were the only channel of communication between the newlyweds (Janardhan 1999, 178, 422).

[3] Bride's parents intercept the groom, who is supposedly on his way to *Kāśī* for higher studies, and invite him to marry their daughter.

[4] General form of address for any man about the same age and social status as the ego, assumed to be a man.

[5] A *Bhāvin* servant accompanying a bride to her new home, and maintaining household expenses for her was also called a *dheḍḍi* in old Goa (Dhume 1985, 73). The *Bhāvins* were literate, whereas most of the brides were not.

[6] Ancient designation for accomplished and cultivated female companions, educated and well-versed in the arts of pleasing men, who had an honorable position in Hindu society. They were like the hetaera of ancient Greece or the geisha of Japan and provided sophisticated, intellectual companionship, which a wife could not do, because she was usually illiterate. The *devadāsīs* as a rule were literate and trained in music and dancing. The current meaning of the word is "common prostitute" and is thus pejorative.

[7] General form of address for any man older than ego.

APPENDIX FIVE

Hindu Rites of Passage

The *saṁskāra* (rites of passage) for Hindus may be defined in very general terms as sacred rites, ceremonies, or sacraments prescribed for Hindus by the *dharmaśāstra* (codes of law) and *gṛhyasūtra* (domestic canon). These rites may also be considered as defining the membership of each individual in the Hindu community and as a general acceptance of its worldview and beliefs. They must have evolved from the tribal customs and usages from the Vedic age and have undergone many changes to suit the economic and social circumstances of the Hindu community. There is no one central religious hierarchy in India that defines the norm for all the Hindus. Most Hindus accept the general authority of the Laws of Manu, or *Manu Dharmaśāstra*; however, the details of their observances are determined by community usage, *gotra* (clan), family traditions, local customs, and variants prescribed by other books of law (Doniger and Smith 1991; Olivelle 1999). In this appendix, I describe the rites and comment on the Gauda Sarasvat Brahmana (GSB) customs of South Kanara District that I am familiar with. The GSB are Ṛgvedis and follow the *Āśvalāyana Gṛhyasūtra* in their rituals. The details of rituals of individual ceremonies are not discussed here; the reader can learn more about them in the works by Rajbali Pandey (1969), P.V. Kane 1974 (2:188–541) and 1973 (4:179–515), R.C. Prasad (1995 and 1997), Venkataraya Narayan Kudva (1978), and Ramabai (alias Ammanna, 2004). However, I do mention the customs and traditions of our family and my own experiences in participating in some of these ceremonies.

Influences on Rites of Passage

The observance of these ceremonies has been influenced to a great extent by the following circumstances: the decline of traditional Sanskrit-based education, the decline of the status of women, the influence of astrology, and a transition from a nonvegetarian to a purely vegetarian diet.

Decline of Traditional Sanskrit-Based Education

Most Hindus have moved away from the traditional Sanskrit-based education to a European or Western English-based education. The East India Company established universities in Bombay, Calcutta, and Madras in 1857, opening a window of opportunity for all Indians to new ideas, Western literature, and the sciences. The original purpose of this move by the British rulers was the training of clerks and other low-level functionaries of the Raj, who would help to perpetuate it. This transition from the local Indian languages or Sanskrit and Persian, the language of Mughal administration, was relatively easy for those communities, such as the Brahmans and the Vaishyas, with a tradition of learning, commerce, or bureaucratic training. I do not claim any special cleverness or aptitude for learning for these communities; the only advantage that they had was their tradition of education and scholarship. I will always remember my elders repeatedly stressing how important it was for all of us to obtain a good education. That was the only way out of our material poverty. The first generation that obtained an English education, like my father did, were high school graduates. The second generation graduated from colleges and became officers in the local government administration or in the civil or the legal establishment. They also entered medicine, engineering, and other professions. The good thing about all these changes was that the Western-educated Indians had skills that were meaningful and salable in a changing society and under changing economic conditions. They ceased to be learned scholars with irrelevant knowledge and skills. The one bad aspect was the contempt that some Western-educated Indians developed for all things traditional and Indian, largely based on Sanskrit, Persian, or one of the other Indian languages. While the West was discovering the ancient Sanskrit India, appreciating and translating its literature into the European languages, most Indians were doing their best to ignore it and to feel proud about their disdain for tradition and their ignorance of it. Some of these were aping the British, who declared traditional Indian knowledge to be unmitigated ignorance, superstition, and thoroughly unscientific. This attitude was also partly initiated and supported by the Christian missionaries in India who wanted to convert Indians to the One True Faith, namely, their own. As a general rule, Hindu children today do not attend any religious classes after regular school hours, to learn to read Sanskrit or to understand it at an elementary level. The result of all these changes has been a sad decline in the understanding of and participation in traditional Hindu rites and ceremonies. In the olden days, when people understood Sanskrit and were knowledgeable about the ceremonies, most of them were conducted by the head of the family. They understood what they were doing and understood the ritual words, and thus they could participate in the ceremonies in a meaningful way. Today, such ceremonies are conducted by an officiating priest who most often recites the sacred texts, the mantra, by rote. Most of the priests do not know enough Sanskrit to appreciate the real significance of these rites, to understand what they are doing, or to explain their actions in the context of the Hindu worldview to an interested participant. The priests are poorly paid, are not properly educated, and eke out a living from the meager *dakṣinā* (ritual gift), the comestibles such as coconuts, rice, and other grains used in the rites that are given to the officiating priest as his dues. Young men, if they have the opportunity to get a good education, do not want to become priests or undergo the lengthy training and education needed for it. These changes are apparent in my own family. My mother's family and quite a few of our relatives used to earn a living as priests and were attached to local GSB temples. In our family, the last Sanskrit scholar who understood the rites and sacrifices was the elder brother of my grandfather, Vasudeva Bhat, who passed away in the 1940s. Only one of his great-grandsons is a practicing priest now. In my mother's family, there is no one who follows the profession. The same holds for our other relatives. As my Aunt Manorama (Mannakka) used to say, "When my children are doing well in school and winning scholarships for further studies, how can I stand in their way of obtaining a higher education and a good job and condemn them to a life of poverty and an uncertain future as a priest?" The GSB community does not want to support or subsidize the priest's profession. Most members of the community are not interested in understanding their sacred rites; they are happy with a pro forma compliance with customs, going through the motions of performing the rites. The community gets the priests it deserves.

Decline of the Status of Women

In the *Ṛgveda*, only a few of the hymns are ascribed to women—16 female seers, or *ṛṣikās*—compared with how many are ascribed to men: 391 male seers, or *ṛṣis* (Sarasvati and Vidyalankara 1977, 1:219–24; Rahurkar 1964; Mookerji 2003, 208–9, 245, 274; Denton 2004). These *ṛṣikās*, called *Brahmavādinīs* (female teachers and expounders of the Vedas), are Lopāmudrā, Romaśā, Viśvavārā Ātreyī, Śaśvatī Āngirasī, Apālā Ātreyī, Yamī Vaivasvatī, Śraddhā Kāmāyanī, Vasukrapatnī Indrasnusā, Ghoṣā Kākṣīvatī, Sūryā Sāvitrī, Indrānī, Urvaśī, Saramā Devaśunī, Juhū Brahmajāyā, Vāk Āmbhṛṇī, and Śacī Paulomī. If the female dog of Indra, Saramā, is left out of this list, there are only fifteen *ṛṣikās*. There are references to female teachers (not teachers' wives), named *Upādhyāyī*,

Upādhyāyā, and *Ācāryā*. In the daily oblations offered to the seers of old (*ṛṣitarpaṇa*), three women, Gārgī Vācaknavī, Vaḍavā Prātitheyī, and Sulabhā Maitreyī, are included. Of these, Gārgī is prominent in the Upaniṣads, arguing on an equal basis with the well-known teacher Yājñavalkya in a public debate. The Bṛhadārṇyaka Upaniṣad mentions a procedure to be followed by parents desirous of begetting a learned daughter (Olivelle 1996, 90). I do not know whether such a procedure worked; however, it should be noted that begetting a learned daughter was considered a worthwhile goal in those days. In the daily rituals of Brahmans, five holy women are invoked: Ahalyā, Draupadī, Sītā, Tārā, and Mandodarī. In the olden days, both boys and girls went through the ceremony of initiation, or *upanayana*, as the beginning of education, which was confined entirely to the Vedic studies (Kane 1974, 2:293–6; Altekar 1999, 200–4; Mookerji 2003, 51, 208–9, 274). At that time it was thought that the discipline of a student life was necessary for both boys and girls (Altekar 1999, 200). If we assume that in the Vedic era the people as a whole were nomadic, without a fixed abode, then it is quite possible that women worked on an equal basis with men, contributed to the general upkeep and support of the family, and enjoyed many rights and privileges. A parallel is to be found in the frontier days of the U.S. West, where women worked along with their men on an equal basis. Later on, under more settled conditions, even the few rights women enjoyed appear to have eroded, reducing them to complete social and economic dependence on the menfolk. In the perpetual jockeying for power and hierarchy, the patriarchal traditions of Hindu society appear to have prevailed. At a later time when the status of women in Hindu society had decreased, we find in the sacred texts derogatory remarks comparing women to different lower life forms and treating them with contempt. Such comments, just because they are in Sanskrit and are part of the codes of law, do not deserve to be treated as holy writ. These misogynistic comments are best ignored as irrelevant. However, traces of some of the former glory days of equality and mutual respect do survive. Hindu rituals demand participation by the legally married wife who is also the *sahadharmiṇī*, meaning that she has the same religious rights and duties as the husband, without whom no ritual is complete (Kane 1974, 2: 429, 526; Mookerji 2003, 208–9, 274). In the eighth or ninth century CE, we hear about Sarasvatī, the wife of Maṇḍana Miśra, acting as a referee in the famous debate between her husband and Śaṅkara. I remember my grandfather Madhava Bhat, born in 1884, mentioning that *upanayana* for girls was prevalent in some orthodox GSB families in the late 1890s and early 1900s. If the girls of these families were keen on getting a traditional education, then their father, uncle, or other members of the family would teach them Sanskrit and related subjects, and they would perform the morning and evening worship, *sandhi*, along with a recitation of Gāyatrī. They would also change the sacred thread, the *jānnuvẽ*, after each menses. My grandfather remembered going to the homes of these women to officiate at this ceremony. The expenses of the *upanayana*, a general decline in Sanskrit studies because of the forced migrations, and the economic hardships of life for the GSB appear to have forced an abandonment of this tradition. The acceptable period for females to marry in the Vedic age was young adulthood; afterward, it became childhood. The justification for child marriage is to be found in the interpretation of some codes of law that the father or guardian incurs the sin of *bhrūṇahatyā* (embryo killing) at each menses as long as his daughter is unmarried (Kane 1974, 2:439–42). This belief ultimately led to women being thoroughly exploited members of Hindu society, with very few rights for property or privileges, essentially no education, and many responsibilities and obligations. Further, this exploitation was glorified by setting it up as an impossible standard to be aimed for by every virtuous wife. The treatment of widows, especially those without sons, was abominable. Widows had very few rights. They had little to no chance of inheriting their husbands' property and were not permitted to remarry. If the family of a dead man was kind and considerate, they allowed his widow to remain in their family house, but she led a barren life, one of religious austerity and deprivation, and she was held vaguely responsible for her husband's untimely death. If the family was inconsiderate, they usually sent the widow back to her parents or threw her out, leaving her to fend for herself and seek the charity of the community. They might even encourage her to burn herself on the funeral pyre of her husband as a convenient solution to the problem of claims on the joint family property. It is not surprising that some widows made this terrible choice instead of waiting for old age and death. This inhuman treatment of widows was excused or justified by the social and religious norms of the time. These were described in great detail by Tryambakayajvan, who was most probably Trayambakarāyamakhin (1665–1750 CE), minister to the Maratha kings of Thanjāvūru, in the book *Strīdharmapaddhati*, translated in the twentieth century as *The Perfect Wife* (Leslie 1995). Of course, this book describes an ideal that is certainly impossible for a real woman to achieve. However, the picture of an exploited woman, with many obligations, few rights, and no authority, comes through clearly (see also Appendix 8: "Goa: A Paradise Lost?"). In patriarchal Hindu society, the status of a *jāti* (birth group) came to be equated with the number of restrictions put on its women. Thus, if divorce, remarriage after widowhood, free choice of husbands, inheritance of property leading to possible economic independence, or any privileges were forbidden to its women, the group could claim a higher status in its ranking. Thus each *jāti* built its "honor and respect" by trampling on its women (see also Appendix 3, "Atri *Gotra*, or Clan *Atri*").

Influence of Astrology

Anxiety about an unknown future is so pervasive that divination by various means appears to have been employed universally to reduce anxiety and give individuals a semblance of control over the future. The flights of birds, livers of sacrificed victims, curious behavior of animals, and celestial phenomena such as eclipses and comets have been used to predict the future. Astrology is an attempt to make the unknown future—the *adṛṣṭa* ("unseen")—known (*dṛṣṭa*, or "seen"). The Sumerians, Babylonians, Chaldeans, Egyptians, Persian Magi, Greeks, Romans, and Hindus—in short, everyone who was anyone amongst the ancient cultures—contributed to astrology, which predicts individuals' futures by the positions of stars and planets at their birth, as recorded in their horoscopes, and by the current positions of the heavenly bodies. It is an offshoot of the science of astronomy and has had a curious position in the Hindu belief system. In the Vedic age, there were vague notions of propitious times, such as the northern progression of the sun (*uttarāyana*) and the bright half of the month, and of not-so-propitious times. Astrology was not fully developed in that age, and practicing astrologers were looked down on. The *Manu Dharmaśāstra* lists astrologers as people who should not be invited to the feasts accompanying sacrifices to the ancestors (*śrāddha*) and expressly forbids people who have renounced this world from practicing astrology (Doniger and Smith 1991, 60, 122, 3.162, 6.50). As time passed, this state of affairs changed. Hindu astronomers/astrologers translated Greek and Roman books on astrology; various deities were assigned to rule the different planets, stars, and constellations; new books on astrology were written in India; and astrology became a full-fledged, so-called science—and very much a part of Hindu orthodoxy. The Hindu genius for the working out minute consequences of the influences of the planets and stars has found its full expression in the present state of astrology in India. It has become an elaborate system that can easily occupy a person's attention for life. Specialization in astrology by some Hindus led to the creation of a new occupation and a family name, *Joiṣi*. Many Hindus are firm believers in astrology and its ability to predict the future. Worship of the nine planets, *navagraha homa*, to ameliorate any of their bad aspects or influences, has become part of most Hindu rituals today. Astrologers are consulted to determine auspicious times for the start of important events such as initiations, marriages, journeys, and founding new businesses. Rites (*śānti*, or "propitiation") are performed to placate the bad influences or conjunctions of planets, and the horoscopes of the intended bride and groom are compared to determine compatibility of temperaments. There have always been both true believers and doubters of astrology, and there are many in between who hedge their bets. The hardheaded Kauṭilya (fourth century BCE) said that for a man who wants to be rich to believe in stars is childish; his guiding star should be wealth only (Rangarajan 1992, 637). Yet Yājñavalkya (first or second century CE) later said, "... the rise and the fall of kings depends on the influences of planets" (Kane 1973, 3:126). Astrology has become very much a part of Hindu orthodoxy; doubting its efficacy is equated with heresy or with being an atheist. One can see skepticism about astrology slowly morphing into belief in the intervening years. Belief and skepticism are both ultimately matters of faith, and each individual has to make a choice that depends on his or her ability to live with an uncertain future.

It should also be noted that the "database" for astrological predictions is the *pañcāṅga* (almanac). There are some thirty almanacs in use in India, and they do not agree with one another. Most are out of step with the seasons because they use different methods of approximations in their calculations. The anarchy of the almanacs continues in spite of proposals to correct these discrepancies, which have not been adopted by the orthodox (see Appendix 6: "Feasts and Festivals"). Hence, the entire premise of astrology is in doubt. This is something that the most ardent believer in astrology should think about when next consulting an astrologer.

Transition From a Nonvegetarian to a Purely Vegetarian Diet

At present, almost all orthodox, religiously observant Hindus are strict vegetarians who avoid eggs, fish, and meat while partaking freely of all dairy products. The exceptions are northern, or *gauḍa*, Brahmans, who include the Sarasvats. Brahmans from Bengal and Kashmir, however, offer to the deity fish and meat dishes at certain religious observances and freely eat them as grace, *prasāda*, afterward. Some Sarasvats eat fish and meat, especially if they are not practicing or officiating Brahmans, hence the epithet "fish-eating Brahmans" used against them.

This was not always so. In the Vedic age, eating meat, including beef, was the norm, without any blame attached to it. Cattle were the most precious possession of the Vedic people, so it made sense that they offered cows as sacrifices to their gods and then ate the meat later. Ox and barren cows were called the food of the god of fire, Agni (Kane 1974, 2:772). A cow was offered as part of the ceremonial reception of honored guests, the *arghya*, and it was up to the guest to decide whether it should be slaughtered or allowed to live (Apte 1954, 84; Jha 2002, 33). Sometimes the guest would make the first ceremonial cut before the host slaughtered the offered cow and served it to the guest. *Madhuparka*, the special mixture of honey, curds, and other ingredients that was served to honored guests and on special occasions such as weddings, contained meat. The expression "cows fit for guests" (*atithinīr*) is used in the *Ṛgveda* (Jha 2002, 33). Beef was also served at the wedding feast to the honored guests. As part of funeral ceremonies, a cow or she-goat was killed, and its limbs were spread over the corpse before cremation. Oblations of fish and meat to the gods and the Manes (dead ancestors) at *śrāddha* were always eaten by the officiating Brahmanas, the man doing the ritual, and his family (Doniger and Smith 1991, 3.123, 3.266–72, 4.213, 5.16).

The reasons behind the transition from a diet including meat to a pure vegetarian diet are many. The virtues of nonkilling, *ahiṁsā*, compared with animal sacrifices were preached in the Upaniṣads (Kane 1974, 5:944). The theory of karma and rebirth warned that an eater of meat in this life would be eaten in the next. Metaphysical speculations looked at the whole universe, from the smallest insect to the most enlightened human being, as a manifestation of the divine, with all beings considered deserving of the same kindness and compassion. The rise of Buddhism and Jainism and the reform movements in Hinduism against animal sacrifices originating from these steered people away from a meat diet. The elaborate Vedic sacrifices had become too expensive and were considered no longer cost-effective, so they went out of fashion for economic reasons (Kosambi 1951, 191–2). Those who sacrificed animals had always been apologetic about shedding blood. The sacrificed animals were strangled, or "quieted," and were supposed to move on to a higher existence in heaven and not really be killed. At a later period in the olden days, the cow was designated as an animal not to be killed. The real reason behind this prohibition could have been economic, because in a settled agricultural society, cattle were very useful and too expensive to be slaughtered for food. The earliest mention of this economic reason is to be found in the shrewd observations of Al-Bīrūnī (973–1048 CE) (Sachau 1971, ch. 68). All of these factors resulted in some authorities on Hindu law declaring meat eating to be forbidden in the Kali age, or *kalivarjya*. The Chinese pilgrim Fa-Hsien, in the fifth century CE, reported that the killing of animals in the Madhyadeśa was unknown, though meat was sold by the *cāṇḍāla* (outcasts) outside cities. Hsüan Tsang, another Chinese traveler of the early seventh century, noted that the flesh of many animals was forbidden and that any person who ate these became an outcast (Jha 2002, 69). In spite of these prohibitions against eating meat, there were exceptions. These were for animals sacrificed at Vedic rituals or meat offered to the Manes at *śrāddha*. As noted by Kane, "it is remarkable that even the Mitākṣarā and the Kalpataru, written about 1100–1120

AD, do not expressly say that in the Kali age flesh-eating at *śrāddha* is totally prohibited at least for Brāhmaṇas" (Kane 1973, 4:424). He also quotes another authority:

> It is noteworthy that even so late as the first half of the seventeenth century, Viśvanātha, a great logician, takes up the cudgels on behalf of flesh-eating by *brāhmaṇas* in sacrifices, *śrāddha*, *madhuparka*, in danger to life and when ordered by a *brāhmaṇa* and charges those who totally forbid flesh-eating with being the followers of the doctrines of the Bauddhas. . . . [Kane 1973, 3:946]

I have given these details to show that Hindu orthodoxy allowed meat eating at some ceremonies and that there was no total prohibition of meat. In spite of these facts, eating of fish and meat by the Sarasvats was held against them and used as evidence to declare them to be non-Brahmans (see Chapter 3: "My Maternal Grandparents"). This is a classic example of a dominant group setting standards to judge a competing group to be inferior, and also thereby declaring its own claims for superiority and dominance. Humans engage in strange behavior under the influence of the primacy conceit.

One more aspect of animal sacrifices as religious ritual should be noted. In the Vedic age when the dominant hierarchy, the Brahman priests, participated in Vedic ritual and animal sacrifices, these were part of Hindu orthodoxy and considered to be high-status rites. At present, almost all of the Hindu high-status groups observing Sanskritic rituals eschew animal sacrifices; such sacrifices are offered only in folk worship in which low-status groups participate. These do not involve Brahman priests or Sanskritic observances of the high-status Hindus. The point I want to make here is that rituals by themselves are not in and of themselves of high or low status. It is the *label* that the high-status group attaches to them that determines their status; status is not intrinsic to what is involved in them. The rites practiced by high-status groups acquire high-status labels by definition. The same situation plays out in the vegetarian–nonvegetarian controversy amongst Hindus. If high-status groups had green ears or blue noses, these would become status symbols. In other words, symbols associated with high-status groups acquire their cachet because of the dominant status of the group that uses them, not the other way around.

Generally Accepted List of *Saṁskāras*

The number of rites of passage varies from eleven to forty-eight, depending on the particular code of law listing them. These lists can be found in the books by Pandey or Kane (Pandey 1969, 15–24; Kane 1974, 2:188–541; 1973, 4:179–551). A number of causes, including a decline in the knowledge of

Sanskrit, adoption of a secular lifestyle, too little time for religion, and the material expenses of these ceremonies, have whittled down number of ceremonies to sixteen. In actual practice, they may be reduced to just four: the birth ceremony combined with naming the baby (numbers 4 and 5), initiation (number 11), marriage (number 15), and the final rites (number 16). In a few cases, the initiation and marriage ceremonies are combined for the simple reason that the parents never got around to performing the initiation ceremony in the first place, and a man cannot marry unless he has undergone initiation.

1. *Impregnation:* Garbhādhāna

The rite of *garbhādhāna* has fallen into abeyance and is no longer observed in most families, except may be those who are ultra-orthodox with an observant paterfamilias. If it is observed at all, the ceremony has become part of the wedding ceremony, provided that the married couple are of age. It is supposed to begin the new life of a baby under ideal sacral conditions, without leaving anything pertaining it to chance (Kane 1974, 2:201–6; Pandey 1969, 48–59).

2. *Causing the Birth of a Male Child:* Puṃsavana

The *puṃsavana* ceremony is no longer performed in most families; the exceptions could be the ultra-orthodox with the means and time to devote to it. Though we now know that the sex of the baby is determined at conception, a few may go through with this ceremony as a bow to tradition. It used to be observed in the olden days at the first indications of a viable pregnancy (Kane 1974, 2:218–22; Pandey 1969, 60–3). The purpose of the ceremony is obvious from its name. For Hindus, the birth of a son is something special for a variety of reasons. Every Hindu is born incurring three debts, *ṛīṇa,* to the gods, to ancestors, and to the sages and other human beings. The only way that a Hindu can repay the debt to ancestors is by begetting a son who performs offerings to the ancestors and carries on the clan (the *gotra*) and family name.

3. *Parting of the Hair:* Sīmanta, *or* Sīmantonnayana

The rite of *sīmanta,* or *sīmantonnayana,* was meant to protect the mother from any and all evil influences and help her to carry the pregnancy to full term and deliver a healthy baby. It was performed in the fourth or fifth month of the pregnancy (Kane 1974, 2:222–6; Pandey 1969, 64–9). It is no longer observed in most families; the exceptions are when there is a rich, doting father; when the one pregnant is the eldest or only daughter; and when the ceremony is a family tradition. I remember my Aunt Mannakka going through this ceremony during her first pregnancy.

4. *Birth Ceremony:* Bāḷāntiro, *or* Jātakarma

The traditional parts of the birth ceremony, *bāḷāntiro* or *jātakarma*, involving the recitation of the appropriate sacred Vedic texts, or mantras, are no longer observed, and there is no participation by an officiating priest. Most fathers would not know the appropriate Vedic mantra to recite anyway. The senior women in the family are in charge in this situation, with the men playing a strictly secondary role. A few decades ago, most of the deliveries were at home, involving a midwife or an experienced woman who had had many babies. Nowadays, babies are born in hospitals or maternity homes maintained by physicians trained in obstetrics and gynecology. Hence, some of the details that follow may be obsolete; they are based on my recollections from my childhood and the birth of my siblings.

The *bāḷāntiryā kūḍa* (birthing room) at our home in Udupi was the small, stuffy, and ill-lit room just off the front veranda, the *jagali*. Now it is used for general storage. Before the advent of electricity, illumination for the room was from an oil lamp. At the suitable time, my grandfather would go to fetch the midwife, a Sarasvat lady named Ammu, by a tonga, a one-horse cart. We children were ordered to be quiet and to not be in the way of people bustling in and out of the birthing room. We were anxious, wondering about all of the moans and groans coming out of it. Finally, we would hear the cries of a baby, heralding the arrival of a new brother or sister. In our family, as in all Hindu families, every new birth was accepted as a gift from the gods, though the boys were more special than the girls. The new baby was cleaned up and put in a *gershi* (winnowing basket, a shallow, square basket, cane-woven, about thirty inches on the side, and about two inches deep) lined with layers of cloth. An oil lamp was kept next to it, so that people could attend to the needs of the baby. The baby was fed with a wick of fine cloth dipped in a solution of sugar or brown sugar, *bōnti*, till it was ready to take its mother's breast. The mother and the baby are considered to be ritually impure, *bhaṣṭa*, till the tenth day after delivery, when they have a bath (Kane 1974, 2:228–37; Pandey 1969, 70–8).

On the sixth day after birth, the Supreme God Brahma is supposed to visit the baby in the middle of the night and write its fate on its forehead. In our family, we used to keep a pen and paper for his use next to the baby's *gershi*, just in case he ran out of writing material. The baby is not bathed the next day, lest one wash away any of Brahma's writing. As a small boy, I used to wonder about the exact mechanism of transfer of the piece of paper to the forehead of the baby, giving rise to many speculative scenarios. I tried keeping awake to catch Brahma in the act. However, sleep got the better of me, and this legend remained unproven till common sense prevailed. Families that can afford the sixth-day rite, the *saṭṭi*, celebrate with an all-night musical performance. When my nephew Śrīnivāsa Prabhu (son of my Uncle Śridhara Bāppā) was born, there was a performance of *tāḷa maddaḷe*, as it is called in Kannada. This is a long reenactment of a well-known incident in one of the Hindu epics, usually in Kannada but occasionally in Konkani, by a troupe of people trained in music and dialogue. There is a narrative in song and a spirited dialogue between the protagonist and his rival, conducted to the accompaniment of a few musical instruments (Karanth 1997). At the end of the performance, sweets and the beverages *pānaka*, *kāpī*, and *cā* were served to the large crowd of invitees. *Saraswats in Kanara* appeared in the *Kanara Gazetteer*, 1883, and is a description of the customs and traditions of our community at that time (Kudva 1978, 276–305). It mentions that the women of the family would perform a circular dance called *phugḍi* as part of the *saṭṭi*. They moved rapidly in a circle, bending at their knees and then straightening up, while holding copper vessels partly filled with water in their hands. They would blow across the openings of these pots to set the air in them vibrating, to produce a pleasant sound. I do not know any other details; I had never heard of this dance or ever seen it performed. It is a tradition that is not observed any longer.

5. *Naming of the Baby:* Cerdā Nāvā̃ Ghālcẽ, *or* Nāmakaraṇa

The baby is given a name on the twelfth day, in the *cerdā nāvā̃ ghālcẽ* (also called *nāmakaraṇa*) ceremony, which is celebrated along with the ceremony of *pāḷḷyāntũ ghālcẽ* (cradling). This ceremony is usually conducted by the women of the family, without involving a priest. However, in some cases, especially if the baby is a firstborn son, a more elaborate version of this twelfth-day naming-and-cradling ceremony, called *bārso*, is observed; it involves a priest (Ramabai, alias Ammanna, 2004, 30). This more elaborate ceremony is not obligatory. Ceremonies to propitiate any bad influence of the planets in the baby's horoscope are also performed at this time. After the baby's bath, it is dressed in festive clothes.

The procedure for the baby's bath, as carried out by my mother, was as follows: The person bathing the baby sits on a low wooden stool in the bathroom, with her feet resting on another stool. The naked baby rests in the hollow formed by the bare legs of the bather, a position guaranteed to hold securely even the most active, squirmy baby. A few drops of oil are applied to the baby's body, and all limbs are stretched, exercised, and thoroughly massaged. Babies enjoy this process a lot and so relax and quiet down. Next, the baby is bathed, swaddled in warm towels, and then dressed.

The *pāḷḷẽ* (cradle) is customarily made of sheet brass and is suspended by chains from the ceiling. It is also decorated, with bunches of mango leaves at a minimum. A smooth piece of granite, usually used for pounding spices and called a *Balabhadra,* after *Balarāma,* the elder brother of Lord Kṛṣṇa, is swaddled in cloth, decorated with some gold chains, and then put in the cradle before the baby is. The origin of this ceremony is obscure and could be one of the following: First, people might have been afraid of any bad influences attendant on the cradling ceremony and thus wished to transfer the malefic aspects to the mythic hero who was strong enough to handle them. Second, in the olden days, the father performed a ceremony to ensure strength and long life for the baby, wishing it to be as permanent as a stone (Pandey 1969, 76). Thus, putting the stone in the cradle might have been a form of sympathetic magic, wishing the baby a long life and much strength, as a last remnant of this custom. The third and perhaps the most satisfactory explanation is that for every Hindu, putting a new baby in a cradle is a reenactment of the cradling of Lord Kṛṣṇa, and thus a stand-in for his elder brother is put into the cradle first.

There are elaborate rules for choosing a baby's name that are based on the time of birth or on astrology and local customs (Kane 1974, 2:234–55; Pandey 1969, 78–85). The customs and traditions of names have changed significantly from the Vedic age to the present. Some of these are discussed in Appendix 3: "Atri *Gotra,* or Clan *Atri.*" The current orthodox GSB custom is to give five names: one based on the family deity, one on the month in which the baby was born, one on the baby's asterism, a secret name, and a customary name for daily use. The secret name is known only to the parents until the age of initiation and is whispered in the baby's ear. The secrecy is to prevent its use by any malefactor who would perform sorcery to harm the baby. Parents have to remember the secret name, which is revealed at the time of the *upanayana.* The custom of using twelve names at a *bārso* is not required by codes of law and has grown to be a tradition in some families. Boys used to be named after their paternal grandfather, whether that ancestor was alive or dead. Nowadays, some of these names are considered old-fashioned and other more modern names are used. There is much greater freedom in choosing a name for a girl. Usually, girls are named after a flower, a desirable virtue, or one of the exemplary women of Hindu epics.

If the great-grandparents are living and the baby is a boy, there is a special ceremony called *poṇti vāti* that is performed on the twelfth day to mark the joyous occasion. My great-grandfather Ananthayya and his wife Śrī Devī, or Hodemma, are supposed to have performed this ceremony after my birth. The great-grandparents do not see the baby till the ceremony. A small gold saucer, like the oil container for a lamp, *poṇti,* is fashioned and filled with clarified butter, ghee, extracted from cow's butter. A cotton wick, *vāti,* dipped in the ghee, is lit, and by that light, the great-grandparents look on the face of their great-grandchild for the first time at an auspicious hour. This fortunate constellation of events, according to Hindu tradition, is paradise on Earth in this life and is supposed to grant the great-grandparents entry into heaven in the next life. The ceremony concludes by the donation of the gold lamp, cash, and other *dakṣiṇā* to the officiating priest.

6. *First Going Out:* Cerdā Bhairi Horcẽ, *or* Niṣkramaṇa

A baby's first going out—the *cerdā bhairi horcẽ*, or *niṣkramaṇa*—can take place any day after the naming of the baby and its first cradling, depending on the weather, the health of the baby, the convenience for the family, and other factors (Kane 1974, 2:255–6; Pandey 1969, 86–9). The tradition is to take the baby to the local temple, bringing along the customary offerings of coconut and bananas, or *nārlu keḷẽ*. The baby is dressed in festive clothes and gold chains, with a dot of collyrium, or *kājjala*, placed on each cheek and the forehead (*gālbottu āni nāma*) to avert evil eyes (*dṛṣṭi*). Other visitors to the temple, especially women, duly admire the baby, pointing out various obscure resemblances to near and dear relatives on either side of the family and making general inquiries about the delivery, and so on. It is considered to be the height of bad manners to make any favorable comments on how good-looking, healthy, or big the baby is, as such comments could draw an evil eye to the baby and make it fall ill. What is proper is a neutral comment such as "May God bless" ("Devu barẽ koro"). Also acceptable are wishing the baby a long life, *dīrghāyuṣya jāvvo*, or a good future, a good education, and a long and exemplary life (*bōdu jāvnu* or *buddhontu jāvkā*). A fat, roly-poly baby is sometimes called a *gurḍāṇo*, beyond, of course, the hearing of the doting mother or grandmother. Some women may stroke the baby's cheeks with both hands and crack their knuckles against their temples to avert any evil eye, much to the satisfaction of the baby's mother and grandmother. It is not a good idea for strangers to kiss the baby's face, for fear of passing on any germs. It is acceptable to kiss its hands or feet. After the visit, any fussiness, crying, temper tantrums, refusal of food, or any other sign of indisposition by the baby is considered to be a sure sign of the evil eye. Of course, this raises the possibility of singling out of a culprit who might have inadvertently praised the baby's looks or said the wrong thing. Usually, the grandmother or the eldest woman in the family then moves a pinch of salt in a clockwise direction over the baby's head, saying all the while, "May this remove any evil eye. May this remove the evil eye of persons known and unknown." Then she puts it in the kitchen fire, which makes the fire crackle and sputter. This bit of folk magic is called *meeṭa uvāḷcẽ*. The sound is supposed to be indicative of the removal of all the evil influences from the baby and their consignment to the fire. The louder the sound, better the outcome of the magic and the longer the list of evils counteracted. If the baby falls sick or is indisposed in spite of all these precautions, the women of the family know whom to blame! Sometimes a little bit of red water, or *vokkuḷa*, is prepared in a shallow copper or brass dish, or *poḷeru*. The grandmother moves this clockwise over the baby's head, *vokkuḷa dākkocẽ*, to remove and drive away any evil eye and any wrong words, spoken or unspoken, just in case the salt doesn't work.

7. *First Feeding with Solid Food:* Cerdā Śīta Jevoncẽ, *or* Annaprāśana

There is no specific ceremony observed amongst the GSB at the first feeding of solid food to a baby, called the *cerdā śīta jevoncẽ* or *annaprāśana* (Kane 1974, 2:256–60; Pandey 1969, 90–3). When a baby is about 6 months old, it is given a homemade preparation of wheat (*gõvũ*) and millet (*nāncaṇo*) called *bōḷu*. The baby may get the *bōḷu* and breast milk at the same time.

When the baby is about a year old, it makes a transition from the wheat–millet preparation to rice ground to a paste with hot milk in a bronze mortar and pestle, or *cāttu-gurḍāṇo*. Both the mortar and the pestle are usually made of cast bronze. The mortar is a deep dish, six to nine inches in diameter and about the same depth, with a flat bottom and a huge curved handle that ends in a small base on the floor to give it additional stability. The flat area where the handle joins the dish is used to hold some salt or hot pickles that accompany the bland milk–rice mixture. The pestle is hollow and sometimes contains a few enclosed pellets of metal that make a pleasing tinkling sound when the pestle is in use. The first condiment used along with this bland food is salt. The baby may also be gradually introduced to hot pickles, called *noṇcā khoḷu*, for which some babies develop a great liking compared with the bland rice. The baby might point its little finger at the hot pickles, just in case the person feeding the baby forgot to alternate the pickles with the bland rice. Indian babies are thus introduced to piquant spicy food at a young age.

Some Indian women may breastfeed as long as they produce milk, even when the baby is quite big, old enough to be fondly called a *ghoṇā* in Konkani. They know that in addition to providing nourishment for the baby, breastfeeding acts as a contraceptive. The weaning of the baby is done by applying a paste of a bitter root, *godkoṣta*, to the nipples. If the baby is old enough to speak and understand, the mother may use psychology, telling the baby repeatedly how unseemly it is for such a big baby to be breastfed and that people will laugh at it. Of course, some babies are not put off by these clever ploys and instead treat them with the contempt that they deserve.

8. *Tonsure:* Caula, Cūḍākarma, *or* Cūḍākaraṇa

The first haircut, or *caula*, for boys usually is after the first year and before the third year. In the olden days, the tonsure consisted of shaving the head or cutting the hair very short, except for a lock of hair, called a *śeṇḍi* or *cūḍā*, left on the crown of the head (Kane 1974, 2:260–7; Pandey 1969, 94–101). Both my grandfather and father wore this tuft of hair. A couple of generations ago, almost all Hindu men had this topknot, and thus they wore a turban or a cap to conceal it. In Maharashtra, Brahmans would wear elaborate scarlet silk headgear, *pagaḍi*, with a hollow crest to accommodate the tuft of hair. In the Vedic age, and even later, the style of wearing this tuft depended on the *gotra* of the person. In those olden days, it was also customary to perform all of the birth ceremonies, including the first haircut, for girls also, according to the traditions of the family (Kane 1974, 2:265). Thus, girls' heads were completely shaved or were shaved except for a tuft of hair or were not shaved at all. Nowadays, only professional priests wear a single tuft, irrespective of the clan; one style fits all. This tuft of hair is one of the three visible signs of a Hindu Brahman, the others being the sacred thread worn diagonally over the left shoulder and the caste mark, *nāma*, on the forehead. During the upheavals in Goa in the 1560s and the forced conversion of Hindus by the state and the Roman Catholic church, one of the favorite methods employed by the members of the religious orders was to cut this tuft of hair, thus rendering the person ritually impure or polluted. This was most often done to minors who were under their control (see Appendix 8: "Goa: A Paradise Lost?").

9. *Ear Piercing:* Cerdā Kānu Vinduco, *or* Karṇavedha

Ceremonial ear piercing, called *cerdā kānu vinduco* or *karṇavedha*, is performed for all children at a point anywhere from the twelfth day (along with the cradling ceremony) to the fifth year of life (Kane 1974, 2:254–5; Pandey 1969, 102–5). I do not remember when my ears were pierced; it must have been done when I was a baby. It is usually done by an *āksāḷānco* (goldsmith). The spot on the ear is marked with a dot of sandalwood paste, or *gopicandana*, used in daily worship (*sandhi*). In addition to the customary fees, the goldsmith gets some rice and coconuts to mark the festive occasion.

I used to sport a pair of diamond studs in my ears and a gold chain round my neck when I was a kid. When I was at Christian High School (1938–1946), I used to take a shortcut, *voḷavāṭa*, to school away from the main road passing in front of my father's law office. My father had repeatedly warned me *not* to use the shortcut, because he was afraid that someone might rob and kill me for the jewelry. I duly ignored his warnings because some of my classmates went that way, and it was a shorter route. Finally, when I was about 10 or 11, he caught me at it and punished me for my disobedience by holding a mini trial. I was asked whether I remembered his warnings, and my wanton disregard for them and the offence committed were pointed out. After some deliberations, he delivered a judgment and a punishment of ten or twelve blows on my palm.

I do not think that my father was happy about all of these proceedings, and he went through the motions reluctantly. Later on when I thought about it, I realized that he did not use a cane, only his own hands. Thus, both of us felt the pain of the punishment. That was the only time my father beat me. The upshot was that the jewelry was retired, and then I looked like other boys of my age.

10. *Beginning of Education:* Vidyārambha, *or* Akṣarārambha

The rite marking the beginning of education or practicing the alphabet, called *vidyārambha* or *akṣarārambha*, is usually conducted in the fifth year of life, before a child begins attending school (Kane 1974, 2:265–7; Pandey 1969, 106–10). I went through it as a firstborn son; people usually skip this rite for later-born children. On an auspicious day and time as determined by astrology, and after a bath, I was seated in the *jagali*, facing east, which is an auspicious direction, with my back to the wall of the front of the house. I held a new slate covered with white rice grains in my lap. My grandfather Madhava Bhat traced in the rice with my forefinger, "Salutations to Ganapathi," "*Om Śri Gaṇapathaye Namah*," in Devanāgarī script. Invoking Lord Ganapathi at the commencement of anything auspicious event is traditional, as he removes any and all obstacles. This ceremony was followed by the customary visit to the local temple with offerings of coconuts and bananas. I had been really looking forward for this ceremony. I remember that the new slate and its pencil, *kāḍḍi*, used to be kept in the right-hand drawer of my father's table in Ananthayya's house. At that time my father (Narayana Bhatji), Ananthayya, and their clerk used to come to Ananthayya's house from work, deposit all of their records there, and then go to their own homes. I used to wait eagerly for my father to unlock the drawer and show me the new slate and *kāḍḍi*; it was so exciting. Standing on my toes, I could barely see over the edge of the drawer to admire my wonderful new slate and *kāḍḍi*. I could not write on it, of course, because I first had to go through the formal ceremony.

11. *Initiation:* Mūñji, *or* Upanayana

The rite of initiation, called *upanayana*, is an important rite and may be considered obligatory for all Hindus (Kane 1974, 2:268–415; Pandey 1969, 111–40; Prasad 1997). It is called *mūñji* in Konkani, from the investiture of the initiate with a girdle of *mūñja* grass of three strands. It marks the admission of the young person into the Hindu religious community, and in the olden days, it also indicated the beginning of Vedic studies. After this ceremony, the person was eligible to participate in the religious life of the community, with all of its rights and obligations. This rite is also supposed to indicate a second birth for the person, so the three castes of priests, warriors, and traders who go through this ceremony are called the twice-born, or *dvija.* All twice-born are obligated to perform three types of rites—studying the Vedas, offering sacrifices, and giving alms—and are therefore called *trikarmi.* It is only the priests who can perform three additional types of sacred actions: teaching the Vedas, officiating at sacrifices for others, and receiving alms. Because these add up to a total of six rites, only priests are called *ṣaṭkarmi.*

Nowadays, the *upanayana* is confined only to boys in a GSB family. I mentioned earlier the fact that in the GSB community in the late 1800s, girls could undergo initiation if they so desired. However, this custom is no longer observed, and in my lifetime I have never heard of any girl undergoing *upanayana* among the Sarasvats. The decline of Sanskrit knowledge, the general decline of interest in rites and religion, and the expense of the ceremony have contributed to this state of affairs. I have heard that the Havik Brahmans, another birth group, used to have upanayana for girls even in modern times. Perhaps there were other birth groups that had similar rites. We need field studies to find out which Brahman communities continued to observe this custom till very recently. Instead, experts who comment on the question of *upanayana* for girls quote the same Manu ad nauseam and claim that girls never went through this ceremony! There are later interpolations and additions to Manu that forbid *upanayana,* as are found in other codes of law also. There is no one monolithic code of law that is followed by all Hindus. Manu is a code of law that can be used as a benchmark or a reference for comparison. The British Raj was looking for one code of law for Hindus, in analogy with Christianity, and they happened to fix their sights on Manu, not realizing that there was a multiplicity of such codes. Some of these customs and traditions predate Manu and might have continued to be observed till very recently. Customs and traditions of a birth group take precedence over any pronouncements of Manu. It is interesting to note that girls of the Parsee community, whose Zoroastrian religion has similarities to the Vedic, continue to be initiated into the religious life of their community in an analogous ceremony (Boyce 1987; 1989).

For some obscure reason, the young boy about to undergo the initiation is told, with some mirth, that the ceremony involves inserting a frog in the thigh—*jāṅgentũ bebbo ghālco*! I have always wondered about the origin of this expression; it should be of interest to an anthropologist. It may be an obscure reference to the vague stirrings of sexual maturity and the trumpet call of hormones that the boy hears at about this age.

Like all auspicious Hindu occasions, the almanac and the boy's horoscope are consulted to fix a *muhūrta* (time) for the ceremony. Invitations that are sent out to relatives and friends clearly specify this time, and unlike what happens for most other ceremonies, most of the guests arrive well ahead of this auspicious moment. The occasion is marked by ceremonial music, *vājjapa*, which starts several hours ahead of time. In the olden days in Goa, before the exile of our community, the local *devadāsīs* (women dedicated to the temple) would dance as befitting an auspicious event. This tradition lasted until as late as 1883; however, it is no longer observed (Kudva 1978, 289 et seq.). The codes of law recommend an age range of 8 to 16 years for priests, 11 to 22 years for warriors, and 12 to 24 years for merchants as the proper time for this ceremony (Kane 1974, 2:274). I had my *mūñji* when I was 9 or 10, and my son Giridhar had his when he was 8. This rite marks the transition of the boy to manhood. Before the ceremony proper, the mother seats the boy on her lap, if he is young enough, and feeds him rice and yogurt for the last time as a child. After this ceremonial feeding, she hands him over to the father, or men of the family, for initiation as an adult. At the climax of the ceremony, the boy sits on the lap of his father or the senior person acting in his stead. Both are covered with a silk cloth, and the father whispers the Gāyatrī or Sāvitrī mantra (*Ṛgveda* 3.62.10) thrice; the boy repeats it after him. This hymn is by Viśvāmitra, son of Gāthī, and is a prayer to Savitṛ, the sun, called the Impeller because all life on the earth originates from the sun. The hymn is in adoration of Savitṛ and prays for mental illumination and knowledge. It literally means "We contemplate that esteemed glory of the divine Savitṛ, who may inspire our intellects or actions" (Kane 1974, 2:302). Hindu tradition considers this particular hymn to be the essence of the *Ṛgveda* and ascribes great sacredness and importance to it in its rites. It is recited daily at the morning and evening *sandhyāvandanam* (twilight worship) and on other special occasions. The unveiling at the end of this part is the symbolic rebirth of the boy as a Brahmana, and the recitation of the Gāyatrī is the beginning of the Vedic studies. Under the guidance of the officiating priest, the boy makes his first sacrifice to the Vedic god Agni. The young novice is then instructed in his duties and obligations as a Brahmana by a senior person. In my case, my instructor was Vasudeva Bhat, my grandfather's elder brother and a Sanskrit scholar; for Giridhar, my father did the honors. The young novice then begins his life as a student by begging from his mother or any close female relative who will not refuse him alms. He then begs alms from other relatives and guests, both male and female. The usual gifts are cash and silver articles. In the olden days, at the conclusion of this ceremony, the boy left his parental home at about age 8 and moved in with his teacher to begin Vedic studies. These studies lasted for quite a few years, with a minimum duration of 12 years. Thus, the parents would see their child leave home as a boy and return at the end of the Vedic studies as a young man. These days, the initiate does not go anywhere away from his parents.

He gets many presents in lieu of alms, and the family and the invited guests sit down for a big dinner. When I had my *mūñji,* I was very much interested in astronomy and badly wanted a telescope. I dropped discreet hints that a telescope would be most welcome; however, there was no telescope among the gifts I received. Such is life!

12. *Beginning of Vedic Studies:* Vedārambha, *or* Upākarma

The beginning of Vedic studies, called *vedārambha* or *upākarma,* is not really a separate rite, because the recitation of the Gāyatrī at the *mūñji* is supposed to be the true beginning of studies. In the olden days, these two rites went together because education meant studies of the Vedas and related six subjects, the Vedāṅga ("limbs of the Veda"): phonetics, rituals of solemn Vedic and domestic sacrifices, grammar, etymology, prosody, and astronomy (Kane 1974, 2:323). A general decline in Vedic education might have been the reason that this separate rite was introduced to mark the occasion for the few who decided to undertake these studies, which were considered worthy of note (Pandey 1969, 141–2). In addition, there was the yearly beginning of the Vedic studies, after the end of the monsoons, designated as *upākarma.* Vedic studies could also be temporarily suspended for varying periods of time if conditions were not propitious because of ritual impurity of the student or the surroundings (Kane 1974, 2:393–402). Amongst the Sarasvats who are Ṛgvedis, the festival of the beginning of the Vedic studies is called Ṛgupākarma. At present, it consists of putting on a new sacred thread (one for bachelors who have undergone *upanayana,* and two for married men who wear the extra sacred thread by proxy for their wives) and visiting the local temple. Special spaghetti-like dishes, *śevāyī̃,* both sweet and piquant, are traditionally served at the feast that follows the ceremony. Amongst most Sarasvats today, there is almost a permanent state of cessation of Vedic studies. There may be a few exceptions, but I am unaware of them. The causes for this state of affairs are many. It should be noted that a life of Vedic studies, if followed strictly, is a full-time job with little time left for other pursuits such as earning a living. Hence, such a life is viable only if it is heavily subsidized by, for example, a local king or a wealthy patron. At one time, that was exactly what happened, with kings donating landed property and other wealth to support the Brahmana devoted to the study and practice of the Vedas, because the ruler felt that such activities benefited the whole kingdom, including the patron. The villages of the donated lands were also the centers of higher education in the olden days. Staying in one location with other practitioners of the Vedic rites to continue this tradition is important. Both of these necessary conditions ceased to exist because of the many migrations of our community. It is also possible that the Sarasvats, being quite pragmatic, could see that a strict adherence to Vedic traditions was not possible with the changing times and that their way of life had to shift. The Vedic rites, which are no longer practiced in their original form, have morphed into the current occasional religious observances.

13. *Haircut:* Keśānta

The first shaving of the beard, a rite called *keśānta*, was performed at the age of 16, when a boy had attained sexual maturity, and marked the beginning of the students' *Brahmacarya*, or life as a celibate. However, there is some confusion as to whether this rite instead marked the *end* of studentship and celibate life (Kane 1974, 2:402–5; Pandey 1969, 143–5). The rite has fallen into abeyance, along with Vedic studies.

14. *Return Home of the Student at the End of Vedic Studies:* Samāvartana

The ceremony marking the student's return home at the end of Vedic studies, called *samāvartana*, has now become part of the wedding and involves a bit of playacting (Kane 1974, 2:405–15; Pandey 1969, 146–52). The bridegroom, dressed as a student and carrying a staff and an umbrella, pretends to be going to Kāśī or Vārāṇasī for further studies; the father of the bride stops him and begs him to change his mind, accompany him to his home, and marry his daughter. The groom obliges, and the wedding proper takes place. Sometimes if the groom is a nephew or someone known to the bride's family, the father of the bride may delay playing his part, letting the groom continue on his way. The young man gets anxious and may begin looking over his shoulder to see whether anyone is going to ask him to return and marry before he wanders off beyond the bounds of the wedding reception area. Finally, the father of the bride hurries to play his part, apologizes to the groom, and puts him out of his misery and embarrassment, much to everyone's merriment.

15. *Marriage:* Vhārḍika, *or* Vivāha

Marriage, called *vhārḍika* or *vivāha*, is perhaps the most important of all the Hindu rites of passage (Kane 1974, 2:427–541; Pandey 1969, 153–233; Prasad 1995). Hindu society has long expected all men to get married; beget children and lead the life of a householder; be a useful, productive member of society; and pay off each of their debts to the gods, ancestors, sages, and the rest of humanity at large. The only exceptions were for those who had taken a vow to be a perpetual student. Some people did bypass this stage of life, renouncing the world to become a *saṁnyāsi* (ascetic). However, the general feeling amongst Hindus was that being a householder and having a family and children was much harder than renouncing such a life, which was considered to be a coward's way out. It was also recognized that it is the householder who supports, by alms, the other three stages of life of a Hindu. The whole system could collapse but for the productive work done by the householders who materially contribute to the wealth of the society.

Hindu marriages are modeled after the sacred marriage of Sūryā, the daughter of the sun god Sūrya who married the moon god Soma, as described in the *Ṛgveda* (O'Flaherty 1981, 267, 10.85; Panikkar 1983, 253). Hence, the ceremonies as well as the sacred mantra accompanying them follow the *Ṛgveda*.

In orthodox Hindu families, astrology plays a great part in the negotiations leading to a Hindu marriage. The horoscopes of the bride and the groom are subject to much scrutiny, and their positive and negative characteristics noted and are classified as tough and hard (*kaṭhīṇa*) or mild and gentle (*saumya*). The future good or bad effects of the bride's horoscope on the intended groom's family are also important. Astrologers claim to predict the compatibility, *meḷā-mēḷi*, of the couple, how many children (read: mostly sons) they will have, whether they will earn much money and acquire the material comforts of life, and so on. Both families appear determined to leave nothing to chance and feel that the future of the young man and the young woman are irrevocably determined by the moment of their birth and the predictions of astrologers. Each of the believers has his or her own favorite astrologer, who is supposed to be specially endowed by education, sanctity of life, special intuition, and so forth, to predict the future. Their many failures are conveniently ignored, any successes due to coincidences are extolled, and the believers feel happy about their supposed control over an uncertain future. In general, the grip of astrology has decreased today. However, in some families, it continues to hold sway, and these people will never undertake important life events such as marriage without consulting their favorite astrologer.

If the two families really want to go through with the wedding, any bad influences of the planets can always be ameliorated by proper religious rites, or the humans involved can be placated by a bigger dowry. The evil of the dowry is a significant presence in these preliminaries. There is a legislative ban on demands for dowries by the groom's side; however, the hard bargaining involved in determining its kind and amount is very much alive in traditional marriages. If the young man and woman meet in college or at work, fall in love, and decide to get married on their own without involving their families, both astrology and dowry generally do not play a significant role. This is a welcome development in the practical mechanics of current Hindu marriages. Other important considerations involved in choosing a bride are her *gotra*, and birth group or caste (*jāti*). In general, Hindus marry outside the clan and in the caste; in other words, they observe clan exogamy and caste endogamy.

The first custom was meant to prevent inbreeding, because a boy and a girl belonging to the same clan were supposed to have a brother–sister relationship. Today, some people do not observe *gotra* exogamy if they want the marriage to take place for other reasons. A few do not even know their *gotra* or care about it. Belonging to the same caste ensures that dietary habits and other everyday customs are the same. These days, when a man and woman decide to get married on their own, these customs may not be observed.

The groom's party goes to the bride's home for the wedding. Astrologers are consulted to determine a *śubha muhūrta* (auspicious time) to begin the journey, the date and time of the wedding, the return after the wedding, and so on. In the olden days, local *devadāsīs* danced in the procession, as befitting an auspicious event (Kudva 1978, 289, 292, 295). This custom has fallen by the wayside. There is a ceremonial welcome, *yedru kāṇsaṇa*, for the groom's party, given by the bride's people. Both groups are led by their respective women and girls—who carry auspicious things such as flowers, saffron powder (*kuṅkuma*), fragrances such as sandalwood paste, and silver sprinklers of rose water—and a company of musicians, or *vājpāñce*. When the two groups meet, they sprinkle rose water on each other; exchange *kuṅkuma*, flowers, and fragrances; and form one group and return to the bride's home, where a ceremonial pavilion, a *vhārḍike mānṭovu*, has been erected. The wedding ceremony proper takes place in a smaller enclosure, a *mānṭvi*, which is the center of all attention. In this small space, the officiating priest establishes the sacred nuptial fire around which all the ceremonies take place, and the wedding is solemnized. The groom is welcomed by the bride's father in the traditional Hindu *arghya* ceremony for receiving an honored guest, which involves activities such as washing and drying his feet to remove the dust of a long journey and offering *madhuparka*. The bride's maternal uncle then leads the bride to the *mānṭvi*. The bride and the groom face each other, with a curtain of cloth between them. The lineages of the each are recited, and the groom presents new garments to the bride. These days, it is the groom's mother who does the honors. This is followed by a rearrangement of the way the bride wears the sari, a *vaarla ghālchẽ*, into the style worn by a married woman. In the formal giving away of the bride, the *kanyādāna*, the groom extends his cupped hands, *añjali*, in a gesture of acceptance, with the bride's hands similarly placed over his as the gift, and the bride's father touches his daughter's hands in a gesture of giving away. The mother of the bride pours water thrice, from a container, *kumbha*, to solemnize the occasion. This is followed by a number of sacrifices in which the couple participate as husband and wife for the first time, including the offering of parched rice, *lāyye homa*. In this ceremony, the bride's brother pours parched rice into the cupped hands of the bride, who offers the rice as an oblation in the nuptial fire, praying for the fecundity and prosperity of the married couple. The bride now belongs to the *gotra* of her husband. This is followed by the bride treading on a stone, *aśmārohaṇa*, at which time her husband exhorts her to be firm as a stone in her devotion to him. According to Hindu law, the marriage is considered to be legally binding and complete at the end of the ceremony of seven steps, *saptapadī* (Kane 1974, 2:534; Panikkar 1983, 263; Doniger and Smith, 1991, 177, 8.227). Seven small heaps of rice are placed north of the nuptial fire, and the groom leads the bride to step on each of these with her right foot, while saying to her, "First step is for vigor, second for potency, third for prosperity, fourth for happiness, fifth for wealth, sixth for longevity, seventh for friendship," and he exhorts her to be devoted to him. He tells his bride, "Having walked seven steps together, we are now friends," and he prays that their friendship is never severed. If the wedding takes place during the day, the bride looks at the sun as a symbol of constancy. If at night, she looks at the pole star, the Big Bear, the Big Dipper, or the Seven Sages (*Saptarṣi*). In this constellation, the second star in the handle of the Big Dipper (ζ Ursa Major, *Ar: Mizar*) and the faint star accompanying it (80 Ursa Major, *Ar: Alcor*) are supposed to represent Vasiṣṭha and his wife Arundhatī (Faithfulness), as an example of wifely devotion (Illingworth and Clark 2000, 45). Somewhere in these proceedings, the new husband also promises to put his earnings in the custody of his wife, as befits a responsible adult with a family to support. At the conclusion of the ceremony, women whose husbands are living, *ayyapaṇā bāila maniṣī*, are invited to bless the couple by sprinkling rice on them, *śesa bhorcē*, which is accompanied by the waving of lights, *ārti dākkocē*. The bride also holds a small young boy, *deḍḍho*, in her lap, or makes him sit by her side, during these ceremonies. This is a bit of sympathetic magic that is supposed to ensure that the couple will have sons. In the olden days, the bride would sit on a red bull's hide (a symbol of fertility and prosperity) during these proceedings; this custom is no longer observed. The young couple receive many gifts, and all of the invited guests sit down for a big dinner to eat more than they should.

These days, a wedding, including the feast, may last for a few hours. In 1583, Linschoten described Hindu weddings in Goa that lasted fourteen days; the brides were about 7 years old, and the grooms were about 9 years old (Burnell and Tiele 1935, 258). In 1883, weddings lasted for ten days, with girls 6 to 11 years old marrying boys 8 to 17 years old (Kudva 1978, 300). By 1912, only the rich had nine-day weddings; most of the weddings for everyone else lasted for five or seven days. There was even a community-wide meeting held in Kochin in December 1908 to end all of this extravagance and reduce weddings to three days. However, the pursuit of status, real or imagined, through the display involved in weddings continues to be a problem for the community. Hindu weddings have been and continue to be synonymous with bankruptcy for the bride's father. The wedding of my Aunt Tucci Mhāva lasted seven days, and I am told that my parents' wedding was a five-day affair. It has long been customary for the bride's father to spend more than he can afford and thus slide into the beginning of lifelong debt or insolvency. Because of the economic realities of life today, these extravagances are mostly in the past. However, even now, many a father equates the birth of a daughter with a grave financial burden.

At the conclusion of the wedding ceremonies, the newly married couple leaves for the groom's house, where they go through a brief ceremony, called *gṛahapraveśa*, of the new bride entering her husband's home. At the main door to the family quarters, there is a brief ceremony in which the groom's sisters sit on the threshold, *humboru*, to block the entrance of the couple, *bāglāri boscẽ*, demanding a promise from the couple that they will give in marriage their children to the sisters' children. The groom's sisters may also get some gifts as part of this ceremony.

The bride is welcomed into her new home, to the accompaniment of *vājjapa*, as the living representative of the Goddess of Prosperity. It is customary to play the Kannada song "*Bhāgyada Lakṣmī Bārammā*," by Sant Purandara Dasa, the title of which may be translated as "Welcome to Lakṣmī, the Embodiment of Prosperity." The bride is asked to enter the house on her auspicious right foot, for good luck. These may be the last few kind words that the new bride hears in her husband's home for some time. This is because unwittingly, she becomes a participant and a victim in the game of power politics at home. The groom's mother, sisters, and other female relatives suddenly find themselves dethroned, and they resent the fact this utter stranger, a mere slip of a girl, suddenly has much greater influence over their beloved son, brother, or favorite nephew, than they ever had (see Chapter 1, "Prabhus of Siddhapur," for details). This fact of life is hard for them to face up to. Though the Ṛgvedic verse says to the new bride, "Be an empress over your husband's father, an empress over your husband's mother; be an empress over your husband's sister and an empress over your husband's brothers" (O'Flaherty 1981, 271, 10.85.46), this exhortation is not well known. Besides, I am sure, every Hindu mother-in-law will question the sanity of the author of this particular Vedic hymn. The poor bride is never aware of her "exalted" status, and in reality, she is at the bottom of the totem pole, or the dominance hierarchy, in her new home. In a joint Hindu family, it used to be customary for the mother-in-law and the sisters-in-law to lord it over the new bride. These days, brides are made of tougher material, are better educated, are more assertive, have spines of steel, and are not prepared to put up with any of this traditional nonsense. These new brides can challenge and best any in-laws whom fate can throw at them!

16. *Last Rites:* Kriyā, *Short for* Antyakriyā, *or* Antyeṣṭi

The last rites, involving cremation, are also called the final sacrifice or final oblations, and are called *kriyā*, short for *antyakriyā*, or *antyeṣṭi*. These may be divided into the funeral ceremonies, the ritual pollution following death and its cleansing, and *śrāddha* (Kane 1973, 4:179–266, 267–333, 334–551; Pandey 1969, 234–74). A few authors do not mention this rite, considered inauspicious, in the general list of the rites of passage (Pandey 1969, 15). The basic purpose of these rites are (1) the expeditious disposal of the body of the deceased for hygienic reasons in a hot climate; (2) to comfort the surviving family members by telling them that the deceased is about to enter a better life and keeping them busy with rites, rituals, and obligations; (3) to specify a fixed period of mourning; and (4) to bring closure to the bereavement process.

In the *Ṛgveda*, there is some evidence for burial of the deceased, as in the "Burial Hymn" (O'Flaherty 1981, 52, 10.18). It is possible that there was a choice and either burial or cremation was observed, depending on a number of circumstances, including the ready availability of wood (Kane 1973, 4:232; Hansen and Mallory 1997). However, cremation must have come into general use even in ancient times except for infants, for ascetics, or in other exceptional cases. Disposal of the dead in the Vedic times was in four stages: cremation, collecting the charred bones and depositing them underground in an urn, expiatory rites including food offerings, and finally, erecting a monument of earth or bricks, which was optional. A cow or a she-goat was killed, and the dead body was covered with its limbs before cremation (Kane 1973, 4:206). There is no animal sacrifice in Hindu cremations now. The bones were collected the day after cremation, or on the third, fifth, or the seventh day by relatives (either men or women) after quenching the funeral pyre with a mixture of milk and water. A winnowing basket was used to separate the bones from ashes, and then the dust and the bones were deposited in an urn. The urn was buried at the bottom of a tree or a monument, the latter being the choice especially in the case of a person who had established the Vedic fires and offered the prescribed sacrifices while alive.

Disposal of the corpse with initial cremation, followed by the collection and burial of bones and then a mourning period of about thirteen days, must have been common amongst the Indo-European tribes of other cultures and environmental surroundings. There are interesting similarities, as well as differences, of details with the death ceremonies of Hittite royalty and the Homeric Greeks. Perhaps this is suggestive of cultural contacts amongst these various tribes before their dispersal to the different countries where we find them at a later date in history (Gurney 1990, 137; Bryce 2002, 176). A plow ox was slaughtered and placed at the feet of the Hittite king. A libation of wine was poured, and the wine cup was smashed to pieces. A male goat was swung to and fro over the dead body to ritually purify it (Bryce 2002, 176). The cremation took place the next day, followed by the collection of the bones by women on the day after. The smoldering remains of the funeral pyre were quenched with beer, wine, and *wahli* (a drink used in Hittite rituals), and then the bones were picked out with silver tongs and deposited in fine oil in a silver jug. The bones were then transferred to a linen cloth of the finest quality and placed in a seat of honor. Libations were poured, animals were sacrificed, and food was offered to the deceased, and then a funeral feast took place. On the sixth day, the bones were taken to a stone house, and a bed in its inner chamber became their final resting place. Mourning amongst the Hittite royalty lasted for not less than thirteen (Gurney 1990) or fourteen days (Bryce 2002).

The funeral of Patroclus and Hector enables us to see the similarities with the Bronze Age rituals of the Greeks and Trojans (Gurney 1990, 137; Rieu 1983, 412–36). The body was cremated, the funeral pyre was quenched with wine, the bones were gathered and placed in a golden urn after being wrapped in a double layer of fat, and the urn, covered with a soft linen cloth, was placed in a hut. The urn containing Hector's bones was buried and a barrow was built over it by the Trojans. The Greeks built a barrow round and about the funeral pyre of Patroclus, holding games in his honor and offering prizes.

I remember the final days of Hodemma, Ananthayya's wife and my father's maternal grandmother, when I was about 6 years old. When it became clear that she was in her final moments, all of her relatives were summoned to her bedside early one morning. She was lying along the east side of the inner bedroom of Ananthayya's house. There was a small bronze lamp, a *divli*, at her head, and her breathing was labored. Each of us put into her open mouth a spoonful of Ganges water brought in a small bottle from one of his pilgrimages to Vārāṇasī (Benares) by my grandfather Madhava Bhat. We were told that we were sending Hodemma to *svarga* (heaven). It is the pious hope of Hindus to have the privilege of such a send-off from their grandchildren. It is customary to cremate the body immediately after death. After she passed away, the body was laid on the blades of the sacred *darbha* grass used in Hindu ceremonies. The body was then brought out and laid in the front courtyard, with the feet of the corpse pointing south, the direction of Yamā, the God of death. Next, the body was bathed and dressed in a new sari by the women of the family, with all the accoutrements of an *ayyapaṇā bāila maniṣī*, including flowers in her hair, a garland of jasmine round her neck, and turmeric and sandalwood paste on her cheeks. For a Hindu woman, to die before her husband is considered to be very fortunate, and quite a few women came to bid ceremonial farewell to her and ask for her blessings for a similar end. The farewell offerings, *hōnti bhorcẽ*, to the dead person consist of a coconut, rice, flowers, and so on. These are carried in a wickerwork basket and are cremated with the body. This custom might have originated in the olden days as a gift of necessities to a traveler setting out on a journey. While these offering were being made, stout pieces of bamboo needed for the bier and wood for the cremation had been brought in. In Udupi, there is a family from our GSB community who specializes in providing all of the necessities for a cremation as a standard package. This is very convenient and efficient; everything needed for the last rites is in the package, and nothing is forgotten. Hodemma's body was then laid on the bamboo framework, the toes of her corpse tied were together with a string with the invocation "May they never tread this earth again," and her body was prepared for the journey to the *śmaśāna* (crematorium). All of these events are part of a religious ceremony; for Hodemma, that ceremony was presided over by my grandfather, as the officiating priest. In the meantime, my Uncle Śrīdhar Bāppā had had his head shaved except for his *śeṇḍī* as a sign of mourning, had bathed, and was ready to perform his duties as an adopted son. Embers from the fire in the kitchen were put in an earthenware pot, *ciḍki*, mounted on a triangular bamboo support that was suspended from three strings, *sūmba*, attached to its corners, to be carried by the son to the cremation grounds. The cooking fires in the house were then put out as a sign of mourning, and no cooking was done for some time. Food cooked in our home was brought to Ananthayya's house. The son covered his head with a white cloth, like a hood, as a sign of mourning, *khoḷa ghālcẽ*, and led the way; he was followed by the bier, which was carried by four stout men, along with other men of the family and friends from the community. While the men lifted the bier and then on their journey to the cremation grounds, all participants invoked God's name, saying, "Nārāyaṇa, Nārāyaṇa." They also carried lighted bundles of joss sticks, *ūdbatti*.

After the cremation, the funeral party stopped at a pond, *talẽ*, to bathe and perform religious ceremonies in which the principal part is played by the son. The funeral procedures explain the strong and persistent desire for at least one son that is evident in Hindu society. These ceremonies continued for the next thirteen days. That is because Hindus believe that the departed soul, the *preta*, hovers around the place of death. During the next few days, in the evening, there was a recitation of one of the sacred Hindu texts, the *Garuḍa Purāṇa*, in the room in which Hodemma had died. Anathayya and I were the only two people who sat through the recitation, which was accompanied by a translation into Konkaṇi by the priest. The sacred text is supposed to be an account of the journey of the dead person's spirit in the hereafter, with the good getting their rewards and the wicked getting a just punishment, and is for the comfort of the bereaved family.

On the third day after cremation, some bones and their ashes were collected, *hāḍa viñcucẽ*, put in an earthenware pot, and buried to the south of the holy basil, or *tulasī*, plant in the front courtyard of Ananthayya's house. Madhava, my grandfather, took these with him next time he went to Vārāṇasī, for immersion in the Ganges with due religious ceremonies. In the religious ceremonies that are performed every day, the departed spirit is supposed to get a subtle body gradually built up by the powers of mantras recited by the priest, and on the twelfth day promoted to be one of the Manes, in a special ceremony (Pandey 1969, 267; Kane 1973, 3:737). On the thirteenth day, there is a grand feast, *vaikuṇṭha samārādhana*, at which the family and friends of the deceased are entertained, to celebrate the entry of the dead person into Vaikuṇṭha, the heavenly abode of Lord Viṣṇu. If the family is very orthodox and rich enough to afford it, these final rites are followed by monthly offerings (*māsika śrāddha*) and finally, on the anniversary of death according to the Hindu calendar, the first end-of-the-year (*varsāntika*) ceremonies for the dead. These days, very few observe the monthly ceremonies in the first year of death, confining themselves only to the yearly offerings (*vārṣika śrāddha*) on the anniversary of death. Observant Hindus perform *śrāddha* to the Manes, covering three generations—parents, grandparents, and great-grandparents—so long as they are alive.

APPENDIX SIX

Feasts and Festivals

The typical Konkani Sarasvat family in the South Kanara District observes many feasts and festivals. Some of these observances are mostly family oriented; the rest are public community festivals centered round the local temple. The family events usually begin with religious rites and ceremonies to fulfill the *vratas* (vowed observances) of a particular member of the family. For annual obligations, *pūjā* (worship) is the climax of the ceremony, and it involves the *nivedya* (offering of food), special dishes and preparations, to the deity, followed by the partaking of these offerings, or *prasāda* (grace), in the form of a grand feast. These could be commemorative events such as the *jayantī* (birthday) of an incarnation, *avatāra*, of God, purificatory ceremonies observed at specified times in a religious year, or occasions to recall important happenings in the Hindu tradition. The Sarasvat community as a whole participates in the public festivals. Most of these are endowed by rich individuals or families at the local Gauda Sarasvat Brahmana (GSB) temple and are conducted annually as their community service, or *sevā*. A few festivals depend on voluntary contributions from individual households. The public functions usually involve a *samarādhanā* (communal feast), in which all Sarasvats who can attend, amounting thousands of people, participate. The food is strictly vegetarian, without eggs, fish, or meat; only dairy products are allowed. Professional cooks prepare huge amounts of rice and accompanying side dishes, including *goḍśẽ* (desserts). These are served on banana leaves to people seated in long *pāṅkti* (rows), in several sittings. This communal feast and the sharing of the food offered to the deity are the ultimate assertion of the unity of the Konkani-speaking Sarasvats groups as one people.

Children play a special part in these feasts and are an integral part of the ceremonies. The firstborn, especially if male, is made much of and is given special treatment. As a child, I remember eagerly looking forward to these celebrations. Schools would be closed, bringing a welcome relief from the tyranny of homework and the autocracy of teachers in the classroom. We could put in requests for special desserts in addition to the obligatory dishes demanded by tradition. Lord Kṛṣṇa's birthday, Kṛṣṇa Janmāṣṭamī, especially calls for children to be the surrogates of his childhood on the Earth. Toy air guns, called *peṭnoḷi* (a word created by the onomatopoeic word *phut*, for the sound produced by an air gun, plus *naḷi*, meaning the tube of bamboo that forms the body of the air gun) that shoot small green berries, or *teppaḷa*, are bought. The neighborhood is filled with the noise of these going off at random intervals. The only factors that limit the use of these toys are the soreness of the right palm that one develops by constant use and running out of the berries to shoot. Friends and strangers are doused with colored water, *vokkuḷa*, celebrating Lord Kṛṣṇa's childhood pranks. Fireworks, with their multicolored illuminations, loud sounds, and acrid smell of sulfur and other chemicals, are eagerly awaited and enjoyed. I used to make elaborate lists of different types and sizes to buy and was always disappointed when the realities of their purchase by my father did not meet my expectations. Though I knew that not always getting what I wanted was one of the facts of life, drawing up these lists, with eager expectations of better dividends every year, was also part of the fun. There are always presents: new clothes, toys, or hard cash. The Indian tradition is always for an older person to give a gift to a younger person, and not the other way around. Hence, children do not have to spend their meager resources on gifts. There was always subtle persuasion from parents for the children to put the money in their *ḍabbi* (piggy bank). However, if the amount was small enough, a child could always spend it on sensible things like candy or toys. I will always be grateful to my relatives, who were generous with their gifts of money and subtly hinted that I should spend it rather than save it. These celebrations are one vehicle through which children absorb the values, traditions, and worldview of Hindus as if by osmosis, in a pleasant family setting. The memories of these happy occasions stay with a person for life and are always pleasant to recall.

The descriptions given here are but a feeble attempt to convey the experience of these festive occasions. To experience these celebrations in full, you have to live through them on location in Udupi or Mulki, using all of your senses to savor the sights, sounds, smells, and tastes that will leave their indelible imprint in your mind. In a few cases, the participants are part of a joyous, fervent, noisy, sweaty, pushing crowd of people, each person trying to outdo others in the noisy expressions of their devotion, or *bhakti*. Though these celebrations are common to all Hindus in different parts of India, they assume overtones and subtle nuances characteristic of the particular region and community where they are observed. There are the different seasons, each with its own ambience and its own particular flavor. The ever-present dust of India, its peculiar smell, and its sudden change when the first few drops of a cooling, refreshing rain fall on it cannot be described adequately. The smells of jasmine, *cāmpẽ* (a yellow flower with an assertive fragrance), and other fragrant tropical flowers of gorgeous colors, plus the tastes and scents of mangoes, jackfruit, berries, and other fruits not available outside the locality, help make these events memorable. The sounds in the neighborhood, the ringing of bells (*ghāṇṭa*), the festive music (*vājjapa*) from the temple, the devotional songs (*bhajana*), the wedding processions, and the occasional funeral all create a matrix of sounds in which memories of the happenings are embedded. Most of these events are family celebrations with or without specific religious connotation; however, these occasions involve a visit to the local Śrī Veṅkaṭaramaṇa Temple or the temple at Mulki, with the traditional offerings of coconut and bananas, or *nārlu keḷẽ*. Then there are the fresh vegetables, with seasonal availability determining the particular dishes that are customary at different festivals. Some main dishes or desserts are obligatory by tradition. In addition, there are the public celebrations, such as the temple procession of a sacred image, or *utsavā mūrti*, that would pass in front of our house. We would put out a bronze lamp, *divli*, at the entrance to the house and proffer handheld *ārti* (lights for waving), as an offering. The *ārti* is a round brass plate or an elongated bronze handle with a shallow round container at one end with a few oil-dipped cotton wicks, *vāti*, in it. The palanquin with the sacred image would come to a stop in front of the house, with its weight resting on two wooden props, and then an assistant would fetch the *ārti*, which the priest would light by the flame of a torch held by an attendant, and wave it clockwise in a circle in front of the image of the deity being carried in procession. A few flowers were then put on the lit *ārti* as a *prasāda* and were returned to the house. The women of the house waved their hand over the flame of the *ārti* to bless themselves, *ārti ghevcẽ*, apply some red powder, *kuṅkuma*, to the *tīḷo* (dot) on their forehead, and take a few flowers to put in their hair. (The dot on a woman's forehead, between her eyebrows, may have originated as a beauty spot, with the added significance of indicating that she was a Hindu, that she was married, and that her husband was alive. A Hindu widow would never wear it in the olden days. It has now reverted back to being just a beauty aid irrespective of religion or married state.) Everyone else similarly blessed themselves and the children.

The timing of the feasts and festivals, which are the highlights of the Hindu religious year, is based on a combination of solar and lunar calendars, or a lunisolar calendar. The solar calendar makes sure that the observances are synchronized with the seasons or the sun, and the lunar calendar ensures sychonization with the moon to define the times appropriate for the celebrations. Hence, it is necessary to have at least some acquaintance with the basic terminology of these calendars. In the next section, a description of the Hindu calendar is followed by a discussion of the different feasts and festivals.

The Hindu Calendar

The *pañcāṅga* (almanac), made of five parts or members, of the Hindu calendar is published every year before the beginning of the new year. The one I have used is called *Mangalore Panchanga* and is in Kannada, the language of the state of Karnataka (Acharya 1996–7). This publication is mostly used for religious or astrological purposes, such as determining auspicious times for performing the different religious rites or social functions such as weddings, *upanayana*, and other rites of passage ceremonies for Hindus (see Appendix 5: "Hindu Rites of Passage"), as well as the casting of horoscopes, matching them for matrimonial alliances, and so on. It also has a list of the popular feasts and festivals. What follows is a description of the contents of the almanac as it pertains to specifying the dates of religious functions.

Era

There are many eras in use in India. The one most commonly used by Hindus is called Śālivāhana Śaka, or Śaka Era (SE), with an epoch or starting date of 78 Common Era (CE) and named after a historical king in North India (Sewell and Dikshit 1996; Richards 2000; Kane 1974, 5:641–718). Thus the year 2000 CE is 1922 SE.

The *saṃvatsara*, or year, is named in a cycle from a group of sixty, which are shown in Table 1. For a discussion of this sixty-year cycle, see the work by Pandurang Vaman Kane (Kane 1974, 5:660). The beginning of the cycle with the year Prabhava follows the current South Indian convention; the North Indian list begins with the year Vijaya (Kane 1974, 5:661; Dershowitz and Reingold 1997, 121). The year 2000 CE was Vikrama, according to the South Indian list (Acharya 1996–7).

The Solar Calendar

The solar calendar is defined by the motion of the sun with respect to the stars and is approximately 365 days in length. The *saura māsa* (solar months) are named after the constellations of stars through which the sun passes. The names of the solar months are given in Table 2 in Sanskrit and Latin, along with the English translation of the Sanskrit names (Kane 1974, 5:562). Their duration varies from 29.3 to 31.6 days.

TABLE 1. Saṃvatsara

1. Prabhava	16. Citrabhānu	31. Hemalambi	46. Paridhāvi
2. Vibhava	17. Subhānu	32. Vilambi	47. Pramādi
3. Śukla	18. Tāraṇa	33. Vikāri	48. Ānanda
4. Pramoda	19. Pārthiva	34. Śārvari	49. Rākṣasa
5. Prajāpati	20. Vyaya	35. Plava	50. Anala/Nala
6. Aṅgiras	21. Sarvajit	36. Śubhakṛt	51. Piṅgala
7. Śrīmukha	22. Sarvadhāri	37. Śobhakṛt	52. Kālayukta
8. Bhāva	23. Virodhi	38. Krodhi	53. Siddhārtha
9. Yuva	24. Vikṛti	39. Viśvāvasu	54. Raudra
10. Dhātṛa	25. Khara	40. Parābhava	55. Durmati
11. Īśvara	26. Nandana	41. Plavaṅga	56. Dundubhi
12. Bahudhānya	27. Vijaya	42. Kīlaka	57. Rudhirodgāri
13. Pramāthi	28. Jaya	43. Saumya	58. Raktākṣa
14. Vikrama	29. Manmatha	44. Sādhāraṇa	59. Krodhana
15. Vṛṣa	30. Durmukha	45. Virodhakṛt	60. Kṣaya

TABLE 2. Solar Months, *Saura Māsa*, and the Signs of the Zodiac

Sanskrit	Latin	English
1. *Meṣa*	Aries	Ram
2. *Vṛṣabha*	Taurus	Bull
3. *Mithuna*	Gemini	Twins
4. *Karka*	Cancer	Crab
5. *Siṁha*	Leo	Lion
6. *Kanyā*	Virgo	Virgin
7. *Tulā*	Libra	Balance
8. *Vṛścika*	Scorpio	Scorpion
9. *Dhanus*	Sagittarius	Archer
10. *Makara*	Capricorn	Goat
11. *Kumbha*	Aquarius	Water carrier
12. *Mīna*	Pisces	Fishes

Uttarāyana and Dakṣiṇāyana The sun is at its southernmost position in the skies at the winter solstice, near December 21. It moves to its northernmost position at the summer solstice, near June 21. This northward progression of the sun is called *uttarāyana* and is considered to be a more auspicious period than the period of its southward movement, or *dakṣiṇāyana*, from the summer solstice to the next winter solstice. In the *Mahābhārata*, the hero Bhishma, who had been vouchsafed by the gods the power to choose the moment of his death, waits till the *uttarāyana*, to die. The Hindu almanac gives the beginning of *uttarāyana* for the 1996–1997 year as 14 January 1997 (Acharya 1996–7). This delay of about 24 days in the beginning of the northward progression of the sun, as given in Hindu calendars, is obviously wrong and is due to the neglect of the precession of equinoxes in the calendar calculations (Kane 1974, 5:222). This lack of synchronization of the calendar with the motion of the sun by about 24 days implies a slippage of the dates of all festivals with respect to the seasons by the same amount (Kane 1974, 5:717). This slippage, if not corrected, will get worse as time progresses.

Saṃkramaṇa, or Saṃkrānti The passage of the sun from one zodiac sign to the next is called a *saṃkramaṇa*, or *saṃkrānti*. Hence, there are 12 *saṃkrāntis* in a solar year. Of these, the solstitial, or *ayana saṃkrāntis*, are Makarasaṃkrānti (winter solstice, about December 21), at the beginning of *uttarāyana*, and Karkasaṃkrānti (summer solstice, about June 21), at the beginning of *dakṣiṇāyana*. Of these, the first is considered to be particularly auspicious, as it is the beginning of the *uttarāyana*. In the Śrī Kṛṣṇa Temple at Udupi, there is a great festival on this occasion every year. Madhvācāya, the founder of the Dvaita sect of Hinduism, established eight *maṭhas*, or monastic orders, and assigned them the responsibility of conducting worship at the Śrī Kṛṣṇa Temple and managing it. They assume this office for a period of two years each, in rotation, or *paryāya*. This transfer takes place during the Makarasaṃkrānti festival every other year. The equinoctial, or *viṣuva*, *saṃkrāntis* are Meṣasaṃkrānti (spring equinox, about March 21) and Tulāsaṃkrānti (autumnal equinox, about September 21), when the day and night are of equal duration. The dates of all the *saṃkrāntis* as given in the traditional almanacs occur 23 to 25 days later than their correct epochs, as mentioned earlier, and are in error.

The Lunar Calendar

In its passage across the skies, the moon passes through 27 asterisms, or *nakṣatras*, also called the lunar mansions. The system of *nakṣatras* is of ancient origin and is mentioned in the Vedic literature (Kane 1974, 5:495). This journey of the moon with respect to the stars (sidereal motion) takes about 27.3 days. The asterisms are listed in Table 3. For purposes of calculation, each of these lunar man-

TABLE 3. Nakṣatras or Lunar Mansions		
1. **Aśvinī**	10. **Maghā**	19. Mūla
2. Bharaṇī	11. Purvā (Phalgunī)	20. Pūrvāṣāḍhā
3. **Kṛttikā**	12. **Uttarā Phalgunī**	21. **Uttarāṣāḍhā**
4. Rohiṇī	13. Hasta	22. **Śravaṇa**
5. **Mṛgaśīrṣa**	14. **Citrā**	23. Dhaniṣṭhā
6. Ārdrā	15. Svātī	24. Śatabhiṣak
7. Punarvasū	16. **Viśākhā**	25. Pūrvā Bhādrapadā
8. **Puṣya**	17. Anurādhā	26. **Uttarā Bhādrapadā**
9. Āśleṣā	18. **Jyeṣṭhā**	27. Revatī

sions is assumed to have the same angular spread of 13°20′. Some of the older listings of the *nakṣatras* give 28, such as in the Atharva Veda with Abhijit added between Uttarāṣāḍhā and Śravaṇa (Kane 1974, 5:497). Also in these older compilations, the list begins with Kṛttikā and ends with Bharaṇī, while lists created after the third century CE follow the order shown in Table 3 (Kane 1974, 5:501–504). For a detailed discussion of the evolution of the *nakṣatra* system, see Kane.

The lunar calendar consists of 12 lunar months, *candra māsa*, of about 30 days each, with an intercalary (*adhika*) thirteenth month added every few years to bring the lunar calendar in step with the seasons. The lunar month ends with the new moon, *amāvāsyā*, according to the South Indian tradition. This convention for month ending is called *amānta*. In North India a convention for ending the month with the full moon is used and is called *pūrṇimānta*. These conventions should always be kept in mind in comparing dates of festivals in different parts of India. The day after the new moon is the beginning of the next month. The months are named by the *nakṣatras* in which a full moon occurs. These are shown in Table 3 in **bold**. Thus in the first month of the lunar year, the full moon occurs in the asterism Citrā and is called Caitra. The next month is Vaiśākha because the full moon occurs in Viśākhā, and so on. The lunar year begins in March/April, with the New Year's celebrations and the names of the lunar months and when they occur in the customary calendar are shown in Table 4.

The *ṛtu*, or seasons, are six in number and are as shown in Table 5. A few listings combine the last two seasons into a long winter, for a total of five seasons.

Each lunar month is divided into two halves: the bright half, *śukla pakṣa*, also called *śuddha*, when the moon is waxing, and the dark half, *kṛṣṇa pakṣa*, also called *bahula*, or *boḷa* in Konkani, when it is waning. The former is considered to be more auspicious than the latter.

TABLE 4. Lunar Months, *Candra Māsa*	
Sanskrit	Common Usage
1. Caitra	March/April
2. Vaiśākha	April/May
3. Jyeṣṭha	May/June
4. Āṣāḍha	June/July
5. Śrāvaṇa	July/August
6. Bhādrapada	August/September
7. Āśvina	September/October
8. Kārtika	October/November
9. Mārgaśira	November/December
10. Puṣya	December/January
11. Maghā	January/February
12. Phālguna	February/March

TABLE 5. Seasons of the Year			
Season	Meaning	Lunar Months	Common Usage
1. Vasanta	Spring	Caitra-Vaiśākha	April/May
2. Grīṣma	Hot	Jyeṣṭha-Āṣāḍha	June/July
3. Varṣa	Rainy	Śrāvaṇa-Bhādrapada	August/September
4. Śarad	Autumn	Āśvina-Kārtika	October/November
5. Hemanta	Winter	Mārgaśira-Puṣya	December/January
6. Śiśira	Frigid	Maghā-Phālguna	February/March

A lunar day is called a *tithi* (Table 6). It is defined as the time required by the moon to gain or lose 12°, or one-thirtieth of a circle, on the sun. The *tithi* allocated to a day is the one prevailing at sunrise. Because the movement of the moon in its orbit is not uniform, the duration of a *tithi* varies; so does the length of a solar day. Because of these variations, it is possible have up to three *tithis* in a single civil day—that is, from sunrise to sunrise—and conversely, a single *tithi* may extend over three days (Kane 1974, 5:68). There are fifteen of them in a *pakṣa*, or fortnight, and they are listed in Table 6 by ordinal numbers, with the fifteenth being called either the full moon, *pūrṇimā*, or *punnava*

TABLE 6. *Tithis* in a Lunar Fortnight
1. *Pratipadī*
2. *Dvitīyā*
3. *Tṛtīyā*
4. *Caturthī*
5. *Pañcamī*
6. *Ṣaṣṭī*
7. *Saptamī*
8. *Aṣṭamī*
9. *Navamī*
10. *Daśamī*
11. *Ekādaśī*
12. *Dvādaśī*
13. *Trayodaśī*
14. *Caturdaśī*
15. *Pūrṇimā* or *Amāvāsyā*

(Konkani), or the new moon, *amāvāsyā*, or *amāsa* (Konkani). The first day of the lunar fortnight is called *pratipadā* or *pratipadī*, which has been Konkanized to *pāḍvo*, as in *Samsāra Pāḍvo* for New Year's Day (Janardhan 1999, 390).

Weekdays, or *vāra*, are named after the visible planets and are as shown in Table 7.

TABLE 7. *Vāra*, or Weekdays	
Common Usage	Sanskrit
Sunday	Ravivāra or Ādityavāra
Monday	Somavāra or Candravāra
Tuesday	Maṅgalavāra or Bhaumavāra
Wednesday	Budhavāra or Saumyavāra
Thursday	Guruvāra or Bṛhaspativāra
Friday	Śukravāra
Saturday	Śanivāra

After having described the various terms used in a Hindu lunisolar calendar, I can now describe the contents of the *pañcāṅga*. For more details, see Kane (Kane 1974, 5:666).

Each page of the almanac covers a period of fifteen days. At the top of a page are given the *saṃvatsara*, the lunar month, the *pakṣa*, the *uttarāyana/ dakṣiṇāyana*, and the *ṛtu*. For each day, the following information, which forms the five members of the almanac, is given: the *tithi*, the *vāra*, the *nakṣatra*, the *yoga*, and the *karaṇa*. I have defined the first three; the last two are strictly of interest for astrology. The *yoga* is not an observable and is calculated from the sum of the longitudes of the sun and the moon. There are 27 *yogas* in a lunar month. A *karaṇa* is half a *tithi*, and there are 60 *karaṇas* in a month. If you are interested in learning more about these, the works by Kane and by Robert Sewell and Sankara Balkrishna Dikshit are good sources (Kane 1974, 5:704; Sewell and Dikshit 1996). In addition, the almanac gives information on the positions of the planets in the zodiac, their retrograde motion, lunar and solar eclipses, and much more data for astrological purposes.

Finally, a few comments on the status of Hindu almanacs in India are in order. There are about 30 calendars in use in India (Kane 1974, 5:641; Richards 2000, 173). As a rule, they do not agree with one another because of different methods of approximations in their calculations. Indian almanacs have not allowed for the precession of equinoxes in the calculation of *saṃkrāntis* for the past 1,600 years or more; hence they have been slipping with respect to the seasons (Sewell and Dikshit 1996, 10). Past suggestions that modern astronomical methods should be used in almanac calculations have not been adopted (Kane 1974, 5:710-3). To resolve almanac anarchy, the government of India appointed a Calendar Reform Committee in 1952. The committee recommendations can be found in its report (1955); Kane summarized them, listing the main recommendations for both the civil and the religious calendars (Kane 1974, 5:714). The report recommends that the present discrepancy of about 24 days between the calendars and the motion of the sun be maintained as a constant difference and that every effort be made to stop its future increase. This recommendation, which perhaps is a compromise between the conservatives and progressives, does not unfortunately solve the problem. If adopted, it would mean that the Indian calendars would never agree with observations and that the present discrepancy of 24 days would be perpetuated. In short, if the recommendation is adopted, it will be an eternal monument to this discrepancy. It makes better sense to admit the present discrepancy as a mistake, zero out the discrepancy, and adopt modern methods of calendar computation that agree precisely with observations. Calculation of the almanac with the inclusion of the precession of equinoxes can be easily programmed on a computer and should not involve much effort. Some degree of uniformity in traditional calendars is highly desirable. However, the multiplicity of discrepant Hindu calendars continues. Part of the reason for allowing this problem to continue without a resolution appears to be financial, because the publication of each version of the calendar is a principal source of livelihood for its author.

Feasts and Festivals

The following is a description of principal feasts and festivals of the Hindu religious year, beginning with New Year's celebrations, including festival date according to the lunar religious calendar. Kane's book is a treasurehouse of information on all of the feasts and festivals and is indispensable for their detailed study. He also lists the rites that are obligatory, *nitya*, and those that are optional, *kāmya*, to Hindus in general. The most extensive list of *vratas* and festivals (*utsava*) is by Kane; they number in thousands, and Kane includes a caveat that even this list should not be considered complete (Kane 1974, 5:253–462). The specific observances vary, depending on the region, the almanac, caste and subcaste, community, and family traditions. Om Lata Bahadur has some interesting observations on North Indian traditions, whereas Kane's approach is all-inclusive (Bahadur 2002). The lunar calendar for dates given in the next section follows the South Indian custom of ending the month with the *amāvāsyā*, or the *amānta* reckoning, while the North Indian tradition ends the month with the full moon, or the *pūrṇimānta* reckoning. Hence, in the two systems, the names of the month could be different for *kṛṣṇa pakṣa* dates, whereas they are the same for the *śukla pakṣa*. This difference, which adds one more qualification to a complex subject, should be kept in mind always.

The names of the special dishes made at the feasts accompanying these religious observances are given in Konkani. Their recipes may be found in the three books by J.V. Shenoy, which are either in Kannada or in Konkani with Kannada script (Shenoy 1988; 1999; 2004). They are usually determined by the fruits and vegetables that are in season and the ubiquity of the coconut, which plays such an important part in all Konkani South Kanara cooking.

Quite a few of the Konkani dishes, such as *āppo* (the *apūpa* of the *Ṛgveda*), *mōdaka*, and *pāyasa*, have ancient names, some going back to the Vedic age. Over time, the ingredients of these dishes as well as their methods of preparation have changed. In *Indian Food: A Historical Companion*, K.T. Achaya discusses the origin and evolution of foods of India from ancient times to the modern age, using a number of sources from literature, archeology, epigraphy, anthropology, philology, botany, and genetics (Achaya 1994). This book is a valuable collection of information on the foods we eat today, in the context of history.

In the following section, *Ś* = *śukla pakṣa*, the bright half of a lunar month, and *K* = *kṛṣṇa pakṣa*, the dark half.

Candra Yugādi, Caitra Pratipadī, or Saṃvatsara Pratipadī, or Savnsāra Pāḍvo (Konkani), Caitra Ś 1 (March/April)

New Year's Day, called Candra Yugādi, Caitra Pratipadī, Saṃvatsara Pratipadī, or Savnsāra Pāḍvo (Konkani), is considered one of the three most auspicious days in the Hindu religious calendar (Kane 1974, 5:81). The other two are Vijay-ādaśamī, Āśvina *Ś* 10, and Dhānya Lakṣmī Pūjā/Bali Pratipadī, Kārtika *Ś* 1 (Kane 1974, 5:189).

In the olden days, when I was young, it was customary to buy new clothes needed for the whole of the new year and wear some of them on the New Year's Day. Some families observed the tradition of symbolic offering, *vāḍappa*, of the new clothes to the Manes (dead ancestors). Usually this offering of new clothes is made only in remembrance of women who died with their husband still alive, or *ayyapaṇā bāila maniṣi*. A thread from the new sari is burned as a symbolic offering to the dead person. A mixture, *panckadāyī*, of beaten rice (*phovu*), brown sugar, grated coconut, cardamom, and other ingredients is offered in front of the family shrine, *devākūḍa*, along with betel leaf, *vīḍo*, to the ancestors, and then all of the family members bow to the family shrine and then partake of the offering. This is a family event carried out without involving a priest or any elaborate ceremony. In some cases, a male ancestor may also be included with the offering of male clothing (*pudvẽ*). In our family home, *mhālgaḍyalẽ ghara*, at Mulki, a *vāḍappa* is made to all the dead unmarried male ancestors, *brahmacāri*, on New Year's Day, and a similar offering of dhoti and *sāri*, *joḍo kāppaḍa*, is made to dead married couples on the second day after New Year's. It is also customary to listen to the highlights of the new year as read aloud from the new almanac (*pañcāṅga āikucẽ*).

An elaborate lunch with many special dishes, and a nap afterward, marks the New Year's celebrations. These dishes are *thenḍlẽ bibbyā upkari*; *āmbaṭa* or *yogyaratna* (*avial* in Kerala, Konkanized to *valvala*) of vegetables in season; and assorted *phoḍis*, *khoṭṭo*, *canẽ daḷicẽ maḍgaṇẽ*, or *goḍśẽ*. A mixture of brown sugar (*gōḍa*) and the bitter neem leaves, symbolic of the joys and sorrows of life, is fried in clarified butter and added to one of the traditional dishes or eaten separately.

Rāma Navamī Mahotsava, from Caitra Ś 4 to Caitra Ś 10 (March/April)

Rāma Navamī Mahotsava (Kane 1974, 5:84) is perhaps the most elaborate and grand function that is observed at the GSB temple in Mulki. Along with customary religious observances, it also involves some elements of modified Vedic ceremonies, or what is left of them. The festival begins five days before the apex of ceremonies on Rāma Navamī proper.

On Caitra *Ś* 5, there is the Dhvaja Ārohaṇa, or Ceremony of Flag-Raising. The flag of Viṣṇu, with images of Hanumān and Garuḍā on either side, is raised to the top of the flagpole (*dhvajastambha*) at the entrance to the temple. It is actually a heavy oblong of beaten silver with these images in relief. The flagpole is a single tree trunk about thirty feet tall, fixed to a concrete base and completely enclosed in silver plate, with mythological figures shown in relief.

Caitra *Ś* 9 is the birthday of Lord Rāma, the seventh incarnation of Viṣṇu, and is the climax of ceremonies with an elaborate cart festival. The processional image, *utsava mūrti*, is taken out on the largest wooden cart, *Brahma ratha*. There are many other subsidiary processions involving other transports, and circumambulations round the main temple.

Concluding ceremonies are held on Caitra *Ś* 10. The sacrificial ceremonies are ended (*yajña visarjana*), the flag of Viṣṇu is lowered, and there are many processions at the end of the festivities (*utsava*). The concluding bath, *avabhṛtha*, at the end of solemn Vedic sacrifices has morphed into the current merrymaking in which devotees douse each other with *vokkuḷa*.

As part of the temple ceremonies, there are *samarādhanā* for thousands of devotees from out of town, the locals, and others. Cooks who specialize in preparations for thousands at a time are brought in, and their dishes have a special flavor, *samrādānyē jevṇā rūci*, that is impossible to duplicate at home. Hence, most people do a minimum of cooking at home during these festivities and instead eat at the communal feast.

Meṣa Saṃkramaṇa corresponds to the spring equinox, on or about March 21. This marks Saura Yugādi, or the solar New Year (Kane 1974, 5:211).

For those who follow the solar calendar, in some parts of India, this marks the beginning of a new year. In our ancestral home in Mulki, yearly offerings are made to the three family spirits: Bhūtās, Brahmaru, and the Gooliga.

Akṣayya Tṛtīyā/Paraśurāma Jayantī, Vaiśākha Ś 3 (April/May)

Akṣayya ("that which is inexhaustible") Tṛtīyā ("third") is a day of fasting and worship of Vāsudeva, another name of Kṛṣṇa (Kane 1974, 5:88–9). People are supposed to obtain inexhaustible rewards for whatever alms that they they give or sacrifices that they make on this day. Paraśurāma Jayantī is the birthday of Paraśurāma (Rāma with the axe), sixth incarnation of Viṣṇu, born a Brāhmaṇa, the fifth son of Jamadagni and his wife, Reṇukā.

There are *utsava* and *samarādhanā* in the temple at Mulki to mark these festivals. There are usually no family rituals in individual homes.

Narasiṁha Caturdaśī or Nṛsiṁha Jayantī, Vaiśākha Ś 14 (April/May)

The epiphany of Lord Narasiṁha (Man-Lion), the fourth incarnation of Viṣṇu, occurred on the evening of the 14 April in the Svātī *nakṣatra* (Kane 1974, 5:329) and is celebrated as Narasiṁha Caturdaśī, or Nṛsiṁha Jayantī.

Hiraṇyakaśipu (Golden Vesture), a Daitya (son of Diti) and a demon, was a devotee of Śiva. After observing many austerities, he obtained from Śiva a boon that protected him from being killed by man or beast, during day or night, inside or outside a house. Armed with this and other boons he had received, he conquered the very heavens, the abode of the gods, drove them out, and ruled there. He also persecuted his son, Prahlāda (Great Joy), who had become an ardent devotee of Viṣṇu, under the following circumstances: When Kayādhu, wife of Hiraṇyakaśipu, was pregnant with Prahlāda, Hiraṇyakaśipu went away to practice austerities. His foes attacked and defeated his armies and were about to kill Kayādhu. Sage Nāradā intervened and sheltered her in his hermitage till the return of her husband. Thus Prahlāda, as a baby in the womb and as a child growing up in Nāradā's hermitage, was exposed to the worship of Viṣṇu and became a great devotee of his, thus invoking his father's wrath. A different version ascribes his devotion to the merit gained in an earlier birth when he was called Soma Śarma, fifth son of Śiva Śarma. His four elder brothers were devotees of Viṣṇu and were ultimately united with him. The youngest son wanted to emulate his brothers and performed many austerities. However, he allowed himself to be disturbed by the atrocities committed by the Daityas and was born as one of them. He sided with his kin in their fight against the gods and was killed in this battle by the discus of Viṣṇu; he was then reborn as a son of Hiraṇyakaśipu. Hiraṇyakaśipu's many attempts to convert his son to the worship of Śiva were in vain. In desperation, he challenged his son's lord to a battle and wanted to know where he could find him. On being told that Viṣṇu was everywhere in the universe, Hiraṇyakaśipu smote a pillar in his palace with his mace. Viṣṇu appeared as Lord Narasiṁha at dusk and on the doorsill killed the evil demon with his claws, freeing his devotee from his persecutor.

For a further discussion of this, the fourth *avatāra* of Viṣṇu, and translations of its accounts in the different *purāṇas* (epics), see the work by Deborah A. Soifer (Soifer 1991).

There are special rituals and sacrifices (*yajña*, or *homa*), followed by an *utsava* and a *samarādhanā*, because the presiding deity at the Mulki temple is Ugra Narasiṁha. There are no family rituals in individual homes.

Buddha Pūrṇimā, or Vaiśākha Pūrṇimā (April/May)

According to the Buddhist tradition, Siddhārta Gautama, the Buddha, was born, attained enlightenment, and entered into *nirvāṇa*, all on the day called Buddha

Pūrṇimā, or Vaiśākha Pūrṇimā (Kane 1974, 5:356). Because the Buddha is now considered to be an incarnation of Viṣṇu, there are special celebrations involving rituals, an *utsava*, and a *samarādhanā* in the Mulki Temple. This marks the end of the *utsava* season in the temple; the next beginning of the *utsava* season is with the Tulasī Pūjā, Kārtika *Ś* 12, which is also the beginning of the marriage season for Hindus.

Daśaharā, Jyeṣṭha Ś 10 (April/May)

Observance of the ritual of Daśaharā is supposed to destroy ten sins listed in Manu 12.5–7 and divided into those of the body (taking things not given, committing violence against the law, having sex with another man's wife), mind (preoccupation with things belonging to others, what is undesirable, and adhering to falsehoods), and speech (verbal abuse, lies, slander, and unbridled chatter) (Kane 1974, 5:90; Doniger and Smith 1991, 278). Note that this ritual is different from the Dasarā festival observed on Vijaya Daśamī.

Vaṭasāvitrīvrata, or Sāvitrīvrata, Jyeṣṭha Pūrṇimā (May/June)

On Vaṭasāvitrīvrata, or Sāvitrīvrata, women whose husbands are living perform a rite in memory of Sāvitrī, considered in Hindu tradition to be an ideal of wifely devotion, or *pativratā*. They pray for good health and long life for their husbands. Sāvitrī married Satyavat, whose death one year after their wedding had been predicted. As a result of the austerities that she observes, she pleases Yama, the god of death, who grants her several boons and restores her husband's life. The *vaṭa* tree is part of the ritual to commemorate the fact that Satyavat took shelter under such a tree when he felt sick and the moment of his death approached (Kane 1974, 5:91–4).

Cāturmāsya Vrata, Āṣāḍha Ś 11 through Kārtika Ś 12, (June/July through October/November)

The observance of Cāturmāsya Vrata extends over four months of the rainy season (Kane 1974, 5: 95, 109–12, 122–3). In ancient India, when most of the land was covered with dense forests, the rains were heavy and made travel and most normal activities difficult or impossible. Hence, for all except the farmers, the rainy season was a time for remaining close to home or the shelter of a monastery and a time for contemplation and study. These reduced activities were later associated with the four-month-long sleep of Viṣṇu. Hence,

1. Āṣāḍha *Ś* 11, Śayana Ekādaśī, or Śayanī: Viṣṇu falls asleep.
2. Bhādrapada *Ś* 11, Parivartinī: He turns around in his sleep.
3. Kārtika *Ś* 11, Prabodhinī: He wakes up.
4. Kārtika *Ś* 12, Puṇyā Utthānadvādaśī: He gets up from his couch, ending Cāturmāsya.

Ekādaśī, the eleventh day of every fortnight, is observed as a day of fasting, *upavasa*, or *upāsa* (Konkani), by pious Hindus. This involves not eating any cooked food; only fruits and milk are allowed, and only in moderation. In practice in South India, where rice is the staple, people abstain from rice for the fast and usually eat wheat preparations, sometimes *not* in moderation.

Karka Saṃkramaṇa, or Dakṣiṇāyana Ārambha (June–July)

Karka Saṃkramaṇa, or Dakṣiṇāyana Ārambha, is the summer solstice that occurs on or about June 21 and marks the beginning of the *dakṣiṇāyana* of the sun (Kane 1974, 5:211).

Guru Pūrṇimā, or Āṣāḍha Pūrṇimā (June–July)

Guru Pūrṇimā, or Āṣāḍha Pūrṇimā, is a day of remembrance of one's gurus and the immeasurable debt owed them. A guru is any person—young, old, wise, foolish, learned, naive—from whom one learns something. The knowledge gained can be simple or sublime, esoteric or exoteric, complex or the simple skills of everyday life. In the Hindu tradition, gurus are to be revered only next to one's parents. While parents give us body and mind, it is the guru who makes a civilized person out of us. Our parents, from whom we learn so many things before the beginning of formal education, are our first gurus. Our gurus are also considered to be our spiritual parents. It is possible that in the olden days, fathers were the teachers of the Vedas for their children (Kane 1974, 2:324). Manu 2.227–237 identifies the father, mother, and teacher as the three highest gurus; extols their virtues; and lists our obligations to them (Doniger and Smith 1991, 40–1). We owe our teachers *guru-śuśrūṣā*: reverence, attentiveness, service, dutifulness, and obedience, not servility (Lipner 1994, 190).

Nāga Pañcamī, Śrāvaṇa Ś 5 (July/August)

Nāga Pañcamī celebrates the worship of cobras or their granite representations, *nāgā phāttoru*, usually established at the roots of an *aśvattha* (*Ficus religiosa*) tree or near a pond of water attached to a temple (Kane 1974, 5:124). The *Ṛgveda* contains no reference to snake worship. As a matter of fact, cobras were killed in a great *yajña*, offered by King Janamejaya in ancient times. It is possible that the worship of cobras as a totem is of ancient origin and pre-Aryan. Such totems were later incorporated into orthodox Hinduism as transports, *vāhana*, of the different gods in the Hindu pantheon. Worship and propitiation of *nāgās* is supposed to be particularly efficacious in begetting children; the phallic symbolism is obvious.

Special dishes prepared for this occasion are *pathraḍo, dhavẽ khirī, pānpāttoḷī*, and *khoṭṭo.*

Bhajana Saptāha Ārambha, Śrāvaṇa Ś 5 (July–August)

Bhajana Saptāha, the continuous worship of Lord Kṛṣṇa as Viṭṭala, by singing songs in his praise, *bhajana*, lasts for seven days (*saptāha*) at the Śrī Venkaṭaramaṇa Temple in Udupi. Groups of people from different parts of the town organize parties that take two-hour shifts singing devotional songs, circumambulating, and dancing around a big bronze lamp set in the middle of the floor. It ends on the seventh day with a celebration of *vokkuḷa* in commemoration of Kṛṣṇa's childhood pranks. Earthenware pots containing colored water and suspended from a high point in front of the temple are broken by milling groups of young men, who get thoroughly doused by the pots' contents.

Ṛg Upākarma, Śrāvaṇa Ś 14 or Ś 15 (July/August)

Upākarma means the opening or beginning of Vedic studies for the year, and *utsarjana*, its cessation, about six months later. For GSBs who are all Ṛgvedins and followers of *Āśvalāyana Gṛhyasūtra*, if the *upākarma* is on Śrāvaṇa *Ś* 15, then the *utsarjana* would be on Maghā *Ś* 15 (Kane 1974, 2:807). In between, Vedic studies were stopped on certain prohibited days for short periods of time for a number of reasons (Kane 1974, 2:393–402). All of these details are only of academic interest these days because amongst most GSBs, formal Vedic studies have ceased.

On *upākarma*, the seven sages, *ṛṣis*, are worshipped, and the sacred threads worn by Brāhmaṇa initiates, one for unmarried men and two for married men, are changed, after a *yajña* in which oblations of ghee are offered. The sacred thread is normally worn diagonally across the chest, over the left shoulder, and passing under the right arm. While one is performing funeral rites or making the annual offerings to ancestors, it is worn over the right shoulder and under the left arm. In some cases, it could also be worn round the neck like a garland.

In the feast that follows these ceremonies, the following special dishes are served: *pathraḍo*, *khoṭṭo*, *śevyã kheeri*, and *goḍśẽ* with cashews.

Vara Lakṣmī Vrata/Rakṣābandhana, Samudrapūjā, Śrāvaṇa Pūrṇimā (July/August)

According to Hindu legends, Brahmā, the creator, assigned a special festival to each of the four classes, *varṇa*, for their very own (Kane 1974, 5:127): Rakṣābandhana (tying an amulet or a bracelet), also called Vara Lakṣmī Vrata, to the Brāhmaṇas; Dasarā to the Kṣatriyas; Divāli to the Vaiśyas; and Holikā to the Śūdras (Kane 1974, 5:200).

Indrāṇī, wife of Indra, tied on her husband's right hand a protective amulet or bracelet that enabled him to vanquish the Asuras (demons). This tradition has continued in parts of India as Śrāvaṇa Pūrṇimā, when women tie silken bracelets on the wrists of their brothers or brother-surrogates, wish them good luck and prosperity, and receive gifts in return.

Kane also mentions the tradition of offering flowers and a coconut to the sea god Varuṇa on Samudrapūjā. On this day the seafaring people, including Muslims and Parsis, of the Konkan and Malabar coasts, pray for calm and safe seas (Kane 1974, 5:128).

Kṛṣṇa Janmāṣṭamī, Śrāvaṇa K 8 (July/August)

Kṛṣṇa Janmāṣṭamī is the birthday of Lord Kṛṣṇa, the eighth incarnation of Viṣṇu (Kane 1974, 5:128). When I was in school in Udupi, the schools were closed in the afternoon on the eve of this festival. One is supposed to fast (that is, not eat rice or rice products) in preparation for the evening festivities. We would spend the afternoon firing our new peṭnoḷi, resulting in many a sore palm. In the evening, after a bath, the men and boys would participate in the main ceremony of the day at the *devākūḍa* and offer *tulasī* (holy basil) leaves while reciting the 1,000 names of Viṣṇu, called Viṣṇu *sahasranāma*. At the conclusion of this part of worship, the officiating priest decorates the huge pile of *tulasī* leaves with flowers. This is followed by a milk offering, *arghya*, to Candra and to Lord Kṛṣṇa. Each person makes this offering thrice.

In this *pūjā*, or worship ritual, all of the preparations for an elaborate feast are offered to him, including many sweets, such as the different *laḍḍūs* (ball-shaped sweets), which are supposed to be his favorites. Afterward, all of us used to sit down for long feast late at night. The special dishes are *gajbajẽ*, *āmbata* (a vegetable dish), *phoḍi* of assorted vegetables, *khoṭṭo*, *tīḷā unḍo*, *navanēta* (fresh butter, flavored with roasted black *til* seeds), *pañckadāyī*, and *rossa phovu* (coconut milk, brown sugar, cardamom, and *phovu*).

Cuḍyeci āni Humbrā Pūjā, Śrāvaṇa Fridays and Sundays (July/August)

The interesting ritual of Cuḍyeci āni Humbrā Pūjā is performed entirely by the women of the family whose husbands are alive, *ayyapaṇā bāila maniṣī*, without involving a professional priest. Most probably, it is special to the GSB community, because I have not been able to find a parallel observance in Kane's opus. The worship of the doorsill, *humboru*, as a seat of Śrī Lakṣmī, the goddess of fortune, is a part of this ritual. That is why one should never step on a doorsill or even accidentally kick it. The ritual is also observed in parts of Karnataka as *hostilu pūje*. Further details may be found in the works by Ramabai, alias Ammanna (2004), and B.K.V. Pai (2003).

The green tips of *darbha* grass, *dirbhāṅkuru*, are collected, along with the many wild and cultivated flowers that grow in profusion in the rainy season, to form small, beautiful bunches of multicolored flowers. These are the *cūḍi*, which play a prominent part in the ritual. The worship takes place round the *tulasī* plant that is in the front yard of every Hindu house. The ceremony is usually performed before midday. After offering the *cūḍi* to *tulasī*, circumambulating it five times, and bowing to the sun, the women worship Śrī Lakṣmī at the doorsill of the main entrance to the house. Similar worship is also conducted at the *devākūḍa*. The younger women in the group then offer the *cūḍi* to the more senior women and ask for their blessings, or *pāyu dorcē*. It is also customary to mail the *cūḍi* to one's relatives in other parts of India or abroad, as a sign of love and affection.

Gaurītṛtīyā, or Vāyṇā Pūjā, Bhādrapada Ś 3, and Gaṇeśa Caturthī (Konkani: Cavati), Bhādrapada Ś 4 (August/September)

The parents of Gaṇeśa, Gaurī and Śiva, are worshipped on the first day of festivities of Gaurītṛtīyā, or Vāyṇā Pūjā (Konkani). The next day is Gaṇeśa Caturthī (or Cavati in Konkani), which marks the epiphany of Lord Gaṇeśa, the god of wisdom, the presiding deity of literature, the giver of success, and the destroyer of obstacles (Kane 1974, 5:145–9, 296; Fuller 2004). The celebrations could last from one to ten days. We did not observe this festival in our home in Udupi, because ours was a cadet branch of the family, so all of the ceremonies took place in the senior branch at our ancestral home in Mulki. The celebrations in Ananthayya's home were grand. A few months before the ceremony, Ananthayya would order the clay image of the god from artisans who specialized in this craft. The wooden seat on which the clay image was formed was given to the artist, with specifications as to its size, body coloring, and so on. Our image always conformed to the traditional specifications, having a deep vermilion (*sindūra*) color, four arms with the proper accoutrements, and a proper benign facial expression. In the 1940s, during India's struggle for independence, the image of Gaṇeśa was used to make political statements without fear of immediate reprisals from the British Raj. The tradition of using the Gaṇeśa festival for political purposes was started in Mahārāṣṭra by Bal Gangadhar Tilak and had spread to other parts of India.

Early on the morning of the festival, I would go with Ananthayya to fetch our Gaṇeśa. In the front yard of the artist's house, there were hundreds of images of different sizes, poses, and colors all ready to go. We would finally locate ours, and a laborer would be hired to carry it home. In Ananthayya's home, the image would be installed in the front veranda, on a large table, and my grandfather Madhava would officiate. There were two *pūjās* during the day, one in the afternoon and the last one at night. The special dishes cooked for the festival were offered to the Lord, and then there was a grand feast. The afternoon was devoted to going round the city, to see as many Gaṇeśas as possible. In each house, the image would be placed in the entrance hall so that visitors had easy access to it. Visitors would step in, look over the display of the image, add it to their statistics, and move on. In some houses, people would offer a *laḍḍu*, a handful of *pañckadāyī*, or a small piece of sugarcane as *prasāda.* Kids would then compare notes, ticking off the number of images they saw, with special mention of some spectacular displays or a politically motivated Gaṇeśa spinning at a wheel or wearing a Gāndhi cap. After the evening worship, it was time to bid good-bye to the Lord till the next year. The image was taken to the back of the house and placed on the wall surrounding a well in the backyard. After some final ceremonies, and an *ārti,* it was consigned to the water in the well, to shouts of "Govindā, Go-ovindā-ā. . . . " As a kid, I always used to feel so sad at Lord Gaṇeśa's departure!

The special dishes for Cavati are *pathraḍo, khoṭṭo, mōdaka, āppo, pañckadāyī, sukrunḍo, cākkulī, tīḷā unḍo* with *lāyye piṭṭo, pāttolī, āmbaṭa, sukhẽ, āmbyā gojju,* and *phovā kheerī.*

Ṛṣi Pañcamī, Bhādrapada Ś 5 (August/September)

The rite of Ṛṣi Pañcamī is in honor of the seven sages, *Saptarṣis,* of Hindu mythology (Kane 1974, 5:149). These legends are of great antiquity and might have been borrowed from the Sumerian tradition. The sages are the sons of Brahma, the creator, and the list of their names varies, depending on the source. Though the original list included only seven, later on it was expanded to include as many as twelve of these worthies. It is customary to include Arundhatī, the wife of Vasiṣṭha, in this list. The list of these sages, who are generally identified with the cosmic principles, is given in the *Mahābhārata* as follows: Marīci ("Light"), Atri ("Devourer"), Aṅgiras ("Fiery"), Pulaha ("Bridger of Space"), Kratu ("Inspiration"), Pulastya ("Smooth Hair"), and Vasiṣṭha ("Owner of Wealth"). Their respective wives are Sambhūti ("Fitness"), Anasūyā ("Without Spite"), Lajjā ("Modesty"), Kṣamā ("Forgiveness"), Sannati ("Humility"), Prīti ("Love"), and Arundhatī ("Faithfulness") (Daniélou 1964, 317). The identification of the seven sages, plus Arundhatī, with the stars of the constellation Big Bear (Ursa Major, or UMa) or the Big Dipper, and as given by astronomer/astrologer Varāhamihira according to Vṛddha Garga, is as follows: starting from the tip of the handle of the Big Dipper in the east, Marīci (UMa η, Alkaid or Benetnasch), Vasiṣṭha (UMa ζ, Mizar) plus Arundhatī (80 UMa, Alcor), Aṅgiras (UMa ε, Alioth), Atri (UMa δ, Megrez), Pulastya (UMa γ, Phachd), Pulaha (UMa β, Marak), and Kratu (UMa α, Dubhe), ending finally with the lip of the dipper in the west (Mitchiner 1982, 274). The additional names in parentheses for each star are those assigned by Arab astronomers (Murdin 2001; Illingworth and Clark 2000). As part of wedding ceremonies, it is customary to point out the polestar (*dhruva nakṣatra*) and Arundhatī to the new bride as models of constancy and wifely devotion (Kane 1974, 2:535). This ceremony is called Dhruvārundhatī Darśana.

Ananta Caturdaśī (Konkani: Nōpi), Bhādrapada Ś 14 (August/September)

Pūjā of Ananta Caturdaśī consists of the worship of Hari ("Remover") as Ananta ("Infinite") while wearing a holy bracelet, *kaṅkaṇa*, of cotton or silk thread twisted into fourteen knots and dyed with saffron (Kane 1974, 5:151). These knots are supposed to symbolize the fourteen worlds created by Hari. An image of Hari made from *darbhā* grass is placed in a silver jar, *anantā kaleśa*, and worshipped.

The special dishes are *theryā āḷāvati*, *mūgā ghaśī*, *āllyā thāmbaḷī*, *kārāte-āmbaḍya ghaśī*, fourteen different types of *phodi*, and fourteen different types of sweets, including *dūdhapāku*, *curmunḍo*, *āppo*, *tīḷā unḍo*, *ceppi roṭṭi*, and *sākre roṭṭi*.

Sarva Pitṛ Śrāddha/Mahālayaśrāddha, Bhādrapada Amāvāsyā (August/September)

The dark half of Bhādrapada, or Mahālaya, is considered to be a festive time for the Manes and particularly propitious for the performance of the rite of Sarva Pitṛ Śrāddha (Kane 1973, 4:530). The Mahālayaśrāddha should follow the procedures of a Pārvaṇaśrāddha—that is, the *śrāddha* that is performed on a full or a new moon (Kane 1973, 4:532). This rite is all-inclusive and is meant for the benefit of paternal and maternal ancestors and their wives, other relatives, married and unmarried men (*brahmacāri*), friends, *ācāryas* (spiritual guides), *upādhyāyas* (teachers), gurus (literally "heavy" or "weighty"; heavy with wisdom), and their pupils (Kane 1973, 4: 530–3).

See "*Śrāddha* Observed on the *Tithi* of the Anniversary of the Death of an Ancestor" in this appendix for special dishes for the feast.

Navarātra or Durgotsava or Durgāpūjā, Āśvina Ś 1–Āśvina Ś 9 (September/October)

1. Navarātri Ārambha, Navē Jevcē (Konkani), Āśvina *Ś* 1
2. Lalithā Pañcamī, Āśvina *Ś* 5
3. Kuladevatā (Mahālasā) Ārādhana, Āśvina *Ś* 6
4. Durgāṣṭamī, Āśvina *Ś* 8
5. Mahānavamī, Āśvina *Ś* 9

Navarātra, or Durgāpūjā, is a nine-day festival celebrating the victory of the goddess Devī ("Resplendent One"), Durgā ("Beyond Reach"), or Lalithā ("Playful") over the evil demons Mahiṣāsura, Caṇḍa, Muṇḍa, Śumbha, and Niśumbha (Kane 1974, 5:154; Kinsley 1988; Fuller 2004). Goddess worship accompanied by animal sacrifices appears to be of ancient origin, certainly pre-Āryan, and it was later incorporated into mainstream Hinduism. The gods of the Vedas were mostly male and were later married onto the various goddesses already in place. Totem worship of different animals was also absorbed into Hinduism, with the animals becoming the transports of the gods. The five days in the preceding list are special in the nine-day festival of Navarātra and are devoted to the special worship of Durgā's different aspects, or *kalā*. Durgāpūjā is perhaps the most important festival in a Bengali year.

Because our family deity, or *kuladevatā*, is Mahālasā, a form of Durgā, there are special rites on Āśvina *Ś* 6 at our ancestral home in Mulki involving her worship, with special honors, called *hōnṭi bhorcẽ*, bestowed on five women (married [*suvāsinī*] or unmarried [*kumārī*]) and appropriate honors bestowed on five men (Brāhmaṇa).

The first day of Navarātri is also called Navẽ Jevcẽ, which means "eating the newly harvested grain," because the new rice crop is brought in, cooked, and eaten. Sheaves of rice stalks are collected and blessed. They are then enclosed in mango, jackfruit, and bamboo leaves and tied to various containers such as jewelry boxes, money boxes, and containers for storing rice, to ensure plenty for the coming year.

The special dishes cooked for this festival are *yogyaratna*, *kheeri* with new rice, *kākkambi*, *punvoḍo*, and *rasvoḍo*.

Vijaya Daśamī, or Dasarā/Āyudha Pūjā, and Śāradā Visarjana, Āśvina Ś 10 (September/October)

Vijaya Daśamī ("Victorious Tenth") is considered to be one of the three most auspicious days in the Hindu religious calendar, the other two being the New Year's Day, Candra Yugādi (Caitra *Ś* 1), and Dhānya Lakṣmī Pūjā/Bali Pratipadī (Kārtika *Ś* 1). In ancient times, kings worshipped their weaponry, Āyudha Pūjā, praying that they would be victorious, and began their military expeditions on this occasion. In modern times, people symbolically worship the tools of their trade and call it Āyudha Pūjā, though no weapons are involved. Lord Rāma conquered Laṅkā on this day, after killing Rāvaṇā. In northern India, the Rāmalīlā celebrations honoring Lord Rāma's triumph are observed for ten days and culminate in the burning of the effigies of Rāvaṇā and his associates and in a display of fireworks. Dasarā celebrations lasting many days used to be observed in the former princely states of Mysore, Barodā, and others, accompanied by religious rites and elaborate processions of pomp and circumstance made possible by the ruling house of the *mahārāja* (Sampath 2008). Dasarā may have its origins as a harvest festival, because new crops are brought in, making military expeditions possible. Later on, it might have become a religious celebration to display the power of the ruling dynasty (Kane 1974, 5:188; Fuller 2004, 114–21; Sampath 2008, 685–8). This is also the day when the Devī Śāradā, invoked during the nine-day festival departs, is sent away (*visarjana*) by her devotees with proper rites and the clay image is consigned to a body of water, such as a river, a lake, or a well (Kane 1974, 5:175–7).

Dīpāvali, or Divāli (Festival of Lights), Āśvina K 13–Kārtika Ś 2 (September/November)

The joyous festival Dīpāvali, or Divāli, can be observed for a maximum of five days but often is celebrated for three days (Āśvina *K* 14–Kārtika *Ś* 1) with displays of decorative lighting, fireworks, feasting, and general celebrations. According to Kane, the whole festival comprises five principal items spread over five days: the worship of wealth, the celebration of Viṣṇu's victory over Narakāsura, worship of Lakṣmī, the celebration of Viṣṇu's victory over Bali, and dice play and the exchange of tokens of brotherly and sisterly affection (Kane 1974, 5:194-207; Bahadur 2002, 208). If it is observed over three days, it is also called Kaumudīmahotsava, perhaps because of the white water lilies, *kumuda*, offered to Bali in this festival (Kane 1974, 5:206).

Dhanteras, Āśvina K 13 (September/October) Dhanteras is usually observed in Gujarat and Saurāṣṭra (Kane 1974, 5:195; Bahadur 2002, 209). Houses are cleaned, painted, decorated, and illuminated, and new utensils are bought to mark the beginning of celebrations.

Naraka Caturdaśī, Āśvina K 14 (September/October) The festival of Naraka Caturdaśī commemorates Kṛṣṇā's victory over the demon Narakāsura. This is also the day when people propitiate Yamā, the lord of death and the underworld, with offerings in hopes of not ending up in his realm. Celebrants usually take a bath after anointing themselves with oil, called an oil bath, or *tellā nhāṇa.*

Dhana Lakṣmī Pūjā, Go Pūjā, Dīpāvalī Amāvāsyā, or Āśvina Amāvāsyā (September/October) For Dhana Lakṣmī Pūjā, Lakṣmī, the goddess of wealth, is worshipped after an oil bath in the morning for the removal of bad luck and penury and for gaining wealth and prosperity. Cattle were the only wealth possessed by the ancient Ārya, and they are worshipped, Go Pūjā, representing Śrī Lakṣmī. Businesspeople close their accounts for the old year and open new accounts for the coming year.

Dhānya Lakṣmī Pūjā/Bali Pratipadī, Bali Pūjā, Kārtika Ś 1 (October/November) Dhānya Lakṣmī Pūjā is one of the three most auspicious days in the Hindu religious calendar; the others are New Year's Day, or Candra Yugādi, and Vijaya Daśamī. This festival celebrates Lakṣmī, the goddess of wealth, as a giver of abundance of the grains, *dhānya.* Shop owners welcome her in a special *pūjā, angaḍi pūje* (Kannada), to their establishments, open new account books, and begin a new business and hopefully, prosperous year. The day is also in memory of Bali, son of Virocana, grandson of Prahlāda, and a great devotee of Viṣṇu. In Viṣṇu's fifth incarnation as Vāmana, or the dwarf, he begged Bali to give him land covering three paces. On agreeing to this request, Vāmana covered the Earth and the heavens in two strides, and then placed the third on Bali's head, thus relegating him to the nether regions, *pātāla*, as its king on this day. According to some traditions, Bali returns to the Earth on this day to see how his subjects are faring. Kerala folk tradition confers special status on Bali, called Mahābali, whose ancient kingdom was supposedly Kerala. For a discussion of the Kerala national festival Ōṇam, and of the Mahābali tradition, see the works by Clifford Hospital (1984) and Soifer (1991). They also give translations and a comparison of the different versions of the Bali narrative as given in the different Purāṇas.

Bhrātṛdvitīyā/Yamadvitīyā, Kārtika Ś 2 (October/November) The festival Bhrātṛdvitīyā celebrates the love and affection between brothers and sisters. Men dine at the homes of their sisters, who wish them long life, good health, and prosperity, and in return, they receive gifts (Kane 1974, 5:207).

For the Dīpāvalī feast on Āśvina *K* 14, the special dishes are assorted *phoḍi, duddaḷī, thouśyā muddho, pañckadāyī, khoṭṭo,* and assorted sweets.

Tulasī Vivāha/Pūjā, Kārtika Ś 12 (October/November)

Tulasī was a beautiful, virtuous woman and the wife of Jālandhara. When Jālandhara was slain by Śiva, she immolated herself on her husband's pyre. She was transformed by Viṣṇu into the Gaṇḍakī River, and her lovely hair became the *tulasī* plant. She is also called Vṛandā, Rādhikā, or Viṣṇupriyā ("Viṣṇu's favorite"). Vṛandāvana is the name of a forest near Mathurā where Kṛṣṇa passed his youth under the name Gopāla ("Cowherd") among the cowherds.

In the front yard of every Hindu house, there is a small brick or mud enclosure, called a *vṛandāvana*, with a *tulasī* plant in it. It is believed by pious Hindus that the *tulasī* is occupied by the spirit of Vṛandā every evening. She is worshipped by lighting a lamp and circumambulatng the plant. Leaves of the plant are plucked only in the morning when her spirit leaves the plant, and never in the evening when she enters it. The Tulasī Pūjā celebrates her marriage to Viṣṇu and marks the beginning of the wedding season for the Hindus (Kane 1974, 5:284, 307).

Special dishes prepared for these festivities are *mūgā ghaśī, ekpānnyẽ chutney, goḍi surnaḷi,* and *dhūdsānnaṇa.*

Vaikuṇṭha Caturdaśī, Kārtika Ś 14 (October/November)

The rites for the festival Vaikuṇṭha Caturdaśī are in the temple only; there are no special ceremonies in individual homes. They mark the end of the rainy season, the beginning of autumn, and the resumption of normal activities (Kane 1974, 5:417). In the Mulki temple, there is Dhātrī Pūjā, or the *pūjā* of the *utsavā mūrti*, under an *āvāḷo*, or gooseberry tree, followed by a communal feast called Vanabhojana (literally, "forest feast" or "a picnic").

Lakṣa Dīpa Festival, Kārtika Pūrṇimā (Konkani: Kārti Punnava) (October/November)

The festival Kārtika Pūrṇimā is celebrated with the lighting of 100,000 lights, *lakṣa dīpa*, and the display of fireworks (Kane 1974, 5:285). On either side of the road chosen for a procession, temporary structures are erected to hold a multitude of lights. Notched posts are driven into the earth at intervals of a few feet, and horizontal slats of split bamboo or areca nut palm are strung across them. At intervals of a few inches on these slats, dollops of fresh cow patties are placed, and small earthenware dishes, *poṇti*, are embedded in them. A little bit of oil in each dish and a wick of cotton produces a readymade lamp. At the southernmost end of Tenkupet, the street where we lived in Udupi, a temporary wooden structure like a stationary chariot, *ratha*, would be erected for supporting hundreds of small lamps lit at the time of the procession. It is indeed a glorious sight to see the multitude of these small lamps glowing in the dark, along with an occasional fireworks display. Children buy and set off fireworks and sparklers. There is a public procession of God's image, which is carried to the *ratha*, with all its lamps lit, and worshipped. A lamp is kept on the front stoop of every Hindu home along the street, and an *ārti* is offered that is lit and waved in front of the sacred image.

The special dishes cooked on this occasion are assorted *phoḍi*, *gajbajẽ*, *tīḷā unḍo*, and assorted sweets.

Kāla Bhairavāṣṭamī, Kārtika K 8 (October/November)

Kāla Bhairava is an "awe-inspiring" manifestation of Śiva, and his cult is associated with the worship of Śiva at Kāśī. He is a form of Śiva who scrutinizes all human activities in the holy city of Kāśī and acts as the superintendent of justice, maintaining law and order there. He is shown carrying a club of peacock feathers and mounted on a dog, which is his transport (Eck 1983, 189–95). In the Oracle at the Mulki temple (see Appendix 7: "The Oracle, or Darshana Seva"), he is the deity that is invoked, and the officiating priest carries a form of club made out of deerskin, *kṛṣṇājinā pāṭṭo*, and a bundle of flexible bamboo canes, *bettā mudrā*, while in a state of possession by Kāla Bhairava. There are no special rites or celebrations to mark Kāla Bhairavāṣṭamī, either in the temple or in individual homes (Kane 1974, 5:285; Eck 1983, 366).

The lunar calendar date given in this discussion follows the *amānta* reckoning of South India and is from the *Mangalore Panchanga* (Acharya 1996–7). Kane, who is supposed to follow the same convention, gives the date as Mārgaśira *K* 8, which is wrong, because this is the correct date if the *pūrṇimānta* convention is followed (Kane 1974, 5:285). Eck gives that date with the *pūrṇimānta* reckoning (Eck 1983, 195).

Ugra Narasiṁha Pratiṣṭhā Pūrṇimā Mahotsava, Mārgaśira Pūrṇimā (November/December)

Ugra Narasiṁha Pratiṣṭhā Pūrṇimā Mahotsava commemorates the installation, *pratiṣṭhā*, of the image, *pratimā*, of Ugra Narasiṁha by His Holiness Vijayendra Tīrta, Swami of the Kāśī Mutt, in 1491 CE, Śukla Saṁvatsara, Mārgaśira Pūrṇimā, or November 23, 1569 CE, at the Mulki Śrī Veṅkaṭaramaṇa Temple, and is called Pratiṣṭe Punnava in Konkaṇi (Pai 1995, 715). I have checked the conversion of the lunisolar date to the Common Era, originally given by M. Govinda Pai, using the book by Sewell and Dikshit (1996). The anniversary of this event is celebrated with special ceremonies, after moving the sacred image of Lord Narasiṁha to the room immediately outside the sanctum called *abhiṣekā kūḍa*. The image is worshipped by pouring water (*abhiṣeka*), including the water of thousands of tender coconuts (*śiyyāḷyā uddāka*), a grand *utsava*, and a *samarādhanā*. In December 2004, these rites were televised on local channels, and a two-CD recording of the ceremony is available from the temple. In it, one can see a closeup of the image, which was not possible formerly.

Dattātreya Jayantī, Mārgaśira Pūrṇimā (November/December)

Dattātreya Jayantī commemorates the birth of Dattātreya, son of Atri and his wife, Anasūyā. His worship is prevalent in Mahārāṣṭra and parts of South India (Rigopoulos 1998). He is considered to have incarnate in him portions of the Hindu Trinity, Brahmā, Viṣṇu, and Śiva (Kane 1974, 5:310). (See also Appendix 3: "*Atri Gotra*, or Clan *Atri*.")

Makara Saṃkramaṇa, Udupi Śrī Kṛṣṇa Temple Paryāyotsava, Uttarāyana Ārambha

Makara Saṃkramaṇa marks the winter solstice on or about December 21, the beginning of *uttarāyana*, or the northward progression of the sun. As mentioned earlier, the lunisolar date given in the Hindu almanacs occurs twenty-three to twenty-five days later than the actual observed northward movement of the sun. In the Śrī Kṛṣṇa Temple in Udupi, there are special celebrations to mark this day. The responsibility for the management and maintenance of the worship at the temple is shared by the heads of eight monasteries established by Madhvācārya, the founder of Dvaita (dualistic) interpretation of Vedānta. Each head of the monastery is assigned a *paryāya*. The transfer of responsibility occurs every second year on this day, and is marked by festivities and celebrations at the temple.

This is celebrated as a harvest festival in Karnataka. It is called Pongal in Tamil Nadu and Andhra Prasdeśa (Andhra Pradesh). Some people perform *gopūjā*, or adoration of the cows as representing Śrī Lakṣmī, also on this day. A rice pudding, or *kheer*, is cooked with the new rice and eaten along with *kiciḍī* and other dishes at a grand feast. Gifts of sweets are exchanged amongst friends and relatives.

The special dishes served are *khoṭṭo*, *kiciḍī*, and *poḷo*, and assorted *phoḍi* and sweets.

Mahāśivarātri, Maghā K 14 (January/February)

The fourteenth of the dark half of every month is called Śivarātri, with the Maghā *K* 14 singled out for special distinction and observances and called the Mahāśivarātri. This is the most important festival celebrated in the cult and worship of Śiva. Fasting the whole day and worshipping Śiva over the whole night by offering the leaves of the *bilva* tree (also called the Bengal quince tree) are obligatory. The *bilva* tree is sacred because it is considered the embodiment of Śiva. Even people who are normally worshippers of Viṣṇu make offerings at Śiva temples and partake of *prasāda* on this holy day (Kane 1974, 5:225).

Holikā, Holi, or Kāma Dahana, Phālguna Pūrṇimā (February/March)

Holikā, also called Holi or Kāma Dahana, is a festival marking the advent of spring and is of ancient origin. It is supposed to be the special festival assigned by Brahmā to the Śudrās as their own (Kane 1974, 5:200). It includes a reenactment, Kāma Dahana, of the burning of Kāma, the god of love, by Śiva, whose austerities had been interrupted by Kāma. Men carry an areca-nut palm and loudly sing ribald songs and engage in much boisterous merriment and loud shouts, modulated by repeated beating of their open mouths by their palms. The palm tree is then burned in a big bonfire for the Kāma Dahana (Kane 1974, 5:237).

Śrāddha Observed on the Tithi of the Anniversary of the Death of an Ancestor

What is *śrāddha*? This is an offering to Brahmanas given with faith, *śraddhā*, for the benefit of the Manes (dead ancestors). Faith in what? Faith in the whole Hindu eschatology, including its beliefs in karma and rebirth, *punarjanma*, and faith that the offerings given to the Brahmanas eventually reach the Manes, to make them contented and happy. There are different types of *śrāddhas*—as many as ninety-six (Kane 1973, 4:380–1). Though all of them are solemn occasions, they are not considered as joyous. The only exceptions perhaps are the *Vṛiddhi-śrāddhas* performed on happy events such as the birth of a son or a marriage in the family. The rites of *śrāddha* are supposed to have been instituted by four ancient sages. In alphabetical order, they are Atri (Rigopoulos 1998, 47), Jamadagni (Rahurkar 1964, 215), Manu, and Viṣṇu (Kane 1974, 4:349). With the passage of time, this rite became the most solemn of household ceremonies and came to influence many aspects of Hindu society and codes of behavior, including the importance attached to having sons as performers of *śrāddha* and thus able to propitiate the Manes, the difficulty of marrying off girls without brothers in ancient times, the Hindu laws of succession and property rights, and the general lack of parity between boys and girls in Hindu society.

On the death of a person, the funeral rites are spread over thirteen days (see Appendix 5: "Hindu Rites of Passage"). These are followed by the monthly rite, *māsika śrāddha*, performed every new moon during the first year of the person's death, culminating in the end-of-the-year rite, *varsāntika śrāddha*, on the first death anniversary. These days, the monthly *śrāddha* is rarely performed, unless the family is both rich and very orthodox. After the first anniversary, it is customary to perform only the annual or *vārṣika śrāddha*, which is called *varṣika* in Konkani. In ancient times, oblations of meat of approved animals were offered to the Manes, and then were later partaken of by the attending Brāhmaṇas and the family of the deceased (Kane 1973, 4:422; Doniger and Smith 1991, 71–2; Achaya 1994). Meat eating, ritual or customary, is of course forbidden now, because it has been declared by the orthodox as a practice to be avoided in the Kali Yuga, *kalivarjya*. Some people who have conveniently forgotten our carnivorous past and are proud of their present religious orthopraxy flaunt it under a banner of vegetarianism. Meat eating has gone the way of solemn Vedic sacrifices, in which partaking of the sacrificial meat offering was obligatory as part of the ritual.

The meal following a *śrāddha* requires some specific special dishes: *ghārī, umbārī, varna*, assorted *phoḍī, koṭṭo, goḍśẽ*, *mūgã ghaśī*, and any items that had been favorites of the deceased in life.

Candra, or Sūrya Grahaṇa

The almanacs note the occurrence of lunar or solar eclipses, which are considered to be polluting events of some religious significance. Pious Hindus do not eat any food a few hours on either side of the eclipse, as specified in the almanac. After the eclipse is over, they bathe to wash away the pollution of the eclipse, and only then do they eat any food. Eclipses are also considered by the very orthodox and by observant Hindus to be particularly propitious occasions for performing *śrāddhas* for the Manes.

I have described here the most important Hindu feasts and festivals. There are many more that are observed by Hindus, depending on family tradition, degree of orthodoxy, convenience, and affordability.

APPENDIX SEVEN

The Oracle, or *Darśana Sevā*

The oracle of Kāla Bhairava, or Darśana Sevā, at the Mulki Śri Veṅkaṭaramaṇa Temple is a religious rite held on appropriate days. It involves trance and possession of a medium, the *darśaṇā pātri,* always a male Gauda Sarasvat Brahmana (GSB), by Kāla Bhairava, who speaks to devotees to answer questions on personal problems, to provide comfort and certainties in an uncertain world. Kāla Bhairava is an "awe-inspiring" manifestation of Śiva. Devotees bare their hearts to the oracle, seeking solace and peace of mind in his words of comfort and reassurance. Some of them have specific problems, such as illness in the family, legal or financial problems, or difficulty in finding a suitable mate for a son or daughter; the list can go on and on. The replies of the oracle, *udāraṇa,* usually in our mother tongue, Konkani, are repeated and explicated by the attending priests. These could be promises of a cure or involve the performance of observances (*vrata*), prayers, expiations, or rites of atonement (*prāyaścitta*). A few people come to pray and receive blessings from the oracle (*darśaṇāri prasādu ghevco*) without having to deal with any immediate problems. The oracle sometimes sprinkles the devotee with consecrated water, *tīrtha mārcẽ,* as a blessing or to ward off evil. For the people of faith, approaching the medium, who is in a state of trance and possession, is to have an audience (*darśan*) with Kāla Bhairava, and an occasion to pay homage. The Darśana Sevā takes place usually on Wednesday, Saturday, and Sunday of every week or on the festive (*utsava*) days, except for the inauspicious days of the Hindu almanac. This ceremony has been going on at the temple since the eighteenth century and has brought it much fame and prosperity. It is in great demand, as can be seen from the 50 to 100 people who attend each of these functions, which form an integral part of temple ceremonies.

The state of trance and possession of the medium of the oracle is called *āveśa*. One outward sign of this state is the quivering of the limbs of the medium, for the duration of the possession. The ancient word *vipra* for a Brahmana etymologically means "quiverer" (Gombrich 1988, 37). There is some controversy as to whether such trance and possession are pre-Vedic or post-Vedic; the evidence is conflicting. It is possible that the states of spirit possession are of ancient origin, may be pre-Arya, and their use in seeking answers to problems of everyday living and in predicting the future are equally old. It is now very much part of Hindu orthodoxy and temple rites. The Konkani word *pātri* may be derived from the Sanskrit *pātram*, for a recipient or a receptacle. The medium is a receptacle for the presence of Kāla Bhairava. The medium at the Mulki temple carries in his right hand a club of black antelope skin (*kṛṣṇājinā pāṭṭo*) with a gold handle, and in his left hand a few flexible bamboo canes (*bettā mudrā*) bound at one end in a gold handle. They are collectively called *pāṭṭo-mudrā* and are the emblems of the oracle.

In sculptures, Kāla Bhairava is usually shown armed with a club of peacock feathers, mounted on a dog as his transport (*vāhana*) (Eck 1983, 189–95). The legend, mythology, and cult of this manifestation of Śiva are discussed by Diana Eck in *Banaras: City of Light*. He is known as the person who maintains law and order in the Holy City of Kāśī, or Benares, where there is a temple dedicated to him. The background and history of this rite at the Mulki temple are given in a small booklet in Kannada, published by the temple management, and all the details given here are from this one source (Anon., n.d.). This rite actually originated at the famous Tirupati Śrī Veṅkaṭaramaṇa Temple in Andhra Pradesh, during a visit by pilgrims from Mulki. In olden days, before the advent of trains and buses, travel to places of pilgrimage like Tirupati was expensive, full of danger, with the chances of a pilgrim returning safely being very small. People traveled by bullock cart or walked in stages of few miles a day, resting along the way at temples or at rest houses (*dharmaśālā*) built by the rich. There were dangers from wild animals, armed robbers, sickness, and accidents. There were no means of long-distance communication, and trying to get any help in an emergency from back home was impossible. People undertook pilgrimages involving such long-distance travel only in the last stages of life, after they had seen their grandchildren born, settled their affairs, and were more preoccupied with the hereafter than with this life. When the prospective pilgrims said their good-byes to their family back home, they did not expect to see them again. With all these problems, pilgrimages were major undertakings, embarked on once in a lifetime. Local temples would collect offerings made to the Tirupati deity to be delivered at a later date. Once every few years, a large party of pilgrims, called *daṇḍa*, or

Rāmdaṇḍa, would travel to Tirupati with all the accumulated offerings. There was always safety in numbers, and they could also afford to take a professional cook to ensure ritual purity and good food on the way. Sometime in the late eighteenth century, Gujjadi Venkata Nayak was a member of a party of pilgrims at Tirupati, from the Mulki temple. At the Tirupati temple, he showed signs of being posessed by a spirit, and an interrogation by the head priest, Mahanta of Tirupati, revealed that the Spirit was indeed Kāla Bhairava. The night before in a dream, the priest had been told by Lord Veṅkaṭaramaṇa to expect these events, and to command Kāla Bhairava, accompany the pilgrims to Mulki and dwell there permanently, and bring solace and comfort to visiting devotees. The priest was also ordered to give a silver-mounted *bettā mudrā* to Venkata Nayak. This artifact still exists at the Mulki temple. After more than two centuries, it is quite fragile and not in everyday use. It is kept enclosed in a silver case in the sanctum. When a new person is installed as a *darśaṇā pātri*, he holds it to mark the passage of the rite to a new generation. The Darśana Sevā at the Mulki temple began with Venkata Nayak, and his successors have all been from the Nayak family (Anon., n.d.). Of these, Rangappa Nayak (1878–1924) stands out for his long tenure of forty-six years, during which the Darśana Sevā attained much fame and a large following amongst the devotees, who enriched the temple with their offerings. People from all over India, including rich Gujarati merchants from Bombay, would come to his Darśana Sevā with their problems. His service at the temple overlapped my grandfather Madhava Bhat's tenure as a priest, and I grew up listening to many a tale of Rangappa Nayak and his famous Darśana Sevā.

At the writing of this book, the *darśaṇā pātri* for the oracle at the Mulki temple is Śrī Palimar Vasantha Devaraya Nayak, son of Palimar Devaraya Narayana Nayak, grandson of Palimar Narayana Nayak, and great-grandson of Palimar Rangappa Nayak. He hails from the village of Palimar, near Mulki. He has been officiating as the *pātri* since 1987. Before that he was the editor of the Kannada newspaper *Hosa Digantha* (*New Horizons*) from 1980 to 1987. He was the subeditor of the Kannada newspaper *Udayavani*, which he began working for after completing his bachelor of science degree in 1970. His ancestors for many generations have been successive mediums at the Mulki temple, and they are an offshoot of the family of Gujjadi Venkata Nayak, who was the first *darśaṇā pātri*. I had the privilege of interviewing him, and tape-recording the conversation, on December 15, 2004, at Mulki, when he told me about his background and the details of the preparations before he assumed his present office (Nayak 2004). The guru, or head of Kāśī Maṭha, His Holiness Shrimad Sudhindra Thirtha Swami, was instrumental in the transformation of Vasantha Nayak from a newspaperman to a *darśaṇā pātri*.

It was he who recruited, guided, and advised the candidate for office, both spiritually and in secular affairs, during this process. Devaraya Nayak, his father, wanted to retire in 1987, and it was time to find a successor. After consulting the horoscopes of possible candidates, the guru decided on Vasantha Nayak as the best choice and asked him to talk to the temple management. At the end of these successful negotiations, he was accepted as a replacement for his father. Vasantha Nayak sees his work at the temple as a sacred calling in which he fulfills his religious obligations for service to the deity. He sees attaining the office of the *darśaṇā pātri* as a form of consecration, involving purity of food, behavior, and thoughts. As part of this process of sanctification, and preparatory to assuming his new duties, Vasantha Nayak went to many places of Hindu pilgrimage. The guru also imparted to him mantras for repeating in prayer, *japa*, as part of his daily worship. Devaraya Nayak conducted his last Darśana Sevā on 5 December 1987, after which he removed the ceremonial gold bracelets (*kaṅkaṇa*) and necklace (*cakra soru*) and put them on his son. These ornaments belong to the temple and are worn by the *darśaṇā pātri* as insignia of his office, during his tenure. Vasantha Nayak's first Darśana Sevā was on 8 December 1987, when he was invested with the *pāṭṭo-mudrā* by his holiness the guru of Kāśī Maṭha.

In the olden days, it was customary for the *pātri* to fast till the end of the Darśana Sevā, having food only at its end. These rules were changed in the 1980s by the guru, who decreed that the *pātri* could have breakfast after the morning worship, or *sandhi*. The sanctum of the temple is divided into three rooms, or *kūḍā*. The innermost room where the sacred images are located is the *garbhagṛaha*. The room just outside it is called the *abhiṣekā kūḍa* because the anointing, or abhiśeka, of the sacred image of Lord Narasimha on the anniversary of its installation takes place here. The room outside it is the *maṇṭapā kūḍa*, outside of which are the steps that lead on to it from the vestibule, *naḍo*, of the temple. The preparatory rites of worship by the *pātri* are performed in the *abhiṣekā kūḍa*, the middle room where all the strict rules of ritual purity are obligatory. After breakfast, he bathes again, changes into the ceremonial dress of deep scarlet silk (*pāṭṭyā toḍopu*), changes his sacred thread (*jānnuvẽ*), sips *pañcagavya* (see Appendix 10, "Glossary"), and performs *sandhi*. He repeats many types of *japa*, and then he recites hymns of praise (*stotra*). He then circumambulates the *garbhagṛaha* five times in prayer, prostrates himself in front of the deity, and sits on a wooden platform (*māṇayī*) facing north, at the entrance to the sanctum. These are the rites of spiritual and mental preparation before the main ceremony.

I will now describe what the devotees attending the Darśana Sevā see from the outside in the *naḍo*, at the main entrance to the temple. When things are ready in the sanctum and the Darśana Sevā is about to begin, a silver-encased staff (*rupyā boḍḍo*) is passed outside to indicate that the ceremony can begin. This staff is one of two kept on either side of the door of the *maṇṭapā kūḍa* as emblems of authority of the temple, and they are also used for crowd control. The auxiliary priest (*parcārike bhaṭṭu*) gives the *pātri tīrtha* to sip three times, or once on the fast day, Ekādaśī. The *pātri* then stands up. The manager of the temple, along with the rest of the devotees (*dhājana*) and several priests, assemble in the vestibule. They pray for God's grace to vouchsafe a successful Darśana Sevā to provide comfort and solace to the devotees. At the end of this prayer, the bells (*ghāṅṭa*) in the temple are rung to an incessant beat, and the temple musicians (*vājpānce*) play on the pipes, or *nāgasvaram*. In the inner sanctum, the main priest (*pūje bhaṭṭu*) begins the waving of lights, the first of five *ārti*, called *darśaṇā ārti*. The *darśaṇā pātri* can be seen at the left of the entrance to the sanctum in a state of *āveśa*. Vasantha Nayak told me in our interview that there is an altered state of consciousness at this point, in which the *pātri* loses awareness of the outside world and does not remember anything that happens later, till the end of the ceremony. He cannot recall any questions asked or replies given during the ceremony. The principal priest waves the fifth and last *ārti*, and then puts it on the doorsill, or *humboru*. The auxiliary priest offers it to the *pātri*, who accepts it (*ārti ghettā*). The auxiliary priest holds a handful of flowers (*puṣpāñjali*) in front of the *darśaṇā pātri*, who symbolically offers it to the deity. The *parcārike bhaṭṭu* puts a garland of flowers round the neck of the *pātri*, and then comes out with the *pāṭṭo-mudrā* in a silver platter (*poḷeru*). The *darśaṇā pātri* appears in the door of the temple, and the pipes play a characteristic fast, shrill trill. The vestibule is flanked by two massive pillars. The one on the left facing the sanctum is called the *tīrthā khāmbo*, because a priest dispensing *tīrtha* and sandalwood paste (*prasādu*) sits next to it. The pillar on the right is called *darśaṇā khāmbo*, because it plays an important role near the end of this ceremony. The *darśaṇā pātri* comes out and stands in the vestibule with his back to the *tīrthā khāmbo*. He is handed the *pāṭṭo* and *mudrā*, the emblems of Kāla Bhairava. With the *pāṭṭo* he strikes himself thrice on the head, and with the *mudrā* thrice on the left side. The pipes and bells fall silent and the part of the rite devoted to questions from the devotees, and answers from the *darśaṇā pātri*, begins. Because of an increase in the size of the crowd, most of the question-and-answer part of the ceremony takes place nowadays at the entrance to the temple, next to the *tulasī kāṭṭē*, the special raised platform for holy basil. Each person or a family, make their offerings, *kāṇika*, according to their means, and seek answers to their problems, blessings, or words of reassurance. The *pātri* blesses by gently touching the heads of devotees with the *pāṭṭo*, or he sprinkles consecrated water (*tīrtha mārcẽ*) as a blessing or to ward off evil. They also get a small ball of sandalwood paste, *gāndhā gūḷi*, as grace (*prasāda*), which the devotee takes home and keeps in the family shrine. Such sessions may last for hours till all the devotees have had a chance to pay their respects or find answers to their problems. Finally, to end the session, the manager or a trustee tells the *pātri*, "*Daya pāvyeta*," requesting an end to the *darśaṇa* ceremony. At this, the *pātri* moves back into the *naḍo* of the temple to the *tīrthā khāmbo*, strikes himself on the head thrice with the *pāṭṭo*, and then gives it to the attending priest. Similarly, he strikes himself thrice on the side with the *mudrā* before handing it over. He accepts some *tīrtha* in his cupped right hand and throws it at the *darśaṇā khāmbo*. He stands still with hands joined in prayer (*pāyam-poṇu rābtā*), the trembling of the limbs slowly subsides, and the state of *āveśa* is over. He turns to the left, bows to the sanctum again, walks away, usually supported by the attending priest, and sits down.

What brings about the trance? No one can be certain; one can only speculate. It could be the final result of a number of rites and ceremonies, spiritual and mental preparation, conditioning, and expectations from all of the people involved. To a devotee full of faith (*bhakti*), the *pātri* is possessed by Kāla Bhairava, who resides on the right hand of the deities in the sanctum of the Mulki temple. To bring about such possession, many contributing preparatory factors are needed. The *pātri* believes that *āveśa* is a sign of God's grace and that he has been called by God to perform an important service to the community of believers. It is up to the deity to ensure the authenticity of the ceremony and to make sure that the words uttered by the *pātri* in the *naḍo* come to pass. The *pātri* has to lead a life of ritual purity and go through a process of mental and spiritual preparation before the ceremony involving *japa* and related rites, so that he can fulfill his expectations and those of the devotees for a successful ceremony. The auditory input of the incessant ringing of bells, the shrill trill of the pipes, and the results expected from them could also contribute to the trance. Finally, the Darśana Sevā is an act of faith for those who believe, and any rational explanations may be superfluous or not pertinent. The following facts related to states of possession, told to me by the current *pātri*, are relevant and attest to the uniqueness of the Darśana Sevā at the Mulki temple. A few *pātris* experience *āveśa* when they are away from their home temples on hearing the ringing of bells and the trill of pipes. Vasantha Nayak told me that this never happens to him when away from the Mulki temple (Nayak 2004). Some other temple had invited his father to be their *pātri* at a higher salary; however, he declined with thanks and told them that it would not work, because he experienced *āveśa* only at the Mulki temple.

APPENDIX EIGHT

Goa: A Paradise Lost?

No future without forgiveness.
—Archbishop Desmond Tutu (1999)

Introduction

Embedded in the minds of the Konkani-speaking Sarasvat community is a story of our past in Goa. It is about the happy life of our people in this paradise on Earth. This idyllic life was interrupted by the conquest of Goa in 1510 by the Portuguese. After a few years under the new rulers, life turned sour for us Hindus. The new rulers wanted to convert all of their subjects to Christianity. The state and church in Goa destroyed Hindu temples, appropriated their wealth and property, and converted some of us to Christianity by force. To save our life and religion, our community, along with other Hindus, fled Goa to live in exile. That, in brief, is the story. Is this story a myth, a product of wishful thinking about a golden past? Was the Goa of the sixteenth and seventeenth centuries really a paradise? What is the truth behind all of these events? If we are looking for truth, whose truth is it? We may never know the answers to all these questions. If we look at current events, recorded for sight and sound, seen on television as part of the evening news, written up by the news media, and analyzed from several different viewpoints, each narrative is different. How, then, can we hope to know what happened nearly five centuries ago? The best we can do is to use the records of events from various sources, assume each source has its own viewpoint, or bias, contrived or incidental, and try to arrive at a connected story.

These events occurred in the territories ruled by the Portuguese in and around Goa. The initial conquest of Goa by the Portuguese in 1510 was confined to the five islands: the island of Goa proper, also called Tiswadi (30 villages); Chorão (Cūḍāmaṇī); Divar (Dīpavti); Vamsim, a small island east of Divar; and Jua. To these were added, in 1543, Bardez (Bārādeśa, twelve villages), Mormugao, and Salcette (Ṣaṣaṣṭi, sixty-six villages). The Sarasvats living in the ninety-six villages of Tiswadi and Salcette together came to be called Ṣeṇvi, short for "Ṣaṇṇavati," or "ninety-six," and people living in Bardez were known as Bardezkars. These territories were called Old Conquests, or *Velhas Conquistas*, by the Portuguese (Map 2). The New Conquests were the following acquisitions: Ponda from the Marathas in 1763; Sanquem, Quepem, and Canacona from the rulers of Sonda in 1764; and Satari, Pernem, and Bicholim from the Bhonsles of Sawantwadi in 1781–1788 (Map 3). Most of the Hindu temples in the Old Conquests were destroyed between 1540 and 1580, and some were relocated to the north and east of the Zuari River in Ponda, which at that time was under the Marathas. All of these regions taken together were known as the Portuguese state of India, or Estado da India Portuguesa (Gune 1979; Xavier 1993; Couto 2004). The city of Old Goa used to be the administrative headquarters and the residence of the viceroy. During the epidemic of 1759, the viceroy moved his residence to Panaji; the administration followed suit in 1827–1835, and in 1843 Panaji was declared the capital of Portuguese Goa (Gune 1979, 797, 816).

Historical records of these troubled times left by the Portuguese, both secular and religious, are the most extensive. These are quite meticulous and describe events from the viewpoint of the power hierarchy, the state and the church. All of us owe the Portuguese a deep debt of gratitude for these records. Some are eyewitness accounts by the participants in these events; others are institutional progress reports to colleagues or superiors in Europe. It is only natural that these letters, reports, and memoranda narrate matters that were of immediate interest to the authors and the recipients of these communications and that they may or may not cover those aspects that interest us. Hence, they are complete to different degrees. We owe an immense debt of gratitude to the scholars who have extracted information from the Portuguese records and made them available to the English-speaking world. In addition, we have accounts of the adventures of travelers from many nations and traditions who visited Goa. Parallel descriptions of the same events by contemporary Hindus, the victims, are not available; perhaps they never existed. Any temple records must have been destroyed and thus are lost. All we have are oral traditions about how bad things were and how we fled Goa to escape persecution, and the grim stories of survival in exile. These stories, of course, change in transmission down successive generations; they are subject to selective memory lapses, embellishments, and exaggerations. Hence, they should be believed with caution. Commercial records of a few wealthy families of Sarasvat merchants who survived those troubled times have been mined for information only recently (Mhamai 2004, 2007). I have not used the eighteenth-century Marathi-language chronicles of the Sarasvats in Goa, titled *Koṅkaṇākhyāna* (*Legends of Konkan*), or the later histories of individual temples, because either I could not get hold of them or they are written in Marathi, which I cannot read (Anon. 2001; Axelrod and Fuerch 1996). These records are capable of exciting intense emotions amongst the people, Hindus or the Catholics, who read or write about them. Some respond to the memory of these events as if they happened yesterday, with the wounds fresh and raw. A few would like to heap scathing censure on the Portuguese state and the Roman Catholic church for their respective actions (Priolkar 1961; book review: Moser 1964); others would like to bend over backward in playing apologist for identical acts (D'Costa 1965; book review: Boxer 1966). Some, while conceding that the Portuguese missionaries' methods were indeed coercive, would like to commend them for being inefficient in enforcing such coercion! In short, the same set of events are viewed from different perspectives. Therefore, stories of past events should always be treated with some degree of skepticism because most probably they are biased. These narrator biases, overt or covert, intentional or not, obvious or not, are to be found in all historical writings. They depend on the perspective, ideology, or explicit political agenda of the historian. In a few cases, the translations from the Portuguese may be wrong, as has been pointed out, or the exact interpretation or number of some events may be in error (de Souza 1975; D'Costa 1965). Pursuing these biases or errors, listing and correcting them, is immensely difficult, time consuming, and beyond my abilities, because I cannot read Portuguese and have no access to primary sources. I am not a professional historian, and even professionals may not be able to correct all errors or biases, including those of first-person narratives. These forensic investigations are also counterproductive because they are usually not conclusive and most probably will not change the minds of people with preset beliefs. Instead, I have done my best to use as many sources as I could, each with its own viewpoint, emphasis, or bias, so that hopefully all points of view will average out in the final narrative. Measurements in the exact sciences always have biases, or systematic errors, to use the correct technical term. The final result, or the "best estimate" of the truth, is obtained by averaging over all measurements, hoping that the biases will cancel out. That is what I have done here. In spite of such averaging, it is quite possible that this narrative has its own set of biases—mine. Hence, a certain modicum of judicious skepticism on the part of the reader of any historical narrative is always in order. In our story, there is no controversy about the main events of sixteenth- and seventeenth-century Goa and later, though one could always quibble about the details. I will leave controversies over details to the historians and confine myself to the principal happenings on which there is a consensus. The specific historical sources I have used are mentioned later, as we go along, in this story. The principal motivation behind this narrative and exploring many of its details has been to rectify my own ignorance about the life of the local people, our GSB community, and the Portuguese in sixteenth-century Goa and later. I wanted to know the facts—the good and the bad. To set the background for the narrative, I will describe what we know about Hindus in Goa, their customs, beliefs, and how they lived. This will be followed by the challenges of the Portuguese conquests and the aftermath. Along with the conquerors came a new religion, a different worldview and customs, new laws and punishments. This will be followed with comments on how these new challenges affected the Hindus, the Portuguese, and the Roman Catholic church. I would like to say a word about the spirit in which this story is told here. The epigraph at the beginning of this appendix, "No future without forgiveness," is the title of a recent book by Archbishop Desmond Tutu (Tutu 1999). The narrative here is written in a spirit of forgiveness, which does not mean forgetting the past or whitewashing it. It is also written with a firm conviction that to practice meaningful forgiveness, it is necessary to know what is being forgiven.

What Can History Teach Us?

Any study of history and its narrative has its own agenda. It is kudos for people and events one admires, and condemnation for those that one does not. The few facts of the narrative could also be used as pegs on which to hang the fabric of one's favorite theory of history. In this story, I will do my best to stick to known historical facts—who, what, when, why, and how; to minimize my personal biases; to praise acts that deserve it; and to criticize those that do not. The intentions and motivations of historical figures will be from their own words if possible, supplemented by any speculations that are clearly labeled as such. I believe that historical events become transparent, and their dynamics clear, if one understands the distribution, devolvement, and pursuit of power and its checks and balances for the dominance hierarchies represented as the main actors of this drama. At least that is the theoretical framework I have found useful in looking at historical events; it is my theory of history. Understanding the intention and motives of the dominant hierarchies—the church and the state—then in power could also go a long way on the road to forgiveness of the past. This is only one aspect of forgiveness; the other is the realization that under similar circumstances of unlimited power and resulting corruption, other humans, including us, could err also. From our vantage point, we can see how misguided the state–church complex was, though motivated by the best of intentions. This does not preclude any judgment of these actions on our part. I will strive to be objective, without righteous anger or condemnation. Understanding the motives of the Portuguese makes them more human and less demonic, though their specific acts were heinous. Just as the Portuguese were motivated by their worldview at that time, it is only natural that we judge their actions by our values now. We could do none other if we are going to be honest with ourselves. If anyone thinks that this is unfair to the past, I disagree. Just as we will be judged by our successors, we will judge those who went before us. If there is no moral or ethical judgment of the past, we will never learn from the mistakes of history.

In this context, it is interesting to recall Lord Acton (John Emerich Edward Dalberg-Acton) and his comments on the whole problem of moral judgment of history. He was a historian, a liberal philosopher, Regius Professor of Modern History at Cambridge University (1895–1902), and a devout Roman Catholic (Macdougall 2003). For him communion with the Roman Catholic church was dearer than life (Hill 2000, 260). However, his religious convictions did not prevent him from being critical of the papacy or the church for its past wrongs, including the Inquisition.

Acton felt that historians had a right as well as an obligation to morally judge past events, in addition to reporting them accurately. His harsh and explicit denunciation of the moral responsibility of the papacy for the evils of the inquisitions is an example. While he acquiesced to the right and obligation of the church to enforce its legitimate authority in spiritual matters, to demand a certain amount of compliance with its rules and enforce its discipline, he felt that it should never transgress the generally accepted code of morality. The question of the boundaries of legitimate authority of the papacy became one of the important problems of the twentieth century. His views on the limits of church authority and the papacy were later vindicated by the heavy internal criticism of the history of the Roman Catholic Church in the wake of the Second Vatican Council, and the substantial reforms following it (Peters 1988, 273).

The problem so clearly stated by Peters is this: Where does ecclesiastical discipline end and where do human rights violations begin? In all human activities, whether those of an individual or an institution, there is an underlying theme of pursuit of power. This is the one viewpoint I have been stressing in the story narrated here and in the rest of this book. Enforcing orthodoxy as opposed to heresy, truth versus falsehood, good against bad—these are all opportunistic scenarios in the struggle for power and dominance. For those pursuing power, the problem is to know how far they can push the envelope of institutional authority without overstepping the boundaries of morality. In this narrative of the state and church in Goa, we will see that both of them transgressed these boundaries of decency, equity, fair play, and justice and are held accountable for their actions. Both of these power structures had unlimited power without checks and balances and were corrupted by it. It is an example of abuse of power, which once again proves the truth of Lord Acton's dictum: Power tends to corrupt, and absolute power corrupts absolutely. In this narrative, I state the historical truth of events truly and objectively to the best of my knowledge, minimize moral judgment on my part, and leave it to the reader.

Forgiveness—An Option?

All religious traditions have accepted human fallibility as a given and have devised means to atone for errors committed because of it: realizing one's error, regretting that it was committed, and begging forgiveness from the injured party. Though formalized by different religious traditions, this process is a purely human transaction between the person who injured and the person who suffered. Confessing one's misdeeds, repenting, and doing penance are expiations for sins prescribed by Hindu codes of law (Doniger and Smith, 1991, 259; Kane 1973, 4:41–2). The Buddha (~fifth to sixth century BCE) preached and practiced forbearance and forgiveness as the only effective way to defuse human conflict. Public confession of one's faults with a resolve not repeat them, the offering and acceptance of explicit apologies, and the use of specific procedures for formal reconciliation between the feuding parties, whether monks or laypersons, have been part of Buddhist tradition for centuries (Harvey 2000). Daily religious practice amongst the Jains includes *pratikramaṇa* (ritual repentance), involving confession of bad thoughts and deeds and seeking forgiveness. The final day of the annual festival Paryuṣa Parvan, called Samvatsarī, is special. On that day, there is a ceremony of communal repentance in which each Jain begs forgiveness from friends and acquaintances (Dundas 2002). In the Jewish tradition, on the eve of the Day of Atonement, people seek forgiveness from one another (Milgrom and Unterman 2007). Jesus asked the wronged person to be generous and forgive many times, serially if necessary. Peter asked Jesus how often he should forgive his brother who has wronged him—perhaps seven times? Jesus replied: Not seven times, but seventy times seven (Matthew 18:21–22). Some of these ideas of forgiveness have had a rebirth in South Africa against a background of the truly monstrous human rights violations of apartheid and a transition to a unified democratic nation of both perpetrators and victims of these crimes. That nation established the Truth and Reconciliation Commission to investigate these atrocities and grant amnesty to political crimes, provided the perpetrators owned up to them with a full disclosure of their offenses (Tutu 1999; James and van der Vijver 2001; Graybill 2002; Eades 1999). The work of the commission and its aftermath are described by Archbishop Tutu, its chairman, in a book, *No Future Without Forgiveness*, the title of which sounds like a trumpet call to sanity in settling conflicts and using forgiveness as an affirmation of our common humanity. I fully agree with the sentiments of the title and the contents of his book and would like to keep it in view at all times when I am discussing past wrongs, big or small, in this story, because forgiveness is the most effective way to put out the fires of hatred and lust for revenge.

Human forgiveness works best and has any meaning at all only when the victim forgives the person who committed the offense, who in turn owns up to it and expresses remorse and a resolve not to repeat it in the future. It is purely a human transaction between these two, without any divine involvement. At least that is my attitude toward forgiveness in this discussion, and it also must have been the sense in which the Buddha taught forgiveness. One of the most revolutionary teachings of the Buddha was that humans could solve their problems themselves, without any divine intervention or help (Schumann 1993, 34; Rahula 1974, 1). The Buddha always liked to keep his teachings simple, without unnecessarily complicating them with additional assumptions if he could help it. It is in this sense that forgiveness is a solution crafted by humans to solve one of their problems. If the victim and or the offender are dead and the offense occurred in the past, the question of forgiveness becomes more complicated. For human offenses, only the victim can forgive; no one else can presume to do so. If those who forgive never experienced the wrongs done, never suffered under them, by what right can they forgive? How can anyone, other than the victims, forgive past crimes without appearing to trivialize their suffering? What exactly will they be forgiving? These and related questions are discussed in Simon Wiesenthal's book *The Sunflower* (Wiesenthal 1998). Simon Wiesenthal, a prisoner in a Nazi concentration camp, is summoned to the bedside of a dying SS (Schutzstaffel) soldier with bandaged eyes, to listen to his confession of atrocities committed against the Jews. The soldier expresses remorse for his past acts and begs Wiesenthal's forgiveness and absolution as a representative Jew. Wiesenthal walks away in silence because he cannot presume to forgive the suffering of other Jews. Wiesenthal was not at peace with himself about his action. Half of the book gives the details of this story, and the other half is devoted to the opinions of fifty-three thoughtful people requested to comment on his action: Did he do right in walking away in silence? Should he have said a few words of even pro forma forgiveness to comfort a dying man? The comments received covered a wide spectrum of opinions. Some felt that what he did was the correct response, a few called for revenge against the perpetrators of the crimes, others would never forgive, and a few invoked God as the only one who could forgive. The religious beliefs of these people seemed to strongly influence their responses. But because it is humans who are cruel to other humans, why drag God into the problem? Forgiveness can be a simple human act without involving God; it is then simple, clear, and devoid of any obscurity, mystification, or theology. If in addition the perpetrator asks for *no* forgiveness, does forgiveness have any meaning? Is it just a hollow mental exercise that means nothing?

As far as I have been able to search, I found no expression of regrets or remorse, or a plea for forgiveness, from either the Portuguese administration or the Roman Catholic church, for all the wrongs done by them or their agents in medieval Goa. A twentieth-century book translated from the original Italian, *When a Pope Asks Forgiveness: The Mea Culpas of John Paul II*, is relevant here (Accattoli 1998). During Pope John Paul's extensive travels all over the world, he met people of many nations, ethnicities, and religions and used these occasions to apologize for some past acts of the Catholic church. This book contains ninety-four instances of his exact words repenting for the past faults of the church or asking for pardon for them. In twenty-ve of these he explicitly said, "I ask forgiveness" or its equal, as an expression of his contrition (Accattoli 1998, xv). Pope John Paul II visited India twice: in February 1986 and in November 1999. He gave many speeches, including two in Goa, in which the heroes of the evangelical activities of the church and the martyrs to their faith in India were eulogized, proving that the church has an excellent institutional memory when it wants (John Paul II 1999b). The text of these speeches is available on the Vatican web site at http://www.vatican.va/holy_father/john_paul_ii/travels/index.htm. In Accattoli's book, the pope's various speeches in India, the exhortation *Ecclesia in Asia* (John Paul II 1999a) given at New Delhi, and the various pronouncements of church hierarchy in India, there is not one expression of contrition for the destruction of Hindu and Muslim places of worship, forcible conversions, the abduction of fatherless children to be brought up as Christians, or the violence committed by the church and the Inquisition against the people of Goa. This collective amnesia on the part of the pope and the church is most regrettable; it is as if these atrocities never occurred. Hence, forgiveness in this case is at best ill-defined and therefore should be taken under what is usually called judicial advisement.

Why is an apology by the pope or the church important? After all, the people who suffered under the state and church in medieval Goa have been dead for a long time and cannot benefit from any apology. It would be a politically correct gesture that would be good for public relations and nothing more. An apology can mean something substantial if it is the result of genuine contrition by the church and indicative of its changed thinking about its attitude to other religions. Has the church learned greater tolerance to other religions accompanied by genuine respect for them and acceptance of them as equals in the pursuit of salvation by humans? Are the happy times of genuine religious pluralism here? Unfortunately, the answer is no, if we were to go by the recent pronouncement of the church. These declarations of the church and the mind-set behind them are be discussed later in this appendix.

However, as a fallible human, I forgive the church and the state. I forgive them the hurt and suffering in me resulting from an account of the atrocities committed by them in Goa. Both the state and the church are power hierarchies that dominate, maintain, and augment the power they have by any means, and perpetuate their hold on power. These hierarchies helped each other, compromising their principles if they had to, so long as they could attain their ultimate goal of dominance—temporal or spiritual. The history of both of these institutions provides ample proof of this assertion. Whether they have a continuing institutional conscience or a "consciousness" is an interesting philosophical question I will not discuss. However, they do have historical records in their archives to support an institutional memory. If they claim credit for all the good things they assert to have done in the past, it is only fair for them to own up to their bad deeds. Whether they actually do so in practice is a separate question. Their reluctance to admit past wrongs is at least proof of the existence of an institutional pride or ego. Perhaps they may show remorse only if the public opinion of their constituency and others is insistent enough to force them to do so. Accountability is the worst nightmare dominance hierarchies have to face. However, a recent statement by Pope Benedict XVI about the conversion of native populations of South America 500 years ago, conceding that "unjustifiable crimes" were committed, is welcome. The pope further added that it is "not possible to forget the suffering and the injustices inflicted by colonizers against the indigenous population, whose fundamental human rights were often trampled" (Fisher 2007a). A similar statement of admission and contrition for the atrocities committed by the state, church, and the Inquisition in Goa is necessary. At least it would go a long way in healing past wounds and educating people who are ignorant of the fact that gross human rights violations that happened in Goa were historical facts. The sacrifices of these many nameless, faceless, and voiceless martyrs to the cause of freedom of conscience, belief, and thought should not be forgotten.

Forgiveness—A Necessity

One may ask: Is it wise to dig up unpleasant past events and discuss people long dead? Why not bury the past and conveniently forget it? Is it not much easier to pretend that nothing out of the ordinary happened and there was peace and harmony all around? The answer is a resounding no! To paraphrase George Santayana: "Those who forget the past are bound to repeat it." Unfortunately, knowing the past in no way immunizes us from repeating it. The question is: What and how much do we learn from the past, and how effectively do we use what we learn? The answer is: Perhaps not much. We keep fighting wars, big and small, for various reasons. The ambient conditions and justifications vary, but the slaughter continues. Lessons learned from the past excesses of the stock market bubbles are forgotten in repeating similar risky ventures, which ultimately lead to disaster and much misery (Ferguson 2008). There are many other examples. Why should the extraordinary events of medieval Goa matter to us today? They matter because they deal with matters of perennial concern: restrictions of individual liberties of thought and belief by the dominant institutional authority. By apologizing for the past, the church would at least acknowledge that it erred and would not repeat such atrocities.

Apologists for these actions can rightly point out that in the sixteenth century, individual human rights were neither known nor accepted. Even if these rights were well known and accepted, it is anybody's guess as to whether they would have stopped the atrocities committed. The commandment "Thou shalt not kill" was accepted by all Christians as applicable to at least other Christians, and as a tacit declaration of their right to life. However, this did not put an end to wars with Christians and their slaughter by other Christian princes. Hence, the defense of human rights violations in Goa because human rights were not generally accepted as such in those days does not wash. Humans have not shown greater compliance with other commandments or respect for the human rights implied by them. That is the reason for laws and judicial systems of rewards and punishments all over the world. The pursuit of power brooks no rivals—individual rights, moral censure, or voice of conscience. The abridgment of individual rights and liberties by organized institutional power occurs time and again in history and merits our continued serious attention and vigilance. Thoughts and beliefs are the most elusive of human attributes; however, their power to motivate action is immense. The power hierarchies saw these liberties as a challenge to their dominance and a threat to their very existence and struck back with all their might. The state and church in Goa and elsewhere played the part of thought police and the agents of thought control to ensure their continued existence as dominance hierarchies. Their avowed good intentions were for the general welfare of people under the care of the mother church for their own good on this Earth and later in the hereafter. To carry out this fight in the most efficient, cost-effective manner, they had to create a whole tool kit of weapons. They first demonized the independence in thoughts and beliefs as "heretical depravity" and the heretics as traitors to God and the state. Rituals of legal procedures that were perversions of due process of law were adopted from the past or invented anew. Practical matters such as seizure of the property of the accused became the norm, anonymous witnesses were used, torture became acceptable, and hearsay evidence became the truth, all backed by a façade of legality. Euphemisms were convenient constructs to salve the voice of conscience and were used as tools of deception. The Inquisition and all its past abuses were not isolated incidents in history never to be repeated. This institution continues to this day under a different name, operates secretly under medieval legal procedures, and asserts its right to monitor and control the faithful of the church (Küng 2001; Collins 2002). There have been other institutions with different names, in different countries and circumstances, but very similar in their abuse of power. The lessons learned from these assaults on individual rights have been unexpected. Instead of forswearing such atrocities forever, states and other power hierarchies have adopted some of these well-tried Inquisition procedures that seem to work as instruments of oppression. These have resulted in large-scale slaughter and extermination of perceived undesirables, show trials of losers in the gamble of politics, and abuse of the weak and powerless (Kirsch 2009). This is indeed a sad case of lessons that should not have been learned from history.

The act of recalling the past as such is not bad; it is the mind-set with which it is done that causes problems. Digging into the past as a prelude to holding its present successors directly responsible, keeping the flame of the lust for revenge alive, flaunting a feeling of moral superiority over these evil perpetrators—all of these are counterproductive and destructive. They are almost as repugnant as the original acts that caused the problem in the first place. However, an objective finding of facts about the past wrongs in a spirit of understanding could lead to a healing of these wounds. We cannot sweep the past under the rug and conveniently forget it; we have to face the truth, however unpleasant. Archbishop Tutu said it most eloquently: "Unless we look the beast in the eye we find it has an uncanny habit of returning to hold us hostage" (Tutu 1999, 28). It is in this spirit that I discuss the persecution of the Hindus and Muslims in medieval Goa by the Portuguese and the Roman Catholic church. The guidelines I have set for myself in this investigation were to find the objective truth about past events, neither enhancing or diminishing it; to avoid inflaming emotions in the present about past wrongs and calling for acts of revenge; to understand the motives of the doers of these deeds and to see them as human, however misguided they might have been; and finally, to permanently work myself out of the cage of a victim by proxy by forgiving the perpetrators of these deeds. Forgiveness is entirely selfish and is meant for the equanimity of my own mind. It is only by forgiving these atrocities that I can forget them. As a descendant of Hindus who were persecuted by the Portuguese in medieval Goa and went into exile, I have empathized with their suffering and the injustice done to them. However, I do not want to dwell on these wrongs forever and live permanently in the cage of a substitute victim. I have never permanently lived in that cage; I have only passed through it a few times. I would like to end this feeling of victimization by proxy. I want to purge myself of anger, hatred, or a desire for revenge, because those emotions are destructive; instead, I would like to adopt constructive understanding and healing forgiveness. Forgiveness posits that all humans are fallible, that cooperation is better than confrontation, and that there is some good in all humans. In short, it is a paean to hope and a ringing affirmation of our common humanity.

Hindus in Pre-conquest Goa

Every literate civilization that has left us a record of its history has thought quite highly of itself while running down and deprecating the "others" (Berreby 2005). This is the primacy pride or primacy conceit, an expression of the primacy drive built into our genome and discussed in the first chapter of this book. This habit of exalting the self over others is another way of asserting our dominance, real or imagined, over them. The Hindus were no exception. Alberuni (973 to ca. 1050), a polymath from Khwārazm, south of the Aral Sea, spent quite a few years in India, learned Sanskrit, and studied and translated scholarly Hindu books on astronomy, mythology, and other subjects. He noted that

> . . . the Hindus believe that there is no country but theirs, no nation like theirs, no kings like theirs, no religion like theirs, no science like theirs. They are haughty, foolishly vain, self-conceited and stolid. . . . According to their belief, there is no other country but theirs, no other race of man but theirs, and no created beings besides them have any knowledge or science whatsoever. Their haughtiness is such that, if you tell them of any science or scholar in Khurâsân or Persiś, they will think you to be both an ignoramus and a liar. If they traveled and mixed with other nations, they would soon change their mind, for their ancestors were not as narrow-minded as the present generation is. [Sachau 1971, 22–3, ch. 1]

Alberuni was a shrewd observer, and even allowing for a bit of exaggeration on his part, there was quite a lot of truth in his observations. The decline of Hindu culture began with such a mind-set, when Hindus felt that they had nothing useful to learn from other people or civilizations. It was much easier to call non-Hindus *mleccha* (barbarians) and, after having given them a pejorative label, ignore them as beneath notice. These attitudes of superiority must have lingered well into the fifteenth to sixteenth century CE in spite of Hindus' interactions with the Muslim culture from the eighth century onward. All of this would change with the arrival of the Portuguese in 1498 CE. The complacency of the Hindus, their worldview, norms of behavior, and religious beliefs, would be challenged aggressively by these and other foreigners who followed. In a way, these challenges were good because they forced the Hindus to look critically at their own society and change it if necessary. It is not clear how much of a critical self-examination of Hindu society took place; perhaps it was not much. They had not been exposed to Western ideas or educated in them and were not conditioned to accept and understand them as possible alternates. Any changes proposed by the Portuguese state were forced on them by fiat, and the Goans tried their best to adapt and survive. Unfortunately, the methods used to effect these changes were reprehensible and caused much misery among the people. The Portuguese were convinced of their racial, cultural, military, and doctrinal superiority over the natives and sought to rule by might. This was an unexpected challenge to the Hindu way of life, and the following material describes how they met this challenge and survived. A feature that was common to both the Portuguese and the largely Hindu society that they encountered in Goa was an absence of any doubt in the correctness of their worldview or its critical self-examination. This certainty of belief meant that both of these groups were totally unable to accept or propose any changes in their behavior or actions on their own. The history of Goa before the advent of the Portuguese Empire and the events leading on to it are described in a number of publications listed in the bibliography (Gune 1979; Kudva 1978; Xavier 1993; de Souza 1979; Angle 1994). The Portuguese state and the Roman Catholic church, in the first flush of the zeal of counter-reformation, knew they could do no wrong. The Hindu society, for its part, was convinced of the verities of their Sanāthana Dharma (eternal law) and the traditions based on it. In considering the interaction between these two power hierarchies, it is proper for us to look critically at both of them to assess them objectively. What were the problems with their worldviews? How did these views influence their mutual interactions? These are the questions we will discuss now. The conditions of the Hindu society will be discussed first, followed by those of the Portuguese state and church.

Village Life of Hindus in Goa

Sixteenth-century Goa was mostly agricultural, built around crop cultivation in its villages. The power structure or the dominance hierarchy of each village was the system of village associations, or *gāvṁkārī*, characteristic of Goa.

These were the cooperative agricultural and welfare associations of great antiquity, which were renamed the *communidades* under the Portuguese regime. Functioning in parallel with such associations were the representative *mahājana* (prominent people), with responsibility for the care, maintenance, and management of local Hindu temples, renamed *mazania* by the Portuguese. The Portuguese policy was to build up *communidades* and undermine the *mazania* in order to transfer temple properties to the church as part of coercive conversion to Christianity (Pereira 1978; 1981). It is possible that there was a certain amount of overlap in the membership of these two groups, attesting to the importance of these two dominance groups in the material and religious life of the whole village.

A village or community is *gāvũ* in Konkani, and *gāvṁkar* can mean either a maker of a village or a person belonging to a particular village. Thus, a person who claimed a particular village to be his "native place," or where his family had lived for generations, and therefore as his place of origin, would take the name of the village ending in the "*kar*" and use it as his family name. The village associations were formed by representatives of clans, or *vāngaḍ*, of the lineal male descendants of the original founders of the villages who had cleared the land of its forests or scrub and cultivated it, built the irrigation system, and maintained it from olden days (de Souza 1979, 1994; Pereira 1978, 1981; Xavier 1993; Mitragotri 1999; Newman 2001; de Bragança Pereira 2008). The earliest record of these associations is from about 1054 CE, in a grant by Jayakeshi, fifth king of the Kadamba dynasty (Periera 1978). Lands belonging to the village, both cultivable or not, were held, administered, and enjoyed jointly by the village association. Most of these associations were formed by the dominant castes of Brahmans, Kshatriyas, or Merchants, and in the process the indigenous tribes of *Gāvḍos*, also called *Kuṇabīs* or *Velips* (Gune 1979; Kosambi 1962, 1969, 1975), had been reduced to a subservient class of serfs or slaves. These were essentially bonded labor attached to the land and the family that owned it, and they were expected to provide work in return for subsistence. However, in a few villages, the original tribes did survive and became part of the dominant hierarchy. The land in Goa was mostly sandy, and only a limited amount of it could be cultivated. In addition to a small amount of rice or legume cultivation, most of the land was devoted to coconut or areca nut plantations. Goa had to import most of its foodstuffs from the rest of India, in exchange for exports of salt, salted fish, copra, and areca nut. The village associations hired people to provide village security, maintained local roads, carried out periodic property surveys to prevent land encroachment, controlled and maintained the irrigation system, settled local disputes, and in general worked by consensus to discharge its municipal functions (Pereira 1978). Cultivable property was auctioned off every few years to the highest bidder among members of the association, and the profits were divided among its members according to an agreed-on formula. Some of these profits were assigned to the care and maintenance of local Hindu temples, which played such an important part in the life of a Goan village. First, the temples were centers of education for the children of the village. Second, some of the priests were also physicians and provided essential health care for the village. Third, the temples were the center of the cultural life of the village, where the reading and exposition in the vernacular of the Hindu mythology, the *purāṇas*; performance of epic stories as *nāṭak* (drama) or the *harikathās* (sacred narratives); and dance performances took place. These temples were also the focus of weekly or seasonal fairs organized around the festivals that played an important part in the village economy. Each temple supported the priests, carpenters, goldsmiths, washermen, ironsmiths, potters, barbers, temple servants who provided various services connected to it including the women dedicated to the temple (*devadāsīs*), musicians, and others (Saraswati 1963; Axelrod and Fuerch 1996). Depending on the wealth of the village that supported the local temples, each temple employed more than 30 to 50 people, directly or indirectly. Temples were the biggest single employer in the whole village. In addition to the power hierarchy of the village owning its lands and the serfs or slaves doing the hard physical labor of cultivation, there was a class of independent artisans and craftsmen who provided the many necessities of life in a village. These are the carpenters who made the furniture and agricultural implements, the leatherworkers and cobblers, metalworkers, barbers, fishermen, masons, potters, washermen and washerwomen, and people who engaged in other crafts.

The houses were built of mud bricks dried in the sun, were thatched, and had little ventilation and a few rooms. Only the well-to-do could afford large joint family homes built around a central courtyard where a few generations lived together. These could support as many as about 150 people in a single family (Kosambi 1962), presided over by the paterfamilias, whose benevolent rule determined every important action of the family members. Such a large family must have been an exception rather than a rule. Joint families of 20 to 30 people living under one roof were more common. Preparing the food for the family, conforming to all the rules of ritual purity, cleaning the house and clothes, and doing other household chores must have been a burden for the women of such large joint families, even if they could afford servants to do work both inside and outside the house. In addition to the daily activities of milking cows and buffaloes and preparing dairy products, there were the summer projects, such as pickling mangoes and jackfruit, drying fruits in season, and preparing various types of sun-dried condiments—*hāppoḷu, pāppoḍu, vōḍi*, and *śevāyı*—for use during the rainy season. The main purpose in life of women was to bear many children (sons preferred, of course) as insurance against childhood diseases and a large infant mortality rate. Surviving childbirth was the major hurdle in every woman's life. In all families, including Hindus, women were the subservient and hence the exploited class, with many responsibilities and few rights. Any rights women might have had were hard earned late in life, after surviving the births of many children, the discipline of their mother-in-law, and finally reaching the pinnacle of life as the mother of grown-up sons and breadwinners. Most men had a single wife; however, there were exceptions, and the right of a man to have more than one wife was never questioned. If the first wife had not produced a single son or if the man had a roving eye and craved variety, he could marry again, with or without the first wife's consent. Sometimes if a man's wife's younger sister could not be married for some reason, her brother-in-law would be expected to step into the breach and marry again. In addition, there was the anomalous situation of extramarital sex involving a *rābbonu ghettili* (mistress). Such liaisons were frowned on by society and gave rise to much local gossip; however, being able to afford the expenses of a second household was a status symbol. The dominance of the patron and the consequent subservience of the woman, or at least a semblance of it, may have added some attraction and piquancy to the relationship. A serially monogamous arrangement, involving a long-term entanglement with a local *kalāvant*, the upper tier of *devadāsī*, was customary for the rich. For the not-so-affluent, the *bhāvin*, the lower class of *devadāsī*, catered to more casual sex. A joint family provided invaluable support in time of trouble; however, it discouraged individual initiative or independent action. It was essential to defer to the judgment of the head of the family, who made sure that the norms of caste, creed, and tradition were faithfully followed. One of the most important duties of the head of the family was the hospitable reception and entertainment of guests, or *atithisatkāra* (hospitality). Guests could drop in at any time, unannounced and without notice, and it was obligatory for the host to entertain them as if their visit had been planned for and eagerly anticipated, even if it meant short rations for some members of the host family (Kosambi 1962). People living in the villages were on the whole more traditional or conservative, with their own beliefs and worldview. In addition to the basic tenets of Hinduism, they believed in astrology; various other forms of divination; the occult and witchcraft, including their favorite *Tāntrik* (adept of Tantras) to cast spells or counteract them; good and bad omens and how to read them; and a universe of related beliefs. The Hindu Āyurvedic system of medicine, with its theory of humors, supplemented with a proper restricted diet and some religious rites in a few cases, was the one sure road for a cure. Whether the theory behind the system of medicine was right or wrong, some local herbs were quite effective in curing some diseases. As for other illnesses, the outcome very much depended on the robust constitution of the sick person whose good genetic heritage had enabled him or her to survive past insults to the body. If the person could not measure up, the fatal outcome was ascribed to the bad karma of the patient, his wife, or the family. From our vantage point, we can label some of these beliefs as questionable. However, it is good to remember that each culture and people, including ours, has its own set of doubtful pet beliefs, not supported by empirical data and equally doubtful. We have very few records of life in Goan villages amongst the Sarasvats of the olden days. As a dominant caste, they must have been living in more comfortable circumstances than most. Most families do not know where or how they lived in Goa. All these memories were wiped clean by the troubled times of Portuguese persecution, and their hurried exile to survival in places outside Goa. Records of trade and other activities of some rich families remain to be mined for information and converted to connected narratives of life for Sarasvat families in those troubled times. There are a few books, however, which give a flavor of life in Goa in the ninteenth century and enable us to guess or extrapolate to earlier times. A biographical novel on the life of a truly remarkable man, Dharmanand Kosambi (1876–1947), author, patriot, a scholar of Buddhism, Pali, and Sanskrit, visiting professor at Harvard and Leningrad University, is highly readable and informative on life and the conditions in late-nineteenth-century and early-twentieth-century Goa, for a family of Sarasvat Brahmans (Sawkar 2001). This book, a biographical novel, is based on an autobiography of the elder Kosambi, their family traditions and collective memory, and the recollections of the author, who is the granddaughter of Dharmanand. *Goa: A Daughter's Story* is written with much love and affection for Goa and Goan life, covering the whole period of Portuguese occupation, leading on to the twentieth century, gives a flavor of life in Goa from the perspective of Christians (Couto 2004). A third book by an anthropologist, *Of Umbrellas, Goddesses, and Dreams: Essays on Goan Culture and Society*, is about present-day Goan society, the changes brought about in Goa after its takeover by India in 1961, and how the different religions coexist today (Newman 2001).

Urban Life of Hindus in Goa

The Gauda Sarasvat Brahmana (GSB) community that lived in the city of Goa worked for the state administration and also participated in various forms of trade, big and small. There was a tradition of learning and scholarship in this community. Many knew Marathi, Sanskrit, Persian, and Hindi in addition to their mother tongue, Konkani, and quickly picked up Portuguese. The Portuguese did not show any marked aptitude for trade and commerce, and this vacant niche was filled by the Gujarati *vania* (traders) and the Sarasvat Brahmans, who had a long tradition as merchants. The overseas trade appears to have been controlled mostly by the Gujarati merchants, who worked in partnership with the Portuguese for various reasons, including favorable concessions in taxes, custom duties, and trade regulations by the state. The inland trade was mostly in the hands of the Sarasvats (Pearson 1973; de Souza 1975), who were involved in a wide spectrum of economic activities, from petty traders to rich merchants financing big shipments of grain or produce and acting as tax farmers and collectors of custom duties. The Sarasvats and their involvement can be recognized by the family names of *Naik*, *Sinai*, *Prabhu*, *Pai*, *Shet*, *Gad*, and others (de Souza 1975). Their education, familiarity with languages and skill in negotiations enabled them to act as ambassadors, interpreters, and general intermediaries between the Portuguese and the local rulers and functionaries. They traded in the import of food grains and spices from the rest of India, farmed revenues from silk and cotton textiles, did gold and silver mining, and bid for contracts on ship building and repairs in the Goa shipyards (de Souza 1975). Jan Huyghen van Linschoten also mentions that these Brahmans controlled most of the land around the town of Goa (Burnell and Tiele 1935). The landed gentry amongst them must have lost their property rights when they went into exile to escape conversion. Some of them returned on promise of better treatment as regards freedom of belief, and they must have gone into trade, because they had lost all their property (Couto 2004, p. 216). A few bid for tax-farming contracts. To be able to bid for these contracts, this group must have had large amounts of capital and must have formed an important section of the whole economy. It is quite possible that at least some of them, the rich and affluent, had some political clout with the state. In the period 1600–1670, 80% of tax farmers were Hindus, 20% were Christians, and of Hindus, 62.7% were Sarasvats. In terms of value, the Hindus held 65.2% of tax revenues, of which the Sarasvats were responsible for 69% of the Hindu total and 44.9% of the whole (Pearson 1973). In the first decade of the seventeenth century, 91.7% of the nonagricultural revenues were administered by Hindus and the remaining by Christians (de Souza 1975). The wealth of some of these Sarasvats can be judged from the substantial amounts of money they loaned and the large tax-farming contracts they bid for. When the state under Prime Minister Pombal expelled the Jesuits in 1759, the Camotim family was left with an unpaid debt of 203,370 *xerafims* owed them by the Jesuits in China (Couto 2004, 219). This was a huge amount of money by any standard!

The largely silver-based Indo-Portuguese coinage was defined in terms of the fictitious unit *reis* (Subrahmanyam 1990, 371–3). The coins in common use were as follows: *xerafim* = 300 *reis*; *tanga* = 60 *reis*; *cruzado* (up to 1560s) =

360 *reis*; *cruzado* (post-1570 and in the early seventeenth century) = 400 *reis*. The *rial* of eight = the silver *pardau* = São Tomé = 360 *reis*. The Mughal rupee was equal to 0.5 *rials* of eight, or 180 *reis*. The approximate purchasing power of a *xerafim* can be understood in terms of the cost of the staples, rice and wheat. A plot of the prices of rice and wheat during 1600–1700, with many gaps in data, is available (de Souza 1979, 172). The following features of this plot should be noted. From 1600–1630, the prices of these food grains were between 6 and 15 *xerafim/khandi*, where 1 *khandi* = 214.3 kg = 472 lb. They peaked around 1630–1635, rising to about 40 *xerafim/khandi*. Between 1660 and 1670, the prices were between 13 and 30 *xerafim/khandi*, peaking at about 40 to 50 *xerafim/khandi* in 1690 and rising higher in 1700. In October 1666, the municipality of Goa set the price of 1 *khandi* of *jirsal* rice = 14.4 *xerafim*; *chamasal* rice = 12.8 *xerafim*; and black rice = 11.2 *xerafim* (de Souza 1979, 281). Quarterly salaries of some professions in the seventeenth century were as follows: barber, 5 *xerafim*; cobbler, 4; washerman, 7; cook, 3; and pandit, or native physician, 15 *xerafim*. At the high end of the economic spectrum in 1654, a large, brand-new galleon weighing 1,000 tons was worth 44,100 rupees, or 26,460 *xerafims*, to a merchant (Pearson 1981, 97). Narsu Naik, an opium revenue farmer, bid for 13,400 *xerafims* (19.5% of total nonagricultural revenues of 68,555 *xerafims*); Damu Sinay was responsible for 12,000 *xerafims* of cloth revenue (17.5% of the total) (de Souza 1975). This reference also mentions Rangana Sinay, a tobacco tax farmer, who bid an astonishing 29,000 *xerafims* in 1683 to collect these revenues.

Hindu Business under the Portuguese

How did the Hindu business fare under the Portuguese? Are there any data from which to extrapolate this information? Information on the financial status of the Hindus, and in particular the Sarasvats, under the Portuguese is available. The data are from an informative paper by T.R. de Souza entitled: "Glimpses of Hindu Dominance of Goan Economy in the 17th Century." This is how the author summarizes the purpose of the article:

> What follows is an attempt to peep into the economic past of Goa during the seventeenth century and to rectify with the help of recorded evidence a half-truth about the Hindu population having received a very raw deal under the Portuguese colonial rule in India. [de Souza 1975, 27]

Let us see what these economic and other data tell us about Hindus in Goa. It is necessary to recall that the rich Sarasvats mentioned here were only a handful in their community, which is a subset of all Hindus. In extrapolating from these few at the economic apex of their society to Hindus at large, we are jumping over two unknowns: the Sarasvat community as a whole and the rest of the Hindus. Imagine an archeologist discovering a building completely covered by sand except for its small visible tip. Trying to guess the shape of the sand-covered part from the visible tip would be as unrealistic as extrapolating from the few rich Sarasvats to Hindus at large. All we know about the Hindus are the census figures given by de Souza. Under these circumstances, such extrapolations could not be reliable because of the paucity of data. Any conclusions drawn from such extrapolations will be speculative at best. The data show that there were some rich Sarasvats who were prominent in trade and commerce in seventeenth-century Goa. These few rich and powerful of the community must have come to some understanding with the state–church power structure, survived their proselytizing zeal, and might even have flourished. It is only another example of the truism that the rich usually survive social upheavals. It does not tell us much about the majority of the other Sarasvats, the petty trader, the well-to-do, or the subsistence farmer from the villages, who were dispossessed of their ancestral property rights and had to go into exile. Census figures for the seventeenth to eighteenth centuries, for different localities in Goa led de Souza to conclude:

> It is obvious from our figures that the Hindus were reduced to a minority group by the end of the seventeenth century. However, not only they were not annihilated, but they were not even reduced to impotence. [de Souza 1975, 30]

Because of the economic clout of the Hindus, the state had to temper its zeal for conversions and moderate its religious and social enforcements. This is supported by a royal instruction to the viceroy, dated 1 March 1704, which said:

> Expulsion of the Hindus will be tantamount to destroying the State, because it is only they who keep our trade going and provide us with all our revenues. However, it will not be right to give them too much freedom and let them have temples within the territories of our jurisdiction. [de Souza 1975, 35]

What do these statements tell us in answer to the original question of whether the Hindus got a raw deal under the Portuguese? The answer has two dimensions to it, one subjective and the other objective. The subjective part deals with individual experiences of the Hindus in those troubled times, and the objective data are measurable quantities available in public records. We may never know the subjective part, because it could be answered only by the people who experienced life under the Portuguese, and they have left us no records. However, as regards the objective component, one could quantify it by the undisputed metrics available from the Portuguese records. These are the number of temples and mosques destroyed, the amount of Hindu property appropriated for churches and Christian institutions built on their sites, the forcible conversions, the kidnapping of minors under the façade of perverse legalisms, and official and legal discrimination against Hindus that have been listed elsewhere in this story. These harsh measures affected all of the Hindus, Sarasvats, and others, rich and poor, and amount to a raw deal by any standard! Two of the rich and prominent Sarasvats, Mhall Pai Vernekar and Krishna Sinai, the chief tax collector, the very pillars of the establishment, later conspired against the state because of its heavy-handed policy of religious conversions (Couto 2004, 85, 196). To take such a drastic step, putting their life and property in jeopardy, they must indeed have been unhappy with the administration. Further, the very economic importance of Hindus seems to have attracted the attention of the state to impose selective taxation on them and use them as cash cows for additional revenues. State bureaucracies can be very imaginative in identifying new sources of taxes, and in spite of the pious sentiments expressed in the royal instructions quoted above, the Portuguese came up with a capitation tax on the *śeṇḍi*, or the tuft of hair on the crown of head worn by all Hindu men, in the same year. The tuft of hair was one unmistakable outward sign that a man was a Hindu. This tax has been called a Portuguese version of the *jizya* imposed on non-Muslims by Muslim kings and some Mughals (de Souza 1994, 106–16). The *śeṇḍi* tax (1704–1841) lasted for nearly a century and half:

> The goldsmiths were to pay 3 *xerafins* per annum, the small shop-keepers (*botiqueiros*) three *xerafins* each, the brokers (*corretores*) also three *xerafins* each, the whole-sale traders (*mercadores*) five *xerafins* each, and all others working in any other profession would pay two *xerafins* each. [de Souza 1994, 110]

This was not a tax on necessities of life such as food or clothing or on luxuries such as tobacco or liquor but one on the very identity of citizens as a Hindu. The state ruled that to live as Hindu under the Portuguese, they had to pay for this privilege with additional monies. This obligation was later extended to Muslims who did not even wear the tuft (de Souza 1994, 110–1): "However, this tax was motivated by the fiscal necessities of the state, though suggested by the religious zealots who belonged to the advisory council of the Portuguese viceroy in Goa" (de Souza 1975, 35). All taxation is ultimately justified by the economics of the state; however, this bit of apologetic does not in any way mitigate the unfairness of such selective taxation. There were many clashes between the Marathas and the Portuguese (Gune 1979, 166–85), including the Maratha hostilities of 1737–1740. The Maratha raids of 1739 and the attempts of the state to repel them gave rise to anti-Hindu feelings, which were used by the clerics to stir up a mob attack on the house of the richest Hindu, Pundu Camotim (Puṇḍarīka or Puṇḍalīka Kāmati), suspected of sheltering enemies. He was also fined 130,000 *xerafims* to pay for the retreat of enemy forces (Couto 2004, 219). There were additional taxes on other Hindus as well to pay for the cost of fighting the Marathas. The Holy Office of the Inquisition kept up its drumbeat of requests to expel Hindus who refused conversion, and later it demanded confiscation of their property as well (Boxer 1960–1961, 88):

> In the upshot, the Hindus of Goa were not expelled at the crisis of the Maratha war, but they were subjected to a forced capital levy which left them with little more than their eyes to weep with.

The Hindus in Portuguese Goa, thus, seem to have been caught between the proverbial rock and a hard place. They had to contend with the evangelical zeal of the state and church, selective taxation, and discrimination in Goa and buy their right to live there. If they migrated to the Adil Shahi states, there was *jizya*, the tax on non-Muslims, and the periodic persecution of the Hindus by the state and Muslims. Each place had its advantages and problems, and both choices were difficult and had its own compromises. The harsh edicts and arbitrary rule of the Portuguese were resented by both the Hindus and the new Christian converts, who appear to have helped each other in surviving those troubled times. This was the beginning of the unique Goan Hindu–Christian society, which though divided by religion has shown remarkable unity and syncretism originating from a memory of common customs and traditions (Dias 1980). A few Hindus made a third choice and migrated to distant Hindu kingdoms such as Kochin, where they hoped to live in peace (Map 1). Kochin and coastal Karnataka were the destinations of many Hindus, including my family, when they left Goa in the sixteenth century. How many people went into exile to escape persecution by the state and church? There are only rough estimates: "Manuel Themudo, S.J., visitor to Kanara missions, reported in 1669 that in the course of the previous 35 years nearly 30,000 Goans, chiefly Hindus, had migrated to Kanara lands due to religious persecutions and other reasons" (de Souza 1979, 54). These estimates should be multiplied by factors of 5 or more to account for exiles to other parts of India, including Bombay, Maratha kingdoms and parts of Maharashtra, Madhya Pradesh, and Kerala, in addition to the Kanara lands. Sudden uprooting of families, loss of goods and property, and hardships of travel to distant and strange parts, and the misery suffered by the exiles must have been incalculable. How did they go into exile? We do not know, because there are no written accounts of their travels. We can only guess. These refugees had two options: to travel by land or by sea, each with its own problems, all bad. The land journey was done on foot, each person carrying a few precious possessions on their head. Perhaps they had a bullock cart, if they could afford one, for children and the older members of the family and goods too heavy to carry. (See the illustration on the cover of this book, strictly based on conjecture.) On the way, they had to face robbers, local wars and upheavals, wild animals, sickness and injury, and the hardship of travel by foot with a heavy load and perhaps little food. They could sail in wooden sailing ships, *macvo*, used in coastal trade with a license from the Portuguese, having to face unpredictable storms and loss of life, pirates, and the problems of travel by sea. According to family tradition, my ancestors went to Kochin in one such coastal ship. Being observant Hindus, they perhaps attributed the hardships of exile to their past bad karma and saw their current suffering as a form of expiation. However, they had hopes for a better future in which their good karma might bear fruit. With this optimism in their hearts, they set out on a journey into the unknown.

Sarasvats Speak Out in Times of Trouble

From extant state and other records, some Sarasvats stand out for their reaction to the happenings around them as personalities in their own right. They were prominent in state service, diplomacy, and large-scale commerce and have left records of their thoughts and feelings. These are important contemporary records of how a few Hindus felt about all of the social and religious upheavals going on around them. Azu Naik (or Naique) was an agent of the state from Bassein (or Baçaim) whose correspondence with Portugal's King John III shows that he was quite well informed about what was happening to people in Goa as well as to Jews and others in Europe. He pleaded for religious tolerance and mitigation of forced conversions that were the state policy. His shrewd observations on governance of the state and separation of religious and civil affairs is worth reproducing (Boxer 1960–1961, 81; D'Costa 1965, 43–4). When the king proposed that Azu Naik should become a Christian, he politely declined. His very diplomatic reply of 18 December 1549 pleaded that he should not be forced to convert because

> . . . there is one only God in whom all believe, and He is indeed very merciful to those whom by His grace He wants to lead in the way of truth, and this belongs to Him alone. When the territories of Your Highness are well peopled and developed by native inhabitants, they are a source of profit and revenue:

> and it is out of this that India and the churches are maintained. There is a great difference between a Friar's life and work and that of a King. There is similar difference between civil government and ecclesiastical affairs. For the main thing is the taxes that are realized from these lands and are paid by the inhabitants of the place: out of these, as I say, churches are maintained. The King's Government ought to care well for such people, and neither allow nor authorize any violence or injury against them. Rather should favour be shown them and authorization given to reside there secure in their customs. And he who freely wishes to become a Christian will do so, as has been happening all along till now. [D'Costa 1965, 43–4]

With reference to the exiling of Hindus in Goa who did not want to become Christians, he mentioned the protection granted by Pope Leo X (1513–1521) to Jewish physicians and musicians in his service and noted:

> For in Rome where the Holy Father is, he permits in his lands all kinds of people, nor does he send them away thence if they do not want to become Christians. Since this is so, why should they act in Goa as they do? [D'Costa 1965, 44]

This wise counsel, however, fell on the deaf ears of the state and church in the zealous pursuit of their evangelizing mission. Krishna Sinai (also called Krishna Rao) was the chief *thanadar*, or tax farmer, between 1523 and 1548 and visited Portugal between 1520 and 1523 (Subrahmanyam 1993). There he secured for himself the posts of *shahbandar* (chief of port) and *corretor dos cavalos* (horse broker), was appointed captain of the native infantry, and was greatly favored by the king of Portugal. In 1543 he negotiated with the Sultan of Bijapur to cede Bardez and Salcette to the Portuguese. In keeping with his wealth, status, and diplomatic connections, he had a large house where he played host to visiting ambassadors and other dignitaries from neighboring states (Couto 2004). However, he became disillusioned with Portuguese rule because of the insistent pressure to convert, and he eventually conspired against the state. He was imprisoned at Bijapur during one of his diplomatic missions and is believed to have died there. He was briefly succeeded by his son Dadji Sinai, who was an interpreter to the viceroy and thus privy to diplomatic correspondence from neighboring states. Loku (Lakṣmaṇa?) Sinai was another rich and prominent tax farmer, well known for his charity and liberal support of good causes, according to Dutch Jesuit Gaspar Berze (D'Costa 1965, 48). In 1548, he fell on hard times and was imprisoned for alleged failure to pay his dues to the state. Though earlier he had been prominent in exhorting Hindus not to convert, while in prison he expressed a desire to become a Christian. We do not know what brought about this change of mind. It may have been prompted by a sincere desire to be baptized, hopes of leniency from the state, or a conviction that he was ritually polluted in prison and could not be reinstated as a Hindu in good standing. He was released from prison and after a brief preparation was baptized as Lucas de Sa (Couto 2004). The ceremony was performed by the bishop of Goa, the governor standing as his godfather; eight days of rejoicing followed (Pearson 1987). Obviously, this was a feather in the cap for the Portuguese. Lucas de Sa was immediately appointed chief tax collector to replace Krishna Sinai, whose family were now dispossessed. Krishna had been imprisoned in Bijapur, where he had been sent with a Portuguese embassy. Lucas apparently wanted to convince himself and others that his conversion was sincere and not motivated by expectations of leniency. Accordingly, his wishes were followed: The legal case against him was not dismissed. There was a trial, followed by an appeal and a final assessment of a fine of 20,000 *pardaus* (*pardau* = 1.2 *xerafim*) against him. The viceroy pleaded with the king to remit two-thirds of this fine. Vithu Sinai was a scribe to the general assembly in 1553 and was in the same post in 1558. He probably became a Christian in 1562, because records indicate that the chief scribe of the whole island requested baptism. Anu Sinai was the commercial agent of the Portuguese, and Gopu Sinai was another important person of the same standing and importance as Krishna Sinai and Loku Sinai (Lucas de Sa). The part played by other Sarasvats in diplomacy, commerce, and in the service of the state in Goa is described by Couto (Couto 2004, Ch. 8; Kudva 1978; Talmaki and Nadkarni 1998). Vithula Sinay (Viṭṭala Śeṇoy) was the envoy of the Nayaks of Ikkeri to the court of Goa. In 1623, he accompanied the Portuguese mission to Ikkeri, consisting of Portuguese Ambassador Fernandes Leitão and Italian traveler Pietro Della Valle (1586–1652) (Lach and Van Kley 1993, 863). Sinay presented Della Valle with a palm-leaf manuscript in Kannada for his library as a curiosity. Ramoji Sinai Cothari was another Sarasvat diplomat who negotiated, from 1645 to 1674, with the kings of Kanara, Bijapur, the Moghul court, and with Shivaji, on behalf of the Portuguese (Couto 2004).

There are many accounts of life in the sixteenth to seventeenth century city of Goa, called "Golden Goa" by many visiting travelers from Europe: the narratives of Dutchman Linschoten (1583–1588), who was an employee of the archbishop of Goa for about five years (Burnell and Tiele 1935; Collingham 2006); Portuguese Augustinian friar Sebastião Manrique, who was in Goa for a few years between 1604 and 1614; Frenchman Francois Pyrard in 1608; and others (Collis 1985; Boxer 1969; Lach and Van Kley 1993; Fonseca 2001).

Hindu Society and Its Problems

The two principal dominance hierarchies in Hindu society are those based on caste and sex. The caste system is cruel, unfair, unjust, and iniquitous and will always be a blot on Hindu society. Any hierarchy, however benevolent, implies exploitation of the weak by the strong, and the caste system of the Hindus is no exception. In rural Goa, the village *gāvṁkārī* system was mostly controlled by the dominant upper castes, as already mentioned. Perhaps the worst part of the caste hierarchy is that it is determined by birth and hence prevents upward mobility, thus not allowing the brightest to move up in the hierarchy. It does not encourage attempts to better oneself or provide opportunities to those with initiative. Other than that, the caste system is neither worse nor better than social stratifications that one finds in every society. This is not meant as an apology for the system; it is just a realistic appraisal of it and stresses the fact that hierarchies of various sorts exist in every society. It is true that the Portuguese society in Goa was casteless; however, as is pointed out later, it was riddled with many gradations of class, enough to satisfy every human conceit and bit of snobbery. Whether one calls it a caste system or social stratification, it is very much part of every society and survives religious conversions to casteless religions. The only way to get rid of the iniquities of this system is to provide a good education to every child, irrespective of caste or class, so that all children have a chance to rise up in society by marketing their useful skills and become part of the dominance group in their turn. This huge change is very much a work in progress both amongst the Hindus and in the rest of India, under a very extensive affirmative-action program of the government.

Hindu society, for the most part, is patriarchal, with males dominant and females subservient. In any society, the dominant group exploits those lower in hierarchy, and this fact of life is true amongst Hindus also. This situation is made worse by the lack of women's property rights in most Hindu *jātis* (birth groups). The property of a joint Hindu family is inherited by the male descendants, who live under the nominal control and authority of the more senior members of the family. The two schools of Hindu family law dealing with inheritance, partition of family property, and related matters are *Dāyābhāga*, in use in Bengal and parts of Assam, and *Mitākṣarā*, applicable in the rest of India. Each of these two schools of law has a tradition of respectable antiquity behind it. The main differences between them depend on the theory behind family property (Kane 1973, 3:558–9) and on arcane points of Hindu law. However, the first school is more favorable to women and minors than the second one is. *Dāyābhāga* assigns right of succession to the husband's share of undivided family property by the wife, even if she is without a son; the *Mitākṣarā* does not. In general, women could not own property, except for the legally sanctioned *strīdhana* (women's property), under her absolute control. *Strīdhana* is a complicated subject of ancient Vedic origin (Kane 1973, 3:770–802; Altekar 1999; Lingat 1973; Derrett 1963, 1968) and is perhaps the only remaining vestige of the olden days when women had property rights and therefore were less subservient to men. These rights also meant greater freedom and control over their persons and sexuality. Evidence for such freedom is found in the rituals of the seasonal Vedic sacrifice of *Varuṇapraghāsa*, in which the wife of the sacrificer, *yajamāna*, is asked by one of the officiating priests to declare the number of lovers she has had (Kane 1974, 2:1098). She can either name them or, if bashful, indicate the number by picking up blades of *darbha* grass from a bunch. If she has none, she says so. Vedic society seems to have been casual about any such extramarital liaisons, accepting confession as expiation. In the *Mahābhārata*, *Pāṇḍu* tells *Kuntī* that from ancient times down to his own days, there was much promiscuity in the land of Uttara Kuru (Sur 1963). In those days, women appear to have been more independent economically. Female artisans could practice their craft and live in the house of a rich person or a king without social censure. These women were called *sairindhrī*, a name adopted by Draupadī, when the Pāṇḍavas were living in disguise for a year in the court of King Virāṭa. While offering food to the Manes (dead ancestors), a person would declare as part of the ritual: "If my mother (or grandmother etc.) has gone astray unmindful of her duty towards her husband, may my father (grandfather, etc.) accept that sperm as his own" (Apte 1954, 87, 243). At a later time, Śvetaketu ("White Light") Āruṇeya, son of Uddalaka Āruṇi, reformed social mores to declare that it was a grave sin for a woman to be false to her husband or for a husband to be false to a chaste wife (Kane 1974, 2:428). Being faithful to one's spouse worked both ways in those days. Early authors of codes of law were also lenient and prescribed penance after repentance for any marital infidelity, though in general they were less forgiving about the sexual peccadilloes of women than those of men (Altekar 1999, 313). After the eleventh century, lack of economic independence for women resulted in strict control over their persons and sexuality by the dominant male hierarchy. No transgressions of strict moral codes were tolerated or allowed; the punishments were harsh. The lives of many heroines of Hindu tradition such as Sītā and Damayanti have been presented to Hindu women as examples of conjugal love, fidelity, self-sacrifice, and other wifely virtues worthy of emulation. Unfortunately, this sets standards for Hindu women that are very high and difficult to live up to, especially when the same social strictures do not expect reciprocity in these sentiments from their husbands. Establishing such norms of behavior is a subtle form of coercion and dominance, where the guilty conscience of individual woman becomes a hard taskmaster. In short, Hindu codes of law have been long on women's duties and obligations and short on their rights and privileges. Women in Hindu society do not enjoy gender equality or economic and sexual freedom. These facts of life have resulted in social customs and traditions that vary from the cruel to the insensitive, such as the self-immolation of the widow with the dead body of the husband (*satī sahagamana*), the harsh treatment of widows, no inheritance or property rights for women, the dedication of women to temples (*devadāsīs*), the lack of education for women, child marriages, and female infanticide. The Portuguese state and church authorities and the religious orders that wanted to spread the Christian gospel in medieval Goa were quick to notice and focus on these problems, and they tried to correct them by fiat or restrictive legislation. To a large extent these laws were opportunistic, because they provided a golden opportunity to advance the program of religious conversion by providing relief from social problems as an incentive to the prospective convert. Women, on conversion to Christianity, acquired inheritance rights in family property and wealth that they had never had under traditional Hindu law (D'Costa 1965; de Mendonça 2002, 170–3; Priolkar 1961). However, most of the Hindu women did not see the traditional customs as particularly unjust; they were not sensitized to their inequity, or they did not have enough education and economic and social independence to fight for their rights and take advantage of the new legislation. Perhaps they were not aware that they had any inherent rights as individuals and or as human beings. The state–church complex deserves commendation for putting an end to the cruel and inhuman practices like *satī*. In the following sections, I will discuss the problems of Hindu society in fifteenth- and sixteenth-century Goa. I will also discuss Portuguese legislation approved by the various provincial councils of Goa and meant to correct these problems. Did such legislation help in the mass conversion of a large number of the Hindus? The answer is no, although it might have been an inducement for conversion in a few cases.

Satī Sahagamana, or *Satī*

Satī sahagamana is the act of a woman of burning herself with her deceased husband's body. *Satī* is a virtuous woman whose act of going together, *sahagamana*, with her dead husband, was much extolled as a sign of love and devotion. It is a painful, cruel death. This fact should never be forgotten despite whatever explanations may be offered, be they cultural, religious, or something else. The only answer I have been able to find is that it was a form of ritual suicide. Ritual suicide and its various ramifications are explained in the next section. Inscribed stelae, *mahāsatīkals*, were erected in honor of these events. In later historical times, there are eyewitness accounts of this rite. In most cases, *satī sahagamana* was voluntary, though there was coercion in a few. This custom might have originated amongst the warrior castes, the royalty, and nobility, who preferred death to capture and enslavement by the victors. Group immolation, *jauhar*, was observed by the Rajput women of Chitor in Rajastan, when defeat and capture by the enemy seemed certain. In some of the Hindu codes of law, Brahman women were specifically forbidden from committing *satī*; such a prohibition might have been a reassertion of an older tradition. However, they too and other dominant social groups must have copied this custom from the warrior class at a later date. It became a status symbol. Relatives of the grieving widow might have brought subtle pressure on her when she was emotionally most vulnerable, as a convenient method of getting rid of a potential joint claimant for family property. Widows have not been treated kindly or with compassion by Hindu society. The woman or her past karma was blamed for the death of her husband, she could not marry again, at least amongst the high-status groups, and her remaining life was a living penance of self-denial and austerity. Under these circumstances, quite a few chose death by burning over life, which was a living hell. The history and growth of this custom, in the different epochs of Indian tradition, have been discussed elsewhere (Altekar 1999; Kane 1973–1990). Books on various aspects of *satī* are listed in the Bibliography (Harran 1987; Datta 1988; Mani 1998; Nanaiah 1992; Narasimhan 1992; Padma 1993; Hawley 1994; Weinberger-Thomas 1999). The cruelty and sheer barbarity of the rite has been an anomaly in Hindu culture, which preached kindness and compassion to all living beings, including animals. The question is why Hindu society tolerated it and even extolled it as a worthy death. One plausible answer is that *satī* came to be considered ritual suicide and hence acceptable.

Ritual Suicide

The Vedas and Hindu codes of law forbid suicide as a major sin. Some codes forbid *satī*, a few accept it, and others do not mention it at all. Most probably, these codes reflect the customs prevalent in the time and place where their authors lived. *Satī* is ritual suicide; Hindu lawgivers have been equivocal about it and have tolerated it only under special circumstances. What is ritual suicide? It is not the act done in the heat of the moment, at times of great sorrow, despair, anger, temporary insanity, or any other emotion that pushes the individual over the edge. Such a suicide is called "fool's death." Rather, it is a deliberate act done with much thought, an assay of the different aspects of the problem, and conforming to the socially accepted norms, and above all having religious motivation. In short, it is done by a person after much thought and preparation. It also has overtones of world renunciation and self-sacrifice, which resonate well in the Hindu psyche. Ritual suicide is also self-immolation for ideological reasons: religious or cultural. It is not possible to separate these two underpinnings, just as it is difficult to separate sacrifice, suicide, and martyrdom. To understand ritual suicide, one has to know the framework of beliefs, especially those about the afterlife, with respect to which the act is carried out. This belief system also demands that specific rituals involving mental and bodily preparations; permission from one's religious guru; and the place, time, and method of suicide are observed. Ritual suicide came to be accepted as part of Hindu culture and was euphemistically called the Great Journey, *mahāprasthāna* (Kane 1974, 2:924). It was committed at holy places such as Prayāga, Benares, and others, to obtain liberation, *mokṣa*, from the succession of births, *saṁsāra*. Incurable diseases, the infirmity of old age (older than 70 years) and its problems, or an inability to observe rules of bodily cleanliness and ritual purification could lead a person to suicide. A few people felt that they had achieved all that they desired in life, were world-weary, had nothing more to live for, and wanted a quick exit from this life. It is recorded by Greek historians that an Indian yogi, perhaps called Kalyāṇa (or Kalanos by the Greeks; c. 326 BCE), who had accompanied Alexander III of Macedon on his return journey, entered fire at Susa because of the problems of old age and intestinal illness (Walker 1968, 1:513, 2:446). A Buddhist monk, Śramaṇācārya (called Sarmanokhegas by the Greeks), who had accompanied a diplomatic mission to the court of Emperor Augustus Caesar in 29 BCE, entered fire in Athens (Walker, 1968, 2:307, 446). Expiatory suicide for major crimes, such as killing a priest or a cow and comitting incest, was recommended. Votive suicide as an act of gratitude, devotion, or in fulfillment of a vow to a deity was also known. There are many other instances of religious suicide carried out by emperors, kings, and the nobility in history. Why did the rich and well-to-do, who had everything to live for, kill themselves? One plausible answer is that they believed that by proper preparation of their mind and body and by choosing a sacred place and an auspicious time to die, they could have a better rebirth. They wanted some *control* over it; at least they believed they could control their rebirth. Sacrificing one's life by bravely fighting against impossible odds for a good cause is respected in all cultures and has given rise to its own customs of ritual suicide. In South India, a professional warrior would accept food from the hands of a king as part of a special ceremony, called the great sacrifice, *mahāmakham*, and vow to die for him (Walker 1968, 2:446; Iyer 1912). This might have originated from recruiting an elite corps of warriors who were prepared to sacrifice their lives for their king in battle. A few people vowed to accompany their king or queen in death, as a mark of their love and devotion. Particular favorites of a king or queen were designated to accompany them in death as a mark of royal favor.

Such persons used to wear a special type of gold jewelry on their left thighs, as a mark of their exalted status (Padma 1993, 129). Monuments called hero stones, *vīrakal*, were erected to commemorate their deaths. When the Meiji emperor of Japan died in 1912, General Nogi Maresuke, a courtier, and his wife, Shizuko, committed ritual suicide—*junshi*, or suicide to follow one's lord in death (Keene 2002, 712). Ritual suicide as an act of protest against grave injustice, including breaking a solemn vow or agreement, was also part of Hindu tradition. The persons of bards who were also the genealogists and panegyrists of royal families, especially in Rajastan, were considered sacred (Walker 1968, 1:125; Snodgrass 2006). They would stand as sureties for legal agreements, including treaties, threatening to wound, mutilate, or kill themselves or their family members in protest if parties to an agreement reneged on it. It was believed that the shedding of their sacred blood in protest would bring about eternal punishment to the family of the person who broke the contract. Burning oneself as an act of protest for a grave injustice was also known. Fasting to death, *sallekhanā*, was practiced by Jain monks or laity as an act of piety in the final stages of life (Sawkar 2001; Dundas 2002). The usual methods employed in these ritual suicides were jumping off of a cliff, entering fire or water, fasting, and being buried in earth or snow; in a few cases, even poison and hanging oneself were allowed. With the tacit acceptance of many such forms of ritual suicide by Hindu society, *satī sahagamana* came to be accepted as just one other means of ending one's life and did not stand out as an act of gross cruelty. This explanation or understanding the motives behind it does not in any way condone the act or make it less inhuman or painful.

The Mogul emperors, Humayun, Akbar, and others, were opposed to *satī*, wanted to abolish it, and were not successful. Akbar did manage to intervene, stop the ceremony, and save a few lives in specific cases. Afonso de Albuquerque, after the conquest of Goa in 1510, passed a law prohibiting this practice in the Portuguese territories. He should be commended for this humane legislation, though he rarely gets credit for it. However, the Portuguese could not completely eliminate this rite even in the small area that they controlled, pointing out the futility of changing social customs by legislation. There was also some laxity in applying the prohibitions of law. We do not have statistics to determine how extensive *satī* was in sixteenth-century Goa and in later years. Perhaps this custom was prevalent only amongst the high-status groups in the Hindu caste hierarchy (Burnell and Tiele 1935; Xavier 1993). There is little evidence for the practice of this rite amongst the GSB (Conlon 1977, 149). However, there is a tradition that three GSB women committed *satī* some six or seven centuries back (Talmaki and Nadkarni 1998, 45–6). These few cases might have been the exceptions rather than the rule. Families that wanted to go through with the rite could always circumvent the law, plead extenuating circumstances, bribe the right people, and literally get away with murder. These rites were carried out in secrecy, according to the accounts of foreign travelers. A few people carried out *satī* in a canoe or a small boat in the middle of the Mandovi or Zuari Rivers in the dead of the night (Xavier 1993, 165), without being bothered by the authorities. It was practiced in Bardez and Salcette till 1560, because Governor Francisco Barreto (1555–1558) had revoked the prohibitions of Albuquerque at the request of the Hindus. The Brahmans of Chorão Island requested the authorities to permit them to take the body of a deceased man and his widow out of the Portuguese territory to perform *satī* during the viceroyalty and governorship of Constantino de Bragança (1558–1561). He denied permission, severely reprimanded them, threatened punishment, and introduced new stringent laws on 30 June 1560, prohibiting the rite in the Goa Island, Bardez, and Salcette. Under these laws, participants in this rite could be sent to the gallows and their property confiscated. In spite of all the legal restrictions, the rite was not completely eliminated and was observed in secrecy. However, the laws discouraged the burning of widows and forced the Hindus to find alternate methods in dealing with the problem. The Hindu codes of law recommended a life of austerity and penance for widows as an alternate to *satī* and was the course of action adopted to suit the new circumstances. The widows had to undergo tonsure, eschew the dress and ornaments of a married woman whose husband is alive, and lead a life of self-denial as an alternative to *satī*. From the travel narratives of foreign observers we find that women who did not go through *satī* were considered a disgrace to the family and were disowned and expelled from it. They had to find shelter and sustenance in temples, live on public charity, and perhaps joined the ranks of *devadāsīs* just to survive (Xavier 1993, 165). I will come to this subject in the section "*Devadāsīs.*" The practice of *satī* is a blot on Hindu traditions and has been mostly eliminated except for a few instances in which it is carried out in the name of tradition, custom, excessive piety, or any other convenient reason. The Portuguese are to be commended for the restrictive legislation that tried to put an end to this rite.

Slavery and Serfs

Slavery in India is of ancient origin and was a part of the social order. It resulted from birth to slave parents, warfare, or judicial punishment. In warfare, the vanquished felt that their lives were forfeit to the victor, who could kill, ransom, or enslave them in perpetuity. The price paid by the defeated to the victorious was dear indeed. Once enslaved, these people lost all of the rights of a free person and became chattel, commodities to be bought and sold by their owner. All human societies and cultures have been guilty of these three evils: warfare, slaughter, and slavery of fellow humans. It is mentioned in the most ancient texts, the Vedas, the Laws of Manu, the Arthaśāstra, and others. Slavery, its type, the degree of bondage and servitude implied by it, and the treatment of slaves are determined by the worldview, religious beliefs, social norms, and economic situation of the dominant elite that own the slaves. The type of work done—domestic, agricultural, mining, or other large-scale production—also determines the fate of slaves. In Greece and Rome, there was a clear-cut dichotomy of the freeman versus the slave. In India there were many degrees of servitude and subtle gradations from one class of slaves to the next. For example, Megasthenes (315–291 BCE), the ambassador of Seleucus to the Mauryan court at Pāṭaliputra, commented on the absence of slavery in India, though we know from other evidence that it was very much a part of life at that time. Perhaps slavery in India was relatively benign compared to its counterpart in Greece, leading the ambassador to think that it did not exist. Slavery in India and neighboring Ceylon, its evolution, economic aspects, and a comparison of the institution in other cultures are discussed in works by the following authors: Gunasinghe (1960–1961), Kosambi (1962, 1969), Patil (1982), Patnaik and Dingwaney (1985), and Sharma (1990). The practice of slavery in India was further complicated by the fourfold caste system. For example, priests could never be enslaved; they were banished by the king for grave offenses for which other castes could be enslaved as punishment. Manu lists seven types of slaves: those captured in war; those who enslaved themselves in return for food; children of slaves; and those bought, given, inherited, or enslaved by the state as a punishment (Doniger and Smith 1991, 196, 8.415). The Arthaśāstra expands this list to nine categories (Patnaik and Dingwaney 1985, 39, 70), and the codes of law—Nāradasmṛti—to fifteen (Patnaik and Dingwaney 1985, 284). Some slaves who were prisoners of war were freed after one year (Auboyer 1988, 36); others could gain their liberty after discharging their debt or other obligations, whereas the rest were slaves in perpetuity. The character of slavery changed, and entirely new classes of slaves were introduced, with Turkish conquests in India and the introduction of Islam with its own worldview, customs, and traditions. A new elite class of slaves were recruited and trained to become part of the Muslim government bureaucracy in its civilian or military administration. Large harems with many wives and concubines increased the demand for eunuchs, slaves cruelly castrated when young, by the royalty and the nobility who could afford these luxuries. The need for slaves was increased by the domestic practice of owning slaves as a status symbol, by the growth of government workshops that produced luxury goods for the power elite, and by the increased use of slaves in agriculture. These changes also produced a need for slaves with specialized skills. These demands were met with new conquests and the enslaving of the non-Muslims, and their later forcible conversion to Islam. Slavery, pre- and post-Islamic, and in general before the arrival of the Portuguese in Goa is discussed by Kosambi (1969, 1975), Patnaik and Dingwaney (1985), Patil (1982), and Sharma (1990). Slavery under the Portuguese took on an entirely different complexion, which again depended on their worldview as Christians versus non-Christians, their hatred of Muslims, attitudes of racial superiority, and general aversion to hard work in the hot tropics. This is discussed as part of Portuguese life and society in Goa later, in the section "Slavery and the Portuguese."

Devadāsīs

A *devadāsī*, God's slave or God's servant, was a woman dedicated for service in a temple. These women were supposed to sing, dance, and perform some minor rituals as part of temple service and worship. Women slaves, or *dāsī*, are mentioned in the *Ṛgveda*; they were given to the officiating priest, *purohita*, as part of his fees by kings or other notables. Slave women carrying jars filled with water are described as dancing and singing as part of some Vedic ceremonies (Kane 1974, 2:181, 1245). It is possible that when temple worship replaced Vedic sacrifices, singing and dancing by *dāsīs* continued and became part of temple ceremonies. The earliest mention of temple dancers is from the Arthaśāstra of Kauṭilya (~third century BCE). One of the responsibilities of the chief textile commissioner of a state was to employ retired temple dancers along with other women in straitened circumstances to spin in state factories (Rangarajan 1992, 69, 333). Kālidāsa describes temple women dancing as part of the evening worship at a temple in Ujjayinī (Altekar 1999, 182). It is quite possible that votive offerings of property to a temple were accompanied by people attached to the land, who thus became serfs or slaves of the temple establishment. Kings and other rich people made votive offerings of female slaves to gain merit, to fulfill a vow, or as a thanks offering for favors granted. Donations of women dedicated to temple service were usually accompanied by gifts of land or property to support them in perpetuity. The temple of the patron deity of a king would be the beneficiary of special favors and grants from the king to make the temple rituals parallel the court ceremonies of great splendor and displays of power. The same women trained in dancing and singing might have taken part in ceremonies both at the court and the temple, especially if they were located in the same city. The economic and devotional origins of this institution were later elaborated into ritual, religious, and mystical aspects mixed with folk traditions and backed by suitable literature in Sanskrit or the vernacular (Kersenboom-Story 1987; Orr 2000; Marglin 1985, 1987; Altekar 1999, Leslie, 1992). The *devadāsīs*, in addition to singing and dancing, came to play an auxiliary role in the ritual of worship; for example, they offered a special form of waving of lights, *kumbhārati*, and offered flowers to the deity, *puṣpāñjali*. The quasi-magical aspect of their participation in temple ceremonies as a special category of women is worth noting and is of great significance. The *devadāsī* became respected members of the temple and court staff, honored as ever auspicious, *nityasumaṅgali*. Their matrilineal lineage became, in effect, a "caste," with its own duties, rights, privileges, rules, and traditions, and very much a part of Hindu society at large. This institution should be understood only in the context of Hindu culture that originated and nourished it. Its description in terms parallel to "temple prostitution" in ancient Sumeria, Babylonia, or other Middle Eastern societies, would be simplistic or downright wrong. New initiates were usually born into the traditional *devadāsī* families, were adopted or dedicated to the temples as votive offerings by parents or rich devotees, or joined the group of their own volition. Before being initiated into their duties at the temple, the novice had to go through training in singing and dancing. These women were usually literate, whereas most of the women of the rest of society were not. They went through a dedication ceremony before becoming a full member of the guild or caste. The dedication ceremony of a young girl involved symbolic wedding to the presiding deity, after which she would accept the patronage of a rich man of her choice who could support her (Kersenboom-Story 1987; Orr 2000; Marglin 1985, 1987). This relationship was usually serially monogamous, with a few long-term commitments sometimes ending in marriage. In a few cases, the quest for money raised its ugly head and the first-night favors of the young initiate were bid for by the local wealthy patrons. Their dedication and duties at the temple meant that the *devadāsīs* were a required presence at auspicious functions, at the king's court or in private homes. Control of their own sexuality outside the bonds of marriage also put them in an ambiguous position in the context of social mores. A few of these women were quite rich, and we know their names and religious affiliations through the epigraphs of their votive offerings to temples or other similar institutions (Padma 1993; Nanaiah 1992; Orr 2000). It should also be mentioned that the characteristics of this institution varied in different parts of India and also evolved over centuries, in step with changes in the local religion, rituals, and political and economic conditions. The conditions that found a niche in Hindu society for the *devadāsī* became untenable with the decline of royalty and the associated rich and powerful nobility, especially with the advent of the East India Company and British rule. The evangelizing Christian missionaries were outspoken in their condemnation of this institution as one more example of the moral degeneracy of Hinduism and Hindu society compared with their own presumed superiority. For the *devadāsī*, life became difficult without the patronage of the local royalty, chiefs, or nobility, compounded by the social opprobrium of the rest of society. Some of them were forced to eke out a living as common prostitutes, indeed a great fall from their once exalted status as cultured, cultivated, attractive, and educated women. In spite of these difficulties, they kept alive the artistic traditions of classical dance and music till modern times. India and humanity at large owe them a debt of gratitude for maintaining the continuity of this cultural tradition and transmitting it to a younger generation.

Devadāsīs in Goa

The *devadāsī* tradition in the Hindu temples of Goa had many similarities to parallel institutions in the rest of South India, as well as important differences. In Goa, it was a two-tiered system, with *kalāvants*, who specialized in singing and dancing, considered superior to the *bhāvins*, who took care of the more menial duties of cleaning, sweeping, trimming and maintaining lamps, weaving garlands of flowers around the temples, and so on. They were given as gifts to the temple to acquire merit by parents, relatives, or rich people; were obtained by sale; or offered themselves for service in the temple voluntarily. The *kalāvants* learned to read, write, sing, dance, and do fine needlework. Both of these groups were entitled to a share in the revenues of the temples, as part of the village *gāvṁkārī* system, in addition to their other earnings. They participated in temple processions, singing the praises of the deity and carrying a special type of *ārati* called *kumbhārati*. On joyous auspicious occasions such as *upanayana* or weddings as late as 1883, they were invited to sing and dance as part of the ceremonies (Kudva 1978). This custom has now fallen into abeyance. The new initiate went through a symbolic wedding ceremony, in which she garlanded a coconut held by another girl or woman dressed as a man and holding a dagger (Xavier 1993, 219). After this ceremony, she could accept the patronage of a rich man of her choice. These relationships were serially monogamous and usually were long-term commitments. The social standing of this community with its origins in a form of slavery in ancient times was low. Its members were exploited by the dominant hierarchies of priests in the temple, the rich propertied or mercantile classes, and the local administrative state functionaries, like any subservient social group. Hindu widows who were unwilling to immolate themselves on the funeral pyre of their dead husband were considered a disgrace to the family, and a few might have been forced by circumstances to join the ranks of the *devadāsīs*. Widows could not marry again because their past bad karma was considered the cause of their husband's death, and hence, they were considered responsible for his death indirectly. Most chose tonsure, gave up all normal comforts, and adopted a pious life of self-denial and religious austerities, including frequent fasts, giving up some types of foods, and were allowed to live with the husband's family or with their parents. However, some were thrown out of the husband's family or did not have parents or other relatives with whom they could live and thus had to fend for themselves. These widows found shelter in local temples and were supported by public charity. Those who chose a life of religious austerity and pious self-denial underwent tonsure, adopted a particular dress that indicated their status, and served as the "nuns" attached to temples like the one of Mahālasā at Verna (later at Mārdol) described by travelers (Xavier 1993, 127, 165, 219). A few might have chosen a secular life and decided to join the ranks of the devadāsīs, just to survive. This is a sad example of the callous cruelty toward women, especially widows, in Hindu society. Lack of property rights for women in Hindu society, especially if they had no male children, and a slavish observance of customs ignoring basic humanity, were perhaps the causes of these cruel practices. Legislation passed by the Portuguese administration gave property rights to widows and their daughters. Though this legislation was meant to provide incentives for religious conversion, it was humane in giving a widow and her children a legal right to the property of her dead husband or father. In May 1925, the leaders of the *devadāsī* community in Goa formed the Gomantak Maratha Samaj, an organization to strive for the betterment of their life and social status. Because of their efforts, the dedication of young girls to temples, *sesha vidhi*, was outlawed by the Goa legislative council in 1930. Young women of the community now marry and have normal families like other Hindus. This community has produced many outstanding practitioners of the performing arts: classical, devotional, and popular music, both vocal and instrumental. The traditional songs sung by the *devadāsīs* at temple processions and other ceremonies must be recorded and documented for posterity; otherwise, alas, they will be lost forever. The Samaj now represents many educated, economically and politically well-off professionals of a vibrant community who have been successful by their own efforts and who form an important part of modern Goa.

Infant Mortality, Child Marriages, and Education of Women

Childhood and adolescence were fraught with many hazards because of the sorry state of medicine in medieval Goa and the lack of community support during hard times such as periodic famines, epidemics, floods, and other disasters. This was further exacerbated by belief in astrology and other traditions. A few may call these beliefs questionable and others may defend them as orthodoxy; however, they did cause quite a few problems. In sixteenth-century

Goa, belief in astrology had become very much a part of Hindu orthodoxy, with the result that babies' horoscopes were cast as soon as they were born. If the astrologer declared that the horoscope of the new baby was good and not harmful to the members of the family, everyone breathed a sigh of relief. For most problems with the horoscope, expiatory rites (*prāyaścitta*) were recommended to propitiate the bad aspects of planets, fate, or whatever else that was supposed to cause a future mishap (Kudva 1978, 286). In Portuguese Goa, some of the more elaborate rites could not be performed because they were forbidden under pain of banishment to the galleys or other harsh punishments. For major problems, some Hindu codes of law advised that a child born under very inauspicious planetary conjunctions should be abandoned and its face should not be seen by members of the family until it was 8 years old (Kane 1974, 2:237). In some such extreme cases, the baby was adopted by people of the same community, and its birth family never had any contact with it. However, it is documented that a few did abandon their babies because of an inauspicious birth. This is a most cruel and heartless thing to do; there is no excuse for such barbarity. A misguided belief in astrology to the level of certainty made these people pass what was almost a sentence of certain death on these poor babies. This was a heinous crime. Other babies were abandoned because of the dire poverty of the parents, who could not afford to feed and clothe them. This situation would have been further exacerbated in times of famine, epidemics, floods, or any other disasters. Under these circumstances, babies were abandoned either because the parents could not bear to see their suffering or with the faint hope that someone might find, feed, and bring them up. We have records of these babies being rescued and brought up by Christian religious orders or laypersons (D'Costa 1965; Priolkar 1961; Lach and Van Kley 1993, 878), who should be commended for a humane act. Many people were too poor to afford a priest or an astrologer to predict a new baby's future, and every additional baby was a problem. These people were the most vulnerable in times of trouble, which were quite common. Periodic droughts and bad crops, famines, epidemics, and starvation without any state or community support were facts of life in medieval Goa. Under these dire straits, parents were known to sell their children or themselves into slavery for a few measures of rice, as noted by Linschoten (Burnell and Tiele 1935). Life was cheap and uncertain, and mere survival was a problem.

For those who could afford them, child marriages were the norm, as described by Linschoten (Burnell and Tiele 1935, 249). Girls of about age 7 and boys as young as 9 were married in the Goa of 1580s. They would live together after attaining puberty. Babies born to mothers not fully mature were sickly and contributed to the high infant mortality. Why and when did this tradition originate? Why this change from adult marriages, which were customary in ancient times (Altekar 1999)? The answer is in the Hindu codes of law (Kane 1974, 2:442), which declare that the father or guardian of an unmarried girl who has attained puberty incurs the sin of embryo killing at each menses. This one Hindu custom had ramifications, all bad, on many other aspects of Hindu society. First, because of the usual childhood diseases and the sorry state of medicine, many of the boys died, leaving child-widows who could not marry and were condemned to a life great suffering and privations. Their life as women and people essentially came to an end even before it had begun and they had experienced any of its pleasures. Second, most girls did not get any education and were illiterate. It was customary to send a *bhāvin* servant, called a *dheḍḍi*, who could read and write, to accompany a young bride to her new home to act as her confidante and handle household expenses, and so on (Dhume 1985, 73). There were a few exceptions, girls who were literate because of their curiosity and eagerness to learn, picking up rudiments of literacy when their brothers or cousins were being educated at home. Third, child marriages essentially did away with the custom of *upanayana* for most Sarasvat girls because there was no education for girls. This further relegated them to a lower status and confirmed their inferior ranking in the family and the social hierarchy. Amongst the Sarasvats, girls could have had *upanayana* performed for them if they were interested in getting a traditional Sanskrit education and would be educated at home by a father or uncles. This was a continuation of the ancient Vedic tradition that survived well into the late nineteenth or early twentieth century in some families with a tradition of Sanskrit learning (see Appendix 5: "Hindu Rites of Passage"). Such cases were the exception rather than the rule. Even if girls could read and write, they were confined to home and were strictly secluded. The ultimate aim of all these restrictions was to guarantee the sexual purity and virtue of the girl. There was no doubt in anyone's mind that girls and women were second-class citizens.

In spite of all these social customs that worked against girls and women achieving a position of authority and responsibility in a Hindu family, there were exceptions. Extant records mention Bhagavtiny Camotim (Bhagavatī Kāmtīṇī), widow of Raulu Camotim (Raul Kāmati), administrator of family property, requesting compensation by the crown for goods worth 96,000 *xerafims* lost in the 1755 Lisbon earthquake. We also know of Rucuminim Camotinin (Rukmiṇī Kāmtiṇī), who by her able management of the family business turned its fortunes around (Couto 2004, 219). There might have been other women who played an active part in helping the males of the family and who took over the responsibility of holding the family together and managing its affairs in times of trouble. We have to mine the rich lode of family records of these merchant families to learn about them.

Linschoten talks of fourteen-day-long wedding celebrations; perhaps only the rich could afford such extravagance. He also mentions that for weddings, it was customary for the father to give his daughter only jewelry, to bear the expenses of the wedding, and to give no household articles. In spite of that, a daughter's wedding usually meant excessive spending by the father of the bride, money he could not afford and loans that he assumed but could not pay back. Unfortunately, being a slave to tradition, many families would have such elaborate weddings anyway, leading to much misery. If the bride's father was rich, all of this extravagance advertised his status; if he could not afford it, it created an illusion of status he did not have. Was it worth all of the debt, insolvency, and misery it caused later? People apparently thought so; they continue to think so now. There were other peculiar beliefs and social customs that caused problems in finding a husband for a daughter. A woman born after three brothers, called a *tikhle*, was considered particularly inauspicious and was supposed to bring calamities to her husband's family (Xavier 1993, 52). A few orthodox men did not want to marry a woman without brothers. This is an old problem going back to Vedic times; under those circumstances, her father could claim his grandson as his heir and designate him to perform his obsequies. A big dowry or other gifts could overcome the bad aspects of all of these problems, provided the father was rich enough to afford it. With all of these problems, girls were a liability, so female infanticide was common. Either girl babies were slowly starved to death or they were fed finger millet, *nāñcaṇo*, in the hope of achieving the same end because of the large amount of roughage in the grain, which most babies could not tolerate (Sawkar 2001, 163). Millet is not completely devoid of nutrition, so the few babies who could tolerate it flourished; however, the intentions behind providing such a diet were evil. This problem continues in some families and localities and is a blot on Hindu society. Educating girls so that they are economically independent and can support themselves is the only solution to these social evils. Economic independence for girls is the only way they can claim their rights as full, cherished members of a Hindu family. Families that educate their girls have mostly eliminated these ancient social evils. However, much remains to be done in traditional families that cling to their customs, do not educate girls, and have not accepted full gender parity.

Intracaste Quarrels and Splinter Groups

The story of our community, the Sarasvats, in Goa is contained in the book *Koṅkaṇākhyāna*, written in *Marāṭi* (Marathi) and dated 1721 CE. I do not read the language, and all of the details that I provide here about this book are from its introduction by Keni (Anon. 2001). It traces the history of the community from antiquity to the author's lifetime, which had seen the destruction of the Hindu temples in Goa, the transfer of the deities and the building of new temples outside Portuguese control, and exile from their homes (Axelrod and Fuerch 1996). The unknown author of this book traveled extensively to places where members of our community were living in exile, and he was quite aware of the new problem of distances separating them. He adopted a question-and-answer format for the book. His purpose was to inform our people about their past before dispersal and to stress the unity of our community to enable them to face and survive the trials and tribulations of exile. The author deplores the internecine quarrels of the community, their jockeying for superiority among sects, and ascribes to them ignorance of our common heritage. His is an eminently wise voice of sanity in the prevailing circumstances. We do not know whether anyone in the Sarasvat community heeded his voice; most probably they did not.

The Sarasvat community in Goa was splintered into groups and subgroups, each considering itself separate and superior to all others (Kudva 1978; Talmaki and Nadkarni 1998). After a while, these groups stopped sharing food or exchanging brides and formed their own community. The reasons for such disunity were many. From our modern vantage point, these reasons seem mostly trivial, some ridiculous, and a few even funny. The following example from *Koṅkaṇākhyāna* should suffice (Kudva 1978, 182; Anon. 2001, 9). During one wedding, when the bride and groom were going round the sacred fire for the seven steps, *saptapadī*, that symbolically bind the couple together and finalize a wedding, the officiating priest warned the bride to be careful near the open flames lest her garment catch fire. The bride said, "I know." A few enemies of the bride's father remarked, "How can she know? Is this perhaps her second marriage?" Some leaders of the community in the assembly, without proper investigation, decreed that the father must perform some expiation. The father refused because he had done nothing wrong. Most people then left the gathering; however, the ceremony was completed. The parties involved felt insulted; this led to open quarrels, which caused formal alienation and separation of people from the rest of the community. There are other similar examples, involving egos, big and small, and exquisitely delicate sensibilities attuned to insults, real or imagined. However, if we consider the time and effort spent by these groups on their mutually destructive quarrels, these reasons must have been important and far from trivial for them.

The community as a whole acted as if it was oblivious to the new and changed circumstances of Portuguese rule, the danger posed by the missionary zeal of the state and the church, and its suffering at their hands. The time was in the 1730s, when Portuguese missionary zeal had peaked and had passed through its worst excesses. However, there were many problems: The *śeṇḍi* tax and the extra capitation tax levied during the Maratha raids were in force, and overt or covert discrimination against the Hindus was a fact of life in Goa. At that time, our community was in a state of social, economic, and political upheaval, fighting for its very existence. A few members had converted to Christianity, either forcibly or voluntarily, in exchange for material advantages accruing from such a step, or for other reasons. Some of the rich and powerful had come to terms with the power structure of the state and were doing quite well (Scammell 1988). Instead of closing their ranks to face these challenges effectively as a group, a significant number of our community continued their mindless quarrels as if it was business as usual. For some, it was time to settle old scores with their enemies and seek revenge by using the dreaded Inquisition. They brought false charges against other members of the community, acted as secret informers to the Inquisition, and reveled in the suffering of the accused. The inquiry period after accusations could be long and protracted and involved confiscation of property and a lengthy period of imprisonment while the wheels of "justice" of the Inquisition turned slowly. Even if the accused was acquitted eventually, the suffering involved and loss of wealth were immense. The problem of such false witnesses before the Inquisition became a grave concern for all Hindus. When the state offered to allow Hindus in exile to return to Goa to live without any religious coercion, the Hindus requested that the king enact laws such that the Inquisition would take no cognizance of charges brought by Hindus against other Hindus, if they were not supported by independent evidence (Priolkar 1961, 109–112). One major communal feud was between the *Smārta* Kushastalikars and Keloshikars and Vaiṣṇava Sasashtikars and Bardezkars. The former considered Śiva as their principal deity, and the latter mainly worshiped Viṣṇu and had minor differences in some customs and observances. The former represented an older tradition, when the whole community worshipped Śiva, and the latter were new converts to the Vaiṣṇava sect. Both of these groups considered themselves as one community, exchanging brides and sharing food. We do not know when the problems between these groups started, when mutual complaints, charges, and recriminations were first exchanged, when the feuds began. A few on each side did not want any reconciliation and continued to fan the flames to achieve their own power-seeking ends. They finally reached a stage in which sometime around 1727, it was decided that their differences could not be reconciled and they could not coexist, so they appealed to the local viceroy or the king in Portugal to act as arbiters (Priolkar 1961, 148, Kudva, 1978; Conlon 1977, 30). The viceroy recommended complete and total separation of the two communities within a month, in which people could opt for one group or the other, with the consequent breakup of close-knit families. These drastic measures and the difficult choices they were forced to make drove some people to despair and suicide, as in the case of at least three women (Priolkar 1961, 148). The mutual separation between these two and other groups persisted well into the twentieth century, when efforts were made to unify them (Conlon 1974). This is indeed a sad chapter in the history of the GSB and indicative of the failure of the community leaders to drum some sense into the heads of the local troublemakers and settle these quarrels amicably. Instead, they indulged in mindless, selfish, internecine quarrels over trivia. Finally, to add insult to injury, these people asked the Portuguese king and viceroy, who had persecuted the whole community, to arbitrate their quarrels! These events do not represent one of the shining moments in the history of the Sarasvats.

The Portuguese in the Age of Exploration and Exploitation

The main driving forces behind the Portuguese voyages of exploration in the fifteenth century were a desire to continue the fight against the Muslims for trade and land, greed for Guinea gold, the search for Prester John, and a desire to break into the trade in spices from the Orient, bypassing all the middlemen (Boxer 1969, 18). Prester John was a mythical rich and powerful Christian ruler somewhere in the East. The Portuguese had hopes of teaming up with him to deliver a final death blow to the Muslims as enemies of Christ. Thus the Age of Discovery was driven by a mixture of greed for gold, slaves, and spices combined with zeal for the spread of the true faith of the Roman Catholic church by the conversion of heathens and the prospect of elimination of the hated Muslims. Historians love to present these explorations as a noble endeavor motivated by a quest for knowledge, the expansion of European horizons beyond their immediate parochial interests, and peaceful trade. The usual impression of the Age of Discovery is that of a number of voyages in pursuit of knowledge for its own sake by Europeans. The harsh reality is that it was a mixture of all of these: the quest for knowledge, exploration of new avenues of trade, slave raids, and exploitation of the "other" by force of arms or trade under duress if they could get away with it (Livermoore 1966; Marques 1972). The mercantile system of commerce in vogue from about the fifteenth to the eighteenth centuries in Europe also encouraged a very aggressive attitude toward foreign trade. The theory and practice of the mercantile system called for a positive export trade balance and an accumulation of gold and silver bullion by the nation-state to fund the waging of wars. The bullion was to be acquired by trade if possible; by conquest if necessary.

In a mercantilistic age, foreign trade was war by other means (Parry 1964, 341). The quest for knowledge was secondary and incidental; the Portuguese were after the fabled riches of the Orient. They used the more advanced European technology to dominate the countries and people they visited, so a more factual name for this period would be the Age of Exploration and Exploitation! If the reader has any doubts on this score, the clear wording of the papal bull *Dum diversas* authorized the king of Portugal to conquer and enslave Saracens, pagans, and other unbelievers, in perpetuity, and acquire their properties (discussed later in this section). This was the beginning of the age of colonialism, which would last for another five centuries.

By the time Vasco da Gama discovered the sea route to India, Portuguese trade in Guinea gold had been going on for quite some years from the middle of the fifteenth century. This was also combined with slave trade from the west coast of Africa beginning in 1441 (Saunders 1982). The quest for Prester John turned out to be a bit of wishful thinking and vanished from their agenda; there were more immediate concerns to face and profits to be made from spices, slaves, precious stones, and other imports. The crusading zeal against the Muslims would be the background against which their dealings in India would be played out. To understand Portuguese behavior in the East, first consider the worldview and mind-set of the Portuguese. They saw themselves as conquerors, not as peaceful merchants. Their demands were backed by superior arms and ships, the best European technology could provide. They could dictate terms from a position of strength, and it was their temperament to prefer *ferro, fogo, e sangue* (iron, fire, and blood) over negotiations and compromise, as mentioned in a different context (Barros 1988, 167). Second, they were racists who were convinced of the superiority of white Europeans over the inferior black, brown, or yellow races of Africa and Asia. Third, there was the continuing strife with the Muslims in the Iberian peninsula that has been going on since the days of Arab expansion in the seventh century, the Crusades, and the Reconquest. The Muslims, Moors, or Saracens, as they were called, were the archenemies of Christ and Christian civilization; they had to be dominated, defeated, enslaved, and eliminated if possible. The Portuguese brought this ancient hatred to the East, and it would color all of their dealings with Muslims of all nationalities. Fourth, they were Christian evangelizers who were zealots, believing ardently in the righteousness of their cause and actions. The Council of Trent (1545–1563) had approved reforms for the church and defined its beliefs as the one true religion in the context of the Protestant Reformation. They were thus energized by the zeal of the Counterreformation, which laid out the agenda of church militants to fight dissent and heresy in all its forms by any and all means. Any religion other than Roman Catholicism had no *legitimacy* either as regards its beliefs or practices. The immediate corollary of this mind-set was the aggressive religious intolerance combined with evangelical zeal that they practiced. Fifth, there was the intermingling of the interests of the Portuguese state and the Roman Catholic church, which were so intimately intertwined that it is useful to think of a state–church complex rather than two separate dominance hierarchies. This intimate relationship was formalized by the church as royal patronage, *padroado real*, by the Portuguese crown of the church missions and establishments in Africa, Asia, and Brazil (Boxer 1969, 228 et. seq.). The rights, privileges, and obligations of the state for the church power structure were defined in a series of papal bulls, discussed later in this section. Sixth, in pursuit of gain, might was right in their dealings with the heathen, who were racially inferior and misguided in religion, especially when these actions of the Portuguese state had been approved by the Roman Catholic church. The words *heathen* and *pagan* are used here interchangeably, without any pejorative connotation, to conform to their dictionary meaning: an unconverted member of a people or a nation that does not acknowledge the God of the Bible. Unfortunately, both of these words in common use do have a negative meaning aiming to disparage or belittle. Each of these themes of the Portuguese worldview is further elaborated in the following sections.

The history of the mutual help and support extended by the power structures of state and church is instructive and should be studied to understand crown patronage and the two groups' idea of the rights and obligations behind it. These were symbiotic dominance hierarchies, each of which helped the other to flourish. The moves of the state and the responses of the church can only be described as an exquisite, intricate minuet beautifully choreographed to achieve their basic aim of dominance. The information on these dealings is extracted from a number of sources on the Portuguese adventures in the Far East (Saunders 1982; Boxer 1963, 1965, 1969, 1978, 1980). The state wanted its actions to be in conformity with current ideas of law and norms of civilized behavior, as a token of which they wanted the approval of the church. The church was only too happy to oblige. If the church's behavior at the time looked Lusocentric—concerned only with what is good for the Portuguese—then that is a correct assessment. The heathen, whether they were black, brown, or yellow, had no rights, and whatever hand was dealt by the white man was the justice that they got and deserved. So long as the state and the church conformed to the legal ritual, the spirit and contents of the documents they approved and adopted did not matter. Prince Henry the Navigator (1394–1460) asked the church to declare the raids in West Africa a crusade so that they could be considered a just war and would also attract soldiers with the promise of indulgences. The church obliged with the papal bull *Illius qui* of 19 December 1442. Some ten years later, the state wanted the church to approve the enslaving of the unbelievers caught in the crusade. Portugal had been importing slaves from West Africa since 1441, and Prince Henry had gotten his royal fifth of the catch. Hence, this approval was supposed to be retroactive. The church responded with the bull *Dum diversas* of 18 June 1452, which authorized the king of Portugal to conquer saracens, pagans, and other non-Christians considered to be the enemies of Christ, reduce them to slavery in perpetuity, and to seize and transfer their lands and wealth to the king and his heirs (Boxer 1969, 21). However, there was a problem because by 1452, the Portuguese had realized that instead of conducting slave raids, it was much more cost effective to let the individual African tribal chiefs do the dirty work of slave capture and then buy slaves from them as intermediaries. This implied peaceful trade with "enemies of Christ," as defined in the earlier papal bulls. Such trade was forbidden; only the pope could provide the necessary dispensation, provided one could show good cause. There were two good reasons to approve this request: First, profits from the trade financed the crusade; second, the slaves thus brought back were converted to Christianity, becoming true believers whose souls were saved in the next world, though they were condemned to perpetual slavery in this one. Papal approval was proclaimed in the bull *Romanus Pontifex* of 8 June 1455, which gave the Portuguese monopoly over all trade and conquest, if necessary, south of Capes Nūn and Bojador. All of these maneuvers made perfectly legal the acquisition of African slaves by war or peaceful trade. Historians have pointed out that this second bull, Romanus Pontifex, may be called the founding charter for the Portuguese empire, because it legalized its trade and conquests (Boxer 1969, 21). By the same token, it can also be called the charter for what later became plantation slavery. Enslaving the conquered people, nonwhite and non-Christian, was part of the Portuguese imperium. These bulls give a true picture of the attitude of Europeans, one of overbearing arrogance toward the others they met in the Age of Discovery (Boxer 1969, 23). Protestant nations such as Great Britain, Holland, and others emulated the Portuguese behavior approved by papal bulls; to do otherwise would have hampered their trade and profits. In their dealings with the natives of Africa, India, or elsewhere in Asia and in the laws they passed and enforced, the Portuguese were punctilious in observing all of the norms of legal requirements as they understood them. Such compliance was enough to satisfy any misgivings of conscience of the ruling authorities of the state and the church. The question of fairness, equity, and justice to the objects of these laws, the African and Asian heathen, did not arise. However, there were a few dissenters, such as the outspoken

Portuguese Padre Fernando Oliveira, who in 1555 criticized the slave trade and its justification, the conversion of the heathen, as just a "pious wash" (Boxer 1969; Saunders 1982). His violent denunciation of "just wars" against Muslims, Jews, or heathens who were prepared to trade peacefully even earned him imprisonment by the Inquisition in Lisbon. These few voices of criticism changed neither state policy nor the treatment of the heathen races; they merely expressed the uneasy voices of the consciences of a few. These people deserve some credit for being bold in expressing contrary opinions in an ocean of conformity.

Early Portuguese Contacts and Trade (1498–1510)

Practical considerations gave trade first priority, and the spread of Christianity amongst the heathen in the East had to wait until the Portuguese had consolidated their position. The trade between the Portuguese and the people of India had many problems. Though it was supposed to be peaceful in theory, it turned out to be more or less a series of hostile encounters in practice. The Portuguese were newcomers on the scene, unfamiliar with local customs, traditions, and etiquette regarding behavior toward or gifts (bribes) for those in power, and they were not particularly keen on learning them. Because of their intense suspicion of the natives and lack of trust, their idea of peaceful trade was to demand a few important local notables as hostages even before beginning any negotiations. They were afraid of walking into a trap and being captured by the local raja, who was equally suspicious that the Portuguese would sail away without paying for purchased goods or having cheated on customs. The Portuguese had a few demands that the locals found to be unreasonable or impossible to meet. However, they had better ships and guns to enforce these demands, and they knew it. Because the Portuguese were dictating terms of trade from a position of strength, they had little patience, were readily angered, touchy about their honor, and wanted respect and were prepared to get it by terrorizing the natives. In addition, the legacy of hatred for Muslims or Moors, nursed over the centuries by the Portuguese, was to color their behavior in India and the Far East. The trade in spices from the Indian ports of Calicut, Kochin, and others, was open to many nationalities, including Arabs, Muslims from Persia and the Middle East, Turks, Chinese, Malays, and others. This trade had been going on for centuries and was open to all who had the silver to pay for the spices they wanted to buy. The Portuguese wanted to eliminate Muslim participation in this activity and to declare trade in spices and some other commodities a Portuguese crown monopoly, and they expected the Hindu ruler of Calicut, Samudri Raja (called Zamorin by the Portuguese), to abide by this edict. Both the spice traders and the coastal suppliers were unhappy with the demands of the newcomers, the Portuguese. However, because they were militarily better equipped, the Portuguese could impose their will by force. This conflict of interests would lead to skirmishes with the ruler of Calicut and with other spice merchants, especially Muslim. For the west coast of India, trade with foreign Muslims had been going on since antiquity, and there were groups of local Muslims, the Mappilas in Kerala and the Navayats in North and South Kanara, who were descendents of Arabs married to native women. The Portuguese adopted a belligerent, overbearing attitude in their dealings with native rulers and local merchants, and they had the might to enforce their dictates. The idea of the "freedom of the seas" began to appear in Europe in the sixteenth century and would be fully articulated by Hugo Grotius in his work *Mare Liberum* (Free Seas, 1609 [Encyclopaedia Britannica 1968]). However, the nation demanding this privilege for its ships and trade had to be strong enough to fight for it. None of the ships trading in the Indian Ocean or the Arabian Sea could challenge the Portuguese; hence, they could enforce their will. The Portuguese introduced a system of license, *cartaz*, to be issued by them on payment of customs on traded goods, and as a passport. Ships without a proper license could be captured or sunk by Portuguese ships, especially if they belonged to Muslim traders. If the ship was loaded with much-desired valuable goods or was in contravention of the various trade edicts imposed by the Portuguese, it was captured anyway in a few cases in spite of carrying a *cartaz*.

It is against this background that we have to look at the excesses and sheer barbarity of behavior of the Portuguese and their leaders (Pearson 1987; Disney 1995; Subrahmanyam 1997; Cliff 2011). The narrative here of these events depends mostly on Pearson, Disney, and Subrahmanyam, who have sifted through the different sources for the "truth" of these atrocities, especially those committed by Vasco da Gama during his second voyage of 1502–1503. He has been described as "violent of temper, and quick to react to perceived insults; he seems scarcely the ideal man to send to make contact with new continents and cultures" (Subrahmanyam 1997, 64). Da Gama's behavior in this voyage was very much conditioned by an earlier event, the Correia affair. This occurred during the 1500–1501 voyage of Pedro Álvares Cabral, who had established a factory at Calicut with Aires Correia in charge. In December 1500 on the advice of Correia, Cabral seized a Muslim-owned ship in port that was about to sail for Jiddah. The immediate reason was that the Portuguese thought that the Samudri Raja had gone back on an agreement with them that gave them first call on loading a cargo of spices. The seizure of the ship enraged the local Muslim merchants, who attacked the Portuguese factory, killing fifty-four men, including Correia, and causing the loss of much valuable goods. Cabral retaliated by seizing ten large ships (or fifteen, according to some reports) in port, and then bombarded Calicut and Pantalayini, a neighboring port, resulting in the slaughter of 400 to 500 people. This was round 1. The Portuguese believed in payback in kind and then some, to compensate for the loss of men and goods and to put fear in the heart of the natives. We do not know whether the two sides felt that this was tit for tat and the scales of justice were then even. However, da Gama, admiral of the Indies and newly ennobled with the title *Dom*, did not. He felt that the Correia affair was an affront to the honor of the king of Portugal, and he was going to avenge it. It is quite possible that the purpose of his second voyage, apart from trade, was revenge. This fact has been used to explain the unnecessary, wanton cruelty of his subsequent acts. On 29 September 1502, off Calicut, the Portuguese stopped the *Mîrî*, a ship returning from pilgrimage to Mecca and carrying a rich cargo and many men, women, and children, variously reported to number between 240 and 380, including some 10 to 12 of the richest merchants of Calicut. The ship's crew did not offer any resistance, despite the ship carrying some artillery. Perhaps the ship owners who were on board felt that there was enough wealth on hand to buy their freedom. They offered a huge ransom and compensation for the loss of goods from the factory in Calicut in the Correia affair in return for being let free (Disney 1995). Da Gama declined these and other offers and offloaded the goods on the ship, and soon it became clear to the passengers that they would not be set free but would be killed. Women held up their children and begged for mercy; they also offered their jewelry and money. When they finally realized that they would not be let go, they fought the Portuguese in a final act of desperation. After a four-day standoff, da Gama ordered the ship to be set afire, killing all on board except for 17 to 20 children and the crippled pilot. The children were saved so that they could be converted to Christianity (Subrahmanyam 1997). Da Gama's justification for his actions, expressed in a letter to the Samudri, was that they were in retaliation for the killing of 40 or so Portuguese in an earlier encounter (the Correia affair) in Calicut and that the children were baptized in retribution for the Muslims' having taken a Portuguese boy to Mecca to be converted to Islam. In these negotiations, the Samudri felt that the loss of goods in the Correia affair was compensated for by the capture of ships by Cabral, just as the loss of life in Calicut was compensated for by the loss of the *Mîrî*. Da Gama did not agree. One of his non-negotiable demands was payment for the loss of goods in the Correia affair. In addition, he demanded that the entire Middle Eastern Muslim settlement in Calicut, numbering more than 4,000 households, be expelled. This demand was both unreasonable and impossible to meet. The Samudri claimed that these Muslims, who had lived in Calicut for a long time, were part of the native population and could not be expelled. Da Gama did not relent; instead he gave the Samudri an ultimatum with a deadline of noon, 1 November 1502. If the Samudri did not satisfy Gama's demands, he could expect retaliation. This was the background to the second notorious event of this voyage, which involved the senseless, barbaric torture of some fishermen in four boats captured off Calicut. According to the various accounts of this incident, critically examined by Disney, the number of fishermen involved was somewhere between 32 and 50, with the 800 quoted by one source being highly improbable. These prisoners have been described as mostly Muslim, Hindu, or a mix of the two. The consensus regarding their fate is as follows: They were distributed amongst the ships of the Portuguese fleet, and after negotiations with the Samudri had broken down and the deadline for da Gama's ultimatum had passed, the prisoners were hanged from the yardarm of the ships around noon. The bodies were taken down; their heads, hands, and feet were cut off; and the mutilated bodies were thrown in the sea to be washed ashore. The severed body parts were loaded in one of the captured boats, which was towed to a point from which it would drift ashore. The eyewitness accounts mention the horrified reactions of the people onshore on seeing the severed limbs. These atrocities were followed by the third major event: the bombardment of Calicut, which lasted from November 1 through November 2 and reportedly killed 467 people onshore. A few more incidents (Pearson 1987) in this litany of cruelty should be mentioned because their aim appears to have been to sow terror in the hearts of the natives rather than win friends. The nephew of a merchant in Cannanore and six other locals were sewn into a sail and thrown overboard to drown. Portuguese pirates seized a few Gujarati *vanias*, cut off their hands, and threw them overboard.

These and other atrocities committed by the Portuguese show the general tenor of their standard operating methods in their dealings with the natives in the East. These methods worked in most confrontations, except where the opposing party was better armed. In those cases, the Portuguese failed miserably, such as in their interactions with the Chinese embassy under the leadership of Tomé Pires, author of *Suma Oriental*, in 1517 (Gordon 2008, 157). The Chinese were not impressed with the bombast and bluster of the Portuguese, declared them to be pirates and imposters bereft of the graces and good manners of diplomats, imprisoned them along with other local Portuguese merchants, and put them on trial. In 1522, they were all sentenced to death as pirates and executed. Their bodies were dismembered and displayed in public as a deterrent. The fate of the Portuguese ambassador-designate, Pires, is not known with certainty. Most probably he was freed and lived in China until he died in 1540 (Gordon 2008, 174). These cruel, aggressive, overbearing acts earned much hatred for the Portuguese in the East. They resulted in the need for the Portuguese to maintain an effective fleet and forts and spend sums on related expenses, which in the long run would undermine the Portuguese Empire and its ambitions. The little people, the local suppliers, retaliated in their own way. They gave the Portuguese substandard spices, sometimes wet or mixed with mud and sand, which when cleaned resulted in weight losses on the order of 30% to 40% (Subrahmanyam 1997). The Portuguese could have had all of the spices and other trade goods that they wanted by adopting peaceful and definitely less expensive methods.

The Portuguese Conquer Goa (1510)

The Portuguese conquered Goa in 1510, under the leadership of Afonso de Albuquerque, with the active participation of Timmayya, a representative of the Hindu kingdom of Vijayanagara. This conquest is an interesting example of the pursuit of dominance by all parties involved, and the games they played to get it. The principal actors in this drama are Timmayya (or Timoja) of Vijayanagar; the Portuguese governor, Afonso de Albuquerque; and Mhall Pai Vernekar (or Mhall Pai, the sardesai of Verna), a prominent spokesman for the local Hindu merchants, the Sarasvats. Military leader Timmayya has been described variously as governor of Honnavar, an admiral of Vijayanagara, married to the princess of Gersoppa, a pirate, a robber leader, a man of low birth, and a man of high office. There was more that is unclear about him: Was he a Maratha, a man of Kanara, a Goan, a Hindu, or a Jain (Couto 2004, 85; Gune 1979, 141)? Shastry has analyzed the many disparate pieces of information about him, the pros and cons; his narrative is the one I follow here (Shastry 1981; 1993; 2000).

The Portuguese describe Timmayya as a man of noble and intelligent bearing whose dignified and honorable behavior gave credence to his claims of representing the emperor of Vijayanagar or the chief of Gersoppa as commander of their navies. His high birth and status are attested to by his marriage to a princess of Gersoppa. His name is that of a man of Kanara, and most probably he was a Jain, because the ruling family of Gersoppa into which he married were Jains. He was not a professional freebooter or a pirate; any ships he captured were on the orders of and as a servant of Vijayanagar. He is best described as an energetic entrepreneur or operator, whose first loyalty was to himself and his interests, second to the emperor of Vijayanagar, and last to the Portuguese as his allies. Shastry lists three of his motives in instigating the capture of Goa. First, he had tried to drive out the Muslims, the Bijapur Adil Shahis, the common enemy of Vijayanagar and the Portuguese, from Goa before, and he had not been successful. If he and the Portuguese allies could capture Goa, he hoped to become its governor and gain by it. Second, he expected to win back his inheritance in Goa that had been usurped by his brother, Chidambara. Third, Krishna Deva Raya, emperor of Vijayanagar, wanted to drive the Muslims from Goa and bring it under his hegemony.

Timmayya incited Albuquerque to attack Goa, providing tactical information and military help and participating in the battle. Timmayya wanted to *use* the Portuguese to attain his ends, which were seizure and governorship of Goa. Albuquerque wanted to *use* the same coalition to obtain his goals, which were the use of a vanquished Goa as a secure naval base and as land for future expansion of the Portuguese Empire. Mhall Pai, the sardesai of Verna, had imprisoned some Navayats, Konkani-speaking descendants of Arabs who had married local women, for harassing Hindus. The Navayats had retaliated and had the support of local Muslim officials, especially Yusuf Gurgi, a Turk and a favorite of Yusuf Adil Shah, the king of Bijapur. Gurgi, along with his entourage of 200 Turks, was notorious for frightful cruelties perpetrated on the local Hindus (Kudva 1978). The Hindu merchants represented by Mhall Pai hoped that the liberation of Goa from Bijapur would mean an end to this persecution, the *jizya* (the tax on non-Muslims), the arbitrary seizure and confiscation of Hindu property, and the power of Arabs and Muslims in trade. They wanted to *use* the conquest for their own ends. The Portuguese–Vijayanagara coalition was successful in capturing Goa after its first attack there in March 1510. However, they were driven out of Goa by Adil Shahi forces and had to retake Goa by another assault in November of the same year. During the second attack, Timmayya was not present on the scene, for a variety of reasons, and one of his captains, Mahlar Rao (Madhava Rao) distinguished himself by his bravery and played a prominent role in the capture of Goa. Timmayya was naïve enough to think that the Portuguese would hand over Goa to him as a *jagir*, in return for an annual payment for his military service. Of course, Albuquerque had his own plans for Goa, and he had the military power to get what he wanted. Timmayya tried to change Albuquerque's mind by winning over his captains to his side. However, Albuquerque was adamant. Timmayya's dreams of becoming the ruler of Goa came to nothing. For all his services to the Portuguese, and as a sop to his ego, Timmayya was appointed *aquazil mor*, or chief judicial and administrative officer of Hindus, not governor of Goa. The second attack had succeeded after hard fighting and considerable loss of life, and Albuquerque allowed the victorious forces to plunder the city and ordered a general massacre of Muslims—men, women, and children. The slaughter is supposed to have lasted for four days, with an estimated massacre of some 6,000 people. This carnage resulted from the age-old Portuguese hatred of Muslims and could have been avoided.

There was a falling out between Timmayya and Albuquerque, who suspected that Timmayya was conspiring against the Portuguese in favor of Vijayanagar. Timmayya was removed from his office, and Mahlar Rao was appointed in his place. Timmayya was of course unhappy with this turn of events. He moved to Vijayanagar, where he died from some illness in about December 1512. His wife and children went back to Goa seeking Portuguese protection, where Albuquerque granted them support in view of Timmayya's services in the capture of Goa. The Hindus in Goa were left essentially unmolested in the initial stages of Portuguese rule. Albuquerque reduced taxes and was benevolent to the Hindus not out of large-hearted religious tolerance; he wanted to consolidate Portuguese power before pushing the religious-conversion agenda. The Hindu power structure, which had invited the Portuguese, hoped to benefit from the destruction of the Muslim power hierarchy and expected good times ahead. Mhall Pai was given a land grant near the capital (Couto 2004, 85).

However, the Portuguese, with their own dominance hierarchies of the state, the Roman Catholic church, and various religious orders, had their own power agenda. They waited until the time was right to strike at the dominant Hindus to destroy them or co-opt the existing power structure. There was, of course, jockeying for power amongst the Portuguese hierarchies and subhierarchies, in the unfolding of the conquest aftermath in Goa. The destruction of Hindu temples began in 1540, and five years later, almost all of them in Portuguese possession were gone (D'Costa 1965, 30). The evangelizing zeal also peaked in the 1560s with many conversions, forced or voluntary. The Inquisition was established in 1560. When life became difficult under the Portuguese, Mhall Pai conspired with Adil Shah to overthrow them. This plot was discovered, and he had to flee to Kochin, where he lived in exile until his death (Couto 2004, 85). The repressive measures against the Hindus, the forced conversions, and the atrocities of the Inquisition forced many of the Hindus to leave Goa and go into exile. The displacement of the Hindus had a disastrous effect on the economy of Goa, because agriculture and trade were mostly in their hands. Any concessions to the Hindus were opposed by the church, the religious orders, and their clergy, who were blind to the ruinous effect of their religious persecution on the state. At about this time, in the seventeenth century, Portuguese power was in decline, seriously challenged by the Dutch and the English. The administrators of the state had to make some tough choices. In fighting for their very existence, they had to compromise with the despised natives, the Muslims and others they had been persecuting all along. In spite of the fulminations of the clerics, the state had to come to terms with the natives and realize that they controlled trade and were needed for tax collection, customs, and the general running of the administrative machinery of the state, as well recruitment material for the army and navy (Scammell 1988).

Casteless Portuguese Meet Caste-Ridden Hindus

The theme of a casteless society versus a caste-based society is a favorite amongst historians, who would like to compare and contrast the virtues of the casteless Europeans, such as the Portuguese, with the burdens of the caste-segregated Hindus. De Mendonça described the situation as follows: "I think that one of the greatest contributions made by the missionaries in their geographical expansion was the possibility they created for an encounter or confrontation of two different societies or cultures: one caste-ridden and the other casteless society, although divided hierarchically" (de Mendonça 2002, 18). It is true that Portuguese society was casteless; however, it was very much stratified, graded, and ranked. Was the difference in societal organization that vast between the two groups? On close examination, the Portuguese appear to have been suspiciously like the caste-ridden Hindus. The Portuguese and the Hindus had the same primacy drive, leading to very similar hierarchies. I compare them here with some care.

The Portuguese were quite color- and race-conscious and jealously guarded their social ranking and status. Linschoten, the Netherlander who lived in Goa, noted the false pride of the Portuguese and the way they treated the natives of Goa with contempt, doing their best to belittle them (Boxer 1969, 23). Their sensitivity to color and race is obvious from the fine gradations and variations of social labels prevalent in Portuguese society. These gradations depended very much on their concept of "purity of blood," or how much of the "pure" Portuguese blood they claimed to have. Initially, purity of blood implied no newly converted Jewish or Moorish ancestors in the family; later this list was extended to include heretics condemned by the Inquisition, members of other heretical Protestant sects, Africans, and Asians. This idea was of such importance that a baby of white parents, nursed by a native wet nurse, was considered contaminated for life and thus not suitable for admission into some religious orders (Boxer 1969, 255). It is *her* milk that contaminated the baby, not that she fed it.

At the top of the heap were the *reinois*, full-blooded Portuguese who came to India as high officials of the state or the church, such as viceroys, governors, archbishops, bishops, army and navy officers, judges, and other functionaries appointed by the king (Xavier 1993). It was customary to recruit them from the higher nobility, *fidalgos* (literally, "son of a someone"), who were considered superior to the lesser nobility, *nobres*. These high officials served for a fixed term in India and returned to Portugal for a posting to other colonies such as those in Brazil or parts of Africa. They did not marry native women, keeping their lineage uncontaminated by native blood. Some of them did indulge in fornication with native women; however, acknowledging any accidental progeny was taboo. Next to the *reinois* were the *casados*, married men or Portuguese nationals who had married Portuguese or local women. The children of the *casados* of pure Portuguese blood were called *castizos* and were considered superior to the *mestizos*, children of mixed parentage, usually Portuguese and Indian. The children of Portuguese and African parentage were mulattos, lower in rank. Portuguese society itself was graded into strata: the ecclesiastics, the nobility, and the common people, or *o povo*. The clergy ranked higher than the nobility, and both wielded spiritual and temporal power. Even the clergy was divided into higher and lower ranks. Indian converts were not admitted to the religious orders as full members; they could only become members of the lower or secular clergy. Attempts by some of the Indian converts to break the race or color barrier were not successful. One such convert, a "Christian Brahmin," Dom Mateus de Castro Mahale, went to Rome in 1625 after being refused ordination by the archbishop of Goa. He was ordained a priest in Rome, and after completing his theological studies with great distinction, he was consecrated bishop of Chrysopolis in 1635 and later appointed vicar-apostolic of Bijapur. Although he had full support of the cardinals of the Congregation for the Propaganda of Faith of Rome, the Portuguese civil and church authorities of Goa refused to allow him to assume his episcopal duties, because they declared his credentials to be fraudulent. His principal enemy was the respected Jesuit patriarch of Ethiopia, Dom Affonso Mendes, who called his fellow bishop and brother in Christ "a bare-bottomed Nigger" (Boxer 1978, 13, Couto 2004, 318–20). This was a disastrous collision of Hindu caste snobbery with Portuguese race superiority, both equally deluded. Below the mulattos and outside the pale of Portuguese society were the *naturais*, the natives. They were divided into Christians and non-Christians, usually Hindus. The Christians were in general favored by the administration as coreligionists or to encourage conversion by the heathen. Side by side with these power elite were the religious orders, who formed their own hierarchies constantly jostling for power and working to the best advantage of their order. Alphabetically, they were the Augustinians, Capuchins, Carmelites, Dominicans, Franciscans, Jesuits, and Theatins (Xavier 1993, 114–21). I have left out the Oratorians, a congregation of native secular priests, because they emerged rather late, near the end of the seventeenth century. Amongst these orders was a hierarchy, with the Jesuits at the top, followed by the Dominicans, who were in charge of the Inquisition, and then the rest of the orders, ranked according to their political, economic, or ecclesiastical power. Some of these orders complemented their spiritual work with moneylending (6%–8% interest was usual [Xavier 1993, 16]), management of acquired property and plantations, and trade, which expressed their power in hard cash. Hence, the presumed superiority of some orders was backed by economic power; the Jesuits were the richest. Proof that these stratifications were real and exercised effective power in Goa can be found by counting the number of prisons they had. These are the ultimate expression of dominance of a few powerful elite over the rest. There were four main prisons: the all-powerful state prison, the prison of the controller of the treasury for economic offenses, the prison of the Inquisition for religious matters (where the alleged offenders and heretics were housed and examined under torture, if necessary, in the gathering of evidence), and the prison of the archbishop for holding Christians for civil and criminal offenses (Xavier 1993, 144). In addition, there were prisons of the religious orders, which in spite of the best efforts of the king and the viceroy were never closed down. In these prisons, the rich and powerful orders, led by the Jesuits, followed by the Franciscans and others, could imprison, fine, and mete out to detainees their own justice independent of the state prison and courts. In spite of the complaints against these prisons, the state was powerless in closing them down. The unlimited power enjoyed by the religious orders naturally corrupted them, leading to various abuses. One such example is narrated by Alexander Hamilton, an English traveler whose *A New Account of the East Indies* was published in 1727 (Collingham 2006). However, his story should be read with caution because, as T.R. de Souza, a historian, says in commenting on Hamilton's travelogue: "Alexander Hamilton paid two short visits to Goa in 1692 and 1704. His account is couched in scurrilous language which reflects the attitude of fanatic Protestant against fanatic Catholic" (de Souza 1979, 211). There may be a hard core of truth mixed with embellishments in this story; unfortunately, we do not know the proportions of this mix or whether there is a core of truth. With all these caveats, this is the story: The clergy in Goa had first call on the fresh fish caught that day; others could buy any left over only after the clergy's needs had been met. A friend of Hamilton's who was expecting a large group of friends for dinner bought the last bit of fresh fish caught that day. A priest who arrived later demanded that this fish be handed over to him. When the man refused, he was berated by the priest using "scurrilous language." A prompt repartee from the man so angered the priest that he threatened to excommunicate him. This matter was resolved only when the man paid a monetary fine and delivered a humiliating apology to the priest on bended knees in front of the archbishop (Collingham 2006, 63–4). If this story is difficult to believe, there are similar accounts of cruel treatment of the locals reported by a bona fide Catholic and a Portuguese man, one of the judges of the Goa high court, and also the acting crown attorney in India in 1619.

> Most unbelievable is the cruel fashion in which these Fathers treat the people of Salcete. It was brought to my notice by Antonio Carniero de Aragao that when he had been to Salcete along with Dom Lourenzo da Cunha and Dr. Antonio Barreto da Silva, a Father had ordered the *canarins* of the locality to supply fish every day. Once they happened to send him less fish, and for that crime they were put into an enclosed place and mercilessly flogged in the presence of the above mentioned Antonio Carniero and other distinguished visitors. The natives do not dare to complain, and even the Portuguese people and the State Ministers remain silent, because they fear to have these Fathers against them. The Fathers were feared because of their ability to write terrible accusations to the home authorities in Portugal. [de Souza 1979, 228]

Looks as though the clergy were a conceited lot, full of themselves. So much for the "casteless" Portuguese society! The concept of castelessness was a comforting illusion, asserting the supposed moral superiority of the Portuguese over the Hindus and nothing more. Human genetic heritage, shared with our cousins the chimps, predates all religions and impels us to dominance, hierarchy, and resulting exploitation. All humans are obsequious to their "betters," just as they condescend to their "inferiors"; only the degree of fawning and bullying varies among situations. All societies, Hindu, Portuguese, Eastern, Western, or any other, have their hierarchies and their pretensions of grandeur and are good examples of this basic insight. Pious exhortations of religions create an illusion of equality, fairness, and justice and are mostly irrelevant to the facts of real life. All human societies are prone to this form of self-delusion that lays claim to the virtue of equality, which none of them possess.

More East–West Encounters

When the East met the West in sixteenth-century Goa, there were surprises for both—some pleasant and a few doubtful. These encounters have left their mark in the local languages as relics. The Europeans were called Franks, or *pharaṅgi*. The word *pharaṅgi* is used in local languages for guns and syphilis also, because the Europeans are supposed to have introduced both of these into India in the age of explorations and exploitations. Another interesting Konkani word is *nasrāṇi*. It is a Konkani form of *nazarene*, or "Christian," and Christians are called by that name in other parts of India too. However, there is also a pejorative meaning of the Konkani word: "dirty, filthy, and smelly." A

Konkani mother who finds that her child is dirty, filthy, and smelly after playing in the dirt may ask the child in exasperation, "What kind of a *nasrāṇi* are you," before giving the child a good bath. I have always been intrigued by the origin of this word and the obvious question: Why foist this calumny of being dirty, filthy, or smelly on Christians? I have a plausible hypothesis that is based on the personal cleanliness and bathing practices in Europe in the Middle Ages, the Age of Exploration, or about the fourteenth through sixteenth centuries, and even much later, down to modern times. The problem was that in those days, Europeans in general and the Portuguese who visited Goa did not bathe daily. They were filthy and must have given off a fetid body odor. (*Note:* This section and the ideas expressed here originated in the following curious way. In September 1988, I was visiting the data centers and research laboratories in China. I was housed with a fellow physicist from Berkeley, California, and his family in the hostel of the China Institute of Atomic Energy, then called the Atomic Energy Institute, in Beijing. Our hosts took us around as a group, sightseeing and dining in fancy restaurants. My friend's wife pointed out how xenophobic Chinese have been throughout history, calling Europeans pejorative names such as *barbarians* and *foreign devils.* Other Asians—Indians, Japanese, Koreans—had similar derogatory names for Europeans. What was the reason behind all of this prejudice? I pointed out that dislike of the "other" is practiced by all nations, tribes, and groups [Berreby 2005]. So what was peculiar about Europeans in their meetings with the Asians? What was it that was characteristic of Europeans but did not apply to Asians? It suddenly struck me that the Europeans in the Age of Exploration must have smelled bad because of their lack of personal hygiene. As a rule, Asians bathed almost every day, while the Europeans did not. This flash of insight made me dig deeper into relevant facts, which substantially supported the initial hunch.) Jews and Muslims were the only people who bathed regularly for religious reasons, while the rest of Europe formed the great unwashed. Though short on baths, the Europeans were long on conceit and felt superior to those of other cultures, washed or unwashed. It is plausible that the Portuguese and other Europeans were responsible for giving all Christians a bad name in Goa and other places. The word *nasrāṇi* must be a relic of those days before Europeans took up bathing, which they eventually did after having had lived in India and the East for some time. This at least appears to be a likely explanation.

The information on this curious subject is mostly from Marques (1971) and Vigarello (1988), supplemented by Wright (1980), Braudel (1981), Duby (1988), Sarti (2002), and Ashenburg (2007). *Daily Life in Portugal in the Late Middle Ages* by Marques tells us about Portugal, and Vigarello discusses mostly the state of affairs in France. It should be emphasized that the habits of cleanliness varied markedly from place to place, and generalizations from few observations to other places could be doubtful or wrong. This caveat should be kept in mind; because the information on this subject is sparse and spotty, we have to make do with what little that is available.

In the middle of sixteenth century, Lisbon alone had about 3,500 women doing laundry, each for about five or six families, thus ensuring clean linen for those who could afford the service. Black and white soap was manufactured using olive oil and ash. Olive-oil soap made in Castile, Spain, was famous, much in demand, and expensive because of its high quality (Ashenburg 2007). This industry was lucrative enough for the profits from it to be assigned as a reward to members of royalty such as Prince Henry the Navigator and his nephew Fernando (Marques 1971). Large cities such as Lisbon and Oporto had public baths open to women only on Sundays, Tuesdays, and Thursdays, and for men the rest of the week. In other places in Europe, there were separate days assigned to men, women, Jews, actors, and others. The segregation of sexes varied according to local customs. In a few places, such as the medicinal springs at Baden, Switzerland, sometime around the 1400s, bathing was a communal activity with naked men and women getting together in hot baths and socializing as at any other public place, such as a church (Duby 1988, 600–610; Greenblatt 2011, 173–176). However, it is not clear how often each individual went to these public baths or how expensive each visit was. These baths were the legacy of the Roman and the Muslim Arab occupations. Bathing was a luxury because it required a certain level of established urban culture, wealth, a good and cheap supply of water, the technology of plumbing or slave labor, and wood or coal for heating in cold weather, all of which were not available to most people. Public steam baths and bathhouses were patronized by most of the locals who were not affluent enough to have them in their homes. We know that the baths were taxed; however, details relating to their use by individuals are lacking. To what extent did the culture of cleanliness of the dominant social class—the Romans and Arabs—become part of the daily life of the rest of the people, the Christians? It is quite possible that when the Christians became dominant in the Roman Empire, or after the Reconquest in Portugal and Spain, they rejected these habits as belonging to the vanquished and hence doctrinally suspect, whereas their unwashed lives mirrored the one true faith (Ashenburg 2007, 71). The conquerers also destroyed the Moorish baths as unnecessary (Ashenburg 2007, 72). This happened in Portugal also (Marques 1971). There was another adverse influence on personal cleanliness, motivated by Christian piety, and a preoccupation with one's immortal soul at the expense of this mortal body. During periods of intense religious fervor, filth and discomfort in one's body or clothing was considered a type of atonement, suffering in this world that would lead to the ennoblement of the soul, with possible increased rewards in the hereafter, and therefore commendable. Odor of sanctity, *olor de santidad*, a euphemism for "foul smell," came to represent one of Christian virtues (Ashenburg 2007, 72). Princess Saint Joana, in the mid-fifteenth century, wore the same chemise months on an end, suffering from the lice bred in it (Marques 1971).

How often did people bathe? Perhaps not very often, if the habits of the rich and affluent of the time are an indicator. Philip the Good (1396–1467), duke of Burgundy, used to bathe once every four to five months (Vigarello 1988, 25). Elizabeth I (1533–1603), queen of England, who lived about 140 years later, bathed once a month, whether she felt she needed it or not (Wright 1980, 53). Jesuit Padre João Rodriguez Tçuzu (c. 1562–1633) was official interpreter to General Toyotomi Hideyoshi and Shogun Tokugawa Ieyeshu and lived in Japan for many years (Schütte 2003a). In one of the early encounters of the East and the West, he remarked on how the Japanese were shocked by the lack of personal cleanliness in the English and the Portuguese, their aversion to hot steam baths, and their habit of eating with unwashed hands (Milton 2003). At the court of Louis XIV (1638–1715), the king and the courtiers bathed only as a cure for sickness (Braudel 1981). The king bathed only once, and only as therapeutic measure, during a period of 65 years, from 1647 to 1711 (Sarti 2002)! This surely must be a record for unwashed royalty! The king and his brother, Philippe, duc d'Orléans, were considered very fastidious because they changed their shirts three times a day (Ashenburg 2007; Spawforth 2008). However, they did not bathe. In Europe from the Middle Ages to the eighteenth century, standards of personal hygiene and body cleanliness were quite different from those of people in other parts of the world. These habits had not become important enough to be part of a person's self-image as an individual in society or for the lack of them to be embarrassing. Lady Mary Wortley Montagu (1689–1762), English letter-writer, poet, essayist, and colorful and eccentric wife of Britain's ambassador to Turkey, was a feminist, a rich, sophisticated, cosmopolitan, and well-traveled medical pioneer who introduced inoculation against smallpox in England; she is a case in point. On seeing her at the opera, someone remarked that her hands were less than clean. Unflappable, she retorted that her feet were much worse (Braudel 1981; Ashenburg 2007). Dr. Samuel Johnson (1709–1784), commenting on the use of clean linen, declared: "I have no passion for it" (Boswell 1960, 1: 246, 24 May 1763). James Boswell, Dr. Johnson's biographer and friend, was averse to baths and hence notorious for his body odor. His friends solved both problems, at least temporarily, by getting their servants to give him a good bath when he was too drunk to object (Ashenburg 2007, 127–8). It is noted that in the Paris of 1788, hardly anyone took baths, and when they did it, was about two per year, in the summer. In the London of 1800, there was not a single bathing establishment (Braudel 1981). These are, of course, orders of magnitude estimates, and they could vary depending on the person, country, local traditions, and any special occasions. The less rich, perhaps, bathed less often, but bathe they did, especially on some special occasions, such as the eve of their own wedding. The public bathhouses also provided wine, food, bed, some gambling, and the company of compliant serving wenches, for a price. Hence, the word *stews* came to mean either "hot baths" or "whorehouses" in English. Similar dual usages are found in Italian and other European languages. The main purpose of going to these bathhouses was to have a good time; cleansing the body was strictly secondary (Vigarello 1988, 34). Some of these steam baths or bathhouses were closed by local civic authorities if they got too rowdy and rambunctious and thus posed a law-enforcement problem. The moral police of society also fulminated against these establishments and the extramarital fornication in them but could not do much to eliminate them entirely. They were also blamed for the spread of syphilis. They were subject to closure by the local authorities, with the support of physicians, during epidemics, especially the bubonic plague, also called the Black Death, because they were blamed for the spread of disease. The earliest plague epidemic was in 1348–1350, with quite a few epidemics occurring later (Marques 1971). The situation was best described in 1526 by Desiderius Erasmus (c. 1466–1536), the great humanist: "Twenty-five years ago, nothing was more fashionable in Brabant than public baths; today, there are none; the new plague has taught us to avoid them" (Vigarello 1988, 27). Brabant is one of the nine provinces of Belgium.

In addition, the medical wisdom at that time was that washing with hot water was a hazardous procedure that upset the delicate balance of humors, opened the pores of the skin, and was likely to expose one's body to the contagion of any pestilence. Physicians recommended that bathing—that is, washing and cleansing the body with water—be avoided if possible and done strictly as a therapeutic measure. Elaborate precautions, such as bleeding, purges, cupping, and enemas, were taken before and after a bath to ameliorate its harmful effects. There was always an attending physician, for those who could afford them, when people embarked on a dangerous bath: If the physician felt that the humors were getting out of balance or if the bather showed any adverse symptoms, the procedure was immediately stopped to prevent further harm. The result was that public or private bathing, however infrequent, almost completely disappeared in sixteenth to eighteenth centuries in Europe. People washed only their hands and faces every day, because these were the visible parts of their bodies, and such cleaning involved the absolute minimum amount of work. Bathing the rest of the body was replaced by vigorous rubbing with scented linen, for those who could afford it. Presumably this procedure masked some body smells with perfume. However, it did not clean the fetid body. Those who could not afford perfumes or the extra linen managed without them as best as they could. Clothing in those days was designed to have a smooth, dense weave, to further protect a porous and vulnerable body against external contagion, and was not changed frequently (Vigarello 1988, 10). Pieces of clothing that were visible, such as linen, were kept clean; changing them replaced bathing. However, this practice did not apply to more private pieces of clothing. All of these strategies, designed to protect the body, resulted instead in people's bodies being hosts to vermin such as nits, fleas, lice, and worms. Physicians ascribed the presence of these parasitic fauna to a lack of equilibrium of bodily humors and did not think that daily baths and frequent change of clothes would eliminate them. Vermin infestation was such a universal problem that rules of etiquette were formulated to provide guidance for dealing with them in a genteel, unobtrusive way in polite society. As a matter of fact, delousing became a socially accepted, pleasurable, semipublic activity:

> . . . delousing went on all the time, a mark of affection and respect; in bed or in front of the fire, mistresses diligently deloused their lovers, serving-maids their masters, daughters their mothers, and mothers-in-law their future sons-in-law. Certain women with particularly nimble fingers even made a profession of it; in summer people sat in the sun and gossiped on the 'flat roofs of low houses' whilst enjoying the services of professional delousers. Vermin were still a daily fact of life at the end of the Middle Ages, for a large part of the population. [Vigarello 1988, 42]

The mental picture of this particular social activity should delight a modern primatologist, for it shows humans reverting to an earlier stage in our evolutionary past and claiming their rightful genetic heritage from our cousins, the chimps and other primates, who delight in grooming. In sixteenth- to eighteenth-century Europe, human infestation by lice and fleas was so pervasive that contemporary painters were not shy in showing it in art. *Woman Catching a Flea* (c. 1638), by French painter Georges de La Tour (1593–1652), and *Mother's Care*, by Caspar Netscher (1639–1684), an artist of the Dutch school, are examples (Ashenburg 2007), the latter showing a prosperous, richly dressed woman hunting for lice on her son's head. Giuseppe Maria Crespi (1665–1747), an Italian artist from Bologna, painted *The Flea* (c. 1709) and *Searcher For Fleas* (c. 1730) (Sarti 2002) on the same subject. In short, flea-bitten Europeans moved around in the fifteenth to eighteenth centuries carrying a personal microsystem of miscellaneous effluvia, which must have been very obvious, extremely offensive, and an insult to the sense of smell. Because they moved in a society where everyone smelled the same, more or less, general sensitivity to offensive smells was lowered to conform to the socially accepted norms. This fact of life called for a recalibration of one's sensibilities.

In the Age of Exploration, when the Europeans visited the East, they might have spent six to eight months or more at sea, with very limited toilet facilities. Their diet was heavy on meat, with the by-products of protein digestion adding pungency to their sweat and leaving its residue on their skins. They must have had a very strong odor. The natives of India, China, or Japan, however poor they were, had a tradition of frequent baths, at least once a day. The powder of soap pods, *śikāye piṭṭi*, and chickpea flour were used in bathing, and soap nuts or soap berries, *riṇṭo*, were used in laundering clothes. Hence, a meeting of the East and the West must have been a clash of sensibilities. Europeans were admired for their fair skin, which has been always associated with high-status groups who did not have to toil in the hot sun of India. Their better-built ships, superior firepower, and more advanced technology were all worthy of respect. However, the deplorable state of their personal hygiene was very obvious and must have earned these early explorers some bad epithets. If the Asians called the Europeans "barbarians," "despised foreigners," or some other pejorative term, bad smell and general filthiness of their person may have been the main reason. Of course, every group or tribe likes to look down on a stranger and consider themselves superior in every way (Berreby 2005). This is the cultural primacy conceit, originating from our built-in need to dominate; it is part of our genetic heritage. However, the outrage to one's sense of smell represented by unwashed strangers must have been very real. This appears to be a reasonable explanation of the Konkani pejorative word *nasrāṇi*. There is documented evidence that the Portuguese in Goa soon worked themselves out of this state of filth and foul smell, learning by the end of the sixteenth century to bathe regularly. When Dutchman Linschoten (1563–1611) arrived in Goa in September 1583, the Portuguese had been in India for about 85 years, or three to four generations, and some had married native women and most probably had learned good new habits. Linschoten worked as a clerk for the archbishop of Goa, Vicente de Fonseca, and lived there for about five years. In his memoirs he notes that the Portuguese bathed once or even twice a day, "from head to foot," changed their linen often, and were scrupulously clean. In addition to washing, the women perfumed themselves with frankincense and sandalwood. These habits stood out because they were so unusual in Europe, especially the daily bathing and the involvement of the *whole* body. Linschoten noted that the Portuguese had learned these habits from the Indian heathens (Burnell and Tiele 1935, 1:193, 212–3). A distinctly positive aspect of the cultural exchange between civilizations!

Professional historians give many details in their narratives of the meeting of the East and the West, except for the obvious dimension of the sense of smell and cleanliness. I am sure that cleanliness is as important as costly dress and general deportment in attempts to impress others and flaunt status. Then why is it that no one talks about it? Are historians too polite or very embarrassed? The missions of ambassadors to get trade concessions, the goal of missionaries to evangelize the heathen, the aim of merchants to extract the maximum profit—were they compromised because one of the parties smelled bad or did not have good hygiene? These are interesting questions on which there is mostly silence in history books. However, there are a few exceptions. Emperor Shah Jahan (r. 1628–1658), while admiring the Franks or Europeans in general, condemned their deplorable toilet habits. He declared that they could be a great nation except for being infidels, eating pork, and not washing after defecating (Hall 1996, 283). Then there was the shrewd Jesuit, Alessandro Valignano (1539–1606), who urged his Jesuit brothers to bathe more often. Valignano was born in Chieti, Italy, and died in Macau, China. Some have suggested that his family was close to Gian Pietro Carafa, bishop of Chieti, and later Pope Paul IV (Ross 1994); others have cast doubts on this relationship. Valignano left Lisbon for Goa in 1574 as a visitor, or supreme authority over all the East Indian Jesuit missions—that is, from the tip of Africa to Japan. In all, he made three voyages to Japan and lived there for a total of ten years (Schütte 2003b). Valignano was a visionary who tried disassociating missionary activities of the Jesuits from the European political and cultural hegemony to include norms of societies of China and Japan, to make Christianity more palatable to the locals. He had to walk a fine line in shifting evangelizing from being too Eurocentric to including Asian values, without being accused of syncretism. He initiated these new guidelines, and they proved to be quite effective in the spread of Christianity in China and Japan (Moran 1993; Ross 1994). He was a thoroughgoing racist who, as a white European, an Italian aristocrat, and a Jesuit, was convinced of his superiority over other people and races, confident of his place at the top of the heap. The fact that his living for thirty-two years away from Europe and amongst many people and races did not in any way change his racist views indicates the tenacity of his bigotry. To him, Africans were a "very untalented race . . . incapable of grasping our holy religion or practicing it"; the people of India were "born to serve rather than command"; they were "miserable and poor beyond measure . . . all of a very low standard of intelligence" (Wright 2004, 93). He also felt that the dark races were stupid, depraved, and barely human mentally (Milton 2003, 86;

Boxer 1969, 254). His strong opposition to the admission of Indians to the Society of Jesus was also expressed in equally blunt language (Boxer 1969, 254). However, he appears to have bestowed a higher status on the Chinese and the Japanese amongst Asians; they were almost "honorary whites." He even conceded that the Japanese were better than the Portuguese in dress, deportment, and knowledge and were definitely not barbarians (Milton 2003, 87). The problem that Valignano faced in Japan was that in spite of the best efforts of the Jesuits, they were not making a significant number of new converts, especially amongst the nobility and the scholars. Valignano wanted to know why. He was enough of a realist to appreciate that the problem could be with the dress, deportment, food, table manners, and personal cleanliness of his Jesuit brothers. He realized that the Japanese must have noticed the rank odor of the Jesuits, because of their aversion to bathing. "It would be an excellent idea, he suggested, if the Jesuits took the time to wash themselves more frequently" (Wright 2004, 118). The Jesuit visitor noted that quite a few of his brothers were uncouth peasants from the backwoods of Europe, less cultured and refined than the Japanese, and even knew very little of the doctrines they were supposed to be preaching. Some Jesuit brothers butchered cows and pigs, made blood sausages, and were involved in activities not done by priests in Japanese society. What was needed was a complete makeover of the Jesuits in Japan. They had to go native, becoming Japanese in their dress, deportment, table manners, etiquette, food, and, above all, in the cleanliness of their persons. He wanted them to acquire the local customs of good breeding and polite manners. To bring about these changes, he wrote a handbook of decorum, *Advertimentos*, with more practical advice and guidance provided by Sumario (1583 with later additions in 1592) and Historia del Principio (Milton 2003, 88). These efforts were meant to "inculturate the Catholic religion," as represented by the Jesuits, in local native cultural traditions and mores and thus make a conversion to Christianity more palatable for the natives. The same strategy was adopted later by another Jesuit, Matteo Ricci (1552–1610), amongst the Confucian bureaucrats of China (Rouleau et al. 2003) and by Roberto de Nobili (1577–1656) in South India amongst the Brahmans (Cronin 2003). These changes in personal cleanliness, amongst other things, appeared to have worked for the Jesuits, if one were to judge by the number of converts they made subsequently. All I want to stress in this narrative is that the local natives were sensitive to the unwritten rules of personal cleanliness and judged the Europeans to be woefully wanting in this respect. No wonder the natives called these unwashed foreigners pejorative names!

The evolution of bathing in Europe, and the acceptance of the idea that it involves cleaning the *whole* body using plenty of water and not just the visible parts such as the hands and face, took a long time. This novel concept of cleanliness came to be generally accepted in Europe only somewhere between the latter half of the eighteenth century and the middle of nineteenth century (Vigarello 1988; Ashenburg 2007). Even then, people ventured into this new territory with some caution. Countess Drohojowska decreed in a book, *On Politeness and Good Taste, or the Duties of a Christian Woman in the World*, published in 1860, that to inculcate genteel manners and good taste in French women, one bath a month was quite adequate (Ashenburg 2007, 188). That was the monthly quota of Elizabeth Tudor nearly three centuries earlier! In nineteenth-century Europe, floundering in a couple of inches of tepid water while going through the motions of a sponge bath was the norm. Luxuriating by immersion up to one's neck in a hot bath was considered to be "pagan, even sinful" (Ashenburg 2007, 188). A bath was not just a bath; it was a moral statement! Europeans knew that too many hot baths had been the ruin of pagan Rome, and they were not going to repeat that experience if they could help it! Luxuriously perfumed baths with hour-long immersion in splendidly appointed, marble-inlaid bathrooms with mirrors and other costly fixtures were known to be the fashion amongst beautiful women—actresses, dancers, and courtesans, who were known under the general rubric of "kept women." Though such baths held great fascination because of the veneer of "sin," respectable society was reluctant to adopt them. A bath of moral rectitude, some discomfort, and dirt was preferable to one of decadent luxury on the slippery slope to sin. Part of the problem was that Victorians were worried about the unspecified moral hazards of a prolonged enjoyable soak in a hot perfumed bath, considered to be more suitable for Asians, foreigners, and such "others" with peculiar, morally compromised habits. In short, the Victorians were afraid of being alone with their own naked bodies! In 1852 the Central Council of Health of Nantes issued this stern warning:

> Bathing is an immoral practice. Unhappy experience has taught us of the moral dangers of spending an hour naked in the bathtub. [Vigarello 1988, 174]

However, habits changed, in Europe and elsewhere. The British rulers of tropical India came to appreciate the virtues of daily bathing, including frequent shampooing and washing of hair, from the despised natives, at about the same time (Collingham 2001). It should be noted that the word shampoo is derived from the Hindi word *cāṃpanā*, "to press." Over the centuries, the East–West dialog has been unfortunately marred by racially motivated name-calling and stereotyping of the "other." The power dynamics of the dominance hierarchy and the primacy drive shaded the "truth" in these meetings. The West had better ships and guns, and they were the aggressors who were after the riches of the Indies and out to dominate the blacks, Moors, and Asians. Under these circumstances, the dominated had to be demeaned, and so their bodies were declared to be dirty and filthy, while the dominant cavorted around unwashed (Noël 1994, 118). However, the very presence of the dominant was an insult and an outrage to everyone's noses, and the citizens retaliated by calling the newcomers barbarians, foreign devils, or *nasrāṇis*. These pejorative names have been quite pervasive and have become part of the myths that the East and West have cobbled together about one another.

Evangelization in Goa

To evangelize is to preach the Christian gospel to non-Christians with hopes of religious conversion. If the preachers respect the preached-to as human beings with the same rights and privileges as themselves, including the right to religious beliefs, evangelization could be a civilized exchange of views on life in this world and claims about the hereafter. The ideal would be for the missionaries to convince the prospective converts to accept their religious beliefs intellectually and emotionally as a free choice. Any other method, based on physical force, financial inducements, offers of medical care, punitive legal procedures, or threats of imprisonment, is coercive. What actually happened in Goa was a mixture of all these. There were some voluntary conversions, and many others were carried out under duress, compulsion, violence, and force. How can one understand all the bloodshed, coercion, cruelty, and violence that occurred in Goa under the name of evangelization? The answer lies in the mind-set and prejudices of the Portuguese in spreading Christianity. These have been mentioned earlier but are worth repeating to understand Portuguese behavior toward the natives. First, they saw themselves as conquerors who, by right of conquest, could dictate and enforce their will on the conquered people of Goa. Second, their racial prejudice was supported by authoritative pronouncements of the Catholic church in the papal bulls confirming their right to plunder and enslave pagans and heathens, so they considered the natives of India fair game for exploitation. Third, it was their firm conviction that the Christianity preached by the Roman Catholic church was the only true religion. Therefore, Hinduism, Jainism, Judaism, and Islam had no legitimacy as religions. They were evil systems of belief that called for devil worship and should be eliminated. Because of its patronage of the church, the crown had a right and obligation to force its beliefs on the non-Christians in Goa. Hence, between the proselytizing preachers and the preached-to heathen, there could never be parity. The heathens had no rights; they could only comply and obey. In other words, the "Portuguese entered, conquered and maintained Goa with a cross in one hand and a sword in the other" (de Mendonça 2002, 125). It should also be noted that there were many problems with Hindu society in medieval Goa. The most notorious was the inhuman custom of self-immolation of widows, or *satī*. Laws of inheritance for widows and daughters amongst Hindus were unjust and unfair, dispossessing women and children and forcing them into a life of poverty and destitution. Some of these ancient wrongs were rectified by humane Portuguese legislation, which should be commended. The fact that such reforms were opportunistic in inducing people to convert, however, should also be noted.

Conversion is a sensitive topic even though it happened centuries ago in Goa. People can get quite emotional about it and have their own perspectives on these past events, as regards fairness, justice, use of force and violence, and whether it was justified at all. In this narrative, I will adopt the viewpoint of an outsider, a neutral observer. I will not discuss the beliefs of either of these religions, leaving that to experts. I will concentrate strictly on what happened to people, what their lives were like, and what their ultimate fate was, according to contemporary records. All Goan Hindus and Muslims were affected by the grinding of the conversion mill. It moved slowly during some periods of history, and then accelerated to produce an abundant harvest of new converts at other times. The lives of these people, whether new converts under the grim shadow of the Inquisition, Hindus permitted to live in Goa under very restricted circumstances, or exiled Hindus, were changed forever. Any person belonging to a particular religion tacitly accepts its worldview and value system and willingly belongs to its dominance and exploitation hierarchies. Change of religion entails uprooting oneself from a large network of support systems and embarking on a new journey of unfamiliar beliefs, customs, traditions, food habits, and value systems. Most people would not do such a thing lightly, for the sake of novelty or experimentation. They would rather coast along in their familiar environment. Church militants believed otherwise: They believed it necessary to spread the gospel of Christ by any expedient method, including force and compulsion. The church and missionaries were not particularly interested in how the heathen felt and were insensitive to the fact that the heathen might love their own religion as much as the militants loved theirs, despite claims of humane kindness by religious missionary orders. That was the crux of the problem, that they believed that Hinduism, Jainism, Judaism, and Islam were not *legitimate* religions. Because those "religions" were evil, in the eyes of the proseltyzers, they were sure to lead the souls of their unfortunate followers to everlasting damnation in hell. Thus the poor misguided heathens had to be "saved" at any cost, as permitted by circumstances. Conversions in Goa were a dynamic process that changed with time, local conditions, and opportunities. Some of its details are not pretty. It was a mixture of many things, good and bad. A few people converted voluntarily; others were persuaded by monetary or material gains, such as state offices, titles, and honors and land grants. There were many dichotomies: high moral intentions versus low practices; the preaching of compassion and the brotherhood of man versus the practice of racism, brute force, and opportunistic cruelty; disinterested compassion versus covetous greed. In all conversion activities, the state–church complex was punctilious about observing a façade of legal minutia and procedural norms. The laws were duly approved and signed by the king, viceroy, governor, or other functionaries; their basic fairness in enforcing them did not matter. The most egregious of the actions of this conversion zeal were three: (1) the people of Goa had to convert to Roman Catholicism or go into exile under the principle of *cuius regio, eius religio* ("whose realm, his religion"), invented at the Peace of Augsburg (1555); (2) the places of worship of non-Catholics should be destroyed, never to be rebuilt; and (3) the Goans' fatherless minors could be legally kidnapped from their guardians to be brought up as Catholics. The one common theme in all these activities was pursuit of dominance and power by the state–church complex at all times: "Conversions created a citizenry for the empire and the Faithful for the church, and conversely these citizens expanded Christendom and the converts strengthened the empire" (de Mendonça 2002, 96). Gaining Christian soldiers to fight for the empire and tithe-paying faithful to support the church in this life were worthwhile goals. Obtaining these—the harvest and the hoped-for fruit of conversions—by any means was perfectly acceptable. The following sections describe the unfolding of events in bringing in this harvest of new converts.

The division of missionary activities into three phases by de Mendonça, beginning in 1510 and ending in 1610, a century later, is useful in providing a time frame for these events (de Mendonça 2002, 106–15). I have adopted this scheme here; the main events of the three phases of conversions are from Délio de Mendonça's *Conversions and Citizenry: Goa under Portugal 1510–1610*. To these I have added two more stages at the end, covering later developments.

Conversions, Phase I (1510–1540)

On the conquest of Goa in 1510, Albuquerque had reassured the Hindus that they had nothing to fear under the Portuguese and that they and their institutions would be protected. However, some Hindu temples in the island of Divar were destroyed by his orders as early as 1513 to build the Church of Our Lady of Serra (Pereira 1978, 48). The Portuguese were consolidating their position in Goa, and though the king of Portugal showed great interest in evangelizing because of crown patronage, there were few conversions. The Hindus must have breathed a sigh of relief to be free at last from the Muslim domination of Goa and its casual atrocities and to be able to live in peace. The

Franciscans had come to India with Vasco da Gama's first voyage and were joined by the Dominicans in 1509. Any conversions in this period were mostly by Franciscans. The diocese of Goa was established in 1534, and the first bishop of Goa was installed in 1538. There was much mixing of the Portuguese and the locals, even syncretistic participation in Hindu religious festivals and celebrations. However, there were protests from the religious and requests that the crown impose restrictions on Hindus and live up to its responsibilities as patron of the church. In 1518, Friar Antonio de Luoro, the Franciscan superior, requested that the king forbid Hindu yogis from visiting the islands of Goa. Four years later, in 1522, the visiting Dominican bishop, Duarte Nunes, complained to the king about the Portuguese and native Christians attending Hindu festivals and requested that he put an end to these idolatrous practices by destroying Hindu temples. Thus the ruling came about that churches should be built to replace the destroyed temples and that Hindus should become Christians or leave the king's dominions (D'Costa 1965, 29; de Mendonça 2002, 13).

Conversions, Phase II (1540–1580)

The Portuguese had expected the Hindus to convert gradually without much persuasion, to destroy their temples of their own accord, and to build churches to replace them. Land grants would be transferred to the new churches, and Christianity would spread peacefully. However, none of that happened. It is estimated that in 1542, there were only about 10,000 new converts in Goa when missionary Francis Xavier and the Jesuits arrived (de Mendonça 2002, 109; Broderick 1987, Broderick and Lapomarda 2003; Wicki 2003). Hence, more forceful measures were needed. The continued occurrence of Hindu worship in temples was seen as a major obstacle to conversions, so most temples were destroyed between 1540 and 1545. On arriving in Goa in 1545, Italian Jesuit Nicolao Lancillotto noted that there were no Hindu temples left in Goa under the Portuguese rule (D'Costa 1965, 30). Vicar General Miguel Vaz and Diogo Barba, a priest, spearheaded the destruction of temples. Conversions increased with the arrival of Jesuits who spearheaded the response of the church militant to the Reformation with such great efficiency that they earned the grudging praise of their rivals, the Protestants (Boxer 1969, 67). There could have been no higher praise, coming as it did from the church's arch foes! In 1557 the Diocese of Goa became an archdiocese, and the Augustinians arrived in 1572. Francis Xavier was shocked by the lax morals of Christians, both the clergy and the laity, in Goa, calling it "Lusitanian concupiscence on a staggering scale" (Boxer 1969, 70), and wrote to the king requesting establishment of the Inquisition to tighten up local Christian discipline. The Inquisition was duly established in 1560 to hunt for dereliction of orthodoxy in longtime Christians, long-established Catholics without any Jewish or Moorish ancestry, European converts from Judaism (*conversos*), and native Christians converted under duress who were suspected of being crypto-Hindus. Though Hindus and Muslims were not the main concern of the Inquisition, they could be hauled in front of it and tried on charges of preventing some infidel from converting. The missionary zeal and intolerance peaked in about 1560. The printing press was established in 1556, and the first book was printed in the same year in support of conversions. Hindus in state service were replaced by new converts. One result of the Council of Trent (1545–1563) was the makeover of the clergy as a "person set apart" from the laity (de Mendonça 2002, 111). Members of the clergy were expected to lead a model life worthy of emulation by the laypeople, to watch over them, and to rebuke them if necessary. The First and Second Provincial Councils were held in 1567 and 1575, respectively, in Goa. They proposed harsh, restrictive legislation on Hindus and Muslims, preventing them from practicing their religion, even in the privacy of their homes. Their homes were searched and any hidden sacred images were confiscated, holy books were burned, and many people were imprisoned. The most severe penalties imposed on the Hindus for performing forbidden religious ceremonies involved being sent to the galleys, being forced to work in a gunpowder factory, or having their property confiscated (de Mendonça 2002, 56, 174). Quite a few converted to Christianity to escape punishment or, as explained in detail later, because they were ritually polluted, had ceased to be Hindus in good standing, or could not be ritually cleansed. There was legislation favoring new converts with jobs and economic incentives. The church had to make sure that the new converts did not lapse into their old religion. These suggestions from the Provincial Council were duly approved into law of the land by the viceroy in 1567 and after the Second Council. Compulsory attendance of Hindus with their families at the preaching of the Christian doctrine became law in 1567, though it was not enforced for some time (Priolkar 1961, 123). According to the guidelines of religious instruction by Alessandro Valignano, a Jesuit visitor in 1575, it "was also necessary to dispel any false opinion they might entertain, by showing them the errors and wickedness of the Hindu religion, and by telling them that Christianity alone was holy and reasonable" (Mendonça 2002, 144). This period also saw the beginning of the decline of the Portuguese state in India, Estado da India, which commenced in the reign of Dom Sebastião (1557–1578 [Boxer 1969, 383; de Mendonça 2002, 113]). This decline was accelerated by the state's spending on the religious orders and churches. Forced conversions and religious persecution lead to the exile of many tax- and revenue-producing Hindus, Muslims, and even Christians from Goa. The state was jeopardizing its own status in its zeal for religion and its patronage; it was cutting its own fiscal throat.

Conversions, Phase III (1580–1610)

The union of Portugal and Spain in 1580 did not in any way diminish missionary activity in Goa, since the Spanish monarch was no less keen on this enterprise. Conversions increased in Salcette, and remaining temples were destroyed and new churches were built in their place. Excesses of missionary zeal resulted in Hindu backlash, which in turn resulted in the massacre of five Jesuits and native Christians in 1583, who became known as the Martyrs of Cuncolim (see the section "Martyrs of Cuncolim" much later in this appendix). The Third, Fourth, and Fifth (and last) Provincial Councils were held in 1585, 1592, and 1606, respectively. The last council ratified the decrees of the earlier two.

Conversions, Phase IV (1610–1774)

The last book printed in Goa was in 1674, a year also saw the closing of the printing press. The press was an important part of the missionary work; Jesuit Visitor Alessandro Valignano, on his arrival in Goa in 1574, had encouraged printing of religious tracts in local languages such as Marathi, Konkani, and Tamil. However, about 100 years later, it was felt that the continued use of native languages encouraged new converts to revert to their old religions, and thus such languages should be banned. Hence, the press was closed in 1674, and the decree of 1684 was passed, which prohibited the use of local languages, including Konkani, and required their replacement by Portuguese in three years. Yet many of the new converts from Hinduism continued to follow their old customs and traditions. The very comprehensive Edict of the Goa Inquisition of 1736 was meant to eradicate any trace of such old habits (Priolkar 1961, 97). This edict dealt with the minutiae of Hindu life in the privacy of the home and thus was difficult or impossible to enforce, even with a system of anonymous informers. Most of these new regulations had nothing to do with Christian faith or doctrine; they were intended to induce a makeover of the converts, with complete elimination of old Hindu habits and customs:

> The same natives of India are hereby ordered that they should not erect pandals with festoons of leaves at the gates of the houses of the bridegroom and the bride.
>
> The said natives of India are hereby ordered that under the bed on which the married couple would sleep, they should not place betel-leaves, areca-nuts or any other edible thing. [Priolkar 1961, 100]

The list of prohibitions went on and on.

Under the reforms of Prime Minister Pombal, the Jesuits were expelled from Goa in 1759, their wealth and lands were confiscated, and the order was dissolved in 1773. The much feared Inquisition in Goa was abolished on 10 February 1774.

Conversions, Phase V (1774–1910)

The Inquisition in Goa was reinstated in 1777, after the fall of Pombal from power, to operate under a new manual of rules and regulations. In 1778, the inquisitor general directed the inquisitors to carry out their work with moderation according to the new manual, "seeking the conversion of the Infidels and sinners with more sweetness and suavity than rigour" (Priolkar 1961, 183). The Inquisition was finally abolished in 1812 as a result of pressure from Great Britain and a call for religious tolerance. Though the reign of terror ended with the abolition, various restrictive laws from the Inquisition that discrimated against the Hindus remained on the books until the Portuguese Revolution of 1910 and the founding of the republic (Pearson 1987). As for the Hindus, after these events, the "move forward after 1910 was dramatic. A community long repressed, marched into the modern age. They had retained their hold on commerce and trade over the centuries but entered professional life through full participation in Portuguese and English education after 1910" (Couto 2004, 308).

Ritual Purity and How It Helped Conversions

What is ritual purity? Hindu tradition demands that many acts of life, such as worship, sacrificial and other offerings to the gods and Manes, everyday meals, and the reading of sacred literature, be done in a state of *anvāḷẽ* or *anvāḷēpaṇa* (ritual purity). A person becomes ritually pure by bathing the whole body, including the head, hence called a "head bath" by some, and changing into freshly washed, ritually clean garments. What I have described applies to normal activities in a Brahman home; for an officiating priest in a temple, there are more elaborate procedures that I will not go into. Ritual purity and its opposite, ritual pollution (*bhaṣṭa*), must have originated as hygienic measures that morphed into a set of do's and don'ts that are part of everyday life in an orthodox Hindu household. These rules are too detailed to be written down and are best learned growing up in an observant household. Such strictures are self-imposed and are part of each family's tradition. Families differ in their observance of all of these rules; most who are secular, or *laukika*, are less strict, while those who are orthodox, belonging to families of professional priests, or *vaidika*, are strictly observant. What are the consequences of these customs? Within a *jāti* (birth group) that conforms to the same rules, food is shared and mates are found, and these customs can lead to stronger social bonds. They also isolate the observant groups from others who do not live by such rules. Such small differences in observance could lead to different subcastes, which result when these groups fragment and separate. Thus in sixteenth- to seventeenth-century Goa, when these observances were more strict than now, Hindu sharing food with Christians or Muslims was out of question. An observant Hindu would get up early and, after a bath, do his daily worship, *pūjā*, and then eat his first meal. Once he left home to attend to his business or trade, where he met Christians, Muslims, and others, he would never eat anything at all. Some might eat fruits, but anything cooked was forbidden. At the end of the day, after the person returned home, he would have another bath, do the evening worship, and then eat the evening meal. It was not that he looked down on others who were "ritually unclean" because they ate beef, drank alcohol, or engaged in other forbidden practices. It was just that observing ritual purity, which meant not partaking in meals with the ritually unclean, was part of the practice of his religious beliefs. However, a few Portuguese and Muslims took offense because Hindus considered them "unclean." In addition to the sense of satisfaction resulting from the observance of these customs, there were the outward signs of being a Hindu and a Brahman. These were the tuft of hair on the crest of the head (*śeṇḍī*), sandalwood paste on the forehead (*nāma*), a string of prayer beads (*japamāḷā*) round the neck, the sacred thread (*jānnuvẽ*) over the left shoulder and under the right and round the torso, and the mode of dress. These were essential in defining each person's self and social identity and place in a hierarchy. I have described these details so that we can understand the havoc played with the life of Hindus, and especially Brahmans, by the new rules and regulations of the Portuguese.

If a person was arrested for any reason either by the Inquisition, the state, or one of the religious orders and lodged in a Portuguese prison, it created many problems whose ramifications were perhaps not completely understood by the confining authorities. Incarceration in Portuguese prisons deprived the prisoners of their ability to maintain their customs, including baths, and relegated them to a state of perpetual pollution. Outward signs of their personhood were confiscated by prison authorities or stolen, and in their own minds they ceased to be Hindus in a state of grace and became nonpersons whose life was one long living death. Prison food was a big problem. The orthodox might have starved themselves to death rather than eat the unclean food cooked by the guards or even drink water in a state of pollution. Such deaths are mentioned in a letter dated 19 December 1729 from the viceroy, João Saldhana da Gama, to the king of Portugal (Priolkar 1961, 185). If hunger got the best of them and they ate the prison food, it was as if their life as an observant Hindu had ended. They could undergo a ceremony of ritual purification and become a Hindu in good standing again if and when they were released from prison. However, these ceremonies were expensive, the Portuguese actively prevented their performance, priests who could perform them were not always available because the Portuguese had exiled them, and prison confinements during tortuous trials were long, extending over months or years. Added to all of these problems was prisoners' shame at having fallen from their life station in the sight of family, caste, or community. This unfortunate situation made many Hindus particularly vulnerable to religious conversion, especially if it was accompanied by a release from prison and any pecuniary advantages of being Christian. Once the Portuguese state, the church, and religious orders such as the Jesuits caught onto these facts, they realized how to take advantage of the situation and used it to the fullest extent to push their program of conversions.

D'Costa expresses surprise that a good number of the Hindus were quite willing to convert after a short imprisonment. Perhaps the reason for this change of mind was that these people felt that they had lost their status as Hindus in good standing, knew that they could not be reinstated without difficult-to-arrange proper ceremonies, and fatalistically accepted their fallen circumstances. They might have blamed their situation on their past karma and decided to convert. The Father of Christians, appointed from among one of the religious orders by the state, could and did take charge of children whose father had died by designating them as orphans even though the mother, grandparents, and other close relatives might have been alive. This was a cruel and cynical use of so-called laws and was much resented by the Hindus. These officials were supposed to bring up these "orphans" as Christians until they were old enough to decide their religion for themselves, at the age of 14 or so. One of the first things that the officials did after getting physical possession of these minors was to cut off their *śenḍi*, shave their heads, and feed them, so that these children were considered doubly polluted ritually and essentially cut off from their kith and kin and the rest of the Hindu community. In a letter to members of his religious order, one such official complained, "Believe me, my brethren, my fingers and arms were paining after all the shaving I did" (de Souza 1994, 108). In a few cases, the mother or other immediate relatives converted to be close to their children. Interdining with converts to Christianity at weddings and other social functions without knowing their changed status caused many people to be declared ritually polluted by the rest of the community and thus excommunicated from it. The only choice of the unfortunates in such cases was to embrace the new religion, even reluctantly. If the sworn testimony of two Spanish Dominican friars is to be believed, the Jesuits were known to get new converts by having their black slaves catch Hindus in the streets of their quarters and smear their lips with beef, thus ritually polluting them (Boxer

1960–1961, 83; 1965; 1978, 100; de Souza 1994, 108; de Mendonça, 2002, 128, 257). Some Hindus would undergo a purification ceremony in adjoining lands outside Portuguese control, even though some other Hindus doubted whether this could really be done (Boxer 1978, 100). Unfortunately for Hindus, and especially the Brahmans, the minutia of ritual pollution made it easy to force them to convert by the organized efforts of the state and the church. The leadership of the Hindu community, however, was not coordinated enough to counteract these forced bogus conversions in any effective way. Manu states emphatically that force vitiates all transactions (Doniger and Smith, 1991, 170, 8.168), making all forced conversions invalid. Unfortunately, the Hindu community either did not know their Manu or would not accept such declarations at face value. There are records of a few such cases of purification after the fact; however, they were rare, expensive, and not convincing to the rest of the community. The incursions of this new religion into the main body of Hindu community were not faced effectively by providing help to the polluted and readmitting them into the caste. Some pro forma ritual, modified to suit the troubled times and declared to be equally effective by the leaders of the community, could have sufficed. Instead, the orthodox adopted the view of declaring the ritually polluted to be lost to the community and writing them off, so that the rest could maintain their integrity and purity. Instead of solving these new problems proactively and effectively, the community tacitly accepted the forced conversions with a sense of resignation, seeing them as caused by the karma of the poor victims. This was a grave failure of leadership of the Hindus, and especially of the Sarasvat community.

Conversions: Voluntary or Coercive?

There are many opinions on the conversion problem, and equally many answers. It is fair to say that the degree of persuasion in conversions varied over the whole spectrum: from the voluntary—no coercion of any kind—at one end to the use of physical force to baptize the heathen at the other extreme. And force was indeed used, especially during jubilees declared by the church. A jubilee was a special occasion, or a definite period of time, during which the faithful could obtain indulgences or forgiveness of their sins if they performed acts specified by the declaration, such as converting a Hindu or a Muslim (de Mendonça 2002, 139–40). During these periods, the conversion zeal of the clergy and the laity reached great heights, and monetary payments or use of physical force to convert were not out of bounds. Quite a few of the religious brothers were ex-soldiers who had no reluctance in using physical force in their new vocation. They would go to villages to hunt their prey—to physically capture village chiefs or high-caste Hindus, whom they forcibly baptized as captives. If these captives could not be purified with proper ceremonies for various reasons, they lost their status as Hindus in good standing. They were shunned by their own people and had no other recourse than to convert to Christianity. In between these extremes, there were financial incentives, promise of state jobs, preferential treatment of new converts, free medical treatment and ministering to the sick in hospitals, and other inducements. All of these methods of persuasion were deemed proper, based as they were on two guiding principles: (1) the subjects of a king should adopt the same religion as the ruler or leave his kingdom and go into exile and (2) compulsion in religious conversion is justified by a scriptural injunction from Jesus Christ—"And the master said to the servant, 'Go out to the highways and hedges, and compel people to come in, that my house may be filled' " (Luke 14:23, Revised Standard Version). Let us look at each of these guiding principles in detail and discuss them as to their applicability to the evangelization in Goa and how they conform to the practice of conversion.

The first principle—*cuius regio, eius religio* ("whose realm, his religion")—came to be accepted in Germany, and later throughout Europe, after the Peace of Augsburg in 1555 (Encyclopaedia Britannica 1968, 19:42). This principle is at the root of all religious intolerance and persecution in Europe, Asia, and the rest of the world, by both Catholics and Protestants (Boxer 1960–1961, 89), and thus it deserves a close examination. This doctrine was first talked about (not adopted) at the Diet of Speyer in 1526 (Encyclopaedia Britannica 1968, 19:478). It was a compromise between the Catholics and the Lutheran estates (members) of the Holy Roman Empire. It was a right won by the Lutherans, members of the Augsburg Confession, by the force of arms, to have their own church and forms of worship to exist side by side with the Catholic church. The agreement even excluded the Zwinglians, Calvinists, and Anabaptists and provided a choice between being either a Catholic or a Lutheran (Holborn 1982, 1:243; Encyclopaedia Britannica 1968, 19:478). It was a limited principle applicable to a restricted set of entities who were party to this treaty. This treaty, like all treaties, is applicable only to the parties who signed it and not to others, who do not have legal or moral standing as far as its application is concerned. To claim that this doctrine, which originated in the context of the Reformation and the European wars, could be transported halfway across the globe to justify the Portuguese conversion zeal against Hindus, Jains, and Muslims is quite a stretch and boggles the imagination. At best it is a legal fiction or humbug crafted in high-sounding Latin to impress the gullible, created by some state functionary to justify arbitrary, cruel, and unjust acts of religious coercion practiced by the state in Goa. It is a bit of casuistry meant to disguise a clear perversion of justice. The only defense was that the state and the church had unlimited power in Goa that they abused, operating on the credo of despots and tyrants all over the world: Might is right. The fallacy of using this principle to justify the actions of the church-state complex is obvious from the fact that all the Hindu temples in the Goa islands had been destroyed by 1545 (D'Costa 1965, 30), ten years before the Peace of Augsburg when this principle was formally accepted. This relic of history lingered on so long as the Portuguese crown existed, because it was considered part of crown responsibility, because of its patronage of the church, and lasted till the founding of the republic in 1910 (de Mendonça 2002, 12).

Let us look more closely at the second principle that compulsion could be used in religious conversion. The church and its evangelizers were ambivalent about it, and there were two schools of thought about it. One group found justification in the scriptural injunction to "compel the heathen to come in." The other group accepted the fact that compulsion in conversion was an act of aggression, admitting that it was morally reprehensible and unacceptable. This second group believed that the desire to convert was an act of grace that was bestowed on a selected few. The compromise was to hold forth with high moral pronouncements that eschewed force in conversion yet to pursue conversion by any method, including force. The Ecclesiastical Council of 1567 stated that conversions should not be made by force or a threat of force; they should be entirely voluntary and should be considered as a sign of grace bestowed by God (Boxer 1969, 68). However, these pious declarations of moderation in conversions were nullified by various other actions of the council that became the law of the land when approved by the vice-regal decree of 4 December 1567 (Boxer 1969, 68). These high moral principles were a salve for the conscience even while coercion brought in the requisite number of new converts. There was no harm in giving Providence a helping hand. The coercive conversions in Goa, other parts of India, and Brazil are best described by the following two examples. Alessandro Valignano, the Visitor and the great reorganizer of Jesuit missions in the East in the sixteenth century, noted that Francis Xavier, one of the greatest missionaries and later canonized a saint, used a mixture of threats and promises in his evangelization (Boxer 1960–1961, 88). Xavier's missionary activities in India over a three-year period were in Malabar and Travancore, on the east coast, up to Madras (now Chennai) and on the neighboring island of Ceylon (now Sri Lanka), mostly amongst the pearl divers and fishermen (Broderick 1987, 15:491; Wicki 2003, 14:877). Valignano states that Francis Xavier, by his spirituality and practical acumen, realized that the natives of India (called Niggers by Valignano) were too primitive to appreciate reason or persuasion but would understand force. By threatening their livelihood of fishing and coastal trade if they did not convert, and by promising the protection of the Portuguese ships if they became Christians, Xavier reaped a rich harvest of converts. This "compel them to come in" school of preachers was not averse to using force in conversions, in spite of the pious admonitions of the Ecclesiastical Council of 1567 against it. There were similar practices in evangelization in other places like Brazil, where Xavier's Jesuit contemporary, Jose de Anchieta, wrote to the Jesuit General in Rome in April 1565 that the sword and the rod of iron were the most efficient mode of spreading Christianity (Boxer 1960–1961, 88–89).

These forced conversions became so egregious that some of the church hierarchy sent a representation to the crown drawn up at Lisbon in February 1563 by the bishops of Ceuta, Lisbon, Tangier, Angra, Portalegre, Lamego, and the Algarve in a memorandum that listed the current abuses in the Portuguese evangelization, including the use of force and the baptism of uninstructed or unwilling. These grave charges by seven leading church dignitaries must have been based on well-established facts (Boxer 1969, 72). These forced conversions and the baptism of uninstructed, unconvinced, unwilling people resulted in their backsliding into their earlier beliefs. This alarmed the church hierarchy and was one of the reasons for the establishment of the Inquisition in Goa. The harsh rule of the Inquisition and the forced conversions sent many of the wealth-producing and tax-paying citizens of Goa into exile, further contributing to the decline of the Portuguese state. The state undermined its power by taking seriously its responsibilities under its patronage of the church.

Legalized Kidnapping of Fatherless Minors

If the state–church complex had any second thoughts about the use of force in the conversion of adults, they had none where the so-called orphans among the Hindus were concerned. Any fatherless Hindu child younger than 14 was declared an orphan under Portuguese civil law, even if the child's mother, grandparents, or other close relatives were alive and willing to take care of the child (de Mendonça 2002, 207). Such an "orphan" came under the jurisdiction of a state official—Father of Christians—usually member of a religious order. The child was indoctrinated in Catholicism but could choose a religion on attaining the "age of reason," at 14. The Hindus were denied the "natural law" of parents to be guardians of their children, because they were declared to have forfeited such rights by worshipping images as Hindus, rather than the true God of the Catholics (de Mendonça 2002, 208). This snatching away of a child from family was accompanied by seizure of the child's share of the family property (Priolkar 1961, 132). With a child from a rich family, such an acquisition of wealth could be substantial. Shorn of its euphemisms, casuistry, legal verbiage, and protocols, assuming control over a fatherless minor, by force if necessary, was legalized kidnapping. These children's parents could remain with them only by converting to Christianity. St. Thomas Aquinas (1225–1274) held without qualifications that

> . . . the natural order of things demands that, before a child comes to the age of discretion, he should be cared for by his parents, in matters both of body and soul. It would therefore be a violation of natural justice if he were taken away from his parents or baptized against their wishes. [D'Arcy 2003, 5:948]

The baptism might have been carried out after the child reached age 14, but indoctrination in the Catholic faith started as soon as the authorities kidnapped the child. St. Thomas Aquinas could be ignored by the religious when his words were not convenient. The history and development of the laws governing this seizure, between 1556 and 1754, and changes in the definition of orphans are available as historical records (de Mendonça 2002, 205–14; D'Costa 1965, 120–5). The original law of 1556, defining a child younger than 14 as an orphan even if the child's mother or other close relatives were alive, was justified under the dubious and selective argument that such a definition was in accordance with Portuguese civil law, which was supposedly applicable to Hindus and Muslims in Goa. The Father of Christians was authorized to enter homes and forcibly remove "orphans" if necessary. Hiding "orphans" or taking them out of Portuguese jurisdiction was widely practiced and could be punished by the perpetrators' being sent to the galleys or having all of their property confiscated (de Mendonça 2002, 207). The state–church dominance hierarchy was cynically certain that a child brought up as a Catholic till 14 would remain Catholic when given a choice. This law remained in force in the Portuguese territories till 1677 and was quite effective in "bringing a rich harvest of boys and girls to the church" (de Mendonça 2002, 207). The law was modified in 1559, and an orphan was redefined as a Hindu or Muslim child younger than 14 who had lost a father, mother, grandparents, and other close relatives. This change was resented by the religious orders because it interfered with their mission of conversion and any ancillary control of the minors' wealth. Though the decree of 1559 did not specify the age below which a Hindu child could be placed into the custody of the Father of Christians, practices varied widely, until the original decree was finally fixed by a vice-regal decree of 1718 specifying age 14 for boys and age 12 for girls (Boxer 1969, 76). There were very few protests against these atrocities or dissenting voices from the power elite. Archbishop D. Aleixo de Meneses was humane enough to respect the rights of parents to take care of their children and decreed that only true orphans could be taken away from their family. However, most of the power hierarchy went along with these doubtful procedures and the conversion zeal of the religious. The problems caused by these zealots are mentioned in a letter, dated 24 January 1728, from the viceroy, João Saldanha da Gama, to the king:

> By the indiscreet zeal and imprudence of some Fathers of Christians the government is many times embarrassed by complaints and mutinies of the Hindus on the ground that orders of His Majesty are not observed. The Father of Christians takes away their children and servants, without waiting orders from Judge Conservator and proceeds immediately to cut their Sendies (tufts of hair at the back of the heads), in order that when they are ordered to be released, they should be considered as unfit for being admitted within their castes. [Priolkar 1961, 136]

Such treatment of "orphans," which sometimes even involved violence, caused much resentment amongst Hindus and Muslims, second only to that engendered by the destruction of their places of worship. The Father of Christians, usually a Jesuit, would feed child food that was ritually polluted, shave off the *śendī*, cut off the child's sacred thread, and wipe off the child's *nāma*, thus removing all outward signs that the child was been an observant Hindu and making the child ritually unclean. Using children as a conduit to the conversion of their elders was one of the methods proposed by Francis Xavier. His insight was indeed correct; this method was successful in producing many new adult converts (de Mendonça 2002, 141, 207). It was a cruel and cynical manipulation of helpless parents, leveraging their love for their children. The Hindus had some religious freedom only after 1754, after which there were no new laws on minors (de Mendonça 2002, 205).

The church and the various religious orders that carried out its evangelizing mission must have felt that while dubious conversion methods were a fact, the end justified the means. As noted by the bishop of Dume, though the new converts might not be good Christians, their descendants would be, which is exactly what happened (Boxer 1969, 73). Once the state–church complex had come to terms with its collective conscience about compulsion in conversions and had gotten used to the idea of abuse of power, the rest was easy. Abuse of power can be addictive, making the next step easier, and with the voice of conscience stilled by the usual casuistry, the holy mission of saving the heathen was well on its way. There were several methods available for evangelization: the destruction of places of worship, coercive laws against non-Christians and their implementation under a program called "rigors of mercy," and economic and other incentives to encourage conversion. The various laws proposed by the five Provincial Councils between 1567 and 1606 are not repeated here but can be found in these sources Priolkar (1961), D'Costa (1965), Boxer (1969, 67–70), Xavier (1993), and de Mendonça (2002).

Destruction of Places of Worship

The most egregious abuse of power in conversions to Christianity was the destruction of places of worship, mostly Hindu temples and a few Muslim mosques. The Portuguese believed that any form of worship other than that sanctioned by the Roman Catholic church was a form of devil worship and should be eliminated. It was hoped that such destruction would stamp out this evil and encourage conversion to the one true Catholic faith. This destruction began in 1513, and its pace accelerated after 1540, till by 1545 it was essentially complete in the old conquests of the island of Goa: *Ilhas* Goa, including Tiswadi; Bardez; and Salcette, including Marmagoa (D'Costa 1965, 30). Vicar General Miguel Vaz and Father Diogo de Borba were the principal representatives of church militants behind these acts of destruction (D'Costa 1965; de Mendonça 2002, 128, 201–4). The destruction of temples would put an end to Hindu worship, rites, and ceremonies and was expected to help the conversion of people at large. Churches would be built, in a few cases on the very sites of former temples, and temple properties would be appropriated to support Christian institutions. The list of these temples in the island of Goa, Bardez, and Salcette, as compiled by noted Goan historian Dr. P(andurang) S(akharam) S(henvi) Pissurlencar from the Portuguese records, is quite extensive and runs into the hundreds (Priolkar, 1961, 69–70, 79–84). It is estimated that a total of about 900 Hindu temples were destroyed in Bardez, Tiswadi, and Salcette (de Souza 1979, 91). The exact number of destroyed temples is immaterial; even one temple destroyed is one too many.

The old Mahālasā temple was in Verna, also called Old Maddol, in the Salcette district of Goa. Verna is a shortened colloquial form of Varuṇapuri, "city of Varuṇa," or Vareṇyapuri, "chief town." We do not know when this temple was built. The legends associated with its founding are recorded in booklets published by the temple management (Anon. 1993; 2005). This temple was destroyed by Diogo Fernandez, captain of Rachol Fort, in two forays, on 7 and 14 March 1567. These dates are from an article written by Dr. Pissurlencar and reproduced in the temple booklets and are most probably reliable (Anon. 1993; 2005). The account of the destruction of this temple is in a letter dated 12 December 1567, from the College of Goa, by Jesuit brother Gomes Vaz. This college, better known as College of St. Paul, was built in 1541 and taken over by the Jesuits in 1544 (de Mendonça 2002, 342). In his letter, Brother Vaz inserts quotes from a letter by Father Luis de Gois (Guoes), now dead, an eyewitness to the destruction of the temple. Extensive quotes from this letter give a flavor of those times, the Portuguese methods and mind-set, and the semblance of legal procedures with which they tried to cloak their actions. I am grateful to Dr. Délio de Mendonça, S. J., former director of the Xavier Centre of Historical Research, for a translation of this letter from the Portuguese (de Mendonça 2008). I have left out the page numbers of the Portuguese text from the translation:

> Having to write now about the conversion of the gentiles of this island (of Goa) and the adjacent ones, it seemed to me wise to insert at this point in the letter about what happened regarding the total destruction of the temples and their idols, still standing then in the lands of Salcete and Bardez which belong to His Majesty, the king of Portugal, near this island (of Goa).
>
> There was in the land a great number of temples, where God our Lord was being greatly offended, and the demon worshipped and served by all gentiles, with honours and offerings and vain sacrifices and due to many works relating to conversion of the gentiles in this island of Goa and surrounding islands, our priests could not directly dedicate themselves wholeheartedly to the work of conversion of the gentiles of the land of Salcete, territory that had been especially allotted to them, just as the land of Bardez is at the care of the fathers of St. Francis. Four or five years ago, when the work of conversion that was started in the island of Goa was considered as concluded, our priests began devoting directly to the conversion of Salcete, and together they decided to destroy the harmful temples, for the success of conversions, but destroying all the temples together would cause some scandal to the resident gentiles and changes in the land, and so it was sought another means, namely, of destroying a few temples at a time, as punishment for some dereliction they might have committed, in this manner some temples were destroyed during these years.
>
> When a priest who resided in the church of Rachol was going to a certain village, with some Christians, to visit a dying man, to speak to him about God and to see whether he could be converted, the entire village revolted against the priest and chased him with stones and arrows, and on the same day they killed a guard of the land who happened to pass by that village, soon after the revolt against the priest. When the viceroy came to know about this revolt, he sent the principal magistrate who after ascertaining about the truth, he burnt down all the temples in the same village.
>
> The same he did with the temples of the other villages, since the gentiles there arose against a Brother who had gone there to take the census of the Christians who resided there. And they surrounded this brother so much so that not having with him but only one catechumen, he was forced to seek shelter at the house of a Christian, which the gentiles cordoned too, but he could finally escape by a door without being noticed. As punishment for this crime, the viceroy ordered the captain to destroy all the temples of that village and forbade under death penalty that no one should dare to rebuild the destroyed temples.

At other times the captain destroyed more temples in other villages since the gentiles refused to obey certain laws, but since this manner of pulling down temples was rather too slow, and Christendom continued to grow, for the last two years our priests insisted with the viceroy that the pulling down of temples should be done more quickly and as they wished to be done, since with temples standing, besides offending God greatly and allowing the demon to be venerated, the priests felt that the gentiles became more stubborn in their conversion and made less impression on the Christians as far as things of faith were concerned.

There was a provision then, as I wrote last year, ordering the gentiles neither to build new temples nor even to repair the existing ones, but in spite of the gentiles refusing to comply, yet that did not stop its execution as ordered by the viceroy and in this way many temples were brought down as a result of the severe winters and strong rains in this land. The gentiles who felt more and more that they were unable to retain these temples for long, and also some newly converts began destroying them secretly.

But because this means was slow and the need to destroy the temples was growing, and the number of Christians increasing, moreover it appeared that the destruction of the temples could be easily executed, the archbishop and our priests represented the matter to the viceroy a few times, which for the viceroy seemed wise to destroy them.

The recommendation that the captain of the land of Salcete made to the viceroy also helped in this purpose to a great extent, facilitating the destruction. The priests also made it clear that the king of Portugal needed timber for the repairs of the artillery, thus impressing upon the viceroy that in some of the main temples, there was fine timber that could meet this need, which prompted the viceroy to write a letter to the gentiles of a main villages where there was a major temple in the entire Salcete, for which the gentiles had great devotion, dedicated to a unmarried woman, called, *Malsadavi*, whom they adored as God and in whose favour the gentiles maintained many public women who lived near the temple exposed for free to all who wished to sin with them, and in the same letter the viceroy asked for the timber of that temple, and at the same time he wrote another letter to the captain, Diogo Fernandez, apprising him this matter.

To better tell about the success of this story it seems to me that it would be pertinent to refer here to certain things from a letter written by Fr. Luis Gois—who now is in heaven, when he resided in one of the churches of those lands, as I mentioned earlier—to Fr. Rector. The letter reads:

> Yesterday the captain of the fort of Rachol went to the temple of Alardor, and I was present when the destruction took place, the destruction

that I wished to see long before, and blessed be God who permitted it, for the sake of timber for the repairs. I decided that before the captain went there, to send a Brother there first with some persons and before any warning to the gentiles he went to that village and when he entered the temple he found a helper of the temple placing silver jewellery on the idols. The Brother took quickly the idol and the jewellery and handed it over to the captain who made an inventory of the entire movable property. I ordered the main idol that was that of a bad woman to be made into pieces and the other idols I asked to be confiscated and taken away.

We ordered a solemn cross to be erected at a prominent place, which was done with some devotion. The cross appeared very majestic and appropriate in that place. This cross is in the middle of a square with tiles, this place being bigger than our garden and located on some steps, and its base is so tall, the height of two men, carved and with battlements, where there were sweet basils. The place where the temple is situated cannot be improved since it is on the lower part of the hill on a large ground, all surrounded by huge tiles, and a road comes out from it similarly tiled that leads to a majestic tank and one of the biggest I have so far seen. The entire road is surrounded by tall stone slabs and steps, and behind there are many trees all planted in rows.

At the entrance of the temple there is an ablution tank, similar to the dome of our Lady of Divar, with a portico of black stone. For certain I have never seen anything so majestic as this one, not even in Portugal, and in which better place could a Church of Our Lady of Conception be situated.

The following are extracts from a letter written by Fr. Luis de G(u)oes:

The temple was not totally pulled down but only the idols were destroyed, and the roofing removed, but everything else remained untouched and standing. Seeing all this the main gentiles of the village, Brahmins, as they are good negotiators and experts in their dealings, after some time asked one Portuguese to approach by all means the viceroy to let them have temple back, even in that dilapidated condition, because they expected that the new viceroy would permit them to rebuild it, and they would b(u)y the temple at any cost.

As soon as the captain came to know the intentions of the gentiles he destroyed the temple to its foundations that they might lose any hope that they might have of being able to worship the demon. And this was the beginning of the total destruction, made this year, of the temples standing in the lands of his Majesty, and by destroying this main temples, the other ones would soon have to suffer the same fate. Some were set on fire, others pillaged, a few razed to

> the ground, in such a way that from the biggest to the smallest not one remained standing. There were more than 280 big temples, and some of them very sumptuous and with excellent finishing touches. They were in prime places and some of them of notable grandeur where the gentiles used to wash themselves before and after performing their ceremonies. All these grandiose temples had big idols in the exterior, since inside, where the main idol was to be found, it was like hell, narrow, low, dark, stinking, dirty, frightening. And to compare everything in one word, it is in everything proportional to the place, which shows perfectly how the demon is enemy of light. The smaller idols/temples are innumerable which stand near these huge temples. Normally the residences of the principal gentiles, like Brahmins and others of the more honoured castes, housed idols in front of the door, perfectly arranged, made of stone or wood or trees which they also worshipped. And these together with all the large temples were pulled down.
>
> The main person responsible for the destruction of the temples was Diogo Fernandez, who at the time was captain of Salcete, whom besides reminding several times the viceroy, for the captain himself was as zealous of the honour of God, with great fervour and diligence executed the provision of the viceroy ordering the destruction of the temples. And knowing that it was the wish of the viceroy that the temples should be destroyed, the captain did not rest until they were demolished. [de Mendonça 2008]

The sacred image of the Goddess apparently had been removed well before the destruction of the temple and had been entrusted to the care of a cowherd, *gorovu*, for safekeeping. It was later installed and reconsecrated in the present temple in Mardol, in the Ponda District. A descendant of this cowherd used to officiate at the new Mahālasā temple in a tradition called *dhūḷi bheṭa*. In this ceremony, the *kuḷāvi* (family of devotees) of the Goddess would visit the temple before washing off the dust, *dhūḷi*, of travel. The *gorovu* would offer three coconuts, everyone would bow down, and he would announce that such-and-such a family, of such-and-such *gotra* (clan), place, lineage, etc., had returned from exile for a visit. I remember being part of this ceremony as late as 1974; it has now been discontinued, and the *gorovu* is nowhere to be seen in the temple. It is a pity that this reminder of the destruction of the temple, the exile of the faithful from Goa, and their travails and troubles has been allowed to lapse.

This drama of destruction, varying in details, must have been enacted at every one of the hundreds of Hindu temples all over Goa. What are the impressions left by this account? First, we should be grateful to the Portuguese for recording these happenings and preserving them. But for such records, these events would have disappeared from our collective memory. Second, the state–church complex and its functionaries were convinced that such destruction was meritorious, was conducive to the spread of Christianity, and saved the souls of the heathens or infidels from eternal damnation. Third, the state–church bureaucracy went through pro forma legal procedures to justify their actions. Either they were carrying out a direct order from the king of Portugal or the viceroy or they were enforcing the laws proposed by the local provincial councils and duly approved by the viceroy in council. Once all of the legalities had been observed, the basic fairness or justice of their actions did not matter. They could always give a reason for their acts, however preposterous. The fact that they destroyed the temple in Verna to get its timber for the king's artillery was perfectly reasonable and did not strain anyone's credulity. Even if it might have occurred to some of the state and church functionaries that such trumped-up reasons were an insult to their own intelligence, it seems that it never occurred to them that those reasons insulted the intelligence of their victims. The Hindus were expected to go through the charade of legality and accept the stupidity of the reasons given by the power hierarchy. History is full of such examples of treatment of the dominated by the dominant (Noël 1994).

What was the Hindus' response to all of the strong-arm tactics of the state–church complex? All they could do was to save their sacred images, take them outside the Portuguese areas of control, build new temples, and install their deities in them. A good account of these activities is given in the journal article "Flight of the Deities: Hindu Resistance in Portuguese Goa" (Axelrod and Fuerch 1996), described in this appendix in the section "Hindu Resistance." Quite a few Hindus left Goa for good and went into exile, giving up their property rights and leaving other possessions behind. Some did not have this option for a number of reasons, and when their backs were against the wall and were about to lose everything they had, including their lives, they decided to fight the oppressor. There were many clashes with the state, the church, and the religious orders in which state officials or members of clergy were killed. The most famous of these led to the Cuncolim Revolt, described in this appendix in the section "The Martyrs of Cuncolim."

The Inquisition or the Holy Tribunal

A discussion of the evangelical activities of the Portuguese state and the Roman Catholic church in Goa from 1510 onward would not be complete without an analysis of the Inquisition or the Holy Tribunal. *Inquisition* is the name for a legal procedure instituted by the Roman Catholic church to detect and eliminate heresy in its hierarchy and enforce clerical discipline. This procedure and the tribunal that used it came to be known by the same name. The Inquisition was not one monolithic institution; there were many in Europe and in the Spanish and Portuguese possessions all over the world. Three main lineages of the institution, traced individually, bring some order in understanding its history and development. The earliest inquisition originated in the late twelfth century as the disciplinary arm of the church to deal with clerical misbehavior and its correction by their superiors, the local bishops. Once Pope Gregory IX (1227–1241) brought it under centralized papal control in 1233–1234, it came to be known as the Papal or Roman Inquisition and was closely connected with the church's attempts at eliminating various types of heresies such as the Cathari and the followers of John Huss (1370–1415), called the Hussites (Roth 1973; Peters 1988, 2003; Roth and Assis 2007; Green 2007). Special representatives of the pope, called papal judge-delegates, who were experts in detecting and eliminating heresy, would be sent to places where their services were needed. Manuals on Inquisitorial procedures were also written in the fifteenth and sixteenth centuries to standardize its functions. Later it spread to many places: Sicily, Malta, Sardinia, Milan, Naples, the papal states, Mantua, Venice, and Tuscany. The Inquisition was revived in 1542 by Pope Paul III (1534–1549) in response to the Reformation. In 1557, Pope Paul IV (1555–1559) assigned responsibility for compiling the Index of Prohibited Books to the Inquisition (Dee and Sheridan 2003). The index was maintained for about four centuries, till it was abolished by Pope Paul VI (1963–1978) in 1966 because it was considered contrary to the teaching of freedom of inquiry by the Vatican Council II. After a few name changes, the Inquisition of Rome is now known as the Congregation for the Doctrine of Faith (CDF); it is the second oldest church-related institution in continuous existence, the oldest being the church itself. The procedure of inquiry was based on Roman law, with a single functionary acting as an investigator to collect evidence, a prosecutor to present it, and a judge to decide the case and mete out punishment. These procedures were later extended to the laity at large because heresy came to be considered equivalent to treason against the state and God. Also, secrecy was imposed on all trial procedures to protect the accusers, and torture could be used to gather evidence. A description of the historical development of these legal formats of inquiry may be found in the works of Edward Peters, who feels that the Inquisition has been "much caricatured and misrepresented between the sixteenth and twenty-first centuries" and tries to correct the record (Peters 1988; 2003, 7:485). He also discusses the Inquisition as represented in art and literature, faithfully or not, and the myths that have grown round it.

The other two lineages of the Inquisition are those of Spain and Portugal, where they were later established by papal bulls at the request of their monarchs. These national Inquisitions acquired a quasi-political character as instruments of the state used to implement its policies. The main motivation behind establishing these national Inquisitions was the problem of the newly converted Jews (*conversos*) and Muslims or Moors (*moriscos*) in these two countries. The Jews and Moors had been converted forcibly and were accused of reverting to their former religion in many cases. Once the tribunal was established, the old Christians and the newly converted Jews, Moors, and an occasional Protestant caught in its net all received its scrutiny, justice, and punishment. The full global spread of the Inquisition essentially covered all countries over the continents of Europe, Asia, Africa, and the Americas where the Roman Catholic church hierarchy ruled under the aegis of the Portuguese and Spanish states (Roth 1973; Roth and Assis 2007; Boyajiyan 1986; Baigent and Leigh 2000; Reston 2005; Green 2007; Kirsch 2009). As regards the organization and administration of the Inquisition, it was one of the earliest multinational corporations (MNCs) that preceded later trade companies. The Spanish Inquisition (1 November 1478 through 15 July 1834) lasted for about three and a half centuries, and the Portuguese Inquisition (23 May 1536 through 31 March 1821) lasted for nearly three centuries, even after allowing for short periods when they were shut down. The first date in these ranges is the date of the papal bull that formed the Inquisition's articles of incorporation, or the charter of its creation, and the second date is the date of its formal abolition. The East India Company (31 December 1600 through 1 June 1874) and the Dutch East India Company (20 March 1602 through 31 December 1799), both motivated by trade, profit, and greed, did not last as long as the Inquisitions, which were driven by religious zeal and general intolerance of other faiths (Robins 2006; Boxer 1977). The many similarities between these MNCs of faith and and the MNCs of trade are worth analyzing to understand their pursuit of power. The suffering of people under the jurisdiction of these institutions, the abuse of power, and the harm done to the natives all over the world are comparable in magnitude for the two groups of MNCs. The papal charter of the Inquisition clearly stated its corporate mission as the search for heresies and heretics and their complete eradication. The Inquisition formed its own bylaws like any legal corporation does, and these were published in books: *Directorium Inquisitorum*; the *Instrucciones* of de Torquemada, the Spanish inquisitor; and others (Roth 1973, 1400; Roth and Assis 2007, 800; Green 2007, 14, 78). There were no shareholders in these corporations, only stakeholders of the church and state hierarchies who wanted to maintain their dominance and power. This corporation was financed partly by the confiscation of property of accused heretics even before they were convicted, and partly by state support. Targeting the rich amongst the "heretics" is a clear indicator of greed as another motive of the Inquisition. However, the final effects of these institutions on their parent countries were entirely different. The East India Company built the British Empire in India, and the Dutch East India Company made the Netherlands rich and powerful; however, the Inquisition was highly detrimental to the intellectual and material progress of the papal states, Spain, and Portugal and set them back by a few centuries. The Inquisition of Goa, a descendant of the Portuguese lineage, was a significant cause of the ultimate ruin of the Portuguese State of India—Estado da India Portuguesa.

The main need for such an institution to detect and eliminate heresy in the laity arose from the expulsion of Jews and Muslims, or Moors, from Spain in 1492 and Portugal in 1497. They were given a choice of conversion to Christianity or expulsion from the country. The fact that quite a few of the power elite both in the state and church owed the Jews money that could be written off or that they had to leave their possessions behind fueled greed, which added an additional incentive to the expulsion. Though the church avowed piously that conversion to Christianity was a "gift of grace" by the Almighty and should never be forced, its militants were not averse to helping the process along by the use of force wherever they could. Young children, too young to decide for themselves, the not-so-rich middle class, and the powerless were particularly vulnerable. Some opted to leave Spain and moved to Portugal, where life was slightly better for the Jews in the beginning. The king of Portugal from 1495 onward, Manuel I, dealt with the Jewish question slightly differently than the way Spain did. He did not want to expel Jews and thus lose their contribution to the wealth and industry of the nation; hence, he baptized them by force without giving them the choice of leaving the country (Roth 1973, Roth and Assis 2007; Reston 2005, Green 2007). It is estimated that in Portugal alone, there were more than 50,000 of these new converts owing doubtful allegiance to their new religion (Boyajiyan 1986, 3). The new converts, *conversos*—also called *marranos*, a pejorative term with various origins and meanings, including "pigs" or "pork" (Cohen 2007a, 2007b)—were never completely accepted as full Christians by the rest of society. They were given a period of grace of twenty years to adjust to the practices of Christianity and would be exempt from any persecution for religious delinquencies. This period of adjustment was later extended to 1534.

However, the new converts were always looked at with suspicion by the longtime Christians, who feared these aggressive, highly mobile individuals. They were accused of practicing their former religion in secret, relapsing back to it covertly, while professing to be Christians in public. The longtime Christians tried their best to prevent an integration of these new converts into mainstream society, enacting many "purity of blood laws" that discriminated against the new converts and prevented their entry into universities, into degree candidacy, into most priestly orders, and into the higher offices of the church, municipality, or state bureaucracies (Boyajiyan 1986, Green 2007, 192–211). "Purity of blood" meant that the lineage of the family was not "contaminated" by any Jewish or Moorish (Muslim) ancestors. Later, the heretic Protestants and African and Asian ancestors were added to this list. The state and the church, by their religious intolerance, racist discrimination, anti-Jewish and anti-Moorish laws, and forced conversions, had created a problem, which they tried to solve by extending the procedures of the Inquisition to the laity at large, especially the new converts. At the request of the state, the church formally constituted an Inquisition in Portugal by a papal bull of 23 May 1536 (Roth 1973). The procedures of the Inquisition, especially the secret accusations and the fact that the accuser and the accused never met face-to-face, the confiscation of the property of the accused, imprisonment during hearings, and the use of torture to extract evidence, could be misused against the innocent to settle old personal scores. Any habits of a person's former religion or observance of any of practices from that religion put that person in jeopardy, liable to be hauled in front of the Inquisition. Ritual purity for Jews and Muslims required them to bathe regularly before prayers, and they were perhaps the cleanest persons in those days compared with Christians. The new converts, who continued to bathe often or on the eve of the Sabbath, were considered suspect and were accused before the Inquisition (Ashenburg 2007). Resting on Sabbath or putting on clean clothes were also reasons for doubting a person's religious sincerity. During the lengthy process of gathering evidence and conducting a trial, many of the accused died or committed suicide because of the harsh conditions in the prisons. Their property was confiscated even before conviction, with a part of it going to the Inquisition. Even if all the charges against an accused person were eventually dropped and the person was set free, they had to face a life of total poverty, with all of their property gone!

The Inquisition, at the end of a trial of a specific case, would formally proclaim its sentence and mete out its punishment at a public ceremony called an auto-da-fé, an act of faith or trial of faith (Burns 2003). The ceremony never included burning heretics at the stake or garroting them before burning as an act of mercy. Autos-da-fé were staged in the main square of the town at the principal church and were ceremonies of immense power as theater to impress, instruct, and caution the community about the fate of heretics, who could never hope to escape the eternal vigilance of the Inquisition. This purpose was clearly stated by one of the inquisitors, who said that the goal of the Inquisition, the trials and death sentences, was terrorizing people to bring about their compliance rather than saving their souls (Green 2007, 14). The ceremony was presided over by the power elite of both the state and the church. In the daylong drama, there was a solemn procession of the accused persons, who were made to wear penitential dress, *sanbenito*, with a miter; then a sermon by the presiding cleric, oaths, and a lengthy reading of sentences; abjurations, followed by reconciliations of the repentant; and as a final resigned measure, "relaxation," or the handing over of the obdurate to the secular authorities for capital punishment, with a solemn injunction to those authorities to carry out the death sentence without spilling blood. These sentences were usually carried out at a separate place and would involve burning the heretic at a stake, which was justified by the New Testament verse "If a man does not abide in me, he is cast forth as a branch and withers; and the branches are gathered, thrown into the fire and burned" (John 15:6 Revised Standard Version). If a heretic repented at the last moment, he or she would be strangled as an act of mercy before being burned. It was considered a great honor and a religious duty to light the brand with which the pyre was kindled, and this task was usually assigned to visiting members of the royalty (Roth 1973). If the condemned heretic was already dead, an effigy or the remains of the person would be dug up and burned. In a few less severe cases, there would be a private ceremony called a *meza* instead of the public auto-da-fé. The first auto-da-fé was held on 20 September 1540 in Lisbon (Roth 1973), and the last, in Mexico in 1850 (Burns 2003). The burning at stake of crypto-Hindus in Goa continued as late as 1768 (Green 2007, 331). The agony and the torment of the heretic ended with his or her death; however, the stigma of heresy devolved on their children and their descendants for many generations. The heretics' *sanbenitos* were hung up in their parish church and their names were inscribed there as a warning in perpetuity to all persons. The relatives of these heretics were tainted forever and could not get state jobs, work for the Inquisition, or be admitted to religious orders under the "purity of blood" laws. One person tried to clear his name 170 years after one of his ancestors was accused of being a Lutheran under doubtful circumstances (Green 2007, 193). The Inquisition's memory was long, its record keeping was meticulous, and forgiveness was not one of its virtues. The Inquisitions in Goa and in Portugal were abolished on 10 February 1774 during the reforms of Prime Minister Pombal. However, after Pombal's fall from power, the Goa Inquisition was revived under a new government in Portugal, with reformed rules of procedure, in 1777. The Inquisition in Goa was finally suppressed in 1812, and the one in Portugal was formally abolished on 31 March 1821 (Roth 1973).

Edgardo Mortara, a Jewish child, was kidnapped by the Roman Inquisition in 1858, two months short of his seventh birthday, because he had been secretly baptized by a maid when he was sick and hence was a Christian according to the church. The Roman Inquisition and Pope Pius IX were unmoved by appeals from his heartbroken parents or the international community to release him to his parents' care. The child was brought up as a Roman Catholic and later became a priest. This episode brought the Roman Inquisition and the Catholic church some unwanted notoriety. The Inquisitor in Rome, Father Pier Gaetano Feletti, a Dominican, was tried for this act and acquitted by a six-judge panel that declared the kidnapping to be within the law in force at that time (Kertzer 1997, 2001). Note the parallel between Edgardo Mortara and the many faceless, nameless, fatherless Hindu children kidnapped by the state–church complex in sixteenth- and seventeenth-century Goa, to be brought up as Catholics. The church was not reluctant to abuse its power so long as it had any in medieval Goa or the papal states.

The Inquisition in Rome lasted till the absorption of the papal or church states into the rest of Italy in October 1870 (Kertzer 1997, 2001). It has morphed into the CDF, its present name, instituted by Pope Paul VI in 1965 (Peters 2003). Though there has been a change of name, the legal procedures of the CDF hark back to the medieval times and the Roman law, according to people who have been tried and disciplined by it in recent times, as described in the book *The Modern Inquisition* (Collins 2002). These prominent Catholics are Tissa Balasuriya, Lavinia Byrne, Paul Collins, Charles Curran, Jeanine Gramick, Hans Küng, and Robert Nugent. This is a sampling of Catholics who, because they were authors, were media personalities, or were involved in doctrinal controversies, became well known; there are others. These people were tried, found guilty, and punished for their deviance from the official teaching of the church on theology; social or political philosophy, including gay and lesbian issues and contraception; or the administration of the church, including papal power and the CDF (Küng 2001; Collins 2002). Neither the church nor any civil government is now willing to garrote or burn anyone at a stake; that is certainly some progress. The secretive Papal or Roman Inquisition, whose decisions are without appeal, is very much alive and functioning today, only under a new name and a different disguise. Its jurisdiction now extends only over Roman Catholics or their clergy, who can be disciplined by it; it is powerless to punish anyone else.

The Inquisition of Goa

The Inquisition of Goa was established in 1560. The reasons for founding it were many. A few people, both secular and clerical, were shocked at the luxury-loving loose life and the immoral behavior of the Portuguese in Goa. Many Jews, forcibly converted to Christianity in Portugal and Spain, had moved to the Portuguese outposts in India to escape the scrutiny of the Inquisition at home. Because their change of religion had been under duress, quite a few of them practiced Judaism in secret or were called Judaizers (Roth and Slutsky 2007). They benefited from better economic opportunities, greater security, and a more tolerant atmosphere in the East (Fischel 1956). Their material and economic success, however, was resented by the long-standing Christians amongst the Portuguese, who were competing with the *marranos* for trade and wealth. The state also believed that these new Christians were encroaching on its trade monopoly and appropriating immense wealth that should have rightfully belonged to it. One effective way of getting back at the *conversos* was to subject them to the justice of the Inquisition. Francis Xavier (1506–1552), cofounder of the Society of Jesus, missionary, and later canonized as a saint of the church in 1622, landed in Goa in May 1542. He was shocked at the behavior of both the laity and some members of the religious orders in Goa. He wrote to the Portuguese king in 1546 to request that the Inquisition be established in Goa. He had the best of intentions: to bring some discipline to the Portuguese laity and clergy and to clean up their behavior. The forcible conversion of Hindus and Muslims in Goa had also created a problem similar to the one on the Iberian peninsula. The new native converts continued to practice their old faiths, because of either conviction or habit, and were viewed as heretics by the church. Preventing the backsliding of new Indian converts and eliminating their old practices became a major concern of the Goa Inquisition. The Inquisition, or the Holy Tribunal of Goa, was established to take care of two main concerns of the state: safeguarding the crown patronage of the church and the orthodoxy of the clergy and laity in the fleshpots of the East and ensuring that the state got what was rightfully its due as owner of a trade monopoly. The Goa Inquisition, because of its excessive zeal and industry, came to be known as "the bloodiest and most prolific of all the Portuguese tribunals" (Green 2007, 154). Pursuing both these objectives resulted in the state and/or the tribunal investigating the new Iberian Jewish converts and bringing them to justice on the slightest proof of any impropriety. There was a large and prosperous Jewish community in India and other parts of Asia. It was feared that the new converts would revert to their old faith by contact with these individuals, and eternal vigilance was called for to prevent it. The threat to the royal monopoly of trade and economic losses from the encroachment of the new converts forced the tribunal to unearth the vast network of family and trade connections all over the world. They were pursued relentlessly from one relative to the next, generations in succession, to Mexico, Peru, Brazil, Macau, the Philippines—in short, all over the civilized world where trade and finance thrived. The reach of the tribunal at a time when sailing ships undertook year-long voyages is truly amazing and illustrates its character as a powerful MNC. The correspondence of members of the Goa Inquisition with their colleagues across the seas is the only evidence we have for many of the trials of the Jewish converts, because the original Goan records have been destroyed. Over a period of many years, the new Christians (or former Jews) came to an understanding with the state and church by paying a colossal "pardon subsidy" of 1.7 million cruzados; by entering into partnership with longtime Christians in state or church offices; by buying titles, indulgences, and pardons; or by acting as bankers to the state and providing it with loans that were never paid back (Boyajiyan 1986, 15, 37). (Note: Up till 1560, 1 cruzado = 360 reis; after 1570, 1 cruzado = 400 reis [Subrahmanyam 1990]. Or 1 cruzado = 1.2 to 1.33 xerafim.) The Inquisition, by state decree, had the exclusive right to investigate and punish crimes against the one true Catholic faith, including blasphemy, sodomy, witchcraft, sorcery, heresy, and Judaizing, committed by any European Christian, noble or commoner, and baptized natives. Initially non-Christians, whether Buddhist, Hindu, Jain, Jew, or Muslim, had nothing to fear from the Inquisition—at least that is what they were told. However, they could be tried by the Inquisition on allegations of preventing other potential converts from changing their faith or on charges of blasphemy. Under this rubric, there were no limits on the power of the Goa Inquisition; it could investigate any non-Christian on secret charges. The Inquisition became a feared tribunal that even the viceroy and other church authorities—and even secular authorities—were afraid to challenge. The extent of this fear may be judged from an incident mentioned in the Goa travel narrative of Niccolao Manucci (Xavier 1993, 125). Manucci was talking to a Portuguese noble at his home when a servant of the Inquisitor brought a letter. The noble turned pale and was visibly trembling with fear when he opened the letter, which turned out to be a request for some excellent mangoes growing in his orchard. The noble immediately sent the mangoes to the Inquisitor via the servant. That very night, he cut down the mango tree in order that he might never again come to the notice of the Inquisitor for any reason.

The church's fight against heresy in Goa had begun earlier in 1543 when Jeronimo Dias, a physician and a *converso*, was tried for blasphemy and burned at the stake. He was strangled as an act of mercy before burning, because of a last-minute repentance. Garcia (Abraham) da Orta (1500–1568) was another famous *converso* (de Carvalho 2007; Fischel 2007; Fischel and Liebowitz 2007). He was a physician trained at the Universities of Salamanca and Alcalá and had taught in Lisbon before he left for Goa in 1534. He prospered in Goa, serving as a physician for the viceroy, church dignitaries, the Muslim ruler Burhān al-Dīn Nizām al-Mulk of Ahamadnagar, and other high officials. He also carried on a trade in spices and precious stones on the side. The viceroy even bestowed on him the island of Bombay, then a small fishing village, in about 1548 in recognition of his services to the state. His book, *Colloquies on the Simples and Drugs of India*, a materia medica of local medicine unknown in Europe, was published in 1563. He performed an autopsy on a victim of the cholera epidemic of 1543. However, Orta and his family practiced Judaism in secret. His sister, Catarina, was sentenced to be burned at the stake in 1568, the year in which he died. Once the Inquisition got a whiff of heresy in the Orta family, the investigation of his relatives, both in Goa and Portugal, continued, and Orta was posthumously sentenced by the Goa Inquisition as a secret Judaizer in 1580. His remains were dug up, burned, and thrown into the sea (de Carvalho 2007; Fischel 2007; Fischel and Liebowitz 2007). Filipe Nery Xavier, a Goan administrator and historian (Priolkar 1961, 59), described the lengths to which the Inquisition in Goa went to eliminate the last traces of heresy and heretics. In 1840, he discovered a stone monument in Bassein on the site of a house ordered razed to the ground by the Goa Inquisition. The occupants of the house and other people belonging to their sect had been tried and condemned by the Holy Office and burned after an auto-da-fé celebrated in December 1747. Their house was demolished and plowed with salt, and the stone monument was erected as witness to their crime and punishment.

Martyrs to Freedom of Thought and Belief

Records of individual trials by the Goa Inquisition have been lost or destroyed and are not available. However, a complete list of people condemned or acquitted by the Inquisition between 1560 and 1774 is available in the National Archives of Lisbon. This list has a total of 16,172 people of different nationalities, of whom nearly three-fourths were Indians, almost equally divided between Christians and non-Christians (de Souza 1994, 75). Priolkar, citing the same data, gives these as 16,172 *cases*. Perhaps *cases* is an infelicitous translation, because it would imply about seventy-five trials per year, or, leaving out Sundays but including holidays and feast days, four days per case, a highly improbable scenario. No bureaucracy can move that fast! The number of trials conducted by the Goa Inquisition in the period 1536–1767 is given as 13,667, which more or less supports the archives' count (Green 2007, 9). Do we have any data on autos-da-fé or people burned at the stake? The data available from different sources are contradictory and should be considered only as estimates and thus used with caution. The earliest auto-da-fé in Goa after the establishment of the Inquisition in 1560 was on 27 September 1563, after which four people, including two Judaizers, were burned (Roth 1973; Roth and Assis 2007). Bartholomew da Fonseca is supposed to have been a particularly zealous Inquisitor, credited with autos-da-fé in 1575 and 1578, after each of which 17 Judaizers were burned, including two Lutherans in the first (Roth 1973; Roth and Assis 2007). After Fonseca returned to Portugal, only twenty people were burned at the stake between 1597 and 1623, of which two were Judaizers. It is estimated that by 1600, the Holy Office had tried, condemned, and burned at least 84 people as Judaizers (Boyajiyan 1986, 7). Imprisonment and trials of other well-known, rich Jews, such as the Almosnino brothers, on charges of having blasphemed against Christianity drove the fear of the tribunal amongst all Jews, converted or not. How many such autos-da-fé took place, and how many victims lost their lives after each of these? Perhaps we will never know the exact number. Because the records of the individual trials of the Inquisition have been lost or were destroyed (Priolkar 1961, 31–5), the number is estimated by the use of summary letters, yearly reports to members of religious orders, or other secondary sources. These numbers do not always cover the same interval of years; they differ widely and may be affected by problems with the original sources or the biases of the narrative. The available data are reproduced here from the references cited. The Goa tribunal tried 3,800 cases and conducted 37 autos-da-fé between 1560 and 1700 and a total of 82 autos by 1773 (Roth 1973, 1391; Roth and Assis 2007, 796). More than 4,000 cases were tried by the Inquisition between 1600 and 1773, and 121 persons were burned at the stake (Maxwell 1995, 129). José da Fonseca, author of the *Historical and Archaeological Sketch of the City of Goa*, mentions that he was unable to make a complete computation of the total number of autos-da-fé that took place during the life of the Inquisition (Fonseca 2001, 220). He found, however, that seventy-one were held between 1600 and 1773, from a book published in Portugal in 1845 that did not give the number of people actually condemned. Actually burned at the stake were 105 men and 16 women; of these, 57 were burned alive and 64 were burned in effigy.

> In the *Biblioteca Nacional* of Lisbon there is a manuscript work called *Repertorio General de Inquisição de Goa* (General Calendar of the Inquisition of Goa) written by João Delgado Figueira, who worked as Promotor, Deputy and later as Inquisitor in the Inquisition of Goa. This deals with the activities of the Inquisition during the period 1561 to 1623 and states that during this period of 63 years 3,800 cases were tried by the Holy Office. Baião writes that during the period 1561 to 1774, 16,172 cases were tried by the Inquisition. A list of the Acts of Faith celebrated by the Goa Inquisition, compiled from the *Reportorio* and other sources by Elkan Nathan Adler, corresponding member of the Royal Academy of History of Spain, is reproduced hereunder . . . [Priolkar 1961, 179]

Priolkar then reproduces a list of about 137 autos-da-fé held between 20 September 1562 and 7 February 1773 from Adler's book *Auto de Fé and Jews* (1908). This list, however, includes a few mezas or private autos-da-fé for less serious offences (Priolkar 1961, 179).

What do all these quotes of disparate data and estimates tell us? The number of people burned at the stake under the auspices of the Inquisition is very subjective. I would like to stress this and refrain from ascribing any sinister motives and/or political agenda to authors for exaggerating, underestimating, or not mentioning at all the number of persons burnt at the stake. Other peoples' motives are difficult to judge; they exist only in our minds and perhaps indicate our own convoluted thinking. Even a single person burned at the stake is one too many; the exact number of such victims is immaterial.

The state–church complex accused these people of "heretical depravity" amounting to treason against the state and God. I look on them as martyrs to freedom of conscience, thought, and belief. They were the true witnesses to these beliefs and paid the ultimate price with their lives. When I think of these victims, whether a handful or a few thousands, I empathize with their sorrow and suffering. I am also sickened at the extremes to which humans can go when motivated by religious zeal. At the same time, I feel a deep sense of gratitude for the sacrifice of these martyrs. Each one of these people contributed in the long run to a change in attitude of humankind toward freedom of conscience, thought, and belief. They made it possible for me to say what I think without fear of reprisal. Deviant thoughts are no longer a crime punishable by death. The precious freedoms of thought and belief have to be guarded at all times to ensure that they are not encroached on.

The Goa Inquisition was abolished on 10 February 1774 during Pombal's term as premier. After his fall from power in 1777, the Inquisition was revived under a new manual of rules and regulations and continued to operate till it was finally abolished on 16 June 1812 under British pressure, and the building where it was housed was razed to the ground (Priolkar 1961; Green 2007, 359). The merchants and traders, driven out of Goa by the Portuguese religious persecution, moved to Bombay, where they could live unmolested under the English (Scammell 1988). Portugal's loss was England's gain. Historians have blamed the Inquisition as one of the causes of the ruin of the Portuguese Empire in India. The administrators in Goa had warned the Portuguese king time and time again about this problem. In a letter to the king dated 19 December 1729 by Viceroy João Saldhana da Gama, who wrote:

> All the ruin of this State consists visibly in the lack of commerce, which lack arises from two reasons; first, the horror with which the merchants, who are only Hindus or Muslims, view the proceedings of the Holy Office, not only on account of the diabolic passion with which they feel their rites have been vilified; but also on account of what they suffer in its prisons where they elect to die by not changing their custom of not eating or drinking in front of the Christians nor any viands prepared by the hands of persons not belonging to their

> caste; and as castes are many, it is not possible to provide separate prisons for different castes. The other is the violence of imprisonment, of which I gave an account to Your Majesty. [Priolkar 1961, 185]

Hindu Resistance

What was the reaction of the Hindus to the high-handed destruction of temples, seizure of their properties, forced conversions, and related atrocities committed by the Portuguese state and church? Did the Hindus offer any effective resistance? If so, what form did it take? These are some of the problems discussed in a very illuminating journal article, "Flight of the Deities: Hindu Resistance in Goa" (Axelrod and Fuerch 1996). In a few cases, Hindus might have accepted the harsh methods of the Portuguese regime passively, as facts of life, with the new rulers replacing the Adil Shahi sultans. Some chose exile, taking with them only the possessions that they could carry. In addition, they saved and reconsecrated the sacred images of deities in new temples in places outside Portuguese control. The Hindu temples were the center of village life before they were destroyed by the Portuguese, and they continued to be so in their new locations. The close ties among the temple, the village, and the families of devotees or *kuḷāvi*, Hindu or the newly converted Catholic, were never forgotten, being kept alive in memories. The history of the Sarasvat community, *Koṅkaṇākhyāna*, describes the destruction of the temples in their old locations, their rebuilding in new villages, and efforts to "secured the honor" of their deities to "confused and spoiled the efforts of the defiled foreigners" (Axelrod and Fuerch 1996). These temples became the focus of life of exiled Hindus, served as centers for reversion to Hinduism for some converts, offered shelter to orphans, and provided priests for secret Hindu ceremonies conducted in areas of Portuguese control, thus frustrating the conversion policies of the Portuguese.

> Like those Muslim rulers in India who pursued policies of forced conversions, the Portuguese mistakenly believed that they could eliminate Hinduism by destroying the temples, implementing draconian conversion policies, and systematically discriminating against Hindus. But more than 450 years after the Portuguese attempted to remove every vestige of Hinduism from Goa, it remains transformed but in remarkably vibrant form. [Axelrod and Fuerch 1996, 391–2]

The Martyrs of Cuncolim

The massacre of 25 July 1583, which resulted in the martyring of Christian priests and civilians at Cuncolim, is an example of the reaction of the natives of Goa to the high-handed methods used by the Portuguese state and church in their missionary activities. This unfortunate incident shows that the docile natives of Goa fought when their backs were against a wall and they expected to lose all that they possessed. It is necessary to narrate briefly the events leading to this revolt to provide a full picture of the situation. Armed uprisings and killing of Christians occurred in some places such as Cortalim in 1564, after the villagers heard that a priest, Father Pedro Colazo, tried to convert a dying Brahman (Axelrod and Fuerch 1996, 388). In a few cases, desperation and the feeling that they did not have much to lose drove whole villages to refuse to pay taxes, cease to cooperate with the new power structure, and opt for armed rebellion. The most famous of these instances is the resistance of the villages of Assolna, Cuncolim, Velim, Veroda, and Ambelim in Salcette, in 1583, which came to be known as the armed rebellion, or uprising, of Cuncolim (Newman 2001; Couto 2004; de Souza 1994; de Souza 1992). It is a classic case of the confrontation between the old power structure in Cuncolim and the new rulers who wanted to impose their hegemony. The property owners and other people of wealth in Cuncolim saw the Portuguese as a threat to their way of life involving religion, land, trade, and livelihood (Newman 2001). They responded by refusing to pay taxes and by harassing and killing low-level functionaries of the state. The rulers retaliated by knocking down temples and burning some buildings, which were rebuilt without permission from the state—a criminal offense. A military force of Portuguese and Indian soldiers, under the leadership of Gilianes Mascarehnas, nephew of the Governor of Goa, was sent in 1583 to quell the unrest. They burned and laid waste to most of Assolna; in Cuncolim, they burned the big temple of *Śāntādurgā* and a few smaller ones, cut down trees, and desecrated temple tanks with the entrails of cows. These attacks were led by a Jesuit priest, Peter (or Pero) Berno. These atrocities were much resented; they form the background in which the next act of the drama unfolded. On 15 July 1583, Rudolfo Acquaviva, Chief of Mission, an Italian of noble birth (nephew of Claudius Acquaviva, the fifth General of the Society of Jesus and a scholar who had spent three years at the court of Akbar), led a party of four other Jesuits, including Peter Berno, involved in earlier acts of destruction and desecration; Gonzalo Rodrigues, a Portuguese émigré; and fourteen other native converts to Cuncolim to erect a cross and select ground for building a church (see "Martyrs of Cuncolim" in the Bibliography for Web sites with more information). Among the converts was Dominic of Cuncolim, a student at the Rachol Seminary, who pointed out the temples that were later destroyed. For having betrayed the villagers to the Jesuits, Dominic was killed by his own uncle, who had not converted. The rest of the party was massacred by an angry mob of Hindus on July 25, and it is claimed that their bodies were thrown into a well. The Portuguese retaliated by using trickery to capture, in the fort at Assolna, sixteen of the main perpetrators of the Cuncolim assault. The Portuguese declared one of the captives innocent of the crime and ordered fifteen others killed. One of them escaped by jumping over a wall, and other rebels involved in the uprising fled into exile. The *Śāntādurgā* temple was destroyed, and the sacred image of the Goddess was installed in a new temple built in the village of Fatorpa. The remaining rebel villagers were forced to become Catholics, and all of the lands of these five villages were confiscated by the state, with the village associations, or *gāvṁkārī* system, being abolished. The lands of the villages of Cuncolim and Veroda were given as a hereditary fief or county to Captain João da Silva, who became Conde de (Count of) Cuncolim (Newman 2001,134). The five Jesuits in the group came to be called the Martyrs of Cuncolim; the process of their canonization began in 1600. However, it was only in 1741 that Pope Benedict XIV declared their martyrdom proved, and the solemn beatification of the five martyrs was celebrated at St. Peter's in Rome on 16 April 1893. It was celebrated in Goa in 1894, and the feast day of July 26 has been observed with great solemnity in Cuncolim ever since. The deaths of the rest of the group, including Gonzalo Rodrigues (who was Portuguese) and fourteen other native converts, were not recognized as martyrdom. Why not? Racism might have been a problem; the church perhaps did not want fourteen brown-skinned members to contaminate the august group of white martyrs. Another reason may be that the missionaries in the East were considered as " . . . true soldiers of Christ ever ready to conquer souls, convert infidels, destroy idols and expel idolatry from India, in order to plant a new Christendom here. . . . According to the missionaries, the local converts were by nature incapable of performing spiritual feats" (de Mendonça 2002, 335). To the church hierarchy in the sixteenth and seventeenth centuries, only the Jesuits merited such distinction and were recommended for elevation to sainthood. De Souza, in his paper "Why Cuncolim Martyrs?" (de Souza 1992, 35), observes that his analysis

> suggests that both the Portuguese rulers and the native dominant class of Cuncolim were using religion for their own vested interests. Religious beliefs were not the main issue, but the economic and political implications of conversion were seen as a threat. The religious feelings of the ordinary people were excited to obfuscate these main implications and to kill the missionaries.

This shrewd observation contains a gem of truth. It exposes the underlying power play beneath all human actions, including this conflict, as the real motivator. The church's agenda for power might have also played an important role in the choice of the Cuncolim Martyrs to be beatified and canonized and in highlighting their sacrifice. From the vantage point of the age when these massacres occurred, beatification of the white European Jesuits looked like a sensible move to support the evangelizing mission of the church. In the meantime, conceits of racial and national superiority have become less relevant and are not "politically correct" in the struggle for power. If the church decides at a later date that the addition of a few brown-skinned martyrs to the roster would help getting new Indian converts and thus extending its power base, it could put their names on a fast track for sainthood. Pursuit of power sets its own priorities and agenda.

Slavery and the Portuguese

The Portuguese imported their first slaves in 1441, and about 1,000 to 2,000 slaves per year entered Portugal after that (Pearson 1987). In those early days, one horse was equivalent in value to fourteen slaves; later on the price rose, and it was equal to six (Hall 1996). Sixteenth-century Portugal had more slaves than any other European nation, and it is estimated that about 10% of Lisbon was made up of slaves (Plumb 1969, xxvi). Between 1450 and 1500, about 150,000 black slaves were secured by the Portuguese (Boxer 1969). Most of the labor in the sugarcane fields of the Algarve in Portugal was made up of slaves. With this background, and familiarity with slave labor, it did not take long for the Portuguese to use the cheap slave labor available in Goa. Slavery had existed in Goa and the rest of India since ancient times, and the Portuguese latched on to this existing system of servitude. However, the Portuguese brought their own particular brand of cruelty. The slaves did the hard, unpleasant manual labor that their masters did not want to do, enabling them to enjoy the good life in the fabled "Golden Goa." The description of this life in 1608 by Frenchman Francois Pyrard gives us some idea of its opulence (Collis 1985). The slaves were mostly blacks from Africa, along with people from Bengal, Assam, Kanara, Malabar, Persia, China, Japan, and Malaya. The Portuguese conducted a few raids into the neighboring states of Bijapur and Sawantawadi, captured their hapless citizens, and sold them as slaves (Xavier 1993, 88). Portuguese slave raids were known to the Mogul historian, who stated that the Portuguese, along with native Arakanese, used to raid Bengal for slaves. It is estimated that on average, they kidnapped 3,400 people from Bengal annually (Collis 1985). On the West coast of India, some of the locals, including Arabs, used to kidnap and sell into slavery helpless people captured in opportunistic raids. Parents were known to sell themselves and or their children into slavery at times of severe famines; life was precarious and cheap. Once these people lost their liberty, they became a commodity to be freely bought and sold. Merchants of all nationalities, religions, and ethnicities traded and profited from the slaves. It was a case of equal-opportunity profit from the misery of their fellow humans. All religious traditions looked on this evil and gave their tacit approval by their deafening silence.

If it is estimated that a Portuguese *casado*, or married householder, had an average of about 10 slaves, then there was a total of about 8,000 slaves in seventeenth-century Goa (Subrahmanyam 1993, 228). In addition, there were state-owned slaves who worked in its galleys and in its gunpowder and naval factories and who were also conscripted into the armed forces as soldiers and sailors in an emergency (Xavier 1993). The household of Garcia de Melo, an important fiscal official, had 19 slaves—6 from Bengal, 6 from China, and 7 from East Africa (Subrahmanyam 1993, 229). Slaves were a status symbol, so the wealthy acquired as many as they could, considering how cheap they were. This status symbol was paraded and displayed in public whenever the owner had an opportunity. Slaves would carry the palanquin in which the owner reclined, an umbrella for shade, and sundry other articles as a display of power and prestige implied by the accompanying number of slaves (Collis 1985, 38–41). The slaves also provided income for their masters, if they had marketable skills. A rich woman was known to have more than 300 slaves, and an unmarried artisan could own 20. The various religious orders, hospitals, and state establishments all had slaves. The Holy House of Mercy and the Jesuit College of St. Paul each had about 200 slaves; the 100 nuns of the convent of Santa Monica complained that their 120 slaves were not nearly enough (Pearson 1987; Xavier 1993). Slaves who had run away from the cruel treatment of their masters used to seek asylum with the religious orders. Slaves were cheap; the most expensive female slave would sell for about 30 cruzados, whereas a fine Arabian or Persian horse would cost about 500 cruzados (Pearson 1987). (*Note:* 1 cruzado = 360 reis (up to the 1560s) = 400 reis (after 1570); 1 xerafim = 300 reis, and the Mughal rupee = 180 reis.) The buying and selling of slaves took place at auctions in the slave market in Goa. These were humiliating and degrading spectacles where the merchandise was paraded almost naked, to be minutely inspected by prospective buyers. Women slaves, if they were good looking or could sew, sing, or dance or had special skills and could prove that they were still virgins, would fetch higher prices. Slaves were either domestic or used for agriculture and other public-works projects such as building roads; clearing forests; transporting goods; and cleaning and maintaining canals, ponds, and related irrigation projects. They were used to fetch and sell in the city of Goa drinking water from the main source of potable water, the natural spring of Banquenim. A proposal to install piped water in the city in 1535 was defeated partly because the slave owners were reluctant to lose this extra income (da Silva Gracias 1994). Slaves with specialized skills could also be used in crafts such as tanning, leather work for shoes or harnesses, weaving, baking, and distilling liquor. Female slaves were mostly used as domestic servants, for sex, as washerwomen, cooks, tailors, and skilled embroiderers. Slaves could be hired out by the day, week, or longer periods. The products of their labor, including fruit preserves, pickles, lace, and embroidery, were sold publicly, sometimes by enticingly or scantily dressed female slaves, and all their earnings enriched their masters. Some female slaves were forced to prostitute themselves and pass on their earnings to their owners. Some of the Portuguese nobility, *fidalgos*, obtained a major part of their earnings in this manner, by the labor of their slaves (Xavier 1993). A few of these *fidalgos* also used their slaves as their private army to harass, intimidate, and settle scores with their enemies.

Slave owners had total and absolute control over everything about their slaves, including their personal lives. Such unlimited power corrupted their masters, leading to abusive treatment and much suffering for the slaves. Some slave owners were kind and humane, whereas others could be cruel and unjust. We know of these abuses of power from the periodic sermons of the clergy, the recommendations of the provincial councils, and fulminations of state authorities. The cruelty of some Portuguese masters extended to withholding food and clothing from their slaves. We learn this from the exhortations of the clergy and their repeated requests to treat slaves humanely and to refrain from their sexual exploitation. The punishments inflicted by the Portuguese on their slaves included cutting off their palms, amputating their arms and legs, scarring their faces, or otherwise maiming them (Xavier 1993, 95–96).

News of the cruelty to slaves in Goa reached the ears of the king of Portugal, who in 1599 wrote:

> I, King, make it known to all who see this decree that I am informed about cruel tortures to which slaves and captives are subjected in the city of Goa and other cities, fortresses and places of Portuguese Indies, about many slaves who die during or after such cruelties, and about their masters who try to hide such evil deeds by burying the victims inside their houses and compounds. I wish to put an end to such cases of homicide and inhuman tortures, and I wish to have the culprits punished as they deserve. Hence, I order my viceroy in India and his successors to hold judicial inquiries every year into the behaviour of the slave owners. [de Souza 1979, 265]

A Theatine missionary, Antonio Lubelli, wrote to his superior in Naples in 1663:

> I shall expatiate only upon the cruelties that are ordinarily perpetrated against the slaves. They are given very little rice to eat, and even this short ration is often reduced to its half or third in order to make them pay for a broken pot or decanter or dish or anything of this sort. . . .

> It is not unusual to punish the carelessness of slaves with imprisonment, or by putting them into stocks, or by caning them face downwards under a ladder. It is to be noted that the cruelty of the females who own slaves is most extravagant. The cruelty against this sort of slave-girls is comparable only to the barbarities employed by tyrants towards martyrs. They often empty cauldrons of boiling water or drop liquefied sealing-wax upon the bare bodies of these slaves. They also flog them until they collapse and then apply restoratives in order to prolong their tortures. The fury of the slave-owning females exceeds all bounds when they are excited by jealousy, and then they prod them with heated iron rods and spikes and subject them to the kind of torture which I feel disgusted to write about. [de Souza 1979, 277]

Slaves were tortured if they were suspected of crimes. Many slaves who could not stand such cruelty ran away and were caught and brought back by people who specialized in such hunts. No wonder slave-catcher was listed as one of the urban professions in Goa! The fact that these guidelines for kind treatment were not effective in practice is obvious from their repetition under different and various rubrics by the state and church from time to time. The state also passed laws that encouraged conversion by non-Christian slaves. If they expressed a desire for conversion to Christianity, they were to be freed. Christian slaves, once they were in Goa, could not be re-exported or sold to infidel masters. There were no effective punishments for acts of cruelty to slaves. It was an example of absolute power corrupting absolutely, to quote Lord Acton. Slavery in Goa, India, and the rest of the world indeed consitute sorry episodes in the history of humans. All of cultures who deprived fellow humans of their liberty as free people, sold them into slavery, and traded them into misery and servitude are guilty of gross crimes against all humanity. Slavery in India under the East India Company was abolished by the Abolition Act of 1843 (Patnaik and Dingwaney 1985). The king of Portugal abolished slavery throughout the Portuguese territories in 1869 (Xavier 1993).

Medicine and Health in Goa

What was the state of medicine and general health of the people in sixteenth- and seventeenth-century Goa? We have to bear in mind that this was the age before the discovery of germs and antibiotics. Medicines used were almost all derived from local herbs that had been found to be effective in treating illness, by trial and error. The theory behind medical practices then was that good health prevailed when the bodily humors were in balance. Any imbalance of these caused a person to fall sick, and the physician used herbs, proper diet, massage, and external application of various herbal mixtures to restore this balance. Indigenous medicine, Hindu Āyurvedic or Muslim *Unānī* (Van Alphen and Aris 1996), was perhaps just as good or as bad as Western medicine of that time. The surgery of the *Suśruta Saṃhitā* (compendium of Āyurvedic medical practices from the third century BCE) had fallen into abeyance, anatomy was not studied by dissecting cadavers, autopsies were no longer carried out, surgeons were not properly trained, and no new knowledge was acquired or added to the traditional corpus (Valiathan 2007). Surgery as such was not practiced by most physicians, neither the Hindu *vaidya* nor the Muslim *hakim*. However, this tradition of surgery was not completely forgotten, and there were isolated pockets of practitioners of surgery as a family tradition. Physicians used the *Caraka Saṃhitā* (third century BCE to third century CE) and other books of later authors (Valiathan 2003). These books represented a revered tradition to be memorized and used by rote, rather than a living medical system of a work in progress. Physicians who knew a few effective cures were very secretive about them because their livelihood depended on their skills. People with a strong constitution or a good genetic heritage survived the latest illness as best as they could in spite of the ministrations of physicians, Eastern or Western. Good habits of cleanliness, though practiced for ritual purity and religious observance rather than for hygiene, were helpful in preventing disease. Frequent bathing by all, including Europeans, because of the hot weather was a definite step toward better health. Herbal medicines might have been helpful in curing illnesses for reasons that no one understood. There were large areas of ignorance, with a proportionate room for belief in astrology, magic, incantations, divine interventions, and other beliefs filled with mystery and awe. If any of these nostrums worked by happenstance, it made believers of most and skeptics of a few. People of the East as well as the West had their own favorite belief systems not supported by objective data. We may refer to these condescendingly as "old superstitions." However, beliefs die hard, they are never completely eliminated so long as our knowledge is incomplete, and there is plenty of room for ignorance. In India, there was an ancient but unfortunate tradition of cutting off a person's nose as a form of criminal punishment. Hence, there was a need for repairing mutilated noses through primitive rhinoplasty, mentioned by *Suśruta*. This is typical case of medical practice evolving to provide a solution to a local problem. The skill of rhinoplasty appears to have survived a general decline of medicine and surgery in India into the eighteenth century. The first recorded historical description of such surgery involved a successful repair job performed by a man of the brickmakers' caste near Poona in 1794 and witnessed by two surgeons of the East India Company, Thomas Cruso and James Trindlay. Inoculation against smallpox in Bengal was known as far back as 1731 and might have existed even earlier (Van Alphen and Aris 1996, 27–9). It is possible that this was used in some parts of India and not known or practiced in general.

The state of health and medicine in medieval Goa under the Portuguese is well documented by de Figueiredo (1967), Xavier (1993), and da Silva Gracias (1994); most of the information given here is derived from these sources. As mentioned earlier, the medicine practiced in Goa was a mixture of the indigenous Hindu Āyurvedic or the Muslim *Unānī* systems along with Western medicine. All of these systems were equally effective or ineffective. However, quite a few people believed that local maladies were better treated by local medicine or herbs rather than by the Western system. But whatever medical system people used, they believed that it worked for them and their illnesses.

Hindu physicians continued their profession, and it appears that they did quite well financially and were much respected in society. A Brahman physician was employed by the Jesuit College of St. Paul in 1548, and a *vaidya* by the name of Rama Boto (Bhat) treated patients at the Convent of Madre de Deus in 1620. Some *vaidyas* were even appointed to the state post of chief physician of Goa. Portuguese physicians, new to Goa, were expected to serve a period of apprenticeship with local physicians before being employed in local hospitals. The state expected the local physicians to pass a qualifying examination and be certified by the head physician of Goa. Because of this requirement, we know the names of some of them. Between December 1613 and May 1622, Sancara Botto (Shankar Bhatta), Madu Pandito (Madhu Pandit), Ganguadara Chatin (Gangadhar Shetti), Banu Botto (Banu Bhatta), Ganesza Naique (Ganesha Nayak), Poquia Chatin (Pakya Shetti), Purcia Parbu (Parashurama Prabhu), Locu Parbu (Lakshmana Prabhu) qualified as physicians (de Figueiredo 1967). From the names, it is obvious that most of them were Sarasvats, with a few Vaishyas thrown in for good measure. French physician C. Dellon's suicide attempt failed while he was imprisoned by the Goa Inquisition; he was treated by a Hindu *vaidya*. Epidemics of smallpox, plague, and cholera were common (da Silva Gracias 1994); they would begin for unknown reasons and end just as mysteriously. From these historical accounts of old Goa, we note that physicians practicing Indian medicine were used by the viceroy and other high administrative officials, as well as church dignitaries, in preference to or sometimes along with European physicians. This patronage of Hindu physicians created professional jealousies amongst the few Portuguese physicians, who might have instigated the various restrictive legislations passed against the *vaidyas*. The First Provincial Council of 1567 forbade Christians to call in a Hindu physician, barber (barbers also acted as surgeons) or midwife without ecclesiastical approval. Therefore, the religious orders made use of their services in secret (Xavier 1993, 118). The wife of Governor Manuel Souza Coutinho (1588–1591) was tried and convicted by the Inquisition and fined 1,000 pardaos for consulting a native physician. There was enough interest in the effectiveness of Indian medicine to collect information on local herbs and potions in *Colloquies on the Simples, Drugs, and Materia Medica of India* (1563) by Garcia da Orta, the Portuguese marrano scientist and physician mentioned in the section "The Inquisition of Goa." We do not know the names of any Indian physicians who might have contributed their knowledge to Orta's book as the usual "native informant." Orta mentions that a *vaidya* named Malupa (Mhala Pai?) used to visit his home and treat his servants; he might have supplied some data on local medicine for Orta's book. When the local physicians were not willing to share their secret cures, the Portuguese were not averse to extracting them by any means, including force. The story of one such case is told by Manucci (Xavier 1993, 118, da Silva Gracias 1994). A Hindu pandit, or physician, knew a cure for scrofula that he would not divulge. The chief physician, who was Portuguese, had this man arrested and put in the prison of the Inquisition, where he preferred to die rather than reveal his secret. What an amazing example of abuse of power by a colonial master; anything possessed by a native was his by right! An Augustinian friar sick with pain and swelling could not be cured by his Portuguese physician. A local woman who cured him was arrested on the orders of the chief physician and had to sell all her possessions to win her freedom (da Silva Gracias 1994).

The Portuguese opened hospitals, some as early as 1511 or immediately after the conquest, and others at later dates (Xavier 1993, 74). The oldest royal hospital was open only to whites; others, such as St. Roque, was open to the local people, even Hindus. In those days of antiquated medicine, a large number of people, especially Portuguese soldiers, died in Goa. It is estimated that in the thirty years between 1604 and 1634, some 25,000 soldiers died in the royal hospital, of whom about 500 died every year because of syphilis or other sexually transmitted diseases (da Silva Gracias 1994). Local folklore credits the Portuguese with the introduction of syphilis, called by its various Konkani names: *pharaṅgi rogu, pharṅgẽ* (European disease), *bhaili pīdā* (foreign sickness). *Bhāvaprakāśa*, a sixteenth-century Āyurvedic book written by Bhāvamiśrā, was the first one to note this bit of information. Some of these institutions were more of a dispensary than a hospital because they offered only outpatient care. All Saints Hospital and of Our Lady of Piety Hospital were also designated as asylums and were meant for native Christians. The Hospital of St. Lazarus, attached to the Jesuit College of St. Paul, and the Hospital of Monte de Guirim in Bardez were two other establishments that helped the sick. In view of the strict laws of ritual purity of food and pollution prevalent at that time for Hindus, accepting food or medicine at these institutions meant a loss of caste and a willingness to be converted. A sick person was faced with a tough choice: to die as a sick Hindu at home or to accept treatment in hopes of a cure and then live as a Christian. Hence, the religious orders were quite aware of the fact that these hospitals provided conduit for the spread of Christianity in Goa while participating in acts of humane kindness.

Hortus Malabaricus (Malabar Garden)

The story of seventeenth-century medicine in India would not be complete without including an account of a compendium of herbs organized by the Dutch. Quite a few of local Indian medicinal herbs were exported to Europe along with spices and then were shipped back for use by local European residents. In many cases, these herbs were the only effective medicine available and were quite valuable. During these long sea voyages, some of the herbs rotted or lost their potency and could not be used. A few people suggested that by knowing and using local herbs, large savings in money and effort were possible. This prompted Hendrik Adriaan van Rheede tot Drakenstein (1636–1691), representative of the Dutch East India Company (usually called VOC, for Verenigde Oost-Indische Compagnie) to the court of the king of Kochin, Vira Kerala Verma, to publish the monumental *Hortus Malabaricus* (*Malabar Garden*) in 12 volumes in 1678–1693 (Manilal 1980; Ram 2005; Lach and Van Kley 1993, 926). The book describes some 725 species (780, according to Manilal) of plants of Malabar in about 794 illustrations. Though the book does not meet modern standards for plant collection of type specimens, the excellent illustrations enable one to identify them, and thus the book is of use even now. An English translation of van Rheede's book by K. S. Manilal, professor of botany at Calicut University, has been published by the university (Ram 2005) to mark the 325th anniversary of the original. This was a large project involving many people with different skills and expertise, including native physicians of traditional medicine, plant collectors, illustrators, translators, and compilers of information, all coordinated by van Rheede. It seem that he got along quite well with all people involved, including the natives of Malabar, for whose life and culture he showed genuine respect and interest. (See the article by Heniger on van Rheede's preface, which appeared in volume 3 of the book [Manilal 1980, 35–69].) They are explicitly acknowledged by name for their assistance, which is quite a rare thing for European authors. The text is in Latin (Roman script), the plant names are in Malayalam, Arabic, Konkani (Devanāgarī script), and Portuguese and Dutch (Roman script). Information on the medical use of the plants was provided by Itty Achuden (Achuthan), a famous hereditary physician of Malabar, and a group of Konkani-speaking Brahmans, Raṅga Bhaṭ, Vināyaka Paṇḍita, and Āpū Bhaṭ, also practitioners of traditional medicine, or *vaidyās*. Emmanuel Carniero, a native convert to Christianity, was the official interpreter, Malayalam to Portuguese, for the VOC. Raṅga Bhaṭ also acted as an interpreter from Konkani to Portuguese. Achuthan's contributions in Malayalam were from palm-leaf manuscripts in his family that recorded the practical experience and knowledge of a lineage of physicians. His testimonial authenticating the medical information in the book is in Malyalam and appears in volume 1. Carniero's testimonial on the contents of the book is also in Malyalam. These are the first examples of the language printed in these scripts; they have been superseded by modern Malayalam (Manilal 1980, 113–20). The three Konkani Brahmans obtained data from medical books used in their families and lineages. Their testimonial attesting to the authenticity of the medical information is in Konkani (Devanāgarī script) and is dated 10 April 1675. The text is one of the earliest extant in Konkani; therefore, the facsimile and the Devanāgarī version (Gomes 2000), its transliteration, and translation (SarDessai 2000) are worth studying. Professor Manilal's attempts to locate Achutan's palm-leaf manuscripts or the books used by the Konkani priest–physicians have proved fruitless. We have to assume that these books are lost, and we should be grateful to van Rheede for having saved the medicinal and botanical knowledge contained in them and passing it on to us. During an inspection trip of the Dutch trading posts on the west coast of India in 1691, van Rheede died on board his ship and is buried in the Dutch cemetery in Surat, Gujarat.

The Printing Press and Educational Institutions

The printing press introduced by the Portuguese in Goa started functioning in 1556. The first book was printed in 1556 and the last in 1674, hence the press was functioning in Goa for about 120 years (Priolkar 1958). The reasons behind closing down the press are discussed in "Conversions, Phase IV (1610–1774)." The press had been sent along with João Nunes Barreto, patriarch-designate of Abyssinia, and was intended for missionary work there. Father João Rodrigues, Jesuit and printer, accompanied the press (Moran 1993). On his way to Abyssinia, the patriarch died in Goa in 1562, and the printing press stayed there. Printing books in the Indian languages was in the interests of the evangelization mission of the church. However, it did have some beneficial effects on the local languages. Printing standardized the script, grammar, and usage of Indian languages and encouraged writing of their dictionaries into European languages. Some 13 books were printed in Goa in the sixteenth century, including the 1563 *Coloquios dos simples, e drogas e causas medicizinaes da India* (*Colloquies on the Simples, Drugs, and Materia Medica of India*) of Garcia da Orta, a Jew newly converted to Christianity. In the seventeenth century, 21 books were printed in Goa, bringing the total number of books to 34; the last book was printed in 1674 (Priolkar 1958, 23). Most of the books printed were religious; in Priolkar's list, 5 of the total of 34 books printed were secular. However, Pearson (1987, 107, 269) gives the total number of books printed between 1556 and 1679 as being 40, mostly religious, with only 3 books being secular. The arrival of Alessandro Valignano, the Jesuit Visitor, in Goa in September 1574 was important for the development of the press in new directions. Before his arrival, books printed were in Portuguese or Latin. He took the initiative in planning and arranging for the publication of various religious books in the native languages (Moran 1993). By 1577, sheets summarizing Christian doctrine were being printed in Tamil. Valignano endorsed both the study of native languages as part of the curriculum in the training of clergy and the printing of religious books in these languages in support of the missionary work. In 1578, the press printed a book on Christian doctrine in Tamil, and in 1588, it printed a book written in Japanese on lectures delivered by a Japanese priest.

Books in the local language, Konkani, or a mixture of Marathi and Konkani were needed to preach and propagate Christian doctrines in a medium that would be readily accepted by the locals. The pioneer in this work was English Jesuit Thomas Stephens (1549–1619), a missionary and a poet in Marathi–Konkani (Iyengar 2003). He landed in Goa in 1579, perhaps the first Englishman to arrive in India, and died in 1619 after spending nearly forty years there. He mastered Sanskrit, Marathi, and Konkani and composed three major works in the last two languages. The first book published in Roman script in 1616 was an epic, *Krista-Purana*, on the life of Jesus Christ, in two parts of thirty-six and fifty-nine cantos, with a total of more than 11,000 strophes in the local ovi meter. It was written in literary Marathi and enlivened with the local Konkani speech to replace the Hindu epics for the new converts. Two more editions appeared in 1649 and 1654, and the last and fourth edition was printed in 1907 in Mangalore. It used to be read as part of church services on certain occasions in Goa till 1776, when the reading was banned by the archbishop of Goa, D. Francisco da Assunzão. Stephens's second book in Konkani, published in 1622, dealt with Christian doctrine: *Doutrina Christã em lingua Bramana-Canarin. Canarin* was what the Portuguese called native Goans, and it was also the name for the local language, which was Konkani. Stephens's third book, published in 1640, was on Konkani grammar, *Arte de Lingua Canarin.* Other books published in Konkani as part of the conversion effort of the state–church complex are listed in the *Historical Essay on the Konkani Language* by Joaquim Heliodoró da Cunha Rivara and translated from the Portuguese by Father Theophilus Lobo (da Cunha Rivara 1857).

There has been some controversy over the question of whether Konkani is a language in its own right or a dialect of Marathi. This question has been ably discussed by a number of experts (da Cunha Rivara 1857; Priolkar 1958; Katre 1966; Pereira 1971; Janardhan 1991; Xavier 1993; SarDessai 2000), so I will not go into the details here. It is a fact that Konkani, the local language of Goa, was never a court language. Thus, it did not have the advantages of robust development resulting from its use as a medium of everyday exchange in a state bureaucracy. It is also not clear whether there was an extensive literature or how much of it was destroyed in Goa during the burning of Hindu religious and secular books by the Catholic church and its religious orders. Translations of the Hindu epics *Rāmāyaṇā*, *Mahābhārata*, and the *Bhagavadgītā* into Konkani and Marathi were made in the fifteenth and sixteenth centuries (Xavier 1993, 178). Because books in the language outside Goa have not survived, perhaps there were not too many such books to start with. However, an anthology of early Konkani literature that has survived has been compiled (Gomes 2000). In the early days of Portuguese occupation, the clergy were expected to learn the language so that the Christian doctrine could be communicated in the local language and the clergy could minister to the spiritual needs of the new converts. It was also taught in Jesuit and other seminaries, as part of the standard curriculum (Xavier 1993, 179–85). It was the only language in which sermons could be preached and that the faithful could use in going to confession. Therefore, the church and the clergy supported the use of the language and its development as part of the conversion work. This state of affairs changed later, resulting in the decree of 1684, which banned the use of Konkani and its replacement by Portuguese. The viceroy decreed that all Goans should learn Portuguese within three years (da Cunha Rivara 1857; Xavier 1993). The motivation behind this drastic change was as follows: Even after years of vigorous and coercive missionary effort, the number of people converted was less than expected. The state–church complex felt that this was partly due to the backsliding by some of the new converts into their earlier beliefs. Exiled Hindu priests, some of whom had returned secretly to Goa and were continuing to preach their doctrines, were blamed for the new converts' change of mind. If the local language was eliminated, it was hoped that this could prevent any such reversion to Hinduism. The Franciscans have been credited in spearheading this effort to ban Konkani. They were either too lazy to learn Konkani or found it too difficult and were able to convince the viceroy that banning its use and totally exterminating the language would be easier. However, the state bureaucracy was being unrealistic in the methods it adopted to eliminate Konkani and replace it with Portuguese. That was the only language most people knew, and the viceroy was not going to replace it with a foreign tongue just by promulgating a decree. Outlawing the local language was part of the state policy to eliminate any traces of Hinduism, as can be seen by the 1736 Edict of the Goa Inquisition (Priolkar 1961, 97). The edict went into great detail, describing many Hindu customs that had nothing to do with Christianity or its practice, and prohibited them just because they were observed by Hindus. All of these fiats by the state–church complex were not effective in meeting their goal, because the laws were not enforceable. The extent of the failure of this policy can be gauged by the further declaration of the archbishop of Goa in 1754 that to receive the sacraments, all Christians had to know Portuguese. In short, the state–church power structure believed in coercion rather than persuasion or provision of any economic incentives to implement such changes. These arbitrary state edicts were imposed on the people through the harsh enforcement techniques of the Inquisition, which has been blamed for the decline of the vernacular as well as of the Portuguese Empire (da Cunha Rivara 1857). These coercive methods have been described as "*ferro, fogo e sangue* (iron, fire and blood)" by another historian (Barros 1988). All of these facts of life in Goa had a very bad effect on Konkani. It split into many dialects: Hindu, Christian, Goan, Manglorean, Maharashtrian, etc. These splits reflected the vicissitudes of life suffered by the speakers of the language, their exile from Goa, and the influence of the local languages through borrowed words and usages. There are currently many valiant efforts to revive Konkani language and publish its literature (SarDessai 2000; Gomes 2000; Pinto 2003), but we must wait and see how successful these activities will be.

Education in Goa before the coming of the Portuguese was mostly for Hindu boys of the three upper castes—priests, warriors, and merchants. This education was part of the local Hindu culture and tradition. The *pāṭhaśālā* (school) was usually attached to the local temple, and some of the temple priests were also its teachers. Basic education in reading, writing, and arithmetic could take a few years. The languages taught were Sanskrit, Konkani, Marathi, and Kannada. Konkani was written either in the Kannada script or the Devanāgarī script, with its cursive or running hand called *moḍī*. Letters were traced in sand smoothed over a level floor, and multiplication tables and word declensions were memorized by repeating after the teacher. There was quite a bit of rote memorizing without much understanding, which was supposed to come later. The basic skills learned after a few years of schooling sufficed for most boys who went into trade and commerce. Advanced education extending over a few more years was available for those who planned to be professional priests and teachers or those who wanted to specialize in traditional medicine, astronomy for preparing almanacs, astrology for reading the future from stars, and other branches of knowledge auxiliary to a study of the Vedas. These were phonetics, rituals of the solemn Vedic and domestic rites, grammar, etymology, and astronomy. Āyurvedic medicine and related medical preparations was another important profession. A student planning on these advanced studies lived in the residence of his teacher, *gurukula*, in villages deeded to priestly families for many years. These villages were called *agrahāra* or *brahmapurī* and were deeded tax free in perpetuity, by kings or local nobility, to learned priestly families in support of advanced education and other services. This system of education, from the basic to advanced, with specialization in medicine and astronomy/astrology, was in place in Goa before the advent of the Portuguese Empire. After the Portuguese conquest of Goa, these schools were destroyed, along with the Hindu temples, starting in the 1540s. They were replaced by schools, seminaries, and colleges on a Western model associated with the Catholic faith (Xavier 1993). These educational institutions thus were part of the evangelization of the church, and the price paid by Hindus for education in them was conversion. Hence, they were avoided by Hindus who wanted to live in their faith. Educating their children became a problem, and a few rich families would invite Hindu teachers from outside the Portuguese territories to live in their homes and educate their children and those of other Hindu families (Couto 2004, 223).

In medieval Goa, most Hindu girls were not educated, and thus they were perhaps illiterate. There were a few exceptions. Girls of the *devadāsī* families, the *Kalāvant* and *Bhāvin*, were educated, literate, and trained in dance and music. Amongst the Sarasvat, the ancient tradition of marking the beginning of education by *upanayana* was continued for girls, provided that the parents could afford the cost of the ceremony and that the girls were interested in getting an education. Some of them were educated along with the boys, by the men of the family. Thus there were a few women who, on being widowed or encountering a family emergency, continued to manage the family business through bad times.

The Portuguese Spread the Bounty of the New and Old Worlds

One beneficial result of the Age of Exploration was the spread of many new and useful plants, fruits, and tubers from the Americas and the reciprocal transport from the Old World to the New. The Portuguese and the Portuguese-Spanish religious orders played an important part in this activity. The result has been that in India today, we find maize (or corn), various pumpkins and squashes, potatoes, sweet potatoes, tomatoes, tapioca, sapodilla (sapota), passion fruit, papayas, avocados, chilies, vanilla, tobacco, rubber, groundnuts (peanuts), and many other food plants native to the Americas being cultivated and forming a significant part of the diet. For some of these, such as the tomato, the pumpkin, the squash, and the maize, all generally accepted to be from the New World, either we do not know who, when, and how they were introduced into India or there is some evidence for their earlier presence on the subcontinent. *Indian Food: A Historical Companion*, by K.T. Achaya (1994), is a treasure trove of information on these questions; the data given here are from this source. The tomato perhaps came late in the eighteenth century via England. Of the pumpkin or squash family, some twenty-five species were known in India by ancient Sanskrit names. We do not know how they arrived.

There is some puzzling evidence for the presence of corn in India long before the voyages of Columbus. Pollen from ancient sites in Kashmir has been identified as that of maize or corn. Sculptures of goddesses in the twelfth-century Somanathpur temple outside Mysore show what look like corn cobs, complete with the silky tassel at their apex. These are interesting and unsolved puzzles as to who, how, and when some foods were introduced into India. However, some plants and fruits can be definitely ascribed to the Portuguese or the Portuguese-Spanish network for introduction to India. A few of these, such as the chili, chile, or chilli (from the Nahuatl word *chilli*) have become so much a part of Indian food and cooking that they deserve special mention. In the earliest records of ancient India, a piquant or pungent (popularly called hot or spicy) taste was obtained with long peppers, called *pippali* (*Piper longum*) in Sanskrit, Bengali, and some other Indian languages. The long peppers are most probably indigenous and were exported from South India 4,000 years ago. The root of the plant was also used in *Āyurvedic* medicine. With the spread of Indo-European culture to South India, the black pepper (*maricam* in Sanskrit, *mīrê* in Konkani) was discovered in about the fourth century BCE, and both these were used in cooking. The Portuguese introduced the chili pepper (*Capsicum annuum* and related varieties) somewhere in the fifteenth to sixteenth century CE. They were called the Pernambuco pepper after the region of Brazil from which they must have been introduced into India. In Bombay they were called *Gowai mirci*, or "Goan pepper," indicating their point of entry in India (Collingham 2006). The long pepper was susceptible to mold spoilage, whereas the chili pepper was not. The chili was similar to the long pepper in appearance, pungency, ease of cultivation, and cheaper; thus it was readily accepted in India as a substitute, and spread all over the country. The earliest record of what are most probably chili peppers in India is in a composition of the saint-poet Puraṇdara Dāsa (1480–1564), who sang their virtues, calling them a friend of the poor in enlivening their food at a low price by their fiery taste (Achaya 1994, 227).

The chili pepper has now completely supplanted the long pepper, which, according to Achaya, now grows wild in Kerala and Assam. Indian cooking today would be unthinkable without the use of chili peppers. Equally popular are the potato and the sweet potato and their varieties, so essential to Indian cooking, also introduced by the Portuguese. Other useful plants or fruits brought over by the Portuguese are papayas, avocados, groundnuts (or peanuts), cashews (called *bādām-i-firaṅgī*, or "European almonds" [Harrison 1975; Basham 1975]), guavas (*peyārā* in Portuguese; *pera* in Konkani), Brazil nuts, pineapples (introduced in 1550, and a favorite of Mughal Emperor Akbar), tobacco (introduced in 1508), and rubber. If I have left out any other New World plant or fruit in this list, either no one knows how it got to India or there is conflicting evidence about it. The Portuguese were also instrumental in transporting native Indian plants and fruits to other parts of the world, a reciprocal gift for the bounty of the New World that India received. The Portuguese state ordered the viceroy in Goa in 1678 to dispatch pepper, cloves, cinnamon, nutmeg, ginger, mango, and jackfruit to Africa, Brazil, and other Portuguese possessions (Russell-Wood 1992; Gollner 2008). The Portuguese religious orders also developed new varieties of mango with all of the desirable properties of flavor, aroma, texture, lack of fiber, long storage life, and others by grafting. The Indian mango, propagated from seed, does not grow true to type; hence, the development of fruit with desirable characteristics is possible by grafted or budded trees. Grafting had been known in India for a long time, being first mentioned in the encyclopedic *Bṛahatsaṃhitā* by Varāhamihira (~fifth century CE), and used for a variety of trees and plants such as jackfruit, plantain, lemon, pomegranate, grape, citron, and jasmine (Achaya 1994, 208). However, it had never been used for mango. The Portuguese developed a number of good varieties of mango, including the famous Alphonso, named after Afonso de Albuquerque, and known by its local names: *Āpus* (Konkani) and *Hāpus* (Marathi). The best varieties of Alphonso are supposed to be from the Ratnagiri and Devgad districts of the Konkan in Maharashtra, and a few fanatical cognoscenti even claim to know the small area in these localities where the ultimate fruit is harvested. The Portuguese introduced the turkey into India (Collingham 2006, 70). In approximately 1612, Jahangir, the Mughal emperor, had ordered Muqarrb Khan, one of his courtiers, to go to Goa and buy from the Franks (the Indians' general name for Europeans) any rare in animals or birds that he could find. He must have brought a breeding pair of turkeys to Delhi, because the court chronicles describe their mating behavior. The bird was so new to India that it did not even have a name. One of these turkeys has been immortalized in a magnificent watercolor by Mansur, one of Jahangir's court painters; it is now in the Victoria and Albert Museum in London (Thackston 1999, 133).

East–West Encounters—The Aftermath

The Hindus

In the encounters between the East and the West, the three main participants were Indian society (mainly Hindu), the Portuguese state, and the Roman Catholic church. Each was influenced and changed by this interaction. Was life for the Hindus, especially the Sarasvats, in sixteenth- to seventeenth-century Goa, a paradise on earth? The reality was much less romantic; it was a mixed bag—some good, some bad. Life was tough and unpredictable. The rule of the Bijapur Adil Shahi dynasty was harsh, the taxes were high, and the Hindus were discriminated against. Quite a few of the state functionaries were Turks, imported mercenaries notorious for their cruelty and harassment of Hindus. This rule was replaced by that of the Portuguese, which in some respects was even worse. Hopes for a better life, which had led some Hindu community leaders such as Mhall Pai of Verna (Couto 2004, 85) to invite a Portuguese takeover of Goa, did not lead to a happy outcome. The events that followed included large-scale destruction of Hindu and Muslim places of worship, forcible conversions, kidnapping of fatherless minors, strange new laws, and cruel punishments such as a lifetime in the galleys or burning at the stake. Life in those days was a big game of chance in more than one way. Historical records show that some Konkani-speaking Sarasvats managed to live through all of the social upheavals of Portuguese rule because they were rich and had the right connections to the power structure. These records do not tell us anything about the hardships of those who had to go into exile to continue to live as Hindus and escape persecution.

How was Hindu society changed by its encounter with the Portuguese? Have all of the problems of Hindu society been eliminated? The caste system is still with us, though it is much attenuated and has become mostly irrelevant because of changed economics and social conditions. Its hold on the Sarasvat urban community as well as the rest of the Hindus is very much less now. People eat in restaurants and in the homes of people of different communities and religions without worrying about ritual purity and other caste-related criteria. They even marry outside their community, religion, or nationality. However, caste may never be completely eliminated. As a status symbol, it is intimately tied up with the human primacy conceit, the desire for power, and the yearning to one-up the neighbors. Caste has its own snob appeal, and all humans are snobs. What are the other significant changes? Satī sahagamana, child abandonment because of an inauspicious birth, infanticide, child marriages, chattel slavery, dedication of *devadāsīs* (a form of subservience and exploitation), the harsh and cruel treatment of women and widows, and the virtual slavery of the serfs who tilled the soil are mostly in the past. Hindu society has changed a lot for the better, in these problem areas and in general. Some of these changes, such as the prohibition of *satī* and better inheritance rights for women, were brought about by Portuguese legislation. The West, which challenged the status quo of Hindu society, its age-old beliefs and customs, did start the foment that eventually changed Hindu society. The Portuguese deserve credit for having started this process of self-examination and change. However, change did not happen overnight; as a matter of fact, it took a long time. The administration in Goa realized that there was resistance to change and resentment against the laws that shook up the status quo. Such progressive reforms could not be achieved by fiat; they had to come from within Hindu society because it wanted to change. Conditions for change had to be right. Exposure to Western ideas and ideals through education, a good understanding of the problems of Hindu society, and critical self-examination resulted from the hard work of many activists and progressives. The reforms and how to achieve them had to come from within Hindu society, with individuals fighting against the orthodoxy, the patriarchy, and other traditionalists who wanted to maintain their hold on power. Such reforms happened in Bengal and other places under British rule at a later time under different circumstances.

Have all of the problems been solved? Certainly not! Hindu society has indeed changed a lot for the better. However, much needs to be done; reform is very much a work in progress. Hindu women, whose education, professional training, and equal rights have long lagged behind those of men, have been a major factor in these changes. Mahatma Gandhi's insistence on including women in the struggle for India's freedom, beginning in 1930, was another important factor in liberating women. Thirty-six years later, India had a woman prime minister, Indira Gandhi (1917–1984). Recent changes in the Hindu legal code, with better inheritance rights for women, are most welcome (Derrett 1963, 1968). Hindu women, especially amongst educated professional urbanites, have worked for and achieved a new sense of power, enabling them to demand gender equality and an end to traditional exploitation and subservience. In most Hindu families, the tyrant of a mother-in-law who once ruled over the joint family no longer exists. She has become part of the past. However, there are many situations in which women are treated as second-class citizens, especially in villages. Until women achieve complete and true parity with men, female feticide and infanticide, dowry murders, and prohibition of remarriage by widows will continue to be problems. The only solution is through the education, gainful employment, and financial independence of women, which will give them equal rights (Parashar 1992; Forbes 1996; Carroll 2009). If all this comes to pass, there will be a renegotiation of the power balance between women and men in Hindu society over the next few generations. It should be of great interest to see how this will come about and what the final result will be. If the traditionalists of Hindu society refuse to be sensitive to women's needs, demands, and rights, they will become irrelevant, and time will pass them by.

The State–Church Complex: The State

The Portuguese state believed that Roman Catholicism was the sole true religion and the unique possessor of eternal truths. The responsibility and the obligations of crown patronage, *padroado real*, the union of "crown and altar," assigned by the church to the state, were taken seriously. The state had a right and a duty to convert people of other faiths to the one true faith of the Roman Catholic church, by force if necessary. This proposition was not acceptable to the Hindus or the Muslims, who went into exile when life became intolerable in Goa. Were there any good things that happened to the Goans as a result of Portuguese rule? There were many.

The Portuguese, and especially the Jesuits, introduced many new fruits and plants, began a tradition of Western educational institutions, and started a printing press, hospitals, and other projects that benefited people at large. If their works and legislation contributed to improved education, better health, and any lessening of human misery, they deserve much praise and our gratitude. On the other hand, the destruction of Hindu temples and Muslim mosques, forcible conversions to Christianity, the seizure of property, long imprisonments, torture, burning at the stake, and other cruel and unusual punishments deserve to be condemned. Hindu temples educated students and its priest–physicians provided medical care to the villages; both these services were destroyed along with the places of worship. Portuguese society was racist, slave-owning, was intolerant, hated Muslims and "heathen" Hindus, and looked down on the non-white people of the East with contempt, except when they could serve as a source of easy wealth. However, later on they had to temper their attitude when they realized that they could hold on to the Portuguese possessions only with much help from these same despised native people, whether in commerce, military operations, or governance (Scammell 1988). The decline of Portuguese power in its struggle with the Dutch and English was a harsh dose of reality that tempered the evangelical zeal of the earlier days. The excessive religious zeal of the state and its persecution of non-Christians certainly contributed to its own demise. This decline in power might have changed their attitudes toward their erstwhile enemies, at least superficially, at a later date. The Portuguese state, involved in Brazil, Africa, and other places, followed the trajectory of history, and what happened in Goa and the East might have had little effect on its development. Some of the inequities of Portuguese rule and the discrimination against non-Catholics lasted till 1910, when the state became a republic, or till 1961, when Goa was liberated from Portuguese rule.

The State–Church Complex: The Church

Where there any changes in the Roman Catholic church and its religious orders? So long as the church hierarchy could convince the secular authorities to support its orthodoxy and its hold on power, it continued to triumph. Once the civil authorities found that they had to temper the harsh commandments of the church to face the realities of life in Goa, the church lost its power. Pombal's rule (1750–1777) and resulting reforms in Portugal and Goa, the suppression of the Society of Jesus, the arrest and transportation of the Jesuits, and attempts to eliminate racial prejudice were movements in the right direction. The Society of Jesus, with its vast plantations in Brazil, large estates in India, and wealth accumulated by trading in the East, had become too powerful and a challenge to the power structure of the state and was thus put down. This development was inevitable; the Jesuits had become too powerful for their own good. The Pombal reforms tried to loosen the stranglehold of the church and move the state toward the Age of Reason (Maxwell 1995; Shastry 1992). The Reformation, followed by the Counterreformation, the Enlightenment, the French Revolution of 1789 with its anti-church program, the Napoleonic wars, the rise of Italian nationalism and the loss of the papal states in 1870, the end of colonialism and the rise of independent states in the East, a better educated and skeptical laity, and the decline of its own hold on the faithful, are a few reasons for changes in the church and its further loss of power (Greeley 2004). This loss of power has been good for the church; it can no longer indulge in sundry military adventures. It has to preserve, protect, and enhance its power by other means.

The Church as a Multinational Corporation To understand the changes in the church and its responses to various current events and challenges, it is instructive to think of it as the oldest continually existing, and one of the most powerful MNCs. One of the main concerns of the church, like any good MNC, is to preserve, protect, and extend its temporal power. Pursuit of power sets its own standards of ethics and morality; there are no other. The conflicts between the ethical teachings of the church and its agenda for power as a corporation, especially in the context of recent problems and challenges, are well documented (Berry 1992; Berry and Renner 2004; Allen Jr. 2004, Goodstein and Halbfinger 2010). The founder, the charter, and its corporate mission are clearly stated in the New Testament (Matthew 16:18–19). St. Peter's Basilica in Rome, the corporate headquarters are unique in the whole world and meant to inspire awe and wonder and impress everyone with its might and to project its power. The corporate bylaws are the canon law of the church. There are no shareholders in the corporation, only the stakeholders of the church hierarchy and the multitudes of the faithful laity. The power base of the corporation is the laity who, in return for a promise of salvation and everlasting life in the hereafter, offers its allegiance and financial support in this world. Upbringing (indoctrination?) in a Catholic home establishes an emotional bond and allegiance to the rites and rituals of the church that is impervious to any of its failings perceived by others. The church has state support in a few nations with a Catholic majority and no wall of separation between the state and church. Some other characteristics of this MNC are perpetual existence independent of officeholders at any particular epoch, limited liability for stakeholders, centralized management, ownership and ease of transfer of property, and tax advantages. One of the driving engines behind the church's temporal power—its finances—is not open to public scrutiny (Berry 2011). The mission of the corporation is an aggressive conversion program of the non-Christian to spread the message of Jesus Christ and also maintain and extend its power base and to conduct associated programs of health, education, and related projects to help the newly converted. The church presents two faces, a dichotomy, in its interaction with the faithful versus its interaction with the rest of the world. There is the compassionate, humane, kind, and warm face of Mother Church, represented by each person's favorite monk, nun, or priest, who, as a mentor, nurtures children as they grow and who devotes his or her life selflessly to caring for the laity. This is the gentle pastoral face of the church. The second face is hard-nosed, a no-holds-barred, all-around pugilist's corporate face, jealous of its power, perks, and privileges and ready to fight for them by any means expedient, legal or political, transparent or secret. The hardball legal tactics adopted by the church and its hierarchy to preserve and protect its reputation and hence its power despite its problems with child abuse by its priests is an example of this (Berry 1992; Berry and Renner 2004; Allen Jr. 2004; Lessig 2010, Goodstein and Halbfinger 2010). Such a dichotomy is a problem as well as an opportunity for the MNC. The problem is a public-relations embarrassment, and its solution lies in trying to ethically reconcile the two contradictory faces of the church. The opportunity is a tactical use of one or the other face of the church to suit the occasion in order to achieve a cost-effective agenda to advance its power. Is it reasonable to ascribe to a corporation the same primacy drive for power as in an individual? The answer is yes, for the following reasons: First, a corporation is made up of individuals, each motivated by a primacy drive, working together to fulfill its mission. Second, even a casual study of church history can provide many past examples of events in which the church successfully fought to enhance its power to achieve primacy. Third, seeing the church as an MNC that fights to conserve and enhance its power can go a long way in explaining its response to current problems, including child abuse and demands by the laity and the clergy for change and reforms.

Extensive education especially in the sciences, the present age of general skepticism, and aggressive evangelization by Protestants, the Church of Latter-Day Saints (popularly called Mormons), and other denominations have diminished the numbers of the Catholic faithful. This decrease is compensated for by a militant conversion program of the church targeting less-educated, not-so-rich, faith-oriented people of developing countries. The faithful have little voice in the governance of the corporation, which is firmly controlled by the pope and the Curia. However, if and when the faithful acquire a significant political clout and are willing to support the teachings of the church, they can become instruments of social change in their home countries by projecting the teachings of the church. The changes they can then implement are prohibition of abortions, restrictions on divorce, and control over subjects taught in schools and over scientific research, such as stem-cell research. Changes in the corporation are rare because of corporate inertia and concerns about safeguarding the power of the corporate management. Reforms by the rarely held councils, such as Vatican II, are possible, though such changes have been essentially set aside or countered by post-conciliar pronouncements of the management (Küng 2001; Collins 2002). However, there have been some real changes in the church and its dealings with the rest of the world, but of course they had to meet certain criteria. Such changes have been those that are seen as beneficial to the church, cost-effective and financially gainful, politically correct, projecting a good corporate image, good for public relations, and good investments for the future, guaranteed to enhance the power and prestige of the church. This is understandable corporate behavior. A few examples of such changes follow.

The Congregation of the Doctrine of Faith as a Modern Inquisition Deviations from the approved teachings of the church, the "heretical depravity" of yesteryear, is handled differently now. There are no imprisonments before convictions, no public theater of auto-da-fé, no state authorities garroting or burning heretics at the stake. Such activities are expensive, messy, not politically correct, and a public relations nightmare today. Instead, the CDF, the lineal successor to the Roman Inquisition, conducts a secret trial using the same procedures of Roman law as of old, without physical torture, and quietly disciplines the guilty. These trials are described in a book: *The Modern Inquisition* (Collins 2002). Some seven prominent intellectuals, all Catholic dissidents, have been thus punished for their deviant opinions on theology; political or social philosophy, including gay and lesbian issues and contraception; and church governance, including papal power and the CDF. There are many other "new heretics" who have been similarly disciplined. Some of them who were teachers in Catholic institutions had their license to teach terminated or were dismissed from their posts. The modern methods are certainly cost-effective and efficient and achieve their ends quietly without much fuss or bad publicity.

Declaration of Religious Freedom One of the solemn declarations at the Vatican Council II was the Declaration on Religious Freedom (*Dignitatis Humanae* [D'Arcy 2003]). It is indeed commendable that the church has newly discovered the virtues of religious freedom and declared it to be a human right enjoyed by all. This is the very freedom that the church denied Buddhists,

Christians of other denominations, Hindus, Jains, Jews, Muslims, and people of other faiths through more than five centuries in many countries under its pastoral care, including Goa, when it had the political and military power to enforce its "one true faith." A cynic might say that this change of heart on the part of the church resulted from its loss of power and a concern for safeguarding its own hierarchy and flock in the brutal totalitarian Communist states that threaten it now. It is all a question of whose ox gets gored, the cynic would say, and the cynic is right. In the newly independent nations in Africa and Asia, the church was quite cozy with the former colonial masters when they were in power; the church is now seen as an agent of these colonial powers. Under the changed circumstances after independence, the church wanted to break with the past and get in bed with the new power elite. However,

> . . . there were in some places suggestions that an unpleasant modern version of the principle *cuius regio, eius religio* was in the making. [D'Arcy 2003, 5:947]

This principle, "whose realm, his religion," had been blithely used in the past to justify forced conversion of non-Christians when the church and the state had unlimited power, as for example in Goa. It has come back to haunt the church in newly independent nations, forcing the church to deal with the new freedom of religion. The church is, of course, loud in complaining when its privileges are encroached on. It is indeed amazing what loss of power for about 100 years has done to diametrically change the attitude of the church. This change is most welcome. The article on freedom of religion in the *New Catholic Encyclopedia* should be read in its entirety, including all of the lawyerly "fine print," so that the reader can appreciate the subtle nuances of this new freedom, including the discussion of the "thesis-hypothesis theory." Those who follow and justify their actions by this theory have been accused of ambivalent speech: "This naturally led to the charge that the attitude of Catholics in regard to religious freedom was highly ambiguous—where they were in a minority they demanded it; where in a majority they refused it" (D'Arcy 2003, 5:948).

Political Lobbying by the Church The loss of the papal states and military power in 1870 and the ensuing inability of the church to convince traditionally Catholic countries to do its bidding and participate in military adventures has resulted in a church that has no military might. The church cannot coerce and enforce its beliefs on anyone by naked physical force as it used to do. However, it continues to make its views known from a moral high ground and enforce them when it can, using other means such as pastoral persuasion or political deals with the dominant groups. The political lobbying by the church has been effective in its containment of damage from the scandal of child abuse by its clergy that was first exposed in the 1980s. After denying the abuse for some time or not reporting the criminal acts to the legal authorities, the church has been forced to face the problem squarely (Berry 1992; Berry and Renner 2004; Allen, Jr. 2004). However, the church, like any good corporation worth its charter, has fought back using all means, in spite of its avowed sympathy for the victims of abuse. One sees the pugnacious corporate face of the church, playing hardball, in this encounter. Lawrence Lessig, a professor of law at Harvard, experienced this behavior of the church when he represented a victim of child sexual abuse in a court of law. Instead of helping the victims of abuse, the church was doing its best to prevent them from getting any compensation they are entitled to offset the effects of past abuse (Lessig 2010).

Law reforms in New York State to extend the statute of limitations for sex-abuse victims to seek legal redress in courts were approved by the state assembly three times; however, the state senate refused to consider them. Opposition comes from the New York Catholic Conference and the expert lobbyists they have hired to kill the bill. Threats to close the schools and parishes in a legislator's district by one bishop have been reported and must have been deterrents to the legislator's support for the new legislation (Lessig 2010).

Recently, the pope and the Curia have been criticized for their slow response to the child abuse scandal by the clergy (Goodstein and Halbfinger 2010). The church has justified this slow response by its concern for the due processes of canon law and civil law to make sure that the priests get justice in individual cases. The church has had a typical corporate response to all criticism: blame the press for exposing the scandal, the greedy laity for demanding monetary compensation, and the cultural norms of countries that exposed the uncomfortable truths as having an anti-church bias. In other words, the church has made every attempt to protect and preserve its corporate power.

The Catholic Church and Other Religions Did the contacts with other religions moderate the views of the Catholic church toward them? The answer, alas, is no. The basic attitude of the church toward other religions remains unchanged; only the talk is more civil. Has the church ever admitted the mistakes of the Inquisition, expressed regret, and asked for forgiveness for the atrocities it was a party to in Goa? The answer is no, as far as I have been able to find. We can judge the current attitude toward other religions from its Declaration on the Church's Attitude toward Non-Christian Religions (*Nostra Aetate*), after the Vatican Council II (1962–1965 [Paul VI 1965; Hastings 1991; Ruokanen 1992; Cornwell 2001]).

Nostra Aetate represented a new beginning. What was missing in this document were the usual pejorative words: *pagan, benighted heathen, idolatry, error, fallacy*, and others of that type that used to be part of interreligious dialog; instead, an attempt is made to find those elements that are common to all faiths and what is good in them (Ruokanen 1992). The Vatican Council II declaration further stated that "the Catholic Church rejects nothing that is true and holy in these religions." Perhaps the church believed that this was a concession on its part to other faiths. However, this statement is full of sophistry and casuistry and created many problems. It is bothersome because the next question that suggests itself concerns who defines what is true and holy. Why does this cause problems? First, for centuries, the church has held that Catholicism is the only one true religion and that other religions represent the worship of false gods. However, by respecting only *some* beliefs of other faiths today, the church still implies that others' beliefs have problems. This is the slippery slope of religious intolerance. The church's habit of passing judgment on other religions has caused problems in the past and is not acceptable now. Such polemics can lead anywhere from endless puerile arguments on the level of "my religion is better than yours" to outright discrimination, prejudice, and mass slaughter. Just as individuals can respect different opinions, beliefs, or viewpoints of others, the church must learn to respect different religious beliefs without presuming to sit in judgment of them. Second, the statement that "the Catholic Church rejects nothing that is true and holy in these religions" is annoying because it is patronizing. Unless the church concedes that all faiths should be respected equally, the road to religious intolerance and discrimination is wide open. The church, however, has never accepted religious pluralism or the equality of all religions. Actually, it has disciplined some clergy for advocating religious pluralism (Cornwell 2001, 214; Collins 2002). Its position on the equality of religions is best summarized by the following quote from a recent declaration by the CDF, *Dominus Iesus*:

> *Equality*, which is a presupposition of inter-religious dialogue, refers to the equal personal dignity of the parties in dialogue, not to doctrinal content, nor even less to the position of Jesus Christ—who is God himself made man—in relation to the founders of other religions. [Ratzinger 2000, 14]

There is no equality of religions as far as the church is concerned; the church is the only possessor of truth. Third, if the church expects followers of other religions to respect its beliefs, simple reciprocity demands that the church do the same to others. Fourth, the church has repeatedly said that Roman Catholics have to accept all of the teachings of the church in totality and not be "cafeteria Catholics" who cherry-pick church teachings. If the church expects this all-or-nothing compliance from its followers, other faiths can expect no less from the Catholics in an interreligious dialog. The document on non-Christian religions, its background, various interpretations and reservations about what it states explicitly or implicitly, and how other religions are graded and ranked by merit into categories further complicate a complex problem (Ruokanen 1992). The general tenor of this document is one of superiority; it is obvious that the church still sits in judgment of other religions. The age-old mind-set has not changed. The church sees believers of other religions as fodder for its evangelizing machinery and nothing more. Their only salvation is to be reborn as newly minted Catholics who, as faithful followers of its teachings, can extend the power base of the church. These declarations of Vatican II have been followed by recent statements by senior clerics who have said that all other religions except the Catholic faith are "gravely deficient" (Ratzinger 2000, 14; Cornwell 2001, 214 et. seq.; Fisher 2007b). With such an attitude, a real dialog between the Catholic church and other faiths is not possible; the church's functionaries will be talking amongst themselves.

Religious Pluralism Versus Syncretism The question remains: What is the real attitude of the church toward other faiths after Vatican II? What is the church's practice compared with its pious declarations of good intentions? A partial answer may be found in the following incident from the biography of Pope John Paul II (Weigel 1999, 511–4). The pope proposed, in 1986, a world day of prayer for peace involving leaders of non-Catholic and non-Christian faiths, to be held at Assisi. This was a progressive, humane gesture toward other faiths in the best tradition of religious pluralism. However, the good intentions behind these suggestions conflicted with the orthodoxy of the church. Alarm bells started ringing at the Vatican because "John Paul understood that this could not mean a universal praying together, which would indeed be syncretism and therefore impossible, for others as well as for him" (Weigel 1999, 512). Though each religious leader would pray according to his or her tradition, their being together at the *same place and time* [my emphasis] was considered syncretism by the Vatican. Syncretism, or mixing of different religious beliefs or practices, could be either inclusive or exclusive. Inclusive syncretism selects elements common to all faiths and emphasizes them as a sign of the common humanity of all peoples and beliefs. Exclusive syncretism, on the other hand, stresses the uniqueness and superiority of one faith and treats the different elements of other faiths as contaminants to be avoided at any cost. Praying with people of other faiths is anathema to the church. The pope was in a tight spot. After much thought and discussion, a procedure acceptable to the orthodox in the Vatican was agreed on. Each religious leader would get together with his or her followers, to pray at a *separate* [my emphasis] site in and around the town of Assisi. The ceremony took place on 27 October 1986. The fasting religious leaders in their various colorful garbs gathered together and then prayed separately so that the pope's prayer would be untainted by syncretism. They met again on a huge elaborately decorated stage, the pope gave a closing speech, they broke their fast, and it was a grand spectacle, religious theater that must have impressed all, including the actor in the pope. This story would be hilarious were it not so sad! The pope, who proposed the idea in the first place, would not pray for world peace together with fellow humans of a different religion, because he was afraid of compromising or contaminating his faith. This proves that all of the rhetoric about the brotherhood of man, human fellowship, and so forth is a lot of empty words. Whatever it is that divides the Catholic church from other religions—beliefs, myths, rituals, theology, or traditions—is alive and well and is in the good hands of the faithful. Solemn declarations at venerable conclaves such as Vatican II are nothing but platitudes for the gullible. They are meant to create an illusion of goodwill amongst faiths, a public-relations ploy that sounds politically correct. The Roman Catholic church concedes nothing and continues to assert its age-old conviction that it is exclusively superior to other faiths. This is sad. The twentieth century showed us, through World War II and the Nazis' "master race," the harm, misery, and bloodshed that can result from people claiming superiority to others. The idea of superiority of one religion over others or of "one true faith" is equally pernicious. It has led to discrimination, injustice, slaughter, and bloodshed in the past and could do so again. Until and unless the simple proposition of equality and legitimacy of all faiths is accepted by the church, there will be no true religious pluralism and there will remain a great likelihood of more hatred, unrest, and bloodshed. It is to be hoped that the Catholic church—and indeed all Christian religions—will one day accept the truth and equality of other religions. The MNC that is the Roman Catholic church may yet see that this proposition is cost-effective, that it is politically correct, and, above all, that it will enhance the church's corporate image and power as a hallmark of superior moral standing.

Popular Christianity in Goa Today The preceding discussion was about Catholic orthodoxy as approved by the hierarchy of the church and the watchdogs of religious purity. What about the religion as practiced by ordinary Goan Catholics in everyday life and their dealings with people of other faiths—popular religion as lived by people with little theology and much faith? Though the church hierarchy has problems with inclusive syncretism, apparently modern Goan Catholics do not (Newman 2001). They have learned to live with Hindus, Muslims, Protestants, and others, all of them with their own history, beliefs, and traditions. There are a few people on the fringes of every faith who would not like to have any contact with those of other beliefs, just because they are of a different religion. If we leave them out, most of the remaining Goans live with pluralism of religions and cultures. Goan Catholics pray at Hindu temples of their family deities before conversion, and Hindus participate in Catholic worship and rituals without worrying about theological correctness. Some Muslims take part in Hindu or Christian festivals and celebrations too. Mutual courtesy amongst Goans is prized higher than doctrinal purity. The two books on life in present-day Goa that were mentioned earlier are very informative on these matters: *Of Umbrellas, Goddesses, and Dreams: Essays on Goan Culture and Society* (Newman 2001) and *Goa: A Daughter's Story* (Couto 2004). Goans are shown, warts and all, in all their humanity, tolerance, and ability to cope with their unique history and traditions. Their attitude is one of enlightened acceptance of the other. We could all learn from it and try to live by it.

The old Mahālasā temple in Verna, destroyed by the Portuguese on 7 and 14 March 1567, has been rebuilt on a windswept plateau, its original site. Like most Hindu temples, it faces east. At the back of the temple, there is a monument to a historic event, a Christian mass celebrated in 1519 in the precincts of a Hindu temple. The monument was built in 1959, in the waning days of the Portuguese Raj, and it faces west away from the temple. It is a cross about three feet high, on a pedestal, surfaced with glazed white tiles. I visited the site in 1999, in 2004, and in 2008. At the last visit, someone had draped a garland of marigolds on the cross as an offering. There was also a metal table with drippings of votive candles in front. At the base of the cross is a tile showing the Crucifixion, and a small marble slab with the following inscription in Portuguese is embedded in the pedestal underneath it:

NESTE ALTO
FOI CELEBRADA A PRIMEIR MISSA
EM TERRAS DE SALSETE
NO ANO DE 1519
MARDOL DE VERNA MAIO DE 1959

Translated, it reads (personal communication, email of July 6, 2005, from Délio de Mendonça):

Here on this height
Was celebrated the first Mass
In lands of Salcete
In the year 1519
Mardol of Verna, May 1959

In 2004 during a second visit, I asked the person in charge of the temple-rebuilding project what the plans were for this monument. He said that it would remain undisturbed as it stood. I would not be surprised if Hindu devotees visiting the temple offer flowers, fruit, and coconuts to it, just as some Catholics make the same offerings at the Mahālasā temple. Goans of all religions are humane, tolerant, and syncretistic. They have no problem in venerating someone else's object of devotion and do not think of this as being untrue to their faith. This bodes well for Goans and their culture, so long as they follow their hearts and do not listen to the zealots and "true believers" of all colors and shades who tell them what to think and how to act. These activists have their own agenda for power.

What have we learned from the story of Portuguese rule in Goa? Many aspects of that rule were an abuse of power fired by religious zeal. It was unlimited power without checks and balances, combined with religious zealotry impervious to doubts or critical self-examination. This proved to be a dangerous combination, with disastrous consequences. Power corrupted, and the certainty of faith drove all actions, however heinous. The dominance hierarchy spent its time justifying its actions behind a screen of empty legalisms or avowed good intentions while perpetuating its power. Abuse of absolute power and being corrupted by it is a recurring theme in human history. The corruption is independent of ethnicity, nationality, or religion. It could happen to any of us. It is general enough to be a law of nature to which all humans and their institutions are subject.

APPENDIX NINE

Guide to Konkani and Sanskrit Pronunciation

This guide to pronunciation makes use of a number of diacritics to supplement the alphabet. Some consider diacritics to be a nuisance, while others see them as essential for a correct pronunciation of Sanskrit or a Sanskrit-derived language such as Konkani. Why do we need them? The Sanskrit phonetic system consists of 49 sounds, each represented by a distinct symbol. Because the English alphabet has only 26 letters, a correct representation of Sanskrit-based words needs additional symbols, which the diacritics provide. Konkani has additional sounds such as the retroflex *ḷ* in *doḷo* (eye), and many nasals. Hence, diacritics are essential to a correct transliteration of Sanskrit or Konkani words to the English alphabet. With a little practice, one can get used to diacritics and pronounce the words correctly. One can also neglect them and plow right through the text as if they did not exist, if they are seen as a bother. For details on the phonology of Sanskrit, see the discussion in a Sanskrit textbook, such as *First Book of Sanskrit* (Bhandarkar 1966), *Devavāṇīpraveśikā: An Introduction to the Sanskrit Language* (Goldman and Sutherland 1987), or *Sanskrit: An Introduction to the Classical Language* (Coulson 1992).

This guide is divided into two tables, one for vowels and the second for consonants. In each table, the second column gives the English word that reproduces the sound of the vowel or the consonant, with the specific part indicated in **bold** letters. It has not been possible to find an English word in every case, because some of the sounds are not part of that language. The fact that a few words such as *dharma*, *karma*, and *bhakti* are now considered standard English has been helpful. Footnotes explain complex situations, where either there is no one word to give as an example or there are differences of opinion on the correct pronunciation. The aspirates—*kha*, *gha*, *cha*, *jha*, *ṭha*, *ḍha*, *tha*, *dha*, *pha*, and *bha*—could be a problem. However, breathing out forcefully after voicing the preceding consonant should achieve the desired result. The third and fourth columns are illustrations of Konkani or Sanskrit words. These examples should clear up any problems in getting the sounds right. If you are not familiar with these words, please go to the glossary (Appendix 10) for their meaning. These guidelines may be used for Kannada also.

TABLE 1. Sounds of Vowels

Vowel	English	Konkani	Sanskrit	Vowel	English	Konkani	Sanskrit
a	c**u**t	*agni*	*agni*	ṛ	**ri**b	*ṛīṇa*	*ṛṇam*
ā	f**a**ther	*ārti*	*ārati*	ḷ	kett**le**	*doḷo*	*īḷ*
i	k**i**t	*ārti*	*ārati*	e	f**a**te	*eka*	*eka*
ī	sl**ee**t	*śrī*	*śrī*	ai	**ai**sle	*airāvatu*	*airāvata*
u	f**u**ll	*upāsu*	*upavāsa*	o	m**o**te	*omkāru*	*omkāra*
ū	t**oo**l	*ūna*	*ūna*	au	m**ou**se	*auṣadha*	*auṣadha*

TABLE 2. Sounds of Consonants

Consonant	English	Konkani	Sanskrit
ka	**k**ey	*kāṅkaṇa*	*kaṅkaṇam*
kha	blo**ckh**ead	*khaḍga*	*khaḍga*
ga	**g**o	*gotra*	*gotra*
gha	do**gh**ouse	*ghāṇṭa*	*ghaṇṭā*
ṅa	ki**ng**	*kāṅkaṇa*	*kaṅkaṇam*
ca	**ch**urch	*cāmpē*	*campak*
cha[1]		*chanda*	*chanda*
ja	**j**oy	*japu*	*japa*
jha[2]	**Jh**ansi	*jhāra, jharī*	*jhara, jharā, jharī*
ña	pi**n**ch	*cañcala*	*cañcala*
ṭa	**t**ent	*ghāṇṭa*	*ghaṇṭā*
ṭha	an**th**ill	*uṣṭhē*	*oṣṭha*
ḍa	**d**ent	*khaḍga*	*khaḍga*
ḍha	han**dh**old	*gūḍha*	*gūḍha*
ṇa	te**n**t	*ṛīṇa*	*ṛṇam*
ta[3]	**th**in	*dāntu*	*danta*

(*continued*)

TABLE 2 (*cont'd*)

CONSONANT	ENGLISH	KONKANI	SANSKRIT
tha[4]	**th**ong	*sthāna*	*sthānam*
da[5]	**D**evanagari	*dayā*	*dayā*
dha	**dh**arma	*dharmu*	*dharma*
na	a**n**ther	*nāgu*	*nāga*
pa	**p**un	*pakṣu*	*pakṣa*
pha	u**ph**old	*phala*	*phalam*
ba	**b**ill	*bala*	*balam*
bha	**bh**akti	*bhakti*	*bhakti*
ma	bu**m**p	*mukti*	*mukti*
ya	**y**oga	*yātrā*	*yātrā*
ra	b**r**acket	*rāyu*	*rāja*
la	**l**ong	*līlā*	*līlā*
va[6]	**v**ine	*vrata*	*vrata*
śa	**sh**een	*śrī*	*śrī*
ṣa[7]		*ṛṣi*	*ṛṣi*
sa	**s**oak	*sevā*	*sevā*
ha	**h**ope	*hasti*	*hastin*
ṁ (nasalized vowel or *anusvāra*[8])		*saṁnyāsi*	*saṁnyāsin*
Konkani nasals are shown by a tilde (~)		*nāvā̃, keḷẽ, māyī̃*	

[1] The *ch* sound in ***ch**urch* with aspiration.
[2] The *j* sound in ***j**oy* with aspiration. This sound is rare even in Sanskrit.
[3] This is a dental sound as in ***th**in*. It is customary to indicate this sound with *th* when written *without* diacritics. When written *with* diacritics, it is indicated by *t*.
[4] The *th* sound in ***th**in* with aspiration.
[5] Pronounce with the tip of the tongue touching the ridge of the upper teeth.
[6] Pronounced as a labiodental—that is, with the upper teeth and the lower lip, as in *vine*. Most Indian languages do not differentiate between the labiodental *v* in *vine* and the labial *w* in *wine*.
[7] Produced with the tip of the tongue further back than when used to sound *ś* or as a retroflex.
[8] In Sanskrit or Devanagari script, this is indicated by a "dot" on the top right of the syllable. The sound is realized by nasalizing the preceding vowel. In transliteration, it is represented either by *ṁ* (Bhandarkar 1966, 1) or by *ṃ* (Goldman and Sutherland 1987, 7; Coulson 1992, 8).

APPENDIX TEN

Glossary

Words are arranged alphabetically, with the standard form of a letter preceding the one with diacritics. Typeface conventions usied in this glossary are as follows: All words with an entry in the glossary are in **bold** if they are English; if they are non-English they are in ***bold italics***; other non-English words used in definitions that do not have their own entry are in *italics* only. Entries of proper names are in **bold** only without *italics*. Word usage or origins are indicated as follows: Ara, Arabic; Eng, English; Heb, Hebrew; Hin, Hindi; Jap, Japanese; Kan, Kannada; Kon, Konkani; Lat, Latin; Mar, Marathi; Pal, Pali; Per, Persian; Port, Portuguese; Pra, Prakrit; San, Sanskrit; Tam, Tamil; Tul, Tulu; Tur, Turkish. Other abbreviations: f, feminine; m, masculine. See also Appendix 9, "Guide to Konkani and Sanskrit Pronunciation," regarding the use of diacritics.

For recipes of Konkani dishes, see the works by Jaya V. Shenoy (1988, 1999, 2004). Works by the following authors were useful in assembling this glossary: Vaman Shivaram Apte (1884, 1998), Pandarinath Bhuvanendra Janardhan (1991, 1999), Monier Monier-Williams (1976), Henk W. Wagenaar et al (1995), and Jennifer Speake (1997).

abhiṣeka: (Kon, San) Annointing, sprinkling; holy ablution or anointment of a sacred image.

adhika māsa: (Kon, San) Intercalary month added to the lunar calendar to bring it into step with the seasons or the solar calendar.

adhikaprasaṅgi: (Kon) Excessive, impertinent questioner on any topic.

adṛṣṭa: (Kon, San) Not seen, not known; fate, destiny.

advaita: (Kon, San) Nonduality in Hindu philosophy, which asserts the identity of the supreme soul Brahman with the universe, including the individual soul, or *ātman*.

aḍavu ghālcẽ: (Kon) To pawn; to give as surety.

aḍgaī: (Kon) A type of pickles.

agni: (Kon, San) Fire; when capitalized, the word is the name for the god of fire.

agrahāra: (Kon, San) A grant of land, usually tax free, given by kings or rich people to **Brāhmaṇas** for sustenance and perpetual performance of Vedic and religious rites for the benefit of the whole kingdom; a village made up of such land gifts. These were also centers of traditional learning in Sanskrit, rituals, medicine, architecture, agriculture, and astronomy/astrology.

aigaḷa śāle: (Kan) School; usually a one-room thatched schoolhouse where one person taught all the grades.

aigaḷu: (Kan) Honorific for a teacher derived from the word *ayyā* (Kan, Tul), meaning "sir."

Airāvata*:* (Kon, San) Name of Indra's elephant.

akṣarārambha: (Kon, San) The beginning of education. *See* rite 10 in Appendix 5, "Hindu Rites of Passage." Also called *vidyārambha* (Kon, San).

akhāḍā: (Pra, Hin, Mar) Wrestling arena. Also called *akhārā.*

akṣata: (Kon, San) Unbroken, whole. Whole grains of rice sprinkled on the head as a blessing. On special occasions, the rice may be colored red by mixing it with ***kuṅkuma***.

alaṅkāra: (Kon, San) Decoration, ornament.

amāsa: (Kon) New moon. From *amāvāsyā* (San).

anattā: (Pal) Not-self. Buddha taught that a living being is made up of only five impermanent aggregates—physical form, sensations, perceptions, volitions, and consciousness—leading to the conclusion that there is no permanent, immortal self. From *anātman* (San).

anāthaśālā: (Kon, San) Orphanage.

anjūra: (Kon) Figs, usually dried. From *añjīra* (San).

anna*:* (Eng) One-sixteenth of a rupee. This coin is no longer in use. Also called *āṇo* (Kon).

annaprāśana: (San) *See* ***cerdā śīta jevoñcẽ***.

antyakriyā: (San) Obsequies, final or funeral rites. Short form: ***kriyā*** (Kon). *See* rite 16 in Appendix 5, "Hindu Rites of Passage."

antyeṣṭi: (San) Final or funeral rites. *See* rite 16 in Appendix 5, "Hindu Rites of Passage."

anuloma: (San) With the hair; regular or in natural accepted order.

anvāḷẽ: (Kon) State of ritual purity; free from dirt, or in a state of purity. This also involves a whole series of do's and dont's connected with ritual purity and pollution. From *anavaskara* (San). *Also called* ***anvāḷpaṇa*** (Kon) and ***anvāḷẽpaṇa*** (Kon).

anvāḷẽpaṇa: (Kon) *See* ***anvāḷẽ*** (Kon).

anvāḷpaṇa: (Kon) *See* ***anvāḷẽ*** (Kon).

anvāḷyā baḍḍi: (Kon) A bamboo staff used to handle ritually clean clothes only.

añjali:* *(San) Cavity formed by cupping open palms in an act of receiving or giving.
aṇṇā: (Kon, Kan) Elder brother.
arghya: (Kon, San) Respectful welcome offering to a god or a venerable person.
aśmārohaṇa: (Kon, San) Ceremony of the bride stepping on a stone while she is exhorted by the groom to be as firm as a stone in her love for him.
aśvattha: (Kon, San) Sacred fig tree (*Ficus religiosa*). Also called bo-tree or pipal, from *pippala* (San).
aṣṭa maṅgala praśna: (Kon) Questions regarding the past, present and the future, pertaining to eight auspicious matters, asked of an astrologer.
Aṣṭamī: (Kon, San) Birthday of Lord Kṛṣṇa. Also called Janmāṣṭamī (Kon, San) and Kṛṣṇāṣṭamī (Kon, San).
atithisatkāra: (Kon, San) Hospitable reception of guests.
auṣadha: (Kon, San) Medicine in general.
avabhṛtha: (San) Bathing at the end of a principal Vedic sacrifice.
avatāra: (Kon, San) Descent; incarnation of God.
ayyapaṇā bāila maniṣī: (Kon) Woman whose husband is living. From *āryapaṇa* (San), "honorable state." *See* ***savvāśiṇī***.
ayyapaṇāri gelleli: (Kon) One who died before her husband, or as a ***suvāsinī***.
ayyapaṇāri morcẽ: (Kon) Dying before one's husband.
ācāru: (Kon) Act or behavior that goes against accepted social or religious norms.
āgama śāstra: (San) Scriptures that specialize in giving details of temple worship and rituals.
ājjā: (Kon) Grandfather. From ***ārya*** (San), "noble," "venerable."
ājjāli jagali: (Kon) Grandfather's veranda.
āksāḷānco: (Kon) Goldsmith.
āḷsando: (Kon) Long beans (*Vigna unguiculata*, subspecies *sesquipedalis*), yard-long beans, long-podded cowpea, asparagus beans.
āmbaṭa: (Kon) A Konkani vegetable dish.
āmbo: (Kon) Mango. From *āmram* (San).
āmbuli: (Kon) Tender mango before being fully mature, used for pickles or a salad (***paccaḍi***).
āni: (Kon) And.
ānnammā: (Kon) Father's mother.
āṅgaḍi: (Kon) Shop. From *aṅgaḍi* (Kan).
āṅgḍi pūjā: (Kon) Yearly sanctification of one's shop or place of business by inviting the goddess of prosperity, Śrī Lakṣmī. From *angaḍi pūje* (Kan).
āṅgaṇa: (Kon) Courtyard. From *aṅgaṇam* (San).
āṅgso: (Kon) Small piece of cloth usually worn round the waist, or to cover the upper body, by males. A similar piece of cloth is draped over the left shoulder and used as a general-purpose handkerchief.

āṅgtena nela pussucẽ: (Kon) *See* ***āṅgṭi pussucẽ*** (Kon).

āṅgṭi pussucẽ: (Kon) Wiping the floor with a wet cloth to remove dust. Also called ***āṅgtena nela pussucẽ*** (Kon).

āṅgvaṇa: (Kon) Religious vow.

āppo: (Kon) Type of cake, a dessert. From *apūpa* (San).

ārti: (Kon) Light waved in a clockwise direction in front of the sacred image in a temple. It is also done in front of the boy being initiated in ***upanayana*** or the bride and groom, as part of the wedding ceremonies. From *ārati* (San).

ārti dākkocẽ: (Kon) Act of waving of an ***ārti***.

ārti ghevcẽ: (Kon) Act of blessing oneself after an ***ārti*** has been sanctified by waving it in front of a sacred image.

Ārya: (Kon, San) Noble, worthy, venerable; name of Indo-European speaking tribes. Also called Vedic people.

āsti: (Kon) Property.

āstika: (San) Asserter; a believer in sacred tradition including God and the hereafter.

āśīrvāda: (Kon, San) Benediction; expression of a wish or prayer as a blessing. From *āśis* (San), "blessing," "benediction." The customary expression in Konkani is "*Devu barẽ koro*," or "May God bless."

ātreya: (San) Male descendant of the sage Atri.

ātreyī: (San) Female descendant of the sage Atri.

āvāḷo: (Kon) Gooseberry (*Ribes uva-crispa*). From *āmalaka* (San). *Also called* ***dhātri*** (San).

āvāhanam: (San) Invoking a deity. The opposite of ***visarjana***, which is bidding good-bye to an invoked deity.

āveśa: (Kon, San) State of trance and possession of a medium of an oracle.

āyudha pūjā: (Kon, San) Sanctification of the weapons of war by the king in the olden days; now, yearly sanctification of the tools of trade by the common people.

Āyurveda: (Kon, San) Traditional Hindu medicine regarded as a supplement to the *Atharvaveda*.

Āyurvedic *vaidya:* (Kon) Practitioner of traditional Hindu medicine.

baccā: (Hin) A kid, child, inexperienced, raw.

Badarikāśrama: (Kon, San) Hermitage at Badarikā, the northernmost monastery founded by the Śaṅkarācārya.

bahiṣkāra: (Kon, San) Excommunication.

bahuḷa: (Kon) Dark half or waning moon. From *bahula* (San).

bailā gāḍi: (Kon) Bullock cart.

bala: (Kon, San) Strength.

balabadhra: A representation or an effigy of Balarāma, assembled from a smooth stone dressed in swaddling clothes, and decorated with some gold chains, used in a cradling ceremony. Also called *balabadhru* (Kon).

basti: (Kon) Jain temple or monastery. From *basadi* (Kan).

baṭāṭo: (Kon) Potato. From *baṭāṭa* (Port).

bayalāṭa: (Kan) Field drama, also known as ***yakṣagāna*** or ***kheḷu*** (Kon).

bāglāri boscẽ: (Kon) Part of the ceremonial entrance of newlyweds into the husband's home. The sisters of the groom sit on the threshold (***humboru***) and extract a promise from the newlyweds that they will give their children in marriage to the children of the sisters. Gifts are given to the sisters.

bāldi: (Kon) Bucket. From *balde* (Port).

bāḷāntiro: (Kon) Childbirth; also, rites associated with childbirth. *See* rite 4 in Appendix 5, "Hindu Rites of Passage." *Also called* ***jātakarma*** (San).

bāḷāntiryācẽ kūḍa: (Kon) Birthing room.

bāmṇā thancẽ: (Kon) Husband's family.

bārhaspatya: (San) A pupil of **Bṛhaspati**, who taught a form of materialism, generally considered heretical.

bāṭlo: (Kon) Converted, as in change of religion; polluted. Probably a short form of ***bhaṣṭelo*** (Kon), "polluted," derived from ***bhraṣṭa*** (San), "ritually polluted." *See also* ***bhaṣṭa*** (Kon).

bāyī: (Kon) Well.

bāyncẽ āḍḍẽ: (Kon) Retaining wall round a well; the front has a flat top for resting the full pot of water, and a niche underneath it for putting ones foot for additional purchase while drawing water. From *bāyiya kāṭṭe* (Kan). *Also called* ***kāṭṭẽ*** (Kon).

BCE: Before the Common Era.

beeḍi: (Kon) Country (*deśī*) smoke.

bettā mudrā: (Kon) One of the emblems,of the oracle at the Mulki temple collectively called ***pāṭṭo-mudrā***. It is made of flexible bamboo canes bound together at one end in a handle of gold and is held in the left hand by the oracle.

bhaiṇi: (Kon) Sister.

bhajana: (Kon, San) Adoration, worship. Singing of devotional music, with or without musical instruments.

bhakti: (Kon, San) Faith, devotion.

Bhanap: (Kon) Nickname of uncertain origin for Chitrapur Sarasvat **Brāhmaṇas**.

bhaṣṭa: (Kon) Ritual impurity.

bhaṣṭi: (Kon) a woman who is ritually unclean, as during menses. From ***bhraṣṭa*** (San), meaning "ritually unclean," "polluted," "fallen." *See also* ***bāṭlo*** (Kon), ***jāti bāṭlo*** (Kon), and ***vholẽ*** (Kon).

bhaṭṭā thañcẽ: (Kon) A Gauḍa Sārasvat Brāhmaṇa priestly family compared to a householder family. Usually, they are more observant of food taboos and rules of ritual purity. *See also* **grasthā thañcẽ** (Kon), ***laukika*** (Kon), and ***vaidika*** (Kon).

bhaṭṭu: (Kon) Academic title of a learned **Brāhmaṇa**, a priest. From *bhaṭṭa* (San), a learned **Brāhmaṇa**. *Also called* ***boṭṭo*** (Goan Kon).

bhaṭṭvyāpti: (Kon) Priestcraft.

bhāgvatu: (Kon) Person who provides continuity to the story of a field drama by introducing the main characters, converses with them, and sings songs that tell the story. From *bhāgavata* (Kan). Also called *bhāgavatu* (Kon).

Bhāgyā Lakṣmī: (Kon) Auspicious goddess of fortune.

Bhāgyada **Lakṣmī** ***bārammā:*** (Kan) "Welcome to the auspicious goddess of fortune"; a Kannada song by Sant Purandara Dasa traditionally played to welcome the new bride to her new husband's home.

bhāṇa: (Kon) Large spherical vessel, about 3 feet in diameter, usually made of copper and used to store hot (*hoona utkā bhāṇa*) or cold (*thanḍa utkā bhāṇa*) water in bathrooms.

bhāṇā muccaḷa: (Kon) Cover for a ***bhāṇa*** (vessel used to store water), usually made of wood.

bhāṇḍi: (Kon) Scaled-down version of a wooden chariot used to take the image of a deity in procession as part of temple festivities.

bhāṅgi: (Kon) Marijuana. From *bhāṅg* (San, Hin).

bhāṅgī pānaka: (Kon) Decoction of marijuana to which are added, milk, unrefined sugar (jaggery), cardamom, etc.

bhāvāji: (Kon) Cousin; brother-in-law.

bhāvin: (Kon) Lower- or second-tier ***devadāsī***, assigned to sweep, clean, trim lamps, and weave flower garlands in a temple. They are usually literate. From *bhāvinī* (San). *See* ***kalāvanta***.

bhiṅgāru: (Kon) White flowers or inflorescence of the betel nut palm (*Areca catechu*).

bhojana śālā: (Kon, San) Dining hall.

bhrūṇahatyā: (Kon, San) Embryo killing.

bhuttā phāththoru: (Kon) Stone dedicated to a spirit and held sacred by its devotees.

bhuuta: (Kon, San) Spirit; a demigod. *Also called* ***bhūta*** (Kon, San).

bhūta: (Kon, San). *See* ***bhuuta*** (Kon, San).

bibbo: (Kon) Cashew nut harvested before it is fully mature and sun-dried. *See* ***kājju bī***.

Bindumādhava: (Kon, San) A form of Lord Viṣṇu as revealed to the sage Agni Bindu (Eck 1983, 206–7). The image used in processions (***utsavā mūrti***) at the Mulki temple.

bīḍāguḍḍo: (Kon) Location of a crematorium in Udupi. From *bīḍu* (Kan), meaning a wild, uncultivated wasteland, and *guḍḍo* (Kon), meaning a hillock, derived from *guḍḍa* (Kan).

bīḷa: (Kon) Hole, cavity, or burrow inhabited by a rat or a snake. Plural: *bīḷā*. From *bilam* (San).

boḷā: (Kon) Simpleton.

bōḷu: (Kon) Extract of wheat and millet fed to babies being weaned.

bombeyāṭa: (Kan) Puppetry.

bōnti: (Kon) Wick of clean linen dipped in a solution of jaggery (brown sugar) or sugar given to a newborn to suck on before it is ready to be breastfed.

boṭṭo: (Goan Kon) *See* ***bhaṭṭu:*** (Kon).

Brahmacāri: (Kon) Unmarried male who has gone through the sacred thread ceremony (***upanayana*** or ***mūñji***). From ***Brahmacārin*** (San).

brahmahatyā: (Kon, San) Priest-killing; killing a **Brāhmaṇa**; one of the five major sins. *See* ***mahāpātaka***.

Brahmara: (Kon) A minor deity. Also called Brahmaru (Kon).

Brahmarā guḍi: (Kon) Small shrine dedicated to a minor deity named Brahmaru.

brahmarākṣasa: (San, Kon) Ogre or demon of gigantic size; fierce, blood-drinking, flesh-eating enemy of humans.

brahmavādinī: (San) Female teacher and expounder of the Vedas.

Brāhmaṇa: (Kon, San) Priest, first of the fourfold ***varṇa*** system of the Hindu religious hierarchy.

Bṛhaspati: (San) Name of a sage, also called Vācaspati, who was a teacher of the gods. Also, name of a philosopher, ca. the sixth century BCE, who advocated materialistic atheism, or humanism, generally considered heretical.

buddhonti jāvkā: (f; Kon) "Be endowed with good behavior or wise counsel," a traditional Konkani blessing and good wishes from an older person to a child. *Also* ***buddhontu jāvkā*** (m; Kon).

bunnā uddāka: (Kon) The term used for coffee in the Konkani community of South Kanara District in the latter half of the nineteenth century. From *bunn* (Ara), "coffee bean."

cakra: (Kon, San) The discus, which is one of the emblems of Śrī Viṣṇu. The other emblems are ***śaṅkha*** (the conch shell), ***gadā*** (the mace), and ***padma*** (the lotus)

cakrasoru: (Kon) A gold necklace of interlocking discs. From *cakrasara* (San).

camcẽ: (Kon) Spoon, ladle. From *camasa, camasam* (San).

canda: (Kon) Beautiful, pleasing, alluring. *From canda* (San), "to shine."

candana: (Kon, San) Sandalwood (*Santalum album*) or any smooth preparation of its paste.

candra śālā: (Kon, San) The building on the left of the main temple in Mulki, where the offices of the temple management are located. *Also called* ***vasantā jagali*** (Kon).

caṇyā upkari: (Kon) A spicy mixture of cooked black chickpeas (*Cicer arietinum*) served as a snack.

cañcala: (Kon, San) Fickle, inconstant.

carambala: (Kon) Starfruit or carambola (*Averrhoa carambola*).

caulu: (Kon) First tonsure or haircut for boys. *See* rite 8 in Appendix 5, "Hindu Rites of Passage." *Also called* **cūḍākarma** (San).

Cavati: (Kon) Birthday of Lord Gaṇeśa. From Caturthī, Gaṇeśa Caturthī (San).

cā: (Kon) Tea.

cāmara: (Kon, San) Bushy tail of a bovine (*Bos grunniens*) mounted on a handle covered with silver or gold plate, used as part of insignia of royalty and accompanying the procession of an image of a deity or a revered guru. It is usually accompanied by a staff of authority, called a *daṇḍa* or ***daṇḍu***.

cāmpẽ: (Kon) Bright yellow flower with an assertive fragrance (*Michelia champaca* or *Magnolia champaca*). From *campak* (San).

cāṇḍāla: (Kon, San) General name for the lowest of the mixed castes originating from a **Śūdra** father and a **Brāhmaṇa** mother.

cāṅga veḷu ghaḍi: (Kon) Auspicious time.

cāri hāttāñ cōgo: (Kon) Robe with four sleeves. Popular name for a robe with elaborate puffed sleeves worn by barristers arguing cases in front of the high courts and a source of pride for their clients.

cārmburo: (Kon) Puffed rice.

Cārvāka: (San) Name of a philosopher, ca. the sixth century BCE, said to have been a pupil of **Bṛhaspati**, who expounded materialistic atheism, generally considered heretical. Also, a follower of this teacher.

cāttu-gurḍāṇo: (Kon) Mortar and pestle. Usually made of cast bronze and used to prepare a mixture of rice and milk (***bōḷu***) for babies. A fat, roly-poly baby is also called, fondly, a ***gurḍāṇo***.

CE: Common Era.

ceḍi: (Kon) Prostitute (pejorative).

ceḍo: (Kon) Manservant.

ceḍũ: (Kon) Maidservant.

celyeka dhāra voththucẽ: (Kon) Act of giving away the bride as a gift to the groom, by her parents or guardian pouring water over her hands. ***Kanyādāna*** (San).

ceṇḍo: (Kon) Drum accompaniment for a field drama, usually played with great vigor. *From* ***ceṇḍe*** (Kan).

cerdā bhairi horcẽ: (Kon) First going out of the baby. *See* rite 6 in Appendix 5, "Hindu Rites of Passage." *Also called* **niṣkramaṇa** (San).

cerdā kānu vinduco: (Kon) Ear piercing of the baby. *See* rite 9 in Appendix 5, "Hindu Rites of Passage." *Also called* ***karṇavedha*** (San).

cerdā nāvā ghālcẽ: (Kon) Naming the baby. *See* rite 5 in Appendix 5, "Hindu Rites of Passage." *Also called* ***nāmakaraṇa*** (San).

cerdā pāḷḷyāntũ ghalcẽ: (Kon) Cradling ceremony for a baby, part of naming the baby, or rite 5 in Appendix 5, "Hindu Rites of Passage."

cerdā śīta jevoñcẽ: (Kon) First feeding of the baby with solid food, usually rice and milk. *See* rite 7 in Appendix 5, "Hindu Rites of Passage." *Also called* ***anna-prāśana*** (San).

cerdũ: (Kon) Baby. From ***cāru dṛśyam*** (San), "pleasant to see."

caṇā: (Kon) Chickpea (*Cicer arietinum*); also called Bengal gram. From *caṇa* (Pra, San).

ciḍki: (Kon) Small unglazed earthenware pot.

ciñcāmba: (Kon) Tamarind (*Tamarindus indica*). From *ciñcā* (San). *Tamarind* is from the Arabic *Tamr-i-Hind*, "dates of India."

cippuṭa: (Kon) Small spoon.

cogo: (Kon) Outer garment, usually upper. From ***cogā*** (Hin).

communidades: (Port) Village community, cooperative agricultural and welfare associations, called ***gāvṁkāri*** before the Portuguese regime.

cūḍākarma: (San) *See* ***caulu*** (Kon).

cūḍi: (Kon) A small boquet of multicolored, wild and cultivated flowers, shoots of grass, ***dirbhāṅkuru***, and other greens used in worship around the holy basil, ***tulasī***, on Fridays and Sundays in the months of ***Śrāvaṇa*** (July/August). From *cūḍā* (San), "crest," "plume," or "diadem."

dakṣiṇā: (Kon, San) Ritual present or gift given to an officiating priest at the conclusion of a religious rite.

dakṣiṇāyaṇa: (Kon) Southward progression of the sun, from the summer solstice (approximately June 21) to the winter solstice (approximately December 21). From *dakṣiṇāyana* (San).

Dakṣiṇa Kannaḍā: (Kon, Kan) South Kanara, name of a district on the west coast of India.

daṇḍu: (Kon) Staff or mace, a wooden staff covered with silver or gold plate, used as a symbol of authority, and part of insignia of royalty, that accompanies procession of an image of a deity or a revered guru. From *daṇḍa* (San). *See* ***cāmara***. A group of piligrims traveling to places of pilgrimage carrying offerings accumulated over a few years is also called ***Rāmadaṇḍu***.

darbha: (Kon, San) Sacred grass used in Hindu sacrificial ceremonies. "Those darbha blades from which no further blades shoot forth are called simply darbhas, blades from which fresh ones sprout forth are called kuśas, blades with their roots are called **kutapas** and those the tips of which are cut off called **tṛṇa** (grass)" (Kane 1974, 2:657). The botanical names in literature are *Poa cynosuroides* (Macdonell and Keith 1995, 1:173) and *Eragrostis cynosuroides* (Janardhan 1999, 167). *Also called* ***kuśa*** or ***munja*** grass.

darśanam: (San) Viewpoint; perspective; opinion; a system of philosophy; viewing.

darśaṇa: (Kon) Audience, view of a deity or a holy person. Also, ceremony in which a medium possessed by a spirit, or oracle, answers questions from devotees regarding their personal problems and prescribes solutions. From *darśanam* (San), "audience"; "seeing," "looking at."

darśaṇā pātri: (Kon) Medium through whom an oracle replies to questions.

darśaṇa sevā: (Kon) Rite or ceremony of the oracle at the Mulki Śrī Venkaṭaramaṇa temple, and other Sarasvat temples considered as a service to the deity. From *darśana sevā* (San).

darśaṇāri prasādu ghevco: (Kon) Receiving blessings and grace, ***prasāda***, from the oracle.

dayā: (Kon, San) Compassion, pity.

dāna: (Kon, San) Gift, donation.

dāntẽ: (Kon) Granite quern for grinding grains. It is made of two discs 3 to 4 inches thick and 18 to 24 inches in diameter. The bottom disc has a central metal axle around which the top disc, which has a central hole of about 3 inches in diameter, rotates. The top disc has an embedded wooden handle near its edge, which is used to rotate it. Grains are fed from the central hole of the top disc, and the ground powder (*pīṭa*) is discharged from the edges of the quern. The top disc is sometimes called ***pāvu***. This device is also used at the ***uḍdā muhurta***, which is part of the ***upanayana*** and wedding ceremonies.

dāntu: (Kon) Tooth. From *danta* (San).

dāntuṇi: (Kon) Comb.

Dāyābhāga: (San) Name of part of a treatise on the codes of law, **Dharmaratna**, by Jīmūtavāhana, dealing with inheritance, partition of family property, and related matters. It is generally applicable in Assam and Bengal. This code favors widows and their inheritance of property, compared with the alternate tradition of **Mitākṣarā**. *See* **Mitākṣarā**.

deśabandhu: (Kon, San) Kin by common nationality; fellow citizen of India.

devadāsī: (San) Female dedicated to service in a temple. *See* ***kalāvant*** and ***bhāvin***.

devasthānā suttā voccẽ: (Kon) Circumambulate round a temple.

devasthānā suttu: (Kon) Circuit round a temple. There may be as many as three depending on the wealth of a temple, its precinct area, how densely it is built, etc. The innermost perimeter is usually called the *devasthānā suttu*. Devotees go round in it with the sanctum on their right—that is, clockwise. The next is called the *utsavā suttu*, and it goes round the main building of the temple on the right, and auxiliary buildings on the left, and is used for most festivals (**utsava**). The outermost perimeter is called *rathā suttu*, and is spacious enough to accommodate the wooden temple carts (**ratha** or **tēru**) during special festivals.

devā kūḍa: (Kon) Family shrine in a private home.

Devu barẽ koro: (Kon) "May God bless"; traditional blessing or good wishes spoken by an elder person to a younger one.

dhamma: (Pal) The teachings of the Buddha. *From* ***dharma*** (San).

dharma: (Kon, San) Law, usage, practice, custom, duty; what is fair and right. This meaning is in the context of Hinduism in general; for the Buddhist context, *see* ***dhamma***.

dharmaśālā: (Kon, San) Charitable institution, a rest-house that provides free accommodation to devotees visiting a temple on a pilgrimage.

dharmaśāsana: (Kon, San) Legal settlement of a gift.

dharmaśāstra: (Kon, San) Code of laws. The **Mānava Dharmasūtra**, or **Manusmṛti**, popularly known as the Laws of Manu or simply Manu, is the best known (Kane 1975, 1:143–149, 306–349; Doniger and Smith 1991); there are many others (Kane 1975, Vol. I; Olivelle 1999). *Also called* ***dharmasūtra*** (Kon, San).

dharmādhikāri: (Kon, San) Title of the Hegde of Dharmasthaḷa, who is in charge of the famous temple there. Also a term used to designate the manager of any temple.

dhājana: (Kon) Ten people; a quorum required at public or religious functions. *See* ***hattu samastaru*** (Kan).

dhākṭi bāila: (Kon) Junior wife, or second wife.

dhāra voththucẽ: (Kon) Formal giving away of the bride by her parents or gaurdian, as a gift to the groom.

dhātri: (San) *See* ***āvāḷo:*** (Kon).

dheḍḍi: (Kon) Girl attendant of a bride. A ***bhāvin*** servant who used to accompany a bride to her new home in Goa in the olden days.

dheḍḍo: (Kon) Boy attendant of a bridegroom.

dhoti: (Kon, Eng) A rectangular piece of cloth, usually white, worn by men.

dhūḷi bheṭa: (Kon) Worship of the family deity, ***kula devatā***, as a returning traveler before washing the dust, ***dhūḷi***, from one's feet. From *dhūli, dhūlī* (San), "dust."

dhvajastamba: (Kon, San) Flagpole at the entrance to a temple.

dirbhāṅkura: (Kon) Tips of the sacred ***darbha*** grass. Also called *darbhāṅkura* (San).

dīrghāyuṣya jāvvo: (Kon) "May you live long."

divli: (Kon) Bronze lamp with a wide round base to catch oil drippings and give it stability. A central column about a couple of feet in length rises from center of the base to end in a circular receptacle for oil at the top. This receptacle has usually, five, seven, or nine spouts, each supporting a cotton wick. There is a central decorative finial or a figure to which some ***kuṅkuma*** is usually applied for auspiciousness.

divṭige salāmu: (Kon) Older name for a ceremony at the Mulki temple, consisting of bowing to the deity with lighted torches, ***divṭigā***, and singing hymns of praise as part of worship. From ***salāmu*** (Kon), "bowing," "salutations," derived from ***salām*** (Ara) and *shālōm* (Heb), "peace," "salutations." It has recently been renamed ***dīpa namaskāra*** (San).

dōṇi: (Kon) Boat. *From* **taraṇī** (San).

drākṣa: (Kon) Raisins or grapes. From *drākṣā* (San).

drishti: (Kon) Evil eye. From *dṛṣṭidoṣa* (San). Also called *dṛṣṭi* (Kon).

dṛṣṭa: (Kon, San) Seen; known.

durbuddhi: (Kon, San) Bad habits.

dvaitam: (San) Duality or dualism in Hindu philosopy, which asserts that the supreme soul, *Brahman*, and the individual soul, ***Ātman***, are different. *Also called dvaita* (San).

dvija: (San) Twice-born—that is, priests, warriors, and traders—who have gone through the sacred thread or initiation ceremony (***upanayana*** or ***mūñji***), which is considered as their second birth.

ḍabbi: (Kon) Piggy bank.

eka (Kon, San) One.

emblems of Lord Viṣṇu: Four in number: ***śaṅkha*** (conch shell), ***cakra*** (discus), ***gadā*** (mace), and ***padma*** (lotus).

entropy: A concept from physics. Spontaneous or natural processes involve a dispersal of energy from a localized to a dispersed state. Such processes take place without the involvement of an external agency. An example is the cooling of a hot object with the transfer of its thermal energy to the surrounding air molecules. Entropy measures such energy dispersal at a specific temperature. Energy dispersal results in the degradation of the quality of energy as measured by its ability to do mechanical work. High-quality energy has low entropy and can deliver more mechanical work. Ultimately, the universe will reach an equilibrium state of maximum entropy from which no work can be extracted.

gadā: (Kon, San) The mace, which is one of the emblems of **Śrī Viṣṇu**. The other emblems are ***cakra*** (the discus), ***śaṅkha*** (the conch shell), and ***padma*** (the lotus).

galāṭo: (Kon) Hubbub.

gammata: (Kon) Jubilation, good times in general.

Gaṇa: (Kon, San) Troop of demigods considered to be attendants of Lord Śiva, under the leadership of Lord Gaṇeśa or Gaṇapati.

Gaṇahoma: (Kon, San) A sacrificial rite to propitiate all the ***Gaṇa***.

garbhagṛaha: (Kon, San) Innermost sanctum of a temple where the sacred images are installed.

garbhādhāna: (Kon, San) Impregnation. *See* rite 1 in Appendix 5, "Hindu Rites of Passage."

Garuḍa Purāṇa: (Kon, San) One of the sacred books of Hindus, recited as part of the funeral rites in the period following death and the final obsequies on the thirteenth day. *Pretakalpa*, or rites of the dead, a section of the book that gives details of what the deceased or departed (*preta*) can expect to find in the next world, is used for this purpose.

Garuḍa rekho: (Kon) Garuda's line. Hindu folklore tells us that people with this line on their palms can handle live cobras without being bitten. From *Garuḍa rekha* (San).

Gauḍa Deśa: (Kon, San) Bengal.

gāddyā mēri: (Kon) Boundary of a field usually raised above the level of the field and used as a footpath. From *gaddeya mēre* (Kan).

gālboṭṭu āni nāma: (Kon) One dot of collyrium on each cheek, ***gālboṭṭu***, and a collyrium mark, ***nāma***, on the forehead of a baby, applied to ward off the evil eye.

gāndha: (Kon) Sandalwood paste given as ***prasāda***, or grace, when a person visits a Hindu temple. From *gandha* (San). It is customary to give a small ball of sandalwood paste (*gāndhā gūḷi*).

Gāvaḍā: (Kon) *See* **Gāvḍo**.

Gāvḍo: (Kon) Aborigines of Goa. *Also called* **Gāvaḍā** (Kon), **Kuṇabī** (Kon), and **Velip** (Kon).

gāvṁkar: (Kon) Maker of village or belonging to a village. *See* ***gāvṁkārī*** for the context and the technical sense in which the term was used in Goa.

gāvṁkārī: (Kon) System of village cooperative agricultural and welfare associations in Goa formed by the lineal descendants of the original settlers in a village. *Also*, the name of such a council. They were renamed *communidades* under the Portuguese regime and called community councils.

gāvũ: (Kon) Village, hamlet, community; a person's native place, where his or her family has lived in the recent past. From *grāma* (San). Also called *gāvuṁ* (Kon).

Gāyatrī: (Kon, San) A very sacred verse, Ṛgveda 3.62.10, to the Sun, Savitṛ, by the sage Viśvāmitra, son of Gāthī, recited at the morning and evening prayers. Also called Sāvitrī (Kon, San). *Also* a Vedic meter.

gershi: (Kon) Winnowing basket; usually lined with cloth and used as a bassinet for a newborn.

gēṇi: (Kon, Kan) Rent.

ghara bharāvaṇi: (Kon) Formal entry of the bride into her husband's home. *See* ***gṛhapraveśa***.

gharjāvāyī: (Kon) In-house son-in-law, or a son-in-law who has overstayed his welcome with the in-laws.

ghaśi: (Kon) A Konkani dish.

ghāṇṭa: (Kon) Bell usually made of bronze, sounded as part of Hindu worship. From *ghaṇṭā* (San).
ghāṇyānco: (Kon) Oil presser.
ghoṇā: (Kon) Older baby who still wants to act like a much younger one and does not want to grow up.
ghosāḷẽ: (Kon) Ribbed gourd (*Luffa acutangula*).
ghuṭṭu: (Kon) Secret. From *gūḍha* (San).
goḍḍā rulāvũ: (Kon) Cream of wheat cooked with jaggery (an unrefined brown sugar).
goḍkoṣta: (Kon) A paste made from a bitter root applied to a mother's nipples to wean a baby.
goḍsẽ: (Kon) Dessert.
goghna: (San) One for whom a cow is killed—that is, a guest. This dictionary meaning conforms to the social custom of the Vedic age, before the prohibition of the slaughter of cattle.
gombeyāṭa: (Kan) Puppetry.
gopicandan: (Kon, San) Yellow clay from Mathura, used in morning and evening worship.
gopūjā: (Kon, San) Worship of Śrī Lakṣmī, goddess of wealth, as represented by cows.
gorovu: (Kon) Cowherd. Also called *goravu* (Kon).
gorũ: (Kon) Cattle.
gotra: (Kon, San) An exogamous clan, usually named after a Vedic sage who is the progenitor of the clan, or a clan totem of pre-Vedic origin. Also, a cow pen. *See* ***pravara***.
gōḍa: (Kon) Brown sugar; jaggery. From *guḍa* (San).
gōvũ: (Kon) Wheat.
grahaṇa: (Kon, San) Eclipse, seizing, grasping.
grahasandhi: (Kon, San) Critical juncture in the life of a person, as determined by a person's horoscope. Some of these are considered to be particularly harmful and need proper expiations or rites, to lessen their bad effects.
grācāru: (Kon) Fate; usually bad luck assumed to be caused by the bad aspects or movements of planets. *From* **grahacāra** (San), "movement of planets." *See* ***nasīb***.
grasthā thañcẽ: (Kon) A **Gauḍa Sārasvat Brāhmaṇa** householder family, compared to a priestly family. They are usually more relaxed about observances of food taboos and rules of ritual purity. From *gṛahasta* (San), "householder." *Also called* *gṛasthā thañcẽ* (Kon) and *gṛhasthā thañcẽ* (Kon). *See also* ***laukika*** and ***vaidika***.
gṛhapraveśa: (Kon, San) Formal entry of the newly married couple into the husband's home. *See* ***ghara bharāvaṇi***.
Gṛhyasūtra: (Kon, San) Domestic canon. They deal with domestic rites and rituals, such as the establishment and maintenance of sacred domestic fires, the

morning and evening oblations, new and full moon sacrifices, sacrifices of cooked food, annual sacrifices, marriage, initiation, birth and related ceremonies, offerings to the **Manes**, and the ceremony of guest reception. The Gauḍa Sārasvat Brāhmaṇa community follows the **Āśvalāyana Gṛhyasūtra**. *See also* **Manes**.

GSB: Gauḍa Sārasvat Brāhmaṇa. *Also* written without diacritics: Gauda Sarasvat Brahmana. The totality of all birth groups, ***jāti,*** that form the GSB cluster or community.

guddo: (Kon) Blow delivered with a closed or clenched fist.

guddo mārco: (Kon) Deliver a blow with a closed or clenched fist.

gumāstu: (Kon) Clerk; accountant. From *gumāśtā* (Per), "agent," "representative," "manager."

gurbiṇī: (Kon) Pregnant woman. From ***gurviṇī*** (San), "a woman heavy with a baby."

gurḍāṇo: (Kon) Pestle; also, a fat roly-poly baby.

gurukula: (Kon, San) Residence of a guru; also a school or college.

guru paraṁpara: (San) Succession or lineage of gurus, usually of a particular monastic establishment (*maṭhu* or *maṭha*) or a lineage.

guru śuśrūṣā: (San) Reverential attendance on one's teacher (guru).

guttu: (Kon, Kan, Tul) Extensive cultivable property.

guttināyā: (Kon, Kan, Tul) Owner of a ***guttu***.

gūḍi: (Kon) Hut or a small hutlike temple. From *kuṭī* (San).

haituka: (San) Skeptic, rationalist.

halvā: (Kon, Ara, Tur) Dessert made from wheat, sugar, and clarified butter, perhaps of Turkish or Arabic origin.

haḷḷentulẽ jena: (Kon) Village folk, supposedly simple and unsophisticated.

hamam: (Tur) Bath.

haridāsa: (Kon, San) God's servant; a person trained to conduct ***harikathā***.

harikathā: (Kon, San) God's stories. A live performance by a ***haridāsa*** of an episode in the Hindu epics (***purāṇas***), accompanied by singing, mime, and exposition of the story.

hasti: (Kon) Elephant. From *hastin* (San).

hattu samastaru: (Kan) Ten prominent people, usually considered a quorum representing the whole community. *See* ***mahājana***.

hāḍa viñcucẽ: (Kon) Collection of bones of the deceased, usually on the third day after cremation and part of the funeral rites. Also called *asthisañcayana* (San).

hāntuḷa: (Kon) Pallet, bed, mattress.

hāppoḷu: (Kon) Thin, circular wafers of dough of black gram (*Vigna mungo*), spices, and salt dried in the sun and served deep-fried and crisp to provide contrast in texture when mixed with rice and curry. Usually, they are red and are pungent or hot. The dough is sometimes mixed with cooked jackfruit, potato, or sweet potato, and the wafers are eaten after deep-frying, as a snack. From *happaḷa* (Kan).

hāsyagāru: (Kon) Comedian. From *hāsyagāra* (Kan) and *hāsya* (San), "jest," "joke," "laughter."

hātti: (Kon) Cubit, equal to the distance between the elbow and the tip of the middle finger, which is usually assumed to be half a yard or 18 inches. From ***hasta*** (San), "cubit," "forearm."

hittala: (Kon) Yard at the back of a house, usually planted with coconut, fruit trees, and flowering shrubs. From *hittalu* (Kan).

hoḍemmā: (Kon) From *hoḍi āmmā* (Kon), "big mother" or "great-grandmother."

hoḍu jāvnu buddhonti jāvkā: (f; Kon) Traditional blessing: "May you live long and be endowed with wise counsel." Also *hoḍu jāvnu buddhontu jāvkā* (m; Kon).

hoḍu māmu: (Kon) Elder uncle.

homa: (Kon, San) Sacrifice. Ceremony offering oblations to the gods by pouring clarified butter into a consecrated fire.

hoona: (Kon) Hot; at a high temperature. From *uṣṇa* (San).

hōṇṭi bhorcẽ: (Kon) Honor bestowed on a ***suvāsinī*** by presenting her with a number of auspicious articles: a coconut with its tuft (***śenḍi***) intact, rice, a blouse piece (*coḷyē khaṇu*), a wooden comb (***dāntuṇi***), a packet of scarlet red powder (***kuṅkuma***), a set of bangles (***kāṅkaṇa***), silver coins, and flowers. The woman so honored receives these in a shallow receptacle made out of the top part of her ***sāri***, or *hōṇṭi*; *bhorcẽ* is the act of filling.

humboru: (Kon) Door sill of the main entrance to a home which is worshipped as a seat of Śrī Lakṣmī. This is the reason why when one crosses a door sill, one makes sure never to touch it with the feet. From *uḍumbara* (San). Also called *hostilu* (Kan).

hummaṇa: (Kon) Liquid at the bottom of a cooking vessel (***kāili***). Also, the essence of a dish, story, or answer to a puzzle.

huththo: (Kon) Anthill. Cobras sometimes inhabit anthills.

iḍḷi: (Kon) Steamed patties of a fermented batter of rice and black gram (***uḍidu***; *Vigna mungo*) or green gram (***mūgu***; *Vigna radiata*). From *iḍli* (Kan).

iskūla: (Kon) School. From *escola* (Port).

iṣṭa devatā: (Kon, San) Favorite god.

īḷ: (San) To praise. Also called *īḍ* (San).

jagali: (Kon, Kan) Veranda.

janma: (Kon, San) Birth.

japa: (Kon, San) Silent or whispered invocation of a prayer or the sacred names of a deity.

jardala: (Kon) Dried apricots.

jaṭkā: (Kon) A light two-wheeled vehicle for two to four people that is drawn by one horse. *See also* ***ṭāṅgā***.

jāti bāṭlo: (Kon) *See* ***bhaṣṭa:*** (Kon).

jauhar: (Hin) Ritual suicide by self-immolation practiced by medieval Rajput women in anticipation of certain defeat and dishonor.

Jayanti: (Kon, San) Day of epiphany of an incarnation of God.

jāṅgentū bebbo ghālco: (Kon) Literally, "inserting a frog in the thigh," a curious, humorous expression of obscure origin describing the sacred thread ceremony (***upanayana*** or ***mūñji***). It may be a reference to the first stirrings of hormones in a teenage boy.

jātakarma: (San) *See* ***bāḷāntiro***.

jānnuvẽ: (Kon) Sacred thread. Also called *yajñopavītam* (San).

jāti: (Kon, San) Birth group. Interdining, marriage, and participating in common social and religious functions are allowed within a birth group.

jāti bātlo: (Kon) Converted to another religion; literally polluted from one's birth group.

jharī: (Kon) A spring of water; a fountain. From *jhara, jharā, jharī* (San). Also called *jhāra* (Kon).

jibbā: (Kon, Ara) Male upper garment, usually of white cotton, with pockets on the side. Also *jubbā* (Ara).

jīrā uddāka: (Kon) Decoction of cumin (*Cuminum cyminum*) seeds (***jīra***) flavored with jaggery (brown sugar) and taken with or without milk as a medicine or as a hot beverage before the advent of tea and coffee.

jīvī kaḍgi: (Kon) Breadfruit (*Artocarpus altilis*); literally, "green jackfruit."

jñāti: (Kon, San) All paternal kinsmen.

joḍo: (Kon) Pair of white **dhoti** (***puḍvẽ***) worn by men.

joiṣi: (Kon) Astronomer or astrologer. From *jyotiṣa* (San).

junshi: (Jap) Ritual suicide by a samurai warrior, with his wife, to follow his liege lord in death.

kaḍgi: (Kon) Unripe jackfruit (*Artocarpus heterophyllus*) that is not fully mature.

kalayi: (Kon) Tin; the wash of tin given to copper vessels to prevent verdigris from forming. From *kastīram* (San), "tin." Also called *kalāyi* (Kon), *kalāya* (Kan), and *kalāyi* (Kan).

kalā: (Kon, San) Aspect; form; also, any practical mechanical or fine art included in the list of the sixty-four arts, such as music and dancing, traditionally described in Hindu culture.

kalāvanta: (Kon) Upper or superior tier of ***devadāsī***, who are trained in singing and dancing, are usually literate, and are dedicated to temple service. Probably derived from *kalāvat* (San), "versed in the arts," usually sixty-four in the Hindu tradition. *See* ***bhāvin***.

kalivarjya: (San) Forbidden in the Kali age (i.e., the present times).

Kali Yuga: (San) Age of Kali; the present; age of strife; age of iron. It is considered the worst of the four ages in Hindu chronology: Kṛta (1,728,000 years), Treta (1,296,000 years), Dvāpara (864,000 years), and Kali (432,000 years). There is supposed to be a progressive physical and moral deterioration of humankind in going from the "golden age" of Kṛta to the "iron age" of Kali. These are also the ancient names, in order, of four throws of a die, with four (Kṛta) being the best and one (Kali) being the worst.

kaḷambi: (Kon) Large wooden chest with a hinged lid, used to store valuables. The head of a household would spread his pallet on top to use it as a bed. The key to the chest would be looped on his sacred thread (***jānnuve*** or *yajñopavītam*) as a symbol of authority.

kamalā phūla: (Kon) Lotus (*Nelumbo nucifera*).

kamaṇḍalu: (Kon, San) Ascetic's waterpot, earthenware or wooden.

kanyādāna: (Kon, San) Formal act of giving away the bride, by the bride's parents or guardian, as a gift to the groom.

kaṅkaṇa: (Kon, San) Bracelet.

kapāṭa: (Kon) Cupboard. Perhaps from *kapāṭam* (San), "door panel."

karbevu: (Kon) Curry leaf (*Murraya koenigii*); sweet neem leaf. From kari bēvu (Kan).

karma: (Kon) Action, work, deed, fate. The certain consequences of acts done in this or previous lives, experienced in this life. From *karman* (San).

karmāṅga: (San) Procedures of religious rites including sacrifices.

karṇavedha: (San) *See* ***cerdā kānu vinduco*** (Kon).

kaṣāyu: (Kon) Decoction of herbs and roots of various kinds, flavored with black pepper, jaggery (brown sugar) or sugar, and cardamom, taken with or without milk as a medicine, tonic, or hot beverage. From *kaṣāyam* (San).

kaṭhīṇa: (Kon) Hard, violent, cruel, ruthless, tough; usually used in reference to a person's nature or horoscope. From *kaṭhina* (San).

kāḍḍi: (Kon) Pencil for writing on a slate.

kāili: (Kon) A hemispherical cooking vessel of iron or some other metal that resembles a Chinese wok.

kāiḷo: (Kon) Crow. Plural: *kāiḷe*. From *kāka* (San).

kājjaḷa: (Kon) Collyrium applied to the eyelashes or eyelids medicinally, or to enhance beauty. From *kajjalam* (San).

kāju: (Kon) Cashew apple (*Anacardium occidentale*). *From caju* (Port).

kājju bī: (Kon) Mature cashew nut. *See* ***bibbo***.

Kāla Bhairava: (Kon, San) One of the demigods considered an attendant of Lord Śiva and who manifests himself through the medium of the oracle at the Mulki temple.

kāmā ceḍū: (Kon) Maid who washes clothes, dishes, cleans the house, etc.
Kāma dahana: (San) Symbolic burning of the god of love, Kāma.
kāmbrānco: (Kon) Carpenter.
kāmya: (San) Optional; a term usually applied to religious rites.
kāṇi: (Kon) Story. From *kahānī* (Hin).
kāṅkaṇa: (Kon) Bracelet, bangles. From *kaṅkaṇa* (San).
kānūna: (Kon) Law; also argumentative, smart-alecky talk. From *kānūn* (Ara, Tur).
kāpi: (Kon) Coffee; *formerly called* **bunnā uddāka**. From *bunn* (Ara), "coffee bean."
kāppaḍa: (Kon) Piece of cloth; *also* a ***sāri***. From *karpaṭa* (San).
kāppḍā kuḍko: (Kon) Remnants of an old ***sāri*** worn while doing housework. Short form: *kuḍko* (Kon). *From kuḍko* (Kon), "piece."
kārṇike devu: (Kon) Deity who answers the prayers of his or her devotees; hence, a powerful deity.
kāsa: (Kon) The end or hem of a lower garment, which, after it is properly gathered in a pleat, is taken between the legs and round the body and is tucked into the waistband at the back. This style of wearing a ***sāri*** is called *sakaccha* ("with a tuck"). A ***sāri*** worn in this style has to be 18 ***hātti*** (9 yards) long. The shorter version is worn *vikaccha* (without a tuck) and is 12 ***hātti*** (6 yards long). A man's **dhoti** worn with tucks is called ***pañcakāsa*** because it is tucked in at five places. It is 8 to 9 ***hātti*** (4 to 4.5 yards) long and worn in a different style. This is a style of dress used mostly at more formal or religious occasions. From *kakṣā, kaccha, kacchaṭikā*, and *kacchāṭī* (San). *See* ***pañcakāsa***.
kāśā divli: (Kon) Bronze lamp.
kāśẽ: (Kon) Bronze. From *kāś* (San), "to shine."
Kāśi Maṭha: (Kon) One of the monastic lineages to which the Gauḍa Sārasvat Brāhmaṇa owe allegiance.
Kāśī *voccẽ:* (Kon) Going to Kāśī or Vārāṇasī. This is a part of the Hindu wedding ceremony in which the bridegroom is supposed to go to Kāśī for higher studies and is importuned on the way, by the bride's father, to go with him to marry his daughter. Also called Kāśī *yātrā* (San).
kāṭṭẽ: (Kon) *See* ***bāyncẽ āḍḍẽ***.
keḷẽ: (Kon) Banana. From *kadalī* (San).
keśānta: (San) Cutting of hair and first shaving of beard. *See* rite 13 in Appendix 5, "Hindu Rites of Passage"; not usually observed now.
khabbara: (Kon) News. From *khabar* (Ara, Per).
khaḍe sākkara: (Kon) Rock sugar.
khaḍga: (Kon, San) Sword.
Khaḍga Rāvaṇu: (Kon) Rāvaṇā brandishing a sword; a very angry person, likely to chop off heads.

khādvā: (Kon) Wooden footwear consisting of a flat platform with a small peg up front, which is grasped between the big and second toes. Worn by those for whom leather footwear is ritually unclean.

khājjuru: (Kon) Dates (*Phoenix dactylifera*) dried partially, with a soft, moist, sticky skin. From *kharjūra* (San).

khārooka: (Kon) Dates dried fully, with a hard, dry, wrinkled skin.

kheḷu: (Kon) Play. Also used for field drama. *Also called* **bayalāṭa** (Kan) or ***yakṣagāna*** (Kan, San).

khoroju: (Kon) "That which itches." Dermatitis, or inflammation of the skin with redness, itching, pus-filled blisters, swelling, scabbing, and scaling.

kīrlu: (Kon) Tender bamboo shoots eaten freshly cooked or pickled.

koddela: (Kon) A Konkani dish.

koḍkẽ: (Kon) Cowshed.

koḷmbi: (Kon) Vessel usually made of a single piece of wood and used for mixing various types of dough, or beaten rice (***phovu***), with grated coconut (***sōyi***), jaggery (brown sugar), etc.

koḷvindūru: (Kon) Bandicoot; a big wild rat that can attack viciously if cornered.

kriyā: (Kon) Last funeral rites. *See* rite 16 in Appendix 5, "Hindu Rites of Passage." *From* **antyakriyā** (San).

kṛṣṇājinā pāṭṭo: (Kon) One of the emblems, a club or strip of black antelope skin mounted on a gold handle, held in the right hand by the oracle at the Mulki temple. *See* ***pāṭṭo-mudrā***.

Kṣatriya: (Kon, San) Warrior, second of the fourfold ***varṇa*** system of the Hindu religious hierarchy.

kuḍko: (Kon) Piece; also, piece of an old ***sāri*** usually worn by women at home while doing household work.

kula devatā: (Kon, San) Family deity.

kuḷār: (Kon) Parental home of a woman.

kuḷāvi: (Kon) Devotees of a particular family deity.

kuḷitu: (Kon) Horse gram (*Macrotyloma uniflorum*). From *kulattha* (San).

kuḷtā kaḍi: (Kon) Dark brown liquid left over after cooking horse gram.

kumārī: (Kon, San) Maiden, virgin.

kumbārānco: (Kon) Potter. Also called *kumbrānco* (Kon).

kumbha: (Kon, San) Water pitcher, jar.

kumbhārati: (San) ***Ārati*** mounted on a water pitcher and customarily carried and waved by a ***devadāsī***. *See* *Nityasumaṅgalī: Devadasi Tradition in South India*, by Saskia C. Kersenboom-Story (1987), for details of its ritual significance.

kumuda: (San) White water lily.

Kuṇabī: (Kon) *See* **Gāvḍo**.

Kuṇḍodhara Bhuta: (Kon, San) An ogre; literally, "a spirit with a pit for a stomach."

kuṅkuma: (Kon, San) Scarlet red powder applied by women to the ***tīḷo***, the auspicious beauty spot on their forehead.
kurbarānco: (Kon) Shepherd.
kuṭumba: (Kon, San) Family.
kuvāḷẽ: (Kon) Ash gourd (*Benincasa hispida*).

labān: (Ara) yoghurt.
lakṣa dīpa: (Kon, San) 100,000 lights.
laukika: (Kon, San) Secular. *See also* **bhaṭṭā thañcẽ** (Kon).
lābhādāyada seve: (Kan) Service or offerings from one's profits.
lālki: (Kon) Conveyance used to take the image of a deity in procession. It is an eight-sided wooden structure with eight pillars and a dome, covered with silver plating and carried on the shoulders of devotees as part of the temple festivities.
lāmbocẽ: (Kon) Hanging, usually from a ceiling.
lāṭi: (Kon) Indigenous irrigation device in vogue before the advent of electric pumps. It consisted of a long wooden beam, supported on a fulcrum at its center, with a metal bucket suspended from a bamboo at one end and a rope at the other. It was operated by two people. One person guided a metal bucket to dip it into a well and collect water. The second person would then jump into a shallow pit, grasping the rope, thus bringing up the full bucket of water, which was emptied into a channel to irrigate a field or a garden. It was labor intensive and primitive but effective.
lāyye homa: (Kon) Sacrifice of parched rice, *lāyi*, offered by a new bride as part of a wedding ceremony. From *lajjā homa* (San).
līlā: (Kon, San) Play, sport.
Lokāyata: (San) World-directed; a materialist and a follower of the philosopher **Cārvāka**.
lośṇe phaṇṇa: (Kon) Garlic seasoning, normally forbidden to priestly families. From *laśuna* (San), "garlic."
luṅgi: (Kon) ***Muṇḍa*** with a colored pattern.

macvo: (Kon) Wooden sailing boat used in coastal trade on the west coast of India. These boats were approximately 60 feet long, with a keel of 33 feet, a beam of 15 feet, a depth of 9 feet, and a bow or prow of 35 feet, with two masts spaced about 25 feet apart and carrying triangular sails. The boats were made of wooden planks sewed together with coconut-fiber yarn (de Bragança Pereira 2008, 90–95). From *machavā* (Hin). Also called *muchuvo* (Goan Kon).
madhucandra: (Kon, Kan, San) Honeymoon. The term is a literal translation, now in vogue, of the English word.

madhuparka: (Kon, San) Honey mixture; a mixture of yoghurt, honey, etc., offered to an honored guest as part of a formal welcome. For example, it is offered by the father of the bride to the groom as part of a wedding ceremony.
maggi: (Kon, Kan) Multiplication tables.
mahanta: (San) Head of a temple or monastery.
mahājana: (Kon, San) Prominent people. Called *mazania* by the Portuguese in Goa, this was a cooperative association with responsibility for the care, management, and maintenance of village Hindu temples. *See* ***hattu samastaru***.
mahāpātaka: (Kon, San) The five major sins: killing a priest, drinking intoxicants, stealing, violating a teacher's marriage bed, or being associated with any of those sinners.
Manes: (Lat) Ancestors who have been venerated and propitiated with proper funeral rites. On death, a person becomes a *preta* ("the departed") with many unfulfilled desires and strong attachments to this world and thus potentially malevolent to the living. After the performance of funeral rites, the *preta* is promoted to join the august company of the *pitara* ("ancestors"), who are always benevolent to their descendants.
mantra: (Kon, San) Sacred text or prayer. Also called *mantra* (Eng).
mantra mudrādhāraṇa: (Kon) Purification ceremony conducted periodically by the head of a monastic lineage for the benefit of his devotees. Metal representations of the emblems of Śrī Viṣṇu—***śaṅkha***, ***cakra***, ***gadā***, and ***padma***—are heated in embers and lightly applied to different parts of the arms and chest of devotees, leaving a mark on the skin that disappears after a time.
mantravādu: (Kon) Sorcery.
Manu Dharmaśāstra: (Kon, San) Code of law according to Manu.
maṇḍala: (Kon, San) Division (book or chapter) of the *Ṛgveda*; there are ten of these.
maṅgaḷa sūtra: (Kon) Auspicious thread or cord worn by a married woman whose husband is alive. It is a piece of jewelry tied by the groom round the bride's neck as part of a wedding ceremony. *From maṅgala sūtra* (San).
maṭha: (Kon, San) Monastery. One of the monastic lineages to which the Gauḍa Sārasvat Brāhmaṇa owe allegiance and by which they are guided in matters of religion.
maṭhādhipati: (Kon, San) Head of a monastery; the final arbiter in matters of religion for his disciples.
mazania: (Port) Village cooperative association of the founders of Hindu temples or their descendants, responsible for the care, maintenance, and management of local Hindu temples in Goa; a Portuguese version of ***mahājana***.
māḍḍyā kāṭṭẽ: (Kon) Enclosure round a coconut tree.
māhpūjā: (Kon) Principal ceremony of worship in a temple, usually at midday. From *mahāpūjā* (San).

māḷi: (Kon) A floor above the ground floor; attic.

mānastambha: (Kon, Kan) Granite pillar erected in front of a Jain temple or monastery.

māndri: (Kon) Plaited rush or grass mat.

māñco: (Kon) Bedstead, usually wooden.

māṇayī: (Kon) Low wooden seat for sitting cross-legged on the floor while performing religious rites or eating.

māṇṭovu: (Kon) A temporary structure, or pandal, erected especially for an ***upanayana*** or a wedding.

māṇṭvi: (Kon) Small eight-sided decorated enclosure, open on all sides, with a canopy supported by eight pillars, in which all rites for a sacred thread ceremony (***upanayana*** or ***mūñji***) or wedding are conducted. From *maṇḍapa* (San).

māshterni: (Kon) Female teacher. From *master* (Eng), meaning "teacher."

māshtru: (Kon) Male teacher. From *master* (Eng), meaning "teacher."

māsika śrāddha: (San) Monthly offerings to the **Manes**. *See* **Manes**.

māsolu: (Kon) Mixture of grated coconut (***sōyi***) and other spices ground to a fine consistency; which spices are included depends on the particular dish. From *masālā* (Hin, Per), "spices," "condiments."

mātyāri hātu kāṇu: (Kon) The act of blessing and the removal of any curse by waving the hand over the head.

meeṭa uvāḷcē: (Kon) Pinch of salt waved over a baby's head and then consigned to the kitchen fire to ward off the evil eye.

mekhalā: (San) Belt, girdle; the triple girdle worn by the "twice-born" at religious functions.

melleḷī: (Kon) The dead who have returned to haunt the living.

meḷā-mēḷi: (Kon) General consonance or dissonance of a boy's and a girl's horoscopes.

mēṇa: (Kon) Sticky wax, usually from a jackfruit.

mhālgaḍyālē ghara: (Kon) Ancestral home.

mhārā̃: (Kon) Dalits, formerly called untouchables.

mhāri: (Kon) Dalit woman, formerly called untouchable.

mhāru: (Kon) Dalit man, formerly called untouchable.

mirsāṅga: (Kon) Chilies. *See also* ***tarni mirsāṅga*** (Kon) and ***sukkhi mirsāṅga*** (Kon).

Mitākṣarā: (San) Name of a commentary on the codes of law, Yājñavalkya Smṛti, by Vijñāneśvara. It has been recognized as the paramount authority in several aspects of Hindu law, representing the essence of its foundations, and is applicable all over India except in Assam and Bengal, where **Dāyābhāga** prevails. In general, this code is less favorable to widows and their inheritance of property than is the **Dāyābhāga**. *See* **Dāyābhāga**.

mleccha: (Kon, San) Barbarian, foreigner, outcast.

mokṣa: (Kon, San) Liberation; release, usually from the cycle of birth and death.

moktesoru: (Kon) Leader of a community; chief officer; trustee of temple management. From *mukhtasar* (Ara). Also called *moktēsara (Kan, Hin).*

mōḍi: (Kon, Kan) Cursive script, beautiful to look at but sometimes difficult to read unless one is properly trained.

mudrā: (Kon, San) Insignia of office. *See* **bettā mudrā.**

muḍo: (Kon) Measure of rice; 42 seers, or 40 kilograms. Name of a spheroidal container of straw about 3 feet in diameter, used to transport rice. These are rarely seen today because they have been replaced by jute bags. From *muḍi* (Kan). Also called *mūḍo* (Kon).

mukha: (Kon, San) Face, or an image of a face.

mukti: (Kon, San) Release; liberation.

muṇḍa: (Kon) Rectangular lightweight piece of cloth, 4 to 4.5 ***hātti*** (cubits) long, or about 2 yards long, worn by men as leisure wear from the waist to the ankles. From *muṇḍita* (San), "cut," because a ***muṇḍa*** is a cut ***veṣṭi***.

muṇḍappā: (Kon, Kan) A variety of mango.

muttaide: (Kan) Woman whose husband is living.

muṭṭāsa: (Kon) Quasi-magical "women's remedy," usually tried when other remedies fail.

mūgu: (Kon) Green gram (*Vigna radiata*), or mung beans used to make bean sprouts. From *mung* (Hin).

mūḷi: (Kon) Roofing thatch. Also called *muḷye taṇa* (Kon).

mūñji: (Kon) Popular name for the sacred thread ceremony. The name is derived from the girdle, *muñja*, of sacred grass, with which the boy is invested as part of the ceremony. *From muñjābandhanam* (San). *Also called* **upanayana**. *See* rite 11 in Appendix 5, "Hindu Rites of Passage."

mysurpāk: (Kon) Dessert made with chickpea flour, sugar, and clarified butter. Perhaps the word is derived from *miśrapāk* (San).

naḍo: (Kon) Vestibule or main entrance to a temple bounded on either side by a raised platform, ***sāḷa*** (Kon), which runs round the inner wall of the main building.

naḷi: (Kon) Tube.

nasīb: (Kon, Ara) Fate; luck.

nasrāṇi: (Kon) Most probably a Konkani version of *Nazarene*, meaning a Christian. Also, it is the name of the St. Thomas Christians, or Syrian-Malabar Christians, of Kerala. It also has a pejorative meaning: a dirty, filthy, smelly, unkempt person.

nattu: (Kon, Kan) Old-fashioned nose ornament, usually worn through a hole in one or both of the nostrils or through the septum. Nose ornaments are of Semitic origin and were not known in India before contacts with Arabs. From *nath* (Hin).

navagraha: (Kon) Nine "planets"; the sun and moon, Mars, Mercury, Jupiter, Venus, Saturn, and the ascending and descending nodes of the moon's orbit where it intersects the ecliptic—Rāhu, Ketu. *From navagrahāha* (San).
navagrahā homu: (Kon) Sacrifice to the nine planets. From navagraha homa (San).
navo: (Kon) Ship. From *nave, navio* (Port).
nāga: (Kon, San) Serpent, cobra.
nāga darśaṇa: (Kon) Ceremony in which a medium possessed by the spirit of Nāga answers questions from devotees regarding their personal problems and prescribes solutions.
nāgakanyakā: (San) Serpent maiden or a medium possessed by the spirit of a serpent maiden.
nāgamaṇḍala: (Kon, Kan) Ritual drawing and or the accompanying ceremony of Nāga worship.
nāgapātri: (Kon) Medium possessed by the Spirit of Nāga.
nāgasvaram: (San, Tam) A South Indian oboe-like wind instrument.
nāgatīrtha: (Kon, San) Pond sacred to and usually inhabited by cobras.
nāgā phāttoru: (Kon) Stone dedicated to Nāga and held sacred by its devotees.
nāma: (Kon) Mark, sign, token that depends on a person's communal affiliation. A vertical U-shaped line of ***gopicandan*** drawn in the center of the forehead for **Vaiṣṇava** men as part of daily worship (***sandhi***). **Śaiva** have horizontal lines on the forehead. Also, a single vertical line of collyrium in the center of a baby's forehead, drawn to ward off the evil eye. From *nāman* (San).
nāmakaraṇa: (San) *See* ***cerdā nāvā ghālce*** (Kon).
nānkā boṭṭu: (Kon) Modern nose ornament, usually worn through a hole in one or both of the nostrils.
nāñcaṇo: (Kon) Finger millets, also called African millets (*Eleusine coracana*), used to prepare baby food (*bōḷu*) and mixed with wheat about fifty-fifty. From *nācaṇā, nācaṇī* (Mar). *Also called* **rāgi** (Kan).
nāñcaṇyā gūḷi: (Kon) Sweets prepared with roasted and ground millets, jaggery (brown sugar), and spices.
nārlā rooku: (Kon) Coconut palm.
nārlu keḷē: (Kon) Offering, taken to a temple, of a whole coconut with its tuft intact (*nārlu*), plus five, seven, or nine ripe bananas (***keḷe***) and flowers. After these are offered to the deity, the flowers are used to decorate the sacred image. The coconut is split into two, and the tip of one of the bananas is opened as symbolic offering to the deity. The coconut, bananas, some sandalwood paste (***gāndha***), and a few flowers offered to the deity are returned to the devotee as ***prasāda***, or grace.
nāstika: (Kon, San) Denier, unbeliever; one who denies the authority of the Vedas and the existence of a creator and an afterlife.
nāti: (Kon) Granddaughter.

nāttu: (Kon) Grandson.

nāṭak: (Kon, Kan, San) Drama.

nhāṇi: (Kon) Bathroom.

nhāṇyẽ māddāḷẽ: (Kon) Rectangular pit, a few feet on each side, in a bathroom, in which the bather stands while bathing.

nirvāṇam: (San) Extinction, dissolution, death.

niścaya tāmbūla: (Kon) Engagement.

niṣkramaṇa: (San) *See* ***cerdā bhairi horcẽ*** (Kon).

nitya: (San) Obligatory, when applied to religious rites.

nivedyu: (Kon) Offerings of eatables to a deity. From *naivedyam* (San).

noṇcẽ: (Kon) Pickles. Most probably from *lavaṇāncẽ* (Kon), "salty," from *lavaṇa* (San), "salt."

noṇcā khoḷu: (Kon) The liquid in which pickles (***noṇcẽ***) are preserved and stored; usually quite piquant.

nureochiba: (Jap) Wet leaf or leaves. Term applied to retired Japanese husbands who want to "help" their wives by making themselves useful around the house and are difficult to get rid of, just as it is difficult to scrape off a wet leaf from the pavement.

omkāra: (Kon, San) Sacred syllable, *AUM*.

paana: (Kon) Pieces of areca nut with betel leaves (*Piper betle*), slaked lime, and spices offered on ceremonial occasions or used as a palate freshener. Also called *tāmbūlam* (San), *phaḍpāna* (Kon), and *phoḍi pāna* (Kon). *See* ***vīḍo***, ***pāna***.

paccaḍi: (Kon) Salad made from fresh, tender, sour mango, or any other sour fruit or vegetable.

padma: (Kon, San) The lotus, which is one of the emblems of Śrī Viṣṇu. The other emblems are ***cakra*** (the discus), ***gadā*** (the mace), and ***śaṅkha*** (the conch shell) (Kon, San).

paika: (Kon) Family name.

pakṣa: (Kon, San) Half of a lunar month.

pallaṅga: (Kon) Bed, usually with rich elaborate woodwork and decorations. From *palyaṅka* (San).

panḍal: (Tam) Temporary canopy of bamboo and woven coconut fronds erected specially for a function like a wedding.

pañcagavya: (Kon, San) Collectively, the five products of a cow—milk, curds, ghee butter, urine, and dung—that are used in worship and in daily life.

pañckadāyī: (Kon) Mixture of beaten rice (***phovu***), brown sugar (***gōḍa***), grated coconut (***sōyi***), cardamom, and sometimes a few other roast grains of *mūng* (mung) or *caṇā* (Bengal gram), usually offered to a deity.

pañcakāsa: (Kon) Style of wearing a **dhoti** on more formal occasions, using five (***pañca***) tucks (***kāsa***). The **dhoti** is 4 to 4.5 yards long, or about twice the length of a standard ***muṇḍa***. The five tucks are as follows: right; left; pleated and in front; loose front end tucked in front; and the remaining part pleated, taken between the legs, and tucked at the back. This description is not a complete explanation of how to wear a **dhoti** in this style; ask someone who knows how to do it properly to demonstrate it. *See* ***kāsa***.

pañcādikā: (Kon) Gossip.

pañcāṅga: (Kon, San) Almanac.

pañcāṅga āikucẽ: (Kon) Listening to the recitation of the highlights of the almanac, usually on New Year's Day. From *pañcāṅga śravaṇam* (San).

pañcāyiti paisalu: (Kon, Kan) Arbitration settlement. From *phaisla* (Ara), "settlement."

paṇḍā: (Kon, Hin) Priests who specialize in the performance of religious rites for visiting pilgrims at sacred sites, such as Kāśī.

papash phaḷa: (Kon) Papaya (*Carica papaya*).

parab: (Kon) Festival. From *parvan* (San).

paraṁpara: (San) Lineage; succession.

parcārike bhaṭṭu: (Kon) Assistant priest who works in the space just outside the inner sanctum of a temple. He does not conduct the ceremony of worship.

pariṣad: (Kon, San) Assembly, meeting, council.

parkaṭa: (Kon) Old, ragged, patched garment. The Konkani word is formed by transposition of parts of the Sanskrit original, a process called metathesis. Also called *karpaṭa* (San).

paryāya: (Kon, San) Regular recurrence, turn, succession. Hereditary right for conducting daily worship and other rites, at a temple for a specific number of years, inherited by a family of priests, or the head of a religious monastery. Also called *paryāyu* (Kon).

pativratā: (Kon, San) Devoted, faithful, loyal wife.

pācci: (Kon) Aunt.

pāje kāṭṭẽ: (Kon) Area leading to the temple precincts in Mulki with a steep slope to the east.

pālki: (Kon) Palanquin. Conveyance used to carry an image of a deity in procession. It is a wooden platform suspended from an omega-shaped support, covered with silver or gold plate, decorated with silk tassels, and carried on the shoulders of devotees as part of temple festivities. From *paryaṅka* (San). Also called *pālaṅki* (Kon).

pāḷḷẽ: (Kon) Cradle.

pāḷḷyāntũ ghālcẽ: (Kon) Cradling ceremony, celebrated along with ***cerdā nāvā ghālce***. *See* rite 5 in Appendix 5, "Hindu Rites of Passage."

pāmāji: (Kon) Moss.

pāna: (Kon) Also called *phaḍpāna.*

pāna ghālcẽ: (Kon) Banana leaves set out in rows for people to eat from at a communal feast.

pānaka: (Kon) Beverage usually made of lemons, sugar or jaggery (brown sugar), cadamom, pepper, etc. From *pānakam* (San).

pāṅgurcẽ: (Kon) Coverlet. Also called *pāṅgurcẽ vaali* or *voli.*

pāṅkti: (Kon) Row; people sitting in a row at a communal feast. From *paṅkti* (San).

pāppoḍu: (Kon) Thin circular wafers of dough made from black gram (*Vigna mungo*), spices, and salt that are dried in the sun and served deep-fried and crisp to provide contrast in texture when mixed with rice and curry. Usually light yellow in color and salty. Also called *pāpaḍ* (Mar) and *pappaḷa* (Kan).

pārāyi: (Kon) A crowbar.

pāsponosu: (Kon) Jungle jackfruit (*Artocarpus pubescens Willd*), with a fruit much smaller than jackfruit, about 6 to 9 inches in diameter. Called *hebbalasu* (Kan).

pāṣaṇḍa: (San) Heretic, unbeliever.

pāṭhaśāla: (Kon, San) School, college.

pāṭṭo: (Kon) A club or strip of black antelope skin mounted on a gold handle that forms the emblem, ***pāṭṭo-mudrā***, of the oracle at Mulki temple. From *paṭṭa* (San).

pāṭṭo-mudrā: (Kon) Emblem of the oracle at the Mulki temple.

pāṭṭyā toḍopu: (Kon) Silk **dhoti** of deep scarlet color with a border of gold thread worn on ceremonial occassions, such as by the ***darśaṇā pātri***. *From paṭṭa* (San), "silk."

pāyampodcẽ: (Kon) A bow to a deity or a sacred person with hands joined in prayer.

pāyamponu rābtā: (Kon) Standing still with hands joined in prayer.

pāyu dorcẽ: (Kon) Showing respect by touching the feet of elders or a worthy person. The person so honored usually responds by saying in Konkani, "*Devu barẽ koro*," or "May God bless." From *pādasevā* (San).

peḍa: (Kon) *See* ***rānye peḍi***.

peja: (Kon) Rice gruel; a comfort food. From *peyā* (San).

peja-mīṭa: (Kon) Rice gruel and salt; considered the absolute minimum for survival, usually because of adverse circumstances.

pejje jevaṇa: (Kon) Meal of rice gruel (***peja***) and pickles (***nonce***) after breakfast and before lunch, usually fed to little children before they go to school. If it is a ceremonial meal for an honored guest, there will be many accompanying dishes (*rāndayo*).

peṇṭa: (Kon) Emporium, mart, where most shops are located. From *pēṭe* (Kan).

pera: (Kon, Por) Guava fruit (*Psidium guajava*).

pēṇḍi: (Kon) Oil cake; residue of seeds/nuts pressed for oil and used as cattle feed. From *piṇyāka* (San).
peṭnoḷi: (Kon) Air gun formed from a hollow bamboo tube with a plunger at one end, and a conical tin funnel as a sound amplifier at the other, used for shooting green berries (***teppaḷa***).
phala: (Kon, San) Fruit in general.
phaḷāru: (Kon) Literally, "fruit meal"; in practice, a meal without rice. From *phalāhāra* (San).
phaṇṇa: (Kon) Seasoning for a dish; usually added immediately before serving it.
phaṇṇa ghālcẽ: (Kon) Applying seasoning. The more idiomatic usage means adding more mischief intentionally to an already tense situation to make it explosive.
phaṇṇā davlo: (Kon) Open ladle used for seasoning.
phaṇṇā upkari: (Kon) A Konkani dish using fresh green vegetables, usually including long beans (*āḷsando*) and snake gourd (*poḍḍāḷẽ*) or ribbed gourd (*ghosāḷẽ*).
pharaṅgi: (Kon) European. Possibly derived from *firaṅgi* (Hin), a word referring to Indian-born Portuguese and later any European.
pharṅge: (Kon) Syphilis. Possibly derived from ***pharaṅgi***, the Konkani term for Europeans, who are supposed to have introduced syphilis into India.
phāṭi: (Kon) Back.
phāṭṭiri: (Kon) On the back.
phāṭṭiri guddo mārco: (Kon) To deliver a blow on the back with a clenched fist.
phāttoru: (Kon) Rock, stone. From *prastara* (San).
phoppaḷa: (Kon) Areca nut (*Areca catechu*). Pieces of the areca nut that have been dehusked and dried are called *phoḍi*.
phoppḷā phula: (Kon) White flowers of the areca nut palm. Also called *bhingāru* (Kon).
phoppḷā rooku: (Kon) Areca nut palm (*Areca catechu*).
phovā upkari: (Kon) A mixture of beaten rice, green chillies, coriander leaves, and other spices served as a snack.
phovu: (Kon) Beaten rice.
phugḍi: (Kon) Name of a dance performed by the women of the house on the night of the sixth day after birth ceremonies, or ***saṭṭi*** (Kudva 1978, 286). This custom is no longer observed in most homes. *See also* ***saṭṭi***.
phullaṭi gurbiṇī jevaṇa: (Kon) Feast in honor of a woman, at her first pregnancy.
piṇḍa: (Kon, San) Ball of rice offered to the **Manes**. *See* **Manes**.
piraṅgi: (Kon, Kan) A big gun or cannon. Possibly derived from ***pharaṅgi*** (Kon) and *firaṅgi* (Hin), "European."
pitrã: (Kon) Manes. From *pitara* (San). *See* **Manes**.
pittaḷi: (Kon) Brass. *Also*, hives from an allergic reaction. From *pittalam* (San).

pīṭa: (Kon) Ground flour; also, batter from wet grinding or powder from dry grinding. From *piṣṭa* (San), "ground," "powdered," "crushed."

piyāvu: (Kon) Onion, which is normally forbidden to priestly families. From *palāṇḍu* (San).

poḍḍāḷẽ: (Kon) Snake gourd; serpent gourd (*Trichosanthes cucumerina*).

poḷeru: (Kon) Round, shallow metal dish.

poḷi pīṭa: (Kon) Ceremonial dishes prepared for an honored guest, such as a new son-in-law.

poḷo: (Kon) Thin pancake. Also called *dōse* (Kan). From *polī* (San), *polikā* (San).

poṇsā sāla: (Kon) Unripe jackfruit pickled in brine. The unripe sheaths enclosing the seeds (*bikkaṇḍa*) are used for this purpose.

poṇosu: (Kon) Jackfruit (*Artocarpus heterophyllus*). If the eatable part is firm, it is called *barko poṇosu*; if it is soft and mushy, it is called *tuḷvo poṇosu*. From *panasam* (San). Also called *halasu* (Kan).

poṇti: (Kon) Small, shallow earthenware dish for oil with a cotton wick in it, used as a lamp when lit. For ceremonial occasions, the dish could be made of gold or silver.

poṇti vāti: (Kon) Ceremonial viewing of, usually, a great-grandson by the great-grandparents.

poṭḷi: (Kon) Package.

pōṭa: (Kon) Belly, stomach, womb.

poṭṭā śīta poḍkā navẽ: (Kon) To fill the belly with rice; one has to eat.

pradakṣiṇa: (Kon, San) Clockwise circumambulation around a sacred object, keeping it always on one's right, such as the sanctum in a temple or a person worthy of great respect.

praḷaya: (Kon) Universal deluge at the end of an epoch. Also called *pralaya* (San).

praṇāma: (Kon, San) Bow, obeisance.

prasaṅga: (Kon, San) Subject or topic of the performance of a field drama (***bayalāṭa***).

prasāda: (Kon, San) Grace; usually sandalwood paste and flowers given to devotees visiting a temple. Also, food offered to a deity and later eaten by the devotees.

praśna: (Kon, San) Question. A formal process, questioning a priest in a prognostication ceremony in a temple or questioning an astrologer.

pratiloma: (San) Against the hair; not regular or in natural order; not favorable.

pratimā: (Kon, San) Image, likeness, representation

pratiṣṭhā: (Kon, San) Installation, consecration.

pravara: (Kon, San) Group of distinguished ancestors of a clan or ***gotra***.

pravāsu: (Kon) Going or journeying abroad, being absent from one's home; a foreign residence. From *pravāsa* (San).

prārthanā: (Kon, San) Prayer.

prāyaścitta: (Kon, San) Atonement, expiation.
preta: (Kon, San) Departed, the dead; the spirit of a dead person before completion of obsequies.
primacy conceit: Cognitive state of an individual or a group that is convinced that it has indeed achieved the dominant or alpha status. This state of mind usually confers a sense of superiority and a desire to flaunt it. It is a subjective feeling of satisfaction, usually based on self-delusion, which is not supported by quantifiable and measurable achievements. *See* **primacy pride**.
primacy drive: A basic need felt by each individual in a group to achieve the dominant or alpha status in it. This hypothesis was suggested by the book *Chimpanzee Politics*, by Frans de Waal, which was based on his observations of the chimpanzees of the zoo in Arnhem, the Netherlands. Primacy drive is a plausible extrapolation from chimp behavior to that of humans, to explain its many aspects.
primacy pride: Similar to **primacy conceit**, except that it is based on measurable hard facts and not on illusions.
puḍvẽ: (Kon) **Dhoti**, a long piece of white cloth worn by men.
puṁsavana: (San) Causing the birth of a male child. *See* rite 2 in Appendix 5, "Hindu Rites of Passage."
punarjanma: (Kon, San) Rebirth.
punnava: (Kon) Full moon. From *pūrṇimā* (San).
puṇya: (Kon, San) Merit.
purāṇa: (Kon, San) Epic; tale containing ancient history, stories, legends, and myths of Hindu tradition, such as the Rāmāyaṇa and the Mahābhārata.
purāṇa sāṅgcẽ: (Kon) Religious rite in which the myths of Hindu tradition are read in Sanskrit and translated into Konkani by a priest. People who participate in such rites acquire merit.
purāṇika: (Kon) Person who reads aloud the Sanskrit text of the epics and translates them into one of the local languages, such as Konkani.
purohita: (Kon, San) Family priest who conducts all religious rites of a family. Also called *puraitu* (Kon).
puruṣārtha: (San, Kon) One or more of the four principal objectives of human life, which are ***dharma*** (virtue), *artha* (wealth), *kāma* (gratification), and ***mokṣa*** (liberation).
pustaka: (Kon, San) Book.
puṣpāñjali: (Kon, San) Handful of flowers; offering of flowers.
pūjā: (Kon, San) Worship; ceremony of worship.
pūje bhaṭṭu: (Kon) Priest who performs rites of worship in the inner sanctum.
pūri: (Kon) Thin, round pieces of dough deep-fried in oil or ghee so that they puff up. Also called *roṭṭi* (Kon).

ragaḍo: (Kon) Granite pestle, or grinding stone, used to prepare a mixture of spices and grated coconut (***sōyi***) into batter (***māsolu*** or *pīṭa*) for ***iḍḷi*** or ***poḷo***. The mortar is a hemisphere about 3 feet in diameter with a concave depression of about 2 to 3 inches and a central dimple about 6 inches in diameter and about 6 to 9 iches deep, in which the pestle (*ragaḍyā dāṇo*) rotates. The pestle is ellipsoidal, with a length of about 12 to 18 inches and a diameter of about 6 inches. The person using the device rotates the pestle with the left hand while feeding the spice mixture or batter with the right.

ratha: (Kon, San) Chariot, carriage, or wooden cart attached to a temple. Temples usually have two to three of these; the biggest of them is usually called the *Brahma Ratha*. *See* ***tēru***.

rathā utsovu: (Kon) Festival in which an image of a deity is taken out in a procession along the outer perimeter of a temple, in a wooden carriage (***ratha***). From *rathotsava* (San).

rābbonu ghettili: (Kon) Kept woman (pejorative); an extramarital entanglement.

rāgi: (Kan) *See* ***nāñcaṇo***.

Rāhu and Ketu*:* (Kon, San) Ascending and descending nodes, respectively, where the moon's orbit intersects the plane of the ecliptic, which is the plane of Earth's orbit round the sun. These are considered to be malevolent "planets" that "swallow" the sun or moon in an eclipse, though their real significance for calculating lunar and solar eclipses was known to Hindu astronomers.

rājju: (Kon) Rope of coir fibers, usually thick. From *rajju* (San). *See* ***sūmba***.

Rāmnām: (Kon, San) Invocation of the name of Lord Rāma repeatedly as a pious religious act.

rāndayi: (Kon) Side dish accompanying the main dish of rice or wheat/millet cakes. From *randhita* (San), "cooked."

rānnaṇi: (Kon) Fireplace for cooking, consisting of the main fireplace (*rānnaṇi*) flanked by two secondary fireplaces (***vāila***).

rānye peḍi: (Kon) Raised platform behind the cooking fires in a kitchen. Also called ***peḍa*** (Kon).

rāṇḍa: (Kon) Slut, whore; also a widow (pejorative). From *raṇḍā* (San). A very offensive, hurtful, obscene term of abuse grossly misused in addressing a woman.

rāyasapatra: (Kon, Kan) Letter from a superior, such as the head of a ***maṭha***.

rāyu: (Kon) King. From *rāja* **(San)**.

riṇṭo: (Kon) Soapnut or soapberry of the genus *Sapindus* and many species, including *delavayi*, *mukorossi*, *trifoliatus*, and *laurifolius*, native to South India. Its outer skin, which is brown or yellow, contains the natural detergent saponin and is ground to a powder for use instead of soap in cleaning jewelry or laundry. Also called *aṇṭavāḷa kāi* (Kan).

rivāj: (Kon, Ara) Custom, vogue, practice. Usually it is used in Konkani as *rīti-rivāj*.

rīti: (Kon, San) Usage, custom, practice. Its customary usage in Konkani is *rīti-rivāj.*

rulāvũ: (Kon) Cream of wheat; spicy or piquant, served at breakfast or with afternoon snacks.

ruppayi (Kon) Rupee (Eng). Monetary unit of India, Pakistan and a few other countries. From *rūpyaka* (San).

ruppẽ: (Kon) Silver. From *rūpyam* (San).

rupyā boḍḍo: (Kon) Staff encased in a plate of silver carried in procession as the insignia of rank and authority. It is used mainly for crowd control.

ruvvi: (Kon) A copper coin, now obsolete, equal to 1/192 of a rupee.

rūḍhi: (Kon, San) Custom, tradition, usage.

ṛīṇa: (Kon) Debt. From *ṛṇam* (San).

ṛṣi: (Kon, San) Inspired sage or poet who is male; a seer of Vedic hymns.

ṛṣikā: (San) Inspired sage or poet who is female; a seer of Vedic hymns.

ṛṣitarpaṇa: (Kon, San) Libations offered to the sages.

sahadharmiṇī: (Kon, San) Lawful wife with the same religious duties and obligations as the husband.

sahagamana: (San) Accompanying, going together. Usually refers to the virtuous wife (***satī***) burning herself on the funeral pyre of the husband.

sahapaṅkti bhojana: (Kon, San) Sitting down to eat in the same row; one of the two signs of acceptance of the participants as one community, the other being intermarriage.

sallekhanā: (San) Ritual suicide by fasting practiced by some Jain monks or laity.

samarādhanā: (Kon) Communal feast. From *samārādhana* (San), "gratification."

samāvartana: (Kon) Student's return home after the completion of Vedic studies. From *samāvartanam* (San). *See* rite 14 in Appendix 5, "Hindu Rites of Passage. It is now part of the wedding ceremony.

sammānu: (Kon) Cermonious hospitality.

samrādānyẽ jevnā rūci: (Kon) Taste of the food at a communal feast; almost impossible to duplicate at home.

saṁnyāsi: (Kon, San) Ascetic; a person who has completely renounced the world.

saṁsāra: (Kon, San) Succession of births; usually denotes the totality of this life.

saṁskāra: (Kon, San) Rites of passage in a Hindu's life, usually sixteen, including birth ceremonies, the thread ceremony, marriage, and the last rites. *See* Appendix 5, "Hindu Rites of Passage."

saṁyuktā galāṭo: (Kon) Hubbub in the Gauḍa Sārasvat Brāhmaṇa community of Mulki, resulting from attempts to unify it by admitting some formerly excommunicated subcastes. *See* the the section in Chapter 3, "My Maternal Grandparents," on the unification movement among the Sarasvats: "The United GSB Conference, or Saṁyukta Gauḍa Sārasvat Brāhmaṇa Pariṣad (1910–1917)."

sandhi: (Kon) Morning and evening twilight prayers. From *sandhyāvandanam* (San).
Santāna Gopāla: (Kon, San) An aspect of Lord Kṛṣṇa. Images of this aspect show Lord Kṛṣṇa holding and granting the boon of a baby.
santāna vṛakṣa: (Kon, San) Family tree; genealogical tree.
Saṅgha: (San, Pal) The Buddhist monastic order of monks and nuns.
saptapadī: (Kon, San) Seven steps, in which the groom leads the bride round the sacred wedding fire. On the completion of the seventh step, the marriage is complete and legally binding.
Saptaṛṣi: (Kon, San) Seven sages. For various lists, see the works by Mitchiner (1982) and Daniélou (1964).
saraḷā mãñco: (Kon) Bed of iron rods, used for cremation.
sarāf: (Kon, Hin, Ara) Dealer in gold and silver; also, a money changer in medieval Goa.
sāri: (Hin) A garment worn usually by women in South Asia. It is a rectangular piece of lightweight cloth, 48 to 54 inches wide and 6 to 9 yards long, worn with one end wrapped round the waist and the other end draped over a shoulder. From *śāṭī* (San), "garment," "cloth." Also called *sari* (Eng).
satī: (San) A virtuous or a good woman, usually refers to a woman who immolates herself on her husband's funeral pyre, in the ceremony of ***satī*** *sahagamana*.
saṭṭi: (Kon) Ceremonies connected with the sixth day after a baby's birth. From *ṣaṣṭhī* (San). *See* rite 4 in Appendix 5, "Hindu Rites of Passage."
saumya: (Kon, San) Gentle, soft; usually used in reference to a person's horoscope or character.
Savnsāra Pāḍvo: (Kon) New Year's Day, which occurs in March/April. From Saṃvatsara Pratipadī (San).
savvāśiṇī: (Kon) A married woman whose husband is alive. *From* ***suvāsinī*** (San).
sāḍḍu: (Kon) Wife's sister's husband.
sākṣi: (Kon) Witness. From *sākṣin* (San).
sāḷa: (Kon) Raised platform that usually runs around the wall of a temple.
sāḷuka: (Kon) Water lily. Different from the lotus (***kamalā phūla***).
Sārasvat: Relating to the goddess Sarasvatī; belonging to the river Sarasvatī; belonging to the Sārasvata country; name of a Vedic sage; name of a particular community. Also used to indicate the Gauḍa Sārasvat Brāhmaṇa (GSB).
sāsama: (Kon) Mustard seeds. From *sarṣapa* (San).
sāvkār: (Kon) Rich merchant. From *sāhūkār* (Hin), meaning a money lender, private banker, a rich man, man of means. Also called *sāvukāru* (Kon).
sevā: (San, Kon) Worship, homage, service.
sharbata: (Kon) Lemonade with sugar or jaggery (brown sugar), sometimes livened up with the addition of black pepper, cardamom, dried ginger, etc. From *ṣerbet* (Tur) and *śerbet* (Per, Ara).

sindūra: (Kon, San) Red lead; also, its vermilion color (*sindūrā baṇṇu*).

sīmanta: (Kon) Parting of the hair; one of the rites observed in the fourth or fifth month of pregnancy for the protection of the fetus. From *sīmantonnayana* (San). *See* rite 3 in Appendix 5, "Hindu Rites of Passage."

smārta: (Kon, San) One who is well versed in and follows traditional laws based on *Smṛti*.

Smṛti: (Kon, San) Canon. A body of traditional remembered codes of laws.

smaśāna: (Kon) Cremation grounds. From *śmaśānam* (San). Also called *śmaśāna* (Kon).

sonnārānco: (Kon) Goldsmith.

sōyi: (Kon) Grated coconut.

sthāna: (Kon, San) Place.

strīdhana: (Kon, San) A woman's private property over which she exercises total control.

stotra: (Kon, San) Hymns of praise.

sudrāñcē ceḍū: (Kon) Maid, generally employed to wash clothes and dishes and clean the house. From ***śūdra*** (Kon, San). Also called *śudrāñcē ceḍū* (Kon).

sukhē: (Kon) A Konkani vegetable dish. Literally, "dry," meaning that the dish contains little liquid sauce.

surai śīta: (Kon) Polished white rice that has been cooked.

suttā punnava: (Kon) Full moon on which new sacred threads (***jānnuve*** or *yajñopavītam*) are worn.

suvāsinī: (San) A married woman whose husband is alive.

sūkta: (Kon) Vedic hymn. From *sūktam* (San).

sūmba: (Kon) String of coir fibers, usually thin. *See* ***rājju***.

svarga: (Kon, San) Heaven.

svāmē: (Kon) Spiritual preceptor. From *svāmin* (San), meaning the head of a monastic lineage to which devotees owe allegiance.

Śaiva: (Kon, San) Hindu whose principal deity is Lord Śiva.

śaṅkha: (Kon, San) The conch shell, which is one of the emblems of Śrī Viṣṇu. The other emblems are ***cakra*** (discus), ***gadā*** (mace), and ***padma*** (lotus).

Śākta: (Kon, San) Hindu whose principal deity is Śakti.

Śāmbhavī: (Kon, San) Name of Pārvati; Sanskrit name for the Mulki River.

śānti: (Kon, San) Peace. Also, propitiatory rite performed to ward off evil by bringing "peace" between warring elements in a person's future that could cause a problem.

Śāntādurgā: (Kon, San) A name of Pārvati; literally "gentle, calm, benevolent Durgā."

śāśvata-vāda: (San) Eternalist view. A belief that the self, or soul, is immortal. *See* ***uccheda-vāda***.

śāstra: (Kon, San) Scriptures, or codes of law.

śāstrōkta: (Kon, San) According to the dictates of the ***śāstra*** (scriptures).

śeṇḍī: (Kon) Tuft of hair on the crown of a boy's or man's clean-shaven head. After a boy's ***caulu***, or ***upanayana***, the tuft was left intact. When a coconut is dehusked, a conical piece of the husk, covering the three "eyes" of the coconut, is left intact. This is also called the *śeṇḍī* of the coconut. From *śikhaṇḍī*, *śikhā* (San).
śesa bhorcẽ: (Kon) Sprinkling of whole rice, sometimes colored with ***kuṅkuma***, *śesa*, as a benediction on the principals at an ***upanayana*** or a wedding by ***suvāsinis*** and others. From *āśis* (San), "blessing," "benediction."
śevãyī: (Kon) Vermicelli, fresh or dried.
śikāyi: (Kon) Powder derived from the pods of a climbing prickly shrub, *Acacia concinna DC*, which contain a natural detergent, saponin, that is used instead of soap. From *sīge kāyī* (Kan). Also called *śikāye piṭṭi* (Kon).
śīrā: (Kon) Sweet cream of wheat, with raisins, cardamon, saffron, etc.
śiyyāḷyā uddāka: (Kon) Water from a green or tender coconut.
śraddhā: (Kon, San) Faith, trust, belief.
śraṅgāru: (Kon) Adornments.
śṛaṅgāra rasa: (Kon, San) Erotic sentiment.
śrāddha: (Kon, San) Funeral rite or ceremony performed for the **Manes**, following death and on the anniversary of death. *See* **Manes**.
śrī: (Kon, San) Wealth, riches; the goddess of wealth, Śrī Lakṣmī. *Also* an honorific that usually precedes a man's name.
śrīkhaṇḍa: (Kon, San) Sandalwood. Also a dessert prepared by straining yoghurt to remove excess water and mixing the residue with sugar, saffron, and cardamom, served with ***pūri***.
śubha muhūrta: (Kon, San) Auspicious time, usually for the performance of a religious function.
sukkhi mirsāṅga: (Kon) Dried chilies.
Śūdra: (Kon, San) Servant, fourth of the fourfold ***varṇa*** system of the Hindu religious hierarchy.
śūnyatā: (San) Emptiness. Buddhist philosophical designation for the ultimate nature of all things. Buddha taught the doctrine of ***anattā*** (not-self), that a person is a combination of physical and mental aggregates without a permanent self. This idea was later extended to the nature of all things, as *śūnyatā*, or emptiness. Also called *suññatā* (Pal).
ṣaṭkarmi: (San) Person entitled to carry out the six duties of a **Brāhmaṇa**: self-study and teaching of the Vedas, offering sacrifices and officiating at them, and giving and receiving gifts. Whether the Gauḍa Sārasvat Brāhmaṇa were entitled to this status of a full-fledged **Brāhmaṇa** has been a controversial subject; these challenges were initiated by other **Brāhmaṇa** communities who questioned this assumption. *See* ***trikarmi***.
taḷẽ: (Kon) Enclosed pond of water usually attached to a temple.

taḷti pustaka: (Kon) Palmyra palm (*Borassus flabellifer*) leaf manuscript.

tamāso: (Kon) Show, spectacle, or entertainment, usually at someone else's expense. From *tamāśā* (Hin).

tambūra: (Kon, Kan) A musical instrument usually with four strings, used as a drone accompaniment in musical performances.

tappu kāṇika: (Kon) Offering to a deity or a guru to make amends for a ritual impropriety. From *tappu kāṇike* (Kan).

tarni mirsāṅga (Kon) Green chilies.

tāla: (San) Palmyra palm tree (*Borassus flabellifer*).

tāla patram: (San) Palmyra palm leaf (*Borassus flabellifer*).

tāḷa maddaḷe: (Kan) Reenactment of a well-known episode from one of the Hindu epics, to the accompaniment of music and a spirited dialog. The artists sit around a conductor, or *bhāgavatu* or *bhāgavata*. There are no costumes or dances, and the dialog is extempore.The topic of a performance is called its ***prasaṅga***.

tāmbiyo: (Kon) Small pitcher, usually made of metal.

tāndulu: (Kon) Uncooked rice after threshing, unhusking and winnowing. *Ukḍo* is parboiled and surai is unhusked without boiling. From *taṇḍula* (San).

tāntrik: (Kon, San) Adept of *Tantra* (a body of spiritual teachings); also, a person who casts spells or counterspells for believing clients.

tellā nhāṇa: (Kon) Oil bath. Usually coconut oil is applied to the whole body, parts of which are thoroughly massaged, finishing off with a cleansing bath with hot water. This is a most enjoyable, relaxing experience.

teppaḷa: (Kon) Green berries of the Indian prickly ash (*Zanthoxylum rhetsa*), often used as projectiles in an air gun (***petnoḷi***). Skins of the dried berries are used as a spice in Konkani dishes such as ***koddela***. The berries are also called *kamtekāi* or *kāḍumeṇasu* (Kan). From *tirphaḷ* (Mar).

tērā utsovu: (Kon) Festival in which image of a deity is taken out in procession in a wooden carriage, called a ***tēru***. *See also* ***ratha***.

tēru: (Kon) Chariot, carriage, wooden cart attached to a temple.

thaṇḍa: (Kon) Cold. From *taṇḍi* (Kan), *ṭhaṇḍā* (Hin).

tīka: (Kon) Piquant, spicy hot. From *tikta* (San).

tīḷo: (Kon) Auspicious beauty spot worn by ***suvāsinī*** (women whose husband is living). From *tilaka* (San).

tīḷo lāvñcē: (Kon) Formal exchange of ***kuṅkuma*** between two ***suvāsinīs***. Each applies a token bit of ***kuṅkuma*** to the ***tīḷo*** of the other.

tīrtha: (Kon) Consecrated water.

tīrtha gandha prasāda: (Kon) Consecrated water (***tīrtha***) usually flavored with sandalwood and camphor, and sandalwood paste (*gandha* or ***gāndha***), with flowers for women or a holy basil leaf for men (***prasāda***), that is given on visiting a Hindu temple.

tīrtha mārcẽ: (Kon) Sprinkling of a devotee with consecrated water, by an oracle or by a priest, as a blessing or to ward off evil.

toranda: (Kon) Pomelo (*Citrus maxima*), a type of large, sweet grapefruit.

trikarmi: (San) Person entitled to carry out the three duties of a twice-born: self-study of the Vedas, offering of sacrifices, and the giving of gifts to charity. The ***trikarmi*** are not entitled to carry out the six duties of a full-fledged **Brāhmaṇa**. *See* ***ṣaṭkarmi***.

tuḷaśi: (Kon) Holy basil (*Ocimum tenuiflorum*), usually planted at the top center of a raised platform (*tuḷaśi kāṭṭẽ*). From *tulasī* (San).

tuḷu: (Kon, Kan, Tul) Local Dravidian language.

tūmbu: (Kon) Outlet for water.

ṭāko: (Kon) Bolt of cloth.

ṭāṅgā: (Kon, Hin) Light two-wheeled vehicle for two to four people that is drawn by one horse. *See also* ***jaṭkā***.

uccheda-vāda: (San) Annihilationist view; belief that the self, or soul, ceases to exist with death. *See* ***śāśvata-vāda***.

udāraṇa: (Kon) Declaration, utterance; reply to devotees' inquiries regarding their personal problems at the *Darśana Sevā*. From *udāharaṇam* (San).

udbatti: (Kon) Joss sticks.

uddāka: (Kon) Water. From *udakam* (San).

uḍgirẽ: (Kon) Ceremonial gift.

uḍidu: (Kon) Black gram (*Vigna mungo*). Also called *urad* (Hin).

ukḍẽ śīta: (Kon) Cooked brown rice, normally not eaten by priestly families, who eat only polished white rice (***surai śīta***).

Umā-Maheśvara: (Kon, San) Iconographic representation of Umā or Pārvati, seated on the lap of Maheśvara or Śiva. See the book *The Presence of Siva* (Kramrisch 1988, 349, *et seq*).

upanayana: (Kon, San) Investing a boy or a girl with a sacred thread (***jānnuve*** or *yajñopavītam*) as a prelude to beginning Vedic studies, popularly called ***mūñji***. *See* rite 11 in Appendix 5, "Hindu Rites of Passage." Investitures for girls are almost unknown these days, though they were celebrated in the Gauḍa Sārasvat Brāhmaṇa community in the olden days. Jñānaprabodhinī, an organization in Pune, is spearheading a movement to revive this ceremony for girls.

upākarma: (San) A rite celebrating the beginning of Vedic studies. It is in abeyance now, along with Vedic studies. *See* rite 12 in Appendix 5, "Hindu Rites of Passage." *Also called* **vedārambha** (San).

upāsu: (Kon) Fast. *From upavāsa* (San).

uśśẽ: (Kon) Pillow.

uṣṭhẽ: (Kon) Food that has touched someone's lip. From *oṣṭha* (San), "lip," "spittle."

utsarjana: (San) Cessation of Vedic studies.
utsava: (Kon, San) Festival.
utsavā mūrti: (Kon) Sacred image taken out in a procession in a temple.
Uttara Kannaḍā: (Kon, Kan) North Kanara, name of a district on the west coast of India, just north of **Dakshina Kannada**, or South Kanara District.
uttarāyaṇa: (Kon) Northward progression of the sun from the winter solstice (~December 21), to the summer solstice (~June 21). From *uttarāyana* (San).
uvāḷi: (Kon) To exorcise.
ūna: (Kon, San) Defective, deficient. "*To ūna soddhitā*": "He is looking for defects."

vaidika: (Kon, San) Religious as opposed to secular or ***laukika***; literally, "conforming to the Vedic tradition"; sacred, scriptural, holy; also, priests. *See also* ***bhaṭṭā thañcẽ*** (Kon).
Vaikuṇṭha: (Kon, San) Heavenly abode of Lord Viṣṇu.
vaikuṇṭha samarādhanā: (Kon) Final, closing, obsequies on the 13th day after death, when the deceased enters the heaven of Lord Viṣṇu. The rituals are followed by a feast for family and friends.
Vaiśya: (Kon, San) Merchant, third of the fourfold ***varṇa*** system of the Hindu religious hierarchy.
Vaiṣṇava: (Kon, San) Hindu whose principal deity is Lord Viṣṇu.
vajrā kuṭkā̃ jōḍu: (Kon) Pair of diamond ear ornaments.
vakil: (Kon, Ara) Lawyer, pleader, advocate. Also called *vakīlu* (Kon, Ara) and *vakīla* (Kan, Hin).
vakdā āṅgaḍi: (Kon) Shop selling medicine, including dried herbs used as medicine.
vakkada: (Kon) Medicine in general.
vanabhojana: (Kon, San) Forest-feast or picnic; also a communal feast held on special occasions at the Mulki temple.
varāha: (Kon, Kan) Gold coin of the Vijayanagara Empire, equal to four rupees in the olden days.
varla: (Kon) End of a ***sāri***, usually ornamented with patterns of gold or silver thread and draped over the left shoulder.
varla ghālcẽ: (Kon) Ceremony in which the mother-in-law changes the bride's mode of wearing a ***sāri***. When the bride enters the wedding enclosure (***māṇṭvi***), she wears the ***sāri*** in the style of an unmarried woman; her mother-in-law changes this to the style of a married woman.
varṇa: (San) Color, class, race, tribe, kind; also used to designate one of the four divisions of Hindu society: **Brāhmaṇa**, **Kṣatriya**, **Vaiśya**, and **Śūdra**.
varsāntika: (Kon) End-of-the-year rites on the first anniversary of death. From *varṣāntika śrāddha* (San).

varṣika: (Kon) Rites for the **Manes** performed on the death anniversary. From *vārṣika śrāddha* (San). *See* **Manes**.

vasantā jagali: (Kon) Where the offices of the Mulki temple management are located. *Also called* ***candra śālā*** (Kon, San).

vassarti: (Kon) A woman in her menses. From *visravati* (San).

vassarte māḷi: (Kon) Upstairs area where women in their menses were segregated to conform to rules of ritual purity.

vāḍappa: (Kon) Symbolic offering of new clothes and eatables to the **Manes** on special occasions. *See* **Manes**.

vāhana: (Kon) Transport, conveyance. Each deity is supposed to have its own characteristic ***vāhana***—a mythic animal, bird, etc. From *vāhanam* **(San)**.

vāila: (Kon) Secondary fireplace, usually on either side of the main fireplace (***rānnaṇi***).

vājjapa: (Kon) Auspicious, festive music (*maṅgala vādyam*). This word refers both to the music as well as to the musical instruments. A double-reeded wind instrument similar to the South Indian ***nāgasvaram***, the North Indian *shahnai*, or the Western oboe is the principal instrument.

vājpāñce: (Kon) Professional musicians who play festive music. *See* ***vājjapa***.

vāḷi: (Kon) Vegetable in the spinach family, not eaten by priestly families.

vāna-kāṇḍaṇa: (Kon) Stationary mortar and pestle used for dehusking grains. The mortar made of granite, is 18 to 24 inches in diameter, and is buried flush with the ground. The pestle is made of wood and is 5 to 6 feet long and about 3 inches in diameter. Its two ends are reinforced with iron bands to prevent the wood from splitting. A person uses this combination while standing and shifts the pestle from one hand to the other on alternate strokes. Also called *kāṇḍāṇẽ* (Kon).

vāna-kuṇṭāṇi: (Kon) Portable mortar and pestle, usually made of cast bronze or brass, used to grind betel nut or spices. Also called *hammandasto-pārāyi* (Kon) in parts of South Kanara.

vāngaḍ: (Kon) Clans that claim descent from the first settlers of a village in Goa and whose male descendants formed the village council. *Also called* ***gāvṁkārī***.

vāsari: (Kon) Kitchen and or inner room of a house. Also called *vāsāro* (Kon).

vāsaram: (San) Inner apartment of a house.

vāti: (Kon) Cotton wick used in a ***divli*** or ***ārti***.

Vedāṅga: (Kon, San) Class of subjects, six in number, considered auxiliary to the study of the Vedas: phonetics, rituals of the solemn Vedic and domestic rites, grammar, etymology, prosody, and astronomy.

vedārambha: (San) *See* ***upākarma*** (San).

Velip: (Kon). *See* **Gāvḍo**.

veṇi: (Kon) The mother-in-law of one's son or daughter.

veṣṭi: (Kon) Cloth that is wound around; a **dhoti**, usually 8 to 9 ***hātti*** (cubits) long, or 4 to 4.5 yards long.
veyu: (Kon) The father-in-law of one's son or daughter.
vhāṇa: (Kon) Open sandals made of leather or plastics.
vhārḍika: (Kon) Marriage. *See* rite 15 in Appendix 5, "Hindu Rites of Passage." *Also called* ***vivāha*** (San).
vhārḍike mānṭovu: (Kon) Enclosure where marriage ceremonies are conducted and the guests welcomed, entertained, and fed.
vholẽ: (Kon) Ritual impurity lasting for a specified number of days, brought on by childbirth or death in the family. *See also* ***bhaṣṭa*** (Kon).
vhoṇṭi: (Kon) *See* ***hōṇṭi bhorcẽ***.
vilāytī: (Kon) Of foreign origin; for example, from England, Europe, or the West in general. *From* *vilāyat* (Ara, Tur), "province"; "foreign land or country."
vilāytāka: (Kon) To the west; Europe or England. From *vilāyat* (Ara, Tur), "province"; "foreign land or country."
vindūru: (Kon) Mouse, rat. From *undaru* (San).
visarjana: (Kon, San) Sending forth; bidding good-bye to an invoked deity. The opposite of ***āvāhanam*** (San), which is invoking a deity.
Viṣṇu *sahasranāma:* (Kon, San) Recitation of the 1,000 names of Lord Viṣṇu as part of Hindu worship.
vivāha: (San) *See* ***vhārḍika***.
vīḍo: (Kon) Pieces of betel nut (*phoḍi*), cloves (*lavaṅga*), slaked lime (*cunno*), and some other spices wrapped in a betel leaf (***pāna***). It is considered auspicious and given as part of a formal welcoming ceremony for an honored guest, to seal an agreement, or given to guests as a digestive after a hearty meal. For many variations on this theme, from the king to the commoner, *see* Achaya 1994. Also called *tāmbūlam* (San) and *phaḍpāna* (Kon).
vōḍi: (Kon) Deep-fried, crunchy morsels of spicy delight whose flavor fills the mouth and tickles the palate, served as an accompaniment to a meal to provide contrast in texture. Also called *saṇḍige* (Kan).
vokkuḷa: (Kon) Colored water, squirted on festival participants using water syringes or carried in earthenware pots that are broken to douse a large number of merrymakers.
vokkuḷa dākkocẽ: (Kon) Ceremonial welcome of a sacred image or an honored guest by waving of a shallow dish (***poḷeru***) containing water colored with red powder (***kuṅkuma***) to ward off the evil eye.
vokkuḷa kheḷcẽ: (Kon) A part of a wedding ceremony in which the groom and the bride hunt for a ring in a container of colored water (*vokkuḷa*). A few of these ceremonies came into fashion when brides and grooms were children.
voḷvāta: (Kon) Shortcut; inner passage.

voṇṭi: (Kon) Male ear ornament with an additional U-shaped yoke of gold joining the front and back of the ornament, seen under the earlobes. The version of this ornament worn by girls and women does not have the appendage. Plural: *voṇṭyō*.

vrata: (Kon, San) Vowed religious observance.

vṛaddhi śrāddha: (San) Offering to the **Manes** on a joyous occasion such as the birth of a son or marriage. *See* **Manes**.

vyāpāri: (Kon) Trader. From *vyāpārin* (San).

vyāpāru: (Kon) Business, trade. From *vyāpāra* (San).

yajamānu: (Kon) Patron; a person who employs a priest or priests to perform religious ceremonies on his behalf. From *yajamāna* (Kon [plural]; San), an old-fashioned term meaning "husband," rarely used now.

yajña: (Kon, San) Sacrifice.

yajñā visarjana: (Kon, San) Ending of the sacrifices, with the departure of the deities invoked.

yakṣagāna: (San, Kan) Field drama. *See* ***kheḷu*** (Kon) and ***bayaḷāṭa*** (Kan).

yātrā: (Kon, San) Pilgrimage, journey.

yedru kāṇsaṇā: (Kon) Ceremonial welcome of the groom's party to the wedding by the bride's party.

Bibliography

Accattoli, Luigi. 1998. *When a pope asks forgiveness: The mea culpa's of John Paul II*, translated by Jordan Aumann, OP. Boston, MA: Pauline Books & Media.

Acharya, Pandit Surendra. 1996–7. *Mangalore panchangam*. (In Kannada). Mangalore, India: Acharya's Math, S.V. Temple Square.

Achaya, K.T. 1994. *Indian food: A historical companion*. Bombay, India: Oxford University Press.

Allchin, Bridget, and Raymond Allchin. 1996. *The rise of civilization in India and Pakistan*. New Delhi, India: Cambridge University Press.

Allen, Jr., John L. 2004. *All the Pope's men: The inside story of how the Vatican really thinks*. New York: Doubleday.

Altekar, A.S. 1999. *The position of women in Hindu civilization: From prehistoric times to the present day*. Reprint. New Delhi, India: Motilal Banarsidas Publishers.

Angle, Prabhakar S. 1994. *Goa: concepts & misconcepts*. Bombay, India: Goa Hindu Association.

Anonymous. n.d. *Mulki Śrī Kālabhairava Stuti*. (In Kannada). Mulki, India: Śrī Venkaṭaramaṇa Devasthāna.

_____. 1847. *Pancayiti paisalu*. (In Kannada). Arbitration settlement dated 28 November 1847, given at the District Collector's Office, Mangalore, South Kanara District, India.

_____. 1993. *Temple informative book*. Mardol, Goa, India: Souvenir Committee, Shri Mahalasa Saunsthan Jeernoddhar Samiti.

_____. 2001. *Koṅkaṇākhyāna*. (In Marati). Reprint of 1909 edition by Shripad Venkatesh Wagle, Vasco-da-Gama, Goa, India: V.M. Salgaocar Foundation.

_____. 2005. *Shri Mahalasa Saunsthan*. Mardol-Ponda-Goa, India: Shri Mahalasa Saunsthan.

Anthony, David W. 2007. *The horse, the wheel, and language: How bronze-age riders from the Eurasian steppes shaped the modern world*. Princeton, NJ: Princeton University Press.

Apte, V.M. 1954. *Social and religious life in the Grihya Sutras*. Reset edition. Bombay, India: The Popular Book Depot.

Apte, Vaman Shivaram. 1998. *The practical Sanskrit–English dictionary*. Reprint of revised and enlarged 1957 edition. Kyoto, Japan: Rinsen Book Co.

_____. 1884. *The student's English–Sanskrit dictionary*. 3rd revised edition. New Delhi, India: Motilal Banarsidass.

Ashenburg, Katherine. 2007. *The dirt on clean: An unsanitized history*. New York: North Point Press.

Auboyer, Jeannine. 1988. *Daily life in ancient India: From 200 BC to 700 AD*. Translated from the French by Simon Watson Taylor. London: Phoenix Press.

Audi, Robert, editor. 1999. *The Cambridge dictionary of philosophy*. 2nd edition. Cambridge, UK: Cambridge University Press.

Axelrod, Paul, and Michelle A. Fuerch. 1996. Flight of the deities: Hindu resistance in Portuguese Goa. *Modern Asian Studies* 30(2):387–421.

Baer, Lee. 2000. *Getting control: Overcoming your obsessions and compulsions*. Revised edition. New York: Plume.

_____. 2002. *The imp of the mind: Exploring the silent epidemic of obsessive bad thoughts*. New York: Plume.

Bahadur, Om Lata. 2002. *The book of Hindu festivals and ceremonies*. Reprint of 2nd revised and enlarged edition of 1997. New Delhi, India: UBS Publishers' Distributors Ltd.

Baigent, Michael, and Richard Leigh. 2000. *The Inquisition*. New York: Penguin.

Barros, Joseph. 1988. Influence of foreign languages on Goan cultural ethos, pp. 165–9, in *Goa: Cultural Trends*, edited by P.P. Shirodkar. Panaji, Goa, India: Directorate of Archives, Archaeology, and Museum.

Basham, A. L, editor. 1975. *A cultural history of India*. New York: Oxford University Press.

_____. 1982. *The wonder that was India: A survey of the history and culture of the Indian sub-continent before the coming of the Muslims*. Reprint of 1954 edition. Bombay, India: Rupa & Co.

_____. 1987. Ājīvikas. *The encyclopedia of religion*, edited by Mircea Eliade, 1:163–5. New York: Macmillan.

Bayly, Susan. 2001. *The new Cambridge history of India: Caste, society and politics in India from the eighteenth century to the modern age*. Reprint of 1999 edition. New York: Cambridge University Press.

Berreby, David. 2005. *Us and them: Understanding your tribal mind*. New York: Little, Brown.

Berry, Jason. 1992. *Lead us not into temptation: Catholic priests and the sexual abuse of children*. New York: Doubleday.

_____. 2011. *Render unto Rome: The secret life of money in the Catholic church*. New York: Crown.

_____, and Gerald Renner. 2004. *Vows of silence: The abuse of power in the papacy of John Paul II*. New York: Free Press.

Bhandarkar, Ramkrishna Gopal. 1966. *First book of Sanskrit*. 34th edition. Bombay, India: Karnatak Publishing House.

Bhat, Mulki Radhakrishna. 1961. The radioactivity of terbium-158 and terbium-157. PhD dissertation, Ohio State University, Columbus, OH.

Bhat, M.R., and M.L. Pool. 1962. Radioactive decay of Tb157 and Tb158. *Physical Review* 127(5):1704–8.

Bhatji, Mulki Narayana. n.d. Miscellaneous notes on our family. Unpublished.

_____. 1983. Tape-recorded interview by M.R. Bhat, August–September, in Udupi, India.

_____. 1990. Tape-recorded interview by Shreedhara Bhat (brother of M.R. Bhat), December, in Udupi, India.

_____. 2007. Mulki Narasimhana Priya Bhaktharu—Śrī Sant Rathanjī Kāṇjī Seṭha (In Kannada), p. 141 in *Śrī Kāśī Maṭha Samsthāna Mattu Gaṇanīya Narasimha Devālayagaḷu*, edited by Kasturi C. Pai. Manipal, India: Manipal Press Ltd.

Bhatt, P. Gururaja. 1975. *Studies in Tuḷuva history and culture*. Manipal, India: Manipal Power Press.

_____. 1977. *Tuḷu nāḍina Nāgamaṇḍala*. (In Kannada). Bangalore, India: IBH Prakashana.

Bhattacharji, Sukumari. 1988. *The Indian theogony: A comparative study of Indian mythology from the Vedas to the Purāṇas*. Reprint of 1970 edition. Delhi, India: Motilal Banarsidass.

Bodhi, Bhikku. 2000. *The connected discourses of the Buddha*. Translation of the *Saṁyutta Nikāya*. Somerville, MA: Wisdom Publications.

Born, Max. 1968. *My life and my views*. New York: Charles Scribner's Sons.

Bose, Abinash Chandra. 1966. *Hymns from the Vedas*. Bombay, India: Asia Publishing House.

Boswell, James. 1960. *Boswell's life of Johnson*. 2 vols; Everyman's Library. Reprint of 1949 edition. New York: E. P. Dutton.

Boxer, C.R. 1960–1. A note on Portuguese missionary methods in the east: 16th–18th centuries. *Ceylon Historical Journal* 10(1–4):77–90.

_____. 1963. *Race relations in the Portuguese colonial empire 1415–1825.* Oxford, UK: Clarendon Press.

_____. 1965. Portuguese society in the tropics: The municipal councils of Goa, Macao, Bahia, and Luanda, 1510–1800. Madison, WI: University of Wisconsin Press.

_____. 1966. Review of *The Christianisation of the Goa Islands, 1510–1567* by Anthony D'Costa. *Bulletin of the School of Oriental and African Studies* 29(2):399–401.

_____. 1969. *The Portuguese seaborne empire*, 1415–1825. New York: Alfred A. Knopf.

_____. 1977. *The Dutch seaborne empire: 1600–1800.* Reprint of 1965 edition. London: Hutchinson & Co.

_____. 1978. *The church militant and Iberian expansion, 1440–1770.* Baltimore: Johns Hopkins University Press.

_____. 1980. *Portuguese India in the mid-seventeenth century.* Delhi, India: Oxford University Press.

Boyajiyan, James C. 1986. Goa Inquisition: A new light on first 100 years (1561–1660). *Purabhilekh–Puratatva* 4(1):1–40.

Boyce, Mary. 1987. *Zoroastrians: Their religious beliefs and practices.* New York: Routledge & Kegan Paul.

_____. 1989. *A history of Zorastrianism.* Vol. 1. *The early period.* 2nd impression with corrections. Leiden, Netherlands: E.J. Brill.

Bradley, Michael J. 2006. *Modern mathematics 1900 to 1950.* New York: Chelsea House.

Braudel, Fernand. 1981. *The structures of everyday life: The limits of the possible.* Vol. 1, *Civilization and capitalism, 15th–18th century.* New York: Harper & Row.

Broderick, John F., S.J. 1987. Xavier, Francis. *The encyclopedia of religion,* edited by Mircea Eliade, 15:491, New York: Macmillan.

_____, and V.A. Lapomarda. 2003. Jesuits. *New Catholic encyclopedia,* 7:779–95. 2nd edition. Farmington Hills, MI: Thomson Gale.

Brough, John. 1953. *The early Brahmanical system of gotra and pravara.* Translation of *The Gotra-Pravara-Mañjarī of Puruṣottama-Paṇḍita.* Cambridge, UK: Cambridge University Press.

_____. 1955. Additional notes on the Brahmin clans. *Journal of the American Oriental Society* 74:263–6.

_____. 1971. Soma and Amanita Muscaria. *Bulletin of the School of Oriental and African Studies of the University of London* 34:331–62.

Bryant, Edwin. 2001. *The quest for the origins of Vedic culture: The Indo-Aryan migration debate*. New York: Oxford University Press

Bryce, Trevor. 2002. *Life and society in the Hittite world*. New York: Oxford University Press.

Bullough, Donald A. 1966. *The age of Charlemagne*. New York: G.P. Putnam's Sons.

Burghardt, W.J. 2003. Cyril of Alexandria, St. *New Catholic encyclopedia*, 4:465–70. 2nd edition. Farmington Hills, MI: Thomson Gale.

Burnell, Arthur Coke, and P.A. Tiele, editors. 1935. *The voyage of John Huyghen van Linschoten to the East Indies: From the old English translation of 1598*. 2 vols. Reprint of 1885 edition published by the Hakluyt Society. New York: Burt Franklin, Publisher.

Burns, R.I. 2003. Auto-da-fé. *New Catholic encyclopedia*, 1:923–4. 2nd edition. Farmington Hills, MI: Thomson Gale.

Carroll, Jamuna, editor. 2009. *India: Opposing viewpoints*. Farmington Hills, MI: Greenhaven Press.

Chakrabarti, Dilip K. 1999. *India: An archaeological history. Palaeolithic beginnings to early historic foundations*. New Delhi, India: Oxford University Press.

Chakravarti, Uma. 2006. *Rewriting history: The life and times of Pandita Ramabai*. 2nd edition. New Delhi, India: Zubaan.

Chanda, Nayan. 2007. *Bound together: How traders, preachers, adventurers, and warriors shaped globalization*. New Haven, CT: Yale University Press.

Chattopadhyaya, Debiprasad, editor. 1982. *Studies in the history of science in India*. 2 vols. New Delhi, India: Editorial Enterprises.

_____. 1986–1991. *History of science and technology in ancient India*. Calcutta, India: Firma KLM Pvt. Ltd.

Chaudhuri, Sukanta, editor. 2004. *Rabindranath Tagore: Selected poems*. New York: Oxford University Press.

Cliff, Nigel. 2011. *Holy war: How Vasco da Gama's epic voyages turned the tide in a centuries-old clash of civilizations*. New York: HarperCollins.

Clough, Arthur Hugh, editor. 2001. *Plutarch's lives*. The Dryden translation edited, with notes and preface by Arthur Hugh Clough. 2 vols. New York: Modern Library.

Cohen, Martin A. 2007a. Marrano. *Encyclopaedia Judaica*, edited by Fred Skolnik, 13:559. 2nd edition. Farmington Hill, MI: Thomson Gale.

_____. 2007b. *Marrano diaspora. Encyclopaedia Judaica*, edited by Fred Skolnik, 13:560–3. 2nd edition. Farmington Hills, MI: Thomson Gale.

Collingham, E.M. 2001. *Imperial bodies: The physical experience of the Raj, c. 1800–1947.* Malden, MA: Blackwell Publishers.

_____. 2006. Curry: a tale of cooks and conquerors. New York: Oxford University Press.

Collins, Paul. 2002. *The modern Inquisition: Seven prominent Catholics and their struggles with the Vatican.* New York: Overlook Press.

Collins, Steven, 1987. *Soul: Buddhist concepts. The encyclopedia of religion,* edited by Mircea Eliade, 13:443–7. New York: Macmillan.

Collis, Maurice. 1985. *The land of the great image.* New York: New Directions.

Conlon, Frank F. 1974. Caste by association: The Gauda Sarasvata Brahmana unification movement. *The Journal of Asian Studies* 33(3):351–65.

_____. 1977. *A caste in a changing world: The Chitrapur Saraswat Brahmans, 1700–1935.* Berkeley: University of California Press.

_____. 1981. The census of India as a source for the historical study of religion and caste, pp. 103–17 in *The census in British India: New perspectives,* edited by N. Gerald Barrier. New Delhi, India: Manohar Publications.

Conze, Edward. 1959. *Buddhist scriptures,* selected and translated by Edward Conze. New York: Penguin.

Cornwell, John. 2001. *Breaking faith: The pope, the people, and the fate of Catholicism.* New York: Viking.

Cotterill, Rodney. 1990. *No ghost in the machine: Modern science and the brain, the mind, and the soul.* London: William Heinemann Ltd.

Coulson, Michael. 1992. *Sanskrit: An introduction to the classical language.* Lincolnwood, IL: NTC Publishing Group.

Couto, Maria Aurora. 2004. *Goa: A daughter's story.* New Delhi, India: Penguin.

Cowell, E.B., and A.E. Gough, translators. 2007. *The Sarva-darśana-saṅgraha of Mādhavāchārya.* Reprint of 2nd revised edition of 1894. Delhi, India: Motilal Banarsidass.

Crease, Robert P. 1999. *Making physics: A biography of Brookhaven National Laboratory, 1946–1972.* Chicago: University of Chicago Press.

Crick, Francis. 1995. *The astonishing hypothesis: The scientific search for the soul.* Reprint of 1994 edition. New York: Touchstone.

Cronin, V. 2003. Nobili, Roberto de. *New Catholic encyclopedia,* 10:407–8. 2nd edition. Farmington Hills, MI: Thomson Gale.

da Cunha Rivara, Joaquim Heliodoro. 1857. An historical essay on the Konkani language. Translated by Fr. Theophilus Lobo. *The printing press in India,* A.K. Priolkar, Part 2, 141–236. Bombay, India: Marathi Samshodhana Mandala.

Damasio, Antonio R. 1994. *Descartes' error: Emotion, reason, and the human brain*. New York: G.P. Putnam.

_____. 1999. *The feeling of what happens: Body and emotion in the making of consciousness*. New York: Harcourt, Brace.

_____. 2003. *Looking for Spinoza: Joy, sorrow, and the feeling brain*. New York: Harcourt.

Danchin, Antoine. 2002. *The Delphic boat: What genomes tell us*. Translated from French by Alison Quayle. Cambridge, MA: Harvard University Press.

Dandekar, R.N., editor. 1976. *Ramakrishna Gopal Bhandarkar as an Indologist*. Poona, India: Bhandarkar Oriental Research Institute.

Daniélou, Alain. 1964. *Hindu polytheism*. Bollingen Series LXXIII. New York: Pantheon Books.

_____. Translated. 1994. *The complete Kāma Sūtra: The first unabridged modern translation of the classic Indian text by Vātsyāyana*. Rochester, VT: Park Street Press.

Danino, Michel. 2010. *The lost river: On the trail of the Sarasvatī*. New Delhi: Penguin.

D'Arcy, E. 2003. Freedom of religion. *New Catholic encyclopedia*, 5:946–54, 2nd edition, Farmington Hills, MI: Thomson Gale.

Das, Gurcharan. 2009. *The difficulty of being good: On the subtle art of dharma*. New Delhi, India: Penguin.

Dasgupta, Surendranath. 1965. *A history of Indian philosophy*. 5 vols. New York: Cambridge University Press.

da Silva Gracias, Fátima. 1994. *Health and hygiene in colonial Goa (1510–1961)*. New Delhi, India: Concept Publishing.

Datta, V.N. 1988. *Sati: A historical, social and philosophical enquiry into the Hindu rite of widow burning*. London: Sangam Books Ltd.

Dawkins, Richard. 2006. *The God delusion*. Boston, MA: Houghton Mifflin.

D'Costa, Anthony, S.J. 1965. *The Christianisation of the Goa islands*. Bombay, India: St. Xavier's College.

Deakin, Michael A.B. 2007. *Hypatia of Alexandria: Mathematician and martyr*. Amherst, NY: Prometheus Books.

D'Souza, Victor S. 1955. *The Navayats of Kanara: A study in culture contact*. Dharwar, India: Kannada Research Institute.

de Bragança Pereira, A.B. 2008. *Ethnography of Goa, Daman and Diu*. Translated by Maria Aurora Couto. New Delhi, India: Penguin.

de Carvalho, Francisco Moreno. 2007. Garcia (Abraham) Da Orta. http://www.vidaslusofonas.pt/garcia_da_horta2.htm. Accessed 6 June 2007.

Dee, D., and D.P. Sheridan. 2003. Index of prohibited books. *New Catholic encyclopedia*, 7:389–91, 2nd edition. Farmington Hills, MI: Thomson Gale.

de Figueiredo, João Manuel Pacheco. 1967. The practice of Indian medicine in Goa during the Portuguese rule, 1510–1699. *Luso-Brazilian Review* 4(1):51–60.

Della Sala, Sergio, editor. 1999. *Mind myths: Exploring popular assumptions about the mind and brain.* New York: John Wiley & Sons.

de Mendonça, Délio. 2002. *Conversions and citizenry: Goa under Portugal 1510–1610.* New Delhi, India: Concept Publishing.

_____. 2008. Personal communication. Letter dated 24 January 2008 and enclosure, which is a translation of pp. 288–294 of a general letter from the College of Goa, written by Brother Gomes Vaz Goa, 12 December 1567. Document 40, pp. 274–308, from António da Silva Rego, editor, *Documentação para a História das Missões do Padroado Português do Oriente*, vol. 10 (*India 1566–1568*). Lisbon, Portugal: Agência Geral do Ultramar, Divisão de Publicações e Biblioteca, 1953.

de Nicolás, Antonio T. 1976. *Meditations through the Ṛg Veda: Four-dimensional man.* Stony Brook, NY: Nicolas Hays Ltd.

de Sélincourt, Aubrey. 1962. *The world of Herodotus.* Boston: Little, Brown.

Denton, Lynn Teskey. 2004. *Female ascetics in Hinduism.* Albany, NY: State University of New York Press.

Derrett, J. Duncan M. 1963. *Introduction to modern Hindu law.* Bombay, India: Oxford University Press.

_____. 1968. *Religion, law and the state in India.* New York: Free Press.

Dershowitz, Nachum, and Edward M. Reingold. 1997. *Calendrical calculations.* New York: Cambridge University Press.

Desai, Sudha Vishwanath. 1980. *Social life in Maharashtra under the Peshwas.* Bombay, India: Popular Prakashan.

Deshpande, Prachi. 2004. Caste as Maratha: Social categories, colonial policy and identity in early twentieth-century Maharashtra. *Indian Economic and Social History Review* 41(1):7–32.

_____. 2007. *Creative pasts: Historical memory and identity in western India 1700–1960.* Ranikhet, India: Permanent Black.

de Souza, Teotonio R. 1975. Glimpses of Hindu dominance of Goan economy in the 17th century. *Indica* 12:27–35.

_____. 1979. *Medieval Goa: A socio-economic history.* New Delhi, India: Concept Publishing.

_____. 1992. Why Cuncolim martyrs? An historical re-assessment, pp. 35–47, in *Jesuits in India: In historical perspective*, edited by Teotonio R. De Souza and Charles J. Borges. Alto Porvorim, Goa: Xavier Center of Historical Research, and Macao, China: Instituto Cultural De Macau.

_____. 1994. *Goa to me.* New Delhi, India: Concept Publishing.

de Tocqueville, A. 2004. *Democracy in America*. A new translation by A. Goldhammer. New York: Library of America.

de Waal, Frans. 1997. *Bonobo: The forgotten ape*. Berkeley: University of California Press.

_____. 1998. *Chimpanzee politics: Power and sex among apes*. Revised edition. Baltimore: Johns Hopkins University Press.

_____. 2005. *Our inner ape: A leading primatologist explains why we are who we are*. New York: Riverhead Books.

_____. 2006. *Primates and philosophers: How morality evolved*. Princeton, NJ: Princeton University Press.

Dhume, Anant Ramkrishna Sinai. 1985. *The cultural history of Goa*. Panaji, Goa, India: Ramesh Anant S. Dhume.

Dias, Mariano Jose. 1980. The Hindu-Christian society of Goa. *Indica* 17(2):109–16.

Dirks, Nicholas B. 2001. *Castes of mind: Colonialism and the making of modern India*. Princeton, NJ: Princeton University Press.

Disney, Anthony. 1995. Vasco da Gama's reputation for violence: The alleged atrocities at Calicut in 1502. *Indica* 32(1):11–28.

Doniger, Wendy. 2009. *The Hindus: An alternative history*. New York: Penguin.

Doniger, Wendy, and Brian K. Smith. 1991. *The laws of Manu*. New York: Penguin.

Doniger, Wendy, and Sudhir Kakar. 2003. *Vatsyayana Mallanaga: Kamasutra*. New York: Oxford University Press.

Dowson, John. 1968. *A classical dictionary of Hindu mythology and religion, geography, history, and literature*. 11th edition. London: Routledge & Kegan Paul.

Duby, Georges, editor. 1988. *A history of private life. II: Revelations of the medieval world*. Translated by A. Goldhammer. Cambridge, MA: Belknap Press.

Dumont, Louis. 1980. *Homo hierarchicus: The caste system and its implications*. Completely revised English edition. Chicago: University of Chicago Press.

Dundas, Paul. 2002. *The Jains*. 2nd edition. New York: Routledge.

Dutta, Krishna, and Andrew Robinson. 1996. *Rabindranath Tagore: The myriad-minded man*. New York: St. Martin's Press.

Dzielska, Maria. 1995. *Hypatia of Alexandria*. 2nd printing. Translated by F. Lyra. Cambridge, MA. London: Harvard University Press.

Eades, Lindsay Michie. 1999. *The end of apartheid in South Africa*. Westport, CT: Greenwood Press.

Eck, Diana L. 1983. *Banaras: City of light*. Princeton, NJ: Princeton University Press.

Eliade, Mircea, editor. 1987. *The encyclopedia of religion*. New York: Macmillan.

Encyclopaedia Britannica. 1968. 24 vols. Chicago: Encyclopaedia Britannica, Inc.

Enthoven, R.E. 1975. *The tribes and castes of Bombay*. 3 vols. Reprint of 1920 edition. Delhi, India: Cosmo Publications.

Fairservis, Jr., Walter A. 1975. *The roots of ancient India*. Second edition, revised. Chicago: University of Chicago Press.

Falk, Harry. 1989. Soma I and II. *Bulletin of the School of Oriental and African Studies, University of London* 52(1):77–90.

Ferguson, Niall. 2008. *The ascent of money: A financial history of the world*. New York: Penguin.

Finegan, Jack. 1989. *An archaeological history of religions of Indian Asia*. New York: Paragon House.

Fischel, Walter J. 1956. Leading Jews in the service of Portuguese India. *Jewish Quarterly Review* 47(1):37–57.

_____. 2007. Goa. *Encyclopaedia Judaica*, edited by Fred Skolnik, 7:651. 2nd edition. Farmington Hills, MI: Thomson Gale.

Fischel, Walter Joseph, and Joshua O. Leibowitz. 2007. Orta, Garcia de. *Encyclopaedia Judaica*, edited by Fred Skolnik, 15:492. 2nd edition. Farmington Hills, MI: Thomson Gale.

Fisher, Ian. 2007a. Pope concedes unjustifiable crimes in converting South Americans. *New York Times*, 24 May. http://www.nytimes.com/2007/05/24/world/americas/24pope.html. Accessed 2 June 2012.

_____. 2007b. Pope, restating 2000 document, cites 'defects' of other faiths. *New York Times*, 11 July. http://www.nytimes.com/2007/07/11/world/europe/11pope.html. Accessed 2 June 2012.

Fonseca, José Nicolau Da. 2001. *An historical and archaeological sketch of the city of Goa*. Reprint of 1878 edition. New Delhi, Madras, India: Asian Educational Services.

Forbes, Geraldine. 1996. *Women in modern India*. Vol.IV.2. *The New Cambridge History of India*. New York: Cambridge University Press.

Freeth, T., Y. Bitsakis, X. Moussas, J.H. Seiradakis, A. Tselikas, H. Mangou, M. Zafeiropoulou, R. Hadland, D. Bate, A. Ramsey, M. Allen, A. Crawley, P. Hockley, T. Malzbender, D. Gelb, W. Ambrisco, and M.G. Edmunds. 2006. Decoding the ancient Greek astronomical calculator known as the Antikythera Mechanism. *Nature* 444:587–591.

Fukazawa, Hiroshi. 1968. State and caste system (*jāti*) in the eighteenth century Maratha kingdom. *Hitotsubashi Journal of Economics* 9(1): 32–44.

Fuller, Christopher John. 2004. *The camphor flame: Popular Hinduism and society in India*. Revised and expanded edition. Princeton, NJ: Princeton University Press.

Furst, Peter T., editor. 1990. *Flesh of the Gods: The ritual use of hallucinogens*. Reissue of 1972 edition. with changes. Prospect Heights, IL: Waveland Press.

Gazzaniga, Michael S. 2008. *Human: The science behind what makes us unique*. New York: HarperCollins.

Gethin, Rupert. 1998. *The foundations of Buddhism*. New York: Oxford University Press.

Ghosh, Amitav. 1992. *In an antique land*. New York: Vintage Books.

Goitein, S.D. 1971. *A Mediterranean Society—the Jewish communities of the Arab world as portrayed in the documents of the Cairo Geniza*. Vol. 17. The community. Berkeley: University of California Press.

_____. 1973. *Letters of medieval Jewish traders*. Princeton, NJ: Princeton University Press.

_____. 1978. *A Mediterranean Society—The Jewish communities of the Arab world as portrayed in the documents of the Cairo Geniza*. Vol. III. *The family*. Berkeley: University of California Press.

_____. 1988. *A Mediterranean Society—The Jewish communities of the Arab world as portrayed in the documents of the Cairo Geniza*. Vol. V. *The Individual*. Berkeley: University of California Press.

Gokhale, Balkrishna Govind. 1988. *Poona in the eighteenth century: An urban history*. Delhi, India: Oxford University Press.

Goldman, Robert P., and Sally J. Sutherland. 1987. *Devavāṇīpraveśikā: An introduction to the Sanskrit language*. Berkeley: University of California Press.

Gollner, Adam Leith. 2008. *The fruit hunters: A story of nature, adventure, commerce, and obsession*. New York: Scribner.

Gombrich, Richard Francis. 1988. *Theravāda Buddhism: A social history from ancient Benares to modern Colombo*. London: Routledge & Kegan Paul.

Gomes, Olivinho J.F., editor. 2000. *Konkani manasagangotri: An anthology of early Konkani literature*. Cavorim Chandor, Goa, India: Konkani Sorospot Prakashan.

Goodall, Jane. 1986. *The chimpanzees of Gombe: Patterns of behavior*. Cambridge, MA: Belknap Press.

Goodstein, Laurie, and David M. Halbfinger. 2010. Amid sexual abuse scandal, an office that failed to act: Pope Benedict's track record called into question. *New York Times,* 2 July.

Gordon, Stewart. 2008. *When Asia was the world.* Philadelphia: Da Capo Press.

Graybill, Lyn S. 2002. *Truth and reconciliation in South Africa: Miracle or model?* Boulder, CO: Lynne Rienner Publishers.

Greeley, Andrew. 2004. *The Catholic revolution: New wine, old wineskins, and the second Vatican council.* Berkeley: University of California Press.

Green, Peter. 1991. *Alexander of Macedon, 356–323 B.C.: A historical biography.* Reprint of revised and enlarged edition first published in 1974 by Pelican Books. Berkeley: University of California Press.

Green, Toby. 2007. *Inquisition: The reign of fear.* New York: Thomas Dunne Books.

Greenblatt, Stephen. 2011. *The swerve: How the world became modern.* New York: W.W. Norton.

Griffith, Ralph T.H. 1963. *The hymns of the Ṛgveda.* 2 vols. Varanasi, India: Chowkhamba Sanskrit Series Office.

Guha, Ramachandra. 2007. *India after Gandhi: the history of the world's largest democracy.* New York: Ecco/HarperCollins.

Gunaratana, Venerable Henepola. 1992. *Mindfulness in plain English.* Boston, MA: Wisdom Publications.

Gunasinghe, P.A.T. 1960–61. Slavery in Ceylon during the period of the Anuradhapura kingdom. *Ceylon Historical Journal* 10(1–4):47–59.

Gune, V.T., editor. 1979. *Gazetteer of the union territory of Goa, Daman and Diu.* District Gazetteer Part 1: Goa. Panaji, Goa, India: Gazetteer Department, Government of the Union Territory of Goa, Daman and Diu.

Gurney, O.R. 1990. *The Hittites.* New York: Penguin.

Hajratwala, Minal. 2009. *Leaving India: My family's journey from five villages to five continents.* Boston, MA: Houghton Mifflin Harcourt.

Hall, Richard Seymor. 1996. *Empires of the monsoon: A history of the Indian ocean and its invaders.* London: HarperCollins.

Hall, Stephen S. 2010. *Wisdom: From philosophy to neuroscience.* New York: Alfred A. Knopf.

Hansen, Leigh Jellison, and J.P. Mallory. 1997. Death beliefs. *Encyclopedia of Indo-European culture.* London: Fitzroy Dearborn Publishers.

Harran, Marilyn J. 1987. Suicide. *The encyclopedia of religion,* edited by Mircea Eliade, 14:125–31. New York: Macmillan.

Harrison, J.B. 1975. The Portuguese. *A cultural history of India*, A.L. Basham, editor. Delhi, India: Oxford University Press.

Harshananda, Swami. 2008. *A concise encyclopaedia of Hinduism*. 3 vols. Bangalore, India: Ramakrishna Math.

Hart, William. 1987. *The art of living: Vipassana meditation as taught by S.N. Goenka*. New York: HarperCollins.

Harvey, Peter. 2000. *An introduction to Buddhist ethics*. New York: Cambridge University Press.

Hastings, Adrian, editor. 1991. *Modern Catholicism: Vatican II and after*. London: SPCK Publishing.

Hawley, John Stratton, editor. 1994. *Sati, the blessing and the curse: The burning of wives in India*. New York: Oxford University Press.

Hicks, David, and Margaret A. Gwynne. 1994. *Cultural anthropology*. New York: HarperCollins College Publishers.

Hill, Roland. 2000. *Lord Acton*. New Haven, CT: Yale University Press.

Hillebrandt, Alfred. 1999. *Vedic mythology*. 2 vols. Translated from the original German by Sreeramula Rajeswara Sarma. Reprint of 1980 English edition. Delhi, India: Motilal Banarsidass.

Hiltzik, Michael A. 1999. *Dealers of lightning: Xerox PARC and the dawn of the computer age*. New York: Harper Business.

Hiorth, Finngeir. 1996. *Introduction to humanism*. Pune, India: Indian Secular Society.

Hiriadka, Muraleedhara Upadhya, and H. Dundiraj, 2001. *Haji Abdulla Saheb*. (In Kannada). Udupi, India: Sakhigita.

Hitchens, Christopher. 2007. *God is not great: How religion poisons everything*. New York: Twelve.

Holborn, Hajo. 1982. *A history of modern Germany: The reformation*. Vol. 1. Princeton, NJ: Princeton University Press.

Hood, Bruce M. 2009. *Supersense: Why we believe in the unbelievable*. New York: HarperCollins.

Hospital, Clifford. 1984. *The righteous demon: A study of Bali*. Vancouver, Canada: University of British Columbia Press.

Hsu, Feng-Hsiung. 2002. *Behind Deep Blue: Building the computer that defeated the world chess champion*. Princeton, NJ: Princeton University Press.

Ifrah, Georges. 2000. *The universal history of numbers: From prehistory to the invention of the computer*. New York: John Wiley & Sons.

Illingworth, Valerie, and John O.E. Clark, editors. 2000. *The facts on file dictionary of astronomy*. 4th edition. New York: Facts on File, Inc.

Inamdar, V.M. 1973. *Shivarama Karanth*. Mysore, India: Institute of Kannada Studies, University of Mysore.

Ingalls, Daniel H.H. 1971. Remarks on Mr. Wasson's soma. *Journal of the American Oriental Society* 91(2):188–191.

Iyengar, K.R. Srinivasa. 2003. Stephens, Thomas. *New Catholic encyclopedia*, 13:526. 2nd edition. Farmington Hills, MI: Thomson Gale.

Iyer, L.K. Anantha Krishna, 1912. *Cochin tribes and castes*. Vol. 2. Madras, India: Higginbotham & Co.

James, Wilmot, and Linda van der Vijver. 2001. *After the TRC: Reflections on truth and reconciliation in South Africa*. Athens, OH: Ohio University Press.

James, William. 1936. *The varieties of religious experience: A study in human nature*. New York: Modern Library.

Jamison, Kay Redfield. 1995. *An unquiet mind*. New York: Alfred A. Knopf.

_____. 1999. *Night falls fast: Understanding suicide*. New York: Alfred A. Knopf.

Jamison, Stephanie W. 1991. *The ravenous hyenas and the wounded sun: Myth and ritual in ancient India*. Ithaca, NY: Cornell University Press.

Janardhan, Pandarinath Bhuvanendra. 1991. *A higher Konkani grammar*. Madras, India: Anantheshwara Print Packs.

_____. 1999. *A practical Konkani–English encyclopaedic dictionary*. Chennai, India: Kay Jay Or Enterprises.

Jayakar, Pupul. 1992. *Indira Gandhi: An intimate biography*. New York: Pantheon.

Jayaraman, A. 1989. *Chandrasekhara Venkata Raman: A memoir*. New Delhi, India: Affiliated East-West Press.

Jensen, Joan M. 1988. *Passage from India: Asian Indian immigrants in North America*. New Haven, CT: Yale University Press.

Jha, D.N. 2002. *The myth of the holy cow*. London: Verso Books.

Jivaji, T. 1919. Judgment pronounced in open court on 17 March 1919 on original suit No. 26 of 1915 in the Court of the Subordinate Judge of South Kanara. Photocopy of original, without attachments, unpublished. Typewritten, 116 legal-size pages.

John Paul II. 1986. Speeches during the India trip: 1–10 February 1986. http://www.vatican.va/holy_father/john_paul_ii/travels/sub_index1986/trav_india.htm. Accessed 21 August 2007.

_____. 1999a. *Ecclesia in Asia: post-synodal apostolic exhortation (November 6, 1999)*. http://www.vatican.va/holy_father/john_paul_ii/apost_exhortations/documents/hf_jp-ii_exh_06111999_ecclesia-in-asia_en.html. Accessed 16 August 2007.

_____. 1999b. Speeches during the India trip: 6–7 November 1999. http://www.vatican.va/holy_father/john_paul_ii/travels/sub_index/trav_india-georgia-1999.htm. Accessed 21 August 2007.

Kamath, Bhaskar Kogga. 1995. *Story of Kogga Kamath's marionettes*. Udupi, India: Regional Resource Centre, M.G.M. College Campus.

Kamath, Suryanath U, editor. 1982. *Karnataka state gazetteer*, in 2 parts. Bangalore, India: Government of Karnataka Publication.

Kane, Pandurang Vaman. 1973–90. *History of Dharmaśāstra: Ancient and medieval religious and civil law in India*. 5 vols. 2nd edition. Poona, India: Bhandarkar Oriental Research Institute.

Kanigel, Robert. 1991. *The man who knew infinity: A life of the genius Ramanujan*. New York: Charles Scribner's Sons.

Karanth, K. Shivarama. 1993. *Ten faces of a crazy mind: Autobiography*. Translated by H.Y. Sharada Prasad. Bombay, India: Bharatiya Vidya Bhavan.

_____. 1997. *Yakṣagāna*. Revised and enlarged edition. New Delhi, India: Indira Gandhi National Centre for the Arts.

Karve, Irawati Karmarkar 1965. *Kinship organization in India*. New York: Asia Publishing House.

Katre, S.M. 1966. *The formation of Koṅkaṇī*. Poona, India: Deccan College, Postgraduate and Research Institute.

Kay, Alan. 1984. Computer software. *Scientific American* 251(3):53–59.

Keene, Donald. 2002. *Emperor of Japan: Meiji and his world*, 1852–1912. New York: Columbia University Press.

Kersenboom-Story, Saskia C. 1987. *Nityasumaṅgalī: Devadasi tradition in South India*. New Delhi, India: Motilal Banarsidass.

Kertzer, David I. 1997. *The kidnapping of Edgardo Mortara*. New York: Alfred A. Knopf.

_____. 2001. *The popes against the Jews: The Vatican's role in the rise of modern anti-Semitism*. New York: Alfred A. Knopf.

Khan, Geoffrey, and Menahem Ben-Sasson. 2007. Genizah, Cairo. *Encyclopaedia Judaica*, edited by Fred Skolnik, 7:460–77. 2nd edition. Farmington Hills, MI: Thomson Gale.

King, Richard. 1999. *Indian philosophy: An introduction to Hindu and Buddhist thought*. Washington, DC: Georgetown University Press.

Kinsley, David. 1988. *Hindu goddesses: Visions of the divine feminine in the Hindu religious tradition*. Berkeley: University of California Press.

Kirsch, Jonathan. 2005. *God against the gods: The history of the war between monotheism and polytheism*. New York: Penguin.

_____. 2009. *The grand inquisitor's manual: A history of terror in the name of God*. New York: HarperCollins.

Kittel, Ferdinand. 1968. *Kittel's Kannada–English dictionary*. 4 vols. Revised and enlarged 1894, edited by M. Mariappa Bhat. Madras, India: University of Madras.

Klostermaier, Klaus K. 1994. *A survey of Hinduism*. 2nd edition. Albany, NY: State University of New York Press.

Koch, Christof. 2004. *The quest for consciousness: A neurobiological approach*. Englewood, CO: Roberts & Co. Publishers.

Kochhar, Rajesh. 2004. *The Vedic people: Their history and geography*. Reprint of 2000 edition. New Delhi, India: Orient Longman Ltd.

Kosambi, Damodar Dharmanand. 1950. On the origin of Brahmin gotras. *Journal of the Bombay Branch of the Royal Asiatic Society* 26:21–0.

_____. 1951. Ancient Kosala and Magadha. *Journal of the Bombay Branch of the Royal Asiatic Society* 27:180–213.

_____. 1953. Brahmin Clans. *Journal of the American Oriental Society* 73:202–8.

_____. 1962. *Myth and reality: Studies in the formation of Indian culture*. Bombay, India: Popular Prakashan.

_____. 1969. *Ancient India: A history of its culture and civilization*. New York: Meridian Books.

_____. 1975. *An introduction to the study of Indian history*. Revised 2nd edition. Bombay, India: Popular Prakashan.

Kosambi, Meera, editor. 2000. *Pandita Ramabai through her own words: Selected works*. Compiled and edited, with translations, by Meera Kosambi. Oxford, UK: Oxford University Press.

Kramrisch, Stella. 1988. *The presence of Śiva*. New Delhi, India: Motilal Banarsidass.

Kudva, V.N. 1978. *History of the Dakshinatya Saraswats*. 2nd edition. Madras, India: Samyukta Gowda Saraswata Sabha.

Küng, Hans. 2001. *The catholic church: A short history*. New York: Modern Library.

Kutumbiah, P. 1962. *Ancient Indian medicine*. Calcutta, India: Orient Longman Ltd.

Lach, Donald F. & Edwin J. Van Kley. 1993. *Asia in the making of Europe*. Vol. 3. *A century of advance*. Chicago: University of Chicago Press.

Laine, James W. 2003. *Shivaji: Hindu king in Islamic India*. New York: Oxford University Press.

LeDoux, Joseph. 2002. *Synaptic self: How our brains become who we are*. New York: Penguin.

Leslie, I. Julia. 1995. *The perfect wife*. Translated from the Sanskrit of Tryambakayajvan, *Strīdharmapaddhati*. Reprint of 1989 edition. New York: Penguin.

Leslie, Julia, editor. 1992. *Roles and rituals for Hindu women*. Reprint of 1991 edition. Delhi, India: Motilal Banarsidass.

Lessig, Lawrence. 2010. A better chance at justice for abuse victims. *New York Times*, 27 April. Also available at http://www.nytimes.com/2010/04/27/opinion/27lessig.html.

Letcher, Andy. 2008. *Shroom: A cultural history of the magic mushroom*. New York: Ecco/HarperPerennial.

Levine, Marvin. 2000. *The positive psychology of Buddhism and Yoga: Paths to a mature happiness*. Mahwah, NJ: Lawrence Erlbaum.

Libet, Benjamin, Curtis A. Gleason, Elwood W. Wright, and Dennis K. Pearl. 1983. Time of conscious intention to act in relation to onset of cerebral activity (readiness-potential): The unconscious initiation of a freely voluntary act. *Brain* 106:623–42.

Libet, Benjamin. 1993. *Neurophysiology of consciousness: Selected papers and new essays by Benjamin Libet*. Boston, MA: Birkhäuser.

Lightman, Bernard V. 1987. *The origins of agnosticism: Victorian unbelief and the limits of knowledge*. Baltimore: Johns Hopkins University Press.

Lingat, Robert. 1973. *The classical law of India*. Translated from the French by J. Duncan M. Derrett. Berkeley: University of California Press.

Lipner, Julius. 1994. *Hindus: Their religious beliefs and practices*. London: Routledge.

Livermoore, H.V. 1966. *A new history of Portugal*. Cambridge, MA: Cambridge University Press.

Macdonell, Arthur Anthony, and Arthur Berriedale Keith. 1995. *Vedic index of names and subjects*. 2 vols. Reprint of 1912 edition. Delhi, India: Motilal Banarsidass.

Macdougall, H.A. 2003. Acton, John Emerich Edward Dalberg. *New Catholic encyclopedia*, 1:84–6. 2nd edition. Farmington Hills, MI: Thomson Gale.

Mahony, William K. 1987. Soul: Indian concepts. *The encyclopedia of religion*, edited by Mircea Eliade, 13:438–43. New York: Macmillan.

Mallory, J.P. 1997a. BMAC (Bactrian-Margiana Archaeological Complex). *Encyclopedia of Indo-European culture*, edited by J.P. Mallory and D.Q. Adams, 72. London: Fitzroy Dearborn Publishers.

Mallory, J.P. 1997b. *Sacred drink. Encyclopedia of Indo-European culture*, edited by J.P. Mallory and D.Q. Adams, 494. London: Fitzroy Dearborn Publishers.

Mani, Lata. 1998. *Contentious traditions: The debate on Sati in colonial India*. Berkeley: University of California Press.

Manilal, K.S. 1980. *Botany and history of Hortus Malabaricus*. New Delhi, India: Oxford & IBH Publishing.

Marchant, Josephine. 2009. *Decoding the heavens: A 2,000-year-old computer-and the century-long search to discover its secrets.* Cambridge, MA: Da Capo Press.

Marglin, Frederique Apffel. 1985. *Wives of the God-king: The rituals of the devadasis of Puri.* New York: Oxford University Press.

_____. 1987. Hierodouleia. *The encyclopedia of religion,* edited by Mircea Eliade, 6:309–13. New York: Macmillan.

Marques, A.H. de Oliveira. 1971. *Daily life in Portugal in the late middle ages.* Translated by S.S. Wyatt. Madison, WI: University of Wisconsin Press.

_____. 1972. *History of Portugal.* 2 vols. New York: Columbia University Press.

Martyrs of Cuncolim. http://www.newadvent.org/cathen/04568a.htm. Accessed 20 July 2007. http://www.catholic-forum.com/saints/define92.htm. Accessed 20 July 2007.

Matilal, Bimal Krishna. 1987. Cārvāka. *The encyclopedia of religion,* Mircea Eliade, editor, 3:105–6. New York: Macmillan.

Maxwell, Kenneth. 1995. *Pombal: Paradox of the enlightenment.* New York: Cambridge University Press.

Mayrhofer, Manfred. 2003. Die personennamen in der Ṛgveda-Saṁhitā: Sichers und zweifelhaftes. *Bayerische Akademie der Wissenschaften, Philosophisch-Historische Klasse Sitzungsberichte.* Heft 3:1–165. Munich: Verlag C.H. Beck.

McGarry, P.S. 2003. Pombal, Sebastião José de Carvalho e Mello. *New Catholic encyclopedia,* 11:466–8. Farmington Hills, MI: Thomason, Gale.

Mhamai, S.K, editor. 2004. *Mhamais of Goa in the network of trade and culture.* Panaji, Goa, India: S.K. Mhamai, Mhamai House.

_____, editor. 2007. *The Mhamai's and Goa's neighbours: Commercial links and allied interests.* Panaji, Goa, India: S.K. Mhamai, Mhamai House.

Milgrom, Jacob, and Alan Unterman. 2007. Forgiveness. *Encyclopaedia Judaica,* edited by Fred Skolnik, 7:127–9. 2nd edition. Farmington Hills, MI: Thomson, Gale.

Milton, Giles. 2003. *Samurai William: The Englishman who opened Japan.* New York: Farrar, Straus & Giroux.

Mitchiner, John E. 1982. *Traditions of the seven ṛṣis.* Delhi, India: Motilal Banarsidass.

Mitragotri, V.R. 1999. *A socio-cultural history of Goa from the Bhojas to the Vijayanagara.* Panaji, Goa, India: Institute Menezes Braganza.

Mittal, Kewal, Krishna. 1974. *Materialism in Indian thought.* New Delhi, India: Munshiram Manoharlal.

Monier-Williams, M. 1976. *English–Sanskrit Dictionary.* 1st Indian edition, reprint of 1851 edition. New Delhi, India: Munshiram Manoharlal.

Montagu, Ashley. 1967. *The anatomy of swearing*. New York: Macmillan.

Mookerji, Radha Kumud. 2003. *Ancient Indian education: Brahmanical and Buddhist*. Reprint of 1951 2nd edition. New Delhi, India: Motilal Banarsidass.

Moran, Joseph Francis. 1993. *The Japanese and the Jesuits: Alessandro Valignano in sixteenth-century Japan*. London: Routledge & Kegan Paul.

Moser, Gerald M. 1964. Review of *The Goa Inquisition*: Being a quatercentenary commemoration study of the Inquisition in Goa by Anant Kakba Priolkar. *Journal of the American Oriental Society* 84(4):483–4.

Murdin, Paul, editor. 2001. *Encyclopedia of astronomy and astrophysics*. Philadelphia: Institute of Physics Publishing.

Nanaiah, N. Saraswati. 1992. *The position of women during Vijayanagara period (1336–1646)*. Mysore, India: Saraswati Publications.

Narasimhan, Sakuntala. 1992. *Sati: Widow burning in India*. New York: Anchor Books.

Navada, A.V., and Denis Fernandes, editors. 2008. *The devil worship of the Tuluvas: From the papers of late A. C. Burnell (1894–1897)*. Mangalore, India: Karnataka Tulu Sahitya Academy.

Nayak, Palimar Vasantha Devaraya. 2004. Tape-recorded interview by M.R. Bhat, 15 December, in Mulki, India.

Newberg, Andrew, Eugene D'Aquili, and Vince Rause. 2001. *Why God won't go away: Brain science and the biology of belief*. New York: Ballantine.

Newman, Robert S. 2001. *Of umbrellas, goddesses and dreams: Essays on Goan culture and society*. Mapusa, Goa, India: Other India Press.

Nikam, N.A., and Richard McKeon, editors and translators. 1978. *The edicts of Asoka*. Midway reprint of 1959 edition. Chicago: University of Chicago Press.

Nilekani, Nandan. 2009. *Imagining India: The idea of a renewed nation*. New York: Penguin.

Ninivaggi, Frank John. 2008. *Ayurveda: A comprehensive guide to traditional Indian medicine for the West*. Westport, CT: Praeger.

Noël, Lise. 1994. *Intolerance: A general survey*. Translated by Arnold Bennett. Montreal: McGill-Queen's University Press.

Nørretranders, Tor. 1998. *The user illusion: Cutting consciousness down to size*. Translated by Jonathan Sydenham. New York: Penguin.

O'Flaherty, Wendy Doniger. 1975. *Hindu myths: A sourcebook translated from the Sanskrit*. Baltimore: Penguin.

_____. 1981. *The Rig Veda: An anthology*. New York: Penguin.

O'Hanlon, Rosalind. 1985. *Caste, conflict, and ideology: Mahatma Jotirao Phule and low caste protest in nineteenth-century Western India.* Cambridge, MA: Cambridge University Press.

Olin, Doris. 2003. *Paradox.* Montreal: McGill-Queen's University Press.

Olivelle, Patrick. 1987. Rites of passage: Hindu rites. *The encyclopedia of religion*, edited by Mircea Eliade, 12:387–92. New York: Macmillan.

_____. 1996. *Upaniṣads.* New York: Oxford University Press.

_____. 1999. *Dharmasūtras: The law codes of Āpastamba, Gautama, Baudhāyana, and Vasiṣṭha.* New York: Oxford University Press.

Orr, Leslie. C. 2000. *Donors, devotees and daughters of God: Temple women in medieval Tamilnadu.* New York: Oxford University Press.

Padakannaya, K.V. et al., editors. 1980. *St. Aloysius College, Mangalore centenary souvenir.* Mangalore, India: St. Aloysius College.

Padma, M.B. 1993. *The position of women in mediaeval Karnataka.* Mysore, India: Mysore University Press.

Pai, B. Kusuma V. 2003. *Karavali Karnatakada Gowda Saraswath Brahmanara samskrithi: Ondu adhyayana.* (In Kannada). Mysore, India: Kusuma Prakashana.

Pai, Manjeshvar Govinda. 1995. *Mūlkiyannu kuritu.* (In Kannada). *A collection of Rastrakavi Govind Pai's (1883–1963) research papers in Kannada.* H.K. Bhat and M. Upadhyaya, editors., 715–7. Udupi, India: Rashtrakavi Govind Pai Samshodhana Kendra, M.G.M. College.

Pais, Arthur J. 2007. Hans Ucko. *India Abroad*, December 7.

_____. 2008. Episcopal Christians apologize to Hindus. *India Abroad*, February 8.

Pandey, Rajbali. 1969. *Hindu saṁskāras: Socio-religious study of the Hindu sacraments.* New Delhi, India: Motilal Banarsidas.

Pandolfini, Bruce. 1997. *Kasparov and Deep Blue: The historic chess match between man and machine.* New York: Fireside.

Panikkar, Raimundo, editor and translator. 1983. *The Vedic experience: Mantramañjarī, an anthology of the Vedas for modern man and contemporary celebration.* Pondicherry, India: All India Books.

Parashar, Archana. 1992. *Women and family law reform in India: Uniform civil code and gender equality.* New Delhi, India: Sage Publications India.

Pargiter, F.E. 1997. *Ancient Indian historical tradition.* Reprint of 1922 edition. Delhi, India: Motilal Banarsidass.

Parry, J.H. 1964. *The age of reconnaissance.* New York: New American Library.

Parry, Jonathan P. 1994. *Death in Banaras*. Cambridge, MA: Cambridge University Press.

Pasricha, Seema. 2006. *Caste based reservation in India*. New Delhi, India: Deep & Deep Publications.

Patil, Sharad. 1982. *Dāsa-Śūdra slavery: Studies in the origins of Indian slavery and feudalism and their philosophies*. New Delhi, India: Allied Publishers.

Patnaik, Utsa, and Manjari Dingwaney. 1985. *Chains of servitude: Bondage and slavery in India*. New Delhi, India: Sangam Books Ltd.

Paul VI. 1965. Nostra aetate: Declaration on the relation of the church to non-Christian religions. The second Vatican council. http://www.newadvent.org/library/docs_ec21na.htm. Accessed 1 June 2007.

Pearson, M.N. 1973. Wealth and power: Indian groups in the Portuguese Indian economy. *South Asia* 3:36–44.

_____. 1981. *Coastal Western India: Studies from the Portuguese records*. New Delhi, India: Concept Publishing.

_____. 1987. *The New Cambridge History of India*. Vol. I.1. *The Portuguese in India*. Cambridge, New York: Cambridge University Press.

Pedersen, Tana L. 2010. *The official guide to Family Tree Maker 2010*. Provo, UT: Ancestry Publishing.

Pereira, José. 1971. *Konkani: A language. A history of the Konkani–Marathi controversy*. Dharwar, India: Karnatak University.

Pereira, Rui Gomes. 1978. *Goa*. Vol. 1. *Hindu temples and deities*. Translated from the Portuguese by Antonio Victor Couto. Panaji, Goa, India: Printwell Press.

_____. 1981. *Goa*. Vol. 2. *Gaunkari (the old village associations)*. Translated from the Portuguese by Angelo das Neves Souza. Panaji, Goa, India: Printwell Press.

Persinger, Michael A. 1987. *Neuropsychological bases of God beliefs*. New York: Praeger.

Peters, Edward. 1988. *Inquisition*. New York: Free Press.

_____. 2003. Inquisition. *New Catholic encyclopedia*, 7:485–92. 2nd edition, Farmington Hills, MI: Thomson Gale.

Pinto, Bennett. 2003. *Konkani bards and musicians of Kanara*. Mangalore, India: R.R. Publishers.

Plumb, J.H. 1969. Introduction, pp. xiii–xxvii, in *The Portuguese Seaborne Empire (1415–1825)*, by C.R. Boxer. New York: Penguin.

Poe, Edgar Allan. 1993. *Tales of mystery and imagination*. Graham Clarke, editor. London: J.M. Dent.

Prabhu, Vilasini. 2005. Tape-recorded interview by M.R. Bhat, 13 January, in Bangalore, India.

Prasad, R.C. 1995. *The Vivāha: The Hindu marriage saṁskāras.* Translated by R.C. Prasad; reprint of 1993 edition. New Delhi, India: Motilal Banarsidass.
_____. 1997. *The Upanayana: The Hindu ceremonies of the sacred thread.* Translated by R.C. Prasad. New Delhi, India: Motilal Banarsidass.
Priolkar, Anant Kakba. 1958. *The printing press in India: Its beginnings and early development.* Bombay, India: Marathi Samshodhana Madala.
_____. 1961. *The Goa Inquisition: Being a quatercentenary commemoration study of the Inquisition in India.* New Delhi, India: Voice of India

Radhakrishna, B.P., and S.S. Merh, editors. 2002. *Vedic Sarasvati: Evolutionary history of a lost river of Northwestern India.* Memoir 42. Bangalore, India: Geological Society of India.
Radhakrishnan, Sarvepalli, and Charles A. Moore, editors. 1989. *A sourcebook in Indian philosophy.* 12th printing of 1957 edition. Princeton, NJ: Princeton University Press.
Rahula, Sri Walpola. 1974. *What the Buddha taught.* 2nd enlarged edition. New York: Grove Press.
Rahurkar, V.G. 1964. *The seers of the Ṛgveda.* Poona, India: University of Poona.
Ram, H.Y. Mohan. 2005. On the English edition of Van Rheede's *Hortus Malabaricus* by K.S. Manilal (2003). *Current Science* 89(10):1672–80.
Ramachandran, V.S., and Sandra Blakeslee, 1998. *Phantoms in the brain: Probing the mysteries of the human mind.* New York: William Morrow.
Ramachandran, V.S. 2004. *A brief tour of human consciousness: From impostor poodles to purple numbers.* New York: Pi Press.
Ramabai alias Ammanna. 2004. *Traditions & customs.* Mangalore, India: Sri Basti Kogganna Cherdappa Shanbouge.
Rangarajan, L.N., editor and translator. 1992. *Kautilya: The arthashastra.* Reprint. New Delhi, India: Penguin.
Rapoport, Judith L. 1991. *The boy who couldn't stop washing: The experience and treatment of obsessive-compulsive disorder.* New York: Penguin.
Ratzinger, Joseph Cardinal, 2000. Declaration "Dominus Iesus." http://www.vatican.va/roman_curia/congregations/cfaith/documents/rc_con_cfaith_doc_20000806_dominus-iesus_en.html. Accessed 12 July 2007.
Reston, James Jr. 2005. *Dogs of God: Columbus, the Inquisition, and the defeat of the Moors.* New York: Doubleday.
Richards, E.G. 2000. *Mapping time: The calendar and its history.* Reprint of 1998 edition, with corrections. New York: Oxford University Press.
Riedlinger, Thomas J., editor. 1997. *The sacred mushroom seeker: Tributes to R. Gordon Wasson.* Rochester, VT: Park Street Press.

Rieu, E.V., translator. 1983. *Homer: The Iliad.* Reprint of 1950 edition. New York: Penguin.

Rigopoulos, Antonio. 1998. *Dattātreya: The immortal guru, yogin, and avatāra.* Albany, NY: State University of New York Press.

Rizzolatti, Giacomo, and Laila Craighero. 2004. The mirror-neuron system. *Annual Review of Neuroscience* 27:169–92.

Robins, Nick. 2006. *The corporation that changed the world: How the East India Company shaped the modern multinational.* London: Pluto Press.

Rogers, Guy MacLean, 2005. *Alexander: The ambiguity of greatness.* New York: Random House.

Ross, Andrew C. 1994. *A vision betrayed: The Jesuits in Japan and China, 1542–1742.* Maryknoll, NY: Orbis Books.

Roth, C. 1973. Inquisition. *Encyclopaedia Judaica,* edited by Cecil Roth, 8:1380–1407. 2nd corrected printing. Jerusalem: Keter Publishing House Ltd.

Roth, Cecil, and Yehuda Slutsky. 2007. Judaizers. *Encyclopaedia Judaica,* edited by Fred Skolnik, 11:520–3. 2nd edition. Farmington Hills, MI: Thomson Gale.

_____, and Yom Tov Assis. 2007. Inquisition. *Encyclopaedia Judaica,* edited by Fred Skolnik, 9:790–804. Farmington Hills, MI: Thomson Gale.

Rouleau, F.A., et al. 2003. Ricci, Matteo. *New Catholic encyclopedia,* 12:223–5. 2nd edition. Farmington, MI: Thomson Gale.

Ruokanen, Miikka. 1992. *The Catholic doctrine of non-Christian religions: According to the Second Vatican Council.* Leiden: E.J. Brill.

Russell, Bertrand. 1957. *Why I am not a Christian.* New York: Simon & Schuster.

Russell-Wood, A.J.R. 1992. *A world on the move: The Portuguese in Africa, Asia, and America, 1415–1808.* New York: St. Martin's Press.

Ryle, Gilbert. 1949. *The concept of mind.* London: Hutchinson.

Sachau, Edward C. 1971. *Alberuni's India.* Translated by Edward C. Sachau; abridged edition. Ainslie T. Embree, editor. New York: Norton.

Sadock, Benjamin J., and Virginia A. Sadock, editors. 2000. *Kaplan & Sadock's comprehensive textbook of psychiatry,* 2 vols. 7th edition. Philadelphia: Lippincott Williams & Wilkins.

Sampath, Vikram. 2008. *Splendours of royal Mysore: The untold story of the Wodeyars.* New Delhi, India: Rupa Co.

Sarasvati, Svami Satya Prakash, and Satyakam Vidyalankara. 1977. *Ṛgveda samhitā.* 12 vols. New Delhi, India: Veda Pratishthana.

Saraswati, Baidyanath. 1963. Temple organization in Goa. *Man in India* 43(2):131–40.

SarDessai, ManoharRai. 2000. *A history of Konkani literature: From 1500 to 1992*. New Delhi, India: Sahitya Akademi.

Sarmah, Thaneswar. 1991. *The Bharadvājas in ancient India*. Delhi, India: Motilal Banarsidass.

Sarti, Raffaella. 2002. *Europe at home: Family and material culture, 1500–1800*. Translated by Allan Cameron. New Haven, CT: Yale University Press.

Sarton, George. 1927. *Introduction to the history of science*. Vol. I. *From Homer to Omar Khayyam*. Baltimore: Williams & Wilkins.

_____. 1959. *A history of science: Hellenistic science and culture in the last three centuries* B.C. Cambridge, MA: Harvard University Press.

Sastri, K.A. Nilakanta. 1966. *A history of south India: From prehistoric times to the fall of Vijayanagar*. 3rd edition. Madras, India: Oxford University Press.

Saunders, A.C. de C.M. 1982. *A social history of black slaves and freedmen in Portugal, 1441–1555*. Cambridge, MA: Cambridge University Press.

Sawkar, Indrayani. 2001. *Man from the sun: The story of the Kosambis*. Mumbai, India: Popular Prakashan.

Scammell, G.V. 1988. The pillars of empire: Indigenous assistance and survival of the 'Estado da India' c. 1600–1700. *Modern Asian Studies* 22(3):473–89.

Schalit, Abraham. 2007. Antipater II or Antipas. *Encyclopaedia Judaica*, edited by Fred Skolnik, 2:205. 2nd edition. Farmington Hills, MI: Thomson Gale.

Schmidt, Hanns-Peter. 1987. *Some women's rites and rights in the Veda*. Poona, India: Bhandarkar Oriental Research Institute.

Schultes, Richard Evans, and Albert Hofmann. 1979. *Plants of the Gods: Origins of hallucinogenic use*. New York: McGraw-Hill.

Schumann, Hans Wolfgang. 1989. *The historical Buddha: The times, life and teachings of the founder of Buddhism*. Translated from the German by M. O'C. Walshe. New York: Penguin.

_____. 1993. *Buddhism: An outline of its teachings and schools*. Translated by Georg Feuerstein. Reprint of 1974 edition. Wheaton, IL: Quest Books.

Schütte, J.F. 2003a. Rodriguez Tçuzu, João. *New Catholic encyclopedia*, 12:281–2. 2nd edition. Farmington Hills, MI: Thomson Gale.

_____. 2003b. Valignano, Alessandro. *New Catholic encyclopedia*, 14:375–6. 2nd edition. Farmington Hills, MI: Thomson Gale.

Searle-Chatterjee, Mary, and Ursula Sharma, editors. 1994. *Contextualising caste: Post-Dumontian approaches*. Oxford: Blackwell Publishers.

Segal, Robert A., editor. 1998. *The myth and ritual theory: An anthology*. Malden, MA: Blackwell Publishers.

Sen, Amartya. 2005. *The argumentative Indian: Writings on Indian history, culture and identity*. New York: Farrar, Straus & Giroux.

Seyffert, Oskar. 1956. *A dictionary of classical antiquities: Mythology, religion, literature, art*. Revised and edited, with additions by Henry Nettleship and J.E. Sandys. New York: Meridian Books.

Sewell, Robert, and Sankara Balkrishna Dikshit. 1996. *The Indian calendar: With tables for the conversion of Hindu and Muhammadan into* A.D. *dates, and vice versa*. New Delhi, India: Motilal Banarsidass.

Sharma, Arvind, et al. 2001. *Sati: Historical and phenomenological essays*. Reprint of 1988 edition. Delhi, India: Motilal Banarsidass.

Sharma, Ram Sharan. 1990. *Śūdras in ancient India: A social history of the lower order down to circa* A.D. *600*. 3rd revised edition. Delhi, India: Motilal Banarsidass.

Shastry, B.S. 1981. *Studies in Indo-Portuguese history*. Bangalore, India: IBH Prakashana.

_____. 1992. Marquês de Pombal and the Jesuits of Goa, pp. 49–59, in *Jesuits in India: In historical perspective*, edited by Teotonio R. De Souza and Charles J. Borges. Alto Porvorim, Goa: Xavier Center of Historical Research, Instituto Cultural De Macau.

Shastry, B.S., editor. 1993. *Goan society through the ages: Seminar papers*. New Delhi, India: Asian Publication Services.

_____. 2000. *Goa–Kanara Portuguese relations, 1498–1763*. Charles J. Borges, editor. New Delhi, India: Concept Publishing.

Shenoy, Jaya V. 1988. *Ūṭa-Upāhāra*. (In Kannada). Revised and enlarged edition of *Āmgelẽ Khāṇa-Jevaṇa*. Udupi, India: Saraswath Prakashan.

_____. 1999. *Āmgelẽ Khāṇa-Jevaṇa*. (In Konkaṇi with Kannada script). Udupi, India: Saraswath Prakashan.

_____. 2004. Sulabha Aḍuge (*Ūṭa-Upāhāra*—Part 2). (In Kannada). Udupi, India: Saraswath Prakashan.

Shiri, Godwin, editor. 1985. *Wholeness in Christ: The legacy of the Basel mission in India*. Mangalore, India: Karnataka Theological Research Institute.

Smith, Daniel B. 2007. *Muses, madmen and prophets: Rethinking the history, science and meaning of auditory hallucinations*. New York: Penguin.

Smith, Houston. 1972. Review: Wasson's *Soma*: A review article. *Journal of the American Academy of Religion* 40(4):480–499.

Snodgrass, Jeffrey G. 2006. *Casting kings: Bards and Indian modernity.* New York: Oxford University Press.

Soifer, Deborah A. 1991. *The myths of Narasiṁha and Vāmana: Two avataras in cosmological perspective.* Albany, NY: State University of New York Press.

Solomon, Andrew. 2001. *The noonday demon: An atlas of depression.* New York: Scribner.

Sorensen, Roy. 2003. *A brief history of the paradox: Philosophy and the labyrinths of the mind.* Oxford, UK: Oxford University Press.

Spawforth, Antony. 2008. *Versailles: A biography of a palace.* New York: St. Martin's Press.

Speake, Jennifer. 1997. *The Oxford dictionary of foreign words and phrases.* Oxford, UK: Oxford University Press.

Srinivas, M.N. 2001. *Indian society through personal writings.* New Delhi, India: Oxford University Press.

_____. 2002. *Collected essays.* New Delhi, India: Oxford University Press.

_____. 2003. An obituary on caste as a system. *Economic and Political Weekly*, February 1, 2003, 455–59.

Staal, Frits. 1975. *Exploring mysticism: A methodological essay.* Berkeley: University of California Press.

Steel, Duncan. 2000. *Marking time: The epic quest to invent the perfect calendar.* New York: John Wiley & Sons.

Stein, Aurel. 1931. On the ephedra, the hūm plant, and the soma. *Bulletin of the School of Oriental Studies, University of London* 6(2) 501–514.

Stern, Menahem. 2007. Hyracanus, John (Johanan). *Encyclopaedia Judaica*, edited by Fred Skolnik, 9:653–4. 2nd edition. Farmington Hills, MI: Thomson Gale.

Subrahmanyam, Sanjay. 1990. *The political economy of commerce: Southern India, 1500–1650.* New York: Cambridge University Press.

_____. 1993. *The Portuguese empire in Asia 1500–1700: A political and economic history.* London: Longman.

_____. 1997. *The career and legend of Vasco da Gama.* New York: Cambridge University Press.

Sur, A.K. 1963. Sex and marriage in the age of the Mahabharata. *Man in India* 43(1):42–54.

Tagore, Rabindranath, 1969. *Our universe.* Translated by Indu Dutt. Bombay, India: Jaico Publishing.

Talmaki, Shripad S., and Pandurang N. Nadkarni. 1998. *Saraswat families: A socio-historical study of Chitrapur Saraswats.* Reprint of 1997 edition. Mumbai, India: Kanara Saraswat Association.

Thackston, Wheeler M., translator, editor, and annotator. 1999. *The Jahangirnama: Memoirs of Jahangir, emperor of India*. Washington, DC: Smithsonian Institution.

Thapar, Romila. 2002. *Early India: From the origins to AD 1300*. Berkeley: University of California Press.

Torrey, E. Fuller, and Michael B. Knable. 2002. *Surviving manic depression: A manual on bipolar disorder for patients, families, and providers*. New York: Basic Books.

Tredennick, Hugh, and Harold Tarrant, translators. 1954. *Plato: The last days of Socrates*. Revised translation with new introduction and notes. New York: Penguin.

Tutu, Desmond Mpilo. 1999. *No future without forgiveness*. New York: Doubleday.

Upadhyaya, U.P., editor. 1996. *Coastal Karnataka: Studies in folkloristic and linguistic traditions of Dakshina Kannada region of the Western coast of India*. Udupi, India: Rashtrakavi Govind Pai Samshodhana Kendra, M.G.M. College.

_____, and Susheela P. Upadhyaya. 2002. *Folk rituals of the Tuluva region of coastal Karnataka*. Udupi, India: Regional Resources Centre of Folk Performing Arts, M.G.M. College.

Valiathan, M.S. 2003. *The legacy of Caraka*. Chennai, India: Orient Longman Ltd.

_____. 2007. *The legacy of Suśruta*. Chennai, India: Orient Longman Ltd.

Van Alphen, Jan, and Anthony Aris, editors. 1996. *Oriental medicine: An illustrated guide to the Asian arts of healing*. Boston, MA: Shambala Publications.

van Buitenen, J.A.B., editor and translator. 1973–8. *The Mahābhārata*. 3 vols. Chicago: University of Chicago Press.

van Nooten, Barend A., and Gary B. Holland. 1994. *Rig Veda: A metrically restored text with an introduction and notes*. Cambridge, MA: Harvard University Press.

Venkataraman, G. 1988. *Journey into light: Life and science of C. V. Raman*. Bangalore, India: Indian Academy of Sciences.

Vigarello, Georges. 1988. *Concepts of cleanliness: Changing attitudes in France since the middle ages*. Translated from the French by Jean Birrell. New York: Cambridge University Press.

Wagenaar, H.W., et al.1995. *Allied Chambers transliterated Hindi-Hindi-English dictionary*. New Delhi, India: Allied Chambers.

Wagle, N.K. 1970. The history and social organization of the Gauḍa Sāraswata Brāhmaṇas of the west coast of India. *Journal of Indian History* 48:7–25; 295–333.

Wagle, Narendra. 1980. A dispute between the Pancal Devajna Sonars and the Brahmins of Pune regarding social rank and ritual privileges: A case-study of *Jati* laws in Maharashtra, 1812–1825, pp. 129–159, in *Images of Maharashtra: A Regional Profile of India*, edited by N.K. Wagle. London: Curzon Press.

Walker, Benjamin. 1968. *Hindu world: An encyclopedic survey of Hinduism.* 2 vols. London: George Allen & Unwin.

Wasson, R. Gordon. 1968. *Soma: Divine mushroom of immortality.* New York: Harcourt Brace Jovanovich.

_____. 1971. The soma of the Rig Veda: What was it? *Journal of the American Oriental Society* 91(2):169–87.

_____. 1972. Soma and the fly-agaric: Mr. Wasson's rejoinder to Professor Brough. *Ethno-Mycological Studies* No. 2. Cambridge, MA: Botanical Museum of Harvard University.

_____, Albert Hofmann, and Carl A.P. Ruck. 1978. *The road to Eleusis: Unveiling the secret of the mysteries.* New York: Harcourt Brace Jovanovich.

_____. 1979. Soma brought up-to-date. *Journal of the American Oriental Society* 99(1):100–5.

_____, Stella Kramrisch, Jonathan Ott, and Carl A.P. Ruck. 1986. *Persephone's Quest: Entheogens and the origins of religion.* New Haven, CT: Yale University Press.

_____. 1990. The divine mushroom of immortality, and what was the soma of the Aryans? pp. 185–200, 201–213, in *Flesh of the Gods: The ritual use of hallucinogens,* edited by Peter T. Furst. Revised with changes in the 1972 edition. Prospect Heights, IL: Waveland Press.

Wegner, Daniel M. 2002. *The illusion of conscious will.* Cambridge, MA: MIT Press.

Weigel, George. 1999. *Witness to hope: The biography of John Paul II.* New York: Cliff Street Books.

Weinberg, Bennett A., and Bonnie K. Bealer. 2001. *The world of caffeine: The science and culture of the world's most popular drug.* New York: Routledge & Kegan Paul.

Weinberger-Thomas, Catherine. 1999. *Ashes of immortality: Widow-burning in India.* Translated by Jeffrey Mehlman and David Gordon White. Chicago, IL: University of Chicago Press.

Weiss, Mitchell G. 1980. Caraka saṁhitā on the doctrine of karma, pp. 90–115, in *Karma and rebirth in classical Indian traditions,* edited by Wendy Doniger O'Flaherty. Berkeley: University of California Press.

Wesson, Robert G. 1967. *The imperial order.* Berkeley: University of California Press.

Wicki, J. 2003. Xavier, Francis, St. *New Catholic encyclopedia,* 14:877. 2nd edition. Farmington Hills, MI: Thomson Gale.

Wikipedia. "Ammembal Subba Rao Pai." http://en.wikipedia.org/wiki/Ammembal_Subba_Rao_Pai. Accessed 31 July 2008.

Wikipedia. "Deshastha Brahmin." http://en.wikipedia.org/wiki/Deshastha_Brahmin. Accessed 19 July 2008.

Wikipedia. "Ephedra." http://en.wikipedia.org/wiki/Ephedra. Accessed 17 December 2010.

Wiesenthal, Simon. 1998. *The sunflower: On the possibilities and limits of forgiveness.* With a symposium edited by Harry James Cargas and Bonny V. Fetterman. Revised and expanded edition. New York: Schocken Books.

World almanac and book of facts 2008. New York: World Almanac Books.

Wrangham, Richard, and Dale Peterson. 1996. *Demonic males: Apes and the origins of human violence.* Boston: Houghton Mifflin.

Wright, J. 2004. *God's soldiers: Adventure, politics, intrigue, and power: A history of Jesuits.* New York: Doubleday.

Wright, Lawrence. 1980. *Clean and decent: The history of the bath and loo.* London: Routledge & Kegan Paul.

Xavier, P.D. 1993. *Goa: A social history (1510–1640).* Panaji, Goa, India: Rajhauns Vitaran.

Acknowledgments

I first heard the stories in this book from my elders—great-grandparents, grandparents, parents, and others. Primed by an attentive audience, inspired by a fresh charge of *pāna* (betel) in a few cases, nostalgic about our past, they made their memories come alive and the events real in our mother tongue, Konkani. I have merely recast them here, in my acquired second language. For this unique gift, I am truly grateful.

I thank Palimar Vasantha Devaraya Nayak, the current *darśaṇā pātri* (medium) for the oracle at the Mulki Śrī Veñkataramaṇa Temple, for granting an interview to answer my many questions. Jayadeva Narayana Bhat was kind enough to check and correct errors in Appendix 7, on the oracle. My thanks are due to Tellicheri Achyuta Shenoy, who lent a copy of the court judgment of 1919 for photocopying. Srinivas Ganapati Bhat answered my questions on Hindu rites and rituals and corrected many errors. Many thanks to Keshava (Keshavu) Bhat, who gave me a copy of the arbitration settlement (*pancayiti paisalu*).

I have made every effort to trace and contact copyright holders of the publications quoted in this book. These are listed in a separate section, "Credits and Permissions," at the end of the book. I thank all those who granted permission to reproduce excerpts from these works. Any inadvertent omissions will be corrected in future editions of this book.

Many thanks to Délio de Mendonça, S.J., former director of the Xavier Centre of Historical Research, Alto Porvorim, Goa, who translated an archival sixteenth-century letter and a Portuguese inscription for me. My grateful thanks are due to Sonja and Jim Santos for another translation of this same Portuguese inscription.

S.N. Sridhar, director of the Center for India Studies, professor of linguistics and India studies, and SUNY Distinguished Service Professor at the State University of New York at Stony Brook (SUNY Stony Brook), allowed me the use of the library of the Center for India Studies. Kamal K. Sridhar, professor in the Department of Asian and Asian American Studies and Linguistics at SUNY Stony Brook, traced the source of the Tagore poem reproduced at the end of Chapter 5, "Immigrants in a New Country." I thank them both for their help. Donna Sammis and Jay Levenson of the interlibrary loan service of the Frank Melville Jr. Memorial Library at SUNY Stony Brook were most helpful in borrowing many hard-to-get books from other institutions. Hanne Tracy of the circulation desk and the librarians at the reference desk there helped in retrieving and printing of many journal articles. Cynthia Dietz, the map librarian, provided much help in locating a few maps. Brandon Pantorno, director of the Comsewogue Public Library, and his staff were always helpful and acquired many of the books I requested.

I have had many interesting discussions with Marvin Levine on Buddhism, yoga, and related matters, and I thank him for his insights. I thank Sanjeev and Jeet Nayak and Merton Reichler for reading an early version of the section on Goa and providing helpful comments.

My classmates K. Vittal Nayak, K. Raghuram Pai, and U. Anandraya Shenoy refreshed my memory of our early years in the Christian High School, recalling many incidents I had forgotten. A list of students and teachers of our high school days, reconstructed entirely from memory by Vittal Nayak, was very helpful. Pangal Rabindra Nayak, through his daughter Kanaka, provided invaluable information on the bus service in the South Kanara District in the early days of its inception.

I received much help from my friends, relatives, and others in assembling this book. Chetan in Mysore, Ganapati in Mangalore, Nitin in Panaji and Pune, Rathnakar in Bangalore, and Suresh in Udupi assisted with copying journal articles or books, buying books, and locating rare or out-of-print sources. Botanical names of a few plants and fruit were provided by Vivekanna and Vasudev in Bangalore. Villa recalled many stories of our family to enrich this book. Many thanks to all of you.

A few of my relatives were kind enough to check the early drafts of Appendix 4, "Kinship Terms in Konkani," and correct errors. They are Rathnakar, Sharada, Chaitra, Sumati, Lalita, Sudhir, Subhalaxmi, Sri Laxmi, Nivedita, and Padma. The lists of special dishes (*poḷi, pīṭa*) that grace our feasts and festivals are from the experts in my family—the women whose hard work in preparing these makes the festive occasions so memorable. Many of my relatives and friends were generous with their time in answering my requests for information and or data, for which I am grateful. They are given here in no particular order: Mannakka, Mohiniakka, Vasanti, Gopalkrishna Bhavaji and Kumuda, Jayadev, Mahesh, Villa, Vivekanna, Vasudev (VTS), Rajendra, Ramakrishna, Kasturi, Lalita, Sathyanath, Saudamini, Shiddha, Suman, Srinivas Bhat, Srinivas Prabhu, Sudhir, Subhalaxmi, Surendra, Suresh, Sri Laxmi, Keshavu, Dipti, Jaya, Pundalik, Yako, and Said. Thank you very much. Any errors or misstatements in the book are all mine.

Katharine O'Moore-Klopf, copyeditor, corrected many errors and infelicitous usage and requested information to fill gaps in the story. Stephen Tiano, book designer and layout artist, created the internal look of the book, assembled all the material of the manuscript, and organized the book. Dick Margulis guided the book production, publication, and marketing. Their efforts have morphed many disjointed bits of the manuscript into the beautiful book you are now holding in your hands. I thank them for their invaluable help.

I thank my wife, Padma, and my son, Giridhar, for their moral and material support and encouragement during the almost twelve years I worked on this book.

Index

U

Credits and Permissions

I thank the owners of copyrights—authors, publishers, and others—for the following publications for granting permission for me to reproduce excerpts from these works in this book. A few of the copyright holders indicated that no permission was needed for short quotes because they met the standards of "fair use" and could be reproduced free of charge. They are included in this list to acknowledge their ownership of copyrights and to thank them for their gracious permission.

The quote from the book by Luigi Accattoli, *When a Pope Asks Forgiveness: The Mea Culpa's of John Paul II*, copyright © 1998 Daughters of St. Paul, translated by Jordan Aumann, OP, and published by Pauline Books & Media, Boston, MA, is reproduced by permission of the publisher.

Permission to reprint a quote from the book by V. M. Apte, *Social and Religious Life in the Grihya Sutras*, published by The Popular Book Depot, Bombay, India, has been requested from the publisher.*

The quotes from the article by Paul Axelrod and Michelle A. Fuerch, "Flight of the Deities: Hindu Resistance in Portuguese Goa," *Modern Asian Studies* 1996;30(2):387–421, copyright © Cambridge University Press, are reproduced with permission of Paul Axelrod and the publisher.

---

* Attempts were made to obtain permission from the copyright holders; however, there was no response to inquiries. If copyright holders subsequently contact the author, the author will be happy to obtain their permission, thank them, and provide full credit on this page in future editions of this book.

Permission to reprint quotes from an article by C.R. Boxer, "A Note on Portuguese Missionary Methods in the East: 16th–18th centuries" *Ceylon Historical Journal* 1960–61;10(1–4):77–90, published by Tisara Press, Dehiwala, Ceylon, has been requested.*

Permission to reprint quotes from the book by C.R. Boxer, *The Portuguese Seaborne Empire, 1415–1825*, copyright © 1969 C.R. Boxer, published by Alfred A. Knopf, has been requested.*

The quote from the book by Maria Aurora Couto, *Goa: A Daughter's Story*, copyright © 2004 Maria Aurora Couto and published by Penguin, New Delhi, India, is reproduced with the author's permission.

The quotes from the article by E. D'Arcy, "Freedom of Religion," *New Catholic Encyclopedia*, 2003;5:946–54, 2nd ed., copyright © by the Catholic University of America, is reproduced with the copyright owner's permission.

The excerpts from the book by Anthony D'Costa, S.J., *The Christianisation of the Goa Islands*, copyright © 1965 A. D'Costa, S.J. are reproduced with the author's permission.

The excerpts from the book by Délio de Mendonça, S.J., *Conversions and Citizenry: Goa under Portugal 1510–1610*, copyright © 2002 Délio Jacinto de Mendonça and published by Concept Publishing, New Delhi, India, are reproduced with the author's permission.

The translation of the Portuguese inscription in Verna is by Délio de Mendonça, S.J.; was provided in an e-mail on July 6, 2005; and is reproduced with the translator's permission.

The letter in Portuguese by Brother Gomes Vaz, written from Goa on 12 December 1567, was translated by Délio de Mendonça, S.J.; was provided with a letter dated 24 January 2008; and is reproduced with the translator's permission.

The "Hymn to Agni and Harmony" from the book by Antonio T. de Nicolás, *Four-dimensional Man: Meditations through the Ṛg Veda*, copyright © 1976 Nicholas Hays Ltd. and published by Nicolas Hays Ltd, Stony Brook, NY, is reproduced with the author's permission.

* Attempts were made to obtain permission from the copyright holders; however, there was no response to inquiries. If copyright holders subsequently contact the author, the author will be happy to obtain their permission, thank them, and provide full credit on this page in future editions of this book.

The quotes from the article by Teotonio R. de Souza, "Glimpses of Hindu Dominance of Goan Economy in the 17th Century," *Indica* 1975;12:27–35, are reproduced with the author's permission.

The quotes from the book by Teotonio R. de Souza, *Medieval Goa: A Socio-economic History*, copyright © 1979 Teotonio R. de Souza, published by Concept Publishing, New Delhi, India, are reproduced with the author's permission.

The quote from the article by Teotonio R. de Souza, "Why Cuncolim Martyrs? An Historical Re-assessment," in *Jesuits in India: In Historical Perspective*, edited by Teotonio R. de Souza and Charles J. Borges and published in Alto Porvorim, Goa, India, by Xavier Center of Historical Research, and in Macao, China, by Instituto Cultural De Macau, is reproduced with permission from the author and the Xavier Center of Historical Research.

The quotes from the book by Teotonio R. de Souza, *Goa to Me*, copyright © 1994 Teotonio R. de Souza, published by Concept Publishing, New Delhi, India, are reproduced with the author's permission.

The quote from the article by Ian Fisher, "Pope Concedes Unjustifiable Crimes in Converting South Americans," copyright © 2007 the *New York Times*, appeared in the *New York Times* on 24 May 2007.

The quote from the book by Peter Green, *Alexander of Macedon, 356–323 B.C: A Historical Biography*, copyright © 1991 Peter Green, published by the University of California Press, Berkeley, is reproduced with the permission of the publisher.

Permission to reprint quotes from the book by Pandurang Vaman Kane, *History of Dharmaśāstra: Ancient and Medieval Religious and Civil Law in India*, 5 vols., 2nd ed., published by the Bhandarkar Oriental Research Institute, Pune, India, has been requested.*

A quote has been used from the book by Robert Kanigel, *The Man Who Knew Infinity: A Life of the Genius Ramanujan*, copyright © 1991 Robert Kanigel, published by Charles Scribner's Sons, New York.

* Attempts were made to obtain permission from the copyright holders; however, there was no response to inquiries. If copyright holders subsequently contact the author, the author will be happy to obtain their permission, thank them, and provide full credit on this page in future editions of this book.

A quote has been used from a book by Joseph LeDoux, *Synaptic Self: How Our Brains Become Who We Are*, copyright © 2002 Joseph LeDoux, published by Penguin, New York.

Quotes have been used from the book by Andy Letcher: *Shroom: A Cultural History of the Magic Mushroom*, copyright © 2007 Andy Letcher, published by Ecco/HarperPerennial, New York.

Maps 1 through 3 were drawn by William L. Nelson, cartographer, of Bill Nelson—Cartography, Accomac, VA, and are copyright © 2010 William L. Nelson. The cartographer has granted exclusive rights to the author, including electronic rights, to use the maps in conjunction with the publication and sale of this book.

Excerpts from a book by N.A. Nikam and Richard McKeon, editors and translators of *The Edicts of Asoka*, copyright © 1959 the University of Chicago, published by the University of Chicago Press, Chicago, are reproduced with the publisher's permission.

Quotes have been used from an English translation of a book originally published in Danish by Tor Nørretranders, *The User Illusion: Cutting Consciousness Down to Size*, copyright © 1991 Tor Nørretranders, translation copyright © 1998 Jonathan Sydenham, published by Penguin, New York.

The quotes from the book by Wendy Doniger O'Flaherty, *The Rig Veda: An Anthology*, copyright © 1981 Wendy Doniger O'Flaherty, published by Penguin Books, New York, are reproduced with the author's permission.

The three charts in Appendix 2: "Family Genealogy" were created using the computer program Family Tree Maker 2010, described by Tana L. Pedersen in *The Official Guide to Family Tree Maker 2010*, copyright © 2009 Ancestryy.com Inc., published by Ancestry Publishing, Provo, UT, a division of Ancestry.com Inc.

The quote from the book by Edward Peters, *Inquisition*, copyright © 1988 Free Press, a division of Simon & Schuster Inc., is reproduced with permission from the author and Simon & Schuster.

---

* Attempts were made to obtain permission from the copyright holders; however, there was no response to inquiries. If copyright holders subsequently contact the author, the author will be happy to obtain their permission, thank them, and provide full credit on this page in future editions of this book.

Permission to reproduce a quote from the Declaration Nostra Aetate, of the Second Vatican Council, promulgated by Pope Paul VI on October 28, 1965, has been requested from the Libreria Editrice Vaticana.*

The excerpts from the book by Anant Kakba Priolkar, *The Goa Inquisition: Being a Quatercentenary Commemoration Study of the Inquisition in India*, copyright © 1961 A.K. Priolkar and published by the Voice of India/ Aditya Prakashan, New Delhi, India, is reproduced with the publisher's permission.

Permission to reprint excerpts from the book by V.G. Rahurkar, *The Seers of the Ṛgveda*, published by the University of Poona, Poona, India, has been requested.*

Quote from the declaration "Dominus Iesus" by Joseph Cardinal Ratzinger, Prefect, Congregation for the Doctrine of the Faith, is reproduced with permission from the Libreria Editrice Vaticana.

Quotes have been used from the book *Alberuni's India*, copyright © 1971 W.W. Norton & Company, Inc., translated by Edward C. Sachau, abridged edition, edited with introduction and notes by Ainslie T. Embree, published by Norton, New York.

Quotes have been used from the book by Sanjay Subrahmanyam, *The Career and Legend of Vasco Da Gama*, copyright © 1997 Cambridge University Press and published by Cambridge University Press, New York.

"The Agnostic," a poem by Rabindranath Tagore from his book *Our Universe*, translated by Indu Dutt, copyright © 1969 Indu Dutt, published by Jaico Publishing House, Bombay, India, is reproduced with permission of the publisher.

Quotes have been used from Desmond Mpilo Tutu's book *No Future Without Forgiveness*, copyright © 1999 Desmond Mpilo Tutu, published by Doubleday, New York.

Quotes have been used from the book by Georges Vigarello, *Concepts of Cleanliness: Changing Attitudes in France Since the Middle Ages*, English

* Attempts were made to obtain permission from the copyright holders; however, there was no response to inquiries. If copyright holders subsequently contact the author, the author will be happy to obtain their permission, thank them, and provide full credit on this page in future editions of this book.